THE
CRICKF

Introduction by
MARK BUTCHER

Edited by
CHRIS MARSHALL

Statistics by
RICHARD LOCKWOOD

Portraits photographed or researched by
BILL SMITH

Queen Anne Press

QUEEN ANNE PRESS
a division of Lennard Associates Limited
Mackerye End, Harpenden, Herts AL5 5DR

Published in association with
The Cricketers' Who's Who Limited

First published in Great Britain 2001

British Library Cataloguing in Publication is available

ISBN 1 85291 636 2

Typeset in Times and Univers Condensed
Editor (for Queen Anne Press): Kirsty Ennever
Quiz compiled by Chris Marshall
Cover design by Paul Cooper

Printed and bound by
Butler and Tanner Limited, Frome and London

PICTURE ACKNOWLEDGEMENTS

Cover photographs (England U19 captains of recent years)
by Allsport UK
(main picture and back cover) Marcus Trescothick
(inset: bottom left) Michael Vaughan
(insets: right, top to bottom)
Ian Bell, Andrew Flintoff, Owais Shah, Alex Morris, Michael Gough

The publishers would also like to thank the county clubs, the players and
their families for their assistance in helping to assemble the information and
photographs in this book. Thanks also to the following for providing
additional photographs: ABC, Allsport UK, BBC, Bournemouth Evening
Echo, Channel 4, David Dawson, Derby Evening Telegraph, Doncaster Star,
Gloucester Citizen, Lincolnshire Echo, SkySports and Roger Wootton

CONTENTS

NO ONE DOES MORE TO PROTECT CRICKET'S MOST VALUABLE ASSETS

The Professional Cricketers Association is responsible for looking after the life and blood of cricket – the players themselves. From increasing accident/injury cover and benevolent support, to providing education and training for new careers after they finish playing. By protecting our members, the PCA is playing its full, prominent and responsible part in the further promotion of cricket towards the Millennium and beyond.

PCA
PROFESSIONAL CRICKETERS ASSOCIATION

Despite England's encouraging change of fortunes during the year 2000, many people within the game will be glad that the year has come to an end. The game has been laid bare by the revelations of match-fixing and all parties, both domestically and in the international arena, have a responsibility to get cricket back on track.

For the international supporter what better remedy can there be than the prospect of judging our recent improvement against Sri Lanka, Pakistan, Australia and India in one calendar year? However, it would be folly for the international authorities to ignore the growing influence of FICA (Federation of International Cricketers' Associations). I fully expect that within the next twelve months all ten Test playing nations will be fully represented. In the short term the players views have to be heard on such issues as the international itinerary, the implementation of the code of conduct, a consistent policy dealing with suspect bowling actions and players' safety. Most importantly we must all ensure that the horrors of the 'Cronje Affair' are never repeated.

On the domestic front, the year 2001 will see the PCA introduce the exciting concept of 'Zone 6' which together with the development of the website *cricnet.com* shows that the players' association is a body that does not stand still. In my mind the two divisional county championship has been an outstanding success, but increased competition brings an even greater need for players and umpires to have better lines of communication. Only recently representatives of the PCA and the umpires met to discuss how this can be achieved.

It can be seen that the PCA has a vital role to play within the game and we, its officers, relish the task ahead.

David Graveney
General Secretary

Glen McGrath
FICA PricewaterhouseCoopers
International Cricketer of the
Year Award 2000

FICA

FEDERATION OF INTERNATIONAL
CRICKETERS' ASSOCIATIONS

PRICEWATERHOUSECOOPERS

INTERNATIONAL
CRICKET AWARDS
2001

Master of Ceremonies
JOHN INVERDALE

In the Company of
SPECIAL GUEST
SPEAKER

THE DORCHESTER
PARK LANE, LONDON

MONDAY 23RD JULY 2001

7PM FOR 7.30PM

BLACK TIE

For enquiries and bookings please call MAIDEN MANAGEMENT
020 7317 1234

INTRODUCTION

The 2000 season will long be remembered by all those involved in English cricket. Long called-for changes and improvements finally approved in the previous year were to be given the task of breathing new life into our ailing summer sport. So, were the rumours of English cricket's death greatly exaggerated? Would the new formats deliver a brave new dawn?

Well, of all the alterations, the most immediately influential has been the introduction of central contracts long resisted by the counties and the 'we used to play every day of t' week and twice on Sundays' brigade. England contracts have allowed the team to rest, prepare, train and practise specifically for each new task. A luxury that has, incidentally, long been afforded to our rivals. Duncan Fletcher has the power to use his rest 'veto' to prolong the potency of his attack, shield the frailty of Atherton's back and ease the workload on Alec Stewart. Consequently England were able to field a full-strength attack in all seven home Tests and the three in Pakistan. Not only were Gough, Caddick et al. available for selection, they were also available for full-throttle spells whenever Nasser required them. Sensibly, the less experienced players or those in need of 'match miles' were given back to their counties.

Even the most churlish of parochial supporters must grudgingly concede that for the good of the game as a whole the England team must be given priority – I am sure the 20,000-strong crowd present on the last day of the Oval Test will agree.

If ever there was any doubt as to whether change was necessary, I believe England's success against Zimbabwe, West Indies and Pakistan has proven it beyond question. When the England team wins English cricket benefits – simple as that.

The new county championship cannot be given credit for these wins – this time. However, I am sure that it will prove its benefit to the national side in years to come. What has been shown is the public enthusiasm and support available to a winning team. Therefore any improvements or changes that will help garner such support are important for the game's future.

The inaugural two-division championship succeeded on many levels. The format ensured that there were no 'dead' matches, and teams fought to the wire to stay up or gain promotion. Home and away ties gave rise to the need for greater attention to research and preparation, and a much tougher mental approach to the season. Teams needed to have a more flexible attitude to tactics and team selection as away points assumed greater significance. All these factors combined to make the championship considerably more competitive than before and, compared to 1999, much harder to win.

However there are still improvements to be made if we are to push standards ever upwards. The goal must be to take English cricket to the top of the new international table and whilst there is evidence of a revival, that is no reason to pat ourselves on the back and snuggle up in the comfy chair. Three up and three down between the two divisions is clearly too many in an overall league of just eighteen teams, and – like it or not – the majority of the best England-qualified players need to be competing in division one.

It has been interesting to be able to view so much international cricket from overseas this winter. Obviously, England's series with Pakistan was the main focal point. However, series from Australia and South Africa provided their own source of interest. Unsurprisingly, Australia dominated proceedings in their own backyard, being far too strong for West Indies and Zimbabwe.

Very peculiar – to the cricket fan weaned on a diet of home Test series – was the quality of the pitches that these no-contests were played on. Even bounce, good pace, limited seam movement and eventual wear and spin were pretty much the basic characteristics, allowing batsmen and bowlers of no little skill to prosper and leaving those that lacked good basics hopelessly exposed. If we are to provide cricketers of the highest quality, the standard of pitches available both for matches and for practice must improve dramatically. The advent of 'pitch liaison officers' acknowledged that fact, but I feel that policing groundsmen is not the answer in the long term. Perhaps centrally contracting them could provide a more satisfactory solution?

All in all, the year 2000 was a successful one for English cricket. Let us hope it will be remembered as a watershed for our game in which the first strides were taken towards world domination. Congratulations to Gloucestershire for their incredible success in one-day cricket, to the England team for their magnificent back to back to back victories … Oh! And of course, long may Surrey continue to win the championship!

If the success of the past year can be thought of as a small step towards an ultimate goal, if excellence is continually striven for and if the traditional practice of resting on our laurels is consigned to history, the future looks very bright indeed.

Mark Butcher
February 2001

THE PLAYERS

THE LAST FORTY YEARS – ENGLAND V AUSTRALIA QUIZ

Throughout the book there are 100 quiz questions based on meetings of the two
countries since 1960. The answers can be found on page 712.

Editor's Notes

The cricketers listed in this volume include all those who played 1st XI cricket for a first-class county at least once last season, in any form of cricket, and all those registered (at the time of going to press) to play for the 18 first-class counties in 2001, even those who have yet to make a first-team appearance. All statistics are complete to the end of the last English season. Figures about 1000 runs, 50 wickets and 50 dismissals in a season refer to matches in England only. All first-class figures include figures for Test matches which are also extracted and listed separately. One-Day 100s and One-Day five wickets in an innings are for the English domestic competitions and all One-Day Internationals, home and abroad. Career records include 'rebel' tours to South Africa. In the interests of space 2000 statistics are not given for those whose appearances in first-class cricket or One-Day competitions were only for teams other than the county to which they are now contracted i.e. universities, Board XIs, minor counties etc (excluding international cricketers on tours to England). These appearances are however reflected in their career statistics and reference is made in the Extras section to the team for which they played.

The following abbreviations apply: * means not out; All First – all first-class matches; 1-day Int – One-Day Internationals; 1-day Lge – National League (including former Sunday leagues); NatWest – NatWest Trophy; B&H – Benson and Hedges Cup (including the Super Cup). The figures for batting and bowling averages refer to the full first-class English list for 2000, followed in brackets by the 1999 figures. Inclusion in the batting averages depends on a minimum of six completed innings, a bowler has to have taken at least 10 wickets. Strike rate refers to a bowler's record of balls bowled per wicket taken. The Stop press section is a home for highlights of close season tours etc. These highlights are not reflected in the statistics in this edition. This year we have also included a stop press page (p. 711) to catch as many late-breaking signings as possible.

Readers will notice occasional differences in the way the same kind of information is presented. This is because it has been decided to follow the way in which the cricketers themselves have provided the relevant information.

Each year in *The Cricketers' Who's Who*, in addition to those cricketers who are playing during the current season, we also include the biographical and career details of those who played in the previous season but retired at the end of it. The purpose of this is to have, on the record, the full and final cricketing achievements of every player when his career has ended.

A book of this complexity and detail has to be prepared several months in advance of the cricket season, and occasionally there are recent changes in a player's circumstances or the structure of the game which cannot be included in time. Many examples of facts, statistics and even opinions which can quickly become outdated in the period between the actual compilation of the book and its publication, months later, will spring to the reader's mind, and I ask him or her to make the necessary commonsense allowance and adjustments.

Chris Marshall, March 2001

ADAMS, C. J.   Sussex

Name: <u>Christopher</u> John Adams
Role: Right-hand bat, right-arm medium
bowler, slip fielder, county captain
Born: 6 May 1970, Whitwell, Derbyshire
Height: 6ft **Weight:** 13st 7lbs
Nickname: Grizzly, Grizwold
County debut: 1988 (Derbyshire),
1998 (Sussex)
County cap: 1992 (Derbyshire),
1998 (Sussex)
Test debut: 1999-2000
Tests: 5

One-Day Internationals: 5
1000 runs in a season: 4
1st-Class 50s: 58
1st-Class 100s: 25
1st-Class 200s: 2
1st-Class catches: 251
One-Day 100s: 15
One-Day 5 w. in innings: 1
Place in batting averages: 40th av. 39.69 (1999 81st av. 32.96)
Place in bowling averages: (1999 113th av. 33.30)
Strike rate: 81.00 (career 92.29)
Parents: John and Eluned (Lyn)
Wife and date of marriage: Samantha Claire, 26 September 1992
Children: Georgia Louise, 4 October 1993; Sophie Victoria, 13 October 1998
Family links with cricket: Brother David played 2nd XI cricket for Derbyshire and
Gloucestershire. Father played for Yorkshire Schools and uncle played for Essex 2nd XI
Education: Tapton House School; Chesterfield Boys Grammar School; Repton School
Qualifications: 6 O-levels, NCA coaching awards, Executive Development Certificate
in Coaching and Management Skills
Off-season: 'Either at home with a paint brush and cordless drill or in Australia
playing grade cricket (the latter hopefully!)'
Overseas tours: Repton School to Barbados 1987; England NCA North to Northern
Ireland 1987; England XI to New Zealand (Cricket Max) 1997; England to South Africa
and Zimbabwe 1999-2000
Overseas teams played for: Takapuna, New Zealand 1987-88; Te Puke, New Zealand
1989-90; Primrose, Cape Town, South Africa 1991-92; Canberra Comets, Australia
1998-99; University of NSW, Australia 2000-01
Cricketers particularly admired: Ian Botham, Malcolm Marshall, Dean Jones,
Michael Atherton
Young players to look out for: Umer Rashid

Other sports played: Football ('mad on it'), golf
Other sports followed: Football (Arsenal FC)
Injuries: Out for one game with a broken finger
Relaxations: 'My kids'
Extras: Beat Richard Hutton's 25-year-old record for most runs scored in a season at Repton. Represented English Schools U15 and U19, MCC Schools U19 and, in 1989, England YC. Took two catches as 12th man for England v India at Old Trafford in 1990. Set county records for the fastest century by a Derbyshire batsman (57 mins) and the highest score in the Sunday League (141*). Whittingdale Young Player Award 1992. His 239 v Hampshire at Southampton 1996 is the highest score by a Derbyshire No. 3. Released by Derbyshire at the end of the 1997 season and joined Sussex for 1998 as captain. Sussex Player of the Year 1998 and 1999. Set individual one-day record score for Sussex of 163 (off 107 balls) v Middlesex in the National League at Arundel 1999; the innings included nine sixes, a Sussex Sunday/National League record. CGU Player of the Month July/August 1999. Top run-scorer in the 1999 National League competition with 798 runs at 79.80. Made Test debut in the first Test v South Africa at Johannesburg, November 1999. Passed 5000 career runs in Sunday/National League v Northamptonshire Steelers at Eastbourne 2000. Sussex 1st XI Fielder of the Season 2000
Opinions on cricket: 'Too many people have too many of them!'
Best batting: 239 Derbyshire v Hampshire, Southampton 1996
Best bowling: 4-29 Derbyshire v Lancashire, Derby 1991

2000 Season

	M	Inns	NO	Runs	HS	Avge	100s	50s	Ct	St	O	M	Runs	Wkts	Avge	Best	5wI	10wM
Test																		
All First	16	26	3	913	156	39.69	1	7	15	-	27	3	110	2	55.00	1-17	-	-
1-day Int																		
NatWest	2	2	0	72	64	36.00	-	1	-	-								
B & H	4	4	0	127	122	31.75	1	-	3	-	10	0	46	0	-		-	-
1-day Lge	14	14	0	483	100	34.50	1	4	11	-	10	0	62	0	-		-	-

Career Performances

	M	Inns	NO	Runs	HS	Avge	100s	50s	Ct	St	Balls	Runs	Wkts	Avge	Best	5wI	10wM
Test	5	8	0	104	31	13.00	-	-	6	-	120	59	1	59.00	1-42	-	-
All First	216	353	27	11850	239	36.34	27	58	251	-	2861	1719	31	55.45	4-29	-	-
1-day Int	5	4	0	71	42	17.75	-	-	3	-							
NatWest	23	22	5	1008	129 *	59.29	4	6	9	-	96	76	1	76.00	1-15	-	
B & H	41	38	5	1318	138	39.93	3	9	17	-	144	120	1	120.00	1-41	-	
1-day Lge	163	156	25	5125	163	39.12	8	34	89	-	710	652	23	28.34	5-16	1	

ADAMS, J. H. K.   Hampshire

Name: <u>James</u> Henry Kenneth Adams
Role: Left-hand bat, left-arm medium bowler
Born: 23 September 1980, Winchester
Height: 6ft 2in **Weight:** 13st 7lbs
Nickname: Jimmy, Padams, Griz
County debut: No first-team appearance
Parents: Jenny and Mike
Marital status: Single
Family links with cricket: 'Dad played a bit
for Kent Schoolboys. Brothers Ben and Tom
played/play for Hampshire age groups'
Education: Hursley Keble Memorial;
Twyford School; Sherborne School
Qualifications: 10 GCSEs, 3 A-levels
Career outside cricket: 'Not a lot. Going to
uni'
Off-season: Playing for Melville in Perth
Overseas tours: England U19 to Sri Lanka
(Youth World Cup) 1999-2000; West of England to West Indies 1995; Sherborne
School to Pakistan
Overseas teams played for: Woodville, Adelaide 1999-2000; Melville, Perth 2000-01
Cricketers particularly admired: Robin Smith, Shane Warne
Young players to look out for: Lawrence Prittipaul 'and a fair few other Hants
youngsters, and brothers Ben and Tom'
Other sports played: Hockey (Dorset age group when 14), football
Other sports followed: Football
Relaxations: Music, 'vegging'
Extras: Played in Lombard World Cup (U15) 1996; called up as an injury replacement
for England U19 tour to Sri Lanka for Youth World Cup 1999-2000. Represented
England U19 v Sri Lanka U19 in 'Test' series 2000
Opinions on cricket: 'Club cricket needs to reach a higher average level and the club
cricketers need to be pushed harder.'

---

1. At Melbourne (third Test), Sydney and Adelaide in 1974-75,
England's opening partnership comprised a current commentator and a county
chief executive. Name them.

ADAMS, K.   Kent

Name: Kristian Adams
Role: Right-hand bat, left-arm medium-fast
swing bowler
Born: 26 November 1976, Cleethorpes
Height: 5ft 11in **Weight:** 12st
Nickname: Grizzle, Grizzly, The Crab
County debut: 2000
One-Day 5 w. in innings: 1
Strike rate: 66.00 (career 66.00)
Parents: Marianne and Kevin
Marital status: Girlfriend Vickie
Education: Thrunscoe Junior School;
Lindsey Comprehensive; Lindsey Sixth Form
Qualifications: 10 GCSEs
Career outside cricket: Professional barman
Overseas tours: MCC A to East and Central
Africa 1998

Cricketers particularly admired: Darren
Gough, Chris Cairns, Wasim Akram
Young players to look out for: Irfan Shah, James Hockley, John Inglis
Other sports played: All sports ('becoming very accustomed to touch rugby!!')
Other sports followed: Football ('I support Grimsby Town – unfortunately!!')
Relaxations: 'Enjoy beating Saggers and Hockley on the PlayStation, then letting
them buy me a drink at "Churchills" in Canterbury'
Extras: On MCC Young Cricketers groundstaff 1997-99. Leading wicket-taker for
Kent 2nd XI 1999. Took 9-27 for Kent 2nd XI v Northamptonshire 2nd XI at
Northampton in the 2000 AON Trophy. Took three wickets in first 11 balls of his
county cricket career, v Leicestershire Foxes in the National League at Leicester 2000,
finishing with 4-19. Won NatWest Man of the Match award for his 6-24 v Cumberland
at Carlisle 2000; his performance included a wicket with his first ball
Opinions on cricket: 'Start giving youth a chance at international level. It's the only
way to bring on the teenagers who at U19 level seem to be world class.'
Best bowling: 2-58 Kent v Surrey, Canterbury 2000

2000 Season

	M	Inns	NO	Runs	HS	Avge	100s	50s	Ct	St	O	M	Runs	Wkts	Avge	Best	5wI	10wM
Test																		
All First	1	0	0	0	0	-	-	-	-	-	22	4	58	2	29.00	2-58	-	-
1-day Int																		
NatWest	2	1	0	2	2	2.00	-	-	-	-	19.1	1	59	6	9.83	6-24	1	
B & H																		
1-day Lge	6	5	3	8	6 *	4.00	-	-	-	-	44	2	195	8	24.37	4-19	-	

Career Performances

	M	Inns	NO	Runs	HS	Avge	100s	50s	Ct	St	Balls	Runs	Wkts	Avge	Best	5wI	10wM
Test																	
All First	1	0	0	0	0	-	-	-	-	-	132	58	2	29.00	2-58	-	-
1-day Int																	
NatWest	2	1	0	2	2	2.00	-	-	-	-	115	59	6	9.83	6-24	1	
B & H																	
1-day Lge	6	5	3	8	6 *	4.00	-	-	-	-	264	195	8	24.37	4-19	-	

ADSHEAD, S. J. Leicestershire

Name: <u>Stephen</u> John Adshead
Role: Right-hand bat, wicket-keeper
Born: 29 January 1980, Worcester
Height: 5ft 9in **Weight:** 12st
County debut: 2000
1st-Class stumpings: 1
Parents: David and Julie
Marital status: Single
Family links with cricket: Father played and brother plays club cricket
Education: Bridley Moor HS, Redditch
Overseas teams played for: Fish Hoek, Cape Town 1998-99; Witwatersrand Technical, Johannesburg 1999-2000
Cricketers particularly admired: Alec Stewart
Other sports played: Football
Other sports followed: Football (Nottingham Forest)
Relaxations: Coarse fishing and scuba diving

Extras: Averaged 90 for Worcester U19 in county U19 competition in 1998, in which Worcestershire reached the semi-finals. Played a few games for Worcestershire 2nd XI. Played for Herefordshire in Minor Counties and NatWest 1999. Top-scored for Leicestershire 2nd XI with 58 in their victory in the AON Trophy Final 2000

2000 Season

	M	Inns	NO	Runs	HS	Avge	100s	50s	Ct	St	O	M	Runs	Wkts	Avge	Best	5wI	10wM
Test																		
All First	1	1	0	0	0	0.00	-	-	-	1								
1-day Int																		
NatWest																		
B & H																		
1-day Lge																		

Career Performances

	M	Inns	NO	Runs	HS	Avge	100s	50s	Ct	St	Balls	Runs	Wkts	Avge	Best	5wI	10wM
Test																	
All First	1	1	0	0	0	0.00	-	-	-	1							
1-day Int																	
NatWest	2	2	0	41	22	20.50	-	-	2	2							
B & H																	
1-day Lge																	

AFZAAL, U.   Nottinghamshire

Name: Usman Afzaal
Role: Left-hand bat, slow left-arm bowler
Born: 9 June 1977, Rawalpindi, Pakistan
Height: 6ft **Weight:** 12st 7lbs
Nickname: Saeed, Usy, Gulfraz
County debut: 1995
County cap: 2000
1000 runs in a season: 1
1st-Class 50s: 21
1st-Class 100s: 6
1st-Class catches: 35
Place in batting averages: 24th av. 44.26 (1999 109th av. 29.57)
Strike rate: 99.55 (career 99.18)
Parents: Mohammad and Firdous
Marital status: Single
Family links with cricket: Older brother Kamran played for NAYC and for

Nottinghamshire U13-U19; younger brother Aqib played for Notts U11-U16, Midlands U15 and England U15

Education: Blue Bell Hill School; Manvers Pierrepont Comprehensive; South Notts College

Qualifications: Coaching certificates

Career outside cricket: Printing business

Off-season: 'Spending time with my loved ones. Working hard on my cricket and fitness to improve all aspects of my game. Concentrating on my business!' England A tour to West Indies

Overseas tours: England U19 to West Indies 1994-95, to Zimbabwe 1995-96; England A to West Indies 2000-01; Nottinghamshire to South Africa; 'ZRK tour to Pakistan with Notts youngsters in 2000'

Overseas teams played for: Victoria Park, Perth

Cricketers particularly admired: David Gower, Graham Thorpe, Saeed Anwar, Phil Tufnell, Imran Khan

Young players to look out for: Aqib Afzaal, Bilal Shafayat, Nadeem Malik, Stephen Randall, 'all the players who toured Pakistan with ZRK tour'

Other sports played: Indoor football, squash, table tennis

Other sports followed: Football (Manchester United 'a little bit')

Relaxations: 'Enjoy listening to music, spending time with my loved ones, and praying to God (Namaz)'

Extras: Played for England U15 against South Africa and, in 1994, for England U17 against India. Broke the U16 bowling record in the Texaco Trophy. 'Broke the back garden indoor record!' Won Denis Compton Award 1996. Awarded Nottinghamshire cap 2000. 'A lot to achieve yet'

Opinions on cricket: 'Always give 150 per cent. Never think you've done enough. Back and believe in yourself. Enjoy the game – it's a top sport.'

Best batting: 151* Nottinghamshire v Worcestershire, Trent Bridge 2000

Best bowling: 4-101 Nottinghamshire v Gloucestershire, Trent Bridge 1998

2000 Season

	M	Inns	NO	Runs	HS	Avge	100s	50s	Ct	St	O	M	Runs	Wkts	Avge	Best	5wI	10wM
Test																		
All First	16	26	3	1018	151*	44.26	3	4	9	-	149.2	46	379	9	42.11	3-26	-	-
1-day Int																		
NatWest	1	1	0	31	31	31.00	-	-	-	-								
B & H	4	4	0	50	45	12.50	-	-	1	-	2	1	4	0	-		-	-
1-day Lge	13	11	3	292	95*	36.50	-	2	6	-	13	0	81	4	20.25	2-30	-	

Career Performances

	M	Inns	NO	Runs	HS	Avge	100s	50s	Ct	St	Balls	Runs	Wkts	Avge	Best	5wI	10wM
Test																	
All First	80	139	13	3692	151 *	29.30	6	21	35	-	4364	2406	44	54.68	4-101	-	-
1-day Int																	
NatWest	4	3	1	70	31	35.00	-	-	1	-	66	57	0	-		-	-
B & H	6	6	1	182	78	36.40	-	2	1	-	12	4	0	-		-	-
1-day Lge	28	22	5	522	95 *	30.70	-	4	11	-	302	272	12	22.66	2-25	-	

ALDRED, P. Derbyshire

Name: Paul Aldred
Role: Right-hand bat, right-arm
medium bowler
Born: 4 February 1969, Chellaston, Derby
Height: 5ft 10in **Weight:** 12st
Nickname: Jack, Aldo, Mr Ed, Dred
County debut: 1995
County cap: 1999
50 wickets in a season: 1
1st-Class 50s: 1
1st-Class 5 w. in innings: 5
1st-Class 10 w. in match: 1
1st-Class catches: 27
Place in batting averages: 259th av. 11.46
(1999 282nd av. 8.13)
Place in bowling averages: 116th av. 36.70
(1999 26th av. 21.26)
Strike rate: 71.82 (career 61.94)
Parents: Harry (deceased) and Lynette
Marital status: Single
Family links with cricket: Father played local cricket
Education: Chellaston and Curbar Primary School; Lady Manners, Bakewell,
Derbyshire
Qualifications: 'None of interest'
Career outside cricket: Builder
Off-season: 'Playing golf, getting fit for 2001; going to the races'
Overseas teams played for: Bentley CC, Melbourne 1994-95
Cricketers particularly admired: Ian Botham, Viv Richards
Young players to look out for: Ben Spendlove, Ian Blackwell
Other sports played: Golf; hockey for Derbyshire U16, U19, U21 and senior squad
Other sports followed: Golf, rugby, horse racing

Injuries: Out for six weeks with broken finger; for one week with rib tip injury

Relaxations: 'Most sports; golf, fishing, rugby, horse racing'

Extras: Played against New Zealand with NCA in 1994. Played for Derbyshire U21 hockey team at the age of 15. His 1999 season included a spell of 27 wickets in three matches

Opinions on cricket: 'Two divisions seems to have improved the standard. You have more to play for at the end of the season; in past years that may not have been the case. Channel 4's coverage of the Test series has made younger people get interested in the game. It makes it easier to understand. They have people presenting the coverage who know about the game.'

Best batting: 83 Derbyshire v Hampshire, Chesterfield 1997

Best bowling: 7-101 Derbyshire v Lancashire, Derby 1999

2000 Season

	M	Inns	NO	Runs	HS	Avge	100s	50s	Ct	St	O	M	Runs	Wkts	Avge	Best	5wl	10wM
Test																		
All First	11	14	1	149	38	11.46	-	-	4	-	203.3	44	624	17	36.70	4-97	-	-
1-day Int																		
NatWest																		
B & H	5	1	0	7	7	7.00	-	-	1	-	41.3	4	157	9	17.44	3-12	-	
1-day Lge	10	8	2	57	25	9.50	-	-	2	-	84	5	348	19	18.31	3-31	-	

Career Performances

	M	Inns	NO	Runs	HS	Avge	100s	50s	Ct	St	Balls	Runs	Wkts	Avge	Best	5wl	10wM
Test																	
All First	50	65	10	646	83	11.74	-	1	27	-	7062	3609	114	31.65	7-101	5	1
1-day Int																	
NatWest	5	3	1	21	17	10.50	-	-	1	-	236	151	7	21.57	4-30	-	
B & H	11	3	1	38	24 *	19.00	-	-	1	-	513	371	16	23.18	3-12	-	
1-day Lge	55	30	10	231	39 *	11.55	-	-	8	-	2058	1799	54	33.31	4-41	-	

2. Which Australian fast bowler was voted Man of the Series in 1982-83 for his 34 wickets at 20.21?

ALI, K.   Worcestershire

Name: Kabir Ali
Role: Right-hand bat, right-arm fast bowler
Born: 24 November 1980, Birmingham
Height: 6ft **Weight:** 12st
Nickname: Taxi, Kabby
County debut: 1999
1st-Class 50s: 1
1st-Class catches: 5
Place in batting averages: 202nd av. 17.75
Place in bowling averages: 132nd av. 40.55
Strike rate: 65.70 (career 62.34)
Parents: Shabir Ali and M. Begum
Marital status: Single
Family links with cricket: Father played
club cricket. Cousin Kadeer Ali also plays for
Worcestershire

Education: Moseley School; Moseley Sixth
Form College; Solihull College
Qualifications: GNVQ (Advanced) Leisure and Tourism
Career outside cricket: Student
Overseas tours: Warwickshire U19 Development Squad to South Africa 1998
Cricketers particularly admired: Ian Botham, Wasim Akram
Young players to look out for: Aatif Ali, Kadeer Ali, Moeen Munir
Other sports played: Badminton, football
Other sports followed: Football (Birmingham City)
Relaxations: 'Spending time with family and friends, watching TV'
Extras: Warwickshire Youth Young Player of the Year award. Won Gold Award on
B&H debut for his 4-29 v Glamorgan 2000. Represented England U19 v Sri Lanka
U19 in one-day and 'Test' series 2000
Opinions on cricket: 'More bouncers to be allowed in one-day games. Neutral
umpiring for international games.'
Best batting: 50* Worcestershire v Nottinghamshire, Worcester 2000
Best bowling: 4-114 Worcestershire v Essex, Kidderminster 2000

> 3. In 1997, which pair of batsmen set the current record
> fourth-wicket partnership of 288 for England in Tests v Australia, and where?

2000 Season

	M	Inns	NO	Runs	HS	Avge	100s	50s	Ct	St	O	M	Runs	Wkts	Avge	Best	5wI	10wM
Test																		
All First	10	15	3	213	50 *	17.75	-	1	5	-	219	41	811	20	40.55	4-114	-	-
1-day Int																		
NatWest	2	1	0	7	7	7.00	-	-	1	-	20	0	97	4	24.25	2-45	-	
B & H	3	0	0	0	0	-	-	-	-	-	15.4	3	94	4	23.50	4-29	-	
1-day Lge	11	7	4	14	7	4.66	-	-	4	-	63.3	4	318	13	24.46	3-19	-	

Career Performances

	M	Inns	NO	Runs	HS	Avge	100s	50s	Ct	St	Balls	Runs	Wkts	Avge	Best	5wI	10wM
Test																	
All First	11	16	3	224	50 *	17.23	-	1	5	-	1434	869	23	37.78	4-114	-	-
1-day Int																	
NatWest	2	1	0	7	7	7.00	-	-	1	-	120	97	4	24.25	2-45	-	
B & H	3	0	0	0	0	-	-	-	-	-	94	94	4	23.50	4-29	-	
1-day Lge	11	7	4	14	7	4.66	-	-	4	-	381	318	13	24.46	3-19	-	

ALI, K.   Worcestershire

Name: Kadeer Ali
Role: Right-hand bat
Born: 7 March 1983, Birmingham
Height: 6ft 2in **Weight:** 10st 7lbs
Nickname: Kaddy
County debut: 2000
1st-Class catches: 1
Place in batting averages: 308th av. 1.85
Parents: Munir Ali and Maqsood Begum
Marital status: Single
Family links with cricket: Father a cricket coach and club cricketer. Cousin Kabir Ali also plays for Worcestershire
Education: Handsworth Grammar; Moseley Sixth Form College
Qualifications: 5 GCSEs
Career outside cricket: Studying
Off-season: England U19 tour of India
Overseas tours: England U19 to India 2000-01
Cricketers particularly admired: Sachin Tendulkar, Vikram Solanki
Young players to look out for: Kabir Ali, Depesh Patel
Other sports played: Football

Other sports followed: Football (Liverpool FC)
Relaxations: Listening to music, going out with friends
Extras: Young Player awards at Warwickshire CCC. Played for the Worcestershire Board XI in the NatWest Trophy in 1999. Represented England U19 v Sri Lanka U19 in 'Test' series 2000
Opinions on cricket: 'Need to play longer version of game more than limited over game.'
Best batting: 8 Worcestershire v Middlesex, Southgate 2000

2000 Season

	M	Inns	NO	Runs	HS	Avge	100s	50s	Ct	St	O	M	Runs	Wkts	Avge	Best	5wl	10wM
Test																		
All First	4	7	0	13	8	1.85	-	-	1	-								
1-day Int																		
NatWest																		
B & H																		
1-day Lge	1	1	0	20	20	20.00	-	-	-	-								

Career Performances

	M	Inns	NO	Runs	HS	Avge	100s	50s	Ct	St	Balls	Runs	Wkts	Avge	Best	5wl	10wM
Test																	
All First	4	7	0	13	8	1.85	-	-	1	-							
1-day Int																	
NatWest	1	1	0	24	24	24.00	-	-	-	-							
B & H																		
1-day Lge	1	1	0	20	20	20.00	-	-	-	-							

ALI, S. M.   Durham

Name: Syed Muazam Ali
Role: Right-hand bat, occasional leg-spin bowler
Born: 23 October 1979, Whipps Cross, London
Height: 5ft 7in **Weight:** 10st 6lbs
Nickname: Muz, Geeze
County debut: 1999 (one-day), 2000 (first-class)
1st-Class catches: 1
Parents: Masroor and Elean
Marital status: Single
Family links with cricket: Father's brother played first-class cricket in Pakistan
Education: St Aubyn's; Chigwell School
Qualifications: 10 GCSEs, 3 A-levels
Overseas tours: Essex U14 to Hong Kong 1993; Essex U15 to Barbados 1994

Cricketers particularly admired:
Graham Gooch, Steve Waugh
Young players to look out for:
Marc Symington, Mike Carberry, Jit Bahl
Other sports followed: Football
(Tottenham Hotspur)
Relaxations: Music, going out with friends
and reading
Extras: MCC Young Cricketer of the Year
1993 (U13), 1995 (U15), 1997 (U19). Man
of the Tour, Essex U15 to Barbados 1994.
Released by Durham at the end of the 2000
season
Best batting: 18 Durham v Somerset,
Riverside 2000

2000 Season

	M	Inns	NO	Runs	HS	Avge	100s	50s	Ct	St	O	M	Runs	Wkts	Avge	Best	5wI	10wM
Test																		
All First	4	5	0	25	18	5.00	-	-	1	-	3	0	9	0	-		-	-	-
1-day Int																		
NatWest	2	2	0	16	11	8.00	-	-	-	-								
B & H																		
1-day Lge	4	4	0	87	36	21.75	-	-	2	-								

Career Performances

	M	Inns	NO	Runs	HS	Avge	100s	50s	Ct	St	Balls	Runs	Wkts	Avge	Best	5wI	10wM
Test																	
All First	4	5	0	25	18	5.00	-	-	1	-	18	9	0	-		-	-	-
1-day Int																	
NatWest	2	2	0	16	11	8.00	-	-	-	-							
B & H																	
1-day Lge	6	6	0	106	36	17.66	-	-	2	-							

4. The conclusion of whose 35-year career was marked by a standing
ovation at the Centenary Test at Lord's in 1980?

ALLEYNE, D.   Middlesex

Name: David Alleyne
Role: Right-hand bat, wicket-keeper
Born: 17 April 1976, York
Height: 5ft 11in **Weight:** 13st
Nickname: Bones, Gears
County debut: 1999 (one-day)
Parents: Jo and Darcy
Marital status: Single
Family links with cricket: Father played
local club cricket
Education: Raglan; Enfield Grammar;
Hertford Regional College; City and Islington
College
Qualifications: GNVQ Leisure and Tourism;
senior cricket coach
Off-season: 'In Perth playing for Midland-
Guildford'
Overseas tours: Middlesex to Johannesburg
2000
Overseas teams played for: Sturt, Adelaide; Stratford, Inglewood, New Zealand;
Midland-Guildford, Perth
Young players to look out for: Carl Greenidge, Ricky Anderson
Other sports played: Football
Other sports followed: Judo, football (Liverpool FC)
Relaxations: Music, reading
Extras: Plays for Winchmore Hill CC. Represented Middlesex U11 to U17.
Represented Middlesex Cricket Board. Played football for Middlesex U15 and U16
and for Enfield Borough U16. Middlesex 2nd XI Player of the Year 2000
Opinions on cricket: 'More time on preparation all year.'

2000 Season

	M	Inns	NO	Runs	HS	Avge	100s	50s	Ct	St	O	M	Runs	Wkts	Avge	Best	5wI	10wM
Test																		
All First																		
1-day Int																		
NatWest	2	2	0	8	7	4.00	-	-	2	-								
B & H																		
1-day Lge	11	11	0	179	58	16.27	-	1	10	5								

Career Performances

	M	Inns	NO	Runs	HS	Avge	100s	50s	Ct	St	Balls	Runs	Wkts	Avge	Best	5wI	10wM
Test																	
All First																		
1-day Int																		
NatWest	2	2	0	8	7	4.00	-	-	2	-							
B & H																		
1-day Lge	12	12	0	192	58	16.00	-	1	12	6							

ALLEYNE, M. W. Gloucestershire

Name: <u>Mark</u> Wayne Alleyne
Role: Right-hand bat, right-arm medium
bowler, occasional
wicket-keeper, county captain
Born: 23 May 1968, Tottenham
Height: 5ft 10in **Weight:** 14st
Nickname: Boo-Boo
County debut: 1986
County cap: 1990
Benefit: 1999
One-Day Internationals: 5
1000 runs in a season: 6
50 wickets in a season: 1
1st-Class 50s: 64
1st-Class 100s: 17
1st-Class 200s: 1
1st-Class 5 w. in innings: 7
1st-Class catches: 230
1st-Class stumpings: 2
One-Day 100s: 4
One-Day 5 w. in innings: 3

Place in batting averages: 212th av. 17.08 (1999 163rd av. 24.00)
Place in bowling averages: 72nd av. 27.36 (1999 138th av. 43.47)
Strike rate: 61.16 (career 63.37)
Parents: Euclid (deceased) and Hyacinth
Wife and date of marriage: Louise Maria, 9 October 1998
Family links with cricket: Brother played for Gloucestershire 2nd XI and Middlesex
YC. Father played club cricket in Barbados and England
Education: Harrison College, Barbados; Cardinal Pole School, East London
Qualifications: 6 O-levels, NCA Senior Coaching Award, volleyball coaching
certificate

Career outside cricket: 'Pursuing Lifestyle Management'

Off-season: Member of England one-day squad on tour to Kenya, Pakistan and Sri Lanka; captain of England A tour to West Indies

Overseas tours: England YC to Sri Lanka 1986-87, to Australia 1987-88; England XI to New Zealand (Cricket Max) 1997; England A to Bangladesh and New Zealand 1999-2000 (captain), to West Indies 2000-01 (captain); England to Australia 1998-99 (CUB Series), to South Africa and Zimbabwe 1999-2000 (one-day series), to Kenya (ICC Knockout Trophy) 2000-01, to Pakistan and Sri Lanka 2000-01 (one-day series)

Cricketers particularly admired: Gordon Greenidge, Viv Richards, Jack Russell, Steve Waugh

Players to look out for: 'Lads at Gloucestershire have got a lot to offer the game. Bodes well for the future'

Other sports played: Basketball, football 'and various ball games interpreted by John Bracewell'

Other sports followed: 'Still follow Tottenham religiously but support our local football and rugby teams'

Injuries: Out for three weeks with irritation of lower lumbar region

Relaxations: 'Sport crazy but also an avid gardener. Keen historian'

Extras: In 1986 became youngest player to score a century for Gloucestershire. In 1990 also became the youngest to score a double hundred for the county. Graduate of Haringey Cricket College. Cricket Select Sunday League Player of the Year 1992. In 1992 struck then highest Sunday League score for Gloucestershire (134*). Scored 112 in the B&H Super Cup final v Yorkshire at Lord's 1999, winning the Man of the Match award. Leading all-rounder in the single-division four-day era of the County Championship with 6409 runs (av. 32.53) and 216 wickets (av. 31.18) 1993-99. Man of the Match in One-Day International v South Africa at East London February 2000 (53, 3-55 and a catch to dismiss Jonty Rhodes). Captain of Gloucestershire's one-day double-winning side (NatWest and B&H Super Cup) 1999 and of treble-winning side (NatWest, B&H and Norwich Union National League) 2000. Played 393 consecutive competitive games, a Gloucestershire record, between 28 July 1990 and 24 June 2000. Gloucestershire captain since 1997

Opinions on cricket: 'It appears that a lot more thought goes into each game now, and the introduction of the divisional format can claim responsibility for this. It certainly has focused teams more, and if we can just reduce the amount of cricket, I think we will have a very good product.'

Best batting: 256 Gloucestershire v Northamptonshire, Northampton 1990

Best bowling: 6-49 Gloucestershire v Middlesex, Lord's 2000

Stop press: Scored 139 and 40 for England A in their Busta Cup match v Leeward Islands at Anguilla 2000-01

2000 Season

	M	Inns	NO	Runs	HS	Avge	100s	50s	Ct	St	O	M	Runs	Wkts	Avge	Best	5wI	10wM
Test																		
All First	16	24	0	410	126	17.08	1	-	14	-	254.5	72	684	25	27.36	6-49	1	-
1-day Int																		
NatWest	4	3	1	53	36 *	26.50	-	-	2	-	30	1	110	2	55.00	1-20	-	
B & H	7	6	1	178	50	35.60	-	1	6	-	45	3	187	5	37.40	2-18	-	
1-day Lge	14	12	3	168	44 *	18.66	-	-	8	-	102	3	415	14	29.64	3-36	-	

Career Performances

	M	Inns	NO	Runs	HS	Avge	100s	50s	Ct	St	Balls	Runs	Wkts	Avge	Best	5wI	10wM
Test																	
All First	277	455	41	12869	256	31.08	18	64	230	2	21168	10753	334	32.19	6-49	7	-
1-day Int	5	4	0	71	42	17.75	-	-	3	-	348	254	10	25.40	3-27	-	
NatWest	38	31	5	577	73	22.19	-	1	14	-	1545	962	38	25.31	5-30	1	
B & H	58	49	10	990	112	25.38	1	2	30	-	2359	1694	52	32.57	5-27	1	
1-day Lge	220	200	43	4609	134 *	29.35	3	19	88	-	7277	6019	197	30.55	5-28	1	

ALTREE, D. A.   Warwickshire

Name: <u>Darren</u> Anthony Altree
Role: Right-hand bat, left-arm
fast-medium bowler
Born: 30 September 1974, Rugby
Height: 5ft 11in **Weight:** 12st
Nickname: Bobby, Bobster, Dazzler
County debut: 1996
1st-Class catches: 1
Strike rate: (career 93.87)
Parents: Tony and Margaret
Marital status: Single
Education: Ashlawn School, Rugby;
carpentry
Career outside cricket: Coil operator
Overseas tours: Warwickshire U19 to Cape
Town 1992-93; Warwickshire to South Africa
1997, 1998, to Zimbabwe 1998
Overseas teams played for: Avendale, Cape
Town 1994-95
Cricketers particularly admired: Dennis Lillee, Allan Donald
Other sports followed: Football (Coventry)
Relaxations: Music, socialising

Extras: Took two 2nd XI hat-tricks in 1996. Released by Warwickshire at the end of the 2000 season
Best batting: 4 Warwickshire v Nottinghamshire, Edgbaston 2000
Best bowling: 3-41 Warwickshire v Pakistan, Edgbaston 1996

2000 Season

	M	Inns	NO	Runs	HS	Avge	100s	50s	Ct	St	O	M	Runs	Wkts	Avge	Best	5wI	10wM
Test																		
All First	1	1	0	4	4	4.00	-	-	-	-	20.1	1	77	0	-		-	-
1-day Int																		
NatWest																		
B & H																		
1-day Lge																		

Career Performances

	M	Inns	NO	Runs	HS	Avge	100s	50s	Ct	St	Balls	Runs	Wkts	Avge	Best	5wI	10wM
Test																	
All First	6	8	3	6	4	1.20	-	-	1	-	751	497	8	62.12	3-41	-	-
1-day Int																	
NatWest	1	1	0	6	6	6.00	-	-	-	-	30	13	0	-		-	-
B & H																	
1-day Lge																	

AMBROSE, T. R.   Sussex

Name: <u>Timothy</u> Raymond Ambrose
Role: Right-hand bat, right-arm medium bowler, wicket-keeper
Born: 1 December 1982, Newcastle, New South Wales
Height: 5ft 7in
County debut: No first-team appearance
Marital status: Single
Family links with cricket: Uncles and cousins played first-grade cricket in Sydney; one uncle represented NSW Colts. Grandfather played first-grade in Outer Sydney. Father a local cricketer
Education: Merewether High School, NSW; TAFE College
Career outside cricket: Greenkeeper (golf courses)
Off-season: Playing cricket in Australia
Overseas teams played for: Nelson Bay, NSW 1999, 2001; Wallsend, NSW 2000
Other sports played: Soccer (NSW Schoolboys invitation; U16 Player of the Year at Highfield Azzurri – Newcastle first-grade club); tennis (junior representative sides)
Other sports followed: Australian Rules (Sydney Swans)

Relaxations: Guitar, golf, surfing
Extras: Captained 1999 Bradman Cup
winning side – NSW U16 Player of the
Series. Scored century for Country v City,
which led to selection for New South Wales
U17 for Australian Championship. Played for
Eastbourne in the Sussex League, Sussex 2nd
XI and Sussex Academy in 2000. Is not
considered an overseas player
Opinions on cricket: 'Teams starting to play
more attacking, attractive cricket.'

AMIN, R. M. Surrey

Name: <u>Rupesh</u> Mahesh Amin
Role: Right-hand bat, slow left-arm bowler
Born: 20 August 1977, Clapham
Height: 5ft 11in **Weight:** 10st 7lbs
Nickname: Idi, Plug
County debut: 1997
1st-Class catches: 4
Strike rate: (career 94.65)
Parents: Mahesh and Aruna
Marital status: Single
Family links with cricket: Father played
club cricket
Education: Stanford Middle School;
Riddlesdown High School; John Ruskin
Sixth Form; Croydon College
Qualifications: 8 GCSEs, 3 A-levels, ECB
Level 1 cricket coaching
Off-season: 'Staying with family and
working to earn more money'

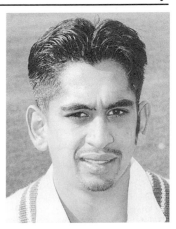

Overseas tours: Bishen Bedi Academy to Sharjah 1999
Overseas teams played for: Manly-Warringah District CC, Sydney 1997-98;
University of New South Wales 1999-2000

Cricketers particularly admired: Saqlain Mushtaq, Sachin Tendulkar
Young players to look out for: Tim Murtagh, Michael Carberry
Other sports played: Snooker ('socially'), five-a-side football (Power League; team name: 'Big Things Squad')
Other sports followed: Football (Liverpool), snooker (Ronnie O'Sullivan), boxing (Prince Naseem Hamed)
Relaxations: Going to cinema, eating good food, going out and seeing places
Extras: Played for Croydon District U15 side that won Hobbs Trophy against London Schools. Attended Bishen Bedi Academy in Delhi for coaching purposes 1998-99
Best batting: 12 Surrey v Leicestershire, The Oval 1998
Best bowling: 4-87 Surrey v Somerset, The Oval 1999

2000 Season

	M	Inns	NO	Runs	HS	Avge	100s	50s	Ct	St	O	M	Runs	Wkts	Avge	Best	5wI	10wM
Test																		
All First	1	1	0	3	3	3.00	-	-	1	-	21	4	67	0	-	-	-	-
1-day Int																		
NatWest																		
B & H																		
1-day Lge																		

Career Performances

	M	Inns	NO	Runs	HS	Avge	100s	50s	Ct	St	Balls	Runs	Wkts	Avge	Best	5wI	10wM
Test																	
All First	11	14	7	34	12	4.85	-	-	4	-	1893	781	20	39.05	4-87	-	-
1-day Int																	
NatWest																	
B & H																	
1-day Lge	2	0	0	0	0	-	-	-	1	-	48	43	2	21.50	2-43	-	

ANDERSON, J. M.   Lancashire

Name: <u>James</u> Michael Anderson
Role: Left-hand bat, right-arm medium-fast bowler
Born: 30 July 1982, Burnley
Height: 6ft 2in **Weight:** 12st 2lbs
Nickname: Jimmy
County debut: No first-team appearance
Parents: Michael and Catherine
Marital status: Single
Family links with cricket: Father and uncle played for Burnley

Education: St Mary's RC Primary School; St Theodore's RC High School; St Theodore's RC Sixth Form Centre (all Burnley)
Qualifications: 10 GCSEs, 1 A-level, 1 GNVQ (Advanced)
Cricketers particularly admired: Michael Atherton, Darren Gough, Courtney Walsh, Shaun Pollock
Young players to look out for: David Brown, Jonathan Clare (both Burnley CC)
Other sports played: Golf, football, 'most active sports'
Other sports followed: Football (Burnley FC), golf
Relaxations: Television, music, all sports
Extras: Played for Lancashire Board XI in the NatWest 2000
Opinions on cricket: 'Too much cricket is

played both at amateur and professional levels in England. The emphasis seems to be on quantity rather than quality.'

2000 Season (did not make any first-class or one-day appearances)

Career Performances

	M	Inns	NO	Runs	HS	Avge	100s	50s	Ct	St	Balls	Runs	Wkts	Avge	Best	5wI	10wM
Test																	
All First																	
1-day Int																	
NatWest	2	1	1	5	5*	-	-	-	-	-	120	98	3	32.66	2-64	-	
B & H																	
1-day Lge																	

---

5. Who reached his century, scored between tea and stumps, by hooking the last ball of the second day for six at Perth in 1974-75?

ANDERSON, R. S. G.   Essex

Name: <u>Ricaldo</u> Sherman Glenroy Anderson
Role: Right-hand bat, right-arm medium-fast bowler
Born: 22 September 1976, Hammersmith, London
Height: 5ft 10in **Weight:** 11st 11lbs
Nickname: Ricky
County debut: 1999
50 wickets in a season: 1
1st-Class 50s: 1
1st-Class 5 w. in innings: 5
1st-Class 10 w. in match: 1
1st-Class catches: 5
Place in batting averages: (1999 281st av. 8.16)
Place in bowling averages: 94th av. 30.37 (1999 60th av. 25.46)
Strike rate: 58.66 (career 49.70)

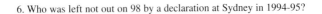

Parents: Heather and Junior
Marital status: Single
Education: Lyon Park School; Alperton High School; Barnet College; NWL College; London Cricket College
Qualifications: 6 GCSEs, BTEC National in Engineering
Overseas tours: Middlesex U16 to Jersey
Overseas teams played for: Coronation CC, South Africa 1996-97
Cricketers particularly admired: Malcolm Marshall, Stuart Law, Carl Hooper
Young players to look out for: James Foster
Other sports followed: Football (Liverpool)
Relaxations: Music
Extras: Took 50 first-class wickets in his first season 1999. Recorded maiden first-class ten-wicket match return (11-111) v Northamptonshire at Ilford 2000; his 6-34 in the first innings included a burst of 5-2 from 14 balls
Best batting: 67* Essex v Sussex, Chelmsford 2000
Best bowling: 6-34 Essex v Northamptonshire, Ilford 2000

6. Who was left not out on 98 by a declaration at Sydney in 1994-95?

2000 Season

	M	Inns	NO	Runs	HS	Avge	100s	50s	Ct	St	O	M	Runs	Wkts	Avge	Best	5wl	10wM
Test																		
All First	9	8	3	170	67 *	34.00	-	1	-	-	234.4	56	729	24	30.37	6-34	3	1
1-day Int																		
NatWest																		
B & H	3	0	0	0	0	-	-	-	-	-	23	1	109	2	54.50	1-33	-	
1-day Lge	3	2	0	2	1	1.00	-	-	-	-	23	2	109	1	109.00	1-31	-	

Career Performances

	M	Inns	NO	Runs	HS	Avge	100s	50s	Ct	St	Balls	Runs	Wkts	Avge	Best	5wl	10wM
Test																	
All First	24	28	5	317	67 *	13.78	-	1	5	-	3678	2002	74	27.05	6-34	5	1
1-day Int																	
NatWest																	
B & H	3	0	0	0	0	-	-	-	-	-	138	109	2	54.50	1-33	-	
1-day Lge	10	7	1	27	10	4.50	-	-	-	-	404	350	5	70.00	3-32	-	

ATHERTON, M. A.   Lancashire

Name: <u>Michael</u> Andrew Atherton
Role: Right-hand bat, leg-break bowler
Born: 23 March 1968, Manchester
Height: 6ft **Weight:** 13st 5lbs
Nickname: Athers, Dread
County debut: 1987
County cap: 1989
Benefit: 1997 (£307,000)
Test debut: 1989
Tests: 102
One-Day Internationals: 54
1000 runs in a season: 7
1st-Class 50s: 101
1st-Class 100s: 50
1st-Class 200s: 2
1st-Class 5 w. in innings: 3
1st-Class catches: 244
One-Day 100s: 12
Place in batting averages: 46th av. 38.14 (1999 17th av. 44.46)
Strike rate: (career 83.15)
Parents: Alan and Wendy
Marital status: Single

Family links with cricket: Father played club cricket

Education: Briscoe Lane County Primary; Manchester GS; Downing College, Cambridge

Qualifications: 10 O-levels, 3 A-levels, BA (Hons) (Cantab)

Off-season: England tours to Pakistan and Sri Lanka

Overseas tours: England YC to Sri Lanka 1986-87, to Australia 1987-88; England A to Zimbabwe 1989-90; England to Australia 1990-91, to India and Sri Lanka 1992-93, to West Indies 1993-94, to Australia 1994-95, to South Africa 1995-96, to India and Pakistan (World Cup) 1995-96, to Zimbabwe and New Zealand 1996-97, to West Indies 1997-98, to Australia 1998-99, to South Africa 1999-2000, to Pakistan and Sri Lanka 2000-01

Cricketers particularly admired: Allan Border

Other sports followed: Golf, squash, football

Injuries: Recurring back injury

Relaxations: 'Decent novels (Heller, Kundera, etc.), good movies, food and wine, travelling, most sports, music'

Extras: First captained England U19 aged 16. In 1987 was first player to score 1000 runs in his debut season since Paul Parker in 1976. Became youngest Lancastrian to score a Test century (151 v NZ at Trent Bridge in 1990); second Lancastrian to score a Test century at Old Trafford (138 v India in 1990). One of *Wisden*'s Five Cricketers of the Year 1991. Appointed England captain in 1993. Cornhill England Player of the Year 1993-94. Voted England's Player of the Series against the West Indies in 1995. Hit 185 not out in the second Test against South Africa in Johannesburg in 1995-96 series; the innings lasted 645 minutes and was the fourth longest by an Englishman in Test matches. Carried bat for 94* in first innings of third Test v New Zealand at Christchurch 1996-97, going on to score 118 in the second innings. Passed Peter May's long-standing record of most Tests as England captain against Australia during the Ashes campaign in 1997. Relinquished England captaincy after 1997-98 Test series v West Indies. Was England's Man of the Series v South Africa 1998. Run of 62 consecutive Test matches ended when he pulled out of the Test v Sri Lanka at The Oval 1998. Selected for England's 1999 World Cup squad but forced to withdraw ahead of Coca-Cola Cup tournament in Sharjah in April 1999 because of back injury. Scored 136 in the second Test v Zimbabwe 2000, thus equalling Denis Compton's record of five Test centuries at Trent Bridge. Shared in Lancashire Sunday/National League record first-wicket partnership (192), with Saurav Ganguly v Somerset Sabres at Taunton 2000. Made 100th Test appearance in third Test v West Indies on his home ground of Old Trafford 2000. Won Man of the Match award for his 83 and 108 v West Indies in the fifth Test at The Oval 2000 – in England's first innings he shared in a new record first-wicket stand for England v West Indies at The Oval (159) with Marcus Trescothick; in England's second innings he was last man out, having scored 108 out of 217

Best batting: 268* Lancashire v Glamorgan, Blackpool 1999

Best bowling: 6-78 Lancashire v Nottinghamshire, Trent Bridge 1990

Stop press: Passed 7000 runs in Test cricket in the first Test v Pakistan at Lahore

2000-01. Scored a 430-ball 125 and a 33-ball 26 in England's victory in the third Test v Pakistan at Karachi, winning the Man of the Match award and moving into fifth place above Wally Hammond in the list of England Test run-scorers

2000 Season

	M	Inns	NO	Runs	HS	Avge	100s	50s	Ct	St	O	M	Runs	Wkts	Avge	Best	5wI	10wM
Test	7	12	0	536	136	44.66	2	2	4	-								
All First	18	29	1	1068	136	38.14	3	6	15	-								
1-day Int																		
NatWest	4	4	1	124	70	41.33	-	2	1	-								
B & H	7	6	1	160	81 *	32.00	-	1	-	-								
1-day Lge	6	6	0	258	105	43.00	1	1	1	-								

Career Performances

	M	Inns	NO	Runs	HS	Avge	100s	50s	Ct	St	Balls	Runs	Wkts	Avge	Best	5wI	10wM
Test	102	187	6	6939	185 *	38.33	15	41	66	-	408	302	2	151.00	1-20	-	-
All First	315	545	45	20598	268 *	41.19	52	101	244	-	8981	4733	108	43.82	6-78	3	-
1-day Int	54	54	3	1791	127	35.11	2	12	15	-							
NatWest	32	32	3	1131	115	39.00	2	9	10	-	188	154	6	25.66	2-15	-	
B & H	67	65	6	2112	121 *	35.79	3	13	34	-	252	228	7	32.57	4-42	-	
1-day Lge	103	100	8	3401	111	36.96	5	19	31	-	216	248	7	35.42	3-33	-	

AUSTIN, I. D. Lancashire

Name: <u>Ian</u> David Austin
Role: Left-hand bat, right-arm medium bowler
Born: 30 May 1966, Haslingden, Lancs
Height: 5ft 10in **Weight:** 14st 7lbs
Nickname: Oscar, Bully
County debut: 1986
County cap: 1990
Benefit: 2000
One-Day Internationals: 9
1st-Class 50s: 20
1st-Class 100s: 2
1st-Class 5 w. in innings: 6
1st-Class 10 w. in match: 1
1st-Class catches: 35
One-Day 5 w. in innings: 1
Place in batting averages: (1999 194th av. 20.83)

Strike rate: 72.00 (career 65.88)
Parents: Jack and Ursula
Wife and date of marriage: Alexandra, 27 February 1993
Children: Victoria, 28 January 1995; Matthew, 26 January 1998
Family links with cricket: Father opened batting for Haslingden CC
Education: Haslingden High School
Qualifications: 4 O-levels, NCA coaching certificate
Overseas tours: NAYC to Bermuda 1985; Lancashire to Jamaica 1986-87, 1987-88, to Zimbabwe 1988-89, to Tasmania and Western Australia 1989-90, 1990-91; England XI to New Zealand (Cricket Max) 1997; England to Bangladesh (Wills International Cup) 1998, to Sharjah (Coca-Cola Cup) 1998-99
Overseas teams played for: Maroochydore, Queensland 1987-88, 1991-92; Randwick, Sydney 1990-91
Cricketers particularly admired: Ian Botham, Hartley Alleyne
Young players to look out for: Andrew Flintoff
Other sports followed: Football (Burnley), golf
Relaxations: Golf, and listening to music
Extras: Set amateur Lancashire League record for highest individual score (147*). Set Lancashire CCC record for most wickets in the Sunday League in 1991. Won the Walter Lawrence Trophy in 1991 for the fastest first-class century of the season, 64 balls off authentic bowling v Yorkshire at Scarborough, batting at No. 10. Man of the Match in the 1996 B&H final and the NatWest semi-final. Lancashire Player of the Year for 1997. Man of the Match in the 1998 NatWest final. One of *Wisden*'s Five Cricketers of the Year 1999. Represented England in the 1999 World Cup
Best batting: 115* Lancashire v Derbyshire, Blackpool 1992
Best bowling: 6-43 Lancashire v Sri Lanka A, Old Trafford 1999

2000 Season

	M	Inns	NO	Runs	HS	Avge	100s	50s	Ct	St	O	M	Runs	Wkts	Avge	Best	5wI	10wM
Test																		
All First	1	1	0	0	0	0.00	-	-	-	-	24	14	32	2	16.00	2-23	-	-
1-day Int																		
NatWest	2	1	1	18	18*	-	-	-	1	-	19	3	52	2	26.00	1-23	-	
B & H	7	4	3	60	24*	60.00	-	-	-	-	59	14	150	9	16.66	3-26	-	
1-day Lge	12	8	3	23	9	4.60	-	-	1	-	92.5	15	313	15	20.86	4-14	-	

7. In the Trent Bridge Test of 1985, the father of a current county cricketer made his one Test appearance. Name him.

Career Performances

	M	Inns	NO	Runs	HS	Avge	100s	50s	Ct	St	Balls	Runs	Wkts	Avge	Best	5wl	10wM
Test																	
All First	124	173	37	3778	115 *	27.77	2	20	35	-	17261	8042	262	30.69	6-43	6	1
1-day Int	9	6	1	34	11 *	6.80	-	-	-	-	475	360	6	60.00	2-25	-	
NatWest	33	23	10	361	97	27.76	-	2	4	-	2133	1203	44	27.34	3-14	-	
B & H	64	41	12	668	80	23.03	-	2	11	-	3652	2276	80	28.45	4-8	-	
1-day Lge	193	117	47	1177	48	16.81	-	-	34	-	8046	5757	216	26.65	5-56	1	

AVERIS, J. M. M. Gloucestershire

Name: James Maxwell Michael Averis
Role: Right-hand bat, right-arm
fast-medium bowler
Born: 28 May 1974, Bristol
Height: 5ft 11in **Weight:** 13st
Nickname: Fish, Avo
County debut: 1994 (one-day),
1997 (first-class)
1st-Class 5 w. in innings: 1
1st-Class catches: 3
One-Day 5 w. in innings: 1
Place in batting averages: 273rd av. 10.00
Strike rate: 124.28 (career 95.39)
Parents: Mike and Carol
Marital status: Single
Family links with cricket: 'Father and
grandfather played and have lots of advice'
Education: Bristol Cathedral School;
Portsmouth University; St Cross College, Oxford University
Qualifications: 10 GCSEs, 3 A-levels, BSc (Hons) Geographical Science, Diploma in
Social Studies (Oxon)
Career outside cricket: 'Financial advisor? (this winter)'
Off-season: 'Doing a computer course at Bristol University. Working and doing
financial planning exams. Keeping fit, playing rugby and catching up on quality time
with Anna Jago'
Overseas tours: Bristol Schools to Australia 1990-91; Gloucestershire to Zimbabwe
1997, to South Africa 1999, to Cape Town 2000; Bristol RFC to South Africa 1996;
Oxford University RFC to Japan and Australia 1997
Overseas teams played for: Union CC, Port Elizabeth, South Africa
Cricketers particularly admired: Jack Russell, Ian Harvey, Malcolm Marshall, Ian
Botham

Young players to look out for: Chris Taylor, Dominic Jago
Other sports played: Rugby (Bristol RFC – first-team debut 1994;
Oxford University – Blue 1996)
Other sports followed: Football (Liverpool FC), rugby (Bristol RFC)
Relaxations: 'Music, films, relaxing with AJ and chewing the cud with MC'
Extras: Double Oxford Blue in 1996-97. Captain of South West U21 rugby in 1995.
Played in every one-day game in Gloucestershire's treble-winning season 2000
Opinions on cricket: 'Professional staffs should be cut to 18 – too much time in
second team cricket can lead to stagnation.'
Best batting: 42 Oxford University v Durham, The Parks 1997
                  42 Oxford University v Sussex, The Parks 1997
Best bowling: 5-98 Oxford University v Hampshire, The Parks 1997

2000 Season

	M	Inns	NO	Runs	HS	Avge	100s	50s	Ct	St	O	M	Runs	Wkts	Avge	Best	5wI	10wM
Test																		
All First	5	7	1	60	25 *	10.00	-	-	1	-	145	36	466	7	66.57	2-40	-	-
1-day Int																		
NatWest	6	2	1	14	12	14.00	-	-	1	-	52.2	4	247	9	27.44	4-36	-	
B & H	7	0	0	0	0	-	-	-	1	-	51.4	3	233	14	16.64	4-8	-	
1-day Lge	16	10	3	65	23 *	9.28	-	-	1	-	126.2	6	537	29	18.51	5-20	1	

Career Performances

	M	Inns	NO	Runs	HS	Avge	100s	50s	Ct	St	Balls	Runs	Wkts	Avge	Best	5wI	10wM
Test																	
All First	19	29	8	382	42	18.19	-	-	3	-	3148	1958	33	59.33	5-98	1	-
1-day Int																	
NatWest	6	2	1	14	12	14.00	-	-	1	-	314	247	9	27.44	4-36	-	
B & H	7	0	0	0	0	-	-	-	1	-	310	233	14	16.64	4-8	-	
1-day Lge	29	18	8	73	23 *	7.30	-	-	2	-	1244	932	42	22.19	5-20	1	

AYMES, A. N.   Hampshire

Name: Adrian Nigel Aymes
Role: Right-hand bat, wicket-keeper
Born: 4 June 1964, Southampton
Height: 6ft **Weight:** 13st
Nickname: Aymeser, Adi, Keeps
County debut: 1987
County cap: 1991
Benefit: 2000

50 dismissals in a season: 5
1st-Class 50s: 34
1st-Class 100s: 7
1st-Class catches: 457
1st-Class stumpings: 41
Place in batting averages: 148th av. 23.41
(1999 61st av. 35.95)
Strike rate: 6.00 (career 43.50)
Parents: Michael and Barbara
Wife and date of marriage: Marie,
14 November 1992
Children: Lucie, 9 November 1994
Family links with cricket: 'Brother bowled
at me in the drive'
Education: Shirley Middle; Bellemoor
Secondary; Hill College
Qualifications: 4 O-levels, 1 A-level, 1 AO-
level, NCA coaching award

Career outside cricket: Building sites, selling cricket equipment
Overseas tours: Hampshire CCC to Isle of Wight 1992, to Portugal 1993,
to Guernsey 1994, to Anguilla 1997
Cricketers particularly admired: Robin Smith, Chris Smith, Peter Haslop, 'and all
the Hursley Park players that made us so successful in the late 1970s-early 1980s'
Young players to look out for: Derek Kenway, Graeme Swann
Other sports followed: Football (Arsenal FC, Southampton FC, 'and all other
Hampshire football sides')
Relaxations: Spending time with friends and family; training
Extras: Half century on debut v Surrey; equalled club record of 6 catches in an
innings and 10 in a match. Hampshire Exiles Young Player of the Year 1990. Was
quickest wicket-keeper to 100 dismissals and 1000 runs in the Sunday League. His
benefit year (2000) got under way at Hambledon with a 13-over game, the opening
delivery of which was bowled a few seconds after midnight on 1 January 2000
Best batting: 133 Hampshire v Leicestershire, Leicester 1998
Best bowling: 2-135 Hampshire v Northamptonshire, Southampton 1998

2000 Season

	M	Inns	NO	Runs	HS	Avge	100s	50s	Ct	St	O	M	Runs	Wkts	Avge	Best	5wI	10wM
Test																		
All First	13	22	5	398	74 *	23.41	-	3	32	6	1	0	13	1	13.00	1-13	-	-
1-day Int																		
NatWest	4	1	1	33	33 *	-	-	-	4	2								
B & H	2	2	0	65	63	32.50	-	1	-	-								
1-day Lge	11	8	1	51	17	7.28	-	-	11	5								

Career Performances

	M	Inns	NO	Runs	HS	Avge	100s	50s	Ct	St	Balls	Runs	Wkts	Avge	Best	5wl	10wM
Test																	
All First	194	288	72	6714	133	31.08	7	34	457	41	174	331	4	82.75	2-135	-	-
1-day Int																	
NatWest	25	11	4	277	73 *	39.57	-	2	38	4							
B & H	39	25	7	370	63	20.55	-	1	37	9							
1-day Lge	150	109	42	1502	60 *	22.41	-	3	134	38							

BAILEY, R. J. Derbyshire

Name: Robert John Bailey
Role: Right-hand bat, off-spin bowler
Born: 28 October 1963, Biddulph,
Stoke-on-Trent
Height: 6ft 3in **Weight:** 14st 7lbs
Nickname: Setter
County debut: 1982 (Northants),
2000 (Derbys)
County cap: 1985 (Northants),
2000 (Derbys)
Benefit: 1993 (Northants)
Test debut: 1988
Tests: 4
One-Day Internationals: 4
1000 runs in a season: 13
1st-Class 50s: 109
1st-Class 100s: 42
1st-Class 200s: 4
1st-Class 5 w. in innings: 2
1st-Class catches: 264
One-Day 100s: 9
One-Day 5 w. in innings: 1
Place in batting averages: 17th av. 48.53 (1999 66th av. 35.38)
Strike rate: 138.00 (career 81.17)
Parents: Marie, father deceased
Wife and date of marriage: Rachel, 11 April 1987
Children: Harry John, 7 March 1991; Alexandra Joy, 13 November 1993
Family links with cricket: Brother plays for Betley-North Staffs with Dominic Cork's
two brothers
Education: Biddulph High School
Qualifications: 6 CSEs, 1 O-level, NCA advanced cricket coach

Career outside cricket: Rob Bailey Ceramics – promotional ceramics for clubs and businesses
Off-season: 'As above!'
Overseas tours: England to Sharjah 1984-85, 1986-87, to West Indies 1989-90; Northants to Durban 1991-92, to Cape Town 1992-93, to Zimbabwe 1994-95; Singapore Sixes October 1994
Overseas teams played for: Rhodes University, South Africa 1982-83; Uitenhage, Melbourne 1983-84, 1984-85; Fitzroy, Melbourne 1985-86; Gosnells, Perth 1987-88
Other sports played: Was schools county badminton champion
Other sports followed: Football (Stoke City, Northampton Town, Rushden & Diamonds), rugby (Northampton Saints)
Injuries: Out for five weeks with torn calf
Relaxations: Walking, and drinking at the local village pub
Extras: Played for Staffordshire. Played for Young England v Young Australia 1983. Selected for cancelled tour of India 1988-89. In 1990 became youngest Northamptonshire player to score 10,000 runs. Won three consecutive NatWest Man of the Match Awards 1995. Took over the Northamptonshire captaincy in 1996 season and held post until the end of the 1997 season. In 1999 v Gloucestershire, passed 20,000 first-class runs for Northamptonshire, becoming only the sixth player to do so. Left Northamptonshire at end of 1999 season and joined Derbyshire for 2000. Recorded his maiden one-day five-wicket return (5-45) v Durham at Riverside in the 2000 B&H. Scored hundred (118) on first-class debut for Derbyshire, v Leics at Derby 2000. Scored 112* v West Indians at Derby 2000; this was the first century by a Derbyshire batsman in matches between the county and the West Indians. Derbyshire Supporters' Club Player of the Year 2000. Awarded Derbyshire cap in 2000
Best batting: 224* Northamptonshire v Glamorgan, Swansea 1986
Best bowling: 5-54 Northamptonshire v Nottinghamshire, Northampton 1993

2000 Season

	M	Inns	NO	Runs	HS	Avge	100s	50s	Ct	St	O	M	Runs	Wkts	Avge	Best	5wI	10wM
Test																		
All First	13	19	4	728	118	48.53	2	5	4	-	46	10	109	2	54.50	1-7	-	-
1-day Int																		
NatWest	1	1	1	20	20*	-	-	-	-	-								
B & H	5	3	2	63	50*	63.00	-	1	2	-	10	0	45	5	9.00	5-45	1	
1-day Lge	11	11	0	243	64	22.09	-	1	3	-	18	0	94	0	-	-	-	

Career Performances

	M	Inns	NO	Runs	HS	Avge	100s	50s	Ct	St	Balls	Runs	Wkts	Avge	Best	5wI	10wM
Test	4	8	0	119	43	14.87	-	-	-	-							
All First	360	603	88	21329	224 *	41.41	46	109	264	-	9254	4899	114	42.97	5-54	2	-
1-day Int	4	4	2	137	43 *	68.50	-	-	1	-	36	25	0	-	-	-	-
NatWest	48	48	13	1595	145	45.57	1	10	18	-	654	407	16	25.43	3-47	-	
B & H	74	69	12	2689	134	47.17	4	20	21	-	450	305	8	38.12	5-45	1	
1-day Lge	240	225	34	6629	125 *	34.70	4	42	63	-	1468	1405	39	36.02	3-23	-	

BAILEY, T. M. B.　　　　Northamptonshire

Name: Tobin Michael Barnaby Bailey
Role: Right-hand bat, wicket-keeper
Born: 28 August 1976, Kettering
Height: 5ft 11in **Weight:** 13st 8lbs
Nickname: Bill, Mad Dog, Scruff
County debut: 1996
1st-Class 50s: 1
1st-Class catches: 19
1st-Class stumpings: 2
Parents: Terry and Penny
Marital status: Single
Family links with cricket: 'Step-dad watches a lot'
Education: Bedford School; Loughborough University
Qualifications: 3 A-levels, BA (Hons) Politics, Level II coaching award
Career outside cricket: Coaching
Off-season: 'Coaching; attending Level III coaching course. Keeping fit; working on my game'
Overseas tours: Bedford to South Africa 1994, to Bermuda; Northamptonshire to Grenada 2000
Cricketers particularly admired: Jack Russell, Mike Atherton, Alan Knott
Young players to look out for: Mark Powell
Other sports played: Hockey and tennis (both for Beds at youth level), golf ('badly')
Other sports followed: Rugby (Bedford RFC), football (Leicester City FC)
Relaxations: 'Watching films, playing golf, spending time with girlfriend Kate and eating out'
Extras: Bedfordshire Young Player of the Year and Northants County League Young Player of the Year in 1995. Holmwoods Schools Cricketer of the Year. Played for England Schools U19 and was a reserve for the England U19 tour to Zimbabwe

1995-96. Won the BUSA cricket cup with Loughborough University in 1996 and captained the university to BUSA cup win in 1998. Represented British Universities 1997 and 1998. Northamptonshire Young Player of the Year 2000. 'Took part in AON Risk game in 2000 that started with 12 players'

Opinions on cricket: 'Three up, three down is too many. I would prefer two up, two down.'

Best batting: 96* Northamptonshire v Worcestershire, Worcester 2000

2000 Season

	M	Inns	NO	Runs	HS	Avge	100s	50s	Ct	St	O	M	Runs	Wkts	Avge	Best	5wI	10wM
Test																		
All First	4	7	2	200	96 *	40.00	-	1	8	1								
1-day Int																		
NatWest																		
B & H																		
1-day Lge	1	0	0	0	0	-	-	-	3	-								

Career Performances

	M	Inns	NO	Runs	HS	Avge	100s	50s	Ct	St	Balls	Runs	Wkts	Avge	Best	5wI	10wM
Test																	
All First	13	15	3	281	96 *	23.41	-	1	19	2							
1-day Int																	
NatWest																	
B & H	10	8	1	97	52	13.85	-	1	5	7							
1-day Lge	7	1	0	10	10	10.00	-	-	9	1							

8. Who was recruited from outside the touring party to play for Australia at Old Trafford in 1981?

BAKER, T. M.   Yorkshire

Name: <u>Thomas</u> Michael Baker
Role: Right-hand bat, right-arm fast-medium bowler
Born: 6 July 1981, Dewsbury, West Yorkshire
Height: 6ft 4in **Weight:** 13st 2lbs
Nickname: Tosh, Helmet
County debut: No first-team appearance
Parents: Mike and Carol
Marital status: Single
Family links with cricket: Brother James represented Notts at junior level
Education: Gomersal First School; Whitcliffe Mount School; Huddersfield Technical College
Qualifications: NCA Level 1 coaching, BTEC Sports Science, GNVQ Sport and Leisure
Career outside cricket: Sports scientist
Off-season: Playing at Edgemead CC, Cape Town
Overseas teams played for: Edgemead CC, Cape Town 2000-01
Cricketers particularly admired: Allan Donald, Jacques Kallis
Young players to look out for: Joe Sayes, 'Chris Brice and his bald head is defnitely one to watch'
Other sports followed: Football (Huddersfield Town)
Injuries: Out for seven weeks with a broken right elbow
Relaxations: 'Socialising, playing any sports (swimming, volleyball, football)'
Extras: Yorkshire CCC Most Promising U17 Cricketer
Opinions on cricket: 'Too many games in such a short time. Will always be the best game in the world.'

BALL, M. C. J.   Gloucestershire

Name: <u>Martyn</u> Charles John Ball
Role: Right-hand bat, off-spin bowler, slip fielder
Born: 26 April 1970, Bristol
Height: 5ft 9in **Weight:** 12st 10lbs
Nickname: Benny, Barfo
County debut: 1988

County cap: 1996
1st-Class 50s: 9
1st-Class 5 w. in innings: 8
1st-Class 10 w. in match: 1
1st-Class catches: 168
One-Day 5 w. in innings: 1
Place in batting averages: 176th av. 20.33
(1999 179th av. 22.20)
Place in bowling averages: 137th av. 43.86
(1999 146th av. 55.61)
Strike rate: 97.26 (career 81.54)
Parents: Kenneth Charles and
Pamela Wendy
Wife and date of marriage: Mona,
28 September 1991
Children: Kristina, 9 May 1990; Alexandra,
2 August 1993; Harrison, 5 June 1997
Education: Stanshawes Court; King Edmund
Secondary School, Yate; Bath College of Further Education
Qualifications: 6 O-levels, 2 A-levels, advanced cricket coach
Career outside cricket: Sports marketing
Overseas tours: Gloucestershire to Namibia 1991, to Kenya 1992, to Sri Lanka 1993,
to Zimbabwe 1996, 1997, to South Africa 1999; MCC to New Zealand 1998-99
Overseas teams played for: North Melbourne, Australia 1988-89; Old Hararians,
Zimbabwe 1990-91
Cricketers particularly admired: Ian Botham, Vic Marks, John Emburey,
Jack Russell
Young players to look out for: Stephen Pope, Alastair Bressington
Other sports played: Rugby, football (both to County Schoolboys level), 'enjoy golf
and skiing'
Other sports followed: 'All sport – massive Man City fan'
Injuries: Broken finger
Relaxations: 'Spending some quality time at home with family'
Extras: Represented county schools. Played for Young England against Young New
Zealand in 1989. Produced best bowling figures in a match for the Britannic County
Championship 1993 season – 14-169 against Somerset
Opinions on cricket: 'The divisional aspect has already shown signs of improvement
to our national team. A form of the game has to be pushed that is quicker, more
thrilling, more exciting and over in a couple of hours if we are to fill stadiums and
attract big sponsors.'
Best batting: 71 Gloucestershire v Nottinghamshire, Bristol 1993
Best bowling: 8-46 Gloucestershire v Somerset, Taunton 1993

2000 Season

	M	Inns	NO	Runs	HS	Avge	100s	50s	Ct	St	O	M	Runs	Wkts	Avge	Best	5wI	10wM
Test																		
All First	9	14	2	244	53	20.33	-	1	13	-	243.1	58	658	15	43.86	3-31	-	-
1-day Int																		
NatWest	6	5	1	33	19	8.25	-	-	3	-	46.3	2	183	10	18.30	3-39	-	
B & H	1	1	1	10	10 *	-	-	-	1	-	8	0	39	2	19.50	2-39	-	
1-day Lge	10	6	1	65	30 *	13.00	-	-	5	-	73	2	347	9	38.55	2-28	-	

Career Performances

	M	Inns	NO	Runs	HS	Avge	100s	50s	Ct	St	Balls	Runs	Wkts	Avge	Best	5wI	10wM
Test																	
All First	142	221	39	3400	71	18.68	-	9	168	-	20957	9891	257	38.48	8-46	8	1
1-day Int																	
NatWest	23	15	4	129	31	11.72	-	-	14	-	1084	716	23	31.13	3-39	-	
B & H	30	19	2	163	28	9.58	-	-	13	-	1566	1055	28	37.67	4-23	-	
1-day Lge	121	86	30	695	36 *	12.41	-	-	40	-	4216	3485	95	36.68	5-42	1	

BANES, M. J. Kent

Name: <u>Matthew</u> John Banes
Role: Right-hand bat (top three)
Born: 10 December 1979, Pembury
Height: 5ft 9in **Weight:** 12st
Nickname: Bano
County debut: 1999
1st-Class 50s: 2
1st-Class catches: 1
Parents: Chris and Jane Ann
Marital status: Single
Education: Holmewood House Prep School;
Tonbridge School; Durham University
Qualifications: 10 GCSEs, 4 A-levels
Off-season: Durham University
Overseas tours: Tonbridge School to
Australia 1996-97; Durham University CC to
Cape Town 2000
Cricketers most admired: Mike Atherton,
Steve Waugh
Young players to look out for: James Foster, Charlie van der Gucht
Other sports played: Hockey, golf
Relaxations: Socialising, films

Extras: Set record for most centuries (11 in three years) for Tonbridge School 1st XI. Made first-class debut v New Zealanders at Canterbury 1999, scoring 53. Played in Old Tonbridgians side that won *The Cricketer* Cup 1999. Represented British Universities 2000

Opinions on cricket: 'Two divisions seems to be the way forward – more competitive. Pitches still need improvement; second-team pitches should be same as first-team.'

Best batting: 53 Kent v New Zealanders, Canterbury 1999

2000 Season

	M	Inns	NO	Runs	HS	Avge	100s	50s	Ct	St	O	M	Runs	Wkts	Avge	Best	5wI	10wM
Test																		
All First	1	1	0	51	51	51.00	-	1	-	-								
1-day Int																		
NatWest																		
B & H																		
1-day Lge																		

Career Performances

	M	Inns	NO	Runs	HS	Avge	100s	50s	Ct	St	Balls	Runs	Wkts	Avge	Best	5wI	10wM
Test																		
All First	3	5	0	111	53	22.20	-	2	1	-								
1-day Int																		
NatWest																		
B & H																		
1-day Lge																		

9. Which England left-hander scored the last of his seven England v Australia centuries at Lord's in 1975?

BARNETT, K. J.   Gloucestershire

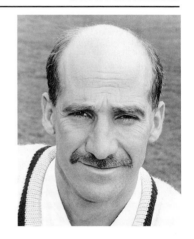

Name: <u>Kim</u> John Barnett
Role: Right-hand bat, leg-break bowler
Born: 17 July 1960, Stoke-on-Trent
Height: 6ft **Weight:** 13st 7lbs
Nickname: The Vicar
County debut: 1979 (Derbyshire),
1999 (Gloucestershire)
County cap: 1982 (Derbyshire),
1999 (Gloucestershire)
Benefit: 1993 (Derbyshire, £37,056)
Test debut: 1988
Tests: 4
One-Day Internationals: 1
1000 runs in a season: 15
1st-Class 50s: 145
1st-Class 100s: 53
1st-Class 200s: 4
1st-Class 5 w. in innings: 3
1st-Class catches: 273
One-Day 100s: 12
One-Day 5 w. in innings: 2
Place in batting averages: 20th av. 45.71 (1999 113th av. 29.08)
Strike rate: (career 75.20)
Parents: Derek and Doreen
Wife: Janet
Children: Michael Nicholas, 24 April 1990; Christina, 11 June 1996
Family links with cricket: 'Father local sportsman, mainly football'
Education: Ipstones C of E; Leek High School, Staffs
Qualifications: 7 O-levels
Career outside cricket: Ex-bank clerk
Off-season: Training
Overseas tours: English Schools to India 1977-78; England YC to Australia 1978-79; England B to Sri Lanka 1985-86 (vice-captain); unofficial English XI to South Africa 1989-90
Overseas teams played for: Boland, South Africa 1980-81, 1982-83
Cricketers particularly admired: Gordon Greenidge
Young players to look out for: Chris Taylor
Other sports followed: Horse racing, football (Stoke City FC), golf
Injuries: Out for three weeks with tendonitis of the knee
Relaxations: Golf
Extras: Played for Northamptonshire 2nd XI when aged 15; also played for

Staffordshire and Warwickshire 2nd XI. Became youngest captain of a first-class county when appointed at Derbyshire in 1983. One of *Wisden*'s Five Cricketers of the Year 1989. Banned from Test cricket after joining tour to South Africa; suspension remitted in 1992. Relinquished Derbyshire captaincy at the end of the 1995 season. Leading century-maker and run-scorer in all competitions in the history of Derbyshire cricket. Left Derbyshire in 1998-99 off-season and joined Gloucestershire for 1999. Has appeared in five successive domestic one-day finals – 1998 NatWest with Derbyshire; 1999 B&H Super Cup and NatWest and 2000 B&H and NatWest, all with Gloucestershire; also holds distinction of having played in the first (1981) and last (2000) NatWest finals. Is second highest run-scorer (2940 runs) in B&H Cup history behind Graham Gooch (5176 runs)

Opinions on cricket: 'We will not produce enough bowlers for the Test arena until we produce pitches that encourage the fast bowlers and leg spinners etc, not just the batsmen.'

Best batting: 239* Derbyshire v Leicestershire, Leicester 1988
Best bowling: 6-28 Derbyshire v Glamorgan, Chesterfield 1991

2000 Season

	M	Inns	NO	Runs	HS	Avge	100s	50s	Ct	St	O	M	Runs	Wkts	Avge	Best	5wI	10wM
Test																		
All First	11	16	2	640	118 *	45.71	2	3	8	-								
1-day Int																		
NatWest	6	6	0	304	86	50.66	-	3	5	-	5	0	27	1	27.00	1-27	-	
B & H	7	7	1	98	39	16.33	-	-	2	-	15	0	73	3	24.33	2-28	-	
1-day Lge	13	13	0	316	62	24.30	-	2	2	-	6	0	24	1	24.00	1-24	-	

Career Performances

	M	Inns	NO	Runs	HS	Avge	100s	50s	Ct	St	Balls	Runs	Wkts	Avge	Best	5wI	10wM
Test	4	7	0	207	80	29.57	-	2	1	-	36	32	0	-	-	-	-
All First	457	744	71	26923	239 *	40.00	57	145	273	-	13989	6999	186	37.62	6-28	3	-
1-day Int	1	1	0	84	84	84.00	-	1	-	-							
NatWest	55	53	3	1992	113 *	39.84	2	14	22	-	766	523	25	20.92	6-24	2	
B & H	95	86	6	2940	115	36.75	4	20	35	-	630	429	16	26.81	3-52	-	
1-day Lge	305	293	43	8447	131 *	33.78	6	46	100	-	1759	1546	56	27.60	4-25	-	

BATES, J. J.   Sussex

Name: <u>Justin</u> Jonathan Bates
Role: Right-hand bat, off-spin bowler
Born: 9 April 1976, Farnborough, Hants
Height: 6ft **Weight:** 11st 7lbs
County debut: 1996 (one-day),
1997 (first-class)
1st-Class 50s: 1
1st-Class 5 w. in innings: 4
1st-Class catches: 17
Place in batting averages: 279th av. 9.00
(1999 211th av. 19.00)
Place in bowling averages: (1999 105th
av. 32.36)
Strike rate: 151.20 (career 73.12)
Parents: Barry and Sandra
Marital status: Single
Family links with cricket: Father played
club cricket and brother Christian played for
Sussex Young Cricketers. Cousin Alan Igglesden played for Kent and England
Education: St Mark's Primary School; Warden Park Secondary School;
Hurstpierpoint College
Qualifications: 8 GCSEs, 3 A-levels, senior coaching award
Career outside cricket: Freelance graphic designer
Overseas tours: Sussex YC to India 1990-91, to Barbados 1992-93, to Sri Lanka 1994-95
Cricketers particularly admired: Carl Hooper, Saqlain Mushtaq
Other sports followed: Golf and rugby
Relaxations: Reading, computing and music
Extras: Released by Sussex at the end of the 2000 season
Best batting: 57 Sussex v Hampshire, Southampton 1999
Best bowling: 5-67 Sussex v Northamptonshire, Northampton 1998

2000 Season

	M	Inns	NO	Runs	HS	Avge	100s	50s	Ct	St	O	M	Runs	Wkts	Avge	Best	5wI	10wM
Test																		
All First	4	6	0	54	17	9.00	-	-	5	-	126	35	374	5	74.80	2-85	-	-
1-day Int																		
NatWest																		
B & H																		
1-day Lge																		

Career Performances

	M	Inns	NO	Runs	HS	Avge	100s	50s	Ct	St	Balls	Runs	Wkts	Avge	Best	5wI	10wM
Test																	
All First	21	32	2	411	57	13.70	-	1	17	-	3583	1528	49	31.18	5-67	4	-
1-day Int																	
NatWest	1	1	0	2	2	2.00	-	-	1	-	38	36	0	-	-	-	-
B & H																	
1-day Lge	6	6	2	20	8	5.00	-	-	4	-	162	165	3	55.00	2-42	-	

BATT, C. J.　　　　　　　　　　Middlesex

Name: <u>Christopher</u> James Batt
Role: Left-hand bat, left-arm fast bowler
Born: 22 September 1976, Maidenhead
Height: 6ft 4in　**Weight:** 13st
Nickname: Batman, Batty, Nora, Closet
County debut: 1998
1st-Class 5 w. in innings: 2
1st-Class catches: 3
Strike rate: 61.50 (career 45.86)
Parents: Clive and Julia
Marital status: Single
Education: Wessex County Primary School,
Cox Green, Maidenhead; Cox Green
Comprehensive School, Maidenhead
Qualifications: 9 GCSEs
Career outside cricket: Gym instructor;
personal fitness instructor/trainer
Overseas tours: Berkshire U19 to Australia
1994; Berkshire U23 to Barbados 1996
Overseas teams played for: Motueka, New Zealand 1998-99
Cricketers particularly admired: Richard Hadlee, Dermot Reeve, Graham Thorpe
Other sports played: Golf (U15 Berkshire Schools champion), football
(Berkshire U16)
Other sports followed: Football (Everton), golf, rugby
Relaxations: Playing golf, 'socialising with friends and women!'
Extras: Local cricket team is Boyne Hill. Colt of the Year 1992 and 1994. Also
member of Julian Cup winning team (senior) in 1993, 1994, 1995 and 1996. Released
by Middlesex at the end of the 2000 season
Opinions on cricket: 'Too many 2nd XI players not having enough aspirations to
further their careers. Compared to overseas teams we are not as strong mentally and
competitively.'

Best batting: 43 Middlesex v Warwickshire, Lord's 1998
Best bowling: 6-101 Middlesex v Nottinghamshire, Trent Bridge 1998

2000 Season

	M	Inns	NO	Runs	HS	Avge	100s	50s	Ct	St	O	M	Runs	Wkts	Avge	Best	5wI	10wM
Test																		
All First	2	3	0	27	21	9.00	-	-	1	-	41	11	146	4	36.50	2-49	-	-
1-day Int																		
NatWest																			
B & H																			
1-day Lge	2	2	2	4	3 *	-	-	-	1	-	13	0	50	3	16.66	2-23	-	

Career Performances

	M	Inns	NO	Runs	HS	Avge	100s	50s	Ct	St	Balls	Runs	Wkts	Avge	Best	5wI	10wM
Test																	
All First	12	17	2	177	43	11.80	-	-	3	-	1697	1092	37	29.51	6-101	2	-
1-day Int																	
NatWest	1	1	0	0	0	0.00	-	-	-	-	48	37	1	37.00	1-37	-	
B & H																	
1-day Lge	6	3	3	12	8 *	-	-	-	1	-	234	161	9	17.88	3-26	-	

BATTY, G. J. Surrey

Name: <u>Gareth</u> Jon Batty
Role: Right-hand bat, off-spin bowler
Born: 13 October 1977, Yorkshire
Height: 5ft 11in **Weight:** 12st
Nickname: Batts, Ian Dowie, Yorkshire Git
County debut: 1997 (Yorkshire),
1998 (one-day, Surrey),
1999 (first-class, Surrey)
Strike rate: (career 48.00)
Parents: David and Rosemary
Marital status: Single
Family links with cricket: 'Dad is Yorkshire
coach; brother played for Yorkshire and
Somerset'
Education: Cullingworth First; Parkside
Middle; Bingley Grammar
Qualifications: 9 GCSEs, BTEC in
Art/Design

Overseas tours: England U15 to South Africa 1993; England U19 to Zimbabwe 1995-96, to Pakistan 1996-97
Cricketers particularly admired: 'Everyone in my team'
Other sports played: Rugby union (Bradford and Bingley), golf
Other sports followed: Rugby (West Hartlepool RFC)
Extras: National U15 bowling award. Made first-class debut for Yorkshire v Lancashire 1997 in non-Championship match. Joined Surrey for 1998. Played for Weybridge side that won Surrey Championship 1999; scored 201* for Weybridge v Spencer 1999
Best batting: 25* Surrey v Sri Lanka A, The Oval 1999
Best bowling: 2-45 Surrey v Sri Lanka A, The Oval 1999

2000 Season

	M	Inns	NO	Runs	HS	Avge	100s	50s	Ct	St	O	M	Runs	Wkts	Avge	Best	5wl	10wM
Test																		
All First																		
1-day Int																		
NatWest	1	1	0	7	7	7.00	-	-	2	-	9.2	0	42	2	21.00	2-42	-	
B & H																		
1-day Lge	2	2	1	46	26 *	46.00	-	-	2	-	11	0	64	0	-		-	-

Career Performances

	M	Inns	NO	Runs	HS	Avge	100s	50s	Ct	St	Balls	Runs	Wkts	Avge	Best	5wl	10wM
Test																	
All First	2	4	1	54	25 *	18.00	-	-	-	-	192	128	4	32.00	2-45	-	-
1-day Int																	
NatWest	1	1	0	7	7	7.00	-	-	2	-	56	42	2	21.00	2-42	-	
B & H																	
1-day Lge	10	10	3	133	37	19.00	-	-	4	-	390	335	4	83.75	1-32	-	

BATTY, J. N.   Surrey

Name: <u>Jonathan</u> Neil Batty
Role: Right-hand bat, 'right-arm fast' bowler,
wicket-keeper
Born: 18 April 1974, Chesterfield
Height: 5ft 10in **Weight:** 11st 7lbs
Nickname: JB, Batts, Zatopek
County debut: 1997
50 dismissals in a season: 1
1st-Class 50s: 5
1st-Class 100s: 1
1st-Class catches: 135
1st-Class stumpings: 23
Place in batting averages: 182nd av. 19.71
(1999 148th av. 25.26)
Strike rate: 36.00 (career 78.00)
Parents: Roger and Gill
Marital status: Single
Family links with cricket: Father played for

Nottinghamshire Schools and played a good standard of club cricket
Education: Repton School; Durham University (St Chad's); Keble College, Oxford
Qualifications: 10 GCSEs, 4 A-levels, BSc (Hons) in Natural Sciences, Diploma in
Social Studies
Overseas tours: Repton School to Holland 1990; MCC to Bangladesh 1996
Overseas teams played for: Mount Cawley CC, Perth 1997-2000
Cricketers particularly admired: David Gower, Bruce French, Alec Stewart
Young players to look out for: David Roberts, Stephen Peters, Alex Tudor
Other sports followed: Football (Nottingham Forest), rugby union (Leicester Tigers)
and squash
Relaxations: Going to the cinema, listening to music and reading
Extras: Oxford Blue in 1996. Has also played Minor Counties cricket for Oxfordshire.
Scored maiden first-class century (100*) v Somerset at The Oval 2000
Opinions on cricket: '2nd XI games should be played on 1st XI wickets.'
Best batting: 100* Surrey v Somerset, The Oval 2000
Best bowling: 1-21 Surrey v Lancashire, Old Trafford 2000

2000 Season

	M	Inns	NO	Runs	HS	Avge	100s	50s	Ct	St	O	M	Runs	Wkts	Avge	Best	5wI	10wM
Test																		
All First	13	16	2	276	100 *	19.71	1	-	29	7	6	0	21	1	21.00	1-21	-	-
1-day Int																		
NatWest																		
B & H																		
1-day Lge	9	3	0	18	8	6.00	-	-	5	1								

Career Performances

	M	Inns	NO	Runs	HS	Avge	100s	50s	Ct	St	Balls	Runs	Wkts	Avge	Best	5wI	10wM
Test																	
All First	59	74	14	1402	100 *	23.36	1	5	135	23	78	61	1	61.00	1-21	-	-
1-day Int																	
NatWest	1	1	0	1	1	1.00	-	-	-	-							
B & H	10	8	3	83	26 *	16.60	-	-	9	-							
1-day Lge	36	26	7	272	40	14.31	-	-	28	7							

BELL, I. R.   Warwickshire

Name: <u>Ian</u> Ronald Bell
Role: Right-hand bat, right-arm medium bowler
Born: 11 April 1982, Coventry
Height: 5ft 10in **Weight:** 11st
Nickname: Belly
County debut: 1999
1st-Class catches: 2
Parents: Terry and Barbara
Marital status: Single
Family links with cricket: Brother has played England for U14
Education: Bilton Middle; Princethorpe College, Rugby
Off-season: Tour to India with England U19; pre-season tour to Cape Town
Overseas tours: England U19 to New Zealand 1998-99, to Malaysia and (Youth World Cup) Sri Lanka 1999-2000, to India 2000-01; Warwickshire U19 to Cape Town 1998-99
Cricketers particularly admired: Michael Atherton, Alec Stewart, Steve Waugh, Graeme Welch

Other sports played: Football (was at Coventry City School of Excellence), rugby
Other sports followed: Football (Coventry City), rugby union (Northampton Saints)
Relaxations: Golf
Extras: Played for England U14, U15, U16, U17 and U19. Scored first international century (115) v New Zealand U19 in Alexandra 1998-99. Player of the Series for England U19 v New Zealand U19 in 'Test' series 1998-99. Scored 190 v Northants 2nd XI and 140 v Glos 2nd XI 1999. Represented England U19 in one-day and 'Test' series v Australia U19 1999. NBC Denis Compton Award 1999. Captained England U19 in one-day and 'Test' series (bar second 'Test') v Sri Lanka U19 2000
Stop press: Scored 109 for England U19 v India U19 in the first 'Test' at Mumbai 2000-01. On his return from India, he was drafted into the England A squad in West Indies as injury cover in the batting department and made his England A debut v Leeward Islands at Anguilla

---

2000 Season (did not make any first-class or one-day appearances)

Career Performances

	M	Inns	NO	Runs	HS	Avge	100s	50s	Ct	St	Balls	Runs	Wkts	Avge	Best	5wI	10wM
Test																	
All First	1	1	0	0	0	0.00	-	-	2	-							
1-day Int																	
NatWest	1	1	0	10	10	10.00	-	-	-	-	3	2	0	-		-	-
B & H																	
1-day Lge																	

10. Who were Shane Warne's hat-trick victims at Melbourne in 1994-95?

BETTS, M. M. Warwickshire

Name: <u>Melvyn</u> Morris Betts
Role: Right-hand bat, right-arm
medium-fast bowler
Born: 26 March 1975, Sacriston
Height: 5ft 11in **Weight:** 12st 9lbs
Nickname: Betsy
County debut: 1993 (Durham)
County cap: 1998 (Durham)
1st-Class 50s: 2
1st-Class 5 w. in innings: 10
1st-Class 10 w. in match: 2
1st-Class catches: 21
Place in batting averages: 240th av. 13.71
(1999 291st av. 6.11)
Place in bowling averages: 16th av. 18.90
(1999 86th av. 29.15)
Strike rate: 48.27 (career 48.81)
Parents: Melvyn and Shirley

Wife and date of marriage: Angela, 3 October 1998
Children: Chloe Grainger
Family links with cricket: Father and uncle played for local club, Sacriston
Education: Fyndoune Comprehensive
Qualifications: 9 GCSEs, plus qualifications in engineering and sports and
recreational studies
Overseas tours: England U19 to Sri Lanka 1993-94; England A to Zimbabwe and
South Africa 1998-99; Durham CCC to South Africa 1995
Cricketers particularly admired: Graham Gooch, David Boon, Jon Lewis
Young players to look out for: Nicky Peng, Chris Hewison
Other sports followed: Football (Newcastle United FC)
Relaxations: 'Local pub with friends outside of cricket'
Extras: Played for England U19 in home series against India in 1994. Left Durham at
the end of the 2000 season and has joined Warwickshire for 2001
Opinions on cricket: 'More time off to keep fitness high and to work on cricketing
skills. First-class pitches need to improve.'
Best batting: 57* Durham v Sussex, Hove 1996
Best bowling: 9-64 Durham v Northamptonshire, Northampton 1997

2000 Season

	M	Inns	NO	Runs	HS	Avge	100s	50s	Ct	St	O	M	Runs	Wkts	Avge	Best	5wI	10wM
Test																		
All First	11	18	4	192	55	13.71	-	1	7	-	354	91	832	44	18.90	7-30	1	1
1-day Int																		
NatWest	2	2	0	2	2	1.00	-	-	1	-	18	1	60	6	10.00	4-34	-	
B & H	3	3	1	4	4	2.00	-	-	-	-	15	1	95	2	47.50	1-44	-	
1-day Lge	6	3	1	22	16	11.00	-	-	2	-	43	3	165	3	55.00	1-14	-	

Career Performances

	M	Inns	NO	Runs	HS	Avge	100s	50s	Ct	St	Balls	Runs	Wkts	Avge	Best	5wI	10wM
Test																	
All First	68	105	23	957	57 *	11.67	-	2	21	-	10983	6248	225	27.76	9-64	10	2
1-day Int																	
NatWest	8	7	1	40	14	6.66	-	-	2	-	510	388	15	25.86	4-34	-	
B & H	12	9	4	51	20 *	10.20	-	-	1	-	511	377	13	29.00	2-26	-	
1-day Lge	49	34	16	195	21	10.83	-	-	9	-	2089	1722	53	32.49	4-39	-	

BEVAN, M. G. Sussex

Name: <u>Michael</u> Gwyl Bevan
Role: Left-hand bat, slow left-arm bowler
Born: 8 May 1970, Canberra, Australia
County debut: 1995 (Yorkshire),
1998 (Sussex)
County cap: 1995 (Yorkshire),
1998 (Sussex)
Test debut: 1994-95
Tests: 18
One-Day Internationals: 144
1000 runs in a season: 3
1st-Class 50s: 62
1st-Class 100s: 45
1st-Class 200s: 2
1st-Class 5 w. in innings: 1
1st-Class 10 w. in match: 1
1st-Class catches: 101
One-Day 100s: 8
One-Day 5 w. in innings: 1
Place in batting averages: 1st av. 74.93
Strike rate: 124.40 (career 73.38)
Wife: Tracy

Education: Australian Cricket Academy
Off-season: Playing for New South Wales and Australia
Overseas tours: Australia to Sharjah 1994, to Pakistan 1994-95, to India and Pakistan (World Cup) 1995-96, to Sri Lanka 1996-97, to India 1996-97, to South Africa 1996-97, to England 1997, to New Zealand 1997-98, to India and Sharjah 1997-98, to Pakistan and Bangladesh 1998-99 (one-day series), to West Indies 1998-99 (one-day series), to UK, Ireland and Holland (World Cup) 1999, to Sri Lanka 1999-2000 (one-day series), to Zimbabwe 1999-2000 (one-day series), to New Zealand 1999-2000 (one-day series), to South Africa 1999-2000 (one-day series), to Kenya (ICC Knockout Trophy) 2000-01
Overseas teams played for: South Australia 1989-90; New South Wales 1990-91 –
Extras: In 1990-91 he became the first player to score a century in five successive Sheffield Shield matches. Made 82 on his Test debut against Pakistan in Karachi, 1994-95. Played for Rawtenstall in the Lancashire League in 1993 and 1994. Played for Yorkshire 1995-96 (vice-captain for the 1996 season). Joined Sussex for 1998 and was appointed vice-captain. Averaged 106.00 in the 1998-99 Australian first-class season. Was in Australia's 1999 World Cup winning side and did not play county cricket that season. Awarded ACB contract for 2000-01. Won Man of the Match award for his 185 from 132 balls for a World XI v an Asia XI in Dhaka 2000; chasing 321 for victory, the World XI lost by just one run, Bevan just failing to hit a six from the final ball. Returned to Sussex as overseas player and vice-captain in 2000. Scored 150-plus (166 and 174) in each innings v Nottinghamshire at Hove 2000; in his next Championship match, v Middlesex at Southgate, he became the first batsman to pass 1000 first-class runs in the 2000 season during his second innings 173*, his fourth score of 150-plus in five Championship innings. Scored 106 for Australia in the inaugural indoor One-Day International v South Africa at Melbourne 2000. Topped English first-class batting averages in 2000 with 1124 runs at 74.93. Top run-scorer in the 2000 National League competition with 706 runs at 117.66. Sussex Player of the Year 2000. Left Sussex at the end of the 2000 season but is expected to return in 2002
Best batting: 203* New South Wales v Western Australia, Sydney 1993-94
Best bowling: 6-82 Australia v West Indies, Adelaide 1996-97
Stop press: Scored 135* in New South Wales's victory over Western Australia in the 2000-01 Mercantile Mutual Cup final at Perth, winning the Man of the Match award

2000 Season

	M	Inns	NO	Runs	HS	Avge	100s	50s	Ct	St	O	M	Runs	Wkts	Avge	Best	5wl	10wM
Test																		
All First	12	18	3	1124	174	74.93	5	1	2	-	103.4	11	400	5	80.00	3-74	-	-
1-day Int																		
NatWest	2	1	0	60	60	60.00	-	1	-	-	7.4	1	45	0	-		-	-
B & H	3	3	2	293	157 *	293.00	1	2	-	-	9	0	62	0	-		-	-
1-day Lge	12	12	6	706	89 *	117.66	-	9	10	-	8.1	0	51	4	12.75	3-17	-	

Career Performances

	M	Inns	NO	Runs	HS	Avge	100s	50s	Ct	St	Balls	Runs	Wkts	Avge	Best	5wI	10wM
Test	18	30	3	785	91	29.07	-	6	8	-	1285	703	29	24.24	6-82	1	1
All First	180	301	54	13796	203 *	55.85	47	62	101	-	8072	4875	110	44.31	6-82	1	1
1-day Int	144	128	44	4763	108 *	56.70	5	32	47	-	1838	1516	33	45.93	3-36	-	
NatWest	11	10	2	456	91 *	57.00	-	5	2	-	223	174	4	43.50	2-47	-	
B & H	16	15	7	1055	157 *	131.87	1	11	1	-	198	185	1	185.00	1-25	-	
1-day Lge	52	50	15	2141	103 *	61.17	2	19	22	-	680	608	36	16.88	5-29	1	

BICHEL, A. J. Worcestershire

Name: Andrew (<u>Andy</u>) John Bichel
Role: Right-hand bat, right-arm fast-medium bowler
Born: 27 August 1970, Laidley, Queensland
Nickname: Bic, Andre
County debut: No first-team appearance
Test debut: 1996-97
Tests: 3
One-Day Internationals: 17
1st-Class 50s: 4
1st-Class 100s: 1
1st-Class 5 w. in innings: 13
1st-Class 10 w. in match: 2
1st-Class catches: 30
Strike rate: (career 48.11)
Family links with cricket: Uncle Donald Bichel played three matches for Queensland in the 1960s

Overseas tours: Queensland Academy of Sport to South Africa; Australia A to Scotland and Ireland 1998; Australia to Kuala Lumpur (Commonwealth Games) 1998, to West Indies 1998-99
Overseas teams played for: Souths, Brisbane 1992-93 – ; Queensland 1992-93 –
Extras: Has played first-grade rugby league. Sheffield Shield Player of the Year 1996-97. Played in Australia's silver medal winning side at the 1998 Commonwealth Games in Kuala Lumpur. Was due to play for Hampshire as their overseas player in 1998 but was selected for Australia A tour of Scotland and Ireland. Took 42 first-class wickets at 22.57 in the 1998-99 Australian season and was Queensland Player of the Year. Took 60 first-class wickets at 20.11 in the 1999-2000 Australian season, including 6-47 for Queensland in Victoria's first innings in the Pura Milk Cup Final. Has same birthday as Sir Donald Bradman
Best batting: 110 Queensland v Victoria, Brisbane 1997-98
Best bowling: 6-45 Queensland v Tasmania, Hobart 1999-2000

Stop press: Recorded maiden Test five-wicket return (5-60) v West Indies at Melbourne 2000-01

2000 Season (did not make any first-class or one-day appearances)

Career Performances

	M	Inns	NO	Runs	HS	Avge	100s	50s	Ct	St	Balls	Runs	Wkts	Avge	Best	5wI	10wM
Test	3	5	0	47	18	9.40	-	-	1	-	519	297	2	148.50	1-31	-	-
All First	57	74	7	1184	110	17.67	1	4	30	-	11500	5612	239	23.48	6-45	13	2
1-day Int	17	11	4	101	29 *	14.42	-	-	2	-	890	701	21	33.38	3-17	-	
NatWest																	
B & H																	
1-day Lge																	

BICKNELL, D. J.   Nottinghamshire

Name: Darren John Bicknell
Role: Left-hand opening bat, occasional slow left-arm bowler
Born: 24 June 1967, Guildford
Height: 6ft 4½in **Weight:** 14st 7lbs
Nickname: Denzil
County debut: 1987 (Surrey), 2000 (Notts)
County cap: 1990 (Surrey), 2000 (Notts)
Benefit: 1999 (Surrey)
1000 runs in a season: 6
1st-Class 50s: 62
1st-Class 100s: 32
1st-Class 200s: 2
1st-Class catches: 81
One-Day 100s: 8
Place in batting averages: 63rd av. 34.32 (1999 96th av. 31.50)
Strike rate: (career 53.82)
Parents: Vic and Valerie
Wife and date of marriage: Rebecca, 26 September 1991
Children: Lauren Elizabeth, 21 October 1993; Sam, 9 November 1995; Emily, 16 December 1997
Family links with cricket: Brother Martin plays
Education: Robert Haining County Secondary; Guildford County College of Technology

Qualifications: 8 O-levels, 2 A-levels, senior coaching award
Off-season: 'Working for Nottingham Forest FC in PR/marketing role'
Overseas tours: Surrey to Sharjah 1988, 1989, to Dubai 1990, to Perth 1995; Nottinghamshire to Johannesburg 2000; England A to Zimbabwe and Kenya 1989-90, to Pakistan 1990-91, to Bermuda and West Indies 1991-92
Overseas teams played for: Coburg, Melbourne 1986-87
Cricketers particularly admired: Wasim Akram, Glenn McGrath, Malcolm Marshall, Saqlain Mushtaq, Martin Bicknell
Young players to look out for: Usman Afzaal, Paul Franks, Guy Welton, David Lucas, Tim Murtagh
Other sports played: Golf 'and any others that I have time to play'
Other sports followed: Football (West Ham United)
Injuries: Knee injury; no time off
Relaxations: 'Spending time with family; golf'
Extras: Shared Surrey record third-wicket stand of 413 with David Ward v Kent at Canterbury in 1990 – both made career bests. Surrey Batsman of the Year four times. Left Surrey and joined Notts for 2000. Became first English cricketer to take part in more than one partnership of 400-plus when he scored 180* in a first-wicket stand of 406* with Guy Welton (200*) v Warwickshire at Edgbaston 2000; the stand broke several records, including that for the highest Nottinghamshire partnership for any wicket, formerly 398 by Arthur Shrewsbury and William Gunn v Sussex at Trent Bridge 1890, and that for the highest unbeaten partnership in Championship history. Awarded Nottinghamshire cap 2000
Opinions on cricket: 'Two divisions an excellent idea; central contracts an excellent idea. Pitches generally improved in 2000. Practice facilities are incredibly poor!! Groundsmen seem to spend more time cutting the outfield than preparing the nets!!'
Best batting: 235* Surrey v Nottinghamshire, Trent Bridge 1994
Best bowling: 3-7 Surrey v Sussex, Guildford 1996

2000 Season

	M	Inns	NO	Runs	HS	Avge	100s	50s	Ct	St	O	M	Runs	Wkts	Avge	Best	5wI	10wM
Test																		
All First	16	28	3	858	180 *	34.32	2	2	3	-	1	1	0	0	-	-	-	-
1-day Int																		
NatWest	1	1	0	1	1	1.00	-	-	-	-								
B & H	4	4	1	75	71 *	25.00	-	1	1	-								
1-day Lge	16	15	2	537	115	41.30	1	5	3	-	1	0	6	0	-	-	-	

Career Performances

	M	Inns	NO	Runs	HS	Avge	100s	50s	Ct	St	Balls	Runs	Wkts	Avge	Best	5wl	10wM
Test																	
All First	227	397	38	14058	235 *	39.15	34	62	81	-	1238	789	23	34.30	3-7	-	-
1-day Int																	
NatWest	21	21	4	779	135 *	45.82	1	5	1	-							
B & H	37	36	4	1316	119	41.12	2	10	13	-							
1-day Lge	119	115	16	3598	125	36.34	5	23	27	-	42	45	2	22.50	1-11	-	

BICKNELL, M. P. Surrey

Name: <u>Martin</u> Paul Bicknell
Role: Right-hand bat, right-arm fast-medium
bowler
Born: 14 January 1969, Guildford
Height: 6ft 4in **Weight:** 15st
Nickname: Bickers
County debut: 1986
County cap: 1989
Benefit: 1997
Test debut: 1993
Tests: 2
One-Day Internationals: 7
50 wickets in a season: 9
1st-Class 50s: 18
1st-Class 5 w. in innings: 32
1st-Class 10 w. in match: 3
1st-Class catches: 78
One-Day 5 w. in innings: 2

Place in batting averages: 84th av. 31.25 (1999 80th av. 33.23)
Place in bowling averages: 13th av. 17.53 (1999 13th av. 18.95)
Strike rate: 41.33 (career 52.22)
Parents: Vic and Val
Wife and date of marriage: Loraine, 29 September 1995
Children: Eleanor, 31 March 1995; Charlotte, 22 July 1996
Family links with cricket: 'Brother plays, but with no luck'
Education: Robert Haining County Secondary
Qualifications: 2 O-levels, NCA coach
Career outside cricket: 'Running "Martin Bicknell Golf"'
Off-season: 'Playing golf, running the business, training'
Overseas tours: England YC to Sri Lanka 1986-87, to Australia 1987-88; England A
to Zimbabwe and Kenya 1989-90, to Bermuda and West Indies 1991-92,
to South Africa 1993-94; England to Australia 1990-91

Cricketers particularly admired: 'All honest county trundlers'
Young players to look out for: Ryan Sidebottom, Tim Murtagh
Other sports played: Golf
Other sports followed: Football (Leeds United), golf
Injuries: Out for one week with back injury
Relaxations: 'Playing golf, reading; spending time with my children'
Extras: His figures of 9 for 45 v Cambridge University at Fenner's in 1988 were the best for the county for 30 years. One of four players on stand-by as reserves for England's World Cup squad 1991-92. Surrey Supporters' Player of the Year 1993, 1999. Surrey Players' Player of the Year 1997, 1998, 1999, 2000. Took 700th first-class wicket (Mark Alleyne) v Gloucestershire at The Oval 1999. Took 7-30 in National League v Glamorgan at The Oval 1999, the best Sunday/National League return by a Surrey bowler. Scored 432 runs to go with his 71 wickets in Surrey's Championship winning season 1999. One of *Wisden*'s Five Cricketers of the Year 2000. Took 800th first-class wicket (Darren Lehmann) v Yorkshire at The Oval 2000. His 16-119 (including 9-47 in the second innings) v Leicestershire in 2000 equalled the Surrey record for wickets taken in a match and is the second best match return in Surrey history behind Tony Lock's 16-83 v Kent at Blackheath 1956. Scored 500 runs to go with his 60 wickets in Surrey's Championship winning season 2000
Opinions on cricket: 'Two divisions does work, as do central contracts. Congratulations to the pitch inspectors who are strong enough to make decisions. However, we do need a degree of uniformity.'
Best batting: 88 Surrey v Hampshire, Southampton 1992
Best bowling: 9-45 Surrey v Cambridge University, The Oval 1988

11. At Brisbane in 1986-87, which current coach and broadcaster became the third Middlesex bowler to take 100 Test wickets?

2000 Season

	M	Inns	NO	Runs	HS	Avge	100s	50s	Ct	St	O	M	Runs	Wkts	Avge	Best	5wI	10wM
Test																		
All First	15	18	2	500	79 *	31.25	-	4	5	-	413.2	115	1052	60	17.53	9-47	3	1
1-day Int																		
NatWest	2	0	0	0	0	-	-	-	1	-	20	4	45	4	11.25	3-19	-	
B & H	4	1	0	25	25	25.00	-	-	-	-	32	6	87	4	21.75	2-15	-	
1-day Lge	11	4	1	37	15 *	12.33	-	-	3	-	87	11	241	15	16.06	3-14	-	

Career Performances

	M	Inns	NO	Runs	HS	Avge	100s	50s	Ct	St	Balls	Runs	Wkts	Avge	Best	5wI	10wM
Test	2	4	0	26	14	6.50	-	-	-	-	522	263	4	65.75	3-99	-	-
All First	228	271	65	4344	88	21.08	-	18	78	-	43136	20143	826	24.38	9-45	32	3
1-day Int	7	6	2	96	31 *	24.00	-	-	2	-	413	347	13	26.69	3-55	-	
NatWest	37	18	8	197	66 *	19.70	-	1	16	-	2295	1286	50	25.72	4-35	-	
B & H	56	29	12	314	43	18.47	-	-	10	-	3203	2091	84	24.89	4-38	-	
1-day Lge	167	81	40	614	57 *	14.97	-	1	36	-	7129	5008	202	24.79	7-30	2	

BISHOP, I. E. Surrey

Name: <u>Ian</u> Emlyn Bishop
Role: Right-hand bat, right-arm
medium-fast bowler
Born: 26 August 1977, Taunton
Height: 6ft 2in **Weight:** 12st 7lbs
Nickname: Bish, Earthworm Jim, Earthy,
Ankles
County debut: 1996 (Somerset),
1999 (Surrey)
1st-Class catches: 4
Strike rate: 87.00 (career 98.57)
Parents: Brian and Jane
Marital status: Single
Family links with cricket: Father and
brother play club cricket
Education: Parkfield Primary School,
Taunton; Castle Secondary School, Taunton;
SCAT, Taunton
Qualifications: GCSEs
Career outside cricket: 'Beer tester for Budweiser'
Off-season: 'Perth, training'
Overseas teams played for: Wanneroo, Perth 1999-2000

Cricketers particularly admired: Darren Gough, Courtney Walsh, Joel Garner

Young players to look out for: Carl Greenidge, Rupesh Amin, Gareth Batty, Tim Murtagh, Joe Porter, Scott Newman, Michael Carberry, 'Alan Butcher'

Other sports played: Football (Spartans & Knight Rangers)

Other sports followed: Football (Liverpool FC)

Injuries: Out for four weeks with shin problems

Relaxations: 'Cigarettes and alcohol. "McCluskies" and "Valbonne"'

Extras: Played for Somerset in 1996. Played for Devon in 1998. Joined Surrey for 1999

Opinions on cricket: 'Not enough floodlit cricket. Playing on too many outgrounds in 2nd XI cricket.'

Best batting: 12 Surrey v Durham, Riverside 2000

Best bowling: 2-45 Surrey v Derbyshire, Derby 1999

2000 Season

	M	Inns	NO	Runs	HS	Avge	100s	50s	Ct	St	O	M	Runs	Wkts	Avge	Best	5wI	10wM
Test																		
All First	2	3	0	14	12	4.66	-	-	-	-	29	8	98	2	49.00	1-24	-	-
1-day Int																		
NatWest																		
B & H	2	0	0	0	0	-	-	-	1	-	11	3	44	2	22.00	2-22	-	
1-day Lge	2	0	0	0	0	-	-	-	-	-	12	1	48	1	48.00	1-22	-	

Career Performances

	M	Inns	NO	Runs	HS	Avge	100s	50s	Ct	St	Balls	Runs	Wkts	Avge	Best	5wI	10wM
Test																	
All First	7	10	4	25	12	4.16	-	-	4	-	690	376	7	53.71	2-45	-	-
1-day Int																	
NatWest	1	1	1	1	1 *	-	-	-	-	-	42	27	0	-	-	-	
B & H	2	0	0	0	0	-	-	-	1	-	66	44	2	22.00	2-22	-	
1-day Lge	10	6	5	23	15 *	23.00	-	-	-	-	457	291	12	24.25	4-34	-	

BISHOP, J. E.   Essex

Name: <u>Justin</u> Edward Bishop
Role: Left-hand middle order bat, left-arm
fast-medium opening bowler
Born: 4 January 1982, Bury St Edmunds
Height: 6ft **Weight:** 13st 2lbs
Nickname: Bish, Bash, Basher, Harold,
Madge
County debut: 1999
Strike rate: (career 86.00)
Parents: Keith and Anne
Marital status: Girlfriend
Family links with cricket: 'Dad plays for
Bury St Edmunds and used to play for
Suffolk'
Education: Ickworth Park Primary School,
Bury St Edmunds; Horringer Court Middle
School; County Upper School, Bury St
Edmunds; Durham University (September
2001)

Qualifications: GCSEs, 1 A-level (PE), GNVQ (Advanced) Science, Level 1 coaching
award
Off-season: England U19 tour to India; getting fit and working for local brewery
Greene King
Overseas tours: England U19 to Malaysia and (Youth World Cup) Sri Lanka
1999-2000, to India 2000-01
Cricketers particularly admired: Mark Ilott ('ability to swing ball back into
right-handers')
Young players to look out for: John Sadler, Chris Nash, Nicky Peng, Jimmy Lofts,
Marco Jeeves, Stuart Fisherman
Other sports played: 'I enjoy an occasional game of golf or snooker'
Other sports followed: Football (Ipswich Town FC)
Relaxations: 'Watching "the Town" win and/or the "Budgies" (NCFC) lose'
Extras: Played football for Suffolk U15 and Bury Town U18. Opening bowler for
England U15 1997. Took 7-42 for England U19 in Sri Lanka U19 first innings in third
'Test' at Worcester, August 2000
Best batting: 17 Essex v Sri Lanka A, Chelmsford 1999
Best bowling: 2-89 Essex v Sri Lanka A, Chelmsford 1999
Stop press: Took 5-64 in India U19's first innings in the third U19 'Test' at
Hyderabad

2000 Season

	M	Inns	NO	Runs	HS	Avge	100s	50s	Ct	St	O	M	Runs	Wkts	Avge	Best	5wI	10wM
Test																		
All First																		
1-day Int																		
NatWest	1	1	0	0	0	0.00	-	-	-	-	7	0	17	1	17.00	1-17	-	
B & H																		
1-day Lge	2	2	2	17	16 *	-	-	-	-	-	4	0	29	1	29.00	1-29	-	

Career Performances

	M	Inns	NO	Runs	HS	Avge	100s	50s	Ct	St	Balls	Runs	Wkts	Avge	Best	5wI	10wM
Test																	
All First	2	1	0	17	17	17.00	-	-	-	-	258	180	3	60.00	2-89	-	-
1-day Int																	
NatWest	1	1	0	0	0	0.00	-	-	-	-	42	17	1	17.00	1-17	-	
B & H																	
1-day Lge	3	3	2	18	16 *	18.00	-	-	-	-	42	53	1	53.00	1-29	-	

BLACKWELL, I. D.   Somerset

Name: Ian David Blackwell
Role: Left-hand bat, slow left-arm bowler
Born: 10 June 1978, Chesterfield
Height: 6ft 2in **Weight:** 16st
Nickname: Blackie, Triflay, Trifle, Pip, Yuf
County debut: 1997 (Derbyshire),
2000 (Somerset)
1st-Class 50s: 6
1st-Class 100s: 1
1st-Class 5 w. in innings: 1
1st-Class catches: 18
Place in batting averages: 115th av. 27.71
(1999 154th av. 24.78)
Place in bowling averages: 138th av. 43.91
(1999 143rd av. 49.58)
Strike rate: 107.34 (career 102.35)
Parents: John and Marilyn
Marital status: Engaged to Clare
Family links with cricket: Father played locally and for Derbyshire Over 50s
Education: Old Hall Primary School; Manor Community School (GCSEs); Brookfield
Community School (A-levels)
Qualifications: 8 GCSEs, 1 A-level, NCA senior coaching award

Off-season: 'Training hard with Daz or Shiney and Bully Swarge'
Overseas teams played for: Delacombe Park CC, Melbourne, Australia 1997, 1999
Cricketers particularly admired: Phillip DeFreitas, Jamie Cox, Steffan Jones, Andrew Caddick, Marcus Trescothick, Matt Bulbeck, Andy Harris, Adrian Rollins
Players to look out for: Matt Bulbeck ('at darts'), Jamie Grove, 'Big Tony' Dorigo, Steve Stubbings
Other sports played: Golf, football ('the Spirettes'), 'gnip gnop with the Swully Barge', any sports
Other sports followed: Football (Chesterfield FC)
Relaxations: PlayStation, using Internet; 'trying to control Little Maximus, playing cards with Dr Manbreast, Closet, Oafe and Yuf'
Extras: Played for Derbyshire from the age of eight through to the 2nd XI. Set record for number of balls lost (7) in a score of 213 not out at Bolsover, which included 23 fours and 15 sixes and equalled the Bassetlaw League 1A record. Left Derbyshire at end of 1999 season and joined Somerset for 2000 on a three-year contract. Scored maiden first-class century (109) v Leicestershire at Taunton 2000
Opinions on cricket: 'Having two divisions has increased competition towards the end of the season as promotion and relegation loom. Central contracts are a good idea and have worked.'
Best batting: 109 Somerset v Leicestershire, Taunton 2000
Best bowling: 5-115 Derbyshire v Surrey, The Oval 1998

2000 Season

	M	Inns	NO	Runs	HS	Avge	100s	50s	Ct	St	O	M	Runs	Wkts	Avge	Best	5wI	10wM
Test																		
All First	18	23	2	582	109	27.71	1	2	6	-	411.3	123	1010	23	43.91	4-18	-	-
1-day Int																		
NatWest	2	2	0	33	32	16.50	-	-	-	-	11	0	47	2	23.50	1-20	-	
B & H	3	2	0	44	41	22.00	-	-	1	-	4	0	29	0	-	-	-	
1-day Lge	16	15	2	267	50 *	20.53	-	1	8	-	105.3	2	478	13	36.76	4-36	-	

Career Performances

	M	Inns	NO	Runs	HS	Avge	100s	50s	Ct	St	Balls	Runs	Wkts	Avge	Best	5wI	10wM
Test																	
All First	43	62	4	1234	109	21.27	1	6	18	-	5220	2356	51	46.19	5-115	1	-
1-day Int																	
NatWest	5	5	1	40	32	10.00	-	-	-	-	216	149	5	29.80	2-34	-	
B & H	8	6	1	90	41	18.00	-	-	3	-	54	67	0	-	-	-	
1-day Lge	37	34	4	724	97	24.13	-	4	13	-	1124	857	30	28.56	4-36	-	

BLAIN, J. A. R.   Northamptonshire

Name: <u>John</u> Angus Rae Blain
Role: Right-hand bat, right-arm
fast-medium bowler
Born: 4 January 1979, Edinburgh
Height: 6ft 2in **Weight:** 13st 7lbs
Nickname: Blainey, Haggis, Hag
County debut: 1997
One-Day Internationals: 5
1st-Class catches: 3
One-Day 5 w. in innings: 1
Strike rate: 132.00 (career 148.00)
Parents: John and Elma
Marital status: Single
Education: Eastfield Primary School;
Penicuik HS; Jewel and Esk Valley College
Qualifications: 8 GCSEs, 1 A-level, HNC
Leisure and Recreation, Level 1 coaching
award

Career outside cricket: 'Maybe some coaching but no other career'
Off-season: 'Spending it mostly at home. May opt to go away after Christmas'
Overseas tours: Northants CCC to Zimbabwe 1997; Scotland U19 to Holland
(International Youth Tournament) 1994-95, to Bermuda (International Youth
Tournament) 1997, to South Africa (Youth World Cup) 1997-98 (captain); Scotland
to Denmark (European Championships) 1996, to Malaysia (ICC Trophy) 1997,
to Malaysia (Commonwealth Games) 1998, to Sharjah 1999
Overseas teams played for: New Plymouth Old Boys, New Zealand 1998-99;
Taranaki Cricket Association, New Zealand 1998-99
Cricketers particularly admired: Devon Malcolm, Steve Waugh
Young players to look out for: Mark Powell
Other sports played: Football (schoolboy forms with Hibernian FC and Falkirk FC,
making youth and reserve team appearances), golf
Other sports followed: Football (Hibernian FC)
Injuries: Out to June 2000 after fusion operation on back in September 1999
Relaxations: 'Listening to music, going out for a drink, going back to Scotland to
spend time with family; watching football, going to the gym and sleeping!'
Extras: Was youngest ever player to play for Scotland national side at 17 years and
114 days. Played for Scotland in the Benson and Hedges and NatWest competitions.
Made his first-class debut for Scotland against Ireland in 1996. Captained Scotland
U19 at U19 World Cup in South Africa 1997-98. Took 5 for 24 on Sunday League
debut for Northants against Derbyshire 1997. Represented Scotland in the 1999 World
Cup, taking 10 wickets and finishing top of the strike rate chart for the tournament

Opinions on cricket: 'The two divisional set-up has been a very beneficial move, creating more competitiveness. Young players expect too much too early once a little success has been gained. There is no substitute for hard work. Second XI cricket should be played at first-class venues more often, where possible. Too many times facilities and wickets are substandard. I prepare myself professionally to play and expect to have professional standards. It sometimes makes the step to first class a little harder.'

Best batting: 31* Northamptonshire v Oxford Universities, The Parks 2000
Best bowling: 1-18 Northamptonshire v Worcestershire, Northampton 1997

2000 Season

	M	Inns	NO	Runs	HS	Avge	100s	50s	Ct	St	O	M	Runs	Wkts	Avge	Best	5wl	10wM
Test																		
All First	1	1	1	31	31*	-	-	-	1	-	22	3	74	1	74.00	1-37	-	-
1-day Int																		
NatWest																		
B & H																		
1-day Lge																		

Career Performances

	M	Inns	NO	Runs	HS	Avge	100s	50s	Ct	St	Balls	Runs	Wkts	Avge	Best	5wl	10wM
Test																	
All First	4	2	1	31	31*	31.00	-	-	3	-	444	282	3	94.00	1-18	-	-
1-day Int	5	5	1	15	9	3.75	-	-	1	-	223	210	10	21.00	4-37	-	
NatWest	1	0	0	0	0	-	-	-	1	-	66	56	2	28.00	2-56	-	
B & H	3	2	1	14	10*	14.00	-	-	-	-	90	140	3	46.66	2-82	-	
1-day Lge	3	0	0	0	0	-	-	-	1	-	144	110	7	15.71	5-24	1	

BLAKEY, R. J. Yorkshire

Name: <u>Richard</u> John Blakey
Role: Right-hand bat, wicket-keeper
Born: 15 January 1967, Huddersfield
Height: 5ft 10in **Weight:** 11st 4lbs
Nickname: Dick
County debut: 1985
County cap: 1987
Benefit: 1998
Test debut: 1992-93
Tests: 2
One-Day Internationals: 3
1000 runs in a season: 4
50 dismissals in a season: 5
1st-Class 50s: 75
1st-Class 100s: 9
1st-Class 200s: 2
1st-Class catches: 668
1st-Class stumpings: 50
One-Day 100s: 3

Place in batting averages: 225th av. 15.52 (1999 147th av. 25.33)
Strike rate: (career 63.00)
Parents: Brian and Pauline
Wife and date of marriage: Michelle, 28 September 1991
Children: Harrison Brad, 22 September 1993
Family links with cricket: Father played local cricket
Education: Woodhouse Primary; Rastrick Grammar School
Qualifications: 4 O-levels, Senior NCA Coach
Career outside cricket: Started own leisure company
Overseas tours: England YC to West Indies 1984-85; Yorkshire to Barbados 1986-87, to Cape Town 1990-91; England A to Zimbabwe and Kenya 1989-90, to Pakistan 1990-91; England to India and Sri Lanka 1992-93
Overseas teams played for: Waverley, Sydney 1985-87; Mt Waverley, Sydney 1987-88; Bionics, Zimbabwe 1989-90
Cricketers particularly admired: Martyn Moxon, Dermot Reeve, Ian Botham, Alan Knott
Other sports followed: All
Relaxations: All sports, particularly golf and squash, eating out, drawing, photography
Extras: Established himself in Huddersfield League. Made record 2nd XI score – 273* v Northamptonshire 1986. Yorkshire's Young Player of the Year 1989. He was awarded a citation by the International Committee for Fair Play in 1995, the only cricketer among the 25 winners worldwide

Best batting: 221 England A v Zimbabwe, Bulawayo 1989-90
Best bowling: 1-68 Yorkshire v Nottinghamshire, Sheffield 1986

2000 Season

	M	Inns	NO	Runs	HS	Avge	100s	50s	Ct	St	O	M	Runs	Wkts	Avge	Best	5wI	10wM
Test																		
All First	12	18	1	264	56	15.52	-	1	41	2								
1-day Int																		
NatWest	2	2	0	41	41	20.50	-	-	-	-								
B & H	6	6	1	130	35	26.00	-	-	6	-								
1-day Lge	16	12	1	290	62	26.36	-	1	21	5								

Career Performances

	M	Inns	NO	Runs	HS	Avge	100s	50s	Ct	St	Balls	Runs	Wkts	Avge	Best	5wI	10wM
Test	2	4	0	7	6	1.75	-	-	2	-							
All First	304	485	72	12760	221	30.89	11	75	668	50	63	68	1	68.00	1-68	-	-
1-day Int	3	2	0	25	25	12.50	-	-	2	1							
NatWest	35	28	10	459	75	25.50	-	2	36	2							
B & H	61	53	13	1153	80 *	28.82	-	6	59	3							
1-day Lge	199	175	38	4766	130 *	34.78	3	25	187	35							

12. Who scored 307 in Australia's only innings in the
fifth Test at Melbourne in 1965-66?

BLEWETT, G.S.   Nottinghamshire

Name: Gregory (<u>Greg</u>) Scott Blewett
Role: Right-hand bat, right-arm
medium bowler
Born: 28 October 1971, Adelaide
Height: 6ft **Weight:** 11st
Nickname: Blewy
County debut: 1999 (Yorkshire)
County cap: 1999 (Yorkshire)
Test debut: 1994-95
Tests: 46
One-Day Internationals: 32
1st-Class 50s: 56
1st-Class 100s: 24
1st-Class 200s: 3
1st-Class 5 w. in innings: 1
1st-Class catches: 115
Place in batting averages: (1999 98th
av. 31.19)
Strike rate: (career 80.34)

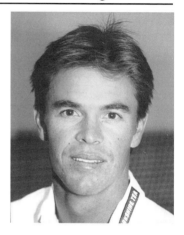

Parents: Bob and Shirley
Wife and date of marriage: Jodie, 26 June 1998
Family links with cricket: Father played for South Australia
Education: Angaston Primary School, Adelaide; Prince Alfred College, Adelaide
Overseas tours: Australian Institute of Sport to Sri Lanka 1990-91; Australia U19
to England 1991; Australia to West Indies 1994-95, to South Africa 1996-97,
to England 1997, to India 1997-98, to West Indies 1998-99, to Sri Lanka 1999-2000,
to Zimbabwe 1999-2000, to New Zealand 1999-2000
Overseas teams played for: Kensington, Adelaide; South Australia 1991-92 –
Cricketers particularly admired: Greg Chappell, Gordon Greenidge, Viv Richards
Other sports played: Golf
Other sports followed: Australian Football League (Adelaide Crows)
Relaxations: Golf, films, socialising
Extras: Scored centuries (102* and 115) in his first two Test matches, v England at
Adelaide and Perth in 1994-95. Scored 214 at Johannesburg 1996-97, sharing in record
fifth-wicket partnership for Australia in Tests v South Africa, 385 with Steve Waugh.
Was due to play for Middlesex in 1997 but was selected for Ashes tour. Was the only
Australian to make 1000 Test runs in 1997 calendar year. Holds the unenviable record
of being the first Australian to be out for 99 twice in Test cricket. In 1998-99, made
1175 first-class runs (av. 146.86 and including five 100s and a 200) before Christmas
in the Australian season, breaking David Hookes' record of 1163 set in 1982-83 and
becoming only the sixth Australian to score four consecutive first-class 100s. Averaged

118.70 in full Australian first-class season 1998-99. Joined Yorkshire as overseas player for 1999 season; released by Yorkshire at end of 1999 season. Awarded ACB contract for 2000-01. Has joined Nottinghamshire as overseas player for 2001
Best batting: 268 South Australia v Victoria, Melbourne 1993-94
Best bowling: 5-29 Australian XI v West Indies, Hobart 1996-97
Stop press: Made match-saving 260* in 10 hours 29 minutes after South Australia had been forced to follow on v Queensland at Brisbane in the Pura Milk Cup

2000 Season (did not make any first-class or one-day appearances)

Career Performances

	M	Inns	NO	Runs	HS	Avge	100s	50s	Ct	St	Balls	Runs	Wkts	Avge	Best	5wI	10wM
Test	46	79	4	2552	214	34.02	4	15	45	-	1436	720	14	51.42	2-9	-	-
All First	154	271	18	11154	268	44.08	27	56	115	-	8034	4141	100	41.41	5-29	1	-
1-day Int	32	30	3	551	57 *	20.40	-	2	7	-	749	646	14	46.14	2-6	-	
NatWest	3	3	0	83	77	27.66	-	1	1	-	100	57	7	8.14	4-18	-	
B & H	3	3	0	84	71	28.00	-	1	-	-	18	23	0	-	-	-	
1-day Lge	11	11	0	178	48	16.18	-	-	6	-	151	116	4	29.00	1-14	-	

BLOOMFIELD, T. F.   Middlesex

Name: Timothy (Tim) Francis Bloomfield
Role: Right-hand bat, right-arm
fast-medium bowler
Born: 31 May 1973, Ashford, Middlesex
Height: 6ft 2in **Weight:** 14st
Nickname: Bloomers, Boof, Frank
County debut: 1997
1st-Class 5 w. in innings: 4
1st-Class catches: 4
Place in batting averages: 307th av. 2.66
(1999 273rd av. 10.00)
Place in bowling averages: 114th av. 36.26
(1999 99th av. 30.51)
Strike rate: 58.04 (career 48.97)
Parents: Richard and Pauline
Marital status: Engaged to Emma
Education: Staines Preparatory School;
Halliford Independent School
Qualifications: 8 GCSEs, NCA coaching award
Off-season: Training; MCC tour to Sri Lanka

Overseas tours: Berkshire U25 to Barbados 1996; Middlesex to South Africa 2000; MCC to Sri Lanka 2001
Cricketers particularly admired: Ian Botham, Viv Richards, Angus Fraser
Young players to look out for: John Maunders, Alan Coleman
Other sports played: Football, golf, tennis, snooker
Other sports followed: Football (Liverpool)
Relaxations: Sport, music
Extras: Has also played for Sussex 2nd XI and Berkshire. Took 4-17 v Somerset at Southgate in the NatWest 2000, winning the Man of the Match award
Opinions on cricket: 'We play too much cricket. The powers-that-be need to be more forward thinking.'
Best batting: 20* Middlesex v Sussex, Hove 1998
Best bowling: 5-36 Middlesex v Glamorgan, Cardiff 1999

2000 Season

	M	Inns	NO	Runs	HS	Avge	100s	50s	Ct	St	O	M	Runs	Wkts	Avge	Best	5wI	10wM
Test																		
All First	10	8	2	16	4*	2.66	-	-	1	-	222.3	35	834	23	36.26	4-46	-	-
1-day Int																		
NatWest	1	0	0	0	0	-	-	-	-	-	8	1	17	4	4.25	4-17	-	
B & H																		
1-day Lge	4	2	2	4	3*	-	-	-	-	-	20	1	65	3	21.66	1-20	-	

Career Performances

	M	Inns	NO	Runs	HS	Avge	100s	50s	Ct	St	Balls	Runs	Wkts	Avge	Best	5wI	10wM
Test																	
All First	33	38	18	137	20*	6.85	-	-	4	-	4457	2759	91	30.31	5-36	4	-
1-day Int																	
NatWest	5	2	1	7	7*	7.00	-	-	-	-	216	140	6	23.33	4-17	-	
B & H	2	0	0	0	0	-	-	-	-	-	84	90	0	-	-	-	
1-day Lge	22	6	3	31	15	10.33	-	-	4	-	864	678	21	32.28	2-8	-	

BOSWELL, S. A. J.   Leicestershire

Name: <u>Scott</u> Antony John Boswell
Role: Right-hand bat, right-arm fast-medium bowler
Born: 11 September 1974, Fulford, York
Height: 6ft 4in **Weight:** 14st 2lbs
Nickname: Bossy, Joey, Grandad
County debut: 1995 (one-day, Northants),
1996 (first-class, Northants), 1999 (Leicestershire)
1st-Class 5 w. in innings: 1

1st-Class catches: 4
Strike rate: 62.44 (career 66.52)
Parents: Tony and Judy
Marital status: Single
Education: Ebor Prep School; Pocklington
School; Wolverhampton University
('Wolly Poly')
Qualifications: 9 GCSEs, 3 A-levels
Overseas tours: Northamptonshire to
Zimbabwe 1998
Overseas teams played for: Hutt Valley,
New Zealand 1994-95; Koeburg CC,
South Africa 1997-98
Cricketers particularly admired: Richard
Hadlee ('for his dedication')
Young players to look out for: Graeme
Swann, Mike Davies
Other sports played: Rugby ('toured
Zimbabwe in '92 with school')

Other sports followed: Football (York City), rugby (York)
Relaxations: Watching TV, socialising and spending time with friends
Extras: Attended Dennis Lillee's Pace Foundation in India 1996. Released by
Northamptonshire at end of 1998 season and joined Leicestershire for 1999. Made
Championship debut for Leics against his former county at Northampton 1999
Best batting: 35 Northamptonshire v Leicestershire, Northampton 1997
Best bowling: 5-94 Northamptonshire v Worcestershire, Northampton 1997

2000 Season

	M	Inns	NO	Runs	HS	Avge	100s	50s	Ct	St	O	M	Runs	Wkts	Avge	Best	5wI	10wM
Test																		
All First	5	7	3	63	20	15.75	-	-	-	-	93.4	21	278	9	30.88	3-39	-	-
1-day Int																		
NatWest																		
B & H																		
1-day Lge	4	1	1	5	5 *	-	-	-	-	-	27	1	109	6	18.16	3-38	-	

Career Performances

	M	Inns	NO	Runs	HS	Avge	100s	50s	Ct	St	Balls	Runs	Wkts	Avge	Best	5wI	10wM
Test																	
All First	20	27	9	229	35	12.72	-	-	4	-	2395	1504	36	41.77	5-94	1	-
1-day Int																	
NatWest																	
B & H	10	6	1	24	14	4.80	-	-	1	-	536	485	6	80.83	3-39	-	
1-day Lge	10	3	2	7	5 *	7.00	-	-	-	-	378	270	11	24.54	3-38	-	

BOULTON, N. R. Worcestershire

Name: <u>Nicholas</u> Ross Boulton
Role: Left-hand bat, right-arm slow-medium
bowler
Born: 22 March 1979, Johannesburg,
South Africa
Height: 6ft 1in **Weight:** 12st 6lbs
Nickname: Boults
County debut: 1997 (Somerset)
Parents: Michael and Pauline
Marital status: Single
Education: Ridge School, Johannesburg;
King's School, Taunton
Overseas tours: King's School 1st XI
to Australia 1995, to South Africa 1997
Overseas teams played for: Wanderers CC,
Johannesburg 1996-98
Other sports followed: Hockey, rugby, golf,
flyfishing, football (Liverpool FC)
Relaxations: Flyfishing, reading, going back to South Africa
Extras: Awarded Holmwoods Schoolboy Cricketer of the Year. Played ESCA U19 and
Transvaal U14. Formerly with Somerset
Best batting: 14 Somerset v Pakistan A, Taunton 1997

2000 Season (did not make any first-class or one-day appearances)

Career Performances

	M	Inns	NO	Runs	HS	Avge	100s	50s	Ct	St	Balls	Runs	Wkts	Avge	Best	5wl	10wM
Test																	
All First	1	2	0	15	14	7.50	-	-	-	-							
1-day Int																	
NatWest																	
B & H																	
1-day Lge																	

BOWEN, M. N.   Nottinghamshire

Name: <u>Mark</u> Nicholas Bowen
Role: Right-hand bat, right-arm
medium bowler
Born: 6 December 1967, Redcar
Height: 6ft 2in **Weight:** 13st 7lbs
Nickname: Bully, Bert, Jim, Grandad, Buster
County debut: 1991-92 (Northamptonshire),
1996 (Nottinghamshire)
County cap: 1997 (Nottinghamshire)
1st-Class 5 w. in innings: 7
1st-Class 10 w. in match: 1
1st-Class catches: 17
Place in batting averages: 238th av. 13.83
(1999 272nd av. 10.00)
Place in bowling averages: (1999 48th
av. 23.56)
Strike rate: 102.00 (career 60.12)
Parents: Keith

Wife and date of marriage: Lesley, 11 October 1997
Family links with cricket: 'Father always played; keen supporter'
Education: St Mary's Junior School, Redcar; Sacred Heart Secondary School, Redcar;
St Mary's Sixth Form College, Middlesbrough; Teesside Polytechnic, Middlesbrough
Qualifications: 8 O-levels, 3 A-levels, BEng (Hons) Chemical Engineering
Career outside cricket: Chemical engineer
Overseas tours: Christians in Sport to Zimbabwe 1994-95; Northamptonshire to
Durban 1992, to Cape Town 1993; Nottinghamshire CCC to Johannesburg 1996-99
Cricketers particularly admired: Ian Botham, Dennis Lillee, Viv Richards
Young players to look out for: Usman Afzaal, Paul Franks, Matt Whiley
Other sports played: Golf ('regularly take Franks and Randall to the cleaners'),
hockey (played for Durham County)
Other sports followed: Football (Middlesbrough FC), rugby
Injuries: Out for two weeks with back injury ('slipped on stairs')
Relaxations: 'Watching TV, DIY, keeping fit, and a good pint of ale'
Extras: Made debut for Northants first team in Natal on 1991-92 tour to South Africa
before playing in the 2nd XI. Released by Northamptonshire at the end of the 1995
season and joined Nottinghamshire for the start of the 1996 season. Retired at the end
of the 2000 season to become a full-time engineer with British Nuclear Fuels
Opinions on cricket: 'I would like to thank the players and staff of Northants and
primarily Nottinghamshire who have made my nine years as a professional very
enjoyable. Thanks for the friendship and support you have offered, and I wish you all
all the best for the future.'

Best batting: 32 Nottinghamshire v Northamptonshire, Northampton 1997
Best bowling: 7-73 Nottinghamshire v Somerset, Taunton 1998

2000 Season

	M	Inns	NO	Runs	HS	Avge	100s	50s	Ct	St	O	M	Runs	Wkts	Avge	Best	5wI	10wM
Test																		
All First	4	6	0	83	24	13.83	-	-	2	-	68	14	208	4	52.00	2-47	-	-
1-day Int																		
NatWest																		
B & H																		
1-day Lge	4	3	0	48	31	16.00	-	-	-	-	25	0	119	3	39.66	2-49	-	

Career Performances

	M	Inns	NO	Runs	HS	Avge	100s	50s	Ct	St	Balls	Runs	Wkts	Avge	Best	5wI	10wM
Test																	
All First	67	92	26	817	32	12.37	-	-	17	-	11003	5925	183	32.37	7-73	7	1
1-day Int																	
NatWest	4	3	2	12	8*	12.00	-	-	2	-	180	129	6	21.50	3-32	-	
B & H	5	3	1	10	9	5.00	-	-	-	-	265	194	5	38.80	2-40	-	
1-day Lge	60	27	12	254	31	16.93	-	-	12	-	2311	2055	63	32.61	4-29	-	

BOWLER, P. D.   Somerset

Name: Peter Duncan Bowler
Role: Right-hand opening bat, occasional
off-spin bowler, occasional wicket-keeper
Born: 30 July 1963, Plymouth
Height: 6ft 2in **Weight:** 13st 10lbs
Nickname: Tom
County debut: 1986 (Leicestershire),
1988 (Derbyshire), 1995 (Somerset)
County cap: 1989 (Derbyshire),
1995 (Somerset)
Benefit: 2000 (Somerset)
1000 runs in a season: 9
1st-Class 50s: 82
1st-Class 100s: 37
1st-Class 200s: 3
1st-Class catches: 174
1st-Class stumpings: 1
One-Day 100s: 5
Place in batting averages: 6th av. 62.14 (1999 11th av. 49.00)

Strike rate: (career 97.33)
Parents: Peter and Etta
Wife and date of marriage: Joanne, 10 October 1992
Children: Peter Robert, 21 September 1993; Rebekah, 25 August 1995
Education: Scots College, Sydney, Australia; Daramalan College, Canberra, Australia; Nottingham Trent University
Qualifications: Australian Year 12 certificate, LLB
Cricketers particularly admired: Gus Valence, Rob Jeffery, Bill Carracher, Phil Russell
Young players to look out for: Matthew Bulbeck, Nick Boulton
Other sports followed: Rugby union
Relaxations: Family and reading
Extras: First Leicestershire player to score a first-class century on debut (100* v Hampshire 1986). Moved to Derbyshire at end of 1987 season and scored a hundred on his debut v Cambridge University in 1988. His 241* v Hampshire at Portsmouth 1992 is the highest score by a Derbyshire No. 1. First batsman to 2000 runs in 1992, finishing equal leading run-scorer (2044) with Mike Roseberry of Middlesex. Derbyshire Player of the Year 1992. Signed a five-year contract with Somerset starting in 1995. Took over the Somerset captaincy mid-season 1997 after Andy Hayhurst was released. Relinquished captaincy after 1998 season. Passed 5000 runs in Sunday/National League, v Durham 1999. Has set up a sports management agency with Nottinghamshire's John Morris. Top-scoring English batsman in first-class cricket in his benefit season (2000) with 1305 runs (av. 62.14)
Best batting: 241* Derbyshire v Hampshire, Portsmouth 1992
Best bowling: 3-25 Somerset v Northamptonshire, Taunton 1998

2000 Season

	M	Inns	NO	Runs	HS	Avge	100s	50s	Ct	St	O	M	Runs	Wkts	Avge	Best	5wI	10wM
Test																		
All First	18	26	5	1305	157 *	62.14	5	4	8	-								
1-day Int																		
NatWest	2	2	0	8	8	4.00	-	-	1	-								
B & H																		
1-day Lge	14	13	0	321	69	24.69	-	2	1	-								

Career Performances

	M	Inns	NO	Runs	HS	Avge	100s	50s	Ct	St	Balls	Runs	Wkts	Avge	Best	5wI	10wM
Test																	
All First	265	453	48	16463	241 *	40.64	40	82	174	1	3212	2009	33	60.87	3-25	-	-
1-day Int																	
NatWest	26	26	0	708	111	27.23	1	3	12	-	36	26	0	-	-	-
B & H	50	49	1	1449	109	30.18	2	11	21	1	309	182	5	36.40	1-15	-
1-day Lge	196	189	19	5567	138 *	32.74	2	45	71	1	308	323	8	40.37	3-31	-

BRESSINGTON, A. N.　　　　　Gloucestershire

Name: <u>Alastair</u> Nigel Bressington
Role: Left-hand bat, right-arm fast-medium bowler; all-rounder
Born: 28 November 1979, Bristol
Height: 6ft 1in **Weight:** 14st
Nickname: Magic, Bressy
County debut: 2000
1st-Class catches: 1
Strike rate: 24.00 (career 24.00)
Parents: Adrian and Marjorie
Marital status: Single
Family links with cricket: Brother Nathan plays for county 2nd XI
Education: Croft School, Painswick; Marling Grammar School, Stroud; UWIC
Qualifications: 12 GCSEs, 4 A-levels
Career outside cricket: Student
Off-season: University
Cricketers particularly admired: Jack Russell, Ian Botham
Other sports played: Rugby (Gloucestershire Colts; Gloucester RFC U21; Newbury – National Division 3)
Other sports followed: Rugby (Bristol RFC), football (Liverpool FC)
Relaxations: Music, reading
Extras: Played for Gloucestershire Board XI in the NatWest 1999 and 2000. Took wicket with third ball in first-class cricket and took five wickets in debut match, including that of Matthew Maynard
Best batting: 2* Gloucestershire v Glamorgan, Bristol 2000
Best bowling: 4-36 Gloucestershire v Glamorgan, Bristol 2000

2000 Season

	M	Inns	NO	Runs	HS	Avge	100s	50s	Ct	St	O	M	Runs	Wkts	Avge	Best	5wI	10wM
Test																		
All First	1	1	1	2	2*	-	-	-	1	-	20	6	49	5	9.80	4-36	-	-
1-day Int																		
NatWest	2	1	0	44	44	44.00	-	-	2	-	19	2	51	4	12.75	3-21	-	
B & H																		
1-day Lge																		

Career Performances

	M	Inns	NO	Runs	HS	Avge	100s	50s	Ct	St	Balls	Runs	Wkts	Avge	Best	5wl	10wM
Test																	
All First	1	1	1	2	2*	-	-	-	1	-	120	49	5	9.80	4-36	-	-
1-day Int																	
NatWest	3	2	0	98	54	49.00	-	1	2	-	150	86	5	17.20	3-21	-	
B & H																	
1-day Lge																	

BRIDGE, G. D.   Durham

Name: <u>Graeme</u> David Bridge
Role: Right-hand bat, slow left-arm bowler
Born: 4 September 1980, Sunderland
Height: 5ft 8in **Weight:** 12st
Nickname: Bridgey, Crag, Brog
County debut: 1999
1st-Class catches: 1
Strike rate: (career 264.00)
Parents: Anne and John
Marital status: Engaged
Family links with cricket: 'Dad played village cricket'
Education: Ryhope Junior School; Southmoor School
Qualifications: 4 GCSEs
Off-season: 'Working'
Overseas tours: England U19 to New Zealand 1998-99, to Malaysia and (Youth World Cup) Sri Lanka 1999-2000

Cricketers particularly admired: Mark Waugh, Phil Tufnell
Young players to look out for: Mark Wallace, Ian Bell, Nicky Peng
Other sports played: Local football
Other sports followed: Football (Sunderland AFC)
Relaxations: Socialising
Extras: Represented England U19 in the one-day series v Australia U19 1999
Opinions on cricket: 'Tea break should be longer.'
Best batting: 6 Durham v Surrey, The Oval 1999
Best bowling: 1-60 Durham v Surrey, The Oval 1999

2000 Season (did not make any first-class or one-day appearances)

Career Performances

	M	Inns	NO	Runs	HS	Avge	100s	50s	Ct	St	Balls	Runs	Wkts	Avge	Best	5wI	10wM
Test																	
All First	1	2	0	11	6	5.50	-	-	1	-	264	110	1	110.00	1-60	-	-
1-day Int																	
NatWest	3	2	1	24	15	24.00	-	-	1	-	162	123	1	123.00	1-49	-	
B & H																	
1-day Lge																	

BRINKLEY, J. E. Durham

Name: <u>James</u> Edward Brinkley
Role: Right-hand bat, right-arm medium-fast bowler
Born: 13 March 1974, Helensburgh, Scotland
Height: 6ft 3in **Weight:** 15st 11lbs
Nickname: JB, Sweat Monster
County debut: 1993-94 (Worcestershire), 1998 (one-day, Essex)
One-Day Internationals: 5
1st-Class catches: 8
1st-Class 5 w. in innings: 2
Strike rate: 50.75 (career 62.86)
Parents: Tom and Sharon
Wife and date of marriage:
Kim, 11 October 1997
Family links with cricket: 'Brother plays club cricket in Worcester and Dad played for the Navy'

Education: Marist College, Canberra; Trinity College, Perth; Manchester Metropolitan University
Qualifications: Fitness instructor, cricket and rugby coach, 'three years into a BSc Sports Science'
Career outside cricket: PE teacher at The Grange and RGS Worcester
Off-season: 'Hopefully back to teaching and spending some time with my wife and the baby that is due in May'
Overseas tours: Worcestershire to Zimbabwe 1993-94, to Barbados 1996; Scotland to Malaysia (Commonwealth Games) 1998, to Sharjah 1999, to Zimbabwe 2000
Overseas teams played for: Scarborough, Perth 1990-93; Western Australian U19 1993; Matabeleland, Zimbabwe 1994-95

Cricketers particularly admired: Glenn McGrath, Darren Gough, 'Dod, Badger and Asim'

Young players to look out for: Thomas Williams ('shame he is Welsh!')

Other sports played: Rugby union, golf

Other sports followed: Rugby union (Worcester RFC)

Relaxations: Good movies, sports science (psychology), 'getting my 2000m rowing time lower'

Extras: Took a hat-trick in both the 2nd XI Championship and the Bain Clarkson Trophy, against Surrey and Somerset respectively. Made first-class debut on Worcestershire tour of Zimbabwe 1993-94. Took 6-98 (the top six) for Worcestershire v Surrey at The Oval 1994 on County Championship debut, the best debut figures for Worcestershire in the 20th century. Coached Zimbabwe U19 in South African provincial Coca-Cola Cup 1994. Joined Essex for part of 1998 season and was released at end of season. Represented Scotland in the 1999 World Cup. Has also represented Scotland in first-class and NatWest cricket. Played for Herefordshire's ECB 38-County Cup winning side 2000. Scottish born but brought up in Australia, where he attended the same school as Simon Katich. Has joined Durham for 2001

Opinions on cricket: 'Great game!'

Best batting: 43* Scotland v Ireland, Ayr 2000

Best bowling: 6-35 Matabeleland v Mashonaland Country Districts, Harare South 1994-95

2000 Season (did not make any first-class or one-day appearances)

Career Performances

	M	Inns	NO	Runs	HS		Avge	100s	50s	Ct	St	Balls	Runs	Wkts	Avge	Best	5wl	10wM
Test																		
All First	19	22	5	189	43	*	11.11	-	-	8	-	3206	1453	51	28.49	6-35	2	-
1-day Int	5	5	0	52	23		10.40	-	-	1	-	168	117	2	58.50	1-29	-	
NatWest	2	2	0	1	1		0.50	-	-	2	-	102	37	3	12.33	2-13	-	
B & H	11	6	3	45	30	*	15.00	-	-	-	-	518	393	11	35.72	2-35	-	
1-day Lge	5	3	1	7	7		3.50	-	-	-	-	174	141	3	47.00	2-26	-	

---

13. In terms of England v Australia Test rubbers, what was unusual about the 1978-79 three-match series?

BROWN, A. D.   Surrey

Name: <u>Alistair</u> Duncan Brown
Role: Right-hand bat, off-spin bowler, occasional wicket-keeper
Born: 11 February 1970, Beckenham
Height: 5ft 10in **Weight:** 12st 6lbs
Nickname: Lordy
County debut: 1992
County cap: 1994
One-Day Internationals: 12
1000 runs in a season: 5
1st-Class 50s: 35
1st-Class 100s: 22
1st-Class 200s: 2
1st-Class catches: 159
1st-Class stumpings: 1
One-Day 100s: 10
One-Day 200s: 1

Place in batting averages: 12th av. 51.94
(1999 9th av. 51.22)
Strike rate: 168.00 (career 660.00)
Parents: Robert and Ann
Wife and date of marriage: Sarah, 10 October 1998
Family links with cricket: Father played for Surrey Young Amateurs in the 1950s
Education: Cumnor House School; Caterham School; 'David Ward's card school for the technically gifted'
Qualifications: 5 O-levels, NCA Senior Coach
Career outside cricket: 'Actor, thespian and all round good egg'
Off-season: 'Working on my chipping and putting'
Overseas tours: England Six-a-side to Singapore 1993, 1994, 1995, to Hong Kong 1997; England to Sharjah (Champions Trophy) 1997-98, to Bangladesh (Wills International Cup) 1998-99
Overseas teams played for: North Perth, Western Australia 1989-90
Cricketers particularly admired: Ian Botham, Viv Richards
Young players to look out for: Jimmy Ormond
Other sports played: Golf, football, snooker, 'winner of the Lanzarote Open Pool Championship 1990'
Other sports followed: Football (West Ham United), rugby league (London Broncos)
Relaxations: 'Watching Jason Ratcliffe play football and Nadeem Shahid comb his hair'
Extras: Scored three of the eight fastest centuries of the 1992 season (71, 78 & 79 balls). Awarded Man of the Match for 118 against India in the third One-Day

International 1996. Recorded the highest-ever score in the Sunday League with 203 off 119 balls against Hampshire at Guildford in 1997 and received an individual award at the PCA Dinner for that achievement. Scored 72-ball 100 v Northamptonshire to become joint winner (with Carl Hooper) of the EDS Walter Lawrence Trophy for the fastest first-class 100 of the 1998 season. Scored 31-ball 50 v South Africa in the Texaco Trophy match at Headingley 1998, the fastest 50 in the history of the Texaco Trophy

Opinions on cricket: 'Two divisions has improved the standard of first-class cricket – there aren't too many dead games any more. Floodlit cricket is still a must, and perhaps we could get the white ball to do a bit more and then go softer earlier!'

Best batting: 295* Surrey v Leicestershire, Oakham School 2000

Best bowling: 1-56 Surrey v Lancashire, Old Trafford 2000

2000 Season

	M	Inns	NO	Runs	HS	Avge	100s	50s	Ct	St	O	M	Runs	Wkts	Avge	Best	5wI	10wM
Test																		
All First	16	23	5	935	295 *	51.94	2	4	16	-	28	9	70	1	70.00	1-56	-	-
1-day Int																		
NatWest	3	3	0	63	59	21.00	-	1	3	-	1	0	9	0	-		-	-
B & H	4	4	0	34	17	8.50	-	-	2	-								
1-day Lge	14	14	0	330	51	23.57	-	1	6	-	11	0	57	4	14.25	3-39	-	

Career Performances

	M	Inns	NO	Runs	HS	Avge	100s	50s	Ct	St	Balls	Runs	Wkts	Avge	Best	5wI	10wM
Test																	
All First	141	221	24	8726	295 *	44.29	24	35	159	1	660	328	1	328.00	1-56	-	-
1-day Int	12	12	0	327	118	27.25	1	1	4	-							
NatWest	25	22	2	549	72	27.45	-	3	8	-	6	9	0	-		-	-
B & H	42	42	6	1282	117 *	35.61	1	6	12	-							
1-day Lge	151	146	4	4361	203	30.71	9	16	45	-	221	198	7	28.28	3-39	-	

14. Which Australian batsman scored his maiden Test century at Headingley in 1981?

BROWN, D. R. Warwickshire

Name: <u>Douglas</u> Robert Brown
Role: Right-hand bat, right-arm
fast-medium bowler
Born: 29 October 1969, Stirling, Scotland
Height: 6ft 2in **Weight:** 14st 2lbs
Nickname: Bullets, Hoots
County debut: 1992
County cap: 1995
One-Day Internationals: 9
50 wickets in a season: 2
1st-Class 50s: 22
1st-Class 100s: 1
1st-Class 200s: 1
1st-Class 5 w. in innings: 12
1st-Class 10 w. in match: 3
1st-Class catches: 68
One-Day 5 w. in innings: 1

Place in batting averages: 45th av. 38.87
(1999 123rd av. 27.75)
Place in bowling averages: 124th av. 38.20 (1999 72nd av. 27.57)
Strike rate: 67.08 (career 49.17)
Parents: Alastair and Janette
Wife and date of marriage: Brenda, 2 October 1993
Children: Lauren, 14 September 1998
Education: St John's Primary, Alloa; Alloa Academy; West London Institute of Higher
Education (Borough Road College)
Qualifications: 9 O-Grades, 5 Higher Grades, BEd (Hons) Physical Education,
NCA Advanced Coach
Career outside cricket: PE teacher
Overseas tours: Scotland XI to Pakistan 1988-89; England VI to Hong Kong 1997;
England A to Kenya and Sri Lanka 1997-98; England to Sharjah (Champions Trophy)
1997-98, to West Indies 1997-98 (one-day series), to Bangladesh (Wills International
Cup) 1998
Overseas teams played for: Primrose, Cape Town 1992-93; Uredenburg Salohana,
Cape Town 1994; Eastern Suburbs, Wellington 1995-96; Wellington, New Zealand
1995-96
Cricketers particularly admired: 'Everyone who gives 100 per cent for the team's
cause'
Young players to look out for: Tony Frost
Other sports played: Golf
Other sports followed: Football (Alloa Athletic), 'most sports'

Relaxations: Golf, music, 'time with Lauren'
Extras: Played football at Hampden Park for Scotland U18. Played first-class and
B&H cricket for Scotland in 1992. His maiden first-class century v Northants on 15 April 1999 is the earliest
Championship 100 in an English season. Scored maiden double century v Sussex at
Hove 2000 (203; the highest score recorded by a Warwickshire No. 7), during which
he shared in a record Warwickshire partnership for 8th wicket (289 with Ashley Giles)
Opinions on cricket: 'Still a great game.'
Best batting: 203 Warwickshire v Sussex, Hove 2000
Best bowling: 8-89 First-Class Counties v Pakistan A, Chelmsford 1997

2000 Season

	M	Inns	NO	Runs	HS	Avge	100s	50s	Ct	St	O	M	Runs	Wkts	Avge	Best	5wl	10wM
Test																		
All First	16	22	6	622	203	38.87	1	2	11	-	268.2	49	917	24	38.20	5-87	1	-
1-day Int																		
NatWest	5	5	1	27	9	6.75	-	-	1	-	42.4	4	182	7	26.00	2-35	-	
B & H	3	1	0	8	8	8.00	-	-	-	-	8	1	44	0	-		-	-
1-day Lge	15	12	2	226	45 *	22.60	-	-	4	-	117	14	447	25	17.88	3-13	-	

Career Performances

	M	Inns	NO	Runs	HS	Avge	100s	50s	Ct	St	Balls	Runs	Wkts	Avge	Best	5wl	10wM
Test																	
All First	114	174	22	4145	203	27.26	2	22	68	-	15098	8052	307	26.22	8-89	12	3
1-day Int	9	8	4	99	21	24.75	-	-	1	-	324	305	7	43.57	2-28	-	
NatWest	18	17	2	275	67	18.33	-	2	2	-	826	544	16	34.00	2-18	-	
B & H	28	20	2	552	62	30.66	-	4	8	-	1295	880	24	36.66	5-31	1	
1-day Lge	103	87	13	1436	78 *	19.40	-	5	27	-	3438	2560	104	24.61	4-42	-	

15. Which Western Australian left-armer was
England's chief tormentor in 1990-91 with 27 wickets in the
four Tests in which he played?

BROWN, J. F.   Northamptonshire

Name: Jason Fred Brown
Role: Right-hand bat, off-spin bowler
Born: 10 October 1974,
Newcastle-under-Lyme
Height: 6ft **Weight:** 13st
Nickname: Cheese, Fish, Brownie
County debut: 1996
County cap: 2000
50 wickets in a season: 1
1st-Class 5 w. in innings: 8
1st-Class 10 w. in match: 3
1st-Class catches: 7
Place in batting averages: 304th av. 3.33
Place in bowling averages: 24th av. 20.62
Strike rate: 50.93 (career 54.50)
Parents: Peter and Cynthia
Wife and date of marriage: Sam,
26 September 1998
Education: St Joseph's RC School, Stoke-on-Trent; St Margaret Ward RC School,
Stoke-on-Trent
Qualifications: 9 GCSEs, Level 1 coaching qualification
Off-season: Coaching; England A tour to West Indies
Overseas tours: Kidsgrove League U18 to Australia 1990; Northants CCC to
Zimbabwe 1998, to Grenada 2000; England A to West Indies 2000-01; England
to Sri Lanka 2000-01
Overseas teams played for: North East Valley, Dunedin, New Zealand 1996-97
Cricketers particularly admired: John Emburey, Carl Hooper
Young players to look out for: Mark Powell, Tim Roberts, James Foster
Other sports played: Golf
Other sports followed: Football (Port Vale)
Relaxations: 'Reading, listening to music, walking my dog Spike'
Extras: Represented Staffordshire at all junior levels and in Minor Counties. Once took
10 for 16 in a Kidsgrove League game against Haslington U18 playing for Sandyford
U18. Played for Staffordshire in the 1995 NatWest competition. Took 100th first-class
wicket in 23rd match, v Sussex at Northampton 2000, going on to take his 50th wicket
of the season in the same game, only his seventh of the summer. Awarded
Northamptonshire cap 2000
Best batting: 16* Northamptonshire v Durham, Northampton 1997
Best bowling: 7-78 Northamptonshire v Sussex, Northampton 2000
Stop press: Drafted into England Test squad for tour to Sri Lanka 2000-01

2000 Season

	M	Inns	NO	Runs	HS	Avge	100s	50s	Ct	St	O	M	Runs	Wkts	Avge	Best	5wl	10wM
Test																		
All First	10	14	5	30	11	3.33	-	-	3	-	517.5	142	1258	61	20.62	7-78	4	2
1-day Int																		
NatWest	3	2	2	1	1 *	-	-	-	-	-	30	2	137	4	34.25	3-35	-	
B & H																		
1-day Lge	12	5	2	10	4	3.33	-	-	4	-	94.3	5	378	13	29.07	2-28	-	

Career Performances

	M	Inns	NO	Runs	HS	Avge	100s	50s	Ct	St	Balls		Runs	Wkts	Avge	Best	5wl	10wM
Test																		
All First	26	35	15	81	16 *	4.05	-	-	7	-	6322		2763	116	23.81	7-78	8	3
1-day Int																		
NatWest	4	2	2	1	1 *	-	-	-	-	-	252		209	5	41.80	3-35	-	
B & H																		
1-day Lge	13	5	2	10	4	3.33	-	-	4	-	609		404	17	23.76	4-26	-	

BROWN, M. J.   Middlesex

Name: <u>Michael</u> James Brown
Role: Right-hand bat, right-arm 'mixture'
bowler, occasional wicket-keeper
Born: 9 February 1980, Burnley
Height: 6ft **Weight:** 11st 5lbs
Nickname: Weasel, Richie Rich, Browny
County debut: 1999
1st-Class catches: 2
Parents: Peter and Valerie
Marital status: Girlfriend Sarah
Family links with cricket: Father played for
Burnley CC (Lancashire League) and some
games for Lancashire 2nd XI in 1970s. Also
played for Southgate CC 1976-78, winning
National Club Knockout in 1977. Brother
David plays for Lancashire U17 and U19
Education: Rosehill Junior School, Burnley;
Queen Elizabeth's Grammar School,
Blackburn; Durham University
Qualifications: 10 GCSEs, 4 A-levels
Career outside cricket: 'Something in business'
Off-season: 'Second year studying at university'

Overseas teams played for: Western Province CC, Cape Town 1998-99
Cricketers particularly admired: Dale Benkenstein
Young players to look out for: James Foster, Will Jefferson, David Brown
Other sports played: Football ('town team')
Other sports followed: Football (Burnley FC)
Injuries: Detached cartilage from right shoulder; 'learning to throw again!'
Relaxations: 'Sleeping, golf'
Extras: Opened batting for Burnley CC in Lancashire League 1995-98. Lancashire League Under-25 Batsman of the Season 1997, 1998. Represented Lancashire Schools at U11, U13, U15 and U17 level 1989-97. Represented Lancashire U19 Federation 1997-98. Played for Lancashire 2nd XI 1997-98. Represented ECB U19 A v Pakistan U19 in two one-day games 1998
Opinions on cricket: 'Second XI games should be played on better wickets. More practice facilities should be available and used more regularly.'
Best batting: 24* Middlesex v Cambridge University, Fenner's 1999

2000 Season (did not make any first-class or one-day appearances)

Career Performances

	M	Inns	NO	Runs	HS	Avge	100s	50s	Ct	St	Balls	Runs	Wkts	Avge	Best	5wI	10wM
Test																	
All First	2	3	2	48	24*	48.00	-	-	2	-							
1-day Int																	
NatWest																	
B & H																	
1-day Lge																	

BROWN, S. J. E.   Durham

Name: Simon John Emmerson Brown
Role: Right-hand bat, left-arm medium-fast bowler, gully fielder
Born: 29 June 1969, Cleadon Village, Sunderland
Height: 6ft 3in **Weight:** 13st
Nickname: Chubby
County debut: 1987 (Northamptonshire), 1992 (Durham)
County cap: 1998 (Durham)
Test debut: 1996
Tests: 1
50 wickets in a season: 7
1st-Class 50s: 2
1st-Class 5 w. in innings: 35
1st-Class 10 w. in match: 2

1st-Class catches: 41
One-Day 5 w. in innings: 2
Place in batting averages: 278th av. 9.11
(1999 269th av. 10.66)
Place in bowling averages: 32nd av. 21.57
(1999 41st av. 22.98)
Strike rate: 47.39 (career 52.30)
Parents: Ernest and Doreen
Marital status: Single
Education: Cleadon Village Junior School;
Boldon Comprehensive, Tyne & Wear; South
Tyneside Marine and Technical College
Qualifications: 6 O-levels, qualified
electrician
Career outside cricket: Electrician
Overseas tours: England YC to Sri Lanka
1986-87, to Australia (Youth World Cup)
1987-88; MCC to Bahrain 1994-95
Overseas teams played for: Marist, Christchurch, New Zealand
Cricketers particularly admired: John Lever, Ian Botham, Dennis Lillee
Young players to look out for: Steve Harmison
Other sports played: Golf
Relaxations: Playing golf
Extras: Offered basketball scholarship in America. Durham Supporters' Player of the
Year 1992. Durham Player of the Year 1994. Took his 500th first-class wicket (Steve
Stubbings caught by Martin Speight) v Derbyshire at Darlington 2000. Granted a
benefit for 2001
Best batting: 69 Durham v Leicestershire, Durham University 1994
Best bowling: 7-51 Durham v Lancashire, Riverside 2000

2000 Season

	M	Inns	NO	Runs	HS	Avge	100s	50s	Ct	St	O	M	Runs	Wkts	Avge	Best	5wI	10wM
Test																		
All First	14	21	12	82	19	9.11	-	-	2	-	442.2	110	1208	56	21.57	7-51	4	-
1-day Int																		
NatWest																		
B & H	2	1	1	3	3*	-	-	-	1	-	18	2	72	2	36.00	1-34	-	
1-day Lge	1	0	0	0	0	-	-	-	-	-	7	0	22	0	-	-	-	

Career Performances

	M	Inns	NO	Runs	HS	Avge	100s	50s	Ct	St	Balls	Runs	Wkts	Avge	Best	5wI	10wM
Test	1	2	1	11	10 *	11.00	-	-	1	-	198	138	2	69.00	1-60	-	-
All First	154	216	70	1732	69	11.86	-	2	41	-	27933	15402	534	28.84	7-51	35	2
1-day Int																	
NatWest	11	7	3	20	8	5.00	-	-	1	-	700	481	19	25.31	5-22	1	
B & H	22	9	5	41	12	10.25	-	-	5	-	1199	726	30	24.20	6-30	1	
1-day Lge	77	36	12	156	18	6.50	-	-	17	-	3297	2746	81	33.90	4-20	-	

BRUNNSCHWEILER, I.   Hampshire

Name: Iain Brunnschweiler
Role: Right-hand bat, wicket-keeper
Born: 10 December 1979, Southampton
Height: 6ft **Weight:** 12st 7lbs
Nickname: Brunchy, Bruno, Rocky, Neo
County debut: 2000
1st-Class catches: 4
Parents: Arthur and Joan
Marital status: Single
Family links with cricket: 'They mostly
dislike it!'
Education: Highfield C of E; King Edward
VI School, Southampton
Qualifications: 9 GCSEs, 3 A-levels, ECB
Level 1 cricket coaching award, UEFA Part B
football coaching award
Off-season: 'Travelling to Perth to train with
Paul Terry and play club cricket'
Overseas tours: England U17 to Bermuda 1997; King Edward VI School
to South Africa 1998
Overseas teams played for: Belmont DCC, Newcastle, NSW 1998-99; Nullamara,
Perth 2000-01
Cricketers particularly admired: Robin Smith, Adi Aymes, Jack Russell, Ian Healy
Young players to look out for: Lawrence Prittipaul, Charlie van der Gucht, James
Adams, Chris Tremlett, John Francis
Other sports played: Football (Southampton Youth), hockey, rugby
Other sports followed: Football (Southampton FC)
Relaxations: *FIFA 2000* on PlayStation, kickboxing
Opinions on cricket: 'The two-divisional structure certainly gave the end of the
season more bite and interest for both players and public. I think that more floodlit
cricket with music and entertainment is the way to interest young people in the game.'
Best batting: 19 Hampshire v New Zealand A, Portsmouth 2000

2000 Season

	M	Inns	NO	Runs	HS	Avge	100s	50s	Ct	St	O	M	Runs	Wkts	Avge	Best	5wI	10wM
Test																		
All First	1	2	0	22	19	11.00	-	-	4	-								
1-day Int																		
NatWest																		
B & H																		
1-day Lge																		

Career Performances

	M	Inns	NO	Runs	HS	Avge	100s	50s	Ct	St	Balls	Runs	Wkts	Avge	Best	5wI	10wM
Test																		
All First	1	2	0	22	19	11.00	-	-	4	-								
1-day Int																		
NatWest																		
B & H																		
1-day Lge																		

BRYAN, R. B.   Middlesex

Name: <u>Russell</u> Barnaby Bryan
Role: Right-hand bat, right-arm medium-fast bowler
Born: 14 February 1981, Maidstone
Height: 6ft 1in **Weight:** 13st
County debut: No first-team appearance
Parents: Ann and Andrew
Marital status: Single
Family links with cricket: 'Father has played club cricket for 30-odd years and is still playing'
Education: Shebbear Primary School; Shebbear College; Brunel University
Qualifications: 10 GCSEs, 2 A-levels, 2 AS-levels
Career outside cricket: Student at Brunel University

Cricketers particularly admired: Darren Gough, Mark Ramprakash, Ian Botham, Allan Donald, Shoaib Akhtar, Justin Langer
Other sports played: Football
Other sports followed: Football (Tottenham Hotspur FC)
Injuries: Out for six months with stress fracture of lower back
Relaxations: Listening to music, going out with friends

Extras: Represented Devon at U17 and U19 level in teams that reached both Texaco finals in 1998. Played in the NatWest for Devon in 2000
Opinions on cricket: 'Pitches need to be better. Tea is too short.'

2000 Season (did not make any first-class or one-day appearances)

Career Performances

	M	Inns	NO	Runs	HS	Avge	100s	50s	Ct	St	Balls	Runs	Wkts	Avge	Best	5wI	10wM
Test																	
All First																		
1-day Int																		
NatWest	1	0	0	0	0	-	-	-	-	-	24	21	0	-		-	-
B & H																		
1-day Lge																		

BULBECK, M. P. L. Somerset

Name: <u>Matthew</u> Paul Leonard Bulbeck
Role: Left-hand bat, left-arm fast-medium bowler
Born: 8 November 1979, Taunton
Height: 6ft 4in **Weight:** 14st 7lbs
Nickname: Bully
County debut: 1998
50 wickets in a season: 1
1st-Class 50s: 1
1st-Class 5 w. in innings: 3
1st-Class 10 w. in match: 1
1st-Class catches: 3
Place in batting averages: (1999 48th av. 37.85)
Place in bowling averages: (1999 79th av. 28.54)
Strike rate: 31.71 (career 41.15)
Parents: Paul and Carolyn
Marital status: Single
Family links with cricket: Father plays for local club; sister plays for same club
Education: Bishops Hall Primary School; Castle School; Taunton School; Richard Huish College
Qualifications: 8 GCSEs
Off-season: 'Recovering from back operation and getting fit for next season'
Overseas tours: West of England U15 to West Indies; Somerset U16 to South Africa; England U19 to New Zealand 1998-99

Cricketers particularly admired: Wasim Akram, Andy Caddick, Graham Rose
Young players to look out for: Ian Blackwell
Other sports played: Football (goalkeeper), golf (12 handicap)
Other sports followed: Football (Manchester United), rugby union (Bath RFC)
Injuries: Out for 14 months with stress fractures of spine
Relaxations: 'PlayStation with Blackie; occasional drink with friends'
Extras: Went to Madras Pace Foundation and was coached by Dennis Lillee and Jeff Thomson in September 1997. Represented England U19 in one-day and 'Test' series v Australia U19 1999. NBC Denis Compton Award 1999
Opinions on cricket: 'Every National League game should be played under floodlights. It brings in bigger crowds and gets the younger people in to watch and gets them interested in cricket.'
Best batting: 76* Somerset v Durham, Riverside 1999
Best bowling: 5-45 Somerset v Northamptonshire, Northampton 1999

2000 Season

	M	Inns	NO	Runs	HS	Avge	100s	50s	Ct	St	O	M	Runs	Wkts	Avge	Best	5wI	10wM
Test																		
All First	3	2	1	6	3*	6.00	-	-	-	-	37	9	109	7	15.57	3-23	-	-
1-day Int																		
NatWest																		
B & H	1	1	1	1	1*	-	-	-	-	-	7	1	27	0	-	-	-	-
1-day Lge	1	1	0	1	1	1.00	-	-	1	-	6	1	23	1	23.00	1-23	-	

Career Performances

	M	Inns	NO	Runs	HS	Avge	100s	50s	Ct	St	Balls	Runs	Wkts	Avge	Best	5wI	10wM
Test																	
All First	26	28	15	412	76*	31.69	-	1	3	-	3704	2174	90	24.15	5-45	3	1
1-day Int																	
NatWest																	
B & H	1	1	1	1	1*	-	-	-	-	-	42	27	0	-	-	-	-
1-day Lge	8	3	0	7	5	2.33	-	-	2	-	264	218	5	43.60	4-40	-	

BURNS, M.   Somerset

Name: Michael Burns
Role: Right-hand bat, right-arm medium
bowler, occasional wicket-keeper
Born: 6 February 1969, Barrow-in-Furness
Height: 6ft **Weight:** 14st
Nickname: George, Ashley, Butch, Onslow
County debut: 1991 (Warwickshire),
1997 (Somerset)
County cap: 1999 (Somerset)
1st-Class 50s: 21
1st-Class 100s: 4
1st-Class catches: 79
1st-Class stumpings: 7
One-Day 100s: 1
Place in batting averages: 36th av. 40.78
(1999 69th av. 35.19)
Place in bowling averages: 73rd av. 27.64
Strike rate: 56.71 (career 72.07)
Parents: Robert and Linda, stepfather Stan
Wife and date of marriage: Carolyn, 9 October 1994
Children: Elizabeth, 12 January 1997; Adam, 3 August 2000
Family links with cricket: 'Grandfather was a great back-garden bowler'
Education: Walney Comprehensive; Barrow College of Further Education
Qualifications: 'Few CSEs, couple of GCEs', qualified fitter at VSEL in Barrow,
coaching award
Career outside cricket: 'Would like to get involved in sports marketing'
Off-season: 'Trying to find a gym. Somebody told me we have one at the ground, but
I have yet to stumble across it'
Overseas teams played for: Gill College, South Africa 1991-92; Motueka, Nelson,
New Zealand 1992-93; Alex Sports Club, Harare 1993-94; Lindisfarne, Tasmania
1999-2000
Cricketers particularly admired: 'King Marcus of Keynsham'
Young players to look out for: Adam Burns ('if he's no good at golf')
Other sports played/followed: Rugby league ('had trials for Barrow RLFC and
Carlisle RLFC') and golf
Relaxations: TV, family, cinema, Indian food
Extras: Had a trial with Glamorgan. Went to La Manga with Lancashire junior side
1984. Played for Cumberland 1989-90. Player of the Tournament at Benson and
Hedges Thailand International Cricket Sixes in 1989. Left Warwickshire and joined
Somerset for the 1997 season. Scored club record of 217 for Lindisfarne in 1999-2000
season. Scored 160 v Oxford Universities at Taunton on 7 April 2000, setting new

record for the earliest ever 100 in a first-class cricket season in this country

Opinions on cricket: 'Although the two division Championship has meant more competitive games, I think it may have become a bit dull for the spectators as teams were less likely to set up a possible result and ended up being satisfied with bonus points. Maybe this was due to many overs being lost to the weather. It would be interesting to see if this is the case during a good summer.'

Best batting: 160 Somerset v Oxford Universities, Taunton 2000

Best bowling: 3-11 Somerset v Lancashire, Taunton 2000

2000 Season

	M	Inns	NO	Runs	HS	Avge	100s	50s	Ct	St	O	M	Runs	Wkts	Avge	Best	5wI	10wM
Test																		
All First	15	20	1	775	160	40.78	2	5	3	-	132.2	33	387	14	27.64	3-11	-	-
1-day Int																		
NatWest	2	2	0	11	11	5.50	-	-	-	-	7	0	60	1	60.00	1-43	-	
B & H	3	3	1	58	40	29.00	-	-	-	-	2	0	14	1	14.00	1-14	-	
1-day Lge	16	15	0	387	97	25.80	-	3	4	-	15	1	90	2	45.00	2-24	-	

Career Performances

	M	Inns	NO	Runs	HS	Avge	100s	50s	Ct	St	Balls	Runs	Wkts	Avge	Best	5wI	10wM
Test																	
All First	78	119	5	3290	160	28.85	4	21	79	7	1874	1091	26	41.96	3-11	-	-
1-day Int																	
NatWest	13	13	3	306	84 *	30.60	-	2	5	-	102	102	2	51.00	1-12	-	
B & H	20	18	1	544	95	32.00	-	5	7	2	160	139	8	17.37	3-18	-	
1-day Lge	94	87	7	1713	115 *	21.41	1	9	46	9	795	743	27	27.51	4-39	-	

16. At Lord's in 1993, who became the first batsman to be given out in England with the assistance of the TV umpire?

BURNS, N. D. Leicestershire

Name: <u>Neil</u> David Burns
Role: Left-hand bat, wicket-keeper
Born: 19 September 1965, Chelmsford
Height: 5ft 10in **Weight:** 12st
Nickname: Burnsie, Ern, George
County debut: 1986 (Essex),
1987 (Somerset), 2000 (Leicestershire)
County cap: 1987 (Somerset)
50 dismissals in a season: 3
1st-Class 50s: 29
1st-Class 100s: 5
1st-Class catches: 352
1st-Class stumpings: 33
Place in batting averages: 129th av. 26.17
Parents: Roy and Marie
Wife and date of marriage: Susan,
26 September 1987
Family links with cricket: Father played
club cricket for Finchley CC; brother Ian captained Essex U19
Education: Mildmay Junior; Moulsham High School
Qualifications: 6 O-levels, advanced cricket coach
Career outside cricket: Neil Burns Company Ltd (NBC), specialising in sports
marketing and PR
Overseas tours: England YC to West Indies 1984-85; Essex to Barbados 1985-86;
Christians in Sport to India 1989-90
Overseas teams played for: Northerns/Goodwood, Cape Town 1984-87, 1992;
Western Province B 1985-86
Cricketers particularly admired: Alan Knott, Bob Taylor, Rod Marsh, Graham
Gooch, Allan Border, Graeme Pollock, David Gower
Other sports followed: Most sports but particularly soccer (West Ham)
Relaxations: Watching/playing sport, reading newspapers, relaxing at home
Extras: Former schoolboy footballer with Tottenham Hotspur and Orient. Once took a
hat-trick of stumpings off Nasser Hussain's leg-breaks for Essex U11 v Berkshire U11.
Took eight stumpings in match v Kent 2nd XI at Dartford in 1984. Joined Somerset in
1987 after spending four years at Essex. Scored maiden first-class 100 v former county
at Chelmsford 1988. Equalled Steve Rhodes' one-day record of four stumpings in an
innings v Kent in Sunday League at Taunton 1991. Stumped Mike Roseberry off a
wide bowled by Ken MacLeay at Lord's in 1992. Retired in 1994. Has also played for
Bucks. Joined Leicestershire for 2000. Took five catches against his former club
Somerset in their first innings at Leicester 2000
Best batting: 166 Somerset v Gloucestershire, Taunton 1990

2000 Season

	M	Inns	NO	Runs	HS	Avge	100s	50s	Ct	St	O	M	Runs	Wkts	Avge	Best	5wI	10wM
Test																		
All First	16	21	4	445	67 *	26.17	-	3	36	1								
1-day Int																		
NatWest	2	2	0	7	7	3.50	-	-	5	-								
B & H	4	4	0	14	9	3.50	-	-	3	2								
1-day Lge	16	11	1	105	29	10.50	-	-	28	2								

Career Performances

	M	Inns	NO	Runs	HS	Avge	100s	50s	Ct	St	Balls	Runs	Wkts	Avge	Best	5wI	10wM
Test																	
All First	172	255	56	5794	166	29.11	5	29	352	33	3	8	0	-	-	-	-
1-day Int																	
NatWest	22	18	3	231	51	15.40	-	1	27	7							
B & H	36	29	9	455	51	22.75	-	1	32	8							
1-day Lge	119	92	23	1161	58	16.82	-	3	131	19							

BUTCHER, G. P. Surrey

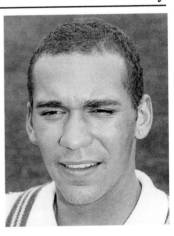

Name: <u>Gary</u> Paul Butcher
Role: Right-hand middle-order bat,
right-arm medium bowler
Born: 11 March 1975, Clapham,
South London
Height: 5ft 9in **Weight:** 12st
Nickname: Butch, Uncle Bib, Robert, 'the
Iron and Steel Business'
County debut: 1994 (Glamorgan),
1999 (Surrey)
1st-Class 50s: 11
1st-Class 100s: 1
1st-Class 5 w. in innings: 2
1st-Class catches: 18
Place in batting averages: (1999 153rd
av. 24.87)
Strike rate: 25.80 (career 56.60)
Parents: Alan and Elaine
Marital status: Girlfriend Roz
Family links with cricket: Brother Mark plays for Surrey and England. Father Alan
played for Surrey, England, and captained Glamorgan. Uncle Ian played for
Gloucestershire and Leicestershire. Uncle Martin played for Surrey

Education: Cumnor House Prep School, South Croydon; Riddlesdown Comprehensive; Heath Clark College
Qualifications: 5 GCSEs, BTEC 1st Diploma in Leisure Studies, badminton coaching award, cricket coaching award
Career outside cricket: 'Varies from off-season to off-season'
Off-season: 'Away in Perth again playing cricket; keeping fit'
Overseas tours: England U18 to Denmark 1993; England U19 to Sri Lanka 1993-94; Glamorgan to Zimbabwe 1995, to Pretoria 1996, to Jersey 1998
Overseas teams played for: Northern Natal, South Africa 1995-96; Hawkesbury Hawks, Sydney 1996-97
Cricketers particularly admired: Brian Lara, Malcolm Marshall, Viv Richards, Curtly Ambrose, Michael Holding, Steve Waugh, David Gower
Young players to look out for: Carl Greenidge
Other sports played: Football
Other sports followed: Football (Liverpool FC)
Relaxations: Music, playing bass guitar, spending time with friends
Extras: Took wicket with first ball on Sunday League debut 1994. Won Glamorgan's Most Improved Player Award 1996. Nominated for Young Player of the Year award 1996. Released by Glamorgan at end of 1998 season and joined Surrey for 1999. Played in three Championship-winning sides in four years (Glamorgan 1997; Surrey 1999, 2000). Took four wickets (Aldred, Munton, Dean, Wharton) in four balls v Derbyshire at The Oval 2000, the first Championship four-in-four since Pat Pocock achieved the feat for Surrey v Sussex at Eastbourne 1972
Opinions on cricket: '2000 was a good year for competitive cricket in the Championship and National League, although it is clear that a majority of pitches that are played on are woeful, so players are finding it harder to improve.'
Best batting: 101* Glamorgan v Oxford University, The Parks 1997
Best bowling: 7-77 Glamorgan v Gloucestershire, Bristol 1996

2000 Season

	M	Inns	NO	Runs	HS	Avge	100s	50s	Ct	St	O	M	Runs	Wkts	Avge	Best	5wI	10wM
Test																		
All First	4	4	1	110	66	36.66	-	1	-	-	21.3	4	65	5	13.00	5-18	1	-
1-day Int																		
NatWest																		
B & H																		
1-day Lge	2	2	0	51	37	25.50	-	-	1	-	8	0	56	0	-	-	-	

Career Performances

	M	Inns	NO	Runs	HS	Avge	100s	50s	Ct	St	Balls	Runs	Wkts	Avge	Best	5wI	10wM
Test																	
All First	49	70	11	1666	101 *	28.23	1	11	18	-	3453	2252	61	36.91	7-77	2	-
1-day Int																	
NatWest	4	3	1	77	48	38.50	-	-	-	-	120	122	4	30.50	2-33	-	
B & H	13	10	3	58	17	8.28	-	-	1	-	199	172	4	43.00	2-21	-	
1-day Lge	42	34	7	487	47	18.03	-	-	5	-	719	842	16	52.62	4-32	-	

BUTCHER, M. A. Surrey

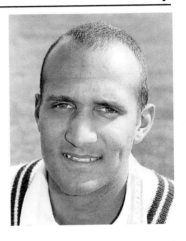

Name: Mark Alan Butcher
Role: Left-hand bat, right-arm medium bowler
Born: 23 August 1972, Croydon
Height: 5ft 11in **Weight:** 13st
Nickname: Butch, Baz
County debut: 1991
County cap: 1996
Test debut: 1997
Tests: 27
1000 runs in a season: 5
1st-Class 50s: 52
1st-Class 100s: 15
1st-Class 200s: 1
1st-Class 5 w. in innings: 1
1st-Class catches: 145
Place in batting averages: 30th av. 42.42
(1999 37th av. 39.88)
Place in bowling averages: (1999 64th
av. 26.17)
Strike rate: 32.40 (career 62.27)
Parents: Alan and Elaine
Wife and date of marriage: Judy, 4 October 1997
Children: Alita, 1999
Family links with cricket: Father Alan played for Glamorgan, Surrey and England
and is now coach with Surrey; brother Gary played for Glamorgan and is now with
Surrey; uncle Ian played for Gloucestershire and Leicestershire; uncle Martin played
for Surrey
Education: Cumnor House School; Trinity School; Archbishop Tenison's, Croydon
Qualifications: 5 O-levels, senior coaching award
Career outside cricket: Singer, guitar player
Overseas tours: England YC to New Zealand 1990-91; Surrey to Dubai 1990 and

1993, to Perth 1995; England A to Australia 1996-97; England to West Indies 1997-98, to Australia 1998-99, to South Africa 1999-2000

Overseas teams played for: South Melbourne, Australia 1993-94; North Perth 1994-95

Cricketers particularly admired: Ian Botham, David Gower, Viv Richards, Larry Gomes, Graham Thorpe, Alec Stewart, Michael Holding

Other sports followed: Football (Crystal Palace)

Relaxations: Music, playing the guitar, novels, wine

Extras: Played his first game for Surrey in 1991 against his father's Glamorgan in the Refuge Assurance League at The Oval, the first-ever match of any sort between first-class counties in which a father and son have been in opposition. Made his maiden Test century v South Africa at Headingley in 1998, earning the Man of the Match award. Captained Surrey during Adam Hollioake's absence on World Cup duty 1999. His 259 v Leicestershire 1999 was the highest score by a left-hander at Grace Road and the fourth highest individual score recorded there overall. Captained England in third Test v New Zealand at Old Trafford 1999, deputising for Nasser Hussain who missed the match through injury. Recorded maiden first-class five-wicket return (5-86, bowling off-spin) v Lancashire at Old Trafford 2000

Opinions on cricket: 'Four-day games are constantly over in two and a half days because home teams understandably use their home advantage. Until surfaces are made to some specification that is centrally controlled, the situation will get worse. You can't produce great cricketers on crap surfaces.'

Best batting: 259 Surrey v Leicestershire, Leicester 1999

Best bowling: 5-86 Surrey v Lancashire, Old Trafford 2000

2000 Season

	M	Inns	NO	Runs	HS	Avge	100s	50s	Ct	St	O	M	Runs	Wkts	Avge	Best	5wI	10wM
Test																		
All First	16	25	4	891	191	42.42	2	3	13	-	27	7	86	5	17.20	5-86	1	-
1-day Int																		
NatWest	2	2	1	92	87 *	92.00	-	1	2	-								
B & H	4	4	2	66	32	33.00	-	-	1	-								
1-day Lge	10	10	0	138	47	13.80	-	-	2	-								

Career Performances

	M	Inns	NO	Runs	HS	Avge	100s	50s	Ct	St	Balls	Runs	Wkts	Avge	Best	5wI	10wM
Test	27	51	1	1253	116	25.06	2	4	21	-	332	169	3	56.33	2-32	-	-
All First	152	263	21	8992	259	37.15	16	52	145	-	6477	3480	104	33.46	5-86	1	-
1-day Int																	
NatWest	17	17	4	568	91	43.69	-	5	9	-	282	196	5	39.20	2-57	-	
B & H	27	23	6	432	67	25.41	-	1	8	-	480	396	7	56.57	3-37	-	
1-day Lge	83	70	13	1259	85 *	22.08	-	3	27	-	1717	1571	37	42.45	3-23	-	

BYAS, D. Yorkshire

Name: David Byas
Role: Left-hand bat, right-arm medium bowler, county captain
Born: 26 August 1963, Middledale, Kilham
Height: 6ft 4in **Weight:** 14st 7lbs
Nickname: Bingo, Gadgett
County debut: 1986
County cap: 1991
Benefit: 2000
1000 runs in a season: 5
1st-Class 50s: 77
1st-Class 100s: 23
1st-Class 200s: 1
1st-Class catches: 313
One-Day 100s: 5
Place in batting averages: 137th av. 24.83
(1999 127th av. 27.34)
Strike rate: (career 93.16)

Parents: Richard and Anne
Wife and date of marriage: Rachael Elizabeth, 26 October 1990
Children: Olivia Rachael, 16 December 1991; Georgia Elizabeth, 30 December 1993; Benjamin, 1997
Family links with cricket: Father played local league
Education: Kilham Primary School; Lisvane School, Scarborough; Scarborough College
Qualifications: 1 O-level (Engineering)
Career outside cricket: Partner in family farming business
Off-season: Farming
Overseas teams played for: Papatoetoe, Auckland 1988-89
Cricketers particularly admired: David Gower, Viv Richards, Ian Botham
Young players to look out for: Matthew Wood, Anthony McGrath, Matthew Hoggard, Ryan Sidebottom
Other sports played: Hockey ('way back in my youth')
Other sports followed: Most other sports
Injuries: Out for three weeks after cartilage operation on right knee
Relaxations: 'Gardening and eating out with my wife and family. Spending time with the family'
Extras: Became youngest captain (aged 21) of Scarborough CC in 1985. Broke John Hampshire's Sunday League record with 702 runs in 1994, which had stood since 1976. Runner-up in the Sunday League averages 1994. Played hockey for Young England (U21) in the European Cup in Portugal. Passed 5000 runs in the

Sunday/National League v Somerset Sabres at Scarborough 2000. Captain of Yorkshire since 1996

Opinions on cricket: 'I believe that the two division system is excellent. However, to win, you should be rewarded with the points of 1998 – too big a reward for drawing a game. Pitches have got to improve all over the country.'

Best batting: 213 Yorkshire v Worcestershire, Scarborough 1995

Best bowling: 3-55 Yorkshire v Derbyshire, Chesterfield 1990

2000 Season

	M	Inns	NO	Runs	HS	Avge	100s	50s	Ct	St	O	M	Runs	Wkts	Avge	Best	5wI	10wM
Test																		
All First	17	26	2	596	84	24.83	-	2	22	-	4.2	0	8	0	-	-	-	-
1-day Int																		
NatWest	2	2	0	48	33	24.00	-	-	3	-								
B & H	6	6	0	106	71	17.66	-	1	2	-								
1-day Lge	12	12	0	230	52	19.16	-	1	10	-								

Career Performances

	M	Inns	NO	Runs	HS	Avge	100s	50s	Ct	St	Balls	Runs	Wkts	Avge	Best	5wI	10wM
Test																	
All First	252	425	37	13545	213	34.90	24	77	313	-	1118	727	12	60.58	3-55	-	-
1-day Int																	
NatWest	31	29	3	868	73 *	33.38	-	8	22	-	18	23	1	23.00	1-23	-	
B & H	51	48	4	1312	116 *	29.81	2	6	14	-	283	155	5	31.00	2-38	-	
1-day Lge	201	195	27	5005	111 *	29.79	3	26	77	-	529	463	19	24.36	3-19	-	

CADDICK, A. R.   Somerset

Name: <u>Andrew</u> Richard Caddick

Role: Right-hand bat, right-arm fast-medium bowler

Born: 21 November 1968, Christchurch, New Zealand

Height: 6ft 5in **Weight:** 14st 13lbs

Nickname: Des, Shack

County debut: 1991

County cap: 1992

Benefit: 1999

Test debut: 1993

Tests: 37

One-Day Internationals: 24

50 wickets in a season: 7

100 wickets in a season: 1

1st-Class 50s: 5

1st-Class 5 w. in innings: 49
1st-Class 10 w. in match: 13
1st-Class catches: 57
One-Day 5 w. in innings: 3
Place in batting averages: 266th av. 10.84
(1999 220th av. 18.38)
Place in bowling averages: 6th av. 15.41
(1999 23rd av. 20.87)
Strike rate: 35.96 (career 48.85)
Parents: Christopher and Audrey
Wife and date of marriage: Sarah,
27 January 1995
Children: Ashton Faye, 24 August 1998
Education: Papanui High School,
Christchurch, New Zealand
Qualifications: Qualified plasterer and tiler
Career outside cricket: Plasterer and tiler
Off-season: England tours to Kenya,
Pakistan and Sri Lanka

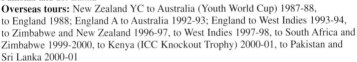

Overseas tours: New Zealand YC to Australia (Youth World Cup) 1987-88,
to England 1988; England A to Australia 1992-93; England to West Indies 1993-94,
to Zimbabwe and New Zealand 1996-97, to West Indies 1997-98, to South Africa and
Zimbabwe 1999-2000, to Kenya (ICC Knockout Trophy) 2000-01, to Pakistan and
Sri Lanka 2000-01
Cricketers particularly admired: Dennis Lillee, Richard Hadlee, Robin Smith,
Jimmy Cook
Players to look out for: Nasser Hussain, Nick Knight, Marcus Trescothick
Other sports followed: 'Mostly all'
Relaxations: Golf
Extras: Rapid Cricketline 2nd XI Championship Player of the Year 1991. Whyte and
Mackay Bowler of the Year 1997. Took 105 first-class wickets in 1998 season.
Leading wicket-taker in the single-division four-day era of the County Championship
with 422 wickets (av. 22.48) 1993-99. England's Man of the Series v New Zealand
1999, taking 20 wickets at an average of 20.60. Returned 7-46, his best Test figures, in
South Africa's first innings of the third Test at Durban, December 1999; shared Man of
the Match award with Gary Kirsten. Cornhill England Player of the Year 1999-2000.
Played for a World XI v an Asia XI in Dhaka 2000. Took 25 wickets in his three
Championship games in 2000, including 12-126 v Hampshire at Southampton and 10-
97 v Kent at Bath. Took 5-16 from 13 overs as West Indies were bowled out for 54 in
their second innings in the second Test at Lord's 2000. Took 5-14 in fourth Test v West
Indies at Headingley 2000, becoming in the process the fifth England bowler to take
four wickets in an over in a Test match and recording the cheapest five-wicket Test
return by an England bowler since Ian Botham's 5-11 v Australia at Edgbaston in
1981. Shared the new ball with Darren Gough in each Test of the West Indies series
2000, the first time the same pair had opened the bowling for England throughout a

series since Fred Trueman and Brian Statham did so v South Africa in 1960
Opinions on cricket: 'Due to the structure change in all forms of county cricket, it's great to see competitive cricket still being played in September.'
Best batting: 92 Somerset v Worcestershire, Worcester 1995
Best bowling: 9-32 Somerset v Lancashire, Taunton 1993

2000 Season

	M	Inns	NO	Runs	HS	Avge	100s	50s	Ct	St	O	M	Runs	Wkts	Avge	Best	5wI	10wM
Test	7	11	1	89	21 *	8.90	-	-	2	-	215.4	66	554	30	18.46	5-14	2	-
All First	10	15	2	141	21 *	10.84	-	-	3	-	329.4	98	848	55	15.41	7-64	5	2
1-day Int	6	3	0	3	2	1.00	-	-	1	-	46	10	128	6	21.33	2-27	-	
NatWest	2	1	0	0	0	0.00	-	-	1	-	20	1	58	0	-	-	-	-
B & H	3	2	1	4	3 *	4.00	-	-	-	-	19	3	62	1	62.00	1-30	-	
1-day Lge	5	3	0	19	16	6.33	-	-	-	-	35.2	8	98	4	24.50	2-15	-	

Career Performances

	M	Inns	NO	Runs	HS	Avge	100s	50s	Ct	St	Balls	Runs	Wkts	Avge	Best	5wI	10wM
Test	37	58	6	611	48	11.75	-	-	16	-	8059	3828	140	27.34	7-46	9	-
All First	163	217	40	2763	92	15.61	-	5	57	-	35076	17397	718	24.22	9-32	49	13
1-day Int	24	13	6	70	21 *	10.00	-	-	6	-	1320	765	32	23.90	4-19	-	
NatWest	23	12	4	29	8	3.62	-	-	5	-	1400	735	41	17.92	6-30	2	
B & H	24	16	9	128	38	18.28	-	-	4	-	1317	891	31	28.74	5-51	1	
1-day Lge	92	36	11	277	39	11.08	-	-	14	-	3977	2882	113	25.50	4-18	-	

CARBERRY, M. A.   Surrey

Name: Michael Alexander Carberry
Role: Left-hand bat, right-arm off-spin bowler
Born: 29 September 1980, Croydon
Height: 6ft **Weight:** 12st 7lbs
Nickname: Carbs
County debut: No first-team appearance
Parents: Maria and Neville
Marital status: Single
Family links with cricket: 'My dad played league cricket during the 1970s and 1980s'
Education: Winterbourne Boys School; St John Rigby RC College
Qualifications: 10 GCSEs, 1 AS-level
Overseas tours: Surrey U17 to South Africa 1997; England U19 to New Zealand 1998-99, to Malaysia and (Youth World Cup) Sri Lanka 1999-2000
Cricketers particularly admired: Alec Stewart, Ricky Ponting, Graham Thorpe, Brian Lara, Saurav Ganguly
Young players to look out for: Carl Greenidge, Michael Gough, Gareth Batty, Paul Franks

Other sports played: Basketball, football
Other sports followed: Football (Tottenham Hotspur)
Relaxations: 'Listening to music, going nightclubbing with my friends, playing for my dad's team (Old Castletonians) on a Sunday'
Extras: Second schoolboy to score a century for Croydon U13 since Ali Brown. Scored century (126*) for ECB U18 v Pakistan U19 at Abergavenny 1998. Scored his first Surrey 2nd XI century v Lancashire. Represented England U19 in one-day and 'Test' series v Australia U19 1999, scoring 50 in the third 'Test' at Chester-le-Street. Played for Surrey Board XI in 1999 NatWest. NBC Denis Compton Award 1999. Represented England U19 v Sri Lanka U19 in one-day series 2000

Opinions on cricket: 'Putting young players onto the full international stage and sticking with them. Allowing young players to play their natural game at the top level and working on their weaknesses. Getting the more senior players to work alongside younger players, so that they are passing on their knowledge.'

2000 Season (did not make any first-class or one-day appearances)

Career Performances

	M	Inns	NO	Runs	HS	Avge	100s	50s	Ct	St	Balls	Runs	Wkts	Avge	Best	5wl	10wM
Test																	
All First																		
1-day Int																		
NatWest	2	2	0	23	19	11.50	-	-	-	-							
B & H																		
1-day Lge																		

17. At The Oval in 1997, no fewer than three bowlers took seven wickets in an innings. Who were they?

CARPENTER, J. R. Sussex

Name: <u>James</u> Robert Carpenter
Role: Left-hand bat, slow left-arm bowler
Born: 20 October 1975, Birkenhead
Height: 6ft 1in **Weight:** 13st
Nickname: Carps
County debut: 1997
1st-Class 50s: 2
1st-Class catches: 5
Strike rate: (career 129.00)
Parents: John and Jo
Marital status: Single
Family links with cricket: Father played
Minor Counties cricket for Cheshire
Education: Gayton Primary School;
Birkenhead School
Qualifications: 9 GCSEs, 4 A-levels
Overseas teams played for: Randwick CC,
Sydney, Australia 1996-99
Cricketers particularly admired: Ian Botham, Allan Border, Steve Waugh
Young players to look out for: Brett Lee, Jamie Keggin (Bootle CC), Adam Warren
Other sports played: Played county schools rugby for Cheshire and schoolboy
football with Liverpool FC. Also had schoolboy forms with Everton and trials with
Bolton Wanderers and played for Runcorn FC in Vauxhall Conference
Relaxations: Golf and 'lying on Coogee beach, Sydney, in the off-season'
Extras: Captained MCC Young Professionals at Lord's. *Daily Telegraph* Bowling
Award. Awarded the Wetherall Trophy by the Cricket Society for the year's
outstanding schoolboy cricketer. Leading catcher in AXA League for 1998 season
Opinions on cricket: 'Two divisions makes the cricket more competitive and more
exciting for the public. More floodlit cricket should be encouraged to attract younger
audience.'
Best batting: 65 Sussex v Nottinghamshire, Trent Bridge 1998
Best bowling: 1-50 Sussex v Nottinghamshire, Hove 1997

2000 Season

	M	Inns	NO	Runs	HS	Avge	100s	50s	Ct	St	O	M	Runs	Wkts	Avge	Best	5wI	10wM
Test																		
All First	1	2	0	8	8	4.00	-	-	-	-								
1-day Int																		
NatWest																		
B & H	3	2	1	53	53*	53.00	-	1	2	-								
1-day Lge	4	4	1	49	29	16.33	-	-	3	-								

Career Performances

	M	Inns	NO	Runs	HS	Avge	100s	50s	Ct	St	Balls	Runs	Wkts	Avge	Best	5wl	10wM
Test																	
All First	13	24	0	383	65	15.95	-	2	5	-	129	81	1	81.00	1-50	-	-
1-day Int																	
NatWest	1	1	0	55	55	55.00	-	1	-	-							
B & H	8	7	2	154	53 *	30.80	-	1	3	-							
1-day Lge	36	29	8	468	64 *	22.28	-	3	22	-	6	15	0	-		-	-

CARTER, N. M. Warwickshire

Name: <u>Neil</u> Miller Carter
Role: Left-hand bat, left-arm fast-medium bowler
Born: 29 January 1975, Cape Town
Height: 6ft 2in **Weight:** 14st 4lbs
Nickname: Carts
County debut: No first-team appearance
1st-Class catches: 1
Strike rate: (career 41.14)
Parents: John and Heather
Marital status: Single
Education: Somerset House Preparatory School; Hottentots Holland High School; Cape Technicon
Qualifications: Level 2 coaching
Off-season: Returning to Boland
Overseas tours: SA Country Schools U15 to England 1992
Overseas teams played for: Boland 1999-2000 –
Cricketers particularly admired: Brad Player, Allan Donald
Young players to look out for: Justin Ontong, Justin Kemp
Other sports played: Golf, swimming
Other sports followed: Rugby (Springboks)
Relaxations: Gym, gricing (steam-train photography)
Extras: Made his first-class debut for Boland during the 1999-2000 season. Is not considered an overseas player
Opinions on cricket: 'Bring the bouncer into one-day cricket, like they do in South African domestic cricket.'
Best batting: 37 Boland v Eastern Province, Port Elizabeth 1999-2000
Best bowling: 3-48 Boland v Gauteng, Paarl 1999-2000

Stop press: Recorded maiden first-class five-wicket return (6-63) in the Supersport Series v Griqualand West in Kimberley 2000-01

2000 Season (did not make any first-class or one-day appearances)

Career Performances

	M	Inns	NO	Runs	HS	Avge	100s	50s	Ct	St	Balls	Runs	Wkts	Avge	Best	5wI	10wM
Test																	
All First	2	4	0	60	37	15.00	-	-	1	-	288	111	7	15.85	3-48	-	-
1-day Int																	
NatWest																	
B & H																	
1-day Lge																	

CASSAR, M. E. Northamptonshire

Name: Matthew Edward Cassar
Role: Right-hand bat, right-arm medium-fast bowler, occasional wicket-keeper
Born: 16 October 1972, Sydney, Australia
Height: 6ft **Weight:** 14st
Nickname: Cass, Chach
County debut: 1994 (Derbyshire)
1st-Class 50s: 9
1st-Class 100s: 1
1st-Class 5 w. in innings: 2
1st-Class catches: 14
One-Day 100s: 4
Place in batting averages: 191st av. 18.94 (1999 214th av. 18.71)
Place in bowling averages: 46th av. 23.40 (1999 91st av. 29.57)
Strike rate: 42.46 (career 51.22)
Parents: Edward and Joan
Wife and date of marriage: Jane, 5 October 1996
Family links with cricket: Wife, Jane, is the England Women's wicket-keeper
Education: Punchbowl Primary School, Sydney; Sir Joseph Banks High School, Sydney; Manchester Metropolitan University
Qualifications: School certificate and senior coaching award
Off-season: 'Moving house, continuing Sports Science degree, playing a game or two for Petersham-Marrickville'
Overseas teams played for: Petersham-Marrickville, Sydney 1988-95, 1999-2001

Cricketers particularly admired: Steve Waugh, Dean Jones, Dennis Lillee, Viv Richards, Ian Botham
Young players to look out for: Ian Blackwell, Trevor Smith, Lian Wharton, Rob Weston, 'Phillip DeFreitas', Kevin Dean
Other sports played: Golf, squash, tennis
Other sports followed: Football (Derby County)
Injuries: Out for six weeks with a groin injury
Relaxations: Sport, music, sleep and food
Extras: Played for New South Wales Colts. Took three wickets in final over of National League match at Southampton 2000, preventing Hampshire scoring the nine runs required for victory; scored 126 in the following National League game v Durham at Derby, being out off the last ball of the match with two runs required for victory. Left Derbyshire at the end of the 2000 season and has joined Northamptonshire for 2001
Opinions on cricket: 'To improve the standard of pitches, groundsmen should be employed by the ECB and not the counties. I like the new two-divisional structure, as I think it does produce more competitive cricket. One overseas player per team is the right balance, because whilst playing with and against the best players in the world is of great benefit, I would hate to see cricket go the same way as football has in this country.'
Best batting: 121 Derbyshire v Sussex, Horsham 1998
Best bowling: 6-76 Derbyshire v Yorkshire, Derby 2000

2000 Season

	M	Inns	NO	Runs	HS	Avge	100s	50s	Ct	St	O	M	Runs	Wkts	Avge	Best	5wI	10wM
Test																		
All First	14	20	2	341	77 *	18.94	-	1	1	-	212.2	54	702	30	23.40	6-76	1	-
1-day Int																		
NatWest																		
B & H	5	4	0	69	43	17.25	-	-	1	-	21	1	82	2	41.00	2-8	-	
1-day Lge	13	13	1	405	126	33.75	1	1	2	-	74.4	1	347	16	21.68	4-29	-	

Career Performances

	M	Inns	NO	Runs	HS	Avge	100s	50s	Ct	St	Balls	Runs	Wkts	Avge	Best	5wI	10wM
Test																	
All First	55	87	11	1803	121	23.72	1	9	14	-	3842	2287	75	30.49	6-76	2	-
1-day Int																	
NatWest	6	6	1	175	90 *	35.00	-	2	-	-	78	63	1	63.00	1-31	-	
B & H	5	4	0	69	43	17.25	-	-	1	-	126	82	2	41.00	2-8	-	
1-day Lge	42	41	4	1165	134	31.48	4	4	13	-	896	781	30	26.03	4-29	-	

CATTERALL, D. N.   Worcestershire

Name: <u>Duncan</u> Neil Catterall
Role: Right-hand bat, right-arm
medium-fast bowler
Born: 19 September 1978, Preston
Height: 5ft 11in **Weight:** 12st 2lbs
Nickname: Cats
County debut: 1998
1st-Class 50s: 2
1st-Class catches: 1
Strike rate: 25.33 (career 46.00)
Parents: David and Christine
Marital status: Single
Family links with cricket: Brother plays and
father played for Leyland DAF in the
Northern League
Education: Horncliffe School, Blackburn;
Queen Elizabeth's Grammar School,
Blackburn; Loughborough University
Qualifications: 11 GCSEs and 4 A-levels
Overseas tours: Queen Elizabeth's Grammar School to Australia, December 1996
Overseas teams played for: Manly CC, Sydney 1999-2000
Cricketers particularly admired: Steve Waugh
Young players to look out for: Kabir Ali
Other sports followed: Football (Preston North End)
Relaxations: Music, socialising
Extras: Represented England Schools U19 in 1998
Opinions on cricket: 'Night cricket needs to be increased to bring in more crowds
and generate interest.'
Best batting: 60 Worcestershire v Essex, Chelmsford 1999
                60 Worcestershire v Middlesex, Worcester 1999
Best bowling: 4-50 Worcestershire v West Indians, Worcester 2000

2000 Season

	M	Inns	NO	Runs	HS	Avge	100s	50s	Ct	St	O	M	Runs	Wkts	Avge	Best	5wl	10wM
Test																		
All First	1	1	0	25	25	25.00	-	-	1	-	25.2	5	92	6	15.33	4-50	-	-
1-day Int																		
NatWest	1	1	0	1	1	1.00	-	-	-	-	9.3	1	40	1	40.00	1-40	-	
B & H																		
1-day Lge	3	2	1	11	9 *	11.00	-	-	1	-	9	0	61	0	-		-	-

Career Performances

	M	Inns	NO	Runs	HS	Avge	100s	50s	Ct	St	Balls	Runs	Wkts	Avge	Best	5wI	10wM
Test																	
All First	4	5	0	157	60	31.40	-	2	1	-	506	308	11	28.00	4-50	-	-
1-day Int																	
NatWest	1	1	0	1	1	1.00	-	-	-	-	57	40	1	40.00	1-40	-	
B & H																	
1-day Lge	10	5	2	27	11 *	9.00	-	-	2	-	312	236	3	78.66	2-35	-	

CAWDRON, M. J.   Gloucestershire

Name: <u>Michael</u> John Cawdron
Role: Left-hand bat, right-arm
medium-fast bowler
Born: 7 October 1974, Luton
Height: 6ft 3in **Weight:** 13st 7lbs
Nickname: Muscles
County debut: 1995 (one-day),
1999 (first-class)
1st-Class 5 w. in innings: 5
1st-Class 10 w. in match: 1
1st-Class catches: 2
Place in batting averages: 224th av. 15.62
(1999 223rd av. 18.00)
Place in bowling averages: 30th av. 21.36
(1999 7th av. 16.62)
Strike rate: 47.96 (career 44.14)
Parents: William and Mandy
Marital status: 'Very single'
Family links with cricket: Father and brother played local village cricket
Education: Cheltenham College
Qualifications: 10 GCSEs, 3 A-levels, NCA coaching award
Overseas tours: West of England U14 to Holland; Cheltenham College to Zimbabwe
1992; Gloucestershire YC to Sri Lanka 1993-94; Gloucestershire Gypsies to
Zimbabwe 1994-95, to Cape Town 1997; Christians in Sport to Zimbabwe 1998
Cricketers particularly admired: Jack Russell, Jeremy Snape, Kim Barnett ('they are
all very tough players who make the most of their talents')
Young players to look out for: David Sales
Other sports followed: Rugby, hockey, rackets, clay-pigeon shooting, golf
Relaxations: Cinema, videos, eating and going out with friends
Extras: Winner of the *Daily Telegraph* Regional Bowling Award 1993. Captain of
MCC Schools and ESCA U19 1993. 'Made 50 off 32 balls on Sunday League debut

against Essex at my old school' (Cheltenham College). Scored 42 and took 5-35 on first-class debut, v Hampshire at Bristol 1999; went on to take two more five-wicket hauls in his next two Championship games. Took part in the Christians in Sport millennium tour to South Africa, the aims of which included distributing cricket kit to disadvantaged youngsters, coaching and playing matches against teams in the townships. Recorded maiden ten-wicket match return (10-74) for First-Class Counties Select XI v New Zealand A at Milton Keynes 2000

Opinions on cricket: 'Twelve-month contracts would be of great benefit to those players who do not wish to winter abroad, as work opportunities are not secure, as other employers are not eager to take on people on such a temporary basis.'

Best batting: 42 Gloucestershire v Hampshire, Bristol 1999
Best bowling: 6-25 First-Class Counties XI v New Zealand A, Milton Keynes 2000

2000 Season

	M	Inns	NO	Runs	HS	Avge	100s	50s	Ct	St	O	M	Runs	Wkts	Avge	Best	5wI	10wM
Test																		
All First	6	8	0	125	32	15.62	-	-	1	-	199.5	64	534	25	21.36	6-25	2	1
1-day Int																		
NatWest	2	2	0	22	17	11.00	-	-	-	-	17	2	56	2	28.00	1-27	-	
B & H	2	0	0	0	0	-	-	-	-	-	10	2	30	3	10.00	3-30	-	
1-day Lge	5	4	0	38	26	9.50	-	-	1	-	34	1	166	4	41.50	2-37	-	

Career Performances

	M	Inns	NO	Runs	HS	Avge	100s	50s	Ct	St	Balls	Runs	Wkts	Avge	Best	5wI	10wM
Test																	
All First	12	17	2	251	42	16.73	-	-	2	-	1810	800	41	19.51	6-25	5	1
1-day Int																	
NatWest	7	4	2	22	17	11.00	-	-	1	-	318	240	8	30.00	4-34	-	
B & H	7	2	2	7	5 *	-	-	-	-	-	265	213	13	16.38	4-28	-	
1-day Lge	27	18	5	215	50	16.53	-	1	4	-	918	761	20	38.05	4-17	-	

CHAPPLE, G.   Lancashire

Name: Glen Chapple
Role: Right-hand bat, right-arm medium-fast bowler
Born: 23 January 1974, Skipton, Yorkshire
Height: 6ft 2in **Weight:** 12st 7lbs
Nickname: Chappy, Boris, Boomor, Cheeky
County debut: 1992
County cap: 1994
50 wickets in a season: 2
1st-Class 50s: 6

1st-Class 100s: 1
1st-Class 5 w. in innings: 11
1st-Class catches: 37
One-Day 5 w. in innings: 4
Place in batting averages: 251st av. 12.11
(1999 149th av. 25.12)
Place in bowling averages: 49th av. 23.97
(1999 134th av. 40.16)
Strike rate: 52.87 (career 56.65)
Parents: Eileen and Michael
Marital status: Single
Family links with cricket: Father played in
Lancashire League for Nelson and was a
professional for Darwen and Earby
Education: West Craven High School;
Nelson and Colne College

Qualifications: 8 GCSEs, 2 A-levels
Overseas tours: England U18 to Canada
1991; England YC to New Zealand 1990-91, to Pakistan 1991-92, to India 1992-93;
England A to India 1994-95, to Australia 1996-97
Cricketers particularly admired: Dennis Lillee, Robin Smith
Other sports followed: Football (Liverpool), golf
Relaxations: 'Watching films, cinema, music, socialising'
Extras: Set record for fastest century in first-class cricket (21 minutes; against
declaration bowling) v Glamorgan at Old Trafford 1993. Man of the Match in the 1996
NatWest final against Essex after taking 6 for 18
Best batting: 109* Lancashire v Glamorgan, Old Trafford 1993
Best bowling: 6-42 Lancashire v Durham, Riverside 2000

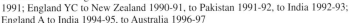

2000 Season

	M	Inns	NO	Runs	HS	Avge	100s	50s	Ct	St	O	M	Runs	Wkts	Avge	Best	5wI	10wM
Test																		
All First	16	19	1	218	41	12.11	-	-	4	-	431.5	101	1175	49	23.97	6-42	1	-
1-day Int																		
NatWest	3	1	0	6	6	6.00	-	-	1	-	27	5	115	2	57.50	2-39	-	
B & H	5	2	1	5	3*	5.00	-	-	-	-	36	2	147	4	36.75	2-34	-	
1-day Lge	14	8	3	62	15*	12.40	-	-	1	-	108	11	454	17	26.70	3-23	-	

Career Performances

	M	Inns	NO	Runs	HS	Avge	100s	50s	Ct	St	Balls	Runs	Wkts	Avge	Best	5wI	10wM
Test																	
All First	117	157	44	2288	109 *	20.24	1	6	37	-	18753	9551	331	28.85	6-42	11	-
1-day Int																	
NatWest	18	9	1	26	7	3.25	-	-	6	-	966	696	25	27.84	6-18	2	
B & H	26	11	6	42	11	8.40	-	-	5	-	1288	991	30	33.03	5-7	1	
1-day Lge	91	35	14	241	43	11.47	-	-	18	-	3564	2803	98	28.60	6-25	1	

CHERRY, D. D.   Glamorgan

Name: <u>Daniel</u> David Cherry
Role: Left-hand bat, right-arm
medium bowler
Born: 7 February 1980, Newport, Gwent
Height: 5ft 9in   **Weight:** 13st
Nickname: Rhino, Banners
County debut: 1998
Parents: David and Elizabeth
Marital status: Single
Family links with cricket: Father is a
qualified coach and played club cricket
Education: Feltonfleet Prep School,
Cobham, Surrey; Tonbridge School, Kent;
University of Wales, Swansea
Qualifications: 10 GCSEs, 3 A-levels
Career outside cricket: Student

Off-season: 'Final year of my history degree'
Overseas tours: Tonbridge School to
Australia 1996-97
Cricketers particularly admired: Michael Atherton, Graham Thorpe,
Steve James
Young players to look out for: Mark Wallace, David Harrison, Simon Jones
Other sports played: Rugby, rackets (Public Schools doubles champion)
Other sports followed: Rugby (Wales), football (Everton)
Relaxations: Reading crime books, 'drinking plenty of pots'
Extras: Played for ECB U19 XI v Pakistan U19 1998
Opinions on cricket: 'Second XI cricket should be played on 1st XI-standard
pitches.'
Best batting: 11 Glamorgan v Derbyshire, Cardiff 1998

2000 Season (did not make any first-class or one-day appearances)

Career Performances

	M	Inns	NO	Runs	HS	Avge	100s	50s	Ct	St	Balls	Runs	Wkts	Avge	Best	5wl	10wM
Test																	
All First	1	1	0	11	11	11.00	-	-	-	-							
1-day Int																	
NatWest																	
B & H																	
1-day Lge																	

CHILTON, M. J. Lancashire

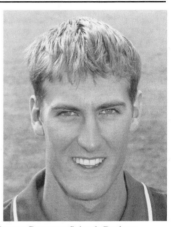

Name: Mark James Chilton
Role: Right-hand top-order bat, right-arm medium bowler
Born: 2 October 1976, Sheffield
Height: 6ft 3in **Weight:** 12st 8lbs
Nickname: Dip, Chill
County debut: 1997
1st-Class 50s: 4
1st-Class 100s: 2
1st-Class catches: 31
One-Day 5 w. in innings: 1
Place in batting averages: 160th av. 22.00 (1999 103rd av. 30.62)
Strike rate: (career 144.00)
Parents: Jim and Sue
Marital status: Single
Family links with cricket: Father played local cricket
Education: Brooklands Primary School; Manchester Grammar School; Durham University
Qualifications: 10 GCSEs, 3 A-levels, BA (Hons) Business Economics, senior coaching award
Off-season: Playing in Adelaide for East Torrens
Overseas tours: Manchester Grammar School to Barbados 1993-94, to South Africa 1995-96; Durham University to Zimbabwe 1997-98
Overseas teams played for: East Torrens, Adelaide 2000-01
Cricketers particularly admired: Alec Stewart, Michael Atherton
Young players to look out for: Stuart Adamson, Jon Humphreys
Other sports played: Golf, tennis

Other sports followed: Football (Manchester United)
Injuries: Out for five weeks with compound dislocation of finger
Relaxations: Music, 'trying to play the guitar'
Extras: Represented England U14, U15, U17. Awarded England U15 Batsman of the Year in 1992. Played for North of England v New Zealand U19 in 1996. Played for British Universities in 1997 Benson and Hedges Cup, winning the Gold Award against Sussex. Awarded 2nd XI cap 1998. His maiden first-class century (106*) v Cambridge University at Fenner's on 9 April 1999 was then the earliest ever 100 in a first-class cricket season in this country (superseded by Michael Burns' century v Oxford Universities on 7 April 2000)
Opinions on cricket: 'Two-divisional structure has increased the competitiveness towards the end of the season.'
Best batting: 106* Lancashire v Cambridge University, Fenner's 1999
Best bowling: 1-1 Lancashire v Sri Lanka A, Old Trafford 1999

2000 Season

	M	Inns	NO	Runs	HS	Avge	100s	50s	Ct	St	O	M	Runs	Wkts	Avge	Best	5wl	10wM
Test																		
All First	10	14	1	286	46	22.00	-	-	10	-	5	1	20	0	-	-	-	-
1-day Int																		
NatWest																		
B & H																		
1-day Lge	7	7	1	95	37	15.83	-	-	-	-	1	0	12	0	-	-	-	

Career Performances

	M	Inns	NO	Runs	HS	Avge	100s	50s	Ct	St	Balls	Runs	Wkts	Avge	Best	5wl	10wM
Test																	
All First	32	51	4	1280	106 *	27.23	2	4	31	-	288	153	2	76.50	1-1	-	-
1-day Int																	
NatWest	3	3	0	112	50	37.33	-	1	2	-	42	42	2	21.00	1-20	-	
B & H	11	11	1	297	56	29.70	-	2	4	-	369	316	14	22.57	5-26	1	
1-day Lge	20	19	1	287	44	15.94	-	-	2	-	180	182	7	26.00	3-41	-	

CLAPP, D. A. Sussex

Name: <u>Dominic</u> Adrian Clapp
Role: Right-hand bat, right-arm medium bowler
Born: 25 May 1980, Southport, Merseyside
Height: 6ft **Weight:** 13st 7lbs
Nickname: Hans, Poppa, Gruber, Rhino, Link, Cornelius
County debut: No first-team appearance
Parents: Adrian and Sarah

Marital status: Single
Family links with cricket: Brother plays for his local club side, Broadwater
Education: Sompting Abbotts Prep School; Lancing College; Worthing Sixth Form College
Qualifications: 6 GCSEs, 1 A-level, Level 1 and 2 cricket coach
Career outside cricket: Coaching/journalism
Off-season: 'I am spending the winter playing club cricket in Melbourne, Australia'
Overseas tours: Sussex U14 to Jersey 1994; Lancing College to Australia 1996; Sussex U19 to Barbados 1997
Cricketers particularly admired: Michael Bevan, Steve Waugh, Mike Atherton, Jacques Kallis, James Kirtley, Ray Belber

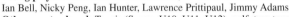

Young players to look out for: Matt Prior, Ian Bell, Nicky Peng, Ian Hunter, Lawrence Prittipaul, Jimmy Adams
Other sports played: Tennis (Sussex U10, U11, U12), golf, two-touch football
Other sports followed: Football (Tottenham Hotspur), rugby, golf, tennis, athletics, boxing
Relaxations: 'Reading newspapers, magazines, books; spending time with my friends; playing cards'
Extras: Sussex U14 Player of the Year 1994. Set record for highest score in Sussex Youth cricket, 189 v Middlesex 1998. Played two Development of Excellence games v Australia U19 1999. Sussex Young Cricketer of the Year 1999. Played for Sussex Board XI in the NatWest 2000
Opinions on cricket: '1. 2nd XI cricket should mirror the first-class game. 2. All pitches should be prepared for what you would expect for a Test match. 3. All groundsmen should be employed by the ECB so home captains do not influence the kind of pitch being prepared. 4. You cannot produce quality Test match batsmen if they continue to play on sub-standard pitches. Batsmen should be able to express themselves rather than playing for survival.'

---

18. At The Oval in 1964, which Australian pace
bowler took 6-47 in England's first innings, then became
Fred Trueman's 300th Test victim?

2000 Season (did not make any first-class or one-day appearances)

Career Performances

	M	Inns	NO	Runs	HS	Avge	100s	50s	Ct	St	Balls	Runs	Wkts	Avge	Best	5wI	10wM
Test																	
All First																	
1-day Int																	
NatWest	2	2	0	14	10	7.00	-	-	-	-	36	46	3	15.33	3-46	-	
B & H																	
1-day Lge																	

CLOUGH, G. D.   Nottinghamshire

Name: <u>Gareth</u> David Clough
Role: Right-hand bat, right-arm medium
bowler
Born: 23 May 1978, Leeds
Height: 6ft **Weight:** 12st
Nickname: Banger, Cloughie
County debut: 1998 (Yorkshire)
1st-Class catches: 1
Parents: David and Gillian
Marital status: Single
Family links with cricket: Brother-in-law
plays local league cricket in Yorkshire
Education: Pudsey Greenside Primary
School; Pudsey Grangefield
Qualifications: 9 GCSEs, 3 A-levels, Level 1
cricket coach
Off-season: Training hard; working for the
Yorkshire Evening Post Promotions
Department; coaching for Notts CCC
Overseas tours: Yorkshire CCC to South Africa 1999
Overseas teams played for: Somerset West, Cape Town 1996-97; Deepdene Bears,
Melbourne 1999-2000
Cricketers particularly admired: Ian Botham, Mike Newell, Steve Waugh
Young players to look out for: Michael Lumb, Wayne Noon
Other sports played: Football, golf 'and most other sports'
Other sports followed: Football ('the Mighty Blues' – Everton FC)
Relaxations: Cinema and socialising with friends
Extras: Formerly with Yorkshire. Played for Nottinghamshire 2nd XI in 2000, topping
the bowling averages with 37 wickets at 19.05 and scoring 400 runs

Opinions on cricket: 'Winter jobs sorted out or 9–12-month contracts'
Best batting: 33 Yorkshire v Glamorgan, Cardiff 1998

2000 Season (did not make any first-class or one-day appearances)

Career Performances

	M	Inns	NO	Runs	HS	Avge	100s	50s	Ct	St	Balls	Runs	Wkts	Avge	Best	5wI	10wM
Test																	
All First	1	2	0	34	33	17.00	-	-	1	-	12	11	0	-	-	-	-
1-day Int																	
NatWest																	
B & H																	
1-day Lge																	

COLLINGWOOD, P. D. — Durham

Name: <u>Paul</u> David Collingwood
Role: Right-hand bat, right-arm medium bowler
Born: 26 May 1976, Shotley Bridge, Tyneside
Height: 5ft 11in **Weight:** 11st 8lbs
Nickname: Colly
County debut: 1995 (one-day), 1996 (first-class)
County cap: 1998
1st-Class 50s: 16
1st-Class 100s: 4
1st-Class catches: 77
Place in batting averages: 134th av. 25.22 (1999 156th av. 24.71)
Place in bowling averages: 129th av. 39.50
Strike rate: 107.16 (career 87.00)
Parents: David and Janet
Marital status: Single
Family links with cricket: Father and brother play in the Tyneside Senior League for Shotley Bridge CC
Education: Benfieldside Junior School; Blackfyne Comprehensive School; Derwentside College
Qualifications: 9 GCSEs and 2 A-levels
Career outside cricket: 'Whatever job I can find'

Off-season: Playing for Richmond CC in Melbourne, Australia
Overseas tours: Durham Cricket Academy to Sri Lanka 1996 (captain)
Overseas teams played for: Bulleen CC, Melbourne 1995-96, 1996-97 ('won flag on both occasions'); Cornwall CC, Auckland 1997-98; Alberton CC, Johannesburg 1998-99; Richmond CC, Melbourne 2000-01
Cricketers particularly admired: Steve Waugh, Simon Katich, Jacques Kallis
Players to look out for: Simon Katich
Other sports played: Golf
Other sports followed: Football ('The Red and Whites' – Sunderland)
Relaxations: 'Watching Sunderland when I'm not away. Reading the *Sports Echo* (SAFC paper) when I am away. Sampling many fine lagers from around the world'
Extras: Took wicket with first ball on first-class debut against Northants, then scored 91. Durham Player of the Year 2000. Awarded the Ron Brierley Scholarship 2000 through the ECB in conjunction with the Victoria Cricket Association, Australia
Opinions on cricket: 'The pitch inspectors should do the job they are asked to do and not back down.'
Best batting: 111 Durham v Derbyshire, Darlington 2000
Best bowling: 3-7 Durham v Glamorgan, Cardiff 1999

2000 Season

	M	Inns	NO	Runs	HS	Avge	100s	50s	Ct	St	O	M	Runs	Wkts	Avge	Best	5wI	10wM
Test																		
All First	16	27	0	681	111	25.22	1	4	19	-	214.2	61	474	12	39.50	2-21	-	-
1-day Int																		
NatWest	2	2	0	6	3	3.00	-	-	-	-	2	0	7	2	3.50	2-7	-	
B & H	6	6	1	109	35	21.80	-	-	3	-	37	1	137	6	22.83	4-31	-	
1-day Lge	15	15	2	607	86	46.69	-	7	11	-	85.5	2	395	12	32.91	3-29	-	

Career Performances

	M	Inns	NO	Runs	HS	Avge	100s	50s	Ct	St	Balls	Runs	Wkts	Avge	Best	5wI	10wM
Test																	
All First	71	121	7	2986	111	26.19	4	16	77	-	3654	1678	42	39.95	3-7	-	-
1-day Int																	
NatWest	8	7	0	105	28	15.00	-	-	1	-	138	78	3	26.00	2-7	-	
B & H	18	17	3	359	49	25.64	-	-	5	-	529	412	13	31.69	4-31	-	
1-day Lge	67	64	6	1617	86	27.87	-	13	35	-	1151	941	29	32.44	3-20	-	

COOK, J. W.   Northamptonshire

Name: <u>Jeffrey</u> William Cook
Role: Left-hand bat, right-arm medium
bowler, slip fielder
Born: 2 February 1972, Sydney
Height: 6ft 4in **Weight:** 14st
Nickname: Cookie
County debut: 2000
1st-Class 50s: 1
1st-Class 100s: 2
1st-Class catches: 4
One-Day 100s: 1
Place in batting averages: 83rd av. 31.37
Parents: Roma and Les
Wife and date of marriage: Fiona,
10 October 1998
Children: Alex, 21 April 2000
Family links with cricket: Mother
represented New South Wales
Education: Rockdale Public School, Rockdale, NSW; James Cook High School,
Kogarah, NSW
Qualifications: NCA Level 2 coaching award, ACB Level 1 coaching award
Off-season: Playing in Australia
Overseas tours: Northamptonshire to Grenada 2000
Overseas teams played for: St George DCC, Sydney 1987-93; Easts CC, Sydney
1999-2000
Cricketers particularly admired: David Gower, Mark Taylor, Steve Waugh
Young players to look out for: Jason Brown
Other sports played: Football, tennis
Other sports followed: Football (Liverpool), rugby league (Parramatta)
Relaxations: 'Spending time with family'
Extras: Represented New South Wales Schoolboys. Represented NSW at U17, U19
and Colts levels. Represented New South Wales and Australia at indoor cricket. Played
for Northants Board XI in 1999 NatWest, scoring 130 v Wiltshire at Northampton.
Scored maiden first-class century (137) v Gloucestershire at Cheltenham 2000 in his
second Championship match
Opinions on cricket: 'More day/night fixtures.'
Best batting: 137 Northamptonshire v Gloucestershire, Cheltenham 2000

2000 Season

	M	Inns	NO	Runs	HS	Avge	100s	50s	Ct	St	O	M	Runs	Wkts	Avge	Best	5wI	10wM
Test																		
All First	11	17	1	502	137	31.37	2	1	4	-	1	0	7	0	-		-	-	-
1-day Int																		
NatWest	3	3	0	105	48	35.00	-	-	-	-								
B & H																		
1-day Lge	14	14	0	186	45	13.28	-	-	5	-								

Career Performances

	M	Inns	NO	Runs	HS	Avge	100s	50s	Ct	St	Balls	Runs	Wkts	Avge	Best	5wI	10wM
Test																	
All First	11	17	1	502	137	31.37	2	1	4	-	6	7	0	-		-	-	-
1-day Int																	
NatWest	4	4	0	235	130	58.75	1	-	-	-	48	50	0	-		-	-
B & H																	
1-day Lge	14	14	0	186	45	13.28	-	-	5	-							

COOK, S. J.   Middlesex

Name: <u>Simon</u> James Cook
Role: Right-hand bat, right-arm
fast bowler
Born: 15 January 1977, Oxford
Height: 6ft 4in **Weight:** 13st
Nickname: Cookie
County debut: 1997 (one-day),
1999 (first-class)
1st-Class 50s: 1
1st-Class catches: 5
Place in batting averages: 234th av. 14.50
(1999 221st av. 18.23)
Place in bowling averages: 95th av. 30.45
(1999 120th av. 35.33)
Strike rate: 74.72 (career 65.31)
Parents: Phil and Sue
Marital status: Single
Education: Botley Primary School;
Matthew Arnold School
Qualifications: GCSEs, NVQ Business Administration II
Career outside cricket: Sales and marketing within the computer industry
Cricketers particularly admired: Angus Fraser, Allan Donald, Mark Waugh

Young players to look out for: Ed Joyce
Other sports followed: Football (Liverpool), 'any other ball sport'
Relaxations: 'Sleeping, playing any sport, watching television and videos'
Opinions on cricket: 'Cut down the number of games that we play and have more short, sharp, quality training sessions.'
Best batting: 51 Middlesex v Hampshire, Lord's 1999
Best bowling: 4-13 Middlesex v Essex, Lord's 2000

2000 Season

	M	Inns	NO	Runs	HS	Avge	100s	50s	Ct	St	O	M	Runs	Wkts	Avge	Best	5wI	10wM
Test																		
All First	7	10	0	145	43	14.50	-	-	2	-	137	41	335	11	30.45	4-13	-	-
1-day Int																		
NatWest	2	2	1	9	7	9.00	-	-	-	-	12	2	39	1	39.00	1-29	-	
B & H																		
1-day Lge	13	9	1	107	28 *	13.37	-	-	4	-	83.5	7	315	14	22.50	3-22	-	

Career Performances

	M	Inns	NO	Runs	HS	Avge	100s	50s	Ct	St	Balls	Runs	Wkts	Avge	Best	5wI	10wM
Test																	
All First	17	26	3	382	51	16.60	-	1	5	-	2482	1289	38	33.92	4-13	-	-
1-day Int																	
NatWest	3	3	1	14	7	7.00	-	-	-	-	120	79	2	39.50	1-29	-	
B & H	1	1	0	6	6	6.00	-	-	-	-	54	71	0	-	-	-	-
1-day Lge	29	21	3	207	28 *	11.50	-	-	6	-	1249	891	38	23.44	3-16	-	

19. What was unusual about the result of the Centenary Test
at Melbourne in 1976-77?

CORK, D. G.   Derbyshire

Name: <u>Dominic</u> Gerald Cork
Role: Right-hand bat, right-arm, fast-medium
bowler, county captain
Born: 7 August 1971,
Newcastle-under-Lyme, Staffordshire
Height: 6ft 3in **Weight:** 13st 4lbs
Nickname: Corky
County debut: 1990
County cap: 1993
Test debut: 1995
Tests: 31
One-Day Internationals: 25
50 wickets in a season: 5
1st-Class 50s: 34
1st-Class 100s: 3
1st-Class 200s: 1
1st-Class 5 w. in innings: 20
1st-Class 10 w. in match: 2
1st-Class catches: 127
One-Day 5 w. in innings: 4

Place in batting averages: 31st av. 41.69 (1999 132nd av. 26.75)
Place in bowling averages: 29th av. 21.09 (1999 35th av. 22.34)
Strike rate: 50.95 (career 53.74)
Parents: Gerald and Mary
Children: Gregory Theodore Gerald, 29 September 1994
Family links with cricket: 'Father and brothers played for Betley CC in local North
Staffs & South Cheshire League with myself'
Education: St Joseph's College, Trent Vale, Stoke-on-Trent; Newcastle College of FE
Qualifications: 3 O-levels, leisure and recreation, qualified coach
Career outside cricket: 'None, but hopefully into commentary'
Off-season: England tours to Pakistan and Sri Lanka
Overseas tours: England YC to Australia 1989-90; England A to Bermuda and West
Indies 1991-92, to Australia 1992-93, to South Africa 1993-94, to India 1994-95;
England to South Africa 1995-96, to India and Pakistan (World Cup) 1995-96, to New
Zealand 1996-97, to Australia 1998-99, to Pakistan and Sri Lanka 2000-01
Overseas teams played for: East Shirley, Christchurch, New Zealand 1990-91
Cricketers particularly admired: Ian Botham, Malcolm Marshall, Imran Khan
Young players to look out for: Trevor Smith, Darren Stevens
Other sports played: Football (Mickleover Sports), volleyball, golf
Other sports followed: Football (Stoke City)
Relaxations: 'Relaxing with my partner and our children'

Extras: In 1990 he took a wicket in his first over in first-class cricket v New Zealanders at Derby and scored a century as nightwatchman for England U19 v Pakistan at Taunton. Played Minor Counties cricket for Staffordshire in 1989 and 1990. Selected for England A in 1991 – his first full season of first-class cricket. The Professional Cricketers' Association (PCA) Young Player of 1991. Took 8-53 on 20th birthday. Achieved first-class hat-trick against Kent 1994. Took 7-43 on Test debut against West Indies at Lord's 1995. Achieved hat-trick against the West Indies at Old Trafford in the fourth Test – the first by an Englishman in Test cricket for 38 years. Voted Player of the Year by the PCA for 1995. Finished at the top of the Whyte and Mackay ratings for bowling in 1995. Cornhill England Player of the Year 1995-96. One of *Wisden*'s Five Cricketers of the Year 1996. Man of the Match in the second Test v West Indies at Lord's 2000; on his recall to the Test side he recorded match figures of 7-52 followed by a match-winning 33* in England's second innings. Scored maiden first-class 200 (200*, the highest score by a Derbyshire No. 8) v Durham at Derby 2000, setting in the process a new record seventh-wicket partnership for Derbyshire (258) with Mathew Dowman; then took wicket with first ball of Durham's second innings. Derbyshire captain since 1998. Granted a benefit for 2001
Opinions on cricket: 'Too many games, too many players, too many counties. We must play our cricket like Test matches – five days, new ball at 80 overs, wicket like a Test pitch.'
Best batting: 200* Derbyshire v Durham, Derby 2000
Best bowling: 9-43 Derbyshire v Northamptonshire, Derby 1995
Stop press: Forced to return early from England's winter tour because of back injury

2000 Season

	M	Inns	NO	Runs	HS	Avge	100s	50s	Ct	St	O	M	Runs	Wkts	Avge	Best	5wI	10wM
Test	4	6	2	90	33 *	22.50	-	-	3	-	109.5	31	245	20	12.25	4-23	-	-
All First	14	17	4	542	200 *	41.69	1	2	10	-	356.4	94	886	42	21.09	6-41	1	-
1-day Int																		
NatWest	2	2	0	99	93	49.50	-	1	2	-	15	1	68	3	22.66	2-40	-	
B & H	4	1	1	26	26 *	-	-	-	4	-	31.2	4	100	6	16.66	3-17	-	
1-day Lge	9	8	0	169	64	21.12	-	2	8	-	80	4	315	15	21.00	4-40	-	

Career Performances

	M	Inns	NO	Runs	HS	Avge	100s	50s	Ct	St	Balls	Runs	Wkts	Avge	Best	5wI	10wM
Test	31	48	8	724	59	18.10	-	2	16	-	6622	3363	118	28.50	7-43	5	-
All First	187	277	41	5963	200 *	25.26	4	34	127	-	31922	15676	594	26.39	9-43	20	2
1-day Int	25	15	2	132	31 *	10.15	-	-	6	-	1440	1071	35	30.60	3-27	-	
NatWest	19	17	4	493	93	37.92	-	5	7	-	1197	726	38	19.10	5-18	2	
B & H	26	19	6	386	92 *	29.69	-	2	15	-	1486	970	29	33.44	5-49	1	
1-day Lge	96	80	8	1278	66	17.75	-	5	41	-	4078	3170	111	28.55	6-21	1	

COSKER, D. A. Glamorgan

Name: <u>Dean</u> Andrew Cosker
Role: Right-hand bat, slow left-arm bowler
Born: 7 January 1978, Weymouth, Dorset
Height: 5ft 11in **Weight:** 12st 8lbs
Nickname: Lurker, Lurks, The Vice, Vas
County debut: 1996
County cap: 2000
1st-Class 5 w. in innings: 2
1st-Class catches: 45
Place in batting averages: 287th av. 8.00
(1999 244th av. 15.14)
Place in bowling averages: 105th av. 32.55
(1999 140th av. 44.42)
Strike rate: 88.93 (career 76.47)
Parents: Des and Carol
Marital status: Single
Family links with cricket: 'Grandad is an
avid supporter and still drives from Swansea
to Cardiff even if it is pouring it down!'

Education: 'Neath Indoor School'; Millfield School; 'had places at Swansea and Cardiff
but for the love of the game of cricket declined them'
Qualifications: 10 GCSEs, 4 A-levels, qualified plumber and carpet designer
Career outside cricket: Interior decorator
Off-season: '1) Two-week crash course in sunbathing in Cape Town; 2) Sitting down
and analysing every other team's batsmen and trying to locate their strengths and
weaknesses!'
Overseas tours: West of England U15 to West Indies 1993-94; Millfield School to Sri
Lanka 1994-95; England U17 to Holland 1995; England U19 to Pakistan 1996-97;
England A to Kenya and Sri Lanka 1997-98, to Zimbabwe and South Africa 1998-99;
Glamorgan CCC to Cape Town and Jersey
Overseas teams played for: Gordon CC, Sydney 1996-97
Cricketers particularly admired: Robert Croft
Young players to look out for: Lee Down
Other sports played: 'Orienteering abroad – distinction in Tenerife; scaling rock
faces; mountain climbing'
Other sports followed: Soccer (Tottenham Hotspur FC)
Relaxations: 'Any physical exercise and entertainment (magic)'
Extras: *Daily Telegraph* Regional Bowling Award. England U15 and U17. Played for
U19 TCCB Development of Excellence XI against South Africa U19 in 1995. Played
for England U19 against Zimbabwe in 1997. Leading wicket-taker on England A tour
of Zimbabwe and South Africa 1998-99. Awarded Glamorgan cap 2000 ('third
youngest Glamorgan player to be capped')

Opinions on cricket: 'The game we play is getting more physically demanding every year. This is why we must place more emphasis on the finer details such as fitness, diet, psychology and mental preparation. All these factors could help fellow professionals reach their personal goals quicker, enabling the England side to compete on a positive, happier plain.'

Best batting: 49 Glamorgan v Sussex, Cardiff 1999
Best bowling: 6-140 Glamorgan v Lancashire, Colwyn Bay 1998

2000 Season

	M	Inns	NO	Runs	HS	Avge	100s	50s	Ct	St	O	M	Runs	Wkts	Avge	Best	5wI	10wM
Test																		
All First	12	15	4	88	14 *	8.00	-	-	9	-	429.5	141	944	29	32.55	4-82	-	-
1-day Int																		
NatWest																			
B & H																			
1-day Lge	6	5	2	26	17	8.66	-	-	-	-	48	1	229	8	28.62	3-36	-	

Career Performances

	M	Inns	NO	Runs	HS	Avge	100s	50s	Ct	St	Balls	Runs	Wkts	Avge	Best	5wI	10wM
Test																	
All First	72	81	23	577	49	9.94	-	-	45	-	13001	5801	170	34.12	6-140	2	-
1-day Int																	
NatWest	5	4	3	16	5	16.00	-	-	-	-	260	152	7	21.71	3-26	-	
B & H	5	4	2	2	1 *	1.00	-	-	1	-	174	128	4	32.00	2-26	-	
1-day Lge	41	23	8	150	27 *	10.00	-	-	10	-	1764	1472	45	32.71	3-18	-	

---

20. Who posted his 200th Test wicket while recording match figures of 10-253 from 89 overs at The Oval in 1981?

COTTERELL, T. P. Gloucestershire

Name: <u>Thomas</u> Paul Cotterell
Role: Left-hand bat, left-arm spinner
Born: 9 March 1977, Isleworth, Middlesex
Height: 6ft 2in **Weight:** 10st
County debut: 1999
1st-Class catches: 2
Place in batting averages: 309th av. 1.16
Strike rate: 151.50 (career 127.63)
Parents: Christopher and Jenny
Marital status: Single
Family links with cricket: Brother Joe has
played U19 and 2nd XI for Gloucestershire
Education: Birdlip CP; Kings School,
Gloucester; Kent University
Qualifications: BA in History
Cricketers particularly admired:
Phil Tufnell, Courtney Walsh, Dennis Lillee
Other sports played: Golf, rugby
Other sports followed: Rugby (Gloucester RFC)
Relaxations: Reading, music

Extras: League bowling prize with Birdlip CC 1993. Kent University Player of the
Year 1998
Best batting: 5* Gloucestershire v Nottinghamshire, Trent Bridge 2000
Best bowling: 3-69 Gloucestershire v Northamptonshire, Northampton 1999

2000 Season

	M	Inns	NO	Runs	HS	Avge	100s	50s	Ct	St	O	M	Runs	Wkts	Avge	Best	5wI	10wM
Test																		
All First	8	10	4	7	5 *	1.16	-	-	2	-	202	48	582	8	72.75	2-69	-	-
1-day Int																		
NatWest	1	0	0	0	0	-	-	-	-	-	10	0	33	2	16.50	2-33	-	
B & H																			
1-day Lge																			

Career Performances

	M	Inns	NO	Runs	HS	Avge	100s	50s	Ct	St	Balls	Runs	Wkts	Avge	Best	5wl	10wM
Test																	
All First	9	11	4	7	5 *	1.00	-	-	2	-	1404	663	11	60.27	3-69	-	-
1-day Int																	
NatWest	1	0	0	0	0	-	-	-	-	-	60	33	2	16.50	2-33	-	
B & H																	
1-day Lge																	

COTTEY, P. A. Sussex

Name: Phillip <u>Anthony</u> Cottey
Role: Right-hand bat, right-arm off-spin bowler, occasional wicket-keeper ('Eastbourne 1997')
Born: 2 June 1966, Swansea
Height: 5ft 5in **Weight:** 10st 7lbs
Nickname: Cotts, TC, Rudy, Tattoo, Seven
County debut: 1986 (Glamorgan), 1999 (Sussex)
County cap: 1992 (Glamorgan), 1999 (Sussex)
1000 runs in a season: 7
1st-Class 50s: 65
1st-Class 100s: 23
1st-Class 200s: 1
1st-Class catches: 161
Place in batting averages: 74th av. 32.17 (1999 121st av. 27.85)
Strike rate: (career 84.87)
Parents: Bernard John and Ruth
Wife and date of marriage: Gail, 5 October 1992
Children: Lowri Rhiannon, 16 October 1993; Seren Nia, 6 August 1997
Family links with cricket: Father played club cricket for Swansea CC
Education: Bishopston Comprehensive School, Swansea
Qualifications: 9 O-levels, advanced coach
Career outside cricket: 'Undecided'
Overseas tours: Glamorgan to La Manga, Barbados, Trinidad, Zimbabwe and Cape Town 1987-96, to Jersey 1998
Overseas teams played for: Penrith, Sydney 1986-88; Benoni, Johannesburg 1990-93; Eastern Transvaal 1991-92
Cricketers particularly admired: Sachin Tendulkar, Ian Botham, Shane Warne, Matthew Maynard

Young players to look out for: Nick Wilton, Robin Martin-Jenkins, Jamie Carpenter, Mike Powell, Simon Jones
Other sports played/followed: Golf, soccer (Swansea City AFC), rugby union (Dunvant RFC) and marathon running
Relaxations: Gym and road running; football for Ammanford FC (Welsh League); spending time with family; golf
Extras: Left school at 16 to play for Swansea City FC for three years as a professional. Three Welsh Youth caps (one as captain). Glamorgan Player of the Year in 1994. Ran the New York Marathon in 1995 and the Athens Marathon in 1996. Left Glamorgan at the end of the 1998 season and joined Sussex on a five-year contract. Sussex Clubman of the Year 1999
Best batting: 203 Glamorgan v Leicestershire, Swansea 1996
Best bowling: 4-49 Glamorgan v Leicestershire, Swansea 1996

2000 Season

	M	Inns	NO	Runs	HS	Avge	100s	50s	Ct	St	O	M	Runs	Wkts	Avge	Best	5wI	10wM
Test																		
All First	16	23	0	740	154	32.17	2	2	8	-	1	1	0	0	-	-	-	-
1-day Int																		
NatWest	2	2	1	30	17	30.00	-	-	-	-								
B & H	4	4	1	6	4	2.00	-	-	1	-								
1-day Lge	13	12	1	134	47	12.18	-	-	4	-								

Career Performances

	M	Inns	NO	Runs	HS	Avge	100s	50s	Ct	St	Balls	Runs	Wkts	Avge	Best	5wI	10wM
Test																	
All First	236	381	50	12139	203	36.67	24	65	161	-	1358	862	16	53.87	4-49	-	-
1-day Int																	
NatWest	29	28	7	567	68	27.00	-	4	8	-	150	96	3	32.00	1-9	-	
B & H	39	37	6	638	96	20.58	-	3	15	-	78	53	1	53.00	1-49	-	
1-day Lge	160	136	27	2790	92 *	25.59	-	16	54	-	509	523	15	34.86	4-56	-	

COUSINS, D. M. Northamptonshire

Name: Darren Mark Cousins
Role: Right-hand bat, right-arm fast-medium bowler, outfielder
Born: 24 September 1971, Cambridge
Height: 6ft 1in **Weight:** 14st
Nickname: Cuz, Mad Dog, The Gimp, Hooks, Vinnie, Roger Ramjet
County debut: 1993 (Essex), 1999 (one-day, Surrey), 2000 (Northants)
County cap: 2000 (Northants)
50 wickets in a season: 1

1st-Class 5 w. in innings: 2
1st-Class catches: 8
Place in batting averages: 244th av. 13.12
Place in bowling averages: 21st av. 19.67
Strike rate: 45.73 (career 53.65)
Parents: Dennis Charles and Deanna
Maureen (deceased)
Marital status: Single
Family links with cricket: Father opened the
bowling for and was capped by
Cambridgeshire
Education: Milton Primary School;
Impington Village College
Qualifications: 7 GCSEs, basic and senior
coaching qualifications
Career outside cricket: 'In the past I've kept
fit by cycle-couriering and PE teaching'
Off-season: 'Having a rest, then going to
Cape Town in January for two months to train and play. Girlfriend is going to show
me there is more to a computer than smut on the Internet'
Overseas teams played for: Gold Coast Dolphins, Queensland 1994-95; Maritzburg
Old Boys, Pietermaritzburg, South Africa 1995-96; Shell Harbour, NSW 1996-97;
Bellville, Cape Town 1999-2000

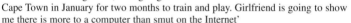

Cricketers particularly admired: 'All the people who have helped me with my
career, especially Alan Butcher, who got me back into first-class cricket'
Young players to look out for: Monty Panesar, Richard Logan, John Blain
Other sports played: Football (represented Cambridgeshire at all youth levels),
swimming (represented Cambridgeshire)
Other sports followed: Football (Liverpool, Cambridge United), rugby union ('I hope
to get to some Northampton games')
Relaxations: 'Censored'
Extras: Represented Cambridgeshire at every level at cricket. Played for a Bull
Development Squad against Australia in 1991, taking four wickets in each innings.
Played 2nd XI cricket for Northants and Worcs. Set record both for number of wickets
in any single Colts festival (21) and for number of wickets taken in the Hilda Overy
Festival overall (74). Spent seven years at Essex, undergoing four back and two knee
operations. Awarded 2nd XI cap and Essex Young Player of the Year 1994. Essex
Cricket Society 2nd XI Player of the Year 1994. Leading Essex wicket-taker in Sunday
League and top of the bowling averages in 1994. Released by Essex at end of 1998
season after only full season on the staff. Played as a pro for Cambridge St Giles and
Cambridgeshire 1999. Played three National League matches for Surrey 1999. Offered
one-year contract at end of 1999 but chose to join Northants for 2000 on two-year
contract. Recorded maiden Championship five-wicket return (5-123) v Middlesex at
Lord's 2000. Awarded Northamptonshire cap 2000
Opinions on cricket: 'I think two divisions has worked very well, as every game is

important. We still need to attract bigger and younger crowds; this could be done with more floodlit cricket. After spending a year out of the game, I realised how much I missed the dressing-room banter and the away trips!'

Best batting: 29* Northamptonshire v Glamorgan, Northampton 2000
Best bowling: 6-35 Essex v Cambridge University, Fenner's 1994

2000 Season

	M	Inns	NO	Runs	HS	Avge	100s	50s	Ct	St	O	M	Runs	Wkts	Avge	Best	5wI	10wM
Test																		
All First	16	23	7	210	29*	13.12	-	-	3	-	510.4	142	1318	67	19.67	5-123	1	-
1-day Int																		
NatWest	2	1	1	10	10*	-	-	-	1	-	19.5	3	81	6	13.50	3-39	-	
B & H	2	1	0	10	10	10.00	-	-	-	-	18	1	73	5	14.60	3-36	-	
1-day Lge	14	9	4	40	18	8.00	-	-	2	-	100	6	415	19	21.84	3-27	-	

Career Performances

	M	Inns	NO	Runs	HS	Avge	100s	50s	Ct	St	Balls	Runs	Wkts	Avge	Best	5wI	10wM
Test																	
All First	31	48	12	369	29*	10.25	-	-	8	-	5044	2456	94	26.12	6-35	2	-
1-day Int																	
NatWest	7	4	2	23	12	11.50	-	-	1	-	329	273	7	39.00	3-39	-	
B & H	8	3	1	32	12*	16.00	-	-	1	-	347	244	7	34.85	3-36	-	
1-day Lge	52	23	9	61	18	4.35	-	-	6	-	2211	1648	71	23.21	3-18	-	

COVERDALE, P. S.   Northamptonshire

Name: <u>Paul</u> Stephen Coverdale
Role: Right-hand bat, right-arm medium bowler
Born: 24 July 1983, Harrogate
Height: 5ft 10in **Weight:** 10st 8lbs
Nickname: Covers, Drill Sergeant, Flaps
County debut: No first-team appearance
Parents: Stephen and Jane
Marital status: Single
Family links with cricket: Father played for Yorkshire CCC and Cambridge University and is now Chief Executive of Northamptonshire
Education: Spratton Hall School; Wellingborough School; 'have applied for university'
Qualifications: 9 GCSEs 'and studying for A-levels'
Career outside cricket: School
Off-season: 'Studying A-levels at Wellingborough School and training with Northants Academy'

Overseas tours: Northamptonshire U19 to South Africa 2000
Cricketers particularly admired: Allan Lamb, Steve Waugh, Michael Atherton
Young players to look out for: Mark Powell, Monty Panesar, Chris Goode
Other sports played: Rugby union
Other sports followed: Rugby (Northampton Saints), football (Aston Villa)
Injuries: Out for a few weeks with 'various injuries, including slicing finger open with a chisel and burning left arm with boiling cooking oil!'
Relaxations: Socialising and going out with friends; listening to music; watching and playing sports
Extras: Progressed through county age groups, captaining at U14, U15, U17 and U19. Represented Northamptonshire Board XI in NatWest ('claiming wicket of Wayne Larkins, caught behind'). Represented East England Schools U18. Academy contract with Northamptonshire for 2001
Opinions on cricket: 'The game has improved dramatically in many areas in the last few years. What a difference success at international level has brought to English cricket! However, I believe there still ought to be further emphasis put upon the format of day/night cricket. I am sure many are eagerly awaiting the time when all first-class grounds will be equipped with their own lights, allowing one of the domestic competitions to be a completely day/night affair.'

21. Which Nottinghamshire opener helped David Gower add 331 for the second wicket at Edgbaston in 1985?

COWAN, A. P.   Essex

Name: <u>Ashley</u> Preston Cowan
Role: Right-hand bat, right-arm
fast-medium bowler, 'benefit-only
wicket-keeper'
Born: 7 May 1975, Hitchin, Hertfordshire
Height: 6ft 5in **Weight:** 15st 3lbs
Nickname: Wallace, Dic Dic
County debut: 1995
County cap: 1997
50 wickets in a season: 1
1st-Class 50s: 5
1st-Class 5 w. in innings: 7
1st-Class catches: 34
One-Day 5 w. in innings: 1
Place in batting averages: 204th av. 17.50
(1999 237th av. 15.80)
Place in bowling averages: 56th av. 25.00
(1999 71st av. 27.54)
Strike rate: 50.91 (career 56.96)
Parents: Jeff and Pam
Marital status: Engaged
Family links with cricket: 'Father tried to play village cricket'
Education: Kingshott Pre-Prep; Framlingham College; 'Essex County Cricket Club'
Qualifications: 8 GCSEs, 3 A-levels, Business Vocational degree
Career outside cricket: IT industry
Off-season: 'Working in the IT industry as a salesman'
Overseas tours: England to West Indies 1997-98
Overseas teams played for: Zingari CC, Durban 1995-97
Cricketers particularly admired: Ian Botham, Curtly Ambrose, Glenn McGrath
Young players to look out for: James Foster, Andy McGarry, Justin Bishop
Other sports played: Golf (single-figure handicap), hockey (Chelmsford), football
(Essex CCC team)
Other sports followed: football (West Ham), rugby (Saracens)
Relaxations: 'Sleeping, music, golf, rugby, business'
Extras: Played rugby and hockey for East of England U18. Was the youngest person
to play for Cambridgeshire. First-class hat-trick at Colchester in 1996. Was the joint
leading scorer in the 1996 NatWest final. Took three wickets in four balls in the final
over of National League match at Southend 2000 to prevent Glamorgan scoring the six
runs needed for victory; the over also contained a run-out
Opinions on cricket: 'More day/night games that attract a young cricket crowd.'
Best batting: 94 Essex v Leicestershire, Leicester 1998
Best bowling: 6-47 Essex v Glamorgan, Cardiff 1999

2000 Season

	M	Inns	NO	Runs	HS	Avge	100s	50s	Ct	St	O	M	Runs	Wkts	Avge	Best	5wl	10wM
Test																		
All First	14	20	6	245	67	17.50	-	1	4	-	398.5	98	1175	47	25.00	5-54	2	-
1-day Int																		
NatWest	2	2	1	1	1 *	1.00	-	-	-	-	14	1	59	1	59.00	1-7	-	
B & H	3	3	2	51	34 *	51.00	-	-	-	-	26.3	0	116	3	38.66	1-24	-	
1-day Lge	13	11	1	76	29 *	7.60	-	-	4	-	103	9	433	22	19.68	4-39	-	

Career Performances

	M	Inns	NO	Runs	HS	Avge	100s	50s	Ct	St	Balls	Runs	Wkts	Avge	Best	5wl	10wM
Test																	
All First	75	110	23	1513	94	17.39	-	5	34	-	11735	6412	206	31.12	6-47	7	-
1-day Int																	
NatWest	12	8	4	43	17 *	10.75	-	-	4	-	685	462	16	28.87	3-29	-	
B & H	16	10	6	99	34 *	24.75	-	-	1	-	873	618	18	34.33	5-28	1	
1-day Lge	63	47	14	385	40 *	11.66	-	-	28	-	2653	2022	73	27.69	4-31	-	

COX, J. Somerset

Name: Jamie Cox
Role: Right-hand bat, off-spin bowler,
county captain
Born: 15 October 1969, Burnie, Tasmania
Height: 6ft **Weight:** 12st 7lbs
Nickname: Buzz, Skippy
County debut: 1999
County cap: 1999
1000 runs in a season: 1
1st-Class 50s: 47
1st-Class 100s: 32
1st-Class 200s: 3
1st-Class catches: 67
One-Day 100s: 3
Place in batting averages: 42nd av. 39.32
(1999 4th av. 57.75)
Strike rate: (career 126.75)
Parents: David and Kaye
Marital status: Single

Family links with cricket: Father played State colts and is life member of local club
Education: Wynyard Primary; Wynyard High; Deakin University (current)
Qualifications: School Certificate, Diploma of Management; currently studying for
Bachelor of Business degree

Career outside cricket: 'Currently exploring'
Off-season: 'Playing for Tasmania, winning Mercantile Mutual and Pura Milk Cups'
Overseas tours: Australia U19 to West Indies 1988; Australia A to Zimbabwe 1989, to Malaysia 1997 (Super 8s); Australia XI to Zimbabwe 1991-92; Tasmania to Zimbabwe 1995-96
Overseas teams played for: Tasmania 1987-88 –
Cricketers particularly admired: Ian Botham, Geoff Marsh, David Boon, Steve Waugh
Young players to look out for: 'Jack Shine, Adam Burns, Fraser Jarvis, Sebastian Pierson, Robert Bowler'
Other sports played: Golf
Other sports followed: Australian Rules football (Western Bulldogs)
Injuries: Out for four days with patella tendonitis
Relaxations: Music, home design
Extras: Scored 1349 runs in the 1996-97 Australian season, with five 100s, including two in one match v New South Wales. Players' Player of the Year 1996-97. Tasmanian Cricket Player of the Year 1996-97. Scored an unbeaten 115 in the first innings of the 1997-98 Sheffield Shield final v Western Australia, becoming the first player to carry his bat in a Shield final. Joined Somerset in 1999 as overseas player and captain. Became the first Somerset player to score a 200 (216) and a 100 (129*) in a match, v Hampshire at Southampton 1999; scored 153 at the same ground in 2000 to make it three successive scores of 100 or more there. Took over captaincy of Tasmania in 1999-2000 in succession to David Boon
Opinions on cricket: 'In good shape. Must be careful not to overprotect centrally contracted players. Points for a draw to be reduced or removed. Unlimited time to get full bowling points; 120 overs for batting points.'
Best batting: 245 Tasmania v New South Wales, Hobart 1999-2000
Best bowling: 3-46 Somerset v Middlesex, Taunton 1999

2000 Season

	M	Inns	NO	Runs	HS	Avge	100s	50s	Ct	St	O	M	Runs	Wkts	Avge	Best	5wl	10wM
Test																		
All First	17	26	1	983	171	39.32	3	3	6	-	14	3	35	0	-	-	-	-
1-day Int																		
NatWest	2	2	0	29	27	14.50	-	-	-	-								
B & H	3	3	0	78	59	26.00	-	1	-	-								
1-day Lge	16	16	0	485	110	30.31	1	3	10	-	9	0	54	0	-		-	-

Career Performances

	M	Inns	NO	Runs	HS	Avge	100s	50s	Ct	St	Balls	Runs	Wkts	Avge	Best	5wI	10wM
Test																	
All First	159	280	17	11476	245	43.63	35	47	67	-	507	319	4	79.75	3-46	-	-
1-day Int																	
NatWest	7	7	0	263	114	37.57	1	1	-	-							
B & H	3	3	0	78	59	26.00	-	1	-	-							
1-day Lge	30	30	0	1078	110	35.93	2	6	16	-	96	82	3	27.33	3-28	-	

CRAVEN, V. J. *Yorkshire*

Name: <u>Victor</u> John Craven
Role: Left-hand bat, right-arm medium bowler
Born: 31 July 1980, Harrogate
Height: 6ft **Weight:** 13st
County debut: 2000
1st-Class 50s: 2
1st-Class catches: 6
Place in batting averages: 135th av. 25.10
Parents: Victor and Susan
Marital status: Single
Family links with cricket: 'Dad played league cricket for 20 years'
Education: Beckwithshaw County Primary; Harrogate Grammar School
Qualifications: GNVQ (Advanced) Business, grades 1 and 2 cricket coaching
Off-season: 'Spending season playing cricket for Deepdene, Melbourne; pre-season tour to South Africa'
Overseas teams played for: Tatura CC, Victoria 1998-99; Deepdene, Melbourne 2000-01
Cricketers particularly admired: Michael Atherton, Graham Thorpe, Alec Stewart
Young players to look out for: Michael Lumb
Other sports played: Golf
Other sports followed: Football (Leeds United), rugby league (Leeds Rhinos)
Relaxations: Cinema 'and my girfriend, Daniela'
Extras: Has Yorkshire 2nd XI cap
Opinions on cricket: 'The game's getting faster and more exciting with the introduction of day/night cricket.'
Best batting: 58 Yorkshire v Derbyshire, Derby 2000

2000 Season

	M	Inns	NO	Runs	HS	Avge	100s	50s	Ct	St	O	M	Runs	Wkts	Avge	Best	5wI	10wM
Test																		
All First	8	11	1	251	58	25.10	-	2	6	-	8	1	15	0	-	-	-	-
1-day Int																		
NatWest																		
B & H	1	1	0	1	1	1.00	-	-	1	-								
1-day Lge	5	5	0	77	28	15.40	-	-	5	-								

Career Performances

	M	Inns	NO	Runs	HS	Avge	100s	50s	Ct	St	Balls	Runs	Wkts	Avge	Best	5wI	10wM
Test																	
All First	8	11	1	251	58	25.10	-	2	6	-	48	15	0	-	-	-	-
1-day Int																	
NatWest																	
B & H	1	1	0	1	1	1.00	-	-	1	-							
1-day Lge	5	5	0	77	28	15.40	-	-	5	-							

CRAWLEY, J. P.   Lancashire

Name: <u>John</u> Paul Crawley
Role: Right-hand bat, occasional wicket-keeper, county captain
Born: 21 September 1971, Maldon, Essex
Height: 6ft 2in **Weight:** 13st 2lbs
Nickname: Creeps, Jonty, JC
County debut: 1990
County cap: 1994
Test debut: 1994
Tests: 29
One-Day Internationals: 13
1000 runs in a season: 7
1st-Class 50s: 83
1st-Class 100s: 33
1st-Class 200s: 4
1st-Class catches: 155
One-Day 100s: 3
Place in batting averages: 22nd av. 45.28 (1999 49th av. 37.82)
Strike rate: (career 126.00)
Parents: Frank and Jean
Marital status: Single

Family links with cricket: Father played in Manchester Association; brother Mark played for Lancashire before moving to Nottinghamshire; other brother Peter plays for Warrington CC and has played for Scottish Universities and Cambridge University; uncle was excellent fast bowler; godfather umpires in Manchester Association
Education: Manchester Grammar School; Trinity College, Cambridge
Qualifications: 10 O-levels, 2 AO-Levels, 3 A-levels, 2 S-levels, BA in History
Off-season: Touring West Indies with England A
Overseas tours: England YC to Australia 1989-90, to New Zealand 1990-91 (captain); England A to South Africa 1993-94, to West Indies 2000-01; England to Australia 1994-95, to South Africa 1995-96, to Zimbabwe and New Zealand 1996-97, to West Indies 1997-98, to Australia 1998-99
Overseas teams played for: Midland-Guildford, Perth 1990
Cricketers particularly admired: Michael Atherton, Neil Fairbrother, Graham Gooch, Alec Stewart, David Gower, Allan Donald, Ian Salisbury
Other sports followed: Football (Manchester United), golf
Relaxations: 'Playing or trying to play the guitar'
Extras: Played for England YC in three home series v New Zealand 1989, Pakistan 1990 and Australia (as captain) 1991. Made his maiden first-class century for Cambridge University on the same day that brother Mark made his for Notts. First to score 1000 runs in U19 Tests. Scored 286 for England A against Eastern Province at Port Elizabeth in 1994, the highest score by an Englishman on an England or England A tour for almost 30 years. Finished top of the first-class batting averages on England's tour to South Africa in 1995-96 with 336 runs at 67.20. Lancashire vice-captain for the 1998 season. Scored century in each innings v Glamorgan 1998. Topped first-class batting averages for 1998 season. Lancashire captain since 1999
Best batting: 286 England A v Eastern Province, Port Elizabeth 1993-94
Best bowling: 1-90 Lancashire v Sussex, Hove 1992

2000 Season

	M	Inns	NO	Runs	HS	Avge	100s	50s	Ct	St	O	M	Runs	Wkts	Avge	Best	5wI	10wM
Test																		
All First	15	22	1	951	156	45.28	5	-	6	-	1	0	19	0	-	-	-	-
1-day Int																		
NatWest	4	3	1	68	41	34.00	-	-	1	-								
B & H	7	7	0	155	61	22.14	-	1	3	-								
1-day Lge	13	13	2	208	71 *	18.90	-	1	1	-								

Career Performances

	M	Inns	NO	Runs	HS	Avge	100s	50s	Ct	St	Balls	Runs	Wkts	Avge	Best	5wI	10wM
Test	29	47	5	1329	156 *	31.64	3	7	26	-							
All First	215	349	32	15259	286	48.13	37	83	155	-	126	199	1	199.00	1-90	-	-
1-day Int	13	12	1	235	73	21.36	-	2	1	1							
NatWest	23	22	3	747	113 *	39.31	1	5	9	-	6	4	0	-		-	-
B & H	44	43	1	1422	114	33.85	1	8	14	-							
1-day Lge	98	95	6	2409	100	27.06	1	15	23	3							

CREESE, M. L. Middlesex

Name: <u>Matthew</u> Leonard Creese
Role: Left-hand bat, slow left-arm bowler
Born: 13 February 1982, Enfield
Height: 6ft 2in **Weight:** 14st
Nickname: Creesey
County debut: 1999
Strike rate: (career 153.00)
Parents: John and Christine
Marital status: Single
Family links with cricket: Father played
club cricket
Education: Millbrook JMI; Goffs GM
School; Durham University
Qualifications: 10 GCSEs, 4 A-levels,
Level 1 cricket coach
Career outside cricket: Student
Off-season: At university
Cricketers particularly admired:
Phil Tufnell, Ian Botham, Steve Waugh
Young players to look out for: James Foster, Will Jefferson, Michael Brown
Other sports played: Rugby, football, golf
Other sports followed: Rugby (Saracens), football (Arsenal)
Relaxations: Listening to music, playing bass guitar, socialising with friends
Extras: Middlesex Seaxe Young Player of the Year 1997. Played for England U15.
Played for ECB U19 XI v Australia U19 1999 and v Sri Lanka U19 2000
Opinions on cricket: 'Further innovations are required to market the county game to
attract a wider audience and provoke media interest. Continued efforts by all
concerned to improve skills level of current players and to attract more youngsters to
take up the game, preferably through schools involvement.'
Best batting: 4 Middlesex v Cambridge University, Fenner's 1999
Best bowling: 1-37 Middlesex v Cambridge University, Fenner's 1999

2000 Season (did not make any first-class or one-day appearances)

Career Performances

	M	Inns	NO	Runs	HS	Avge	100s	50s	Ct	St	Balls	Runs	Wkts	Avge	Best	5wI	10wM
Test																	
All First	1	1	0	4	4	4.00	-	-	-	-	153	98	1	98.00	1-37	-	-
1-day Int																	
NatWest																	
B & H																	
1-day Lge																	

CROFT, R. D. B. Glamorgan

Name: <u>Robert</u> Damien Bale Croft
Role: Right-hand bat, off-spin bowler
Born: 25 May 1970, Morriston, Swansea
Height: 5ft 11in **Weight:** 13st 10lbs
Nickname: Crofty
County debut: 1989
County cap: 1992
Benefit: 2000
Test debut: 1996
Tests: 17
One-Day Internationals: 46
50 wickets in a season: 5
1st-Class 50s: 29
1st-Class 100s: 2
1st-Class 5 w. in innings: 28
1st-Class 10 w. in match: 4
1st-Class catches: 116
One-Day 5 w. in innings: 1
Place in batting averages: 162nd av. 21.69 (1999 212th av. 18.94)
Place in bowling averages: 113th av. 35.80 (1999 102nd av. 31.37)
Strike rate: 87.92 (career 79.62)
Parents: Malcolm and Susan
Wife: Marie
Children: Callum James Bale Croft
Family links with cricket: Father and grandfather played local league cricket
Education: Hendy CP School; St John Lloyd Catholic School, Llanelli; Neath Tertiary College; West Glamorgan Institute of Higher Education
Qualifications: 6 O-levels; OND Business Studies; HND Business Studies; NCA senior coaching certificate

Career outside cricket: 'Who knows?'
Overseas tours: England A to Bermuda and West Indies 1991-92, to South Africa 1993-94; England to Zimbabwe and New Zealand 1996-97, to West Indies 1997-98, to Australia 1998-99, to Sharjah (Coca-Cola Cup) 1998-99, to Sri Lanka 2000-01
Overseas teams played for: 'England'
Cricketers particularly admired: Alan Jones, Tom Cartwright, Don Shepherd, John Steele, John Emburey
Young players to look out for: 'Too many Welsh youngsters to mention'
Other sports played: Golf, squash
Other sports followed: Rugby (Hendy and Wales)
Relaxations: Fishing and shooting
Extras: Captained England South to victory in International Youth Tournament 1989 and was voted Player of the Tournament. Glamorgan Young Player of the Year 1992. Represented England in the 1999 World Cup. Made his 16th England Test appearance v West Indies at Edgbaston 2000, passing Jeff Jones' total of 15 Tests to become the most capped Welshman
Best batting: 143 Glamorgan v Somerset, Taunton 1995
Best bowling: 8-66 Glamorgan v Warwickshire, Swansea 1992
Stop press: Drafted into England party for tour to Sri Lanka 2000-01

2000 Season

	M	Inns	NO	Runs	HS	Avge	100s	50s	Ct	St	O	M	Runs	Wkts	Avge	Best	5wI	10wM
Test	2	3	1	46	27 *	23.00	-	-	-	-	76	17	177	3	59.00	2-53	-	-
All First	14	17	4	282	56	21.69	-	2	4	-	586.1	153	1432	40	35.80	5-26	2	-
1-day Int	2	2	1	10	5 *	10.00	-	-	-	-	5	0	30	1	30.00	1-30	-	
NatWest	3	1	1	30	30 *	-	-	-	1	-	24	1	117	4	29.25	2-17	-	
B & H	6	6	0	95	35	15.83	-	-	-	-	35	1	148	5	29.60	3-42	-	
1-day Lge	14	12	2	139	24	13.90	-	-	4	-	106.3	1	446	11	40.54	2-22	-	

Career Performances

	M	Inns	NO	Runs	HS	Avge	100s	50s	Ct	St	Balls	Runs	Wkts	Avge	Best	5wI	10wM
Test	17	27	7	341	37 *	17.05	-	-	8	-	3935	1557	39	39.92	5-95	1	-
All First	234	339	67	6704	143	24.64	2	29	116	-	50560	23002	635	36.22	8-66	28	4
1-day Int	46	33	12	309	32	14.71	-	-	9	-	2274	1597	42	38.02	3-51	-	
NatWest	30	24	6	405	64	22.50	-	3	5	-	1804	1068	36	29.66	4-47	-	
B & H	33	29	7	675	77	30.68	-	5	8	-	1727	1093	37	29.54	4-30	-	
1-day Lge	137	110	27	1716	68	20.67	-	5	38	-	5726	4229	131	32.28	6-20	1	

CROWE, C. D.   Leicestershire

Name: <u>Carl</u> Daniel Crowe
Role: Right-hand bat, 'waste of space off-spinner!'
Born: 25 November 1975, Leicester
Height: 6ft **Weight:** 12st 7lbs ('probably heavier now, as new McDonald's has opened round the corner')
Nickname: Crozzer
County debut: 1995
1st-Class catches: 10
Place in batting averages: 211th av. 17.16
Place in bowling averages: 93rd av. 30.20 (1999 104th av. 31.63)
Strike rate: 74.20 (career 64.15)
Parents: Jeannette and Eddie
Wife and date of marriage: Helen, 14 October 2000

Family links with cricket: Brother Craig plays for Leicestershire 2nd XI
Education: Lutterworth High School; Lutterworth Grammar School
Qualifications: 11 GCSEs, 2 A-levels, NCA Senior Coach
Career outside cricket: 'Wheeling and dealing'
Off-season: 'Taking Leicester City to the top of the Premiership on *LMA Manager*/PlayStation'
Overseas tours: Leicestershire U19 to South Africa 1993-94; Leicestershire to Holland 1996, 1998, to Barbados 1998, to Sri Lanka 1999, to Anguilla 2000
Overseas teams played for: Old Mentonians, Melbourne 1997-99
Cricketers particularly admired: Mark and Steve Waugh, Saqlain Mushtaq
Other sports played: 'Try all sports.' 'Had a hole in one'
Other sports followed: 'Support Leicester at everything and follow Spurs'
Relaxations: 'Like to sleep, but rooming with Neil Burns I don't get a chance. Also really enjoy bowling in nets for hours to then get five minutes' batting at the end'
Extras: Played for Leicestershire U12-U19 and Midlands Schools U14-U19. One of the Cricketers of the Festival at Cambridge U19 Festival 1994. Won Leics 2nd XI batting award 1998. Played in Leicestershire's victory in the AON Trophy final 2000
Opinions on cricket: 'Things are beginning to look up!'
Best batting: 44* Leicestershire v Northamptonshire, Northampton 1999
Best bowling: 4-55 Leicestershire v Hampshire, Southampton 2000

2000 Season

	M	Inns	NO	Runs	HS	Avge	100s	50s	Ct	St	O	M	Runs	Wkts	Avge	Best	5wl	10wM
Test																		
All First	8	8	2	103	30	17.16	-	-	4	-	185.3	50	453	15	30.20	4-55	-	-
1-day Int																		
NatWest	1	1	0	5	5	5.00	-	-	-	-	2	0	19	0	-		-	-
B & H																		
1-day Lge	1	1	1	5	5 *	-	-	-	-	-	1	0	10	0	-		-	-

Career Performances

	M	Inns	NO	Runs	HS	Avge	100s	50s	Ct	St	Balls	Runs	Wkts	Avge	Best	5wl	10wM
Test																	
All First	19	23	5	336	44 *	18.66	-	-	10	-	2053	1006	32	31.43	4-55	-	-
1-day Int																	
NatWest	1	1	0	5	5	5.00	-	-	-	-	12	19	0	-		-	-
B & H																	
1-day Lge	3	2	2	9	5 *	-	-	-	-	-	6	10	0	-		-	-

CULLINAN, D. J. Kent

Name: <u>Daryll</u> John Cullinan
Role: Right-hand bat, off-spin bowler
Born: 4 March 1967, Kimberley, South Africa
Height: 5ft 10in
County debut: 1995 (Derbyshire)
Test debut: 1992-93
Tests: 59
One-Day Internationals: 132
1st-Class 50s: 62
1st-Class 100s: 32
1st-Class 200s: 2
1st-Class 300s: 1
1st-Class catches: 189
One-Day 100s: 5
Strike rate: (career 101.20)
Family links with cricket: Elder brother Ralph (R. E. Cullinan) played for Border and Orange Free State B from 1984-85 to 1990-91
Education: Queens College, Queenstown, South Africa; Stellenbosch University
Overseas tours: South Africa to Sri Lanka 1993-94, to Australia 1993-94, to England 1994, to New Zealand 1994-95, to Zimbabwe 1995-96, to India and Pakistan (World

Cup) 1995-96, to India 1996-97, to Pakistan 1997-98, to Australia 1997-98, to England 1998, to New Zealand 1998-99, to UK, Ireland and Holland (World Cup) 1999, to Zimbabwe 1999-2000, to India 1999-2000, to Sri Lanka 2000-01, to West Indies 2000-01

Overseas teams played for: Border 1983-84 – 1984-85, 1994-95 – 1995-96; Western Province 1985-86 – 1990-91; Transvaal/Gauteng 1991-92 – 1993-94, 1996-97 –

Other sports played: Rugby union (as schoolboy)

Extras: Represented South African Schools in 1983 and (as captain) 1984. In 1983-84 became the youngest player to score a first-class century in South Africa. In 1993-94 set the record for the highest first-class score in South African cricket, 337* for Transvaal v Northern Transvaal at Johannesburg. Set record individual Test score for South Africa, 275* v New Zealand at Eden Park 1999 (since equalled by Gary Kirsten). Was Derbyshire's overseas player in 1995; has joined Kent as overseas player for 2001. Is contracted to the UCBSA

Best batting: 337* Transvaal v Northern Transvaal, Johannesburg 1993-94

Best bowling: 2-27 Border v Natal B, East London 1983-84

Stop press: His 112 v Sri Lanka at Cape Town in January 2001 (his fourth successive Test 100 at that ground) was his 12th Test century, edging him to the top of the list of South African Test century-makers ahead of Gary Kirsten

---

2000 Season (did not make any first-class or one-day appearances)

Career Performances

	M	Inns	NO	Runs	HS	Avge	100s	50s	Ct	St		Balls	Runs	Wkts	Avge	Best	5wI	10wM
Test	59	96	9	3748	275 *	43.08	11	17	50	-		120	71	2	35.50	1-10	-	-
All First	203	347	50	13126	337 *	44.19	35	62	189	-		506	289	5	57.80	2-27	-	-
1-day Int	132	128	16	3804	124	33.96	3	23	61	-		174	124	5	24.80	2-30	-	
NatWest	3	3	2	148	119 *	148.00	1	-	2	-								
B & H	3	3	2	106	101 *	106.00	1	-	1	-								
1-day Lge	12	11	3	365	76 *	45.62	-	3	4	-								

22. What was unusual about Graham Gooch's dismissal in England's second innings at Old Trafford in 1993?

CUNLIFFE, R. J.   Gloucestershire

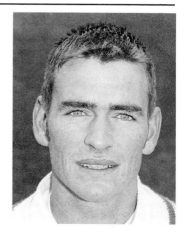

Name: <u>Robert</u> John Cunliffe
Role: Right-hand bat, cover fielder
Born: 8 November 1973, Oxford
Height: 5ft 10in **Weight:** 12st 8lbs
Nickname: 'Forrest Gump for some reason'
County debut: 1993 (one-day),
1994 (first-class)
1st-Class 50s: 10
1st-Class 100s: 3
1st-Class catches: 47
One-Day 100s: 3
Place in batting averages: 219th av. 16.35
(1999 86th av. 32.38)
Parents: Barry and Janet
Marital status: Engaged to Claire
Family links with cricket: 'Dad played in
his younger days for his wife's village team
and was groundsman for nine years at
Banbury Twenty CC'
Education: Grimsbury Primary; Banbury School; Banbury Technical College
Qualifications: Carpentry course, coaching award
Career outside cricket: Coaching
Overseas tours: England U19 to India 1992-93
Overseas teams played for: Richmond City CC, Melbourne 1995-97
Cricketers particularly admired: Robin Smith
Other sports played: Football
Relaxations: Walking the dog, watching TV
Extras: Played in England U19 home series against West Indies in 1993
Best batting: 190* Gloucestershire v Oxford University, Bristol 1995

23. Two wicket-keepers scored their maiden first-class 100s
in Ashes Tests at Old Trafford. Name them.

2000 Season

	M	Inns	NO	Runs	HS	Avge	100s	50s	Ct	St	O	M	Runs	Wkts	Avge	Best	5wI	10wM
Test																		
All First	9	14	0	229	74	16.35	-	1	10	-								
1-day Int																		
NatWest	2	2	0	69	69	34.50	-	1	-	-								
B & H	2	2	0	95	71	47.50	-	1	1	-								
1-day Lge	5	4	0	49	34	12.25	-	-	1	-								

Career Performances

	M	Inns	NO	Runs	HS	Avge	100s	50s	Ct	St	Balls	Runs	Wkts	Avge	Best	5wI	10wM
Test																	
All First	57	95	5	2280	190 *	25.33	3	10	47	-							
1-day Int																	
NatWest	12	10	0	234	69	23.40	-	1	2	-							
B & H	20	19	3	810	137 *	50.62	3	4	10	-							
1-day Lge	33	31	4	591	66	21.88	-	5	5	-							

DAGNALL, C. E. Warwickshire

Name: <u>Charles</u> Edward Dagnall
Role: Right-hand bat, right-arm
fast-medium bowler
Born: 10 July 1976, Bury, Lancashire
Height: 6ft 3in **Weight:** 14st 13lbs
Nickname: Baggo, Dog-face, Elvis, Slagnall,
Daggers, Dr Evil
County debut: 1999
Strike rate: 65.60 (career 44.45)
Parents: Mike and Jackie
Marital status: 'Very single'
Family links with cricket: Parents both
umpires; 'Dad ran town team U13'
Education: Bolton School; Bridgwater
School, Worsley; UMIST
Qualifications: 9 GCSEs, 3 A-levels,
BSc (Hons) Chemistry
Off-season: Singer (alias Thelonius Phonq)

with soul-funk band Frisco Crabbe and the Atlantic Frantics
Overseas teams played for: Newtown, Geelong, Australia 1994-95; St Josephs,
Geelong 1998-99

Cricketers particularly admired: Ian Botham, Paul Killey, Andy Cumberbatch, Gladstone Small, Allan Donald
Other sports played: Volleyball
Other sports followed: Football (Burnley FC), golf, tennis
Relaxations: Meeting new people, golf, listening to music from the '70s; 'cooking for A. Richardson'
Extras: Played for Cumberland. Man of the Match, Board XI final 1999 (Warwickshire v Essex). Topped 2nd XI batting averages 1998 and was second in bowling averages. Awarded 2nd XI cap 1999. Took a wicket with his fourth ball in first-class cricket v Oxford University at The Parks 1999. Has been presenter on Sky Digital shopping channel
Opinions on cricket: 'Two division competition has made normally mundane end of season fixtures into potentially very competitive and exciting games. However, too much cricket is still being played, and injuries take their toll on players because of this.'
Best batting: 6* Warwickshire v Essex, Chelmsford 2000
Best bowling: 4-20 Warwickshire v Oxford University, The Parks 1999

2000 Season

	M	Inns	NO	Runs	HS	Avge	100s	50s	Ct	St	O	M	Runs	Wkts	Avge	Best	5wI	10wM
Test																		
All First	2	2	2	11	6*	-	-	-	-	-	54.4	16	181	5	36.20	2-57	-	-
1-day Int																		
NatWest																		
B & H																		
1-day Lge	5	1	0	1	1	1.00	-	-	1	-	42	7	142	12	11.83	4-34	-	

Career Performances

	M	Inns	NO	Runs	HS	Avge	100s	50s	Ct	St	Balls	Runs	Wkts	Avge	Best	5wI	10wM
Test																	
All First	3	3	2	11	6*	11.00	-	-	-	-	489	269	11	24.45	4-20	-	-
1-day Int																	
NatWest	1	1	0	4	4	4.00	-	-	-	-	54	37	1	37.00	1-37	-	
B & H																	
1-day Lge	5	1	0	1	1	1.00	-	-	1	-	252	142	12	11.83	4-34	-	

DAKIN, J. M.   Leicestershire

Name: <u>Jonathan</u> Michael Dakin
Role: Left-hand bat, right-arm
medium-fast bowler, 'benefit wicket-keeper'
Born: 28 February 1973, Hitchin, Herts
Height: 6ft 6in **Weight:** 16st 4lbs
Nickname: JD, Brutus, Worby, Barney
County debut: 1993
County cap: 2000
1st-Class 50s: 9
1st-Class 100s: 5
1st-Class catches: 15
One-Day 100s: 1
One-Day 5 w. in innings: 1
Place in batting averages: 32nd av. 41.63
(1999 118th av. 28.37)
Place in bowling averages: 140th av. 45.78
(1999 98th av. 30.26)
Strike rate: 90.71 (career 81.18)
Parents: Fred John and Gloria May
Marital status: Single
Family links with cricket: Brother plays for Ivanhoe
Education: King Edward VII School, Johannesburg, South Africa
Qualifications: Matriculation
Off-season: Playing in Wellington, New Zealand
Overseas tours: Rutland Tourists to Jersey 1992; Leicestershire CCC to South Africa
1996, 1997, to Barbados, to Sri Lanka, to Anguilla
Overseas teams played for: Wanderers, South Africa 1986-92; Alberts, South Africa
1993; Kaponga CC, New Zealand 1995-96
Cricketers particularly admired: Darren 'Roaster' Maddy, Tim Mason, Cliff Eaton,
Phil ('Old Boy') DeFreitas
Young players to look out for: James Ormond, Greg King, Ash Wright
Other sports followed: Rugby union (Leicester Tigers), football (Man City)
Injuries: Out for two weeks with broken finger and shin splint
Relaxations: Eating out
Extras: Won three Bain Hogg trophies in four years. Scored 193 against Middlesex in
the Bain Hogg in 1996. Won the Gold Award against Durham in the 1996 B&H.
Awarded Leicestershire cap 2000
Opinions on cricket: 'Get NCL back to 40 overs. Physios must travel with their club
to every game.'
Best batting: 190 Leicestershire v Northamptonshire, Northampton 1997
Best bowling: 4-27 Leicestershire v Worcestershire, Worcester 1999

2000 Season

	M	Inns	NO	Runs	HS	Avge	100s	50s	Ct	St	O	M	Runs	Wkts	Avge	Best	5wI	10wM
Test																		
All First	9	12	1	458	135	41.63	1	3	2	-	211.4	39	641	14	45.78	2-20	-	-
1-day Int																		
NatWest	2	2	0	5	5	2.50	-	-	-	-	11	2	40	2	20.00	1-5	-	
B & H	4	3	0	19	10	6.33	-	-	-	-	24	1	77	3	25.66	2-28	-	
1-day Lge	9	8	3	130	68*	26.00	-	1	1	-	67.3	7	348	9	38.66	2-36	-	

Career Performances

	M	Inns	NO	Runs	HS	Avge	100s	50s	Ct	St	Balls	Runs	Wkts	Avge	Best	5wI	10wM
Test																	
All First	42	60	6	1746	190	32.33	5	9	15	-	4709	2323	58	40.05	4-27	-	-
1-day Int																	
NatWest	7	7	0	68	26	9.71	-	-	-	-	228	159	3	53.00	1-5	-	
B & H	16	12	3	314	108*	34.88	1	-	5	-	471	394	13	30.30	3-68	-	
1-day Lge	90	79	11	1062	68*	15.61	-	1	18	-	2364	2091	78	26.80	5-30	1	

DALE, A.   Glamorgan

Name: Adrian Dale
Role: Right-hand bat, right-arm medium bowler, county vice-captain
Born: 24 October 1968, Johannesburg
Height: 5ft 11in **Weight:** 11st 11lbs
Nickname: Arthur
County debut: 1989
County cap: 1992
1000 runs in a season: 3
1st-Class 50s: 49
1st-Class 100s: 16
1st-Class 200s: 1
1st-Class 5 w. in innings: 4
1st-Class catches: 76
One-Day 100s: 2
One-Day 5 w. in innings: 2
Place in batting averages: 60th av. 34.87 (1999 99th av. 31.11)
Place in bowling averages: 78th av. 28.04 (1999 67th av. 27.13)
Strike rate: 62.78 (career 67.95)
Parents: John and Maureen
Wife and date of marriage: Ruth, 9 January 1999

Children: Jessica, 12 January 2001
Family links with cricket: Father played occasionally for Glamorgan 2nd XI
Education: Chepstow Primary School; Chepstow Comprehensive; Swansea University
Qualifications: 9 O-levels, 3 A-levels, BA (Hons) Economics
Career outside cricket: Estate agency. Glamorgan Marketing Department
Off-season: 'Spending a month in New Zealand and working for Glamorgan CCC on a membership drive'
Overseas tours: Welsh Schools U16 to Australia 1986-87; Combined Universities to Barbados 1988-89; Glamorgan to Trinidad 1989-90, to Zimbabwe 1990-91, to Trinidad 1991-92, to Cape Town 1992-93, 1999; England A to South Africa 1993-94
Overseas teams played for: Bionics, Zimbabwe 1990-91; Cornwall, New Zealand 1991-93, 1995-97
Cricketers particularly admired: Ian Botham, Michael Holding, Mike Gatting
Other sports followed: Football (Arsenal), rugby union (Wales)
Relaxations: Travelling, eating out
Extras: Played in successful Combined Universities sides of 1989 and 1990. Only batsman to score two half-centuries against the West Indies tourists in the same match in 1991. Took a wicket with his first delivery at Lord's. Recorded Glamorgan's then best one-day bowling figures, 6-22, against Durham 1993. Shared in Glamorgan's highest ever partnership, 425*, with Viv Richards against Middlesex, 1993. Scored two centuries in Championship match v Gloucestershire at Cardiff 1999. Took 5-25 from 22.4 overs v Middlesex at Southgate 2000. Glamorgan CCC Player of the Year 2000. Appointed vice-captain of Glamorgan for 2001
Opinions on cricket: 'A great deal seems very positive in moving towards a stronger national team.'
Best batting: 214* Glamorgan v Middlesex, Cardiff 1993
Best bowling: 6-18 Glamorgan v Warwickshire, Cardiff 1993

2000 Season

	M	Inns	NO	Runs	HS	Avge	100s	50s	Ct	St	O	M	Runs	Wkts	Avge	Best	5wI	10wM
Test																		
All First	17	27	3	837	81	34.87	-	5	8	-	240.4	54	645	23	28.04	5-25	2	-
1-day Int																		
NatWest	3	3	1	11	4*	5.50	-	-	-	-	20	4	78	2	39.00	2-23	-	
B & H	6	6	2	182	63*	45.50	-	1	1	-	40.5	5	165	4	41.25	2-11	-	
1-day Lge	16	15	3	306	73*	25.50	-	1	3	-	96	2	434	13	33.38	2-20	-	

Career Performances

	M	Inns	NO	Runs	HS	Avge	100s	50s	Ct	St	Balls	Runs	Wkts	Avge	Best	5wI	10wM
Test																	
All First	198	326	27	9803	214 *	32.78	17	49	76	-	13659	7204	201	35.84	6-18	4	-
1-day Int																	
NatWest	32	29	3	793	110	30.50	1	3	6	-	1262	903	26	34.73	3-54	-	
B & H	39	38	6	940	100	29.37	1	2	11	-	1513	1067	43	24.81	5-41	1	
1-day Lge	160	143	19	3506	82	28.27	-	20	36	-	5013	4343	132	32.90	6-22	1	

DALEY, J. A.   Durham

Name: <u>James</u> Arthur Daley
Role: Right-hand bat
Born: 24 September 1973, Sunderland
Height: 5ft 11in **Weight:** 12st
Nickname: Bebs, Jonty
County debut: 1992
County cap: 1999
1st-Class 50s: 18
1st-Class 100s: 3
1st-Class catches: 42
One-Day 100s: 1
Place in batting averages: 233rd av. 14.52
(1999 136th av. 26.47)
Strike rate: (career 126.00)
Parents: William and Christine
Marital status: Single
Family links with cricket: Brother played
representative cricket for Durham
Education: Hetton Comprehensive
Qualifications: 5 GCSEs
Career outside cricket: Travel agent
Overseas tours: Durham to Zimbabwe 1991-92; England U19 to India 1992-93;
England XI to Holland 1993
Cricketers particularly admired: David Graveney, Wayne Larkins, Jimmy Adams
Other sports followed: Most sports
Relaxations: Socialising, listening to all types of music
Extras: Scored three centuries in 1991 for MCC Young Cricketers at Lord's. Northern
Electric Foundation for Sport award winner 1992
Best batting: 159* Durham v Hampshire, Portsmouth 1994
Best bowling: 1-12 Durham v Cambridge University, Fenner's 1998

2000 Season

	M	Inns	NO	Runs	HS	Avge	100s	50s	Ct	St	O	M	Runs	Wkts	Avge	Best	5wI	10wM
Test																		
All First	10	17	0	247	50	14.52	-	1	4	-	7	0	20	0	-		-	-
1-day Int																		
NatWest																		
B & H	4	4	0	27	15	6.75	-	-	-	-								
1-day Lge	8	8	0	261	105	32.62	1	2	1	-								

Career Performances

	M	Inns	NO	Runs	HS	Avge	100s	50s	Ct	St	Balls	Runs	Wkts	Avge	Best	5wI	10wM
Test																	
All First	82	142	11	3714	159 *	28.35	3	18	42	-	126	81	1	81.00	1-12	-	-
1-day Int																	
NatWest																	
B & H	11	10	0	106	33	10.60	-	-	-	-	12	19	0	-		-	-
1-day Lge	46	42	8	1136	105	33.41	1	7	11	-	1	4	0	-		-	-

DALRYMPLE, J. W. M.   Middlesex

Name: <u>James</u> William Murray Dalrymple
Role: Right-hand bat, off-spin bowler
Born: 21 January 1981, Nairobi, Kenya
Height: 6ft **Weight:** 13st 3lbs
County debut: 2000 (one-day)
Parents: Dougie and Patricia
Marital status: Single
Family links with cricket: 'Dad played lots of club cricket'
Education: Ashfold School, Dorton; Radley College, Abingdon; St Peter's College, Oxford University
Qualifications: 10 GCSEs, 5 A-levels
Career outside cricket: Student
Cricketers particularly admired:
Ian Botham, Mark Waugh, Mike Atherton, Courtney Walsh, Viv Richards
Other sports played: Rugby, hockey (county), golf, tennis
Other sports followed: Rugby (Northampton RUFC), football (Tottenham Hotspur)
Relaxations: Golf, tennis, flying, reading, music
Extras: Represented England U19 v Sri Lanka U19 in one-day and 'Test' series 2000

2000 Season

	M	Inns	NO	Runs	HS	Avge	100s	50s	Ct	St	O	M	Runs	Wkts	Avge	Best	5wI	10wM
Test																		
All First																		
1-day Int																		
NatWest																		
B & H																		
1-day Lge	1	0	0	0	0	-	-	-	-	-	7	1	37	1	37.00	1-37	-	

Career Performances

	M	Inns	NO	Runs	HS	Avge	100s	50s	Ct	St	Balls	Runs	Wkts	Avge	Best	5wI	10wM
Test																	
All First																	
1-day Int																	
NatWest																	
B & H																	
1-day Lge	1	0	0	0	0	-	-	-	-	-	42	37	1	37.00	1-37	-	

DAVIES, A. P.   Glamorgan

Name: <u>Andrew</u> Philip Davies
Role: Left-hand bat, right-arm medium-fast bowler
Born: 7 November 1976, Neath
Height: 6ft **Weight:** 13st
Nickname: Diver
County debut: 1995
1st-Class catches: 1
Strike rate: (career 69.68)
Parents: Philip and Anne
Marital status: Single
Family links with cricket: 'Phil plays with BP Llandarcy, as does brother Mark'
Education: Coedffranc; Dwr-y-Felin Comprehensive School; Christ College, Brecon
Qualifications: 6 GCSEs, 1 A-level; two coaching awards
Career outside cricket: 'Tracking down and suing whoever designed A.D. Shaw's attire!!!'
Off-season: 'Recovering from yet another operation'
Overseas tours: Wales MC to Barbados; Glamorgan to Pretoria, to Cape Town

Overseas teams played for: Marist CC, Whangarei, New Zealand 1995-96
Cricketers particularly admired: Glenn McGrath, Steve Watkin, Steve Waugh
Young players to look out for: Dave Harrison, Mark Wallace
Other sports followed: Football (Swansea City)
Injuries: Out for two months with wrist injury
Relaxations: 'Interests and concerns are where exactly Adrian Shaw gets his clothes from'
Extras: Trials at Birmingham City FC. Rugby trials for Wales U17. Welsh U19 Player of the Year 1995. Wales Player of the Year 1996. 2nd XI cap 1998. 2nd XI Player of the Year 1998-99. 1st XI Player of the Month August-September 1998
Opinions on cricket: 'Great improvement with the two divisions. Sides should try to play more day/night games to attract greater crowds and add more excitement!'
Best batting: 34 Glamorgan v Essex, Chelmsford 1998
Best bowling: 2-22 Glamorgan v Sussex, Hove 1998

2000 Season (did not make any first-class or one-day appearances)

Career Performances

	M	Inns	NO	Runs	HS	Avge	100s	50s	Ct	St	Balls	Runs	Wkts	Avge	Best	5wI	10wM
Test																	
All First	9	9	2	79	34	11.28	-	-	1	-	1115	603	16	37.68	2-22	-	-
1-day Int																	
NatWest																	
B & H																	
1-day Lge	10	7	3	27	18	6.75	-	-	1	-	370	281	12	23.41	2-17	-	

24. What feat of captaincy did Mark Taylor achieve in the 1998-99 series?

DAVIES, M. A. Durham

Name: <u>Mark</u> Anthony Davies
Role: Right-hand bat, right-arm medium-fast
bowler
Born: 4 October 1980, Stockton-on-Tees
Height: 6ft 3in **Weight:** 13st 6lbs
Nickname: Davo
County debut: 1998 (one-day)
Parents: Howard and Mandy
Marital status: Single
Family links with cricket: Grandfather keen
fan of Durham
Education: Billingham C of E School;
Northfield School, Billingham
Qualifications: 5 GCSEs, NVQ Level 3
Sport and Recreation
Off-season: 'In Australia working on
my game'
Overseas teams played for: North
Kalgoorlie CC, Western Australia
Cricketers particularly admired:
Andrew Caddick, Glenn McGrath
Young players to look out for: Nicky Peng, Ian Bell
Other sports played: Football, golf, boxing
Other sports followed: Football (Middlesbrough)
Injuries: Out for two weeks with punctured right lung
Relaxations: Socialising, golf
Extras: Represented England U19 in one-day series v Sri Lanka U19 2000. Is a
Durham Academy player

2000 Season

	M	Inns	NO	Runs	HS	Avge	100s	50s	Ct	St	O	M	Runs	Wkts	Avge	Best	5wI	10wM
Test																		
All First																		
1-day Int																		
NatWest																		
B & H																		
1-day Lge	1	0	0	0	0	-	-	-	-	-	6	0	15	3	5.00	3-15	-

Career Performances

	M	Inns	NO	Runs	HS	Avge	100s	50s	Ct	St	Balls	Runs	Wkts	Avge	Best	5wl	10wM
Test																	
All First																	
1-day Int																	
NatWest																	
B & H																	
1-day Lge	2	1	0	0	0	0.00	-	-	1	-	84	59	5	11.80	3-15	-	

DAVIES, M. K. Northamptonshire

Name: <u>Michael</u> Kenton Davies
Role: Right-hand bat, slow left-arm bowler
Born: 17 July 1976, Ashby-de-la-Zouch
Height: 6ft **Weight:** 12st
Nickname: Dicky
County debut: 1997
1st-Class 5 w. in innings: 5
1st-Class catches: 8
Place in batting averages: 274th av. 9.87
(1999 283rd av. 7.85)
Place in bowling averages:
(1999 27th av. 21.42)
Strike rate: 88.66 (career 66.98)
Parents: Lyndon and Ann
Marital status: Single
Education: Fairfield Primary School,
Loughborough; Loughborough Grammar
School; Loughborough University

Qualifications: 8 GCSEs, 4 A-levels, BSc PE, Sports Science and Recreation
Management
Overseas tours: England A to Bangladesh and New Zealand 1999-2000
Overseas teams played for: Techs CC, Cape Town 1999
Cricketers particularly admired: Nick Cook, Steve Waugh
Young players to look out for: Mark Powell, Monty Panesar
Other sports played: Golf
Other sports followed: 'Wales at anything, especially rugby'
Relaxations: Music, cinema, socialising
Extras: Leicestershire U19 Player of the Year. Represented British Universities; was a
member of BUSA's cricket squad in the 1997 Benson and Hedges Cup. NBC Denis
Compton Award 1999. Released by Northants at the end of the 2000 season
Opinions on cricket: 'Two divisions is a good idea. Tea should be longer.'

Best batting: 32* Northamptonshire v Durham, Northampton 1999
Best bowling: 6-49 Northamptonshire v Hampshire, Northampton 1999

2000 Season

	M	Inns	NO	Runs	HS	Avge	100s	50s	Ct	St	O	M	Runs	Wkts	Avge	Best	5wI	10wM
Test																		
All First	5	8	0	79	25	9.87	-	-	2	-	133	45	339	9	37.66	3-25	-	-
1-day Int																		
NatWest																		
B & H																		
1-day Lge	2	2	1	4	4	4.00	-	-	-	-	12	0	57	3	19.00	2-29	-	

Career Performances

	M	Inns	NO	Runs	HS	Avge	100s	50s	Ct	St	Balls	Runs	Wkts	Avge	Best	5wI	10wM
Test																	
All First	31	44	13	316	32 *	10.19	-	-	8	-	6230	2425	93	26.07	6-49	5	-
1-day Int																	
NatWest																	
B & H	6	3	2	4	2 *	4.00	-	-	-	-	272	238	5	47.60	3-11	-	
1-day Lge	2	2	1	4	4	4.00	-	-	-	-	72	57	3	19.00	2-29	-	

DAVIS, M. J. G.   Sussex

Name: Mark Jeffrey Gronow Davis
Role: Right-hand bat, right-arm off-spin bowler
Born: 10 October 1971, Port Elizabeth, South Africa
Height: 6ft 2in **Weight:** 12st 8lbs
Nickname: Doxy, Davo, Sparky
County debut: No first-team appearance
1st-Class 50s: 4
1st-Class 5 w. in innings: 3
1st-Class 10w. in match: 1
1st-Class catches: 45
Strike rate: 186.00 (career 78.10)
Parents: Jeremy and Marilyn
Wife and date of marriage: Candice, 8 April 2000
Family links with cricket: Father supported Sussex
Education: Woodridge Preparatory School; Grey High School; University of Pretoria
Qualifications: BA Psychology and English
Off-season: Playing league cricket in South Africa and Australia
Overseas tours: South Africa U24 to Sri Lanka 1995; Northern Transvaal to

Zimbabwe 1992-93, to Kenya 1994-95, 1995-96
Overseas teams played for: Northern Transvaal/Northerns 1991-92 –
Cricketers particularly admired: Malcolm Marshall, Tim May, Roy Pienaar, Shane Warne
Players to look out for: Herschelle Gibbs
Other sports played: Golf, tennis
Other sports followed: Rugby ('support the Springboks'), football (Middlesbrough)
Relaxations: 'Golf, music, going out with friends, watching good movies'
Extras: Made first-class debut for Northern Transvaal B 1990-91. Captain of Northern Transvaal/Northerns 1997-2000, during which time the province won the first two trophies in its history. Represented South

Africa A v Zimbabwe 1995. Member of MCC; played for MCC against Sri Lanka A at Shenley in 1999 and against New Zealand A at The Parks in 2000. Is not considered an overseas player
Opinions on cricket: 'Still the best game in the world.'
Best batting: 71 Northerns v Free State, Bloemfontein 1995-96
Best bowling: 8-37 Northerns B v North West, Potchefstroom 1994-95

2000 Season (did not make any first-class or one-day appearances)

Career Performances

	M	Inns	NO	Runs	HS	Avge	100s	50s	Ct	St	Balls	Runs	Wkts	Avge	Best	5wI	10wM
Test																	
All First	70	111	17	1514	71	16.10	-	4	45	-	11013	4731	141	33.550	8-37	3	1
1-day Int																	
NatWest																	
B & H																	
1-day Lge																	

DAWSON, R. K. J.   Yorkshire

Name: <u>Richard</u> Kevin James Dawson
Role: Right-hand bat, right-arm off-spin
bowler
Born: 4 August 1980, Doncaster
Height: 6ft 4in **Weight:** 11st 4lbs
Nickname: Billy Dog
County debut: No first-team appearance
Strike rate: 204.00 (career 204.00)
Parents: Kevin and Pat
Marital status: Single
Family links with cricket: Brother Gareth
plays for Doncaster Town CC
Education: Hill House Preparatory School;
Batley Grammar School; Exeter University
Qualifications: 10 GCSEs, 4 A-levels
Career outside cricket: Student
Overseas tours: England U18 to Bermuda
1997; England U19 to New Zealand 1998-99

Cricketers particularly admired: Steve Waugh, Graeme Swann
Young players to look out for: Graeme Bridge, Ian Bell
Other sports played: Football
Other sports followed: Football (Doncaster Rovers FC)
Relaxations: Sleeping, listening to music
Extras: Sir John Hobbs Jubilee Memorial Prize 1995. Captained England U15. Played
for Devon 1999 and 2000. Represented England U19 in one-day and 'Test' series v
Australia U19 in 1999. Has Yorkshire 2nd XI cap. Captained British Universities 2000
Opinions on cricket: 'The wickets should be better. Tea should be made longer.'
Best batting: 1 British Universities v Zimbabweans, Fenner's 2000
Best bowling: 1-115 British Universities v Zimbabweans, Fenner's 2000

2000 Season (did not make any first-class or one-day appearances)

Career Performances

	M	Inns	NO	Runs	HS	Avge	100s	50s	Ct	St	Balls	Runs	Wkts	Avge	Best	5wI	10wM
Test																	
All First	1	1	0	1	1	1.00	-	-	-	-	204	115	1	115.00	1-115	-	-
1-day Int																	
NatWest	3	3	0	14	7	4.66	-	-	1	-	131	88	4	22.00	2-32	-	
B & H																	
1-day Lge																	

DEAN, K. J.   Derbyshire

Name: <u>Kevin</u> James Dean
Role: Left-hand bat, left-arm
medium bowler ('still swing it, though')
Born: 16 October 1975, Derby
Height: 6ft 5in **Weight:** 14st
Nickname: Deany, Red Face, The Wall
County debut: 1996
County cap: 1998
50 wickets in a season: 1
1st-Class 5 w. in innings: 9
1st-Class 10 w. in match: 1
1st-Class catches: 5
One-Day 5 w. in innings: 1
Place in batting averages: 302nd av. 4.08
Place in bowling averages: 14th av. 17.84
(1999 6th av. 16.50)
Strike rate: 33.54 (career 39.89)
Parents: Ken and Dorothy
Marital status: Single
Education: Waterhouses Primary School; Leek High School; Leek College of Further
Education
Qualifications: 8 GCSEs, 3 A-levels, 1 AS-level
Career outside cricket: Working for Ladbrokes
Off-season: 'Working hard on trying to hit a six next season. Loads of swimming
(again) and working for Ladbrokes whilst cheering on the Super Rams'
Overseas teams played for: Sturt CC, Adelaide 1996-97
Cricketers particularly admired: Wasim Akram, Courtney Walsh, Dominic Cork,
'also any member of the "Left Arm Union": Mullally, Ilott, Smith, Lewry, Sheriyar,
Taylor, Brown, Bulbeck, Hutchison, Sidebottom etc'
Young players to look out for: Ed Joyce, Graham Napier
Other sports played: Football (Blue Circle), golf, tennis, squash ('I will beat you, Cas')
Other sports followed: Football (Derby County), horse racing
Injuries: 'Back after back op; a few niggles but nothing serious'
Relaxations: 'Going horse racing. Talking with Sutts and trying to keep it vaguely
interesting. Trying to stay one step ahead of the practical jokers, Aldred, Wells, Krikken.
Playing golf and trying to get my handicap down so less people think I am a bandit'
Extras: A member of the Staffordshire U16 Texaco winning team. Achieved first-class
hat-trick against Kent at Derby 1998. Took second first-class hat-trick (Habib,
Kumble, Ormond) v Leicestershire at Leicester 2000. His 8-52 v Kent at Canterbury
2000 included a spell of 6-6. Took 31 wickets in his last seven innings of the 2000
season

Opinions on cricket: 'As many one-day games as possible should be played under floodlights, as so far they have proved to be a great success. Children should also be admitted free in Championship cricket. The away team should decide whether they want to bat or bowl; this would eradicate pitch doctoring.'

Best batting: 27* Derbyshire v South Africans, Derby 1998
Best bowling: 8-52 Derbyshire v Kent, Canterbury 2000

2000 Season

	M	Inns	NO	Runs	HS	Avge	100s	50s	Ct	St	O	M	Runs	Wkts	Avge	Best	5wI	10wM
Test																		
All First	12	15	3	49	22	4.08	-	-	-	-	246	57	785	44	17.84	8-52	4	-
1-day Int																		
NatWest	1	0	0	0	0	-	-	-	-	-	10	3	14	3	4.66	3-14	-	
B & H																		
1-day Lge	13	11	8	48	8 *	16.00	-	-	1	-	97.2	7	461	15	30.73	4-30	-	

Career Performances

	M	Inns	NO	Runs	HS	Avge	100s	50s	Ct	St	Balls	Runs	Wkts	Avge	Best	5wI	10wM
Test																	
All First	48	58	23	330	27 *	9.42	-	-	5	-	6942	3837	174	22.05	8-52	9	1
1-day Int																	
NatWest	11	3	2	8	8	8.00	-	-	4	-	630	421	20	21.05	3-13	-	
B & H	6	2	1	20	14 *	20.00	-	-	-	-	240	211	5	42.20	2-62	-	
1-day Lge	50	22	15	103	16 *	14.71	-	-	9	-	2105	1618	56	28.89	5-32	1	

25. Which non-wicketkeeping fielder took a world record
(since equalled) seven catches at Perth in 1974-75?

DEFREITAS, P. A. J.   Leicestershire

Name: <u>Phillip</u> Anthony Jason DeFreitas
Role: Right-hand bat, right-arm
fast-medium bowler
Born: 18 February 1966, Scotts Head,
Dominica
Height: 6ft **Weight:** 13st 7lbs
Nickname: Daffy, Lunchy
County debut: 1985 (Leics),
1989 (Lancs), 1994 (Derbys)
County cap: 1986 (Leics),
1989 (Lancs), 1994 (Derbys)
Test debut: 1986-87
Tests: 44
One-Day Internationals: 103
50 wickets in a season: 12
1st-Class 50s: 46
1st-Class 100s: 8
1st-Class 5 w. in innings: 54
1st-Class 10 w. in match: 5
1st-Class catches: 110
One-Day 5 w. in innings: 6
Place in batting averages: 23rd av. 45.13 (1999 141st av. 25.94)
Place in bowling averages: 108th av. 33.48 (1999 29th av. 21.76)
Strike rate: 83.51 (career 57.42)
Parents: Sybil and Martin
Wife and date of marriage: Nicola, 10 December 1990
Children: Alexandra Elizabeth Jane, 5 August 1991
Family links with cricket: Father played in Windward Islands. All six brothers play
Education: Willesden High School
Qualifications: 2 O-levels
Overseas tours: England YC to West Indies 1984-85; England to Australia 1986-87,
to Pakistan, Australia and New Zealand 1987-88, to India (Nehru Cup) and West
Indies 1989-90, to Australia 1990-91, to New Zealand 1991-92, to India and Sri Lanka
1992-93, to Australia 1994-95, to South Africa 1995-96, to India and Pakistan
(World Cup) 1995-96; England XI to New Zealand (Cricket Max) 1997
Overseas teams played for: Port Adelaide, South Australia 1985; Mosman, Sydney
1988; Boland, South Africa 1993-94, 1995-96
Cricketers particularly admired: Ian Botham, Graham Gooch, Geoff Boycott,
Mike Gatting
Other sports followed: Football (Manchester City) and rugby league (Warrington)
Relaxations: 'Golf, gardening, visiting stately homes, spending spare time with wife
and daughter Alexandra'

Extras: Left Leicestershire and joined Lancashire at end of 1988 season. Man of the Match in 1990 NatWest Trophy final. One of *Wisden*'s Five Cricketers of the Year 1992. Man of the Tournament in the Hong Kong Sixes 1993. Left Lancashire at the end of the 1993 season and joined Derbyshire. Player of the Series against New Zealand 1994. Captained Derbyshire for part of 1997 season after the departure of Dean Jones. Is the only playing English cricketer to have appeared in two World Cup finals. Took 1000th first-class wicket (Usman Afzaal caught by Karl Krikken) v Notts at Trent Bridge 1999. Left Derbyshire at end of 1999 season and rejoined Leicestershire for 2000. Scored 97 and 123* v Lancashire at Leicester 2000 (also bowled 47 overs in Lancashire's only innings)
Best batting: 123* Leicestershire v Lancashire, Leicester 2000
Best bowling: 7-21 Lancashire v Middlesex, Lord's 1989

2000 Season

	M	Inns	NO	Runs	HS	Avge	100s	50s	Ct	St	O	M	Runs	Wkts	Avge	Best	5wI	10wM
Test																		
All First	14	18	3	677	123 *	45.13	1	4	1	-	459.2	122	1105	33	33.48	4-41	-	-
1-day Int																		
NatWest	1	1	0	15	15	15.00	-	-	-	-	10	0	29	1	29.00	1-29	-	
B & H	4	3	0	24	20	8.00	-	-	1	-	20	1	78	3	26.00	2-32	-	
1-day Lge	13	10	0	115	40	11.50	-	-	3	-	100	10	374	11	34.00	2-24	-	

Career Performances

	M	Inns	NO	Runs	HS	Avge	100s	50s	Ct	St	Balls	Runs	Wkts	Avge	Best	5wI	10wM
Test	44	68	5	934	88	14.82	-	4	14	-	9838	4700	140	33.57	7-70	4	-
All First	314	444	42	9177	123 *	22.82	8	46	110	-	60874	29368	1060	27.70	7-21	54	5
1-day Int	103	66	23	690	67	16.04	-	1	26	-	5712	3775	115	32.82	4-35	-	
NatWest	38	25	4	378	69	18.00	-	1	6	-	2367	1211	52	23.28	5-13	4	
B & H	63	43	9	736	75 *	21.64	-	3	16	-	3427	1960	87	22.52	5-16	1	
1-day Lge	188	143	23	2283	72 *	19.02	-	6	36	-	7674	5592	202	27.68	5-26	1	

26. Which pair of West Indian-born pace bowlers opened the bowling for England at Melbourne in 1986-87?

DIVENUTO, M. J.   Derbyshire

Name: <u>Michael</u> James DiVenuto
Role: Left-hand (No. 3) bat, right-arm
medium/leg-break bowler
Born: 12 December 1973, Hobart, Tasmania
Height: 5ft 11in **Weight:** 12st 12lbs
Nickname: Diva
County debut: 1999 (Sussex),
2000 (Derbyshire)
County cap: 1999 (Sussex),
2000 (Derbyshire)
One-Day Internationals: 9
1000 runs in a season: 1
1st-Class 50s: 47
1st-Class 100s: 13
1st-Class catches: 87
One-Day 100s: 1
Place in batting averages: 70th av. 32.95
(1999 29th av. 41.03)

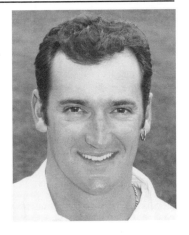

Strike rate: (career 116.25)
Parents: Enrico and Elizabeth
Marital status: Single
Family links with cricket: 'Dad and older brother Peter both played grade cricket in Tasmania'
Education: St Peter's School, Hobart; St Virgil's College, Hobart
Qualifications: HSC (5 x Level III subjects), Level III cricket coach
Career outside cricket: Part-time sports journalist with Southern Cross TV, Hobart
Off-season: Playing first-class cricket for Tasmania
Overseas tours: Australian Cricket Academy to India and Sri Lanka 1993, to South Africa 1996; Australia A to Malaysia (Super 8s) 1997 (captain), to Scotland and Ireland 1998 (captain), to Los Angeles 1999; Australia to South Africa 1996-97 (one-day series), to Hong Kong (Super 6s) 1997, to Malaysia (Super 8s) 1998; Tasmania to Zimbabwe 1995-96
Overseas teams played for: North Hobart CC, Tasmania; Kingborough, Tasmania; Tasmania 1991-92 –
Cricketers particularly admired: David Boon, Dean Jones, Kepler Wessels, Mark and Steve Waugh
Young players to look out for: Lawrence Prittipaul
Other sports played: Australian Rules (Tasmanian U15, U16 and Sandy Bay FC)
Other sports followed: Australian Rules football (Geelong Cats)
Injuries: Missed a day in the field with back spasms
Relaxations: Golf, sleeping and eating

Extras: Scored career-best 189 v Western Australia in 1997-98 Sheffield Shield final, contributing more than 50 per cent of Tasmania's total in their second innings. Joined Sussex as overseas player for 1999. Joined Derbyshire as overseas player for 2000. Scored 173* v Derbyshire Board XI at Derby in NatWest 2000, a record for Derbyshire in one-day cricket. Awarded Derbyshire cap 2000

Opinions on cricket: 'I think that divisional cricket was a success last season. I don't think the standard of pitches improved at all last year. Are the PLOs a bit scared to report a Test venue for a poor pitch? There probably should be more central contracts, and it was great to see England play with pride, passion and aggression last year against the West Indies. They will need that and more to beat the Aussies.'

Best batting: 189 Tasmania v Western Australia, Perth 1997-98
Best bowling: 1-0 Tasmania v Queensland, Brisbane 1999-2000

2000 Season

	M	Inns	NO	Runs	HS	Avge	100s	50s	Ct	St	O	M	Runs	Wkts	Avge	Best	5wI	10wM
Test																		
All First	16	25	3	725	92 *	32.95	-	6	12	-	8.3	3	19	0	-		-	-	-
1-day Int																		
NatWest	2	2	1	257	173 *	257.00	1	1	-	-								
B & H	5	4	1	120	61 *	40.00	-	1	1	-								
1-day Lge	16	16	0	372	84	23.25	-	1	5	-								

Career Performances

	M	Inns	NO	Runs	HS	Avge	100s	50s	Ct	St	Balls		Runs	Wkts	Avge	Best	5wI	10wM
Test																		
All First	110	188	9	7207	189	40.26	13	47	87	-	465		247	4	61.75	1-0	-	-
1-day Int	9	9	0	241	89	26.77	-	2	1	-								
NatWest	4	4	1	330	173 *	110.00	1	2	1	-								
B & H	7	6	1	223	62	44.60	-	2	1	-								
1-day Lge	30	30	4	968	94 *	37.23	-	7	11	-								

DOBSON, M. C.   Northamptonshire

Name: <u>Martyn</u> Colin Dobson
Role: Right-hand bat, off-spin bowler
Born: 28 May 1982, Scunthorpe
Height: 6ft **Weight:** 14st 6lbs
Nickname: Bonz
County debut: No first-team appearance
Parents: David and Susan
Marital status: 'Very single'
Family links with cricket: 'Dad played 2nd XI cricket with Yorkshire and

Warwickshire and was a club pro for many years. Brother Michael was with Northants and is this year club captain at Loughborough University'

Education: Bottesford Primary School; Frederick Gough Comprehensive; Oundle School, Northampton

Qualifications: 9 GCSEs, 2 A-levels

Off-season: 'Playing National League rugby union with Morley RUFC. Working in the office furniture business in Leeds'

Cricketers particularly admired:
Carl Hooper, Viv Richards

Young players to look out for:
Michael Dobson, John Sadler

Other sports played: Rugby (Morley 1st XV)

Other sports followed: Rugby, football (Scunthorpe Utd, Liverpool)

Relaxations: Music, socialising

Extras: Played rugby for Lincs County Schools U15 and U16. Captain of ESCA U14 and U15. Sir John Hobbs U16 prize from the Cricket Society 1997. Top of both batting and bowling averages for Yorkshire U19 1998

Opinions on cricket: 'Still no opinions – not been playing for long enough yet. Still enthusiastic about the game and all aspects – batting, bowling, fielding and practising. I want to play for a long time and maintain my enjoyment.'

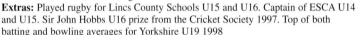

27. What part did Robin Sims play in the Lord's Test in 1989?

DONALD, A. A.   Warwickshire

Name: <u>Allan</u> Anthony Donald
Role: Right-hand bat, right-arm fast bowler
Born: 20 October 1966, Bloemfontein,
South Africa
Height: 6ft 3in **Weight:** 14st
County debut: 1987
County cap: 1989
Benefit: 1999
Test debut: 1991-92
Tests: 62
One-Day Internationals: 121
50 wickets in a season: 5
1st-Class 50s: 2
1st-Class 5 w. in innings: 66
1st-Class 10 w. in match: 9
1st-Class catches: 109
One-Day 5 w. in innings: 10
Place in batting averages: 275th av. 9.85
Place in bowling averages: 66th av. 26.50
Strike rate: 61.65 (career 47.75)

Parents: Stuart and Francine
Wife and date of marriage: Tina, 21 September 1991
Children: Hannah and Oliver
Family links with cricket: Father and uncle played club cricket
Education: Grey College High School; Technical High School, Bloemfontein
Qualifications: Matriculation
Off-season: Playing for South Africa
Overseas tours: South Africa to India (one-day series) 1991-92, to Zimbabwe (one-day series) 1991-92, to Australia and New Zealand (World Cup) 1991-92, to West Indies 1991-92, to Sri Lanka 1993-94, to Australia 1993-94, to England 1994, to New Zealand 1994-95, to Zimbabwe 1995-96, to India and Pakistan (World Cup) 1995-96, to India 1996-97, to Pakistan 1997-98, to Australia 1997-98, to England 1998, to New Zealand 1998-99, to UK, Ireland and Holland (World Cup) 1999, to Zimbabwe 1999-2000, to India 1999-2000, to Kenya (ICC Knockout Trophy) 2000-01, to West Indies 2000-01
Overseas teams played for: Free State, South Africa 1985-86 –
Cricketers particularly admired: Richard Hadlee, Malcolm Marshall, Gladstone Small, Andy Lloyd, Eddie Barlow
Other sports followed: Rugby, golf, tennis
Relaxations: 'Listening to music, having a barbecue, playing golf and having a few beers with my friends'

Injuries: Broke two ribs in a collision with a boundary board while attempting a catch at Southampton

Extras: Played for South African XI v Australian XI in 1986-87 and v English XI in 1989-90. Toured with South Africa on first-ever visit to India and to West Indies in 1991-92. One of *Wisden*'s Five Cricketers of the Year 1992. Took his 100th Test wicket against England in Johannesburg 1995-96. Voted Man of the Series against England finishing with 19 wickets at an average of 26.15. Took his 500th wicket for Warwickshire during the 1997 season. Was awarded his country's highest sporting honour when he was presented with a Gold Medal by Nelson Mandela at an awards ceremony in Pretoria on 15 August 1997. Took his 200th Test wicket (Sanath Jayasuriya) v Sri Lanka in 1998 in his 42nd Test, becoming the first South African to reach this landmark. Was South Africa's Man of the Series v England 1998. Took his 200th One-Day International wicket v Zimbabwe at Chelmsford in the 1999 World Cup. Played for Warwickshire 1987-2000 (except 1994, 1996, 1998). Retired from county cricket at the end of the 2000 season; is contracted to the UCBSA until April 2002

Best batting: 55* South Africans v Tasmania, Devonport 1997-98

Best bowling: 8-37 Orange Free State v Transvaal, Johannesburg 1986-87

Stop press: Took 300th Test wicket (Shayne O'Connor) in the first Test v New Zealand at Bloemfontein (his home city) in November 2000; he became the first South African to reach this mark, achieving the feat in his 63rd Test

2000 Season

	M	Inns	NO	Runs	HS	Avge	100s	50s	Ct	St	O	M	Runs	Wkts	Avge	Best	5wI	10wM
Test																		
All First	8	9	2	69	18	9.85	-	-	3	-	205.3	61	530	20	26.50	4-59	-	-
1-day Int																		
NatWest	5	0	0	0	0	-	-	-	-	-	43.3	5	163	12	13.58	4-42	-	
B & H	3	1	0	2	2	2.00	-	-	-	-	9	0	50	0	-		-	-
1-day Lge	7	5	3	19	11	9.50	-	-	-	-	52	8	148	11	13.45	3-9	-	

Career Performances

	M	Inns	NO	Runs	HS	Avge	100s	50s	Ct	St	Balls	Runs	Wkts	Avge	Best	5wI	10wM
Test	62	78	29	540	34	11.02	-	-	16	-	13564	6415	297	21.59	8-71	20	3
All First	295	337	127	2562	55 *	12.20	-	2	109	-	55011	25759	1152	22.36	8-37	66	9
1-day Int	121	30	13	84	13	4.94	-	-	16	-	6438	4336	206	21.04	6-23	2	
NatWest	35	11	6	39	14 *	7.80	-	-	4	-	2150	1239	87	14.24	5-12	5	
B & H	30	16	8	89	23 *	11.12	-	-	4	-	1595	1086	39	27.84	5-25	1	
1-day Lge	82	29	15	158	18 *	11.28	-	-	18	-	3571	2354	119	19.78	6-15	2	

DOWMAN, M. P.   Derbyshire

Name: <u>Mathew</u> Peter Dowman
Role: Left-hand bat, right-arm medium
bowler
Born: 10 May 1974, Grantham, Lincs
Height: 5ft 10in **Weight:** 12st
Nickname: Doomer
County debut: 1993 (one-day,
Nottinghamshire), 1994 (first-class,
Nottinghamshire), 2000 (Derbyshire)
County cap: 1998 (Nottinghamshire),
2000 (Derbyshire)
1000 runs in a season: 1
1st-Class 50s: 16
1st-Class 100s: 8
1st-Class catches: 46
Place in batting averages: 78th av. 32.03
(1999 74th av. 34.33)
Strike rate: 79.50 (career 86.64)
Parents: Clive and Jackie
Marital status: Engaged to Joanne. 'Get married October 2001'
Family links with cricket: 'Dad and three brothers all used to play for Grantham
Town; two brothers represented Lincolnshire Schools and Lincolnshire U19'
Education: Earlsfield County Primary; St Hugh's Comprehensive; Grantham College
Qualifications: 3 GCSEs, national sports award, senior coach
Career outside cricket: 'Decorating the house'
Off-season: 'Play golf; look to further my education'
Overseas tours: Lincolnshire U16 to Zimbabwe 1988-89; England U19 to India
1992-93; Nottinghamshire to Cape Town 1992-93, to Johannesburg 1996-97, 1997-98,
1998-99; Derbyshire to Portugal 2000
Overseas teams played for: South Barwon, Geelong, Melbourne 1995-96; East
Shirley, Christchurch, New Zealand 1997-98 ('didn't complete season')
Cricketers particularly admired: Robin Smith, Mike Gatting, Malcolm Marshall,
Jimmy Adams
Young players to look out for: Luke Sutton
Other sports played: Golf ('single-figure handicap'), squash
Other sports followed: Ice hockey (Nottingham Panthers), football, golf
Injuries: Out for two weeks with unstable shoulder
Relaxations: 'Golf, ice hockey, watching films, music, spending time at home'
Extras: Played in winning Midlands team at ESCA Festival 1989. Set record for most
runs in a season for Lincolnshire Schools and record for most runs in Lincolnshire
Schools career. Played for England U19 in home series against West Indies in 1993,

scoring 267 in second 'Test'. Winner of the 1997 Uncapped Whyte and Mackay Batting Award. Released by Nottinghamshire at end of 1999 season and joined Derbyshire for 2000 on a two-year contract. Scored 140 v Durham at Derby 2000, in the process sharing (with Dominic Cork) in a new record seventh-wicket partnership for Derbyshire (258). Awarded Derbyshire cap 2000

Opinions on cricket: 'The improvement in the England side suggests the central contracts system helps the bowlers recover. Even if you are out of the one-day competitions early, you still have things to play for with promotion and relegation. Players seem to be happy with it which is always important.'

Best batting: 149 Nottinghamshire v Leicestershire, Leicester 1997

Best bowling: 3-10 Nottinghamshire v Pakistan A, Trent Bridge 1997

2000 Season

	M	Inns	NO	Runs	HS	Avge	100s	50s	Ct	St	O	M	Runs	Wkts	Avge	Best	5wI	10wM
Test																		
All First	17	29	3	833	140	32.03	2	4	11	-	53	11	155	4	38.75	2-46	-	-
1-day Int																		
NatWest	2	1	0	18	18	18.00	-	-	1	-	19	0	71	2	35.50	2-49	-	
B & H	5	4	1	78	65	26.00	-	1	-	-	11	0	51	3	17.00	2-28	-	
1-day Lge	14	14	1	164	33	12.61	-	-	2	-	29	0	149	6	24.83	2-16	-	

Career Performances

	M	Inns	NO	Runs	HS	Avge	100s	50s	Ct	St	Balls	Runs	Wkts	Avge	Best	5wI	10wM
Test																	
All First	79	138	10	3783	149	29.55	8	16	46	-	2166	1118	25	44.72	3-10	-	-
1-day Int																	
NatWest	8	7	0	145	47	20.71	-	-	3	-	222	134	4	33.50	2-49	-	
B & H	19	14	3	407	92	37.00	-	3	5	-	398	299	14	21.35	3-21	-	
1-day Lge	75	75	4	1284	74 *	18.08	-	5	17	-	989	933	21	44.42	2-16	-	

28. Who replaced Steve Waugh to make his Test debut
(and score a century) at Adelaide in 1990-91?

DRAKES, V. C.   Warwickshire

Name: <u>Vasbert</u> Conniel Drakes
Role: Right-hand bat, right-arm fast bowler
Born: 5 August 1969, St Michael's, Barbados
Height: 6ft 2in **Weight:** 12st
County debut: 1996 (Sussex),
1999 (Nottinghamshire)
County cap: 1996 (Sussex),
1999 (Nottinghamshire)
One-day Internationals: 5
50 wickets in a season: 1
1st-Class 50s: 14
1st-Class 100s: 4
1st-Class 5 w. innings: 21
1st-Class 10 w. in match: 3
1st-Class catches: 36
One-Day 5 w. in innings: 2
Place in batting averages: (1999 236th
av. 15.81)

Place in bowling averages: (1999 38th av. 22.42)
Strike rate: (career 46.12)
Parents: Leon and Caroline
Family links with cricket: 'Sir Francis Drake is the famous bowler in the family – the only bowler to receive a knighthood. Introduced cricket to Barbados on an away day'
Education: St Lucy Secondary and College School, Barbados
Qualifications: NCA coach
Career outside cricket: Electrician
Overseas tours: Barbados U19 to UK 1987; Barbados U21 to UK 1990; Barbados to South Africa 1992; West Indies to England 1995
Overseas teams played for: Barbados 1991-92 – ; Border, South Africa 1996-97 –
Cricketers particularly admired: Desmond Haynes, Malcolm Marshall, 'and all successful fast bowlers throughout the world'
Other sports followed: Tennis, golf, basketball, football (Arsenal) and volleyball
Relaxations: Listening to music
Extras: Played for West Indies in One-Day International series against Australia in 1994-95. Once took 9-2 for Lamhey CC. Was Sussex overseas player in 1996 and 1997. Took 56 wickets for Border 1998-99, two short of the South African record shared by Peter Pollock and Sylvester Clarke. Joined Nottinghamshire as overseas player for 1999 on one-year contract. Took nine wickets on Championship debut for the county, v Worcestershire at Trent Bridge 1999. Took four wickets in four balls for Nottinghamshire in the final over of their National League victory v Derbyshire at Trent Bridge 1999; Derbyshire started the over needing ten runs with five wickets in

hand. Awarded Nottinghamshire cap 1999; released by Nottinghamshire at end of 1999 season. Has joined Warwickshire as overseas player for 2001

Best batting: 180* Barbados v Leeward Islands, Anguilla 1994-95
Best bowling: 8-59 Border v KwaZulu-Natal, Durban 1996-97

2000 Season (did not make any first-class or one-day appearances)

Career Performances

	M	Inns	NO	Runs	HS	Avge	100s	50s	Ct	St	Balls	Runs	Wkts	Avge	Best	5wl	10wM
Test																	
All First	108	176	20	3457	180*	22.16	4	14	36	-	19603	10336	425	24.32	8-59	21	3
1-day Int	5	2	0	25	16	12.50	-	-	1	-	239	204	3	68.00	1-36	-	
NatWest	8	5	1	111	35	27.75	-	-	-	-	501	297	18	16.50	4-62	-	
B & H	8	6	1	130	58	26.00	-	1	-	-	396	289	11	26.27	5-19	1	
1-day Lge	38	32	6	394	40	15.15	-	-	6	-	1638	1373	48	28.60	5-31	1	

DRAVID, R. Kent

Name: Rahul Dravid
Role: Right-hand bat, off-spin bowler
Born: 11 January 1973, Indore
Height: 5ft 11in
County debut: 2000
County cap: 2000
Test debut: 1996
Tests: 37
One-Day Internationals: 128
1st-Class 50s: 56
1st-Class 100s: 25
1st-Class 200s: 3
1st-Class catches: 140
1st-Class stumpings: 1
One-Day 100s: 8
Place in batting averages: 9th av. 55.50
Strike rate: 80.75 (career 130.25)
Education: St Joseph's High School; Bangalore University
Overseas tours: India to England 1996, to South Africa 1996-97, to West Indies 1996-97, to Sri Lanka 1997-98, to Zimbabwe 1998-99, to New Zealand 1998-99, to UK, Ireland and Holland (World Cup) 1999, to Australia 1999-2000, to Kenya (ICC Knockout Trophy) 2000-01, to Bangladesh 2000-01

Overseas teams played for: Karnataka, India 1990-91 –
Extras: Captained India U19 v New Zealand U19. Became the third Indian to score 100s in each innings of a Test with his 190 and 103* v New Zealand at Hamilton in January 1999. Shared in a stand of 318 for the second wicket with Saurav Ganguly for India v Sri Lanka at Taunton in the 1999 World Cup, a record for any wicket in One-Day International cricket. Was leading run-scorer and topped the batting averages in the 1999 World Cup with 461 runs at 65.85. Was named CEAT International Cricketer of the World Cup 1999. One of *Wisden*'s Five Cricketers of the Year 2000. Joined Kent as overseas player for 2000 on a one-year contract. Took first first-class wicket (Alec Stewart) v Surrey at The Oval 2000. Left Kent at the end of the 2000 season
Best batting: 215 Karnataka v Uttar Pradesh, Bangalore 1997-98
Best bowling: 2-16 Kent v Surrey, The Oval 2000
Stop press: Scored 200*, 70* and 162 in his three innings in the two-match Test series v Zimbabwe in India 2000-01

2000 Season

	M	Inns	NO	Runs	HS	Avge	100s	50s	Ct	St	O	M	Runs	Wkts	Avge	Best	5wl	10wM
Test																		
All First	16	25	3	1221	182	55.50	2	8	15	-	53.5	11	128	4	32.00	2-16	-	-
1-day Int																		
NatWest	2	2	0	76	54	38.00	-	1	-	-								
B & H	2	2	0	50	27	25.00	-	-	1	-								
1-day Lge	13	13	3	437	104	43.70	1	2	6	-	11	0	56	0	-		-	-

Career Performances

	M	Inns	NO	Runs	HS	Avge	100s	50s	Ct	St	Balls	Runs	Wkts	Avge	Best	5wl	10wM
Test	37	64	4	2821	190	47.01	6	16	39	-	24	6	0	-	-	-	-
All First	136	221	30	10453	215	54.72	28	56	140	1	521	240	4	60.00	2-16	-	-
1-day Int	128	120	9	4083	153	36.78	7	25	69	1	186	170	4	42.50	2-43	-	
NatWest	2	2	0	76	54	38.00	-	1	-	-							
B & H	2	2	0	50	27	25.00	-	-	1	-							
1-day Lge	13	13	3	437	104	43.70	1	2	6	-	66	56	0	-			

DRIVER, R. C.   Lancashire

Name: Ryan Craig Driver
Role: Left-hand bat, right-arm medium bowler
Born: 30 April 1979, Truro
Height: 6ft 3in **Weight:** 15st
Nickname: Bambi
County debut: 1998 (Worcestershire)
1st-Class 50s: 1

1st-Class catches: 3
Place in batting averages: 149th av. 23.25
Strike rate: 34.00 (career 34.00)
Parents: Les and Jan
Marital status: Single
Family links with cricket: Grandfather and uncle played club cricket. Father was captain of Truro CC for six years and still plays in Cornwall League. Mother and girlfriend keen supporters
Education: St Gluvias CP and Trewirgie School, Redruth; Redruth Technology College; Durham University
Qualifications: 9 GCSEs, 3 A-levels, 2.2 degree in Sport in Community, NCA Level 2 coaching award
Off-season: Relaxing and staying fit
Overseas tours: ESCA West U14 to West Indies 1993-94; Cornwall Colts to South Africa 1996, 1997
Cricketers particularly admired: Graeme Hick, Glenn McGrath
Young players to look out for: Kadeer Ali
Other sports played: Squash
Other sports followed: Football (Derby County)
Relaxations: Music, 'getting beaten at squash by Tim Roberts'
Extras: CSCA Batting Award 1993-96. Played for ESCA U19 and MCC Schools in 1997. Played for Cornwall CCC from 1995. West Region *Daily Telegraph* Batsman of the Year 1995. England Schoolboy Cricketer of the Year 1997. Opening bat for Truro CC (Cornwall champions in 1996 and 1997). 2nd XI Player of the Month August/September 1998. Durham University 1st XI 1998-2000; played in Durham University's BUSA Championship winning side 1999. Won Man of the Match award in NatWest Trophy v Gloucestershire 2000 (the game was later declared void and replayed but award stood). British Universities 1999-2000. Durham University Sportsman of the Year 2000. Released by Worcestershire at the end of the 2000 season and has joined Lancashire for 2001
Opinions on cricket: 'Introduction of two divisions has added an edge to county cricket in both four-day and one-day competitions.'
Best batting: 64 Worcestershire v Sussex, Worcester 2000
Best bowling: 1-13 Worcestershire v Northamptonshire, Worcester 2000

2000 Season

	M	Inns	NO	Runs	HS	Avge	100s	50s	Ct	St	O	M	Runs	Wkts	Avge	Best	5wI	10wM
Test																		
All First	11	20	4	372	64	23.25	-	1	2	-	11.2	2	44	2	22.00	1-13	-	-
1-day Int																		
NatWest	2	2	1	61	61 *	61.00	-	1	-	-								
B & H																			
1-day Lge	8	8	0	128	52	16.00	-	1	1	-	6	0	42	1	42.00	1-17	-	

Career Performances

	M	Inns	NO	Runs	HS	Avge	100s	50s	Ct	St	Balls	Runs	Wkts	Avge	Best	5wI	10wM
Test																	
All First	15	27	4	480	64	20.86	-	1	3	-	68	44	2	22.00	1-13	-	-
1-day Int																	
NatWest	3	3	1	61	61 *	30.50	-	1	-	-							
B & H																		
1-day Lge	9	9	0	131	52	14.55	-	1	1	-	36	42	1	42.00	1-17	-	

DUMELOW, N. R. C.   Derbyshire

Name: Nathan Robert Charles Dumelow
Role: Right-hand bat, right-arm off-spin bowler
Born: 30 April 1981, Derby
Height: 5ft 10in **Weight:** 10st 7lbs ('I think')
Nickname: Piggy ('I am the "babe" at Derbyshire so because of the film they call me "Piggy"')
County debut: No first-team appearance
Parents: Kate and Robert
Marital status: Single
Family links with cricket: 'Father plays for Derbyshire Over 50s; is an excellent club cricketer and qualified coach'

Education: Foremark Hall ('prep to Repton'); Denstone College; 'attended Brooksby Agricultural College because my parents are farmers'
Qualifications: 7 GCSEs, coach
Career outside cricket: 'None; only working at home'
Off-season: 'I am going to South Africa in the winter'

Overseas tours: U15 and U16 tours to South Africa and Barbados
Overseas teams played for: Schoeman Park CC, Bloemfontein
Cricketers particularly admired: 'Lance Klusener for his attacking play;
Chris Cairns for his all-round ability; Mark Waugh just for playing cricket at the top
for so long'
Young players to look out for: 'Hopefully myself'
Relaxations: Fishing, shooting, golf
Extras: Won all Derbyshire age-group awards. 'I was the player that Derbyshire
would not let play for the Board against my own county, even though I had played
every other round; this question was on *A Question of Sport*.' Played for Derbyshire
Board XI in the NatWest 1999 and 2000
Opinions on cricket: 'Two divisions excellent – created more fighting spirit right to
the end of the season. I think some young cricketers play too much and I think I did
last year.'

2000 Season (did not make any first-class or one-day appearances)

Career Performances

	M	Inns	NO	Runs	HS	Avge	100s	50s	Ct	St	Balls	Runs	Wkts	Avge	Best	5wl	10wM
Test																	
All First																	
1-day Int																	
NatWest	2	2	0	56	32	28.00	-	-	-	-	90	63	2	31.50	2-21	-	
B & H																	
1-day Lge																	

29. Which Australian captain spun his side to victory with 6-70
in England's second innings at Old Trafford in 1961?

DUTCH, K. P.   Somerset

Name: <u>Keith</u> Philip Dutch
Role: Right-hand bat, off-spin bowler
Born: 21 March 1973, Harrow, Middlesex
Height: 5ft 9in **Weight:** 11st 4lbs
Nickname: Dutchy, Oik
County debut: 1993 (Middlesex)
1st-Class 50s: 3
1st-Class 5 w. in innings: 1
1st-Class catches: 22
One-Day 5 w. in innings: 1
Place in batting averages: 151st av. 22.85
(1999 262nd av. 11.90)
Place in bowling averages: 31st av. 21.52
Strike rate: 50.70 (career 64.71)
Parents: Alan and Ann
Marital status: Single
Children: Lauren Beth-Amy,
15 January 1999
Family links with cricket: Father coached
Education: Nower Hill High School, Pinner; Weald College, Harrow
Qualifications: 5 GCSEs, 1 AS-level, staff tutor coach
Off-season: Coaching
Overseas tours: MCC to Central and East Africa 1997, to Canada 2000-01
Overseas teams played for: Worcester United, South Africa 1992-93; Geelong City,
Australia, 1994; Rygersdal CC, Cape Town 1997-98
Cricketers particularly admired: Mark Ramprakash, John Emburey
Young players to look out for: Owais Shah, David Nash, Stephen Peters, Ed Joyce
Other sports followed: Football (Arsenal FC)
Relaxations: Music, TV and shopping for clothes
Extras: On MCC groundstaff for one year before becoming a contracted player.
Middlesex 2nd XI Player of the Year 1995. In 1996 scored over 1,000 2nd XI
Championship runs and took 65 wickets. During this time he set a record for the
highest-ever batting total and best bowling figures by a Middlesex player in the history
of the 2nd XI Championship with 261 against Somerset and 15 for 157 against
Leicestershire – each was the fourth highest in the championship record books. 2nd XI
Championship Player of the Year in 1993, 1996 and 1999. Took five catches in
Cambridge University's first innings at Fenner's 2000. Scored 91 and took 6-62 (both
career bests) in a single day v Essex at Chelmsford 2000. Released by Middlesex at
the end of the 2000 season and has joined Somerset for 2001
Best batting: 91 Middlesex v Essex, Chelmsford 2000
Best bowling: 6-62 Middlesex v Essex, Chelmsford 2000

2000 Season

	M	Inns	NO	Runs	HS	Avge	100s	50s	Ct	St	O	M	Runs	Wkts	Avge	Best	5wI	10wM
Test																		
All First	5	7	0	160	91	22.85	-	2	9	-	143.4	45	366	17	21.52	6-62	1	-
1-day Int																		
NatWest	3	3	2	67	29 *	67.00	-	-	1	-	14	1	58	2	29.00	2-37	-	
B & H																		
1-day Lge	7	6	1	32	17	6.40	-	-	-	-	50	4	211	6	35.16	1-18	-	

Career Performances

	M	Inns	NO	Runs	HS	Avge	100s	50s	Ct	St	Balls	Runs	Wkts	Avge	Best	5wI	10wM
Test																	
All First	27	35	2	497	91	15.06	-	3	22	-	2459	1191	38	31.34	6-62	1	-
1-day Int																	
NatWest	9	8	4	160	49 *	40.00	-	-	5	-	462	302	8	37.75	2-30	-	
B & H	6	6	1	48	20	9.60	-	-	2	-	186	152	7	21.71	4-42	-	
1-day Lge	62	53	14	695	58	17.82	-	2	15	-	2023	1581	68	23.25	5-35	1	

EALHAM, M. A.   Kent

Name: <u>Mark</u> Alan Ealham
Role: Right-hand bat, right-arm medium bowler; all-rounder
Born: 27 August 1969, Ashford, Kent
Height: 5ft 10in **Weight:** 14st 4lbs
Nickname: Ealy, Skater, Boarder, Ealberg
County debut: 1989
County cap: 1992
Test debut: 1996
Tests: 8
One-Day Internationals: 55
1000 runs in a season: 1
1st-Class 50s: 42
1st-Class 100s: 5
1st-Class 5 w. in innings: 14
1st-Class 10 w. in match: 1
1st-Class catches: 56
One-Day 100s: 1
One-Day 5 w. in innings: 4
Place in batting averages: 155th av. 22.53 (1999 101st av. 30.78)
Place in bowling averages: 86th av. 29.29 (1999 52nd av. 23.92)
Strike rate: 67.95 (career 59.76)

Parents: Alan and Sue
Wife and date of marriage: Kirsty, 24 February 1996
Family links with cricket: Father played for Kent
Education: Chartham; Stour Valley Secondary School
Qualifications: 9 CSEs
Career outside cricket: Plumber
Off-season: England one-day squad to Kenya, Pakistan and Sri Lanka
Overseas tours: England A to Australia 1996-97, to Kenya and Sri Lanka 1997-98; England VI to Hong Kong 1997; England to Sharjah (Champions Trophy) 1997-98, to Bangladesh (Wills International Cup) 1998, to Australia 1998-99 (CUB Series), to Sharjah (Coca-Cola Cup) 1998-99, to South Africa and Zimbabwe 1999-2000 (one-day series), to Kenya (ICC Knockout Trophy) 2000-01, to Pakistan and Sri Lanka 2000-01 (one-day series)
Overseas teams played for: South Perth, Australia 1992-93; University, Perth 1993-94
Cricketers particularly admired: Ian Botham, Viv Richards, Robin Smith, Steve Waugh, Paul Blackmore and Albert 'for his F and G'
Young players to look out for: Pete Trego, James Hockley
Other sports followed: Football (Manchester United) and most other sports
Injuries: Out for four weeks with broken index finger
Relaxations: Playing golf and snooker, watching films
Extras: Set record for fastest Sunday League century (44 balls), v Derbyshire at Maidstone 1995. Represented England in the 1999 World Cup. Returned a new England best One-Day International bowling analysis with his 5-15 v Zimbabwe at Kimberley in January 2000; all five were lbw
Opinions on cricket: 'In the one-day competitions where fixtures are "drawn", give the visiting side the choice of the toss to ensure the best possible surfaces are prepared. Two-divisional cricket is a success, but only two teams from each division to go up and down.'
Best batting: 139 Kent v Leicestershire, Canterbury 1997
Best bowling: 8-36 Kent v Warwickshire, Edgbaston 1996

2000 Season

	M	Inns	NO	Runs	HS	Avge	100s	50s	Ct	St	O	M	Runs	Wkts	Avge	Best	5wI	10wM
Test																		
All First	11	14	1	293	83	22.53	-	2	3	-	271.5	67	703	24	29.29	5-35	1	-
1-day Int	7	4	1	74	32	24.66	-	-	1	-	60	7	203	5	40.60	2-37	-	
NatWest	2	2	1	8	8 *	8.00	-	-	-	-	20	3	52	5	10.40	4-36	-	
B & H	2	2	0	78	61	39.00	-	1	-	-	17.2	6	49	8	6.12	4-17	-	
1-day Lge	12	10	1	175	49 *	19.44	-	-	3	-	91.4	11	313	10	31.30	3-38	-	

Career Performances

	M	Inns	NO	Runs	HS	Avge	100s	50s	Ct	St	Balls	Runs	Wkts	Avge	Best	5wI	10wM
Test	8	13	3	210	53 *	21.00	-	2	4	-	1060	488	17	28.70	4-21	-	-
All First	149	240	38	6337	139	31.37	5	42	56	-	19963	9592	334	28.71	8-36	14	1
1-day Int	55	39	4	648	45	18.51	-	-	8	-	2799	1874	61	30.72	5-15	2	
NatWest	21	20	6	402	58 *	28.71	-	2	6	-	1145	584	26	22.46	4-10	-	
B & H	41	38	9	859	75	29.62	-	7	14	-	2080	1358	65	20.89	4-17	-	
1-day Lge	141	116	31	2157	112	25.37	1	9	36	-	5489	4089	131	31.21	6-53	2	

ELLIOTT, M. T. G. Glamorgan

Name: <u>Matthew</u> Thomas Gray Elliott
Role: Left-hand bat, 'pseudo left-arm
orthodox' bowler
Born: 28 September 1971, Chelsea, Victoria,
Australia
Height: 6ft 3in **Weight:** 12st 7lbs
Nickname: Herb
County debut: 2000
County cap: 2000
Test debut: 1996-97
Tests: 20
One-Day Internationals: 1
1000 runs in a season: 1
1st-Class 50s: 40
1st-Class 100s: 31
1st-Class 200s: 2
1st-Class catches: 130
One-Day 100s: 1
Place in batting averages: 13th av. 51.23
Strike rate: (career 110.33)
Parents: John and Glenda
Wife and date of marriage: Megan, 11 December 1994
Children: Zachary, 22 December 1997
Family links with cricket: Father played district cricket with Northcote (Melbourne)
Education: Lancaster Primary School; Kyabram Secondary College
Qualifications: VCE certificate
Off-season: Playing for Victoria in Australia's domestic season
Overseas tours: Australia to South Africa 1996-97, to England 1997, to West Indies
1998-99
Cricketers particularly admired: Steve Waugh
Young players to look out for: Matthew Inness, Michael Klinger (Victoria)

Other sports followed: Australian Rules football (Collingwood FC)
Relaxations: Reading biographies/true stories; fishing
Extras: One of *Wisden*'s Five Cricketers of the Year 1998. Sheffield Shield Player of the Year 1995-96 and 1998-99. Awarded ACB contract for 2000-01. Scored century (117) in his first Championship innings for Glamorgan, v Warwickshire at Edgbaston 2000. Scored 177 in helping to set county record first-wicket partnership of 374 with Stephen James v Sussex at Colwyn Bay 2000; James went on to score 309*. Left Glamorgan at the end of the 2000 season
Opinions on cricket: 'Generally in pretty good shape.'
Best batting: 203 Victoria v Tasmania, Melbourne 1995-96
Best bowling: 1-3 Victoria v Tasmania, Melbourne 1998-99

2000 Season

	M	Inns	NO	Runs	HS	Avge	100s	50s	Ct	St	O	M	Runs	Wkts	Avge	Best	5wI	10wM
Test																		
All First	13	21	0	1076	177	51.23	4	4	19	-	20	5	43	0	-		-	-	-
1-day Int																		
NatWest	3	3	0	181	156	60.33	1	-	-	-								
B & H	6	6	0	60	29	10.00	-	-	5	-								
1-day Lge	11	11	2	429	94	47.66	-	4	5	-	3	1	10	0	-		-	-

Career Performances

	M	Inns	NO	Runs	HS	Avge	100s	50s	Ct	St	Balls	Runs	Wkts	Avge	Best	5wI	10wM
Test	20	34	1	1171	199	35.48	3	4	13	-	12	4	0	-		-	-
All First	114	208	16	9712	203	50.58	33	40	130	-	993	562	9	62.44	1-3	-	-
1-day Int	1	1	0	1	1	1.00	-	-	-	-							
NatWest	3	3	0	181	156	60.33	1	-	-	-							
B & H	6	6	0	60	29	10.00	-	-	5	-							
1-day Lge	11	11	2	429	94	47.66	-	4	5	-	18	10	0	-		-	-

ELSTUB, C. J.   Yorkshire

Name: Christopher John Elstub
Role: Right-hand bat, right-arm medium-fast bowler
Born: 3 February 1981, Dewsbury
Height: 5ft 11in **Weight:** 12st
Nickname: Shrub, Elly
County debut: 2000
1st-Class catches: 1
Strike rate: 52.62 (career 52.62)
Parents: Richard and Susan
Marital status: Single

Family links with cricket: Father played club cricket and for Yorkshire 2nd XI
Education: Gomersal Middle School; Whitcliffe Mount School; Leeds Metropolitan University
Qualifications: 9 GCSEs, 1 A-level, GNVQ (Advanced) Leisure and Tourism, NCA coaching award Levels 1 and 2
Career outside cricket: Teacher
Off-season: Studying at university and keeping fit
Cricketers particularly admired: Darren Gough, Darren Lehmann, Courtney Walsh
Young players to look out for: Michael Lumb, Joe Sayers
Other sports played: Hockey (Bradford)
Other sports followed: Football (Emley FC and Manchester United)
Injuries: Out for six weeks with stress fracture of tibia
Relaxations: Sleeping, listening to music, socialising with friends
Opinions on cricket: 'There are too many games played in the season, which leads to injuries. More National League matches should be played under floodlights.'
Best batting: 4* Yorkshire v Lancashire, Headingley 2000
Best bowling: 3-37 Yorkshire v West Indians, Headingley 2000

2000 Season

	M	Inns	NO	Runs	HS	Avge	100s	50s	Ct	St	O	M	Runs	Wkts	Avge	Best	5wI	10wM
Test																		
All First	4	4	3	6	4 *	6.00	-	-	1	-	70.1	13	175	8	21.87	3-37	-	-
1-day Int																		
NatWest																		
B & H																			
1-day Lge	2	0	0	0	0	-	-	-	-	-	12.2	0	67	0	-		-	-

Career Performances

	M	Inns	NO	Runs	HS	Avge	100s	50s	Ct	St	Balls	Runs	Wkts	Avge	Best	5wI	10wM
Test																	
All First	4	4	3	6	4 *	6.00	-	-	1	-	421	175	8	21.87	3-37	-	-
1-day Int																	
NatWest																	
B & H																		
1-day Lge	2	0	0	0	0	-	-	-	-	-	74	67	0	-		-	-

EVANS, A. W.   Glamorgan

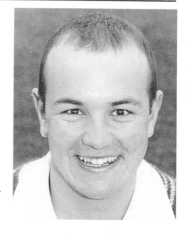

Name: <u>Alun</u> Wyn Evans
Role: Right-hand bat, right-arm
medium bowler
Born: 20 August 1975, Glanamman, Dyfed
Height: 5ft 8in **Weight:** 12st
Nickname: Troll
County debut: 1996
1st-Class 50s: 6
1st-Class 100s: 1
1st-Class catches: 23
One-Day 100s: 1
Place in batting averages: 190th av. 19.00
(1999 159th av. 24.38)
Parents: Gareth and Lynfa
Marital status: Single
Family links with cricket: Father played for
Ammanford CC. Brother Huw plays for
Ammanford; has also played for Glamorgan
2nd XI
Education: Fishguard Primary School; Fishguard High School; Neath Tertiary College
Qualifications: 11 GCSEs, BTEC National Diploma in Sports Science, Senior Cricket
Coaching Award
Career outside cricket: 'Not decided'
Off-season: 'Decorating my new house in Cardiff; playing rugby'
Overseas tours: Welsh Schools U17 to Sydney, Australia 1992-93
Overseas teams played for: Marist CC, Whangarei, New Zealand 1995, 1996, 1997;
Gordon, Sydney 1999-2000
Cricketers particularly admired: Wasim Akram, Matthew Maynard, Steve James
Young players to look out for: John Derrick ('seems to be getting younger each
year'), Carl Roberts
Other sports played: Rugby, golf, fly fishing
Other sports followed: Rugby (Cardiff), football (Tottenham Hotspur FC)
Relaxations: Playing golf, running
Extras: Welsh Schools Player of the Year 1994. MCC Young Cricketer 1995.
Balconiers 2nd XI Player of the Year 1996. ASW Young Player of the Year
Opinions on cricket: 'I got stuck playing 2nd team cricket for most of the season last
year and most of the wickets that we played on, on club grounds, were well below the
standard expected. Second team games should be played on first-class grounds.'
Best batting: 125 Glamorgan v Cambridge University, Fenner's 1998

2000 Season

	M	Inns	NO	Runs	HS	Avge	100s	50s	Ct	St	O	M	Runs	Wkts	Avge	Best	5wI	10wM
Test																		
All First	4	6	0	114	58	19.00	-	1	-	-								
1-day Int																		
NatWest																		
B & H																		
1-day Lge	2	2	0	11	6	5.50	-	-	1	-								

Career Performances

	M	Inns	NO	Runs	HS	Avge	100s	50s	Ct	St	Balls	Runs	Wkts	Avge	Best	5wI	10wM
Test																	
All First	36	60	7	1449	125	27.33	1	6	23	-	6	3	0	-	-	-	-
1-day Int																	
NatWest	3	3	0	93	52	31.00	-	1	-	-							
B & H	2	2	0	24	14	12.00	-	-	-	-							
1-day Lge	35	30	5	541	108	21.64	1	2	12	-							

FAIRBROTHER, N. H.   Lancashire

Name: <u>Neil</u> Harvey Fairbrother
Role: Left-hand bat, left-arm medium bowler
Born: 9 September 1963, Warrington, Cheshire
Height: 5ft 8in **Weight:** 11st 4lbs
Nickname: Harvey
County debut: 1982
County cap: 1985
Benefit: 1995
Test debut: 1987
Tests: 10
One-Day Internationals: 75
1000 runs in a season: 10
1st-Class 50s: 103
1st-Class 100s: 38
1st-Class 200s: 3
1st-Class 300s: 1
1st-Class catches: 264
One-Day 100s: 6
Place in batting averages: 19th av. 45.72 (1999 137th av. 26.47)
Strike rate: 38.00 (career 120.50)
Parents: Les and Barbara
Wife and date of marriage: Audrey, 23 September 1988

Children: Rachael Elizabeth, 4 April 1991; Sam, 3 April 1994
Family links with cricket: Father and two uncles played local league cricket
Education: St Margaret's Church of England School, Oxford; Lymm Grammar School
Qualifications: 5 O-levels
Overseas tours: England A to Pakistan 1990-91; England to Sharjah 1986-87, to India and Pakistan (World Cup) 1987-88, to Australia and New Zealand 1987-88, to New Zealand 1991-92, to India 1992-93, to Australia 1994-95, to South Africa 1995-96, to India and Pakistan (World Cup) 1995-96, to Bangladesh (Wills International Cup) 1998-99, to Australia 1998-99 (CUB Series), to Sharjah (Coca-Cola Cup) 1998-99
Cricketers particularly admired: Clive Lloyd, Allan Border, David Gower
Other sports followed: Football, rugby union, rugby league
Relaxations: Music and playing sport
Extras: 'I was named after the Australian cricketer Neil Harvey, who was my mum's favourite cricketer.' Played for England YC v Australia 1983. His 366 in 1990 was the third highest score ever made in the County Championship, the second highest first-class score by a Lancashire batsman and the best at The Oval. Appointed Lancashire captain for 1992 but resigned in 1993. Has appeared in ten domestic one-day finals, a record he shares with Derek Underwood. Represented England in the 1999 World Cup
Best batting: 366 Lancashire v Surrey, The Oval 1990
Best bowling: 2-91 Lancashire v Nottinghamshire, Old Trafford 1987

2000 Season

	M	Inns	NO	Runs	HS	Avge	100s	50s	Ct	St	O	M	Runs	Wkts	Avge	Best	5wl	10wM
Test																		
All First	15	23	5	823	138	45.72	2	3	16	-	6.2	2	11	1	11.00	1-5	-	-
1-day Int																		
NatWest	4	2	0	22	15	11.00	-	-	1	-								
B & H	7	6	2	197	74	49.25	-	2	2	-								
1-day Lge	15	14	3	354	75	32.18	-	3	5	-								

Career Performances

	M	Inns	NO	Runs	HS	Avge	100s	50s	Ct	St	Balls	Runs	Wkts	Avge	Best	5wl	10wM
Test	10	15	1	219	83	15.64	-	1	4	-	12	9	0	-	-	-	-
All First	342	542	75	19267	366	41.25	42	103	264	-	723	453	6	75.50	2-91	-	-
1-day Int	75	71	18	2092	113	39.47	1	16	33	-	6	9	0	-	-	-	
NatWest	45	42	8	1576	93 *	46.35	-	12	22	-	48	44	1	44.00	1-28	-	
B & H	82	78	23	2795	116 *	50.81	1	23	36	-	54	67	1	67.00	1-17	-	
1-day Lge	237	220	56	6571	116 *	40.06	4	46	70	-	48	48	1	48.00	1-33	-	

FELLOWS, G. M.   Yorkshire

Name: <u>Gary</u> Matthew Fellows
Role: Right-hand bat, right-arm
medium bowler
Born: 30 July 1978, Halifax, West Yorkshire
Height: 5ft 9in **Weight:** 11st
Nickname: Mousey, Mick
County debut: 1998
1st-Class 50s: 1
1st-Class catches: 9
Place in batting averages: 164th av. 21.31
Strike rate: 92.66 (career 90.00)
Parents: Eric and Tina
Marital status: Single
Family links with cricket: Dad and two
brothers play league cricket
Education: Whitehill Primary School,
Illingworth, Halifax; North Halifax Grammar
School, Illingworth, Halifax

Qualifications: 10 GCSEs, 1 A-level, coaching award
Overseas teams played for: Bulawayo Athletic Club, Zimbabwe 1996-97
Cricketers particularly admired: Craig White, Mark Waugh
Other sports played: Football (on Bradford City books for one season)
Other sports followed: Football (Halifax Town)
Relaxations: Most sports 'and a laugh with the lads after the game'. Golf
Extras: Set record for most catches by a fielder in a season (11) for Yorkshire Schools
U15 1993. Awarded Yorkshire 2nd XI cap 1998
Best batting: 50 Matabeleland v Mashonaland, Bulawayo 1996-97
Best bowling: 2-27 Yorkshire v Surrey, Scarborough 2000

2000 Season

	M	Inns	NO	Runs	HS	Avge	100s	50s	Ct	St	O	M	Runs	Wkts	Avge	Best	5wI	10wM
Test																		
All First	14	20	4	341	46	21.31	-	-	8	-	139	32	403	9	44.77	2-27	-	-
1-day Int																		
NatWest	2	2	0	20	18	10.00	-	-	-	-								
B & H	6	5	2	82	28	27.33	-	-	-	-	3	0	12	0	-		-	-
1-day Lge	15	12	0	232	65	19.33	-	2	7	-	13	1	54	2	27.00	1-16	-	

Career Performances

	M	Inns	NO	Runs	HS	Avge	100s	50s	Ct	St	Balls	Runs	Wkts	Avge	Best	5wI	10wM
Test																	
All First	20	31	5	502	50	19.30	-	1	9	-	900	467	10	46.70	2-27	-	-
1-day Int																	
NatWest	4	3	0	47	27	15.66	-	-	-	-	18	20	0	-		-	-
B & H	7	6	2	116	34	29.00	-	-	-	-	18	12	0	-		-	-
1-day Lge	30	23	2	380	65	18.09	-	2	9	-	147	133	2	66.50	1-16	-	

FERLEY, R. S.   Kent

Name: <u>Robert</u> Steven Ferley
Role: Right-hand bat, left-arm spin bowler
Born: 4 February 1982, Norwich
Height: 5ft 8in **Weight:** 12st 4lbs
Nickname: Deadly, Bob Turkey
County debut: No first-team appearance
Parents: Pam and Tim (divorced)
Marital status: Single
Education: North Wootton CP; King Edward
VII High School; Sutton Valence School
(A-levels); Grey College, Durham University
Qualifications: 10 GCSEs, 3 A-levels
Career outside cricket: Student
Off-season: England U19 tour to India;
studying at Durham University
Overseas tours: England U17 to Northern
Ireland (ECC Colts Festival) 1999; England
U19 to India 2000-01
Cricketers particularly admired: Steve Waugh, Mike Atherton, Derek Underwood
Young players to look out for: Paddy Bush, Ian Bell, Mark Wallace, Rob Joseph
Other sports played: Rugby, hockey, tennis, football
Other sports followed: Football (Liverpool)
Relaxations: Socialising with friends, sleeping, running, snooker
Opinions on cricket: 'I love the game. I want to be involved as long as possible. I have
not experienced any first-class cricket, so difficult to comment.'
Stop press: Took 4-32 (including 3-2 in nine balls) on his 19th birthday to help
England U19 to victory over India U19 in the second 'One-Day International' at
Vijayawada 2000-01

FISHER, I. D.   Yorkshire

Name: <u>Ian</u> Douglas Fisher
Role: Left-hand bat, slow left-arm bowler
Born: 31 March 1976, Bradford
Height: 5ft 11in **Weight:** 13st 12lbs
Nickname: Fish, Flash, Yoda, Flick
County debut: 1995-96
1st-Class 50s: 2
1st-Class 5 w. in innings: 2
1st-Class catches: 1
Place in batting averages: 153rd av. 22.62
(1999 166th av. 23.72)
Place in bowling averages: 117th av. 36.75
(1999 115th av. 34.00)
Strike rate: 79.18 (career 68.59)
Parents: Geoff and Linda
Marital status: Single
Family links with cricket: Father played
club cricket
Education: Denholme First School; Parkside Middle School; Beckfoot Grammar
School
Qualifications: 9 GCSEs, NCA coaching award, Sports Leaders Award, Lifesaver
(bronze), YMCA Gym Instructor
Off-season: 'Training, resting, doing a college course'
Overseas tours: Yorkshire to Zimbabwe 1996, to South Africa 1998, 1999, to Perth
2000
Overseas teams played for: Somerset West, Cape Town 1994-95; Petone Riverside,
Wellington, New Zealand 1997-98
Cricketers particularly admired: Darren Lehmann, Shane Warne
Young players to look out for: Tom Baker, Michael Lumb
Other sports played: Five-a-side football, squash
Other sports followed: Football (Leeds United), rugby league (Leeds Rhinos)
Relaxations: Watching movies, eating out, socialising with friends, shopping
Extras: Played England U17 and Yorkshire Schools U15, U16 and Yorkshire U19.
Has Yorkshire 2nd XI cap
Opinions on cricket: 'I thought the two division Championship was a success,
although this did not stop teams preparing pitches that allowed games to be over in
two and three days. Something needs to be done to stop this if our game is to keep
going forward.'
Best batting: 68* Yorkshire v Somerset, Taunton 2000
Best bowling: 5-35 Yorkshire v Mashonaland, Harare 1995-96

2000 Season

	M	Inns	NO	Runs	HS	Avge	100s	50s	Ct	St	O	M	Runs	Wkts	Avge	Best	5wI	10wM
Test																		
All First	6	10	2	181	68 *	22.62	-	1	1	-	211.1	48	588	16	36.75	3-40	-	-
1-day Int																		
NatWest																		
B & H																		
1-day Lge	7	4	0	29	20	7.25	-	-	-	-	44.3	2	171	10	17.10	3-20	-	

Career Performances

	M	Inns	NO	Runs	HS	Avge	100s	50s	Ct	St	Balls	Runs	Wkts	Avge	Best	5wI	10wM
Test																	
All First	23	31	8	517	68 *	22.47	-	2	1	-	2881	1352	42	32.19	5-35	2	-
1-day Int																	
NatWest	3	1	0	5	5	5.00	-	-	2	-	150	87	3	29.00	1-21	-
B & H	1	0	0	0	0	-	-	-	1	-	48	26	1	26.00	1-26	-
1-day Lge	22	10	3	63	20	9.00	-	-	3	-	753	509	24	21.20	3-20	-

FLANAGAN, I. N. Essex

Name: Ian Nicholas Flanagan
Role: Left-hand bat, right-arm medium bowler
Born: 5 June 1980, Colchester
Height: 6ft 1in **Weight:** 13st 5lbs
Nickname: Bud
County debut: 1997
1st-Class 50s: 3
1st-Class catches: 19
Place in batting averages: 262nd av. 11.12 (1999 233rd av. 16.50)
Strike rate: (career 93.00)
Parents: Roy and Anita
Marital status: Single
Family links with cricket: Father played club cricket for Colchester and Carlisle. Mother makes teas
Education: Millfield County Primary, Wivenhoe; Colne Community School, Brightlingsea
Qualifications: 10 GCSEs, Level 2 coach
Off-season: Playing and coaching in Perth
Overseas tours: England U19 to Pakistan 1996-97, to South Africa (including Youth World Cup) 1997-98, to New Zealand 1998-99

Overseas teams played for: North Perth, Western Australia 1999-2000
Cricketers particularly admired: Sachin Tendulkar, Stuart Law
Young players to look out for: Ian Bell
Other sports played: Squash, golf
Other sports followed: English rugby, football (Tottenham Hotspur and Colchester United)
Relaxations: Watching films, sleeping
Extras: Represented England U19 in one-day and 'Test' series v Australia U19 1999. Also played for England U17 and U18. Released by Essex at the end of the 2000 season
Opinions on cricket: 'Two divisions is a success. There should only be central contracts for the core of the England team (only five or six contracts).'
Best batting: 61 Essex v Warwickshire, Edgbaston 1998
Best bowling: 1-50 Essex v Sri Lanka A, Chelmsford 1999

2000 Season

	M	Inns	NO	Runs	HS	Avge	100s	50s	Ct	St	O	M	Runs	Wkts	Avge	Best	5wI	10wM
Test																		
All First	4	8	0	89	23	11.12	-	-	7	-								
1-day Int																		
NatWest																		
B & H																		
1-day Lge																		

Career Performances

	M	Inns	NO	Runs	HS	Avge	100s	50s	Ct	St	Balls	Runs	Wkts	Avge	Best	5wI	10wM
Test																	
All First	18	32	1	580	61	18.70	-	3	19	-	93	51	1	51.00	1-50	-	-
1-day Int																	
NatWest																	
B & H																	
1-day Lge																	

FLEMING, M. V.　　　　　　　　Kent

Name: <u>Matthew</u> Valentine Fleming
Role: Right-hand bat, right-arm
medium bowler, county captain
Born: 12 December 1964, Macclesfield
Height: 5ft 11ins **Weight:** 13st
Nickname: Jazzer
County debut: 1988
County cap: 1990
One-Day Internationals: 11
1st-Class 50s: 41
1st-Class 100s: 10
1st-Class 5 w. in innings: 2
1st-Class catches: 77
One-Day 100s: 3
One-Day 5 w. in innings: 2
Place in batting averages: 100th av. 29.43
(1999 41st av. 39.52)
Place in bowling averages: 68th av. 26.89
(1999 103rd av. 31.56)

Strike rate: 59.60 (career 75.82)
Parents: Valentine and Elizabeth
Wife and date of marriage: Caroline, 23 September 1989
Children: Hannah, 9 October 1992; Victoria, 16 June 1994; Mathilda, 13 February 1997
Family links with cricket: Great-grandfather C.F.H. Leslie played four Tests for England on 1882-83 tour of Australia; once hit an all-run seven at Lord's. Father played for Eton 2nd XI; mother opened the bowling for Heathfield School
Education: St Aubyns School, Rottingdean; Eton College
Qualifications: 8 O-levels, 3 A-levels, granted short-service commission in Royal Green Jackets 1985
Career outside cricket: 'Sadly I am going to have to decide very soon!'
Off-season: 'Recovering and preparing. Reintroducing myself to my children'
Overseas tours: England VI to Hong Kong 1997; England to Sharjah 1997-98, to West Indies 1997-98 (one-day series), to Bangladesh (Wills International Cup) 1998
Overseas teams played for: Avendale, Cape Town 1983-84
Cricketers particularly admired: 'This year Mike Atherton and Alec Stewart, Courtney Walsh and Curtly Ambrose, Steve Waugh'
Other sports played: 'Most sports; none with distinction'
Other sports followed: Football (Arsenal), rugby union (London Wasps)
Injuries: Out for two matches with pulled calf; for one game with fractured thumb
Relaxations: 'Field sports, bonfiring, my family'

Extras: First two scoring shots in Championship cricket were sixes. Chairman of the Professional Cricketers' Association. Out twice before lunch batting at number three for Kent against West Indies in 1995. Took 4-13 and scored a 20-ball 63* (reaching 50 from 16 balls) in a reduced (ten-over) AXA League match v Yorkshire at Canterbury in 1996. Player of the Tournament in the 1997 Hong Kong Sixes. Director of *The Cricketer* magazine. Shared in a new NatWest record sixth-wicket stand of 226 with Nigel Llong v Cheshire at Bowdon 1999, scoring 117* in the process; the second 50 of his 100 came off 13 balls. Captain of Kent since 1999. Granted a benefit for 2001

Opinions on cricket: 'Whilst we are making some progress on the pitch and our series victory over West Indies was thrilling, I remain convinced that English cricket has serious problems off it. We appear to be constitutionally challenged.'

Best batting: 138 Kent v Essex, Canterbury 1997
138 Kent v Worcestershire, Worcester 1999

Best bowling: 5-51 Kent v Nottinghamshire, Trent Bridge 1997

2000 Season

	M	Inns	NO	Runs	HS	Avge	100s	50s	Ct	St	O	M	Runs	Wkts	Avge	Best	5wI	10wM
Test																		
All First	14	18	2	471	47	29.43	-	-	4	-	278.1	72	753	28	26.89	4-77	-	-
1-day Int																		
NatWest	2	1	0	8	8	8.00	-	-	-	-	16	4	46	0	-		-	-
B & H	2	1	0	4	4	4.00	-	-	2	-	14	0	63	1	63.00	1-19	-	
1-day Lge	14	12	2	302	79	30.20	-	2	2	-	86.4	7	306	16	19.12	3-7	-	

Career Performances

	M	Inns	NO	Runs	HS	Avge	100s	50s	Ct	St	Balls	Runs	Wkts	Avge	Best	5wI	10wM
Test																	
All First	197	317	37	8602	138	30.72	10	41	77	-	19865	9213	262	35.16	5-51	2	-
1-day Int	11	10	1	139	33	15.44	-	-	1	-	523	434	17	25.52	4-45	-	
NatWest	24	22	2	467	117 *	23.35	1	1	11	-	951	584	23	25.39	3-28	-	
B & H	49	45	3	1067	105 *	25.40	1	5	16	-	2314	1647	66	24.95	5-27	2	
1-day Lge	185	161	21	3332	112	23.80	1	14	41	-	6631	5677	223	25.45	4-13	-	

FLEMING, S. P.   Middlesex

Name: <u>Stephen</u> Paul Fleming
Role: Left-hand bat, occasional right-arm
slow-medium bowler
Born: 1 April 1973, Christchurch, New
Zealand
Height: 6ft 3in
County debut: No first-team appearance
Test debut: 1993-94
Tests: 51
One-Day Internationals: 125
1st-Class 50s: 41
1st-Class 100s: 12
1st-Class catches: 142
One-Day 100s: 3
Education: Cashmere High School;
Christchurch College of Education
Overseas tours: New Zealand to England
1994, to South Africa 1994-95, to India 1995-

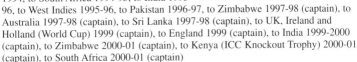

96, to West Indies 1995-96, to Pakistan 1996-97, to Zimbabwe 1997-98 (captain), to
Australia 1997-98 (captain), to Sri Lanka 1997-98 (captain), to UK, Ireland and
Holland (World Cup) 1999 (captain), to England 1999 (captain), to India 1999-2000
(captain), to Zimbabwe 2000-01 (captain), to Kenya (ICC Knockout Trophy) 2000-01
(captain), to South Africa 2000-01 (captain)
Overseas teams played for: Canterbury 1991-92 –
Extras: Captain of New Zealand since 1996-97. Led New Zealand to their series
victory in England in 1999, which included the Kiwis' first wins at Lord's and The
Oval. Topped New Zealand Test batting averages (52.20) on tour of India 1999-2000.
Averaged 66.50 in two-match Test series v West Indies 1999-2000. Has joined
Middlesex as overseas player for 2001
Best batting: 174* New Zealand v Sri Lanka, Colombo 1997-98
Stop press: Led New Zealand to victory in the ICC Knockout Trophy in Kenya 2000-
01. Made 57 and 99 in the first Test v South Africa at Bloemfontein 2000-01

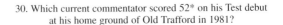

30. Which current commentator scored 52* on his Test debut
at his home ground of Old Trafford in 1981?

2000 Season (did not make any first-class or one-day appearances)

Career Performances

	M	Inns	NO	Runs	HS	Avge	100s	50s	Ct	St	Balls	Runs	Wkts	Avge	Best	5wl	10wM
Test	51	90	6	3121	174 *	37.15	2	24	84	-							
All First	110	182	17	6750	174 *	40.90	12	41	142	-	90	110	0	-	-	-	-
1-day Int	125	121	13	3465	116 *	32.08	3	21	57	-	29	28	1	28.00	1-8	-	
NatWest																	
B & H																	
1-day Lge																	

FLINTOFF, A. Lancashire

Name: Andrew Flintoff
Role: Right-hand bat, right-arm medium bowler
Born: 6 December 1977, Preston
Height: 6ft 4in **Weight:** 13st 10lbs
County debut: 1995
County cap: 1998
Test debut: 1998
Tests: 9
One-Day Internationals: 15
1st-Class 50s: 18
1st-Class 100s: 6
1st-Class 5 w. in innings: 1
1st-Class catches: 82
One-Day 100s: 2
Place in batting averages: 59th av. 35.05
(1999 45th av. 38.26)
Place in bowling averages: 20th av. 19.33
(1999 74th av. 27.93)
Strike rate: 54.13 (career 73.71)
Parents: Colin and Susan
Family links with cricket: Brother Chris and father both play local league cricket
Education: Greenlands County Primary; Ribbleton Hall High School
Qualifications: 9 GCSEs
Off-season: Touring Kenya, Pakistan and Sri Lanka with England
Overseas tours: England Schools U15 to South Africa 1993; England U19 to West Indies 1994-95, to Zimbabwe 1995-96, to Pakistan 1996-97 (captain); England A to Kenya and Sri Lanka 1997-98, to Zimbabwe and South Africa 1998-99; England to Sharjah (Coca-Cola Cup) 1998-99, to South Africa and Zimbabwe 1999-2000, to Kenya (ICC Knockout Trophy) 2000-01, to Pakistan and Sri Lanka 2000-01

Cricketers particularly admired: Jason Gallian, John Crawley, Stephen Titchard, Warren Hegg
Other sports followed: Football (Preston North End and Liverpool FC)
Relaxations: Listening to music and sleeping
Extras: Won a *Daily Telegraph* regional award for batting. Represented England U14 to U19 and played for U17 against India in 1994. Captained England U19 in the series against Zimbabwe in 1997. Scored 61 off 24 balls in Championship match v Surrey at Old Trafford in June 1998, including 34 from one over by Alex Tudor. Became the 50th recipient of the Cricket Writers' Club Young Player of the Year award in September 1998. Professional Cricketers' Association's Young Player of the Year 1998. Topped England A batting averages for tour to Zimbabwe and South Africa 1998-99 with 542 runs at an average of 77.42. Struck 50 (including four sixes) on One-Day International debut, v Pakistan, Sharjah 1998-99. Scored 143 off 66 balls, including nine sixes, in National League v Essex at Chelmsford 1999. His 160 v Yorkshire at Old Trafford 1999 included 111 runs before lunch, the first century before lunch by a Lancashire batsman in a Roses match. Won the EDS Walter Lawrence Trophy 1999 (for the fastest first-class century of the season) for his 100 off 61 balls for Lancashire v Gloucestershire at Bristol. Represented England in the 1999 World Cup. Forced to return home early from England tour of South Africa and Zimbabwe 1999-2000 after breaking a foot in the fourth Test at Cape Town. Won Man of the Match award for his 135* from 110 balls in the NatWest quarter-final v Surrey at The Oval 2000
Opinions on cricket: 'Cricket should be promoted more in state schools.'
Best batting: 160 Lancashire v Yorkshire, Old Trafford 1999
Best bowling: 5-24 Lancashire v Hampshire, Southampton 1999
Stop press: Struck 84 from 60 balls to win Man of the Match award in England's victory in the first One-Day International v Pakistan at Karachi 2000-01. Returned home early from Pakistan because his long-standing back problem prevented him from bowling; later recalled as cover for the injured Michael Vaughan and for one-day series in Sri Lanka

2000 Season

	M	Inns	NO	Runs	HS	Avge	100s	50s	Ct	St	O	M	Runs	Wkts	Avge	Best	5wI	10wM
Test	3	5	0	61	16	12.20	-	1	-	-	36	15	83	1	83.00	1-48	-	-
All First	13	19	1	631	119	35.05	1	4	12	-	135.2	49	290	15	19.33	4-18	-	-
1-day Int	6	5	1	70	42 *	17.50	-	-	3	-	4	0	20	0	-	-	-	-
NatWest	4	3	1	200	135 *	100.00	1	-	-	-	18	2	63	2	31.50	2-21	-	
B & H	7	6	1	143	70	28.60	-	1	4	-	60	7	192	7	27.42	2-30	-	
1-day Lge	9	9	0	191	64	21.22	-	1	1	-	53	5	218	10	21.80	3-39	-	

Career Performances

	M	Inns	NO	Runs	HS	Avge	100s	50s	Ct	St	Balls	Runs	Wkts	Avge	Best	5wl	10wM
Test	9	14	0	233	42	16.64	-	-	4	-	827	385	7	55.00	2-31	-	-
All First	65	100	9	3255	160	35.76	6	18	82	-	3833	1676	52	32.23	5-24	1	-
1-day Int	15	11	1	170	50	17.00	-	1	3	-	266	248	7	35.42	2-3	-	
NatWest	13	11	2	385	135 *	42.77	1	1	7	-	287	168	4	42.00	2-21	-	
B & H	16	14	1	321	92	24.69	-	2	7	-	462	253	9	28.11	2-30	-	
1-day Lge	41	40	2	1013	143	26.65	1	5	12	-	870	629	31	20.29	4-24	-	

FORDER, D. J. Gloucestershire

Name: <u>Damian</u> Joseph Forder
Role: Right-hand bat, left-arm seam bowler
Born: 11 March 1979, Bristol
Height: 6ft 3in **Weight:** 13st 7lbs
Nickname: Damo
County debut: No first-team appearance
Parents: Helen and Stephen
Marital status: Girlfriend Carrie Anne
Family links with cricket: Brothers played
for Thornbury
Education: Olveston Primary School;
Marlwood School; City of Bristol College
Qualifications: 1 GCSE, BTEC National
Diploma Sports Science, GNVQ Leisure and
Tourism, Level 1 coaching award
Career outside cricket: Coaching
Off-season: 'Working on my batting/fitness;
clearing up a back injury I have; going on a
weightlifting course etc, so I can work in a gym'
Overseas tours: Pre-season tours to South Africa
Cricketers particularly admired: Mike Smith, Courtney Walsh, Allan Donald
Young players to look out for: Tom Cotterell, Chris Taylor
Other sports played: Tennis
Other sports followed: Football (Man Utd, Bristol City), rugby (Bristol, Thornbury)
Injuries: Out for three months with back injury
Relaxations: 'Music, cinema, gym; being at home, playing with my niece and
nephew, spending time with my family and girlfriend'
Extras: Two-week trip to Dennis Lillee Pace Foundation in India, courtesy of *Daily
Telegraph* Fast Bowler 1997. Played for England U19 v Pakistan U19 1998. Played for
the Gloucestershire Board XI in the NatWest 1999 and 2000
Opinions on cricket: 'I think one-day cricket is the key for the future, as it is more

exciting and you get a result the same day. Also, more people seem to watch, especially day/night matches.'

Career Performances

	M	Inns	NO	Runs	HS	Avge	100s	50s	Ct	St	Balls	Runs	Wkts	Avge	Best	5wl	10wM
Test																	
All First-																	
1-day Int																	
NatWest	2	2	2	4	3*	-	-	-	1	-	96	92	0	-	-	-	
B & H																	
1-day Lge																	

FOSTER, J. S. Essex

Name: James Savin Foster
Role: Right-hand bat, wicket-keeper
Born: 15 April 1980, Whipps Cross, London
Height: 6ft **Weight:** 12st
Nickname: Fozzy
County debut: 2000
1st-Class 50s: 1
1st-Class catches: 6
Parents: Martin and Diana
Marital status: Single
Family links with cricket: 'Dad played for Essex Amateurs'
Education: Forest School; Durham University
Qualifications: 10 GCSEs, 3 A-levels
Career outside cricket: 'Unsure'
Off-season: Touring West Indies with England A; also at university
Overseas tours: BUSA to South Africa 1999; Durham University to South Africa 1999, to Vienna (European Indoor Championships) 1999; England A to West Indies 2000-01
Cricketers particularly admired: Nasser Hussain, Stuart Law, Robert Rollins, Ian Healy, Jack Russell
Young players to look out for: John Chambers, Adnan Akram, Tony Palladino
Other sports played: Hockey (Essex U21), tennis (played for GB U14 v Sweden U14; national training squad)

Other sports followed: Football (Wimbledon FC)

Relaxations: Socialising, 'Klute and Rixy's'

Extras: Essex U17 Player of the Year 1997. Represented ECB U19 v Pakistan U19 1998. Represented England U19 v Australia U19 in 'Test' series 1999. Represented BUSA v South Africa Universities 1999 and v New Zealand A and Zimbabweans 2000. Awarded 2nd XI cap at end of 2000 season. Voted Essex Cricket Society 2nd XI Player of the Year 2000. Scored 52 on debut v Glamorgan at Southend 2000

Opinions on cricket: 'Wickets need to be improved. Two division cricket has made the Championship a lot more competitive.'

Best batting: 52 Essex v Glamorgan, Southend 2000

Stop press: Scored 53 on England A debut v Guyana in Grenada 2000-01

2000 Season

	M	Inns	NO	Runs	HS	Avge	100s	50s	Ct	St	O	M	Runs	Wkts	Avge	Best	5wI	10wM
Test																		
All First	4	5	2	125	52	41.66	-	1	6	-								
1-day Int																		
NatWest																		
B & H																		
1-day Lge	6	6	3	81	22 *	27.00	-	-	6	1								

Career Performances

	M	Inns	NO	Runs	HS	Avge	100s	50s	Ct	St	Balls	Runs	Wkts	Avge	Best	5wI	10wM
Test																	
All First	4	5	2	125	52	41.66	-	1	6	-							
1-day Int																	
NatWest																	
B & H																	
1-day Lge	6	6	3	81	22 *	27.00	-	-	6	1							

FRANCIS, J. D. — Hampshire

Name: <u>John</u> Daniel Francis
Role: Left-hand bat, slow left-arm bowler
Born: 13 November 1980, Bromley, Kent
Height: 5ft 11in **Weight:** 13st
Nickname: Fred
County debut: No first-team appearance
Parents: Linda and Daniel
Marital status: Single
Family links with cricket: Brother Simon plays for Hampshire. Father plays club cricket. Grandfather played for the Navy
Education: Yardley Court, Tonbridge; King Edward VI, Southampton; Durham and Loughborough Universities
Qualifications: 10 GCSEs, 3 A-levels
Off-season: Studying at Loughborough University

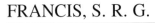

Overseas tours: Twyford School to Barbados 1993; West of England U15 to West Indies 1995; King Edward VI, Southampton to South Africa 1998; Durham University to South Africa 2000
Cricketers particularly admired: Robin Smith, Graham Thorpe, Olly Broom
Young players to look out for: Lawrence Prittipaul, Andy Hollingsworth, Richard Cooper
Other sports played: Hockey (England U18), golf, squash
Injuries: Out for 'a couple of weeks' with a lower back injury
Relaxations: Drawing and painting, socialising
Extras: Won the Sir John Hobbs Silver Jubilee Memorial Prize. Leading run-scorer in Lombard U15 World Cup 1996. Hampshire Young Sportsman of the Year 1995

FRANCIS, S. R. G. — Hampshire

Name: <u>Simon</u> Richard George Francis
Role: Right-hand bat, right-arm fast-medium bowler
Born: 15 August 1978, Bromley, Kent
Height: 6ft 2in **Weight:** 14st 7lbs
Nickname: Franky
County debut: 1997
1st-Class catches: 1
Place in batting averages: 269th av. 10.66
Place in bowling averages: 130th av. 40.13

Strike rate: 68.13 (career 84.08)
Parents: Daniel and Linda
Marital status: Single
Family links with cricket: Brother John is contracted to Hampshire. Father played club cricket. Grandfather played for the Navy
Education: Yardley Court, Tonbridge; King Edward VI, Southampton; Durham University
Qualifications: 9 GCSEs, 1 A/O-Level, 3 A-levels, BA (Hons) Sport, Level 1 coaching in cricket and hockey
Career outside cricket: Gym instructor/lifestyle consultant
Off-season: Working as gym instructor in central London; training in South Africa for three months ('and returning for summer')
Overseas tours: England U17 to Holland (International Youth Tournament) 1995; England U19 to Pakistan 1996-97; Durham University to Zimbabwe 1997-98
Overseas teams played for: Stellenbosch University-Maties 1999
Cricketers particularly admired: Malcolm Marshall, Allan Donald, Curtly Ambrose, Courtney Walsh
Young players to look out for: Lawrence Prittipaul, John Francis
Other sports played: Golf (second in PCA Players' Team Competition 2000)
Injuries: Out from August 2000 to January 2001 with a stress fracture in right elbow
Relaxations: Playing golf 'and sleeping!'
Extras: *Daily Telegraph* West Region Bowling Award U15. Played hockey for England U18 1995. Played in Durham University's BUSA Championship-winning side 1999. Put on 90 for the tenth wicket with Dimitri Mascarenhas v Surrey at The Oval 2000, the pair falling just two runs short of pulling off a remarkable Championship victory
Opinions on cricket: 'More day/night games – more entertaining; bigger crowds.'
Best batting: 30* Hampshire v Surrey, The Oval 2000
Best bowling: 4-95 Hampshire v Surrey, The Oval 2000

2000 Season

	M	Inns	NO	Runs	HS	Avge	100s	50s	Ct	St	O	M	Runs	Wkts	Avge	Best	5wI	10wM
Test																		
All First	9	13	7	64	30 *	10.66	-	-	1	-	170.2	37	602	15	40.13	4-95	-	-
1-day Int																		
NatWest	1	0	0	0	0	-	-	-	-	-	6	1	10	0	-		-	-
B & H																		
1-day Lge	5	4	3	17	8 *	17.00	-	-	2	-	27	4	118	1	118.00	1-22	-	

Career Performances

	M	Inns	NO	Runs	HS	Avge	100s	50s	Ct	St	Balls	Runs	Wkts	Avge	Best	5wI	10wM
Test																	
All First	16	22	10	91	30 *	7.58	-	-	1	-	2102	1232	25	49.28	4-95	-	-
1-day Int																	
NatWest	1	0	0	0	0	-	-	-	-	-	36	10	0	-		-	-
B & H																	
1-day Lge	10	5	3	18	8 *	9.00	-	-	2	-	348	242	6	40.33	2-28	-	

FRANKLIN, G. D. Warwickshire

Name: <u>Gavin</u> David Franklin
Role: Right-hand bat, off-spin bowler
Born: 9 January 1978, Wolverhampton
Height: 6ft **Weight:** 12st 12lbs
Nickname: Franko
County debut: No first-team appearance
Parents: David and Helen
Marital status: Single
Family links with cricket: Father qualified coach who represented the Veterinary College XI at Edinburgh University and played for Wolverhampton CC
Education: Birchfield Preparatory School; Malvern College; Durham University
Qualifications: 3 A-levels, BA (Hons) Social Sciences, NCA coaching Levels 1 and 2
Career outside cricket: 'Not yet decided'
Off-season: 'Coaching, training, socialising'
Overseas tours: British Universities to South Africa 1999-2000; Durham University Indoor VI to Vienna 1999, 2000; Durham University to South Africa 2000
Overseas teams played for: Newtown and Chilwell CC, Geelong, Australia 1996-97
Cricketers particularly admired: David Gower, David Nash, Graeme 'Pop' Welch, 'Foxy'
Young players to look out for: Mark Hardinges
Other sports played: Golf, football
Other sports followed: Football (Aston Villa)
Relaxations: Playing golf and listening to Stone Roses
Extras: Was captain of the most successful post-war 1st XI at Malvern College. Represented Staffordshire U11-U19 and in Minor Counties. Captained Staffs U19 to victory at 1996 Oxford Festival. Represented British Universities 2000
Opinions on cricket: 'Happy with two division structure. Cricket should be played for

enjoyment; everything else stems from there. Very disappointing to see the element of sportsmanship drifting away from the game.'
Best batting: 12 British Universities v Zimbabweans, Fenner's 2000

2000 Season (did not make any first-class or one-day appearances)

Career Performances

	M	Inns	NO	Runs	HS	Avge	100s	50s	Ct	St	Balls	Runs	Wkts	Avge	Best	5wI	10wM
Test																	
All First	1	1	0	12	12	12.00	-	-	-	-	60	78	0	-		-	-	-
1-day Int																	
NatWest																	
B & H																	
1-day Lge																	

FRANKS, P. J.   Nottinghamshire

Name: <u>Paul</u> John Franks
Role: Left-hand bat, right-arm fast-medium bowler; bowling all-rounder
Born: 3 February 1979, Sutton-in-Ashfield
Height: 6ft 1½in **Weight:** 13st 6lbs
Nickname: Pike, Franno, Franksie, 'The General'
County debut: 1996
County cap: 1999
One-Day Internationals: 1
50 wickets in a season: 2
1st-Class 50s: 7
1st-Class 5 w. in innings: 8
1st-Class catches: 24
One-Day 5 w. in innings: 2
Place in batting averages: 126th av. 26.29 (1999 246th av. 14.50)
Place in bowling averages: 92nd av. 29.69 (1999 49th av. 23.63)

Strike rate: 56.23 (career 53.82)
Parents: John and Patricia
Marital status: Single
Family links with cricket: 'Dad played for far too long!!'
Education: Walter D'Ayncourt Primary School; Minster School, Southwell; West Notts College

Qualifications: 8 GCSEs, GNVQ (Advanced) Leisure Management
Career outside cricket: 'PGA Tour golf pro – just ask Bickers'
Off-season: England A tour to West Indies. 'Consistently beating Denzil and Johnners by three shots'
Overseas tours: England U19 to Pakistan 1996-97, to South Africa (including Youth World Cup) 1997-98; England A to Zimbabwe and South Africa 1998-99, to Bangladesh and New Zealand 1999-2000, to West Indies 2000-01; Notts CCC to South Africa 1998, 1999
Cricketers particularly admired: Allan Donald, Glenn McGrath, Chris Cairns, Saqlain 'which way is it going?' Mushtaq
Young players to look out for: Steve Randall, Matt Whiley, Chris Hewison, Mark Wallace
Other sports played: Golf, 'Aussie Rules', 'resident Notts CCC go-karting champion!!'
Other sports followed: Football (Mansfield Town 'the future of football')
Relaxations: Sleeping, golf
Extras: Became youngest ever Notts player (and third-youngest player ever, aged 18 years 163 days) to take a hat-trick, v Warwickshire in July 1997. Won Youth World Cup winner's medal in Johannesburg 1998. Attended Dennis Lillee coaching school, Chennai (Madras), March 1997, February 1998 and March 1999. NBC Denis Compton Award 1999. Made One-Day International debut v West Indies at his home ground of Trent Bridge 2000. Cricket Writers' Young Player of the Year 2000
Opinions on cricket: 'Two divisions created greater competition between teams that would otherwise have been playing dead games. We ought to use a bright orange ball instead of a white one for NCL games.'
Best batting: 66* Nottinghamshire v Kent, Canterbury 1998
Best bowling: 7-56 Nottinghamshire v Middlesex, Lord's 2000

2000 Season

	M	Inns	NO	Runs	HS	Avge	100s	50s	Ct	St	O	M	Runs	Wkts	Avge	Best	5wl	10wM
Test																		
All First	13	18	1	447	60	26.29	-	3	5	-	393.4	81	1247	42	29.69	7-56	2	-
1-day Int	1	1	0	4	4	4.00	-	-	1	-	9	0	48	0	-	-	-	-
NatWest	1	1	0	7	7	7.00	-	-	-	-	10	0	47	2	23.50	2-47	-	
B & H	4	4	2	32	14	16.00	-	-	-	-	24	5	87	4	21.75	2-14	-	
1-day Lge	16	11	8	146	32 *	48.66	-	-	4	-	130.3	4	562	25	22.48	6-27	1	

Career Performances

	M	Inns	NO	Runs	HS	Avge	100s	50s	Ct	St	Balls	Runs	Wkts	Avge	Best	5wI	10wM
Test																	
All First	62	93	15	1566	66 *	20.07	-	7	24	-	11358	5766	211	27.32	7-56	8	-
1-day Int	1	1	0	4	4	4.00	-	-	1	-	54	48	0	-	-	-	
NatWest	9	7	3	110	26 *	27.50	-	-	3	-	480	329	15	21.93	3-7	-	
B & H	4	4	2	32	14	16.00	-	-	-	-	144	87	4	21.75	2-14	-	
1-day Lge	47	35	13	364	40	16.54	-	-	6	-	2094	1594	67	23.79	6-27	2	

FRASER, A. R. C. Middlesex

Name: <u>Angus</u> Robert Charles Fraser
Role: Right-hand late-order bat, right-arm
fast-medium bowler, outfielder 'specialist',
county captain
Born: 8 August 1965, Billinge, Lancashire
Height: 6ft 6in **Weight:** 'Should be under
16st'
Nickname: Gus, Lard, Wiggy, Recall
County debut: 1984
County cap: 1988
Benefit: 1997
Test debut: 1989
Tests: 46
One-Day Internationals: 42
50 wickets in a season: 7
1st-Class 50s: 2
1st-Class 5 w. in innings: 33
1st-Class 10 w. in match: 4
1st-Class catches: 50
One-Day 5 w. in innings: 1
Place in batting averages: 236th av. 14.18 (1999 258th av. 12.90)
Place in bowling averages: 44th av. 23.14 (1999 81st av. 28.76)
Strike rate: 59.31 (career 62.60)
Parents: Don and Irene
Wife and date of marriage: Denise, March 1996
Children: Alexander Charles Mitchell, May 1993; Bethan Louise, July 1995
Family links with cricket: 'Mum and dad keen followers. Brother Alastair played for
Middlesex, Essex, then Middlesex again'
Education: Weald First School; Gayton High School, Harrow; Orange Hill Senior
High School, Edgware
Qualifications: 7 O-levels, qualified cricket coach

Career outside cricket: Writing for *The Mail on Sunday*; commentating/summarising for Sky TV and *TMS*

Off-season: 'Relaxing as much as I can with my family, but as captain of Middlesex next year I can see a lot of hard work ahead of me this winter'

Overseas tours: Thames Valley Gentlemen to Barbados 1985; Middlesex to La Manga 1985, 1986, to Portugal 1991-93; England to India (Nehru Cup) 1989-90, to West Indies 1989-90, to Australia 1990-91, to West Indies 1993-94, to Australia 1994-95,
to South Africa 1995-96, to West Indies 1997-98, to Australia 1998-99, to Sharjah (Coca-Cola Cup) 1998-99

Overseas teams played for: Plimmerton, Wellington 1985-86, 1987-88; Western Suburbs, Sydney 1988-89, 1994-95

Cricketers particularly admired: Allan Border, Graham Gooch, Curtly Ambrose, Courtney Walsh

Young players to look out for: Michael Powell (Glamorgan) 'pick him for England', Ed Joyce

Other sports played: 'Golf with a sombrero on'

Other sports followed: 'Follow Liverpool FC keenly. Enjoy watching rugby internationals at my local rugby club, Harrow'

Injuries: Out for one game with Achilles tendon trouble

Relaxations: Spending time with family, golf, Liverpool FC, drinking good red wine

Extras: Middlesex Player of the Year 1988 and 1989. Took a hat-trick in the Benson and Hedges Cup in 1989. Took his 100th Test wicket (Brian Lara) against West Indies in 1995. Finished 2nd in the Whyte and Mackay bowling ratings for 1995. One of *Wisden*'s Five Cricketers of the Year 1996. His 8-53 v West Indies at Trinidad in 1998 is the best return by an English bowler in the West Indies. Peter Smith Award 1998. Winner of the KUMALA Cape Wines 'Century of Bottles' award for the best individual performance against the 1998 South Africans. Awarded MBE in New Year honours list 1999. Represented England in 1999 World Cup. Appointed captain of Middlesex for 2001

Opinions on cricket: 'Two divisional cricket is a success. Middlesex played first-class cricket on good wickets last year, but I still feel the standard of batting in this country needs to improve. There seems a real lack of patience amongst young players, both on and off the field. They want everything to happen now, whether it be to score runs, take wickets or earn money. Unless you are extremely lucky, consistent success and wealth take a long time to achieve, with a lot of hard work on the way. Well done England last summer! It was great to watch. Let's enjoy it. I only wish I was there.'

Best batting: 92 Middlesex v Surrey, The Oval 1990

Best bowling: 8-53 England v West Indies, Port of Spain 1997-98

2000 Season

	M	Inns	NO	Runs	HS	Avge	100s	50s	Ct	St	O	M	Runs	Wkts	Avge	Best	5wI	10wM
Test																		
All First	15	22	6	227	30	14.18	-	-	4	-	474.3	150	1111	48	23.14	6-64	1	-
1-day Int																		
NatWest	3	1	1	8	8*	-	-	-	-	-	24	5	61	4	15.25	2-19	-	
B & H	1	1	0	3	3	3.00	-	-	1	-	10	3	30	1	30.00	1-30	-	
1-day Lge	13	7	4	28	7	9.33	-	-	2	-	92.5	14	322	18	17.88	4-18	-	

Career Performances

	M	Inns	NO	Runs	HS	Avge	100s	50s	Ct	St	Balls	Runs	Wkts	Avge	Best	5wI	10wM
Test	46	67	15	388	32	7.46	-	-	9	-	10876	4836	177	27.32	8-53	11	1
All First	275	330	82	2749	92		-	2	50	-	53025	22883	847	27.01	8-53	33	4
1-day Int	42	20	9	141	38*	12.81	-	-	5	-	2392	1412	47	30.04	4-22	-	
NatWest	35	13	10	80	19	26.66	-	-	6	-	2241	1117	49	22.79	4-34	-	
B & H	45	24	12	117	30*	9.75	-	-	10	-	2655	1564	55	28.43	4-49	-	
1-day Lge	181	74	34	460	33	11.50	-	-	29	-	8052	5238	198	26.45	5-32	1	

FROST, T.   Warwickshire

Name: Tony Frost
Role: Right-hand bat, wicket-keeper
Born: 17 November 1975, Stoke-on-Trent
Height: 5ft 10in **Weight:** 10st 6lbs
County debut: 1997
County cap: 1999
1st-Class 50s: 3
1st-Class 100s: 1
1st-Class catches: 71
1st-Class stumpings: 3
Place in batting averages: (1999 199th av. 20.47)
Parents: Ivan and Christine
Marital status: Single
Family links with cricket: Father played for Staffordshire
Education: James Brinkley High School; Stoke-on-Trent College
Qualifications: 5 GCSEs
Overseas tours: Kidsgrove U18 to Australia 1990-91
Cricketers particularly admired: Ashley Giles 'could be described as a legend', 'Pop' Welch and George Burns 'in the JT bracket'

Other sports followed: Football, golf
Relaxations: Listening to music, watching films, reading aircraft magazines
Extras: Represented Staffordshire at all levels from U11 to U19. Won Texaco U16 competition with Staffordshire in 1992. Played for Development of Excellence XI U17 v South Africa and U18 v West Indies and U19 v India. Awarded Warwicks cap 1999
Best batting: 111* Warwickshire v Oxford University, The Parks 1998

2000 Season

	M	Inns	NO	Runs	HS	Avge	100s	50s	Ct	St	O	M	Runs	Wkts	Avge	Best	5wI	10wM
Test																		
All First	1	0	0	0	0	-	-	-	-	-								
1-day Int																		
NatWest																		
B & H																		
1-day Lge	1	1	0	18	18	18.00	-	-	-	-								

Career Performances

	M	Inns	NO	Runs	HS	Avge	100s	50s	Ct	St	Balls	Runs	Wkts	Avge	Best	5wI	10wM
Test																	
All First	30	43	5	895	111 *	23.55	1	3	71	3	6	6	0	-	-	-	-
1-day Int																	
NatWest	2	2	0	5	5	2.50	-	-	4	1							
B & H	3	2	1	11	10 *	11.00	-	-	3	-							
1-day Lge	22	9	3	88	22 *	14.66	-	-	15	3							

FULTON, D. P.   Kent

Name: David (<u>Dave</u>) Paul Fulton
Role: Right-hand top-order bat, left-arm spin bowler, occasional wicket-keeper
Born: 15 November 1971, Lewisham
Height: 6ft 2in **Weight:** 12st 7lbs
Nickname: Rave, Tav, Bozo
County debut: 1992
County cap: 1998
1st-Class 50s: 27
1st-Class 100s: 6
1st-Class 200s: 1
1st-Class catches: 158
Place in batting averages: 159th av. 22.26 (1999 133rd av. 26.74)
Strike rate: (career 169.00)
Parents: John and Ann
Marital status: Single

Children: 'Millie' ('Staffordshire bull terrier; 13 February 2000')

Family links with cricket: Father used to play for village side

Education: Otford County Primary; The Judd School, Tonbridge; University of Kent at Canterbury

Qualifications: 10 GCSEs, 3 A-levels, BA (Hons) Politics and International Relations, advanced cricket coach, rugby coach, gym instructor qualification

Career outside cricket: 'Journalist, politician, "Dr Love" for *For Me* magazine in Australia'

Off-season: 'Working for papers or magazines, freelancing; business ventures; "Dr Love"; PCA tour to Malta; coaching'

Overseas tours: Kent U17 to Singapore and New Zealand 1987-88; Kent to France 1998

Overseas teams played for: Avendale CC, Cape Town 1993-94; Victoria CC, Cape Town 1994-95; University of WA, Perth 1995-96; Petersham-Marrickville CC, Sydney 1998-99, 1999-2000

Cricketers particularly admired: Graham Gooch, Gordon Greenidge, Courtney Walsh, Andrew Harrison, Dave Townsend

Young players to look out for: Gavin Burt, David Skuthorpe

Other sports played: Chess (England junior), table tennis ('top 10 in UK as a junior'; played for South England juniors); rugby, football, tennis, golf, squash

Other sports followed: Football (Nottingham Forest), rugby (Harlequins)

Relaxations: 'Searching for Mrs Right; walking Millie, my dog'

Extras: Was the last person to catch Viv Richards in a first-class match, in 1993. Opened the batting and the bowling against South Africa in their first county game 1994. Helped Dean Headley's hat-trick against Derbyshire 1996 by catching Kim Barnett and Chris Adams. Set record for the longest innings ever played by a Kent batsman in scoring his 207 against Yorkshire at Maidstone in 1998

Opinions on cricket: 'Pitches... Cricket is a business. Let's move with the times and run it like one.'

Best batting: 207 Kent v Yorkshire, Maidstone 1998

Best bowling: 1-37 Kent v Oxford University, Canterbury 1996

2000 Season

	M	Inns	NO	Runs	HS	Avge	100s	50s	Ct	St	O	M	Runs	Wkts	Avge	Best	5wI	10wM
Test																		
All First	14	24	1	512	115	22.26	1	1	29	-	17	5	45	0	-		-	-	-
1-day Int																		
NatWest	2	2	0	23	14	11.50	-	-	1	-								
B & H																		
1-day Lge	6	6	0	104	69	17.33	-	1	3	-								

Career Performances

	M	Inns	NO	Runs	HS	Avge	100s	50s	Ct	St	Balls	Runs	Wkts	Avge	Best	5wI	10wM
Test																	
All First	107	190	12	5293	207	29.73	7	27	158	-	169	110	1	110.00	1-37	-	-
1-day Int																	
NatWest	8	8	0	88	19	11.00	-	-	1	-	6	9	0	-		-	-
B & H	2	2	0	42	25	21.00	-	-	3	-							
1-day Lge	19	19	0	204	69	10.73	-	1	8	-							

GALLIAN, J. E. R.   Nottinghamshire

Name: <u>Jason</u> Edward Riche Gallian
Role: Right-hand bat, right-arm
medium bowler, county captain
Born: 25 June 1971, Manly, NSW, Australia
Height: 6ft **Weight:** 14st
Nickname: Gal
County debut: 1990 (Lancashire),
1998 (Nottinghamshire)
County cap: 1994 (Lancashire),
1998 (Nottinghamshire)
Test debut: 1995
Tests: 3
1000 runs in a season: 2
1st-Class 50s: 36
1st-Class 100s: 17
1st-Class 300s: 1
1st-Class 5 w. in innings: 1
1st-Class catches: 112
One-Day 100s: 7
One-Day 5 w. in innings: 1
Place in batting averages: 62nd av. 34.60 (1999 92nd av. 31.77)
Strike rate: 110.40 (career 71.40)

Parents: Ray and Marilyn
Wife and date of marriage: Charlotte, 2 October 1999
Family links with cricket: Father played for Stockport
Education: The Pittwater House Schools, Australia; Oxford University
Qualifications: Higher School Certificate, Diploma in Social Studies
(Keble College, Oxford)
Off-season: 'Becoming computer literate'
Overseas tours: Australia U20 to West Indies 1989-90; England A to India 1994-95,
to Pakistan 1995-96, to Australia 1996-97; England to South Africa 1995-96;
Nottinghamshire to Johannesburg 2000
Overseas teams played for: NSW and Australia U19 1988-89; NSW Colts and NSW
2nd XI 1990-91; Manly 1993-94
Cricketers particularly admired: Desmond Haynes, Mike Gatting
Young players to look out for: Usman Afzaal, David Lucas
Other sports followed: Rugby league and union, football
Injuries: Out for one game with a bruised hand
Relaxations: Listening to music, playing golf
Extras: Captained Australia YC v England YC 1989-90. Represented Australia U20
and U21 1991-92. Took wicket of D. A. Hagan of Oxford University with his first ball
for Lancashire in first-class cricket 1990. Played for Oxford University in 1992 and for
Combined Universities in the B&H Cup. Captained Oxford University 1993. Left
Lancashire during the 1997-98 off-season and joined Nottinghamshire for 1998, being
appointed captain after resignation of Paul Johnson
Opinions on cricket: 'Two-tiered cricket in four-day and one-day games has been a
positive move and has created interest during all of the season.'
Best batting: 312 Lancashire v Derbyshire, Old Trafford 1996
Best bowling: 6-115 Lancashire v Surrey, Southport 1996

2000 Season

	M	Inns	NO	Runs	HS	Avge	100s	50s	Ct	St	O	M	Runs	Wkts	Avge	Best	5wI	10wM
Test																		
All First	16	26	3	796	150	34.60	3	-	23	-	92	24	278	5	55.60	2-42	-	-
1-day Int																		
NatWest	1	1	0	8	8	8.00	-	-	-	-								
B & H	4	4	0	85	47	21.25	-	-	1	-	10	0	73	2	36.50	2-34	-	
1-day Lge	15	14	0	439	84	31.35	-	2	3	-	10	0	73	0	-		-	-

Career Performances

	M	Inns	NO	Runs	HS	Avge	100s	50s	Ct	St	Balls	Runs	Wkts	Avge	Best	5wI	10wM
Test	3	6	0	74	28	12.33	-	-	1	-	84	62	0	-	-	-	-
All First	140	244	22	8101	312	36.49	18	36	112	-	6712	3825	94	40.69	6-115	1	-
1-day Int																	
NatWest	14	14	1	442	101 *	34.00	1	3	8	-	162	122	1	122.00	1-11	-	
B & H	34	33	2	995	134	32.09	2	6	6	-	725	621	17	36.52	5-15	1	
1-day Lge	89	87	9	2655	130	34.03	4	14	32	-	844	825	28	29.46	2-10	-	

GANGULY, S. C. Lancashire

Name: <u>Saurav</u> Chandidas Ganguly
Role: Left-hand bat, right-arm medium bowler
Born: 8 July 1973, Calcutta
Height: 5ft 11in
County debut: 2000
Test debut: 1996
Tests: 35
One-Day Internationals: 145
1st-Class 50s: 49
1st-Class 100s: 14
1st-Class 200s: 1
1st-Class 5 w. in innings: 2
1st-Class catches: 91
One-Day 100s: 16
One-Day 5 w. in innings: 1
Place in batting averages: 79th av. 31.95
Strike rate: 125.50 (career 67.15)
Education: St Xavier's College

Overseas tours: India to Australia 1991-92, 1999-2000; to England 1996, to South Africa 1996-97, to West Indies 1996-97, to Sri Lanka 1997-98, to Zimbabwe 1998-99, to New Zealand 1998-99, to UK, Ireland and Holland (World Cup) 1999, to Kenya (ICC Knockout Trophy) 2000-01 (captain), to Bangladesh 2000-01 (captain)
Overseas teams played for: Bengal 1989-90 –
Extras: Scored century (131) on Test debut, v England at Lord's 1996, and another (136) in the following Test at Trent Bridge to become the third player, after Lawrence Rowe and Alvin Kallicharran, to score a century in his first two Test innings. Shared in a stand of 318 for the second wicket with Rahul Dravid for India v Sri Lanka at Taunton in the 1999 World Cup, a record for any wicket in One-Day International cricket; his 183 scored in that innings is the second-highest individual score in World Cup cricket behind Gary Kirsten's 188. Appointed captain of India February 2000.

Played for an Asia XI v a World XI in Dhaka 2000. Won Man of the Match awards in his first two NatWest games 2000. Shared in Lancashire Sunday/National League record first-wicket partnership (192), with Michael Atherton v Somerset Sabres at Taunton 2000. Left Lancashire at the end of the 2000 season

Best batting: 200* Bengal v Bihar, Calcutta 1994-95
Best bowling: 6-87 Bengal v Delhi, Delhi 1997-98
Stop press: Scored 141* v South Africa in the semi-finals of the ICC Knockout Trophy in Kenya 2000-01 and 117 v New Zealand in the final. Named CEAT International Player of the Year 2000

2000 Season

	M	Inns	NO	Runs	HS	Avge	100s	50s	Ct	St	O	M	Runs	Wkts	Avge	Best	5wI	10wM
Test																		
All First	14	21	0	671	99	31.95	-	6	10	-	83.4	11	311	4	77.75	2-39	-	-
1-day Int																		
NatWest	4	4	1	272	120 *	90.66	1	2	3	-	30	4	123	3	41.00	3-26	-	
B & H	6	6	1	62	22 *	12.40	-	-	2	-	36	3	149	7	21.28	3-7	-	
1-day Lge	13	13	2	569	102	51.72	2	4	4	-	55	2	242	7	34.57	3-22	-	

Career Performances

	M	Inns	NO	Runs	HS	Avge	100s	50s	Ct	St	Balls	Runs	Wkts	Avge	Best	5wI	10wM
Test	35	60	5	2505	173	45.54	7	12	21	-	1263	692	20	34.60	3-28	-	-
All First	122	194	25	7789	200 *	46.08	15	49	91	-	6447	3691	96	38.44	6-87	2	-
1-day Int	145	140	12	5569	183	43.50	13	32	43	-	2212	1848	50	36.96	5-16	1	
NatWest	4	4	1	272	120 *	90.66	1	2	3	-	180	123	3	41.00	3-26	-	
B & H	6	6	1	62	22 *	12.40	-	-	2	-	216	149	7	21.28	3-7	-	
1-day Lge	13	13	2	569	102	51.72	2	4	4	-	330	242	7	34.57	3-22	-	

31. Who scored his 20th Test century – and the 200th for Australia v England – at Perth in 1986-87?

GANNON, B. W.   Gloucestershire

Name: <u>Benjamin</u> Ward Gannon
Role: Right-hand lower order bat, right-arm medium bowler
Born: 5 September 1975, Oxford
Height: 6ft 3in **Weight:** 13st 7lbs
Nickname: Vamous
County debut: 1999
1st-Class 5 w. in innings: 3
1st-Class catches: 7
Place in batting averages: 249th av. 12.33 (1999 278th av. 8.75)
Place in bowling averages: 60th av. 25.24 (1999 96th av. 30.06)
Strike rate: 41.75 (career 44.64)
Parents: Martin and Jane
Marital status: Single
Education: Dragon School, Oxford; Abingdon School; Cheltenham and Gloucester College of Higher Education
Qualifications: 3 A-levels, BSc (Hons) Physical Geography and Sports Science
Career outside cricket: 'None. Getting fit for new season'
Off-season: Fitness work; club cricket in South Africa
Overseas tours: Gloucestershire to Zimbabwe 1997, to South Africa 1999, 2000; Forest Nomads to Zimbabwe 1999
Overseas teams played for: Waverley, Sydney 1993-94; Union CC, Port Elizabeth 2000
Cricketers particularly admired: Courtney Walsh, Curtly Ambrose, Glenn McGrath
Young players to look out for: Simon Jones, Steve Harmison
Other sports followed: Boxing, athletics, tennis, rugby
Injuries: Out for two weeks with a hamstring injury
Relaxations: Listening to music, keeping fit
Extras: Took seven wickets in his first-class debut match, v Glamorgan at Cardiff 1999. NBC Denis Compton Award 1999
Opinions on cricket: 'The standard of pitches has got to improve to start producing better cricketers to compete against the best in the world. At the moment the Aussies are the best in the world and generally play on better pitches than the other Test-playing nations.'
Best batting: 28 Gloucestershire v Essex, Colchester 2000
Best bowling: 6-80 Gloucestershire v Glamorgan, Cardiff 1999

2000 Season

	M	Inns	NO	Runs	HS	Avge	100s	50s	Ct	St	O	M	Runs	Wkts	Avge	Best	5wI	10wM
Test																		
All First	8	10	4	74	28	12.33	-	-	3	-	201.5	38	732	29	25.24	5-58	1	-
1-day Int																		
NatWest																			
B & H																			
1-day Lge																			

Career Performances

	M	Inns	NO	Runs	HS	Avge	100s	50s	Ct	St	Balls	Runs	Wkts	Avge	Best	5wI	10wM
Test																	
All First	19	22	8	144	28	10.28	-	-	7	-	2768	1724	62	27.80	6-80	3	-
1-day Int																	
NatWest																	
B & H																	
1-day Lge																	

GAZZARD, C. M.   Somerset

Name: <u>Carl</u> Matthew Gazzard
Role: Right-hand bat, wicket-keeper
Born: 15 April 1982, Penzance
Height: 6ft **Weight:** 12st 5lbs
Nickname: Gazza
County debut: No first-team appearance
Parents: Paul and Alison
Marital status: Single
Family links with cricket: Father and
brother both played for Cornwall Schools;
mother's a keen follower
Education: St Mary's Roman Catholic,
Penzance; Mounts Bay Comprehensive;
Richard Huish College, Taunton
Qualifications: 10 GCSEs, 2 A-levels,
Level 1 and 2 coaching
Career outside cricket: 'Not yet known'
Off-season: Playing and training in Perth,
Australia
Overseas tours: Cornwall Schools U13 to Johannesburg; West of England U15 to
West Indies; Somerset Academy to Durban 1999
Cricketers particularly admired: Ian Allen, Shakil Ahmed, Ian Healy, Alec Stewart,
Marcus Trescothick

Young players to look out for: Matthew Wood, Peter Trego
Other sports played: Football (played through the age groups for Cornwall)
Other sports followed: Football (West Ham United)
Relaxations: Any sport, watching TV, socialising
Extras: Played for England U13, U14, U15. Won the Graham Kersey Award for Best Wicket-keeper at Bunbury Festival. Played for Cornwall in Minor Counties aged 16 and in the NatWest Trophy 1999. Played in England U19 3-0 'One-Day International' series victory over Sri Lanka U19 in 2000 and in the win in the first 'Test'
Opinions on cricket: 'The game is becoming quicker and harder to force your way into, but with the right attitude and self-belief we can add to the quality and entertainment already provided. Second XI playing regulations should be the same as in first-class matches.'

2000 Season (did not make any first-class or one-day appearances)

Career Performances

	M	Inns	NO	Runs	HS	Avge	100s	50s	Ct	St	Balls	Runs	Wkts	Avge	Best	5wI	10wM
Test																	
All First																		
1-day Int																		
NatWest	1	1	0	16	16	16.00	-	-	2	-							
B & H																		
1-day Lge																		

GIDDINS, E. S. H. Surrey

Name: Edward (Ed) Simon Hunter Giddins
Role: Right-hand bat, right-arm
medium-fast bowler
Born: 20 July 1971, Eastbourne
Height: 6ft 4in **Weight:** 13st 10lbs
Nickname: The Chief
County debut: 1991 (Sussex), 1998 (Warwickshire)
County cap: 1994 (Sussex), 1998 (Warwickshire)
Test debut: 1999
Tests: 4
50 wickets in a season: 4
1st-Class 5 w. in innings: 21
1st-Class 10 w. in match: 2
1st-Class catches: 19
One-Day 5 w. in innings: 1
Place in batting averages: 305th av. 3.12 (1999 280th av. 8.44)

Place in bowling averages: 77th av. 28.03
(1999 33rd av. 21.96)
Strike rate: 59.13 (career 51.50)
Parents: Simon and Pauline
Marital status: Single
Family links with cricket: 'A keen interest'
Education: St Bede's School, Eastbourne;
Eastbourne College
Qualifications: O-levels, A-levels, national
coaching certificate
Career outside cricket: 'In the process of
opening a bar/restaurant in London's West
End'
Off-season: 'Organising the bar'
Overseas tours: England A to Pakistan 1995-
96; Rumsey Tours to Barbados 2000
Overseas teams played for: Mosman,
Sydney 1994-95
Cricketers particularly admired: Graham Gooch, Eddie Hemmings, Ian Gould
Young players to look out for: Nad Shahid, Nick Warren
Other sports played: 'Love golf'
Other sports followed: Football (Fulham FC)
Injuries: Out for one month with a hamstring injury
Relaxations: Travel
Extras: Joined Warwickshire for the 1998 season. Recorded maiden Test five-wicket
return (5-15; 7-42 in match) in the first Test v Zimbabwe, Lord's 2000, winning the
Man of the Match award. Left Warwickshire during the 2000-01 off-season and has
joined Surrey for 2001
Opinions on cricket: 'Sunday League cricket should not be 40 overs; it should be 10
overs a side but on a "best of three" basis – i.e. first to secure two wins gets the four
points.'
Best batting: 34 Sussex v Essex, Hove 1995
Best bowling: 6-47 Sussex v Yorkshire, Eastbourne 1996

2000 Season

	M	Inns	NO	Runs	HS	Avge	100s	50s	Ct	St	O	M	Runs	Wkts	Avge	Best	5wI	10wM
Test	3	5	2	10	7	3.33	-	-	-	-	48	14	161	8	20.12	5-15	1	-
All First	12	11	3	25	14	3.12	-	-	1	-	285.5	92	813	29	28.03	5-15	1	-
1-day Int																		
NatWest	3	0	0	0	0	-	-	-	1	-	26	1	109	1	109.00	1-34	-	
B & H	3	1	1	0	0 *	-	-	-	-	-	18	2	51	5	10.20	3-22	-	
1-day Lge	9	2	1	0	0 *	0.00	-	-	3	-	57.4	7	182	5	36.40	2-15	-	

Career Performances

	M	Inns	NO	Runs	HS	Avge	100s	50s	Ct	St	Balls	Runs	Wkts	Avge	Best	5wl	10wM
Test	4	7	3	10	7	2.50	-	-	-	-	444	240	12	20.00	5-15	1	-
All First	125	150	61	465	34	5.22	-	-	19	-	21273	11388	413	27.57	6-47	21	2
1-day Int																	
NatWest	17	6	3	27	13	9.00	-	-	3	-	1043	630	19	33.15	3-24	-	
B & H	22	7	5	6	4 *	3.00	-	-	5	-	1196	734	30	24.46	5-21	1	
1-day Lge	95	37	15	37	9 *	1.68	-	-	13	-	3990	3158	103	30.66	4-23	-	

GILES, A. F. Warwickshire

Name: <u>Ashley</u> Fraser Giles
Role: Right-hand bat, slow left-arm bowler
Born: 19 March 1973, Chertsey, Surrey
Height: 6ft 4in **Weight:** 15st 7lbs
Nickname: Splash, Skinny
County debut: 1993
County cap: 1996
Test debut: 1998
Tests: 1
One-Day Internationals: 5
50 wickets in a season: 2
1st-Class 50s: 13
1st-Class 100s: 3
1st-Class 5 w. in innings: 13
1st-Class 10 w. in match: 2
1st-Class catches: 36
One-Day 100s: 1
One-Day 5 w. in innings: 2
Place in batting averages: 39th av. 40.36 (1999 195th av. 20.83)
Place in bowling averages: 42nd av. 23.07 (1999 53rd av. 24.05)
Strike rate: 60.76 (career 66.78)
Parents: Michael and Paula
Wife and date of marriage: Stine, 9 October 1999
Children: Anders Fraser, 29 May 2000
Family links with cricket: 'Dad played and brother Andrew still plays club cricket at Ripley, Surrey'
Education: Kingfield Primary School, Old Woking; George Abbott County Secondary, Burpham, Guildford
Qualifications: 9 GCSEs, 2 A-levels, coaching certificate
Career outside cricket: 'Baby sitting'
Off-season: Touring with England to Kenya, Pakistan and Sri Lanka

Overseas tours: Surrey U19 to Barbados 1990-91; Warwickshire to Cape Town 1996, 1997, to Bloemfontein 1998; England A to Australia 1996-97, to Kenya and Sri Lanka 1997-98; England to Sharjah (Champions Trophy) 1997-98, to Bangladesh (Wills International Cup) 1998, to Australia 1998-99 (CUB Series), to South Africa and Zimbabwe 1999-2000 (one-day series), to Kenya (ICC Knockout Trophy) 2000-01, to Pakistan and Sri Lanka 2000-01

Overseas teams played for: Vredenburg/Saldanha, Cape Town 1992-95; Avendale CC, Cape Town 1995-96

Cricketers particularly admired: Dermot Reeve, Tim Munton, Dougie Brown, Ian Botham

Young players to look out for: Ian Bell

Other sports played: Golf (14 handicap), football ('Klinsmann')

Other sports followed: Football (QPR)

Injuries: Out for one week with Achilles tendon injury

Relaxations: 'Cinema, music, spending lots of time with Stine and Anders'

Extras: Surrey Young Cricketer of the Year 1991. Shared in record Warwickshire partnership for 10th wicket, 141 with Tim Munton v Worcestershire at Worcester 1996. NBC Denis Compton Award for Warwickshire in 1996. Warwickshire Player of the Year in 1996 and 2000. Warwickshire Most Improved Player 1996. Cricket Society Young Allrounder of the year 1996. Scored 100 (123*) and took five wickets (5-28) in an innings in same match (v Oxford University at The Parks) in 1999, the first time this feat had been performed by a Warwickshire player since Tom Cartwright achieved it v Lancashire at Edgbaston in 1961. Shared in record Warwicks partnership for 8th wicket (289 with Dougie Brown v Sussex at Hove 2000), scoring 128*, the best by a Warwicks No. 8, in the process. Scored maiden one-day century (107) v Derbyshire at Edgbaston in the NatWest 2000, batting at No. 3. Took 23 wickets (12-135 and 11-196) in two games v Northants 2000. Followed first innings score of 98 with five wickets in an innings (6-58) v Sussex at Edgbaston 2000

Opinions on cricket: 'Two divisions pulling the game in the right direction. Central contracts are the future of our game.'

Best batting: 128* Warwickshire v Sussex, Hove 2000

Best bowling: 8-90 Warwickshire v Northamptonshire, Northampton 2000

Stop press: Recorded maiden five-wicket return in Tests (5-75) in the second Test v Pakistan at Faisalabad 2000-01; finished the series with 17 wickets, the highest total by an England bowler in a series in Pakistan

2000 Season

	M	Inns	NO	Runs	HS	Avge	100s	50s	Ct	St	O	M	Runs	Wkts	Avge	Best	5wI	10wM
Test																		
All First	13	14	3	444	128 *	40.36	1	1	4	-	526.4	163	1200	52	23.07	8-90	5	2
1-day Int																		
NatWest	5	4	0	189	107	47.25	1	1	2	-	45	0	188	7	26.85	2-34	-	
B & H	3	1	0	15	15	15.00	-	-	-	-	3	0	25	0	-	-	-	
1-day Lge	13	11	0	221	45	20.09	-	-	7	-	115	9	435	22	19.77	3-32	-	

Career Performances

	M	Inns	NO	Runs	HS	Avge	100s	50s	Ct	St	Balls	Runs	Wkts	Avge	Best	5wI	10wM
Test	1	2	1	17	16 *	17.00	-	-	-	-	216	106	1	106.00	1-106	-	-
All First	93	124	28	2890	128 *	30.10	3	13	36	-	18633	7154	279	25.64	8-90	13	2
1-day Int	5	3	2	17	10 *	17.00	-	-	1	-	228	197	5	39.40	2-37	-	
NatWest	17	13	3	354	107	35.40	1	2	2	-	893	584	29	20.13	5-21	1	
B & H	19	14	3	188	37	17.09	-	-	9	-	712	554	22	25.18	3-22	-	
1-day Lge	76	48	8	739	57	18.47	-	1	25	-	2723	1943	99	19.62	5-36	1	

GOLDING, J. M.　　　　　　　　　　　　　Kent

Name: <u>James</u> Matthew Golding
Role: Right-hand bat, right-arm
medium-fast bowler
Born: 19 July 1977, Canterbury
Height: 6ft 4in　**Weight:** 16st
Nickname: Jingo, Goldie
County debut: 1999
Strike rate: 102.00 (career 117.00)
Parents: Marilyn and Adrian
Marital status: Single
Education: St Anne's, Sturry; Kent College,
Canterbury; University College, Worcester
Qualifications: 8 GCSEs, 3 A-levels, BSc
Geography with Sports Studies
Overseas teams played for: Kensington
District CC, Adelaide
Cricketers particularly admired: Graeme
Hick, Ian Botham, Allan Donald,
Jacques Kallis
Other sports played: Hockey, tennis, golf, squash
Other sports followed: Hockey (Canterbury HC)
Relaxations: Golf, socialising with friends, all sports
Extras: Man of the Match playing for Kent Cricket Board v Hampshire in NatWest
third round 1999. Made first-class debut for Kent v New Zealand 1999 while still an
amateur; his first wicket was New Zealand captain Stephen Fleming
Best batting: 18* Kent v Zimbabweans, Canterbury 2000
Best bowling: 1-38 Kent v Zimbabweans, Canterbury 2000

2000 Season

	M	Inns	NO	Runs	HS	Avge	100s	50s	Ct	St	O	M	Runs	Wkts	Avge	Best	5wl	10wM
Test																		
All First	1	1	1	18	18 *	-	-	-	-	-	17	7	38	1	38.00	1-38	-	-
1-day Int																		
NatWest																		
B & H	2	1	0	7	7	7.00	-	-	2	-	14	4	69	4	17.25	3-20	-	
1-day Lge	3	2	0	0	0	0.00	-	-	-	-	13	2	38	1	38.00	1-18	-	

Career Performances

	M	Inns	NO	Runs	HS	Avge	100s	50s	Ct	St	Balls	Runs	Wkts	Avge	Best	5wl	10wM
Test																	
All First	2	3	2	21	18 *	21.00	-	-	-	-	234	112	2	56.00	1-38	-	-
1-day Int																	
NatWest	3	2	0	52	47	26.00	-	-	2	-	150	141	0	-	-	-	-
B & H	2	1	0	7	7	7.00	-	-	2	-	84	69	4	17.25	3-20	-	
1-day Lge	3	2	0	0	0	0.00	-	-	-	-	78	38	1	38.00	1-18	-	

GOODE, C. M.   Northamptonshire

Name: <u>Chris</u> Martin Goode
Role: Right-hand bat, right-arm fast bowler; all-rounder
Born: 12 October 1984, Kettering
Height: 6ft 3in **Weight:** 12st 3lbs
Nickname: Goodey
County debut: No first-team appearance
Parents: Martin and Carla
Marital status: Girlfriend
Education: Finedon Mulso C of E School; Huxlow
Career outside cricket: Full-time education
Overseas tours: Northamptonshire U17-U19 to South Africa 1999-2000; Northampton Town FC U14 to Italy 1998-99
Cricketers particularly admired: Allan Donald
Young players to look out for: Samit Patel (Nottinghamshire U16)
Other sports played: Football ('used to play for Northampton Town U10-U16')
Other sports followed: Football (Man Utd)
Injuries: Out for one month with a groin injury

Relaxations: 'Music, women, football'
Extras: Represented England U15 in Costcutter U15 World Challenge 2000, taking 4-22 v India
Opinions on cricket: 'Enjoy it!'

GOODWIN, M. W. Sussex

Name: <u>Murray</u> William Goodwin
Role: Right-hand bat, right-arm medium/leg-spin bowler
Born: 11 December 1972, Harare, Zimbabwe
Height: 5ft 9in **Weight:** 11st 2lbs
Nickname: Muzz, Goodie
County debut: No first-team appearance
Test debut: 1997-98
Tests: 19
One-Day Internationals: 71
1st-Class 50s: 17
1st-Class 100s: 6
1st-Class catches: 33
One-Day 100s: 2
Place in batting averages: 5th av. 65.10
Strike rate: (career 82.14)
Parents: Penny and George
Wife and date of marriage: Tarsha, 13 December 1997
Family links with cricket: 'Brother also played for Zimbabwe before it was a Test-playing nation. Father coached me throughout my childhood. Whole family involved in cricket'
Education: St Johns Primary, Harare, Zimbabwe; Newton Moore SHS, Bunbury, Western Australia
Qualifications: Fitness trainer, Level 2 coach
Career outside cricket: 'To still be involved in the game in some way'
Overseas tours: Australian Cricket Academy to South Africa 1992, to Sri Lanka and India 1993; Zimbabwe to Sri Lanka 1997-98, to Pakistan 1998-99, to South Africa 1999-2000, to West Indies 1999-2000, to England 2000
Overseas teams played for: Excelsior, Holland 1997; Western Australia 1994-95 – 1996-97, 2000-01 –
Cricketers particularly admired: Steve Waugh
Young players to look out for: Shaun Marsh
Other sports played: Golf, hockey, tennis
Other sports followed: Aussie Rules football, rugby
Relaxations: 'I enjoy spending time with close friends'

Extras: Emigrated to Australia aged 13. Attended Australian Cricket Academy. Scored 148* for Zimbabwe v England in second Test at Trent Bridge 2000, winning Man of the Match award. Scored 112* v West Indies in NatWest Triangular Series at Riverside 2000, winning Man of the Match award. Retired from international cricket in 2000. Has joined Sussex as overseas player for 2001

Opinions on cricket: 'One must never lose sight of the fact that the game is always bigger than the player.'

Best batting: 194 Zimbabweans v Gloucestershire, Gloucester 2000

Best bowling: 2-23 Zimbabweans v Lahore City, Lahore 1998-99

Stop press: Scored 167 for Western Australia v New South Wales at Perth in the Mercantile Mutual Cup 2000-01, setting a new record for the highest individual score in Australian domestic one-day cricket

---

2000 Season

	M	Inns	NO	Runs	HS	Avge	100s	50s	Ct	St	O	M	Runs	Wkts	Avge	Best	5wI	10wM
Test	2	4	2	178	148 *	89.00	1	-	-	-								
All First	8	12	2	651	194	65.10	3	1	3	-	4	1	19	0	-	-	-	-
1-day Int	7	7	1	189	112 *	31.50	1	-	-	-								
NatWest																		
B & H																		
1-day Lge																		

Career Performances

	M	Inns	NO	Runs	HS	Avge	100s	50s	Ct	St	Balls	Runs	Wkts	Avge	Best	5wI	10wM
Test	19	37	4	1414	166 *	42.84	3	8	10	-	118	69	0	-	-	-	-
All First	48	83	8	3483	194	46.44	6	17	33	-	575	297	7	42.42	2-23	-	-
1-day Int	71	70	3	1818	112 *	27.13	2	8	20	-	248	210	4	52.50	1-12	-	
NatWest	1	1	0	4	4	4.00	-	-	-	-	30	28	1	28.00	1-28	-	
B & H																	
1-day Lge																	

---

32. What happened to prevent the final day's play taking place at Headingley in 1975?

GOUGH, D. Yorkshire

Name: Darren Gough
Role: Right-hand bat, right-arm fast bowler
Born: 18 September 1970, Barnsley
Height: 5ft 11in **Weight:** 13st 4lbs
Nickname: Dazzler
County debut: 1989
County cap: 1993
Test debut: 1994
Tests: 43
One-Day Internationals: 81
50 wickets in a season: 4
1st-Class 50s: 11
1st-Class 100s: 1
1st-Class 5 w. in innings: 25
1st-Class 10 w. in innings: 3
1st-Class catches: 40
One-Day 5 w. in innings: 6
Place in batting averages: 245th av. 13.10
Place in bowling averages: 18th av. 18.98 (1999 12th av. 18.76)
Strike rate: 38.90 (career 50.43)
Parents: Trevor and Christine
Wife and date of marriage: Anna Marie, 16 October 1993
Children: Liam James, 24 November 1994; Brennan Kyle, 9 December 1997
Education: St Helens Junior; Priory Comprehensive; Airedale and Wharfdale College (part-time)
Qualifications: 2 O-levels, 5 CSEs, BTEC Leisure, NCA coaching award
Off-season: England tours to Kenya, Pakistan and Sri Lanka
Overseas tours: England YC to Australia 1989-90; Yorkshire to Barbados 1989-90, to South Africa 1991-92 and 1992-93; England A to South Africa 1993-94; England to Australia 1994-95, to South Africa 1995-96, to India and Pakistan (World Cup) 1995-96, to Zimbabwe and New Zealand 1996-97, to Australia 1998-99, to Sharjah (Coca-Cola Cup) 1998-99, to South Africa and Zimbabwe 1999-2000, to Kenya (ICC Knockout Trophy) 2000-01, to Pakistan and Sri Lanka 2000-01
Overseas teams played for: East Shirley, Christchurch, New Zealand 1991-92
Cricketers particularly admired: Ian Botham, Steve Waugh, Shane Warne, Michael Atherton ('mental strength')
Young players to look out for: Marcus Trescothick, Andrew Flintoff, Graeme Swann, Paul Hutchison, Ryan Sidebottom, Rob Cunliffe, Darren Stevens
Other sports played: Golf
Other sports followed: Football (Tottenham Hotspur and Barnsley)
Relaxations: Golf, cinema, 'spending time with family'

Extras: Scored 65 in his first Test innings, v New Zealand at Old Trafford 1994, batting at No. 9. Cornhill England Player of the Year 1994. Yorkshire Sports Personality of the Year 1994. Took a hat-trick against Kent in 1995. Cornhill England Player of the Year 1994-95. Whyte and Mackay Bowler of the Year in 1996. England Player of the Series in the Texaco one-day rubber v South Africa 1998. Took 100th Test wicket (Jonty Rhodes) v South Africa at Headingley 1998. Took Test hat-trick v Australia at Sydney in January 1999, the first Ashes hat-trick by an England bowler since J. Hearne's at Leeds in 1899. Was third English cricketer to reach 100 One-Day International wickets. *Sheffield Star* Sports Personality of the Year. Cornhill England Player of the Year (for the second time) 1998-99. One of *Wisden*'s Five Cricketers of the Year 1999. Represented England in the 1999 World Cup. Won Freeserve Fast Ball award 2000 (for the fastest recorded ball bowled in a televised match) for a delivery timed at 93.1 mph at Lord's on 20 May during the first Test v Zimbabwe. Shared the new ball with Andrew Caddick in each Test of the West Indies series 2000, the first time the same pair had opened the bowling for England throughout a series since Fred Trueman and Brian Statham did so v South Africa in 1960. Took 25 Test wickets v West Indies 2000 and was named England's Man of the Series. Granted a benefit for 2001

Opinions on cricket: 'Divisions improving the intensity of the matches, which in the long run will improve the standards. County cricket rewards mediocrity too well. Too many pros; four too many teams. Central contracts a must for at least 30 players – a target for everybody else to reach. "A" tours must be reserve Test team except for one or two young "could-bes".'

Best batting: 121 Yorkshire v Warwickshire, Headingley 1996
Best bowling: 7-28 Yorkshire v Lancashire, Headingley 1995

2000 Season

	M	Inns	NO	Runs	HS	Avge	100s	50s	Ct	St	O	M	Runs	Wkts	Avge	Best	5wI	10wM
Test	7	11	3	103	23 *	12.87	-	-	2	-	223.2	40	704	34	20.70	5-109	1	-
All First	10	13	3	131	23 *	13.10	-	-	3	-	324.1	62	949	50	18.98	6-63	2	-
1-day Int	7	4	3	7	3 *	7.00	-	-	-	-	56	5	213	9	23.66	3-20	-	
NatWest	2	1	0	3	3	3.00	-	-	-	-	18.5	2	66	9	7.33	5-30	1	
B & H	6	2	1	4	4	4.00	-	-	-	-	45	9	132	8	16.50	4-17	-	
1-day Lge	6	3	3	36	15 *	-	-	-	-	1	-	47	8	136	7	19.42	3-19	-	

Career Performances

	M	Inns	NO	Runs	HS	Avge	100s	50s	Ct	St	Balls	Runs	Wkts	Avge	Best	5wI	10wM
Test	43	65	12	635	65	11.98	-	2	11	-	9062	4809	173	27.79	6-42	7	-
All First	175	236	41	3070	121	15.74	1	11	40	-	31775	16682	630	26.47	7-28	25	3
1-day Int	81	51	19	347	45	10.84	-	-	12	-	4476	3083	133	23.18	5-44	2	
NatWest	24	13	0	228	46	17.53	-	-	3	-	1523	851	54	15.75	7-27	2	
B & H	35	18	6	164	48 *	13.66	-	-	11	-	1808	1096	42	26.09	4-17	-	
1-day Lge	104	68	19	644	72 *	13.14	-	1	19	-	4467	3238	131	24.71	5-13	2	

GOUGH, M. A.   Durham

Name: <u>Michael</u> Andrew Gough
Role: Right-hand bat, off-spin bowler,
specialist gully fielder
Born: 18 December 1979, Hartlepool
Height: 6ft 5in **Weight:** 14st
Nickname: Goughy
County debut: 1998
1st-Class 50s: 7
1st-Class 100s: 1
1st-Class catches: 35
Place in batting averages: 231st av. 14.66
(1999 191st av. 21.20)
Strike rate: 91.40 (career 102.09)
Parents: Michael and Jean
Marital status: Single ('soon to be engaged
to Nicola Reed')
Family links with cricket: 'Dad played
Minor Counties cricket for Durham. Cousin
Paul played for Durham U19. Uncle John was a good opening bat'
Education: Sacred Heart RC Primary School, Hartlepool; English Martyrs School and
Sixth Form College, Hartlepool
Qualifications: 10 GCSEs, cricket coaching award
Off-season: 'Watching England on TV; training, nets, rest; hopefully Sri Lanka tour
pre-season with Durham'
Overseas tours: Durham U21 to Sri Lanka November 1996; Durham to Sri Lanka
2001; England U17 to Bermuda (International Youth Tournament) June 1997; England
U19 to South Africa (inc Youth World Cup) 1997-98, to New Zealand 1998-99
(captain); England A to Bangladesh and New Zealand 1999-2000
Cricketers particularly admired: Mike Atherton, Steve Waugh, Jacques Kallis,
Shane Warne, Simon Katich, Saqlain Mushtaq, Ronnie Irani
Young players to look out for: Gary Pratt, Nicky Peng, James Foster, Ian Hunter,
Chris Lawson (Hartlepool CC)
Other sports played: Football (had trials with Arsenal, Sheffield United and
Hartlepool, and attended Middlesbrough FC School of Excellence)
Other sports followed: Football (Hartlepool United season-ticket holder – 'for my
sins!!!')
Injuries: Out for two months with a back injury; for six weeks after removal of a non-
malignant cyst from breast; for two weeks with a chest infection – 'a season to
forget!!'
Relaxations: 'Music, TV, sport, socialising, spending time with girlfriend Nicola,
cinema, eating out, spending time with friends, football'

Extras: Captained North of England and England U15. Part of winning England U17 team at the International Youth Tournament in Bermuda 1997. Durham CCC Young Player of the Year 1997. Scored 62 on first-class debut, against Essex 1998. Became youngest player to score a century for Durham, against Cambridge University 1998. Captained England U19 v Australia U19 in one-day and 'Test' series 1999. 'Hit Shane Warne for a four!!!'

Opinions on cricket: 'Far too much cricket played, therefore players lose hunger and desire. Extend tea break by ten minutes. Should play more day/night cricket – great to play in, great spectacle for spectators, great attraction for kids, therefore more involvement in game. Should follow examples of South Africa, New Zealand and Australia and set up national cricket academy. More fast bowlers on central contracts for monitoring progress and injury prevention.'

Best batting: 123 Durham v Cambridge University, Fenner's 1998
Best bowling: 4-49 Durham v Nottinghamshire, Riverside 1999

2000 Season

	M	Inns	NO	Runs	HS	Avge	100s	50s	Ct	St	O	M	Runs	Wkts	Avge	Best	5wI	10wM
Test																		
All First	7	12	0	176	33	14.66	-	-	3	-	76.1	14	280	5	56.00	4-106	-	-
1-day Int																		
NatWest	1	1	0	10	10	10.00	-	-	-	-								
B & H																		
1-day Lge	5	5	1	92	36	23.00	-	-	1	-	5	0	30	0	-		-	-

Career Performances

	M	Inns	NO	Runs	HS	Avge	100s	50s	Ct	St	Balls	Runs	Wkts	Avge	Best	5wI	10wM
Test																	
All First	33	57	1	1302	123	23.25	1	7	35	-	1123	660	11	60.00	4-49	-	-
1-day Int																	
NatWest	1	1	0	10	10	10.00	-	-	-	-							
B & H																	
1-day Lge	8	7	1	108	36	18.00	-	-	2	-	72	75	0	-		-	-

GRAYSON, A. P.   Essex

Name: Adrian Paul Grayson
Role: Right-hand opening bat, slow left-arm
bowler
Born: 31 March 1971, Ripon
Height: 6ft 1in **Weight:** 12st
Nickname: Larry
County debut: 1990 (Yorkshire),
1996 (Essex)
County cap: 1996 (Essex)
1000 runs in a season: 3
1st-Class 50s: 36
1st-Class 100s: 8
1st-Class catches: 102
Place in batting averages: 114th av. 27.82
(1999 60th av. 36.10)
Place in bowling averages: 139th av. 44.30
(1999 125th av. 38.59)
Strike rate: 106.80 (career 93.02)
Parents: Adrian and Carol
Wife and date of marriage: Alison, 30 September 1994
Children: Oliver, 30 January 1997; Beth, 3 February 1999
Family links with cricket: 'Father is a staff coach; brother Simon plays when free
from football commitments'
Education: Bedale; Bedale Comprehensive School
Qualifications: 8 CSEs, BTEC in Leisure Studies, advanced cricket coach
Career outside cricket: Working for Ridley's Brewery
Off-season: 'Working for Ridley's for five months; keeping fit'
Overseas tours: England YC to Australia 1989-90; England to Kenya (ICC Knockout
Trophy) 2000-01, to Pakistan 2000-01 (one-day series); Yorkshire to Barbados 1989-
90, to Cape Town 1991, 1992, 1993, to Leeward Islands 1994
Overseas teams played for: Petone, Wellington 1991-92, 1995-96
Cricketers particularly admired: Graham Gooch, Martyn Moxon, Darren Gough
Young players to look out for: James Foster, Oliver Grayson
Other sports played: Golf (16 handicap), football (Essex CCC charity side; was
offered apprentice forms with Middlesbrough FC at 16 but signed for Yorkshire)
Other sports followed: Football (Leeds United)
Relaxations: 'Spending time with my wife and children; playing golf; watching
football'
Extras: Played for England YC v New Zealand 1989 and Pakistan 1990. Brother plays
professional football. Scored 1000 runs for first time in 1994. Yorkshire Player of the
Year 1994. Released by Yorkshire at end of 1995 and joined Essex for 1996 season.

Essex Player of the Year 1997

Opinions on cricket: 'Two divisions an excellent idea and is working well. Central contracts have worked and should be applauded. County staffs should be reduced, but there should be an increase in wages for retained players.'

Best batting: 159* Essex v Hampshire, Ilford 1999

Best bowling: 4-16 Essex v Middlesex, Southend 1999

Stop press: Drafted into England one-day squad for ICC Knockout Trophy in Kenya 2000-01 as cover for the injured Ashley Giles, making One-Day International debut v South Africa, and for one-day element of tour to Pakistan

2000 Season

	M	Inns	NO	Runs	HS	Avge	100s	50s	Ct	St	O	M	Runs	Wkts	Avge	Best	5wI	10wM
Test																		
All First	17	31	2	807	144	27.82	1	5	10	-	178	39	443	10	44.30	3-55	-	-
1-day Int																		
NatWest	2	2	0	21	18	10.50	-	-	-	-	7	0	34	1	34.00	1-34	-	
B & H	3	3	0	28	17	9.33	-	-	-	-	19	0	95	1	95.00	1-39	-	
1-day Lge	15	15	3	309	64	25.75	-	1	5	-	90.2	2	394	19	20.73	3-21	-	

Career Performances

	M	Inns	NO	Runs	HS	Avge	100s	50s	Ct	St	Balls	Runs	Wkts	Avge	Best	5wI	10wM
Test																	
All First	142	232	20	6318	159 *	29.80	8	36	102	-	10233	4640	110	42.18	4-16	-	-
1-day Int																	
NatWest	22	18	1	409	82 *	24.05	-	3	7	-	869	682	21	32.47	3-24	-	
B & H	28	23	6	353	49 *	20.76	-	-	7	-	1017	733	25	29.32	3-30	-	
1-day Lge	126	103	16	1601	69 *	18.40	-	5	33	-	4094	3619	112	32.31	4-25	-	

> 33. Whose 123 constituted 66.84 per cent of Australia's runs
> in their second innings at Sydney in 1998-99?

GREEN, R. J.   Lancashire

Name: <u>Richard</u> James Green
Role: Right-hand bat, right-arm
medium-fast swing bowler
Born: 13 March 1976, Warrington, Cheshire
Height: 6ft **Weight:** 13st 4lbs
Nickname: Greeny, Slime
County debut: 1995
1st-Class 50s: 1
1st-Class 5 w. in innings: 1
1st-Class catches: 7
Place in bowling averages: (1999 117th
av. 34.60)
Strike rate: 288.00 (career 73.69)
Parents: Jim and Christine
Marital status: Single
Family links with cricket: 'Grandfather and
father were both league legends, so I am
told!'

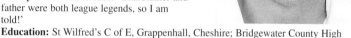

Education: St Wilfred's C of E, Grappenhall, Cheshire; Bridgewater County High
School, Appleton, Cheshire; Mid-Cheshire College (studied Business Studies)
Qualifications: 5 GCSEs, experienced qualified coach
Career outside cricket: House letting agent. 'Would love to own a successful wine
bar'
Off-season: 'Gaining IT qualifications and sales experience; expanding my network of
contacts'
Overseas tours: Lancashire to Jamaica 1996, to Cape Town 1997
Overseas teams played for: Waratah-Mayfield CC, Newcastle, NSW 1994-95;
Prahran CC, Melbourne, Australia 1996-97; Cape Town CC, South Africa 1999
Cricketers particularly admired: Stephen Titchard, Ian Austin, Warren Hegg
Other sports played: Snooker
Other sports followed: Football (Manchester United), 'all sports'
Injuries: 'Constant back pain and sore knees; no time off'
Relaxations: 'Joining up with ex-colleague Stephen Titchard and friends in the local'
Extras: Cheshire County League's youngest century-maker. Played for England
U17 and England U19. Denis Compton Award winner in 1997
Opinions on cricket: 'Would like to see more youngsters with correct side-on actions
rather than coached, ugly, robotic ones. Second XI cricket should be abolished and
probably will be soon. Choose from academy and premier leagues. Just make sure the
cricket is played on good wickets, unlike at present. Also, less cricket so there's more
squad training. In that way everyone feels involved, so when they're called upon they
feel part of it and can perform to their best.'

Best batting: 51 Lancashire v Essex, Old Trafford 1997
Best bowling: 6-41 Lancashire v Yorkshire, Old Trafford 1996

2000 Season

	M	Inns	NO	Runs	HS	Avge	100s	50s	Ct	St	O	M	Runs	Wkts	Avge	Best	5wI	10wM
Test																		
All First	3	3	1	29	29 *	14.50	-	-	2	-	48	9	175	1	175.00	1-68	-	-
1-day Int																		
NatWest																			
B & H																			
1-day Lge	1	1	1	3	3 *	-	-	-	-	-	4.5	1	24	0	-		-	-

Career Performances

	M	Inns	NO	Runs	HS	Avge	100s	50s	Ct	St	Balls	Runs	Wkts	Avge	Best	5wI	10wM
Test																	
All First	30	31	12	324	51	17.05	-	1	7	-	4053	2209	55	40.16	6-41	1	-
1-day Int																	
NatWest	1	1	0	0	0	0.00	-	-	-	-	66	35	1	35.00	1-35	-	
B & H	5	3	1	13	7	6.50	-	-	1	-	249	231	6	38.50	2-33	-	
1-day Lge	21	4	3	31	14 *	31.00	-	-	2	-	827	716	25	28.64	3-18	-	

GREENFIELD, K.   Sussex

Name: Keith Greenfield
Role: Right-hand bat, off-spin bowler
Born: 6 December 1968, Brighton
Height: 6ft   **Weight:** 13st 7lbs
Nickname: G-Man, Grubby
County debut: 1987
1st-Class 50s: 13
1st-Class 100s: 9
1st-Class catches: 65
One-Day 100s: 2
Strike rate: (career 162.80)
Parents: Leslie Ernest and Sheila
Wife and date of marriage:
Caroline Susannah, 22 February 1992
Children: Bethany Hannah,
18 December 1998
Family links with cricket: Father keen
spectator, as is father-in-law, who played club
cricket for 20 years

Education: Coldean First and Middle Schools; Falmer High School
Qualifications: 3 O-levels, BTEC National Diploma in Leisure and Business, ECB Level 3 coach and Level 1 and 2 tutor
Off-season: 'Admin and coaching at Hove'
Overseas tours: Sussex U16 to Guernsey 1985; Select XI to Malaga 1994, 1995; MCC to SE Asia and Far East 1994-95, to Bangladesh 1996, to New Zealand 1999 (captain); Sussex U19 to Barbados 1997 (as coach)
Overseas teams played for: Cornwall and Districts, Auckland 1988-90
Cricketers particularly admired: Ian Botham, Paul Parker, Derek Randall, Allan Border
Young players to look out for: Krishna Singh
Other sports played: Golf
Other sports followed: Golf, football (Liverpool FC, Brighton & HA FC), 'any sport'
Relaxations: 'Spending time with family (Caz and Beth); concerts, eating out, having quiet drink with friends; golf'
Extras: First person taken on Youth Training Scheme to become a professional cricketer at Sussex. Only uncapped player to have captained Sussex in first-class match, at Hove (v Cambridge U) 1991; scored century in this game. Captained 2nd XI to 2nd XI Championship title in 1990. Sussex Young Player of the Year 1990. Sussex Team Man of the Year 1990, 1993. Is now 2nd XI captain/coach at Sussex
Opinions on cricket: 'Our Test team will only really start to improve when teams in the Championship start to prepare the best possible pitches, not ones to suit their bowlers, and certainly not ones that at the start of a four-day game are such that a draw will never happen. Otherwise our cricket will not go forward.'
Best batting: 154* Sussex v India, Hove 1996
Best bowling: 2-40 Sussex v Essex, Hove 1993

2000 Season (did not make any first-class or one-day appearances)

Career Performances

	M	Inns	NO	Runs	HS		Avge	100s	50s	Ct	St	Balls	Runs	Wkts	Avge	Best	5wI	10wM
Test																		
All First	78	135	15	3550	154	*	29.58	9	13	65	-	814	524	5	104.80	2-40	-	-
1-day Int																		
NatWest	15	14	3	431	129		39.18	1	2	7	-	402	303	3	101.00	2-35	-	
B & H	25	24	3	611	93	*	29.09	-	4	8	-	432	354	2	177.00	1-17	-	
1-day Lge	117	115	11	2751	102		26.45	1	16	34	-	994	978	22	44.45	3-34	-	

GREENIDGE, C. G. Surrey

Name: <u>Carl</u> Gary Greenidge
Role: Right-hand bat, right-arm
fast bowler
Born: 20 April 1978, Basingstoke
Height: 5ft 10in **Weight:** 12st 7lbs
Nickname: Carlos, Carlito, G
County debut: 1998 (one-day),
1999 (first-class)

1st-Class 5 w. in innings: 1
1st-Class catches: 3
Place in bowling averages: (1999 24th
av. 21.00)
Strike rate: 210.00 (career 55.83)
Parents: Gordon and Anita
Marital status: Single
Family links with cricket: Father Gordon
played for Hampshire and West Indies, as did
cousin (on mother's side) Andy Roberts
Education: St Paul's, Barbados; St Michael's, Barbados; Heathcote School,
Chingford; City of Westminster College
Qualifications: GNVQ Leisure and Tourism, NCA senior coaching award
Cricketers particularly admired: Malcolm Marshall, Dennis Lillee, Carl Hooper,
Mark Waugh, Graham Thorpe, Ricaldo Anderson, Muazam Ali, Gareth Batty,
Rupesh Amin, 'and many more'
Other sports followed: Football (Arsenal), basketball (LA Lakers)
Relaxations: 'Music, kung fu movies, PlayStation, and my bed'
Extras: Spent a year on Lord's groundstaff. Took eight wickets on his Championship
debut for Surrey, v Yorkshire at The Oval 1999
Opinions on cricket: 'There is just too much cricket being played. Cut down the
number of games played and have longer intervals (lunch and tea). This one bouncer
per batsman per over is just ridiculous. In Championship and Test cricket, batsmen
should learn to deal with it, or something. When is bowling going to get a little
easier??!!'
Best batting: 14 Surrey v Sri Lanka A, The Oval 1999
Best bowling: 5-60 Surrey v Yorkshire, The Oval 1999

2000 Season

	M	Inns	NO	Runs	HS	Avge	100s	50s	Ct	St	O	M	Runs	Wkts	Avge	Best	5wI	10wM
Test																		
All First	3	2	0	9	6	4.50	-	-	-	-	35	13	106	1	106.00	1-35	-	-
1-day Int																		
NatWest	2	0	0	0	0	-	-	-	-	-	14	0	87	0	-		-	-
B & H	1	0	0	0	0	-	-	-	-	-	4	0	22	0	-		-	-
1-day Lge	6	1	1	3	3 *	-	-	-	3	-	34.2	1	185	4	46.25	2-43	-	

Career Performances

	M	Inns	NO	Runs	HS	Avge	100s	50s	Ct	St	Balls	Runs	Wkts	Avge	Best	5wI	10wM
Test																	
All First	5	5	0	29	14	5.80	-	-	3	-	670	337	12	28.08	5-60	1	-
1-day Int																	
NatWest	2	0	0	0	0	-	-	-	-	-	84	87	0	-		-	-
B & H	1	0	0	0	0	-	-	-	-	-	24	22	0	-		-	-
1-day Lge	9	2	2	5	3 *	-	-	-	4	-	314	291	4	72.75	2-43	-	

GRIFFITHS, P. Leicestershire

Name: Paul Griffiths
Role: Right-hand bat, right-arm medium-fast bowler
Born: 14 September 1975, Wolverhampton
Height: 6ft 7in **Weight:** 14st
Nickname: Kinder, Egg, Express, Longshanks, Gimp, Useless
County debut: 2000
Strike rate: 126.00 (career 126.00)
Parents: Tony and Val
Marital status: Single
Family links with cricket: 'Dad played club cricket. Brother plays for Wolverhampton CC and has played for Staffordshire'
Education: St Nicholas School, Codsall, Wolverhampton; Codsall High School; Cheltenham and Gloucester College of Higher Education
Qualifications: 3 A-levels, BSc (Hons) Physical Geography and Sports and Exercise Science
Career outside cricket: 'Professional gambler'
Off-season: Fitness training

Cricketers particularly admired: Michael Holding, Allan Donald, Ian Botham, Curtly Ambrose
Young players to look out for: Steve Adshead, Ashley Wright, 'my brother Simon', Amer Khan
Other sports played: Golf (Staffordshire Boys' Champion 1991)
Other sports followed: Football (Wolverhampton Wanderers)
Injuries: Out for seven weeks with a broken bone in foot
Relaxations: Socialising, cinema, gambling
Extras: Took wicket (Adrian Griffith) with his third ball in first-class cricket, v West Indians at Leicester 2000
Opinions on cricket: 'Second XI cricket should be played on first-class grounds. More day/night games to bring in the crowds.'
Best bowling: 1-65 Leicestershire v West Indians, Leicester 2000

2000 Season

	M	Inns	NO	Runs	HS	Avge	100s	50s	Ct	St	O	M	Runs	Wkts	Avge	Best	5wI	10wM
Test																		
All First	1	0	0	0	0	-	-	-	-	-	21	3	65	1	65.00	1-65	-	-
1-day Int																		
NatWest																		
B & H																		
1-day Lge																		

Career Performances

	M	Inns	NO	Runs	HS	Avge	100s	50s	Ct	St	Balls	Runs	Wkts	Avge	Best	5wI	10wM
Test																	
All First	1	0	0	0	0	-	-	-	-	-	126	65	1	65.00	1-65	-	-
1-day Int																	
NatWest																	
B & H																	
1-day Lge																	

34. Who holds the record for the highest score by an England captain in Australia?

GROVE, J. O.   Somerset

Name: <u>Jamie</u> Oliver Grove
Role: Right-hand bat, right-arm
fast-medium bowler
Born: 3 July 1979, Bury St Edmunds
Height: 6ft 1in   **Weight:** 12st 1lb
Nickname: Grover, Groover
County debut: 1998 (Essex),
2000 (Somerset)
1st-Class 5 w. in innings: 1
Place in bowling averages: 112th av. 34.90
Strike rate: 55.09 (career 58.45)
Parents: Christopher John and Patricia Susan
Marital status: Single

Family links with cricket: 'Father played
Minor Counties cricket, brother plays for
local club and mother follows us all'
Education: Whepstead Primary School;
St James Middle School, Bury St Edmunds;
County Upper School, Bury St Edmunds
Qualifications: 9 GCSEs, City and Guilds in Basic Engineering, Modern
Apprenticeship in Mechanical Engineering
Career outside cricket: Engineer ('Happy now, dad?')
Off-season: 'Working until Christmas, then going to Tasmania'
Overseas tours: England U19 to South Africa (inc Youth World Cup) 1997-98
Cricketers particularly admired: Shoaib Akhtar, Allan Donald
Young players to look out for: Matthew Wood (Somerset), Samuel Waterson
Other sports played: 'All sports'
Other sports followed: Football (West Ham United)
Relaxations: Going out with friends; listening to music
Extras: Played for England at U15, U17 and U19 level. Was part of the successful
England U19 World Cup-winning squad in South Africa in 1997-98. Released by
Essex at end of 1999 season and joined Somerset for 2000. Recorded maiden first-
class five-wicket return (5-90) v Leicestershire at Leicester 2000
Opinions on cricket: 'It's great!!'
Best batting: 33 Essex v Surrey, Chelmsford 1998
Best bowling: 5-90 Somerset v Leicestershire, Leicester 2000

2000 Season

	M	Inns	NO	Runs	HS	Avge	100s	50s	Ct	St	O	M	Runs	Wkts	Avge	Best	5wl	10wM
Test																		
All First	10	10	5	56	17	11.20	-	-	-	-	192.5	27	733	21	34.90	5-90	1	-
1-day Int																		
NatWest																		
B & H																		
1-day Lge																		

Career Performances

	M	Inns	NO	Runs	HS	Avge	100s	50s	Ct	St	Balls	Runs	Wkts	Avge	Best	5wl	10wM
Test																	
All First	18	22	7	161	33	10.73	-	-	-	-	2046	1384	35	39.54	5-90	1	-
1-day Int																	
NatWest																	
B & H																	
1-day Lge																	

GUY, S. M.   Yorkshire

Name: Simon Mark Guy
Role: Right-hand bat, wicket-keeper, also leg-spin bowler
Born: 17 November 1978, Rotherham
Height: 5ft 7in **Weight:** 10st 6lbs
Nickname: Roland Rat, Shy Guy, Fez, Psycho
County debut: 2000
1st-Class catches: 21
1st-Class stumpings: 2
Place in batting averages: 184th av. 19.42
Parents: Darrell and Denise
Marital status: Engaged to Suzanne Riley
Family links with cricket: 'Two brothers and father play cricket. Elder brother played Yorkshire Senior Schools U19 (when 17). Father played for Notts and Worcs 2nd XI and for Rotherham Town in the Yorkshire League'
Education: Listerdale Junior School; Wickersley Comprehensive School
Qualifications: Pass in GNVQ Leisure and Recreation, qualified cricket coach, 'two years at the Yorkshire Cricket School under Ralph Middlebrook'

Career outside cricket: 'Coaching or sports management'
Off-season: 'Stay at home with my fiancée; reach my physical peak for the start of the season and work hard on my batting'
Overseas tours: Yorkshire to South Africa 1999
Overseas teams played for: Orange Cyrus, NSW 1999-2000
Cricketers particularly admired: Keith Piper, Karl Krikken, Darren Lehmann
Young players to look out for: John Sadler, Richard Dawson
Other sports played: 'All sports', rugby (played for South Yorkshire and Yorkshire)
Other sports followed: Rugby (Rotherham RUFC), 'Treeton Welfare CC, where all my family play'
Relaxations: 'Playing all sports, socialising with friends, watching cartoons, and eating a lot'
Extras: Set fifth-wicket partnership record in Yorkshire League (199 unbroken). Topped Yorkshire 2nd XI batting averages 1998 (106.00). Scored first 50 for Yorkshire 2nd XI in 1998; followed up with 112 not out in next game. Awarded 2nd XI cap 2000. Took off pads to bowl on his Championship debut v Somerset at Taunton 2000. Took five catches in an innings for first time for Yorkshire 1st XI 2000
Best batting: 42 Yorkshire v Somerset, Taunton 2000

2000 Season

	M	Inns	NO	Runs	HS	Avge	100s	50s	Ct	St	O	M	Runs	Wkts	Avge	Best	5wI	10wM
Test																		
All First	6	9	2	136	42	19.42	-	-	21	2	4	1	8	0	-		-	-
1-day Int																		
NatWest																		
B & H																		
1-day Lge																		

Career Performances

	M	Inns	NO	Runs	HS	Avge	100s	50s	Ct	St	Balls	Runs	Wkts	Avge	Best	5wI	10wM
Test																	
All First	6	9	2	136	42	19.42	-	-	21	2	24	8	0	-		-	-
1-day Int																	
NatWest																	
B & H																	
1-day Lge																	

HABIB, A.   Leicestershire

Name: Aftab Habib
Role: Right-hand bat, right-arm
slow bowler
Born: 7 February 1972, Reading, Berks
Height: 5ft 11in **Weight:** 12st 7lbs
Nickname: Afie, Tabby, Yaar, Habiby, Inzie
County debut: 1992 (Middlesex),
1995 (Leicestershire)
County cap: 1998 (Leicestershire)
Test debut: 1999
Tests: 2
1000 runs in a season: 2
1st-Class 50s: 21
1st-Class 100s: 11
1st-Class 200s: 1
1st-Class catches: 37
One-Day 100s: 1
Place in batting averages: 18th av. 47.18
(1999 32nd av. 40.57)

Parents: Hussain and Tahira
Marital status: Single
Family links with cricket: Cousin of Zahid Sadiq (ex-Surrey and Derbyshire)
Education: Alfred Sutton Primary School; Millfield Junior School; Taunton School
Qualifications: 7 GCSEs, NCA coaching awards
Career outside cricket: 'I would like to teach PE'
Off-season: 'Spend some time with my girlfriend; do some courses in the winter;
relax and have a break.' England A tour to West Indies
Overseas tours: Berkshire CCC to South Africa 1996; England YC to Australia
1989-90; England U19 to New Zealand 1990-91; England A to Bangladesh and New
Zealand 1999-2000, to West Indies 2000-01
Overseas teams played for: Globe Wakatu, Nelson, New Zealand 1992-93,
1996-97; Riccarton CC, Christchurch, New Zealand 1997-98
Cricketers particularly admired: Sachin Tendulkar, Steve Waugh, Vikram Solanki
Young players to look out for: Paul Franks, Chris Taylor, Umer Rashid
Other sports played: Golf
Other sports followed: Football ('follow Reading FC and enjoy watching
Liverpool'), rugby ('enjoy watching All Blacks')
Relaxations: 'Music, pictures; spending time with girlfriend Kezia; dining out'
Extras: Played for England U15-U19. Played football for Reading Schools. Middlesex
2nd XI Seaxe Player of the Year 1992. Released by Middlesex at end of 1994 season.
Played for Berkshire and had trials with Essex and Somerset. Leicestershire 2nd XI Player

of the Year in 1995. Championship medal with Leicestershire in 1996 and 1998. Gold Award winner in the Benson and Hedges Cup with 111 against Durham in 1997. With James Whitaker, set then record partnership for Leicestershire for fifth wicket of 320, v Worcestershire at Leicester in 1996. Scored 101* for England A v New Zealand A to help save the first 'Test' at Lincoln 1999-2000

Opinions on cricket: 'Better wickets needed. Too many low-scoring games, both one-dayers and four-dayers. More day/night games. Start on Fridays.'

Best batting: 215 Leicestershire v Worcestershire, Leicester 1996

Stop press: Forced to return home early from England A tour of West Indies with a shoulder injury

2000 Season

	M	Inns	NO	Runs	HS	Avge	100s	50s	Ct	St	O	M	Runs	Wkts	Avge	Best	5wI	10wM
Test																		
All First	17	23	1	1038	172 *	47.18	2	8	8	-								
1-day Int																		
NatWest	2	2	0	28	27	14.00	-	-	2	-								
B & H	4	4	1	96	70 *	32.00	-	1	2	-								
1-day Lge	15	14	2	384	70	32.00	-	2	1	-								

Career Performances

	M	Inns	NO	Runs	HS	Avge	100s	50s	Ct	St	Balls	Runs	Wkts	Avge	Best	5wI	10wM
Test	2	3	0	26	19	8.66	-	-	-	-							
All First	87	125	19	4738	215	44.69	12	21	37	-	48	52	0	-	-	-	-
1-day Int																	
NatWest	10	9	0	201	67	22.33	-	2	4	-	4	5	2	2.50	2-5	-	
B & H	17	13	2	381	111	34.63	1	2	9	-							
1-day Lge	60	55	13	1164	99 *	27.71	-	5	18	-	1	4	0	-	-	-	

HAMBLIN, J. R. C.   Hampshire

Name: James Rupert Christopher Hamblin

Role: Right-hand bat, right-arm fast-medium bowler

Born: 16 August 1978, Pembury, Kent

Height: 6ft **Weight:** 13st 9lbs

Nickname: Hambo, Tombstones, Cheeseboard

County debut: No first-team appearance

Parents: Bryan and Amanda

Marital status: Single

Family links with cricket: 'Father played for Oxford University 1971-73 and scored a first-class hundred'

Education: Vinehall Preparatory School; Charterhouse School; University of the West of England, Bristol
Qualifications: 9 GCSEs, 2 A-levels, BA (Hons) Economics
Off-season: Playing and coaching in Johannesburg
Overseas tours: British Universities to South Africa 1999
Overseas teams played for: Harare Sports Club, Zimbabwe 1996-97
Cricketers particularly admired: James Kirtley, James Williams
Young players to look out for: James Kirtley, Lawrence Prittipaul, Matt Windows
Other sports played: Golf, rackets, real tennis
Other sports followed: 'All sports'

Injuries: Out for two months with a broken wrist
Relaxations: Playing golf and snooker
Extras: Voted 2nd XI Cricketer of August/September 1999. Played in Charterhouse Friars' *The Cricketer* Cup winning side 2000
Opinions on cricket: 'Second XI cricket should mirror the first-class game. There is too much cricket played on poor pitches and on poor grounds with poor facilities when the counties' main grounds could be used instead.'

---

35. At Sydney in 1962-63, which Australian left-armer took a wicket with his last delivery in Test cricket?

Name: <u>Gavin</u> Mark Hamilton
Role: Left-hand bat, right-arm medium-fast bowler
Born: 16 September 1974, Broxburn
Height: 6ft 3in **Weight:** 13st
Nickname: Hammy, Jock, Dits, 'anything Scottish'
County debut: 1994
County cap: 1998
Test debut: 1999-2000
Tests: 1
One-Day Internationals: 5
50 wickets in a season: 1
1st-Class 50s: 14
1st-Class 100s: 1
1st-Class 5 w. in innings: 8
1st-Class 10 w. in match: 2
1st-Class catches: 26
One-Day 5 w. in innings: 2

Place in batting averages: 106th av. 28.71 (1999 15th av. 47.25)
Place in bowling averages: 33rd av. 21.65 (1999 14th av. 19.18)
Strike rate: 47.05 (career 48.98)
Parents: Gavin and Wendy
Marital status: Single
Family links with cricket: Father 'long-term fast bowler at club level' (Sidcup, Kent; West Lothian, Scotland). Brother opening bat for Sidcup CC and has opened batting for Scotland
Education: Dulverton Primary School, New Eltham; Hurstmere School, Sidcup
Qualifications: 10 GCSEs and two coaching awards
Overseas tours: England to South Africa and Zimbabwe 1999-2000; Yorkshire pre-season tours to South Africa, Zimbabwe and West Indies
Overseas teams played for: Welling, Municipals, and Stellenbosch University – all South Africa; Spotswood, Melbourne
Cricketers particularly admired: Craig White, Mark Robinson, Chris Adams
Young players to look out for: Matthew Wood, Vikram Solanki, Gary Fellows
Other sports played: Golf ('a lot of it'), football (Arsenal YTS)
Other sports followed: Football (Falkirk FC)
Relaxations: Listening to music and reading the paper
Extras: Took 10 wickets and scored 149 runs v Glamorgan at Cardiff in 1998, the second best all-round contribution in Yorkshire history. First-class All-rounder of the Year 1998; Yorkshire Players' Player of the Year 1998; Yorkshire Supporters' Player of

the Year 1998. Scored 76 for Scotland v Pakistan at Chester-le-Street in the 1999 World Cup, the first 50 scored by a Scotland player in World Cup cricket. Scored 217 runs (av. 54.25) in the 1999 World Cup, more than any England batsman. Finished in top 15 of first-class batting and bowling averages 1999. Made Test debut v South Africa in the first Test, Johannesburg 1999. Scored maiden first-class century (125) v Hampshire at Headingley 2000. Scored 57* and took 5-34 v Sussex Sharks in the National League at Scarborough 2000

Best batting: 125 Yorkshire v Hampshire, Headingley 2000
Best bowling: 7-50 Yorkshire v Surrey, Headingley 1998

2000 Season

	M	Inns	NO	Runs	HS	Avge	100s	50s	Ct	St	O	M	Runs	Wkts	Avge	Best	5wl	10wM
Test																		
All First	13	16	2	402	125	28.71	1	2	7	-	313.4	80	866	40	21.65	5-22	1	-
1-day Int																		
NatWest	2	2	1	2	1*	2.00	-	-	-	-	17	3	63	5	12.60	3-39	-	
B & H	6	3	1	36	28*	18.00	-	-	-	-	36	5	107	5	21.40	3-24	-	
1-day Lge	14	10	3	222	57*	31.71	-	1	1	-	76.5	4	319	20	15.95	5-34	1	

Career Performances

	M	Inns	NO	Runs	HS	Avge	100s	50s	Ct	St	Balls	Runs	Wkts	Avge	Best	5wl	10wM
Test	1	2	0	0	0	0.00	-	-	-	-	90	63	0	-	-	-	-
All First	70	94	20	2116	125	28.59	1	14	26	-	10384	5330	212	25.14	7-50	8	2
1-day Int	5	5	1	217	76	54.25	-	2	1	-	214	149	3	49.66	2-36	-	
NatWest	9	7	2	89	39	17.80	-	-	3	-	462	293	17	17.23	3-27	-	
B & H	16	8	4	106	28*	26.50	-	-	1	-	648	413	17	24.29	4-33	-	
1-day Lge	61	40	11	541	57*	18.65	-	1	8	-	2153	1812	72	25.16	5-16	2	

36. On which Ashes tour did Sunday Test cricket first take place in England? Was it a) 1977; b) 1981; c) 1985?

HANCOCK, T. H. C.   Gloucestershire

Name: <u>Timothy</u> Harold Coulter Hancock
Role: Right-hand bat, right-arm medium
bowler, short-leg or cover fielder, county
vice-captain
Born: 20 April 1972, Reading
Height: 5ft 11in **Weight:** 12st 7lbs
Nickname: Herbie
County debut: 1991
County cap: 1998
1000 runs in a season: 1
1st-Class 50s: 39
1st-Class 100s: 5
1st-Class 200s: 1
1st-Class catches: 88
One-Day 100s: 1
One-Day 5 w. in innings: 1
Place in batting averages: 186th av. 19.38
(1999 116th av. 28.60)

Strike rate: 62.25 (career 63.00)
Parents: John and Jennifer
Wife and date of marriage: Rachael, 26 September 1998
Children: George, 30 January 2000
Family links with cricket: 'Dad and brother very keen players'
Education: St Piran's, Maidenhead; St Edward's, Oxford; Henley College
Qualifications: 8 GCSEs, senior coaching award
Career outside cricket: 'None as yet'
Overseas tours: Gloucestershire to Kenya 1991, to Sri Lanka 1992-93, to Zimbabwe
(two visits)
Overseas teams played for: CBC Old Boys, Bloemfontein 1991-92; Wynnum
Manley, Brisbane 1992-93; Harlequins, Durban 1994-95
Cricketers particularly admired: Viv Richards, Gordon Greenidge, Ian Botham
Young players to look out for: Alastair Bressington
Other sports played: Hockey, golf
Other sports followed: 'I like to play and watch rugby, but don't do either enough'
Injuries: Out for a month with a broken hand
Relaxations: 'Family life and a round of golf'
Extras: Played hockey for Oxfordshire U19. Appointed vice-captain of
Gloucestershire for 2000. Scored maiden one-day century (110) to win Man of the
Match award in the NatWest quarter-final v Northamptonshire at Bristol 2000
Opinions on cricket: 'I'm all for the introduction of central contracts. England
players are England players and that's their priority for 12 months of the year.'

Best batting: 220* Gloucestershire v Nottinghamshire, Trent Bridge 1998
Best bowling: 3-5 Gloucestershire v Essex, Colchester 1998

2000 Season

	M	Inns	NO	Runs	HS	Avge	100s	50s	Ct	St	O	M	Runs	Wkts	Avge	Best	5wI	10wM
Test																		
All First	15	22	1	407	85	19.38	-	1	7	-	83	23	209	8	26.12	3-24	-	-
1-day Int																		
NatWest	3	3	0	154	110	51.33	1	-	2	-	10	1	34	2	17.00	2-34	-	
B & H	7	7	0	186	60	26.57	-	1	2	-								
1-day Lge	13	12	0	238	50	19.83	-	1	5	-	7.1	0	39	1	39.00	1-10	-	

Career Performances

	M	Inns	NO	Runs	HS	Avge	100s	50s	Ct	St	Balls	Runs	Wkts	Avge	Best	5wI	10wM
Test																	
All First	144	251	16	6507	220 *	27.68	6	39	88	-	2709	1558	43	36.23	3-5	-	-
1-day Int																	
NatWest	16	15	0	630	110	42.00	1	5	6	-	233	178	13	13.69	6-58	1	
B & H	36	33	3	739	71 *	24.63	-	3	7	-	319	243	10	24.30	3-13	-	
1-day Lge	112	102	2	1807	73	18.07	-	7	43	-	684	641	22	29.13	3-18	-	

HARDEN, R. J.   Yorkshire

Name: Richard John Harden
Role: Right-hand bat, left-arm medium bowler
Born: 16 August 1965, Bridgwater
Height: 5ft 11in **Weight:** 13st 7lbs
Nickname: Sumo, Curtis
County debut: 1985 (Somerset), 1999 (Yorkshire)
County cap: 1989 (Somerset)
1000 runs in a season: 6
1st-Class 50s: 70
1st-Class 100s: 28
1st-Class catches: 189
One-Day 100s: 4
Place in batting averages: (1999 126th av. 27.37)
Strike rate: (career 73.90)
Parents: Chris and Anne
Wife and date of marriage: Nicki Rae, 25 September 1992

Family links with cricket: Grandfather played club cricket for Bridgwater
Education: King's College, Taunton
Qualifications: 8 O-levels, 2 A-levels, coaching award
Overseas teams played for: Central Districts, New Zealand 1987-88
Cricketers particularly admired: Viv Richards, Jimmy Cook
Other sports followed: Squash, golf, rugby
Relaxations: 'Love my domestic duties (dusting, Hoovering, etc.) rather than golf. Good food and the odd drink'
Extras: Joined Yorkshire for the 1999 season on a two-year contract after 13 years with Somerset. Retired during the 2000 season because of injury
Best batting: 187 Somerset v Nottinghamshire, Taunton 1992
Best bowling: 2-7 Central Districts v Canterbury, Blenheim 1987-88

2000 Season

	M	Inns	NO	Runs	HS	Avge	100s	50s	Ct	St	O	M	Runs	Wkts	Avge	Best	5wI	10wM
Test																		
All First	2	3	0	1	1	0.33	-	-	-	-								
1-day Int																		
NatWest																		
B & H																		
1-day Lge	1	1	1	2	2*	-	-	-	-	-								

Career Performances

	M	Inns	NO	Runs	HS	Avge	100s	50s	Ct	St	Balls	Runs	Wkts	Avge	Best	5wI	10wM
Test																	
All First	253	417	63	13336	187	37.67	28	70	189	-	1478	1023	20	51.15	2-7	-	-
1-day Int																	
NatWest	27	24	2	848	108*	38.54	3	3	14	-	18	23	0	-	-	-	-
B & H	59	56	4	1126	76	21.65	-	6	15	-							
1-day Lge	180	172	32	4385	100*	31.32	1	27	52	-	1	0	0	-	-	-	-

HARDINGES, M. A. Gloucestershire

Name: <u>Mark</u> Andrew Hardinges
Role: Right-hand bat, right-arm medium bowler
Born: 5 February 1978, Gloucester
Height: 6ft 1in **Weight:** 13st
Nickname: Dinges
County debut: 1999
Strike rate: 100.00 (career 109.50)
Parents: David and Jean
Marital status: Single

Family links with cricket: 'Uncle played for Glamorgan 2nd XI; Dad played club cricket; brother played for Loughborough Uni first team'
Education: Hillstone; Malvern College; Bath University
Qualifications: 10 GCSEs, 3 A-levels
Career outside cricket: Student
Off-season: At university
Overseas tours: Malvern College to South Africa 1995
Overseas teams played for: Newtown and Chilwell, Geelong, Australia
Cricketers particularly admired: Steve Waugh, Mark Alleyne
Young players to look out for: Gavin Franklin, David Nash, Ben Knowles
Other sports played: Tennis (Gloucester U14), football (university first team)
Other sports followed: Football (Tottenham), golf, 'most sports really'
Relaxations: 'Golf, going out with my friends'
Extras: Represented British Universities 2000
Opinions on cricket: 'Not been in the game long enough, although I do believe that two divisions is the way forward because it keeps interest going throughout the season.'
Best batting: 3 British Universities v Zimbabweans, Fenner's 2000
Best bowling: 2-16 Gloucestershire v Essex, Bristol 2000

2000 Season

	M	Inns	NO	Runs	HS	Avge	100s	50s	Ct	St	O	M	Runs	Wkts	Avge	Best	5wI	10wM
Test																		
All First	2	3	0	3	3	1.00	-	-	-	-	50	17	99	3	33.00	2-16	-	-
1-day Int																		
NatWest																		
B & H																		
1-day Lge																		

Career Performances

	M	Inns	NO	Runs	HS	Avge	100s	50s	Ct	St	Balls	Runs	Wkts	Avge	Best	5wl	10wM
Test																	
All First	3	4	0	4	3	1.00	-	-	-	-	438	159	4	39.75	2-16	-	-
1-day Int																	
NatWest																	
B & H																	
1-day Lge																	

HARMISON, S. J.   Durham

Name: <u>Stephen</u> James Harmison
Role: Right-hand bat, right-arm
fast-medium bowler
Born: 23 October 1978, Ashington,
Northumberland
Height: 6ft 4in **Weight:** 14st
Nickname: Harmy
County debut: 1996
County cap: 1999
50 wickets in a season: 2
1st-Class 5 w. in innings: 2
1st-Class catches: 9
Place in batting averages: 280th av. 8.66
(1999 294th av. 5.26)
Place in bowling averages: 102nd av. 31.61
(1999 73rd av. 27.73)
Strike rate: 70.19 (career 58.69)
Parents: Margaret and James

Wife and date of marriage: Hayley, 8 October 1999
Children: Emily Alice, 1 June 1999
Family links with cricket: Brothers (James and Ben) play for Northumberland and,
with father, for Ashington
Education: Ashington High School
Overseas tours: England U19 to Pakistan 1996-97; England A to Zimbabwe and
South Africa 1998-99
Sportsmen particularly admired: Alan Shearer, David Boon, Courtney Walsh
Young players to look out for: Neil Killeen
Other sports played: Football, snooker, golf
Other sports followed: Football (Newcastle United season ticket holder)
Relaxations: Socialising and spending time with family
Extras: Represented Northumberland U17. Played football for Ashington in the

Northern League. Was selected for England A tour of Bangladesh and New Zealand 1999-2000 but was forced to withdraw with a knee injury. Included in the England party for the two Tests v Zimbabwe and for the first Test v West Indies 2000 before developing shin problems.

Best batting: 36 Durham v Kent, Canterbury 1998

36 Durham v Worcestershire, Worcester 1998

Best bowling: 5-70 Durham v Gloucestershire, Riverside 1998

Stop press: Was selected for England A tour of West Indies but was forced to withdraw with a shin problem

2000 Season

	M	Inns	NO	Runs	HS	Avge	100s	50s	Ct	St	O	M	Runs	Wkts	Avge	Best	5wI	10wM
Test																		
All First	11	15	3	104	33 *	8.66	-	-	2	-	304.1	69	822	26	31.61	4-74	-	-
1-day Int																		
NatWest	1	1	0	0	0	0.00	-	-	-	-	3	0	34	1	34.00	1-34	-	
B & H	6	4	2	17	8 *	8.50	-	-	-	-	42	2	195	8	24.37	2-34	-	
1-day Lge	6	2	1	3	2	3.00	-	-	-	-	50.5	2	258	8	32.25	3-45	-	

Career Performances

	M	Inns	NO	Runs	HS	Avge	100s	50s	Ct	St	Balls	Runs	Wkts	Avge	Best	5wI	10wM
Test																	
All First	46	67	18	443	36	9.04	-	-	9	-	8687	4491	148	30.34	5-70	2	-
1-day Int																	
NatWest	2	2	1	2	2 *	2.00	-	-	1	-	72	76	2	38.00	1-34	-	
B & H	7	4	2	17	8 *	8.50	-	-	-	-	288	231	8	28.87	2-34	-	
1-day Lge	14	6	4	6	2	3.00	-	-	2	-	635	538	11	48.90	3-45	-	

37. Who scored 95 as England's nightwatchman at Sydney in 1982-83?

HARRIS, A. J.   Nottinghamshire

Name: <u>Andrew</u> James Harris
Role: Right-hand bat, right-arm fast-medium bowler
Born: 26 June 1973, Ashton-under-Lyne, Lancashire
Height: 6ft **Weight:** 11st 9lbs
Nickname: AJ
County debut: 1994 (Derbyshire), 2000 (Nottinghamshire)
County cap: 1996 (Derbyshire), 2000 (Nottinghamshire)
1st-Class 5 w. in innings: 8
1st-Class 10 w. in match: 1
1st-Class catches: 20
One Day 5 w. in innings: 1
Place in batting averages: 228th av. 15.30
Place in bowling averages: 96th av. 30.86
(1999 84th av. 28.92)

Strike rate: 52.43 (career 54.34)
Parents: Norman (deceased) and Joyce
Wife and date of marriage: Kate, 7 October 2000
Education: Tintwistle Primary School; Hadfield Comprehensive School; Glossopdale Community College
Qualifications: 6 GCSEs, 1 A-level
Career outside cricket: 'Running my own video rental company'
Off-season: 'Running Letterbox Video Rentals will take up most of my time when I return from my honeymoon'
Overseas tours: England A to Australia 1996-97
Overseas teams played for: Ginninderra, West Belconnen, Australia 1992-93; Victoria University of Wellington CC, New Zealand 1997-98
Cricketers particularly admired: Merv Hughes, Allan Donald
Young players to look out for: Ed Joyce, David Lucas
Other sports played: Golf, snooker, football, 'but as I'm average at them, they are definitely played for enjoyment rather than in the hope of winning anything'
Other sports followed: 'I follow Leigh RMI as that's who my brother plays for, as well as Man City, the only Premiership team to come from Manchester'
Injuries: Out for four weeks with a badly broken index finger
Relaxations: 'Following the football results, especially Man City as they push for a place in Europe. I will probably get a couple of rounds of golf in as I try to lower my 17 handicap'
Extras: Left Derbyshire at end of 1999 season and joined Notts for 2000. 'Those who

wonder why I wear No. 13 in the National League after the luck with injuries I have had over the past couple of years may wish to know that it was my father's birthday. It is in memory of him (he died in 1998) that I wear this number.' Awarded Nottinghamshire cap 2000

Opinions on cricket: 'Those sceptics who thought two division Championship cricket would not work should have been at Bristol as both ourselves and Gloucestershire chased promotion. It produced a great final day's play, and although neither of us won promotion due to results elsewhere, it was edge-of-your-seat stuff.'

Best batting: 39 Nottinghamshire v Worcestershire, Trent Bridge 2000

Best bowling: 6-40 Derbyshire v Middlesex, Derby 1996

2000 Season

	M	Inns	NO	Runs	HS	Avge	100s	50s	Ct	St	O	M	Runs	Wkts	Avge	Best	5wI	10wM
Test																		
All First	11	14	4	153	39	15.30	-	-	4	-	384.3	62	1358	44	30.86	6-110	4	-
1-day Int																		
NatWest	1	1	1	3	3 *	-	-	-	-	-	10	0	77	0	-	-	-	-
B & H	2	1	0	1	1	1.00	-	-	-	-	10.3	2	39	1	39.00	1-23	-	
1-day Lge	13	4	2	21	9	10.50	-	-	4	-	102	8	520	11	47.27	5-35	1	

Career Performances

	M	Inns	NO	Runs	HS	Avge	100s	50s	Ct	St	Balls	Runs	Wkts	Avge	Best	5wI	10wM
Test																	
All First	57	79	22	545	39	9.56	-	-	20	-	9837	5893	181	32.55	6-40	8	1
1-day Int																	
NatWest	7	4	3	21	11 *	21.00	-	-	1	-	397	275	9	30.55	3-10	-	
B & H	12	4	1	12	5	4.00	-	-	4	-	612	474	17	27.88	3-41	-	
1-day Lge	55	19	10	66	10 *	7.33	-	-	13	-	2304	1962	69	28.43	5-35	1	

---

38. Who deputised as wicket-keeper for the indisposed Alec Stewart on the third day of the second Test at Lord's in 1997?

HARRISON, D. S.   Glamorgan

Name: <u>David</u> Stuart Harrison
Role: Right-hand bat, right-arm fast-medium
bowler; all-rounder
Born: 31 July 1981, Newport
Height: 6ft 4in **Weight:** 13st 6lbs
Nickname: Harry, Haza, Mensa, Rodney
County debut: 1999
Strike rate: (career 192.00)
Parents: Stuart and Susan
Marital status: Single
Family links with cricket: 'Dad played for
Glamorgan in early 1970s; brother played for
England U15s in U15 World Cup last year;
mum does teas for club 1st XI'
Education: Greenlawn Primary, New Inn,
Pontypool; West Monmouth Comprehensive,
Pontypool; Usk College, Pontypool
Qualifications: 5 GCSEs, BTEC National
Diploma in Sports Science, Levels 1 and 2 coaching awards
Career outside cricket: 'Coaching young cricketers in the Gwent area'
Off-season: 'Working on fitness and strength and learning how to control the white
ball!!'
Overseas tours: Gwent U15 to Cape Town 1996; Wales to Jersey 1996, 1997;
England U19 to Malaysia and (Youth World Cup) Sri Lanka 1999-2000
Cricketers particularly admired: Matthew Maynard, Rob Bailey, Steve Watkin
Young players to look out for: Nicky Peng, Ian Bell, Mark Wallace
Other sports played: Squash ('played for Wales until I was 16'), rugby union
('played for Wales Schools until I was 14'; represented Pontypool Schools XV in
Welsh Cup final)
Other sports followed: Rugby union (Pontypool), football (Manchester United)
Relaxations: 'Sleeping, driving, golf; taking my dog for a walk'
Extras: Represented Wales from 12 to 16. Represented England at U17, U18 and U19
levels. Represented England U19 v Sri Lanka U19 in 'Test' series 2000, 'nearly saving
one "Test" with my best mate Mark Wallace'
Opinions on cricket: 'Day/night cricket was a success last summer and it should
continue. Two divisions was also a success, the season being more competitive, with
games going to the last day of the season.'
Best batting: 27 Glamorgan v Gloucestershire, Bristol 2000
Best bowling: 1-15 Glamorgan v Oxford University, The Parks 1999

2000 Season

	M	Inns	NO	Runs	HS	Avge	100s	50s	Ct	St	O	M	Runs	Wkts	Avge	Best	5wI	10wM
Test																		
All First	1	2	0	27	27	13.50	-	-	-	-	10	2	45	0	-		-	-
1-day Int																		
NatWest																		
B & H																		
1-day Lge	3	3	1	11	5 *	5.50	-	-	1	-	14	1	96	0	-		-	-

Career Performances

	M	Inns	NO	Runs	HS	Avge	100s	50s	Ct	St	Balls	Runs	Wkts	Avge	Best	5wI	10wM
Test																	
All First	3	4	0	56	27	14.00	-	-	-	-	192	109	1	109.00	1-15	-	-
1-day Int																	
NatWest																	
B & H																	
1-day Lge	3	3	1	11	5 *	5.50	-	-	1	-	84	96	0	-		-	-

HARTLEY, P. J.   Hampshire

Name: <u>Peter</u> John Hartley
Role: Right-hand bat, right-arm
fast-medium bowler
Born: 18 April 1960, Keighley
Height: 6ft **Weight:** 14st 3lbs
Nickname: Jack, PJ
County debut: 1982 (Warwickshire),
1985 (Yorkshire), 1998 (Hampshire)
County cap: 1987 (Yorkshire),
1998 (Hampshire)
Benefit: 1996 (Yorkshire)
50 wickets in a season: 7
1st-Class 50s: 14
1st-Class 100s: 2
1st-Class 5 w. in innings: 23
1st-Class 10 w. in match: 3
1st-Class catches: 68
One-Day 5 w. in innings: 5
Place in batting averages: 210th av. 17.16 (1999 200th av. 20.33)
Place in bowling averages: 141st av. 46.46 (1999 30th av. 21.77)
Strike rate: 81.73 (career 54.33)
Parents: Thomas and Molly

Wife and date of marriage: Sharon Louise, 12 March 1988
Children: Megan Grace, 25 April 1992; Courtney, 25 July 1995
Family links with cricket: Father played local league cricket
Education: Haworth; Hartington Middle/Greenhead Grammar School;
Bradford College
Qualifications: City & Guilds in Textile Design and Management, NCA coaching award
Career outside cricket: Sales consultant
Overseas tours: Yorkshire pre-season tours to Barbados 1986-87, to South Africa 1991-92, 1992-93, to Zimbabwe
Overseas teams played for: Melville, New Zealand 1983-84; Adelaide, Australia 1985-86; Harmony and Orange Free State, South Africa 1988-89
Cricketers particularly admired: Malcolm Marshall, Richard Hadlee
Other sports played: Golf (4 handicap)
Other sports followed: Football (Chelsea FC)
Relaxations: Gardening, walking
Extras: Returned 8-65, his best figures for Hampshire, against Yorkshire, his former county, at Basingstoke 1999. Recorded his highest B&H score (32*) and best one-day analysis (5-20) v Sussex at Hove 2000. Retired at the end of the 2000 season
Opinions on cricket: 'Poor pitches. Grounds should be under the control of the ECB (pitches doctored too much). Reduce the amount of cricket played.'
Best batting: 127* Yorkshire v Lancashire, Old Trafford 1988
Best bowling: 9-41 Yorkshire v Derbyshire, Chesterfield 1995

2000 Season

	M	Inns	NO	Runs	HS	Avge	100s	50s	Ct	St	O	M	Runs	Wkts	Avge	Best	5wI	10wM
Test																		
All First	9	11	5	103	23 *	17.16	-	-	-	-	204.2	33	697	15	46.46	3-91	-	-
1-day Int																		
NatWest	3	0	0	0	0	-	-	-	-	-	26.4	5	93	3	31.00	2-20	-	
B & H	4	2	2	33	32 *	-	-	-	1	-	32	7	102	12	8.50	5-20	1	
1-day Lge	5	3	1	18	14	9.00	-	-	-	-	42	8	161	8	20.12	3-41	-	

Career Performances

	M	Inns	NO	Runs	HS	Avge	100s	50s	Ct	St	Balls	Runs	Wkts	Avge	Best	5wI	10wM
Test																	
All First	232	283	66	4321	127 *	19.91	2	14	68	-	37109	20635	683	30.21	9-41	23	3
1-day Int																	
NatWest	36	18	8	250	83	25.00	-	2	2	-	2125	1349	56	24.08	5-46	1	
B & H	53	33	13	269	32 *	13.45	-	-	13	-	2853	1838	80	22.97	5-20	2	
1-day Lge	178	119	41	1246	52	15.97	-	2	31	-	7584	5831	217	26.87	5-36	2	

HARVEY, I. J.   Gloucestershire

Name: <u>Ian</u> Joseph Harvey
Role: Right-hand bat, right-arm fast-medium
bowler
Born: 10 April 1972, Wonthaggi, Victoria,
Australia
Nickname: Freak
County debut: 1999
County cap: 1999
One-Day Internationals: 18
1st-Class 50s: 21
1st-Class 100s: 4
1st-Class 5 w. in innings: 8
1st-Class 10 w. in match: 1
1st-Class catches: 57
One-Day 5 w. in innings: 4
Place in batting averages: 89th av. 30.38
(1999 176th av. 22.57)

Place in bowling averages: 9th av. 16.45
(1999 76th av. 28.25)
Strike rate: 38.15 (career 59.80)
Overseas tours: Australian Academy to New Zealand 1994-95; Australia to Sharjah
1997-98, to New Zealand 1999-2000 (one-day series), to Kenya (ICC Knockout
Trophy) 2000-01
Overseas teams played for: Dandenong, Victoria; Victoria 1993-94 –
Extras: The nickname 'Freak' is a reference to his brilliant fielding and was
reportedly coined by Shane Warne. Took a wicket (Jonty Rhodes) with his second ball
in One-Day International cricket in 1997-98. Top scorer (57) for Victoria in their
Mercantile Mutual Cup final victory over New South Wales 1998-99. Joined
Gloucestershire in 1999 as overseas player. Won NatWest Man of the Match award v
Durham Cricket Board XI at Riverside 1999. Top wicket-taker in the 1999 National
League competition with 30 wickets at 15.80. Awarded ACB contract for 2000-01.
Had match figures of 10-32 from 25 overs (and scored 60 in Gloucestershire's only
innings) v Sussex at Hove 2000
Best batting: 136 Victoria v South Australia, Melbourne 1995-96
Best bowling: 7-44 Victoria v South Australia, Melbourne 1996-97

2000 Season

	M	Inns	NO	Runs	HS	Avge	100s	50s	Ct	St	O	M	Runs	Wkts	Avge	Best	5wl	10wM
Test																		
All First	10	14	1	395	79	30.38	-	4	10	-	254.2	79	658	40	16.45	6-19	3	1
1-day Int																		
NatWest	5	5	0	109	47	21.80	-	-	4	-	48	8	184	12	15.33	4-37	-	
B & H	3	2	0	123	88	61.50	-	1	-	-	29.2	3	95	9	10.55	5-34	1	
1-day Lge	14	14	1	400	66	30.76	-	3	4	-	112.1	11	372	34	10.94	5-19	2	

Career Performances

	M	Inns	NO	Runs	HS	Avge	100s	50s	Ct	St	Balls	Runs	Wkts	Avge	Best	5wl	10wM
Test																	
All First	74	125	9	3359	136	28.95	4	21	57	-	11483	5559	192	28.95	7-44	8	1
1-day Int	18	15	4	177	43	16.09	-	-	6	-	794	611	13	47.00	3-17	-	
NatWest	10	9	0	158	47	17.55	-	-	6	-	535	309	22	14.04	4-29	-	
B & H	6	4	0	171	88	42.75	-	1	-	-	320	200	16	12.50	5-34	1	
1-day Lge	28	28	2	697	66	26.80	-	3	5	-	1320	846	64	13.21	5-19	3	

HATCH, N. G.   Durham

Name: <u>Nicholas</u> Guy Hatch
Role: Right-hand bat, right-arm medium-fast bowler
Born: 21 April 1979, Darlington
Height: 6ft 7in **Weight:** 14st 10lbs
Nickname: Snatchy, Hatchy, Hurricane
County debut: No first-team appearance
Parents: Mike and Paula
Marital status: Single
Family links with cricket: Father played club cricket with Darlington CC for over 20 years. Brother plays club cricket in London
Education: Raventhorpe Prep School; Barnard Castle School; Hull University
Qualifications: 11 GCSEs, 5 A-levels, BA History and Politics
Off-season: Playing club cricket in Perth, Western Australia, for Claremont-Nedlands
Overseas teams played for: Claremont-Nedlands CC, Perth 2000-01
Cricketers particularly admired: Courtney Walsh, Steve Waugh, Curtly Ambrose
Young players to look out for: Nicky Peng, Gordon Muchall
Other sports played: Rugby union (played for North of England U19)

Other sports followed: All sports
Injuries: Out for eight weeks with a hamstring tear
Relaxations: Reading, socialising with friends
Extras: Represented British Universities v New Zealand A in one-day match 2000
Opinions on cricket: 'Too much cricket. Should be less, and cricket played both at club and county level more competitive.'

HAVELL, P. M. R. Sussex

Name: <u>Paul</u> Matthew Roger Havell
Role: Left-hand bat, right-arm fast bowler
Born: 4 July 1980, Melbourne, Australia
Height: 6ft 3in **Weight:** 13st
Nickname: Trigger
County debut: No first-team appearance
Parents: Roger
Marital status: Single
Family links with cricket: Brother played for Sussex U19
Education: Mentone Grammar, Melbourne; Warden Park School; Haywards Heath College
Qualifications: 9 GCSEs, Level 1 coaching award
Off-season: 'Training and working on my game!'
Overseas tours: Sussex U19 to Barbados 1997-98
Overseas teams played for: East Doncaster CC, Australia 1998-99; Carlton CC, Melbourne 2000
Cricketers particularly admired: 'All players at Sussex CCC'
Young players to look out for: 'Matthew Prior and me'
Other sports played: Hockey, tennis
Other sports followed: 'I love Gaelic football in Ireland'
Injuries: Out for two months with a knee injury
Relaxations: 'Chilling out watching TV at home'
Extras: Sussex Young Cricketer of the Year 1995
Opinions on cricket: 'If everyone works hard on their game, everyone will improve, thus improving the state of English cricket in general. If we play on harder, faster wickets that produce high-scoring cricket, this will then make our national side more successful.'

HAYDEN, M. L.   Northamptonshire

Name: <u>Matthew</u> Lawrence Hayden
Role: Left-hand bat, right-arm medium bowler
Born: 29 October 1971, Kingaroy, Australia
Height: 6ft 2in **Weight:** 15st 1lb
Nickname: Haydos
County debut: 1997 (Hampshire), 1999 (Northamptonshire)
County cap: 1997 (Hampshire), 1999 (Northamptonshire)
Test debut: 1993-94
Tests: 8
One-Day Internationals: 19
1000 runs in a season: 2
1st-Class 50s: 60
1st-Class 100s: 40
1st-Class 200s: 4
1st-Class catches: 150
One-Day 100s: 4
Place in batting averages: 8th av. 57.72 (1999 5th av. 57.30)
Strike rate: 90.00 (career 57.31)
Parents: Moya and Lawrence
Wife and date of marriage: Kellie, 5 May 1996
Education: Saint Mary's Catholic College; Marist College, Ashgrove; Queensland University of Technology
Qualifications: Marketing/public administration
Career outside cricket: Fishing
Off-season: 'Australian summer'
Overseas tours: Australia A to Scotland and Ireland 1998; Australia to England 1993, to Sharjah 1993-94, to South Africa 1993-94, 1996-97, to Sri Lanka 1999, to New Zealand 1999-2000, to India 2000-01
Overseas teams played for: Queensland 1991-92 –
Cricketers particularly admired: Allan Border, Steve Waugh
Young players to look out for: Simon Katich, David Sales
Other sports played: Fishing, surfing
Other sports followed: Rugby league (London Broncos), football (Man U)
Relaxations: Beach, travelling
Extras: Scored 149 on his first-class debut for Queensland against South Australia and went on to become the first Australian to score 1000 runs in his debut season 1991-92. Toured England with Australia in 1993, scoring 1000 runs but not playing in a Test. Scored two 100s (165 and 116) for Queensland v South Australia at Adelaide 1993-94.

Has played league cricket for Greenmount in the Bolton League, breaking the club record with an aggregate of 1483 runs. Hampshire's overseas player 1997, scoring 1438 runs with an average of 57.52. Scored a 200 (235*) and a 100 (119) for Hants v Warwicks at Southampton 1997; David Hemp scored two 100s in the game for Warwicks. Joined Northants for 1999 on a two-year contract as overseas player. Scored a century before lunch v Notts at Northampton 1999, going on to make 170. County captain 1999-2000. Awarded ACB contract for 2000-01. Left Northamptonshire at the end of the 2000 season

Opinions on cricket: 'Sessions should be two hours. New ball taken at 80 overs. Umpires don't get enough support from players or administration. PLOs are inconsistent and require a more specific approach to marking wickets.'

Best batting: 235* Hampshire v Warwickshire, Southampton 1997
Best bowling: 3-10 Northamptonshire v Worcestershire, Northampton 1999

2000 Season

	M	Inns	NO	Runs	HS	Avge	100s	50s	Ct	St	O	M	Runs	Wkts	Avge	Best	5wl	10wM
Test																		
All First	15	22	0	1270	164	57.72	4	6	21	-	15	2	56	1	56.00	1-8	-	-
1-day Int																		
NatWest	3	3	1	151	77 *	75.50	-	2	4	-								
B & H	1	1	0	67	67	67.00	-	1	-	-								
1-day Lge	15	15	2	462	96 *	35.53	-	2	6	-	11	0	73	1	73.00	1-16	-	

Career Performances

	M	Inns	NO	Runs	HS	Avge	100s	50s	Ct	St	Balls	Runs	Wkts	Avge	Best	5wl	10wM
Test	8	14	0	300	125	21.42	1	-	8	-							
All First	171	296	31	13870	235 *	52.33	44	60	150	-	917	548	16	34.25	3-10	-	-
1-day Int	19	18	2	477	67	29.81	-	5	7	-	6	18	0	-	-	-	
NatWest	8	8	1	424	107	60.57	1	3	6	-							
B & H	6	6	1	283	120 *	56.60	1	1	3	-	54	45	2	22.50	2-45	-	
1-day Lge	39	38	2	1344	118	37.33	2	6	16	-	147	151	3	50.33	2-38	-	

HAYNES, J. J.   Lancashire

Name: <u>Jamie</u> Jonathan Haynes
Role: Right-hand bat, wicket-keeper
Born: 5 July 1974, Bristol
Height: 5ft 10in **Weight:** 12st 7lbs
Nickname: JJ, Champ, The Mole
County debut: 1996
1st-Class 50s: 1
1st-Class catches: 21
1st-Class stumpings: 2
Parents: Steve Haynes and Moiya Ford
Marital status: Single
Family links with cricket: Father and uncle
both played for Gloucestershire CCC
Education: Garran Primary, Canberra,
Australia; Padua High School, Canberra;
St Edmunds College, Canberra; University of
Canberra

Qualifications: Year 12 Certificate, coaching
certificate
Career outside cricket: 12-month contract at Lancashire
Overseas tours: Lancashire CCC to Cape Town 1999
Overseas teams played for: Tuggeranong Valley CC, Australia 1995-96; South
Canberra CC, Australia 1996-97
Cricketers particularly admired: Mike Watkinson, Gary Yates, Mike Atherton,
Warren Hegg
Young players to look out for: Chris Schofield, James Anderson
Other sports played: Australian Rules football
Other sports followed: Football (Manchester United, Burnley)
Relaxations: Golf, shopping, eating (Thai food), 'going to the movies'
Extras: Top scorer with 80 as nightwatchman in Lancashire's first innings v Sri Lanka A
at Old Trafford 1999
Opinions on cricket: 'Day/night cricket is the way forward. National League should
be exclusively day/night cricket. Coloured clothing should be worn for all limited over
competitions.'
Best batting: 80 Lancashire v Sri Lanka A, Old Trafford 1999

	M	Inns	NO	Runs	HS	Avge	100s	50s	Ct	St	O	M	Runs	Wkts	Avge	Best	5wI	10wM
Test																		
All First	1	2	2	34	27 *	-	-	-	1	-								
1-day Int																		
NatWest																		
B & H																		
1-day Lge	2	1	0	12	12	12.00	-	-	2	1								

Career Performances

	M	Inns	NO	Runs	HS	Avge	100s	50s	Ct	St	Balls	Runs	Wkts	Avge	Best	5wI	10wM
Test																	
All First	6	9	3	215	80	35.83	-	1	21	2							
1-day Int																	
NatWest																	
B & H																	
1-day Lge	3	1	0	12	12	12.00	-	-	3	1							

HAYWOOD, G. R.   Nottinghamshire

Name: <u>Giles</u> Ronald Haywood
Role: Left-hand bat, right-arm
medium bowler
Born: 8 September 1979, Chichester
Height: 6ft 1in **Weight:** 12st
Nickname: Porno, Chopper, Lord Lucan
County debut: 1996 (one-day, Sussex),
1999 (first-class, Sussex),
2000 (one-day, Notts)
Parents: Ron and Shirley
Marital status: Single
Family links with cricket: Father and
brother both play club cricket
Education: The Prebendal, Chichester;
Lancing College; Sussex University
Qualifications: 11 GCSEs, 3 A-levels
Overseas tours: Sussex U19 to Sri Lanka
1995; England U17 to Bermuda (International

Youth Tournament) 1997; England U19 to South Africa (including Youth World Cup)
1997-98, to New Zealand 1998-99
Cricketers particularly admired: Chris Broad, Desmond Haynes, Sachin Tendulkar
Young players to look out for: Paul Havell, Paul Robbins

Other sports played: Golf, squash
Other sports followed: Football (Brighton & Hove Albion FC)
Relaxations: Eating out, watching sport on TV, sleeping, 'VH-1'
Extras: Played for ESCA U15, England U16. Made Sunday League debut at age 17.
Represented England U19 in one-day series v Australia U19 1999. Released by Sussex
at end of 1999 season and joined Nottinghamshire for 2000; released by
Nottinghamshire at the end of the 2000 season
Best batting: 14 Sussex v Leicestershire, Arundel 1999

2000 Season

	M	Inns	NO	Runs	HS	Avge	100s	50s	Ct	St	O	M	Runs	Wkts	Avge	Best	5wI	10wM
Test																		
All First																		
1-day Int																		
NatWest																		
B & H	2	2	0	6	5	3.00	-	-	2	-	4	0	15	0	-		-	-
1-day Lge	2	2	1	24	16 *	24.00	-	-	-	-	8.5	0	34	2	17.00	2-34	-	

Career Performances

	M	Inns	NO	Runs	HS	Avge	100s	50s	Ct	St	Balls	Runs	Wkts	Avge	Best	5wI	10wM
Test																	
All First	1	2	0	15	14	7.50	-	-	-	-	80	66	0	-		-	-
1-day Int																	
NatWest	2	2	1	20	18 *	20.00	-	-	-	-	60	37	1	37.00	1-18	-	
B & H	4	4	0	6	5	1.50	-	-	2	-	132	78	2	39.00	1-24	-	
1-day Lge	11	9	1	92	24	11.50	-	-	4	-	324	258	6	43.00	2-34	-	

HEADLEY, D. W.   Kent

Name: <u>Dean</u> Warren Headley
Role: Right-hand bat, right-arm fast-medium bowler
Born: 27 January 1970, Stourbridge
Height: 6ft 4in **Weight:** 14st 3lbs
Nickname: Froggy
County debut: 1991 (Middlesex), 1993 (Kent)
County cap: 1993 (Kent)
Test debut: 1997
Tests: 15
One-Day Internationals: 13
50 wickets in a season: 2
1st-Class 50s: 6
1st-Class 5 w. in innings: 25

1st-Class 10 w. in match: 2
1st-Class catches: 60
One-Day 5 w. in innings: 3
Place in batting averages: (1999 216th av. 18.56)
Place in bowling averages: (1999 129th av. 38.97)
Strike rate: (career 55.37)
Parents: Ron and Gail
Marital status: Single
Family links with cricket: Grandfather (George) and father (Ron) both played for West Indies
Education: Gigmill Junior School, Stourbridge; Oldswinford Hospital School; Royal Grammar School, Worcester
Qualifications: 7 O-levels
Career outside cricket: 'Various'
Overseas tours: RGS Worcester to Zimbabwe 1988; Christians in Sport to India 1989-90; England A to Pakistan 1995-96, to Australia 1996-97; England to Sharjah (Champions Trophy) 1997-98, to West Indies 1997-98, to Australia 1998-99, to South Africa 1999-2000
Overseas teams played for: Melbourne, Jamaica 1991-92; Primrose CC, South Africa 1993-95
Cricketers particularly admired: Malcolm Marshall, 'my dad', Ian Botham, Gavin O'Hanlon, Adam Patrick, Min Patel
Other sports played: 'Have a go at anything'
Other sports followed: Football (WBA)
Injuries: Missed entire 2000 season with back injury
Relaxations: Socialising, watching films, playing golf and eating out
Extras: Played for Staffordshire. Took five wickets on debut including a wicket with his first ball in Championship cricket 1991. Played for Worcestershire 2nd XI 1988-89. Left Middlesex at the end of 1992 season and signed for Kent. Took a record-breaking three hat-tricks during the summer of 1996. The third generation of his family to play Test cricket, both his father and grandfather played Test cricket for West Indies. Received Man of the Match award for his 6-60 in Australia's second innings in the fourth Test at Melbourne 1998-99, which included a burst of 5-9. Forced to return home early from England tour to South Africa 1999-2000 with stress fracture of back
Best batting: 91 Middlesex v Leicestershire, Leicester 1992
Best bowling: 8-98 Kent v Derbyshire, Derby 1996
Stop press: Forced to retire through injury during the 2000-01 off-season

2000 Season (did not make any first-class or one-day appearances)

Career Performances

	M	Inns	NO	Runs	HS	Avge	100s	50s	Ct	St	Balls	Runs	Wkts	Avge	Best	5wI	10wM
Test	15	26	4	186	31	8.45	-	-	7	-	3026	1671	60	27.85	6-60	1	-
All First	139	187	44	2373	91	16.59	-	6	60	-	25803	13293	466	28.52	8-98	25	2
1-day Int	13	6	4	22	10 *	11.00	-	-	3	-	594	520	11	47.27	2-38	-	
NatWest	16	8	4	46	24 *	11.50	-	-	2	-	960	569	28	20.32	5-20	1	
B & H	27	10	3	62	26	8.85	-	-	6	-	1505	1007	30	33.56	4-19	-	
1-day Lge	100	33	19	160	29 *	11.42	-	-	17	-	4216	3173	128	24.78	6-42	2	

HEGG, W. K.   Lancashire

Name: <u>Warren</u> Kevin Hegg
Role: Right-hand bat, wicket-keeper
Born: 23 February 1968, Manchester
Height: 5ft 9in **Weight:** 12st 10lbs
Nickname: Chucky
County debut: 1986
County cap: 1989
Benefit: 1999 (£178,000)
Test debut: 1998-99
Tests: 2
50 dismissals in a season: 6
1st-Class 50s: 44
1st-Class 100s: 5
1st-Class catches: 663
1st-Class stumpings: 76
Place in batting averages: 55th av. 35.50
(1999 90th av. 31.90)
Parents: Kevin (deceased) and Glenda
Wife and date of marriage: Joanne, 29 October 1994
Children: Chloe Louise, 13 November 1998
Family links with cricket: Brother Martin plays in local leagues
Education: Unsworth High School; Stand College, Whitefield
Qualifications: 5 O-levels, 7 CSEs, qualified coach
Off-season: 'Marketing course at Lancs University'
Overseas tours: NCA North U19 to Bermuda 1985; England YC to Sri Lanka 1986-87, to Australia (Youth World Cup) 1987-88; England A to Pakistan and Sri Lanka 1990-91, to Australia 1996-97; England to Australia 1998-99
Overseas teams played for: Sheffield, Tasmania 1988-90, 1992-93

Cricketers particularly admired: Ian Botham, Alan Knott, Bob Taylor, Gehan Mendis, Ian Healy

Young players to look out for: Peter Devaney, Jamie Haynes ('for his fine glovework'), Gordon Howarth ('right-arm fast bowler at Whitefield')

Other sports played: Football (Old Standians)

Other sports followed: Rugby league (Salford City Reds), football (Manchester United)

Relaxations: 'Golf, golf, golf'

Extras: Became youngest player for 30 years to score a century for Lancashire with his 130 v Northamptonshire in his fourth first-class game. Took 11 catches in match v Derbyshire at Chesterfield in 1989, equalling world first-class record. Wombwell Cricket Lovers' Society joint Wicket-keeper of the Year 1993. Vice-captain of Lancashire in 1999

Opinions on cricket: 'Prize money should not be given for runners-up in division two – the reward of promotion is enough!! – enabling monies to be awarded to third place in division one.'

Best batting: 134 Lancashire v Leicestershire, Old Trafford 1996

2000 Season

	M	Inns	NO	Runs	HS	Avge	100s	50s	Ct	St	O	M	Runs	Wkts	Avge	Best	5wI	10wM
Test																		
All First	17	23	5	639	128	35.50	1	4	39	6								
1-day Int																		
NatWest	4	1	0	3	3	3.00	-	-	3	3								
B & H	7	5	1	70	36	17.50	-	-	11	-								
1-day Lge	14	10	1	133	33	14.77	-	-	10	2								

Career Performances

	M	Inns	NO	Runs	HS	Avge	100s	50s	Ct	St	Balls	Runs	Wkts	Avge	Best	5wI	10wM
Test	2	4	0	30	15	7.50	-	-	8	-							
All First	275	401	77	8742	134	26.98	5	44	663	76	6	7	0	-	-	-	-
1-day Int																	
NatWest	38	21	1	351	37	17.55	-	-	48	6							
B & H	68	35	14	562	81	26.76	-	2	93	6							
1-day Lge	201	119	48	1473	52	20.74	-	1	203	32							

HEMP, D. L.   Warwickshire

Name: <u>David</u> Lloyd Hemp
Role: Left-hand bat, right-arm
medium bowler, county vice-captain
Born: 15 November 1970,
Hamilton, Bermuda
Height: 6ft 1in **Weight:** 13st
Nickname: Hempy, Jonesy
County debut: 1991 (Glamorgan),
1997 (Warwickshire)
County cap: 1994 (Glamorgan),
1997 (Warwickshire)
1000 runs in a season: 3
1st-Class 50s: 42
1st-Class 100s: 13
1st-Class catches: 95
One-Day 100s: 4

Place in batting averages: 47th av. 37.90
(1999 70th av. 34.96)
Strike rate: 60.00 (career 55.76)
Parents: Clive and Elisabeth
Wife and date of marriage: Angie, 16 March 1996
Family links with cricket: Father plays for Ffynone CC; brother Tim captains
Swansea and plays for Wales Minor Counties; sister Charlotte played for Parklands
Junior School
Education: Parklands Junior; Olchfa Comprehensive School; Millfield School; West
Glamorgan Institute of Higher Education; Birmingham University
Qualifications: 5 O-levels, 2 A-levels, NCA coaching awards
Off-season: Continuation of MBA degree at Birmingham University and Level III
coaching award
Overseas tours: Welsh Cricket Association U18 to Barbados 1986; Welsh Schools
U19 to Australia 1987-88; Glamorgan to Trinidad 1990; South Wales Cricket
Association to New Zealand and Australia 1991-92; England A to India 1994-95
Overseas teams played for: Hirsh Crusaders, Durban 1992-98
Cricketers particularly admired: David Gower, Viv Richards
Young players to look out for: Ian Bell
Other sports followed: Football (Swansea City, West Ham United)
Relaxations: Golf, listening to music, reading
Extras: Scored 258* for Wales v MCC 1991. In 1989 scored 104* and 101* for Welsh
Schools U19 v Scottish Schools U19 and 120 and 102* v Irish Schools U19. Left
Glamorgan at the end of the 1996 season and joined Warwickshire. Scored two 100s
(138 and 114*) for Warwicks v Hants at Southampton 1997; Matthew Hayden scored a

200 and a 100 for Hants in the same match. Appointed vice-captain of Warwickshire for 2001

Opinions on cricket: 'Reduce amount of cricket played, which would allow for more quality practice in between games. Bowlers would remain fairly fresh all season. Batters should become more disciplined because of less innings, which would hopefully raise standard and competitiveness of cricket played. Away captain should have choice of whether to bat or bowl. Cricketers are only as good as the surface they play on. Improve the wickets, which will improve the standard of players. Pitch inspectors less tolerant; more points deducted for poor surfaces.'

Best batting: 157 Glamorgan v Gloucestershire, Abergavenny 1995
Best bowling: 3-23 Glamorgan v South Africa A, Cardiff 1996

2000 Season

	M	Inns	NO	Runs	HS	Avge	100s	50s	Ct	St	O	M	Runs	Wkts	Avge	Best	5wI	10wM
Test																		
All First	17	24	2	834	129	37.90	1	5	9	-	20	3	80	2	40.00	2-29	-	-
1-day Int																		
NatWest	3	3	0	38	35	12.66	-	-	1	-								
B & H	3	2	0	10	9	5.00	-	-	-	-								
1-day Lge	9	8	0	106	45	13.25	-	-	1	-								

Career Performances

	M	Inns	NO	Runs	HS	Avge	100s	50s	Ct	St	Balls	Runs	Wkts	Avge	Best	5wI	10wM
Test																	
All First	144	243	19	7478	157	33.38	13	42	95	-	948	741	17	43.58	3-23	-	-
1-day Int																	
NatWest	19	18	2	742	112	46.37	3	3	5	-	48	43	1	43.00	1-40	-	
B & H	22	20	0	546	121	27.30	1	4	2	-	49	32	4	8.00	4-32	-	
1-day Lge	98	86	10	1543	83 *	20.30	-	7	43	-	74	86	3	28.66	2-43	-	

39. Who won the Man of the Match award in the 1976-77 Centenary Test for his 174 as England chased 463 for victory?

HEWISON, C. J.   Nottinghamshire

Name: Christopher (<u>Chris</u>) Jon Hewison
Role: Right-hand bat, right-arm medium bowler
Born: 6 October 1979, Gateshead
Height: 6ft 1in **Weight:** 13st
Nickname: Spuggy, Hewey, Mutly, Houston
County debut: 2000
1st-Class catches: 5
Parents: Neil and Kay
Marital status: Single
Family links with cricket: 'Dad played for Durham (when Minor County) 1974-75 and was a professional in local leagues'
Education: Marley Hill Primary; Whickham Comprehensive; Whickham Comprehensive Sixth Form

Qualifications: 9 GCSEs, 2 A-levels
Off-season: Playing cricket in Melbourne
Overseas tours: Durham U21 to Sri Lanka 1997; England U18 to Bermuda (International Youth Tournament) 1998
Overseas teams played for: Hallam Kallora Park 1998-99, 2000-01
Cricketers particularly admired: Viv Richards, Robin Smith, Curtly Ambrose
Young players to look out for: Paul Armstrong, Ian Hunter, Imran Shah
Other sports played: Football, tennis, snooker
Other sports followed: Football (Newcastle United FC), rugby league (Wigan)
Relaxations: 'Watching or playing any sports; snooker against my dad; socialising with my mates'
Extras: *Daily Telegraph* U14 Cricketer of the Year. North East Junior Cricketer of the Year. Colin Milburn Trophy. Formerly with Durham. Played for Durham Board XI in the NatWest 1999. Top run-scorer for Nottinghamshire 2nd XI 2000
Opinions on cricket: 'Still too much cricket, especially one-dayers, but the two divisions proved to be a good idea, as the end of last season showed.'
Best batting: 24 Nottinghamshire v Glamorgan, Trent Bridge 2000

---

40. Which current international match referee captained
Australia in the fourth Test at Headingley in 1968 in the absence
of the injured Bill Lawry?

2000 Season

	M	Inns	NO	Runs	HS	Avge	100s	50s	Ct	St	O	M	Runs	Wkts	Avge	Best	5wI	10wM
Test																		
All First	1	2	0	30	24	15.00	-	-	5	-								
1-day Int																		
NatWest																		
B & H																		
1-day Lge																		

Career Performances

	M	Inns	NO	Runs	HS	Avge	100s	50s	Ct	St	Balls	Runs	Wkts	Avge	Best	5wI	10wM
Test																		
All First	1	2	0	30	24	15.00	-	-	5	-								
1-day Int																		
NatWest	2	2	0	19	19	9.50	-	-	1	-								
B & H																		
1-day Lge																		

HEWITT, J. P. Middlesex

Name: <u>James</u> Peter Hewitt
Role: Left-hand bat, right-arm
medium-fast bowler
Born: 26 February 1976, Southwark, London
Height: 6ft 3in **Weight:** 12st 8lbs
Nickname: Shoes, Hewey, Danny,
Bambi, Dumbo
County debut: 1995 (one-day),
1996 (first-class)
County cap: 1998
50 wickets in a season: 1
1st-Class 50s: 3
1st-Class 5 w. in innings: 5
1st-Class catches: 22
Place in batting averages: (1999 230th
av. 17.50)
Place in bowling averages: (1999 87th
av. 29.20)
Strike rate: (career 48.94)
Parents: Gillian Underhay and Terry Hewitt
Marital status: Single
Family links with cricket: Father played club cricket and had trials with Surrey.
Grandfather 'played a bit'

Education: Buckingham Primary School, Hampton; Teddington Secondary School, Middlesex; Richmond College; Kingston College; City of Westminster College
Qualifications: GCSEs; City and Guilds Part I, II and III in Recreation and Leisure; GNVQ Leisure and Tourism; coaching awards in cricket (intermediate and advanced), squash, basketball, hockey, gymnastics, badminton, football, volleyball, plus referee qualifications; Community Sports Leadership Award
Overseas teams played for: Western Australia University 1997-98
Cricketers particularly admired: Richard Hadlee, David Gower, Curtly Ambrose, Dominic Cork, Richard Johnson, Philip Hudson
Other sports played/followed: Athletics ('represented South of England at cross-country'), football ('played for Chelsea Youth'), badminton, volleyball, rugby (Harlequins)
Relaxations: Watching and playing a number of sports and sports quiz programmes
Extras: 'I was invited back to my old school, Teddington, to present the sports awards to the pupils – I consider this to be an honour'
Best batting: 75 Middlesex v Essex, Chelmsford 1997
Best bowling: 6-14 Middlesex v Glamorgan, Cardiff 1997

2000 Season

	M	Inns	NO	Runs	HS	Avge	100s	50s	Ct	St	O	M	Runs	Wkts	Avge	Best	5wI	10wM
Test																		
All First																		
1-day Int																		
NatWest																		
B & H	1	1	0	8	8	8.00	-	-	-	-	8	3	40	1	40.00	1-40	-	
1-day Lge	5	3	0	17	12	5.66	-	-	2	-	24	1	115	1	115.00	1-24	-	

Career Performances

	M	Inns	NO	Runs	HS	Avge	100s	50s	Ct	St	Balls	Runs	Wkts	Avge	Best	5wI	10wM
Test																	
All First	56	76	11	1194	75	18.36	-	3	22	-	7831	4470	160	27.93	6-14	5	-
1-day Int																	
NatWest	5	3	2	23	14 *	23.00	-	-	2	-	234	174	3	58.00	1-26	-	
B & H	9	5	0	30	14	6.00	-	-	2	-	444	384	6	64.00	2-49	-	
1-day Lge	54	30	11	244	32 *	12.84	-	-	18	-	1923	1418	52	27.26	4-24	-	

HEWSON, D. R. Gloucestershire

Name: <u>Dominic</u> Robert Hewson
Role: Right-hand bat, right-arm medium bowler
Born: 3 October 1974, Cheltenham
Height: 5ft 9in **Weight:** 12st 7lb
Nickname: Chopper
County debut: 1996
1st-Class 50s: 9
1st-Class catches: 17
Place in batting averages: 156th av. 22.40 (1999 248th av. 14.40)
Strike rate: (career 54.00)
Parents: Robert and Julie
Wife and date of marriage: Amy, 14 October 2000
Education: Cheltenham College; University of West of England

Qualifications: 10 GCSEs, 3 A-levels, City and Guilds in Tree Surgery
Career outside cricket: Works for Treework Services, near Bristol
Overseas teams played for: Constantia, Cape Town 1995-96; Central, Hawkes Bay, New Zealand 1998-99
Cricketers particularly admired: Jon Lewis, Jack Russell, Courtney Walsh, Mark Snape
Other sports followed: Rugby, ice hockey, Aussie Rules, football
Relaxations: Seeing friends
Extras: Made debut for Gloucestershire 2nd XI in July 1993
Best batting: 87 Gloucestershire v Hampshire, Southampton 1996
Best bowling: 1-7 Gloucestershire v Kent, Bristol 1998

2000 Season

	M	Inns	NO	Runs	HS	Avge	100s	50s	Ct	St	O	M	Runs	Wkts	Avge	Best	5wI	10wM
Test																		
All First	11	21	1	448	67	22.40	-	3	5	-	5	1	30	0	-	-	-	-
1-day Int																		
NatWest	2	2	0	49	38	24.50	-	-	-	-								
B & H	4	3	1	51	30 *	25.50	-	-	1	-								
1-day Lge	5	4	0	85	45	21.25	-	-	1	-								

Career Performances

	M	Inns	NO	Runs	HS	Avge	100s	50s	Ct	St	Balls	Runs	Wkts	Avge	Best	5wI	10wM
Test																	
All First	37	69	5	1356	87	21.18	-	9	17	-		54	37	1	37.00	1-7	-	-
1-day Int																	
NatWest	4	4	0	106	45	26.50	-	-	1	-							
B & H	4	3	1	51	30 *	25.50	-	-	1	-							
1-day Lge	12	8	0	114	45	14.25	-	-	1	-							

HICK, G. A. Worcestershire

Name: <u>Graeme</u> Ashley Hick
Role: Right-hand bat, off-spin bowler, county captain
Born: 23 May 1966, Harare, Zimbabwe
Height: 6ft 3in **Weight:** 14st 7lbs
Nickname: Hicky, Ash
County debut: 1984
County cap: 1986
Benefit: 1999
Test debut: 1991
Tests: 60
One-Day Internationals: 112
1000 runs in a season: 15
1st-Class 50s: 122
1st-Class 100s: 100
1st-Class 200s: 9
1st-Class 300s: 1
1st-Class 400s: 1
1st-Class 5 w. in innings: 5
1st-Class 10 w. in match: 1
1st-Class catches: 491
One-Day 100s: 27
One-Day 5 w. in innings: 1
Place in batting averages: 57th av. 35.13 (1999 12th av. 48.31)
Strike rate: 270.00 (career 89.05)
Parents: John and Eve
Wife and date of marriage: Jackie, 5 October 1991
Children: Lauren Amy, 12 September 1992
Family links with cricket: Father has served on Zimbabwe Cricket Union Board of Control since 1984 and played representative cricket in Zimbabwe
Education: Banket Primary; Prince Edward Boys' High School, Zimbabwe
Qualifications: 4 O-levels, NCA coaching award

Off-season: England tours to Kenya, Pakistan and Sri Lanka

Overseas tours: Zimbabwe to England (World Cup) 1983, to Sri Lanka 1983-84, to England 1985; England to New Zealand and Australia (World Cup) 1991-92, to India and Sri Lanka 1992-93, to West Indies 1993-94, to Australia 1994-95, to South Africa 1995-96, to India and Pakistan (World Cup) 1995-96, to Sharjah 1997-98, to West Indies 1997-98 (one-day series), to Bangladesh (Wills International Cup) 1998-99, to Australia 1998-99, to Sharjah (Coca-Cola Cup) 1998-99, to South Africa and Zimbabwe 1999-2000 (one-day series), to Kenya (ICC Knockout Trophy) 2000-01, to Pakistan and Sri Lanka 2000-01

Overseas teams played for: Old Hararians, Zimbabwe 1982-90; Northern Districts, New Zealand 1987-89; Queensland, Australia 1990-91; Auckland 1997-98

Cricketers particularly admired: Duncan Fletcher (former Zimbabwe captain; now England coach) for approach and understanding of the game, David Houghton, Basil D'Oliveira

Other sports followed: Football (Liverpool FC), golf, tennis, squash, hockey

Relaxations: 'Leaning against Steve Rhodes at first slip'

Extras: Made first century aged six for school team. Youngest player participating in 1983 Prudential World Cup (aged 17); youngest player to represent Zimbabwe. Scored 1234 runs in Birmingham League and played for Worcestershire 2nd XI in 1984 – hitting six successive centuries. In 1986, at age 20, he became the youngest player to score 2000 runs in an English season. One of *Wisden*'s Five Cricketers of the Year 1987. In 1988 he made 405* v Somerset at Taunton, the highest individual score in England since 1895, and scored 1000 first-class runs by end of May, hitting a record 410 runs in April. In 1990 became youngest batsman ever to make 50 first-class centuries and scored 645 runs without being dismissed – a record for English cricket. Also in 1990 became the fastest to 10,000 runs in county cricket (179 innings). Qualified as an English player in 1991. Scored first Test century v India in Bombay 1992-93 and was England's leading batsman, bowler and fielder. Published *Hick 'n' Dilley Circus* and *A Champion's Diary*. Also played hockey for Zimbabwe. Finished third in the Whyte and Mackay batting ratings in 1995 and top of the first-class batting averages in 1997. Scored hundredth first-class 100 v Sussex at Worcester in 1998 with his second 100 of the match; at the age of 32, he became the second youngest player after Wally Hammond to score one hundred 100s; received an Individual Performance Award from the PCA in recognition of his achievement. Represented England in the 1999 World Cup. Scored two centuries in a match for the fourth time, v Essex at Chelmsford 1999; the second 100, his 108th, put him level with Zaheer Abbas at 15th in the all-time century-scoring list. Won One-Day International Man of the Match awards v Zimbabwe, the country of his birth, for his match-winning 87* at Bulawayo and his 80 and 5-33 at Harare, February 2000. Captain of Worcestershire since 2000. Scored 101 in England's only innings in his first Test v Zimbabwe at Lord's 2000; it was his first Test century at Lord's

Best batting: 405* Worcestershire v Somerset, Taunton 1988

Best bowling: 5-18 Worcestershire v Leicestershire, Worcester 1995

Stop press: Scored 40 in match-winning partnership with Graham Thorpe in third Test at Karachi 2000-01

2000 Season

	M	Inns	NO	Runs	HS	Avge	100s	50s	Ct	St	O	M	Runs	Wkts	Avge	Best	5wI	10wM
Test	6	10	0	252	101	25.20	1	1	8	-								
All First	14	24	2	773	122	35.13	3	3	16	-	45	6	135	1	135.00	1-13	-	-
1-day Int	7	6	1	126	50	25.20	-	1	1	-	8	0	43	2	21.50	2-37	-	
NatWest	2	2	0	36	23	18.00	-	-	3	-	5	0	27	0	-		-	-
B & H	3	2	1	55	55 *	55.00	-	1	3	-								
1-day Lge	7	6	0	148	101	24.66	1	-	7	-	19	0	126	1	126.00	1-50	-	

Career Performances

	M	Inns	NO	Runs	HS	Avge	100s	50s	Ct	St	Balls	Runs	Wkts	Avge	Best	5wI	10wM
Test	60	104	6	3257	178	33.23	6	18	84	-	2985	1256	22	57.09	4-126	-	-
All First	397	653	62	32082	405 *	54.28	111	122	491	-	19859	9789	223	43.89	5-18	5	1
1-day Int	112	110	14	3639	126 *	37.90	5	25	59	-	1165	962	30	32.06	5-33	1	
NatWest	40	40	6	1692	172 *	49.76	4	9	22	-	1241	775	23	33.69	4-54	-	
B & H	65	63	13	2772	127 *	55.44	7	19	41	-	732	562	12	46.83	3-36	-	
1-day Lge	200	191	33	7183	130	45.46	11	51	64	-	2650	2295	80	28.68	4-21	-	

HOCKLEY, J. B.   Kent

Name: <u>James</u> Bernard Hockley
Role: Right-hand bat, right-arm
off-spin bowler
Born: 16 April 1979, Stone Park, Beckenham
Height: 6ft 2in **Weight:** 13st
Nickname: Ice, Hockers, Casper, Ghost
County debut: 1998
1st-Class 50s: 1
1st-Class catches: 2
Strike rate: (career 90.00)
Parents: Bernard and Joan
Marital status: Engaged to Wendy
Education: Churchfields Primary School,
Beckenham; Kelsey Park School, Beckenham
Qualifications: 7 GCSEs, NCA coaching
award
Career outside cricket: 'Trying to find one
at the moment'
Off-season: 'Paying off my house; staying at home and working on fitness and
technique'
Overseas tours: Kent to Jamaica 1999
Overseas teams played for: North City, Wellington 1999-2000

Cricketers particularly admired: Ian Botham, Aravinda De Silva, Carl Hooper
Young players to look out for: Martin Saggers, Kristian Adams, Robert Grummitt
Other sports played: Football, golf, snooker, rugby
Other sports followed: Football (Arsenal)
Injuries: Out for eight weeks with strained hamstring
Relaxations: Listening to music, watching TV, shopping
Extras: AKCL Player of the Year Award in 1995. Equalled Trevor Ward's Kent U15 batting record with a total of 1,000 runs in the season. Kent Schools Player of the Year in 1996
Opinions on cricket: 'Two divisional system seems to be a success; lots of competitive cricket to make better, tougher players.'
Best batting: 74 Kent v Zimbabweans, Canterbury 2000
Best bowling: 1-57 Kent v Gloucestershire, Canterbury 1999

2000 Season

	M	Inns	NO	Runs	HS	Avge	100s	50s	Ct	St	O	M	Runs	Wkts	Avge	Best	5wI	10wM
Test																		
All First	5	5	0	111	74	22.20	-	1	2	-	3	3	0	0	-	-	-	-
1-day Int																		
NatWest	1	1	0	8	8	8.00	-	-	-	-								
B & H	1	1	0	14	14	14.00	-	-	-	-								
1-day Lge	9	8	2	236	64	39.33	-	1	3	-								

Career Performances

	M	Inns	NO	Runs	HS	Avge	100s	50s	Ct	St	Balls	Runs	Wkts	Avge	Best	5wI	10wM
Test																	
All First	7	8	0	175	74	21.87	-	1	2	-	90	57	1	57.00	1-57	-	-
1-day Int																	
NatWest	1	1	0	8	8	8.00	-	-	-	-							
B & H	1	1	0	14	14	14.00	-	-	-	-							
1-day Lge	11	10	2	263	64	32.87	-	1	5	-							

41. Whose 196 at The Oval in 1985 was his first century against
Australia in his 40th innings against them?

HOGG, K. W. Lancashire

Name: <u>Kyle</u> William Hogg
Role: Left-hand bat, right-arm fast-medium
bowler
Born: 2 July 1983, Birmingham
Height: 6ft 3in **Weight:** 11st 7lbs
Nickname: Hoggy
County debut: No first-team appearance
Parents: Sharon Ramadhin and William
Hogg
Marital status: Single
Family links with cricket: 'Dad played for
Lancs and Warwickshire; grandad Sonny
Ramadhin played for Lancs and West Indies'
Education: St Anne's, Oldham; Saddleworth
High School

Qualifications: GCSEs
Career outside cricket: 'Don't know yet'
Off-season: England U19 tour to India
Overseas tours: England U19 to India 2000-01
Cricketers particularly admired: Brian Lara, Curtly Ambrose, Andrew Flintoff
Young players to look out for: Nicky Peng
Other sports played: Football
Other sports followed: Football (Man Utd)
Relaxations: Going out, golf, listening to music
Opinions on cricket: 'The day/night cricket excites me!!'

HOGGARD, M. J. Yorkshire

Name: <u>Matthew</u> James Hoggard
Role: Right-hand bat, right-arm fast-medium bowler
Born: 31 December 1976, Leeds
Height: 6ft 2in **Weight:** 14st 7lbs
Nickname: Hoggie
County debut: 1996
County cap: 2000
Test debut: 2000
Tests: 1
50 wickets in a season: 1
1st-Class 5 w. in innings: 5

1st-Class catches: 9
One-Day 5 w. in innings: 2
Place in batting averages: 293rd av. 7.35
(1999 288th av. 6.62)
Place in bowling averages: 65th av. 26.46
(1999 34th av. 22.10)
Strike rate: 60.20 (career 51.60)
Parents: Margaret and John
Marital status: Living with girlfriend Sarah
Education: Lowtown Primary; Pudsey
Grangefield; Pudsey Grangefield Sixth Form
Qualifications: GCSEs and A-levels
Career outside cricket: 'Eating'
Off-season: England tours to Kenya,
Pakistan and Sri Lanka
Overseas tours: Yorkshire CCC to South
Africa; England U19 to Zimbabwe 1995-96;
England to Kenya (ICC Knockout Trophy)
2000-01, to Pakistan and Sri Lanka
2000-01

Overseas teams played for: Pirates, Johannesburg 1996-98; Free State 1998-2000
Cricketers particularly admired: Allan Donald
Young players to look out for: Matthew Wood
Other sports played: Rugby
Other sports followed: Rugby league (Leeds Rhinos)
Relaxations: Dog walking
Extras: Made Test debut in the second Test v West Indies at Lord's 2000. Top wicket-taker in the 2000 National League competition with 37 wickets at 12.37. Awarded Yorkshire cap 2000. PCA Young Player of the Year 2000
Opinions on cricket: 'Better wickets are needed to prepare players for Test cricket. More day/night games to get the public interested in the game, but we need to improve the lights.'
Best batting: 21* Free State v Gauteng, Johannesburg 1999-2000
Best bowling: 5-47 Yorkshire v Derbyshire, Derby 1999
Stop press: Drafted into England one-day squad for Kenya and Pakistan 2000-01 as replacement for the injured Alan Mullally; was already selected for Test squads. Returned match figures of 8-30 (4-13 and 4-17) from 22.3 overs v Pakistan Board XI at Lahore and took 17 wickets in total in his two matches in Pakistan

2000 Season

	M	Inns	NO	Runs	HS	Avge	100s	50s	Ct	St	O	M	Runs	Wkts	Avge	Best	5wI	10wM
Test	1	1	1	12	12 *	-	-	-	1	-	13	3	49	0	-	-	-	-
All First	16	18	4	103	20 *	7.35	-	-	3	-	501.4	134	1323	50	26.46	5-50	2	-
1-day Int																		
NatWest																		
B & H	5	1	1	2	2 *	-	-	-	-	-	36	7	124	5	24.80	4-39	-	
1-day Lge	15	7	4	4	2 *	1.33	-	-	1	-	121.3	18	458	37	12.37	5-28	2	

Career Performances

	M	Inns	NO	Runs	HS	Avge	100s	50s	Ct	St	Balls	Runs	Wkts	Avge	Best	5wI	10wM
Test	1	1	1	12	12 *	-	-	-	1	-	78	49	0	-	-	-	-
All First	42	54	17	258	21 *	6.97	-	-	9	-	7482	3542	145	24.42	5-47	5	-
1-day Int																	
NatWest	1	0	0	0	0	-	-	-	-	-	30	6	0	-	-	-
B & H	7	1	1	2	2 *	-	-	-	-	-	301	176	8	22.00	4-39	-
1-day Lge	20	11	6	8	2 *	1.60	-	-	1	-	921	608	43	14.13	5-28	2

HOLLIOAKE, A. J.   Surrey

Name: <u>Adam</u> John Hollioake
Role: Right-hand bat, right-arm
medium bowler, county captain
Born: 5 September 1971,
Melbourne, Australia
Height: 5ft 11in **Weight:** 13st 10lbs
Nickname: Smokey
County debut: 1992 (one-day),
1993 (first-class)
County cap: 1995
Test debut: 1997
Tests: 4
One-Day Internationals: 35
1000 runs in a season: 2
1st-Class 50s: 38
1st-Class 100s: 13
1st-Class 5 w. in innings: 1
1st-Class catches: 115
One-Day 100s: 1
One-Day 5 w. in innings: 4
Place in batting averages: 96th av. 29.95 (1999 79th av. 33.37)
Strike rate: 84.66 (career 73.09)

Parents: John and Daria
Marital status: Single
Family links with cricket: Brother plays
Education: St Joseph's College, Sydney; St Patrick's College, Ballarat, Australia; St George's College, Weybridge; Surrey Tutorial College, Guildford
Qualifications: 'Some GCSEs and A-levels'
Career outside cricket: 'None'
Off-season: Coaching Hong Kong cricket team
Overseas tours: School trip to Zimbabwe; Surrey YC to Australia; England YC to New Zealand 1990-91; England A to Australia 1996-97 (captain); England VI to Hong Kong 1997 (captain); England to Sharjah (Champions Trophy) 1997-98 (captain), to West Indies 1997-98 (captain in one-day series), to Bangladesh (Wills International Cup) 1998-99 (captain), to Australia 1998-99 (CUB Series), to Sharjah (Coca-Cola Cup) 1998-99
Overseas teams played for: Fremantle, Western Australia 1990-91; North Shore, Sydney 1992-93; Geelong, Victoria; North Perth, Western Australia 1995-97
Cricketers particularly admired: 'Every cricketer who gives their best and takes up the challenge to compete'
Young players to look out for: Tim Murtagh, Nicky Peng, Joe Porter, Michael Carberry
Other sports played: 'Boxing – grappling'
Other sports followed: 'No holds barred fighting'
Injuries: 'Numerous shoulder problems'
Extras: Played rugby for London Counties, Middlesex and South of England as well as having a trial for England U18. Scored a century on first-class debut against Derbyshire 1993. Surrey Young Player of the Year 1993. Scored fastest ever one-day 50 – in 15 balls v Yorkshire in the Sunday League at Scarborough 1994. Surrey Supporters' Player of the Year 1996 and Surrey Players' Player of the Year 1996. His 39 wickets in the Sunday League in 1996 was a record for the competition. Man of the Match in the first One-Day International against Australia at Headingley in 1997. He and brother Ben became the first brothers to make their England Test debut together this century in the fifth Test against Australia at Trent Bridge 1997. Captained England in the Texaco Trophy one-day series v South Africa 1998. Represented England in the 1999 World Cup. His 111 from 98 balls v Glamorgan Dragons in the National League at The Oval 2000 was his maiden one-day century. Coached Hong Kong in the Asian Cricket Council Trophy in Sharjah 2000. Has been Surrey captain since 1997
Opinions on cricket: 'We are lucky to have such a good game to play, and it is an honour for me to have the opportunity to compete every day.'
Best batting: 182 Surrey v Middlesex, Lord's 1997
Best bowling: 5-62 Surrey v Glamorgan, Swansea 1998

2000 Season

	M	Inns	NO	Runs	HS	Avge	100s	50s	Ct	St	O	M	Runs	Wkts	Avge	Best	5wl	10wM
Test																		
All First	16	23	0	689	80	29.95	-	3	27	-	42.2	12	119	3	39.66	1-8	-	
1-day Int																		
NatWest	3	2	1	30	17	30.00	-	-	-	-	11	0	55	4	13.75	3-23	-	
B & H	4	3	0	27	16	9.00	-	-	1	-	20	1	93	5	18.60	3-36	-	
1-day Lge	14	13	4	346	111	38.44	1	-	7	-	59.4	1	263	23	11.43	5-29	1	

Career Performances

	M	Inns	NO	Runs	HS	Avge	100s	50s	Ct	St	Balls	Runs	Wkts	Avge	Best	5wl	10wM
Test	4	6	0	65	45	10.83	-	-	4	-	144	67	2	33.50	2-31	-	-
All First	126	192	16	6780	182	38.52	13	38	115	-	7309	3994	100	39.94	5-62	1	-
1-day Int	35	30	6	606	83 *	25.25	-	3	13	-	1208	1019	32	31.84	4-23	-	
NatWest	22	17	3	468	88	33.42	-	3	9	-	716	555	21	26.42	4-53	-	
B & H	33	26	3	649	85	28.21	-	4	11	-	1148	1014	33	30.72	4-34	-	
1-day Lge	112	101	14	2302	111	26.45	1	9	27	-	3692	3470	162	21.41	5-29	4	

HOLLIOAKE, B. C. Surrey

Name: <u>Ben</u> Caine Hollioake
Role: Right-hand bat, right-arm
medium-fast bowler
Born: 11 November 1977,
Melbourne, Australia
Height: 6ft 2in **Weight:** 14st
Nickname: Pely, Big Dog
County debut: 1996
County cap: 1999
Test debut: 1997
Tests: 2
One-Day Internationals: 7
1st-Class 50s: 10
1st-Class 100s: 2
1st-Class 5 w. in innings: 1
1st-Class catches: 49
One-Day 5 w. in innings: 1
Place in batting averages: 264th av. 10.92
(1999 131st av. 26.90)
Place in bowling averages: 118th av. 37.00 (1999 119th av. 34.82)
Strike rate: 64.27 (career 55.49)
Parents: John and Daria

Marital status: Single

Family links with cricket: 'Dad played for Victoria; mum played for fun; brother played badly'

Education: Edgarley Hall; Millfield School; Wesley College, Perth, Western Australia; 'Joey Benjamin's house'

Qualifications: 'A couple of GCSEs and NCA coaching award'

Career outside cricket: 'I'm having to think harder and harder about that'

Off-season: 'Playing for Rest of World v Asia in November; after that, options…'

Overseas tours: Millfield to Zimbabwe 1992; West of England to West Indies 1992; England U19 to Pakistan 1996-97; England A to Kenya and Sri Lanka 1997-98; England VI to Hong Kong 1997; England to Sharjah (Champions Trophy) 1997-98, to West Indies 1997-98 (one-day series), to Australia 1998-99

Overseas teams played for: Melville, Perth 1992-95; North Perth 1996-97; South Perth 1999-2000

Cricketers particularly admired: 'Waqar and Wasim, Waugh Bros, Mr G. Dilley, Surrey team-mates, Tony Lock and grumpy old Carly'

Young players to look out for: Alex Tudor ('I mean really look!'), Quintin Pickles

Other sports played: Golf ('first of three holes-in-one at the Belfry 10th 1996'), 'goat racing'

Other sports followed: Football (Chelsea), Aussie Rules (West Coast Eagles), beach football ('France and Brazil funnily enough are very entertaining')

Injuries: Out for three weeks with 'useless ankle'; for one month with torn muscle

Relaxations: 'Walking the dog'

Extras: Played England U14 and U15. Played Western Australia U17 and U19. Became the youngest player to take five wickets in a Sunday League game when he took 5-10 v Derbyshire at The Oval in 1996. His first two appearances at Lord's both resulted in him winning Man of the Match awards – his 63 off 48 balls in the third One-Day International against Australia in 1997 (his England one-day debut) and his 98 off 113 balls for Surrey against Kent in the Benson and Hedges Cup final in 1997. Became the youngest player (aged 19 and after only 11 first-class games) to make his Test debut for England since Brian Close in 1949 and he and brother Adam became the first brothers to make their Test debuts together for England this century. Was voted the Young Cricketer of the Year by both the Cricket Writers' Club and the PCA in 1997. Scored 100s (103 and 163) for England A in the second and third 'Tests' v Sri Lanka A 1997-98. Played for a World XI v an Asia XI at The Oval 2000

Opinions on cricket: 'More could be done to market the game. England are still approaching that golden era. Just when we thought that Sky Sports was the only place to watch cricket, Channel 4 came and saved the day.'

Best batting: 163 England A v Sri Lanka A, Moratuwa 1997-98

Best bowling: 5-51 Surrey v Glamorgan, The Oval 1999

2000 Season

	M	Inns	NO	Runs	HS	Avge	100s	50s	Ct	St	O	M	Runs	Wkts	Avge	Best	5wI	10wM
Test																		
All First	10	14	1	142	29	10.92	-	-	8	-	117.5	25	407	11	37.00	4-41	-	-
1-day Int																		
NatWest	2	1	0	0	0	0.00	-	-	-	-	7	0	52	0	-		-	-
B & H	3	3	0	49	44	16.33	-	-	3	-	19.1	0	102	2	51.00	1-10	-	
1-day Lge	8	5	0	93	42	18.60	-	-	3	-	47.4	0	181	11	16.45	4-42	-	

Career Performances

	M	Inns	NO	Runs	HS	Avge	100s	50s	Ct	St	Balls	Runs	Wkts	Avge	Best	5wI	10wM
Test	2	4	0	44	28	11.00	-	-	2	-	252	199	4	49.75	2-105		
All First	63	95	6	2208	163	24.80	2	10	49	-	6493	3684	117	31.48	5-51	1	-
1-day Int	7	6	0	122	63	20.33	-	1	1	-	150	122	2	61.00	2-43	-	
NatWest	12	8	0	95	33	11.87	-	-	6	-	474	376	8	47.00	2-28	-	
B & H	20	18	1	556	98	32.70	-	4	5	-	808	731	22	33.22	3-23	-	
1-day Lge	53	45	3	753	61	17.92	-	1	16	-	1852	1529	63	24.26	5-10	1	

HOLLOWAY, P. C. L.   Somerset

Name: Piran Christopher Laity Holloway
Role: Left-hand bat, off-spin bowler,
wicket-keeper
Born: 1 October 1970, Helston, Cornwall
Height: 5ft 8in **Weight:** 11st 5lbs
Nickname: Oggy, Leg, Piras
County debut: 1988 (Warwickshire),
1994 (Somerset)
County cap: 1997 (Somerset)
1st-Class 50s: 24
1st-Class 100s: 9
1st-Class catches: 79
1st-Class stumpings: 1
One-Day 100s: 2
Place in batting averages: 180th av. 19.84
(1999 87th av. 32.18)
Parents: Chris and Mary
Marital status: 'Engaged to the lovely Nikki'
Family links with cricket: 'Mum and Dad are keen'
Education: Nansloe CP School, Helston; Millfield School; Taunton School;
Loughborough University
Qualifications: 7 O-levels, 2 A-levels, BSc (Hons) Sports Science

Career outside cricket: Coaching
Overseas tours: Millfield School to Barbados 1986; England YC to Australia 1989-90; Warwickshire CCC to Cape Town 1992 and 1993; Somerset CCC to Holland 1994
Overseas teams played for: North Perth, 1993-94; Nedlands, Perth 1994-96; Claremont Nedlands 1996-98
Cricketers particularly admired: Ian Botham, David Gower
Young players to look out for: Matt Bulbeck, Steve Harmison
Other sports followed: Squash, football, rugby, tennis, surfing
Relaxations: Music, surfing, travel
Extras: Won the Jack Hobbs Trophy in 1990. Played Young England for three years. Was fourth in the county averages in 1991. Somerset Young Player of the Year 1995. Scored the most runs in A-grade cricket in Perth in 1997-98 season in which Claremont Nedlands won the Bank West Cup
Best batting: 168 Somerset v Middlesex, Uxbridge 1996

2000 Season

	M	Inns	NO	Runs	HS	Avge	100s	50s	Ct	St	O	M	Runs	Wkts	Avge	Best	5wl	10wM
Test																		
All First	13	20	1	377	113	19.84	1	1	9	-	2	0	4	0	-	-	-	-
1-day Int																		
NatWest	2	2	0	33	22	16.50	-	-	1	-								
B & H	3	3	0	152	78	50.66	-	2	1	-								
1-day Lge	9	9	1	58	15	7.25	-	-	3	-								

Career Performances

	M	Inns	NO	Runs	HS	Avge	100s	50s	Ct	St	Balls	Runs	Wkts	Avge	Best	5wl	10wM
Test																	
All First	107	179	27	4791	168	31.51	9	24	79	1	52	50	0	-	-	-	-
1-day Int																	
NatWest	15	14	3	537	90	48.81	-	4	8	1							
B & H	10	10	1	219	78	24.33	-	2	8	-							
1-day Lge	88	79	16	1723	117	27.34	2	10	36	7							

HOUSE, W. J. Sussex

Name: William (<u>Will</u>) John House
Role: Left-hand top-order bat, right-arm
medium bowler
Born: 16 March 1976, Sheffield
Height: 5ft 10in **Weight:** 12st 6lbs
Nickname: Housey, Etna, Wendy
County debut: 1997 (Kent), 2000 (Sussex)
1st-Class 50s: 7
1st-Class 100s: 2
1st-Class catches: 19
One-Day 5 w. in innings: 1
Place in batting averages: 248th av. 12.44
Strike rate: 198.00 (career 361.25)
Parents: Bill and Anna
Marital status: Girlfriend Felicity
Family links with cricket: 'Dad played
Yorkshire League'
Education: British School in the
Netherlands, The Hague; Sevenoaks School;
University of Cambridge (Gonville and Caius College)
Qualifications: 11 GCSEs, International Baccalaureate, NCA coaching award
Career outside cricket: 'Sports business'
Off-season: 'Working in London and netting in Hove'
Overseas tours: MCC to Australia 1999, to Bangladesh 2000
Overseas teams played for: Royal Hague CC 1985-89; University CC, Adelaide
1994-95
Cricketers particularly admired: Ian Botham, David Gower
Young players to look out for: Matt Prior, Tim Ambrose
Other sports played: Rugby (Cambridge University U21 XV 1996-97), football
(Cambridge Blue 1998)
Other sports followed: Rugby, football (Sheffield Wednesday), golf
Injuries: 'Nothing major, just little niggles'
Relaxations: Music, history
Extras: Cricket Society's leading all-rounder in schools cricket in 1993. Kent CCC's
Most Improved Player 1996. Cambridge University's Player of the Year 1996 and
1998. Benson and Hedges Gold Awards for British Universities v Surrey 1997 (93
runs) and v Gloucestershire 1998 (5-34). Left Kent at end of 1999 season and joined
Sussex for 2000 on a two-year contract
Opinions on cricket: 'Playing in two divisional cricket (both one-day and
Championship) in 2000 was a very positive experience. More points for a
Championship win may encourage some sides to play more positively throughout the

season, but generally the changes helped to ensure competitive, intense, meaningful cricket right up to the end of the season.'

Best batting: 136 Cambridge University v Derbyshire, Fenner's 1996
Best bowling: 1-34 Cambridge University v Oxford University, Lord's 1998
1-34 Sussex v Glamorgan, Colwyn Bay 2000

2000 Season

	M	Inns	NO	Runs	HS	Avge	100s	50s	Ct	St	O	M	Runs	Wkts	Avge	Best	5wI	10wM
Test																		
All First	6	10	1	112	35	12.44	-	-	3	-	33	7	104	1	104.00	1-34	-	-
1-day Int																		
NatWest	2	1	0	5	5	5.00	-	-	3	-								
B & H	4	4	0	20	8	5.00	-	-	-	-	16	0	94	5	18.80	4-41	-	
1-day Lge	14	13	4	259	80 *	28.77	-	1	2	-	55.5	2	254	10	25.40	3-34	-	

Career Performances

	M	Inns	NO	Runs	HS	Avge	100s	50s	Ct	St	Balls	Runs	Wkts	Avge	Best	5wI	10wM
Test																	
All First	33	51	8	1313	136	30.53	2	7	19	-	1445	947	4	236.75	1-34	-	-
1-day Int																	
NatWest	3	2	0	20	15	10.00	-	-	3	-	24	23	0	-	-	-	
B & H	15	15	0	334	93	22.26	-	2	3	-	185	190	10	19.00	5-58	1	
1-day Lge	35	30	5	580	80 *	23.20	-	1	4	-	386	308	11	28.00	3-34	-	

42. At Headingley in 1993, who became the first Australian batsman since Bradman to score centuries in three successive Ashes Tests?

HUMPHRIES, S. Sussex

Name: Shaun Humphries
Role: Right-hand bat, right-arm 'slow inswing' bowler, wicket-keeper
Born: 11 January 1973, Horsham, West Sussex
Height: 5ft 11in **Weight:** 11st
Nickname: Stan, Gooner
County debut: 1993
1st-Class 50s: 2
1st-Class catches: 56
1st-Class stumpings: 3
Place in batting averages: (1999 266th av. 11.00)
Parents: Peter and Marilyn
Marital status: Engaged to Kate Arnold
Family links with cricket: Parents avid watchers

Education: Itchingfield CP; The Weald School, Billingshurst; Kingston College of Further Education
Qualifications: 5 GCSEs, BTEC National Diploma in Leisure Studies, Level 2 cricket coach
Career outside cricket: 'Still looking! Currently painter and decorator'
Off-season: 'Following the Arsenal and planning the next boxing trip following Lennox Lewis'
Overseas tours: Sussex U13 to Barbados 1987; Sussex U18 to India 1990-91; Keith Greenfield Malaga Tour 1994-95
Overseas teams played for: Sutherland CC, Sydney 1994-95
Cricketers particularly admired: Jack Russell ('different level!!'), Geoff Kirkham, Mark Hamilton
Young players to look out for: 'Any one of Dr Dew's Wednesday night production line!'
Other sports played: 9-ball pool, golf ('poorly')
Other sports followed: 'Going to see the Arsenal', cycling, rugby league (Cronulla Sharks)
Injuries: Out for four weeks with an ('alcohol-induced') twisted ankle
Relaxations: 'Music, chilling with the Mrs and travelling to any sporting events (Las Vegas Lewis v Holyfield 2 1999)'
Extras: Released by Sussex at the end of the 2000 season
Best batting: 66 Sussex v Kent, Tunbridge Wells 1998

2000 Season

	M	Inns	NO	Runs	HS	Avge	100s	50s	Ct	St	O	M	Runs	Wkts	Avge	Best	5wl	10wM
Test																		
All First	2	4	1	41	18	13.66	-	-	4	1								
1-day Int																		
NatWest																		
B & H	1	1	0	0	0	0.00	-	-	-	-								
1-day Lge																		

Career Performances

	M	Inns	NO	Runs	HS	Avge	100s	50s	Ct	St	Balls	Runs	Wkts	Avge	Best	5wl	10wM
Test																	
All First	31	47	5	555	66	13.21	-	2	56	3							
1-day Int																	
NatWest	3	2	0	11	10	5.50	-	-	4	1							
B & H	4	3	0	16	16	5.33	-	-	2	1							
1-day Lge	25	11	3	58	13	7.25	-	-	15	11							

HUNT, T. A.   Middlesex

Name: <u>Thomas</u> Aaron Hunt
Role: Left-hand bat, right-arm
medium-fast bowler
Born: 19 January 1982, Melbourne, Australia
Height: 6ft 3in **Weight:** 13st 7lbs
Nickname: Thos
County debut: No first-team appearance
Parents: Jennifer Hunt and Tim Woodbridge
Marital status: Single
Education: Brackenberry, Hammersmith;
Acton High; St Clement Danes
Qualifications: 8 GCSEs, 1 A-level, 1st level
coaching award
Cricketers particularly admired: Brian
Lara, Curtly Ambrose, Waqar Younis,
Sachin Tendulkar

Other sports played: 'Keen skier, also
played school and Sunday league football'
Other sports followed: Basketball (LA Lakers), football (Man Utd)
Injuries: Out for five months with a knee injury
Relaxations: 'Music; following and playing a wide range of sports'

HUNTER, I. D.   Durham

Name: Ian David Hunter
Role: Right-hand bat, right-arm
fast-medium bowler
Born: 11 September 1979, Durham City
Height: 6ft 2in **Weight:** 11st 9lbs
Nickname: Hunts, Sticks, Figo, Silvinho
County debut: 1999 (one-day),
2000 (first-class)
1st-Class 50s: 1
Strike rate: 69.50 (career 69.50)
Parents: Ken and Linda
Marital status: Single
Family links with cricket: Brother plays for
local village side

Education: Sacriston Junior School;
Fyndoune Community College, Sacriston;
New College, Durham
Qualifications: 9 GCSEs, 1 A-level (PE),
BTEC National Diploma in Sports Science,
Level I and II cricket coaching awards
Off-season: 'Relaxing/socialising; preparing for next season'
Overseas tours: Durham U21 to Sri Lanka 1996
Cricketers particularly admired: Allan Donald, Steve Waugh
Young players to look out for: Nicky Peng, 'Luis Daley, Jimmy Figo'
Other sports played: Football, golf
Other sports followed: Football (Newcastle United FC)
Relaxations: Socialising with friends; keeping fit, golf, football
Extras: Set a new Durham best analysis for the 2nd XI Championship with his 11-155 v
Lancashire 2nd XI 1999. Represented England U19 in 'Test' series v Australia U19
1999. Scored 63 as nightwatchman on Championship debut v Leicestershire at Riverside
2000
Opinions on cricket: 'Two divisions has made county cricket much more competitive.
The standard of pitches still has to improve; not enough Championship matches go the
distance.'
Best batting: 63 Durham v Leicestershire, Riverside 2000
Best bowling: 4-73 Durham v Yorkshire, Riverside 2000

2000 Season

	M	Inns	NO	Runs	HS	Avge	100s	50s	Ct	St	O	M	Runs	Wkts	Avge	Best	5wI	10wM
Test																		
All First	3	4	0	83	63	20.75	-	1	-	-	69.3	12	228	6	38.00	4-73	-	-
1-day Int																		
NatWest	1	1	0	1	1	1.00	-	-	-	-	4	0	18	0	-		-	-
B & H																		
1-day Lge	14	7	3	30	14 *	7.50	-	-	2	-	93.5	3	430	17	25.29	4-29	-	

Career Performances

	M	Inns	NO	Runs	HS	Avge	100s	50s	Ct	St	Balls	Runs	Wkts	Avge	Best	5wI	10wM
Test																	
All First	3	4	0	83	63	20.75	-	1	-	-	417	228	6	38.00	4-73	-	-
1-day Int																	
NatWest	1	1	0	1	1	1.00	-	-	-	-	24	18	0	-		-	-
B & H																	
1-day Lge	18	9	3	37	14 *	6.16	-	-	2	-	756	562	21	26.76	4-29	-	

HUSSAIN, N.   Essex

Name: Nasser Hussain
Role: Right-hand bat, county club captain
Born: 28 March 1968, Madras, India
Height: 6ft **Weight:** 12st 7lbs
Nickname: Nashwan
County debut: 1987
County cap: 1989
Benefit: 1999 (£271,500)
Test debut: 1989-90
Tests: 53
One-Day Internationals: 45
1000 runs in a season: 5
1st-Class 50s: 81
1st-Class 100s: 42
1st-Class 200s: 1
1st-Class catches: 308
One-Day 100s: 5
Place in batting averages: 263rd av. 11.06
(1999 7th av. 52.00)
Strike rate: (career 153.00)
Parents: Joe and Shireen
Wife and date of marriage: Karen, 24 September 1993

Family links with cricket: Father played zonal cricket in India. Played for Madras in Ranji Trophy 1966-67. Brother Mel played for Hampshire. Brother Abbas played for Essex 2nd XI

Education: Forest School, Snaresbrook; Durham University

Qualifications: 10 O-levels, 3 A-levels, BSc (Hons) in Natural Sciences, NCA cricket coaching award

Off-season: Touring Kenya, Pakistan and Sri Lanka with England

Overseas tours: England YC to Sri Lanka 1986-87, to Australia (Youth World Cup) 1987-88; England A to Pakistan and Sri Lanka 1990-91, to Bermuda and West Indies 1991-92, to Pakistan 1995-96 (captain); England to India (Nehru Cup) 1989-90, to West Indies 1989-90, to West Indies 1993-94, to Zimbabwe and New Zealand 1996-97, to West Indies 1997-98, to Australia 1998-99, to South Africa and Zimbabwe 1999-2000 (captain), to Kenya (ICC Knockout Trophy) 2000-01 (captain), to Pakistan and Sri Lanka 2000-01 (captain)

Overseas teams played for: Madras 1986-87; Petersham, Sydney 1992-93; Adelaide University 1990; Stellenbosch University, South Africa 1994-95; Primrose, Cape Town

Cricketers particularly admired: Mark Waugh, Graham Gooch, Sachin Tendulkar

Other sports played: Golf (10 handicap), football

Other sports followed: Football (Leeds United)

Relaxations: Listening to music. Listening to Mark Ilott. Watching television

Extras: Played for England Schools U15 for two years (one as captain). Became youngest player to play for Essex Schools U11 at the age of eight and U15 at the age of 12. At 15, was considered the best young leg-break bowler in the country. Cricket Writers' Club Young Cricketer of the Year, 1989. Set records for third (347* v Lancashire at Ilford 1992), fourth (314 v Surrey at The Oval 1991) and fifth (316 v Leicestershire at Leicester 1991) wicket partnerships for Essex (with Mark Waugh, Salim Malik and Mike Garnham respectively). Essex Player of the Year 1993. Appointed Essex's vice-captain 1996. Finished 2nd in the Whyte and Mackay batting ratings in 1995. Appointed England's vice-captain in 1996-97. Shared in record fourth-wicket partnership for England in Tests v Australia (288) with Graham Thorpe at Edgbaston 1997. Appointed Essex's captain for 1999. Represented England in the 1999 World Cup. Appointed England captain after 1999 World Cup. Topped England batting averages in the 1999-2000 Test series v South Africa with 370 runs at 61.66; during the series he became the first player to bat for 1000 minutes in Test cricket without being out. Handed over Essex team captaincy to Ronnie Irani at the start of the 2000 season but remains Essex club captain. Played for a World XI v an Asia XI at The Oval 2000. In 2000 led England to victory in the NatWest triangular one-day series, to a Test series win over Zimbabwe, and to a first Test series win over West Indies for 31 years

Best batting: 207 England v Australia, Edgbaston 1997

Best bowling: 1-38 Essex v Worcestershire, Kidderminster 1992

2000 Season

	M	Inns	NO	Runs	HS	Avge	100s	50s	Ct	St	O	M	Runs	Wkts	Avge	Best	5wI	10wM
Test	6	10	1	92	22	10.22	-	-	2	-								
All First	10	16	1	166	33	11.06	-	-	7	-								
1-day Int	3	3	1	46	34	23.00	-	-	2	-								
NatWest	1	1	0	8	8	8.00	-	-	-	-								
B & H	3	3	0	72	40	24.00	-	-	-	-								
1-day Lge	6	6	0	256	60	42.66	-	3	3	-								

Career Performances

	M	Inns	NO	Runs	HS	Avge	100s	50s	Ct	St	Balls	Runs	Wkts	Avge	Best	5wI	10wM
Test	53	94	9	3066	207	36.07	8	13	38	-	30	15	0	-	-	-	-
All First	270	435	43	16664	207	42.51	43	81	308	-	306	322	2	161.00	1-38	-	-
1-day Int	45	45	8	978	93	26.43	-	6	25	-							
NatWest	27	25	3	903	108	41.04	2	4	18	-							
B & H	50	45	8	1726	118	46.64	2	15	21	-							
1-day Lge	143	132	18	3664	114	32.14	1	25	63	-							

HUSSEY, M. E. K.   Northamptonshire

Name: Michael (<u>Mike</u>) Edward Killeen Hussey
Role: Left-hand bat, right-arm medium bowler
Born: 27 May 1975, Perth, Western Australia
Height: 6ft   **Weight:** 12st 7lbs
Nickname: Huss
County debut: No first-team appearance
1st-Class 50s: 22
1st-Class 100s: 12
1st-Class catches: 38
Strike rate: (career 75.33)
Parents: Helen and Ted
Marital status: Engaged to Amy
Family links with cricket: Brother Dave is in the Western Australia state squad
Education: Whitfords Catholic; Prendiville; Curtin
Career outside cricket: Teacher
Overseas tours: Australia U19 to India 1994; Australian Commonwealth Cricket Academy to Pakistan 1995; Australia A to Scotland and Ireland 1998
Overseas teams played for: Wanneroo, Western Australia (captain 1999-2000); Western Australia 1994-95 –

Cricketers particularly admired: Steve Waugh, Mark Taylor, Sachin Tendulkar, Dennis Lillee

Young players to look out for: Shaun Marsh

Other sports played: Golf, squash, tennis

Other sports followed: Australian Rules (West Coast Eagles), football (Man Utd)

Relaxations: Movies, beach

Extras: Attended the Australian Academy in 1995. Finished third in the Sheffield Shield Player of the Year award in his first full season 1995-96. Played league cricket in Scotland for Ferguslie CC in 1998. Sir Donald Bradman Young Cricketer of the Year 1998. Excalibur Award (Western Australia) 1998-2000. Scored maiden Mercantile Cup century (100*) v Victoria at Melbourne 1999-2000, sharing in a competition record sixth-wicket partnership of 173 with Brad Hogg. Carried his bat for 172* v South Australia in the Pura Milk Cup 1999-2000. Awarded ACB contract for 2000-01. Has joined Northamptonshire as overseas player for 2001

Best batting: 187 Western Australia v Tasmania, Perth 1998-99

Best bowling: 2-21 Western Australia v Queensland, Perth 1998-99

2000 Season (did not make any first-class or one-day appearances)

Career Performances

	M	Inns	NO	Runs	HS	Avge	100s	50s	Ct	St	Balls	Runs	Wkts	Avge	Best	5wI	10wM
Test																	
All First	61	110	7	4777	187	46.37	12	22	38	-	226	107	3	35.66	2-21	-	-
1-day Int																	
NatWest																	
B & H																	
1-day Lge																	

HUTCHISON, P. M.   Yorkshire

Name: Paul Michael Hutchison

Role: Left-hand bat, left-arm swing bowler

Born: 9 June 1977, Leeds

Height: 6ft 4in **Weight:** 12st 4lbs ('nearer 14 stone in April 2001, hopefully')

Nickname: Hutch, Big Boy!

County debut: 1996

County cap: 1998

50 wickets in a season: 1

1st-Class 5 w. in innings: 7

1st-Class 10 w. in match: 1

1st-Class catches: 9

Place in batting averages: 310th av. 0.50

Place in bowling averages: 64th av. 26.25 (1999 17th av. 20.23)

Strike rate: 48.56 (career 42.16)

Parents: David Hutchison and Rita Laycock

Marital status: Engaged to Emma

Family links with cricket: Brother Richard plays at Pudsey St Lawrence in the Bradford League

Education: Pudsey Greenside; Pudsey Crawshaw High; 'the Yorks changing room!!'

Qualifications: 8 GCSEs, GNVQ Leisure and Tourism, qualified cricket coach, basic IT ('thanks to PCA')

Career outside cricket: 'Yes – and probably soon, with my injury record!!'

Off-season: 'Playing for South Perth, then joining Yorks on pre-season in South Africa'

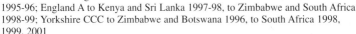

Overseas tours: England U19 to Zimbabwe 1995-96; England A to Kenya and Sri Lanka 1997-98, to Zimbabwe and South Africa 1998-99; Yorkshire CCC to Zimbabwe and Botswana 1996, to South Africa 1998, 1999, 2001

Overseas teams played for: South Perth CC, Perth 2000-01

Cricketers particularly admired: Matt Maynard, Neil Fairbrother, Craig White

Young players to look out for: Michael Lumb, Matthew Wood

Other sports played: Golf, football

Other sports followed: 'Most sports; anything on Sky Sports; any team from my area (Leeds/Bradford)'

Injuries: Out for two months with a bad back ('again'); for two months with a dislocated left shoulder

Relaxations: 'Going out with Big Sid and the lads. Couch, TV controller and Sky Digital! Gardening!'

Extras: Represented England at U17, U18 and U19 levels. Played for Pudsey St Lawrence in the Bradford League. Had a place at the Yorkshire Academy. Took 7 for 50 on county debut against Hampshire at Portsmouth, only bettered by Wilfred Rhodes 99 years previously. Took 7 for 38 on first first-class appearance of 1997, against Pakistan A. Voted Wombwell Cricket Lovers' Young Player of the Year for 1997. PCA representative for Yorkshire CCC

Opinions on cricket: 'Great game to be involved with. Two divisions is good; would probably change it to two up, two down in National League. Floodlit cricket is a plus. Off-the-field problems still a worry.'

Best batting: 30 Yorkshire v Essex, Scarborough 1998

Best bowling: 7-31 Yorkshire v Sussex, Hove 1998

2000 Season

	M	Inns	NO	Runs	HS	Avge	100s	50s	Ct	St	O	M	Runs	Wkts	Avge	Best	5wI	10wM
Test																		
All First	7	8	2	3	3 *	0.50	-	-	3	-	129.3	32	420	16	26.25	3-62	-	-
1-day Int																		
NatWest																		
B & H																		
1-day Lge	5	2	2	1	1 *	-	-	-	1	-	31.3	4	141	5	28.20	3-27	-	

Career Performances

	M	Inns	NO	Runs	HS	Avge	100s	50s	Ct	St	Balls	Runs	Wkts	Avge	Best	5wI	10wM
Test																	
All First	41	42	22	178	30	8.90	-	-	9	-	6240	3338	148	22.55	7-31	7	1
1-day Int																	
NatWest	3	1	1	4	4 *	-	-	-	-	-	132	62	5	12.40	3-18	-	
B & H	6	2	2	6	4 *	-	-	-	-	-	191	112	10	11.20	3-14	-	
1-day Lge	20	8	5	8	2 *	2.66	-	-	2	-	782	568	21	27.04	4-34	-	

HUTTON, B. L.   Middlesex

Name: <u>Benjamin</u> Leonard Hutton
Role: Left-hand bat, right-arm
medium bowler
Born: 29 January 1977,
Johannesburg, South Africa
Height: 6ft 2in **Weight:** 12st
Nickname: Gibbs
County debut: 1999
1st-Class 50s: 3
1st-Class catches: 13
Place in batting averages: 235th av. 14.46
(1999 180th av. 22.06)
Strike rate: 79.60 (career 97.75)
Parents: Richard and Charmaine
Marital status: Single
Family links with cricket: 'Both my father
and grandfather were very keen cricketers!!'
Education: Holmewood House Prep School;
Radley College; Durham University
Qualifications: 10 GCSEs, 3 A-levels, BA (Hons) Social Sciences, NCA
coaching award
Career outside cricket: 'None as yet'

Off-season: 'Spending winter 2000-01 playing for Gosnells, Perth; finding part-time work to tide me over'

Overseas tours: Durham University to Zimbabwe 1997-98; Middlesex to South Africa 2000

Overseas teams played for: Wanderers CC, Johannesburg 1995-96; Pirates CC, Johannesburg 1995-96; Gosnells, Perth 2000-01

Cricketers particularly admired: 'Both father [Richard Hutton] and grandfather [Sir Leonard Hutton]', Justin Langer, Mark Ramprakash, Michael Atherton

Young players to look out for: Michael Vaughan, Michael Powell (Glamorgan), Marcus Trescothick, Ed Joyce

Other sports played: Golf (12 handicap), rackets

Other sports followed: Football, 'all sports'

Injuries: 'None of any severity'

Relaxations: 'Reading, listening to music, surfing the web'

Extras: BUSA Halifax medal 1997. Palatinate at Durham University. Opened for Middlesex v Essex at Southend 1999 with Andrew Strauss, his former opening partner at Radley. Played in Durham University's BUSA Championship winning side 1999

Opinions on cricket: 'The two divisional Championship has been a huge success. Players feel that there is more to play for. Promotion and relegation battles will provide more meaningful matches where sides have to risk more to win games, which inevitably will lead to improved standards across the board.'

Best batting: 59 Middlesex v Nottinghamshire, Southgate 1999

Best bowling: 2-9 Middlesex v Glamorgan, Southgate 2000

2000 Season

	M	Inns	NO	Runs	HS	Avge	100s	50s	Ct	St	O	M	Runs	Wkts	Avge	Best	5wI	10wM
Test																		
All First	10	15	2	188	55	14.46	-	1	8	-	66.2	17	217	5	43.40	2-9	-	-
1-day Int																		
NatWest																		
B & H																		
1-day Lge	7	4	1	97	49	32.33	-	-	1	-	25	2	134	5	26.80	4-32	-	

Career Performances

	M	Inns	NO	Runs	HS	Avge	100s	50s	Ct	St	Balls	Runs	Wkts	Avge	Best	5wI	10wM
Test																	
All First	19	31	2	529	59	18.24	-	3	13	-	782	485	8	60.62	2-9	-	-
1-day Int																	
NatWest																	
B & H	4	2	0	4	4	2.00	-	-	1	-	127	101	4	25.25	2-43	-	
1-day Lge	15	10	2	172	49	21.50	-	-	8	-	186	196	6	32.66	4-32	-	

HYAM, B. J.   Essex

Name: <u>Barry</u> James Hyam
Role: Right-hand bat, wicket-keeper
Born: 9 September 1975, Romford, Essex
Height: 5ft 11in **Weight:** 11st 7lbs
Nickname: Bazza
County debut: 1993
County cap: 1999
50 dismissals in a season: 1
1st-Class 50s: 2
1st-Class catches: 147
1st-Class stumpings: 10
Place in batting averages: 268th av. 10.66
(1999 170th av. 23.36)
Parents: Peter and Gloria
Wife and date of marriage: Villene,
30 September 2000
Family links with cricket: 'Mum and Dad
are keen fans; brother Matthew is captain of
Harold Wood CC; brother Richard plays for
Harold Wood U17'

Education: Marshalls Park; Havering Sixth Form College; Westminster College
Qualifications: 9 GCSEs, 1 A-level, NCA coaching award
Career outside cricket: Coaching
Off-season: 'Coaching at Essex CCC Cricket School; drawing; trying to sell my
limited edition prints (of Nasser Hussain and Ronnie Irani)'
Overseas tours: MCC to Bangladesh 1999-2000
Cricketers particularly admired: Jack Russell, Nasser Hussain
Young players to look out for: Justin Bishop, Tim Phillips
Other sports played: Golf, football
Other sports followed: Football (West Ham United)
Relaxations: Drawing
Extras: Made first-class debut on his 18th birthday. Made the equal highest number of
first-class wicket-keeping dismissals in the 2000 season (55 with Steve Rhodes)
Opinions on cricket: 'I think the two divisions worked well. There was something on
all the games, right down to the last one in the season.'
Best batting: 53 Essex v Gloucestershire, Bristol 2000

2000 Season

	M	Inns	NO	Runs	HS	Avge	100s	50s	Ct	St	O	M	Runs	Wkts	Avge	Best	5wl	10wM
Test														-				
All First	15	24	0	256	53	10.66	-	1	49	6								
1-day Int																		
NatWest	2	2	0	5	4	2.50	-	-	2	-								
B & H	3	3	0	42	24	14.00	-	-	1	-								
1-day Lge	9	6	1	27	16 *	5.40	-	-	6	3								

Career Performances

	M	Inns	NO	Runs	HS	Avge	100s	50s	Ct	St	Balls	Runs	Wkts	Avge	Best	5wl	10wM
Test																	
All First	53	85	9	1230	53	16.18	-	2	147	10	12	8	0	-	-	-	-
1-day Int																	
NatWest	3	2	0	5	4	2.50	-	-	2	-							
B & H	3	3	0	42	24	14.00	-	-	1	-							
1-day Lge	30	20	4	177	37	11.06	-	-	26	4							

ILLINGWORTH, R. K.   Derbyshire

Name: <u>Richard</u> Keith Illingworth
Role: Right-hand bat, slow left-arm bowler
Born: 23 August 1963, Bradford
Height: 6ft **Weight:** 13st 7lbs
Nickname: Lucy, Harry
County debut: 1982 (Worcestershire)
County cap: 1986 (Worcestershire)
Benefit: 1997 (Worcestershire, £271,275)
Test debut: 1991
Tests: 9
One-Day Internationals: 25
50 wickets in a season: 5
1st-Class 50s: 20
1st-Class 100s: 4
1st-Class 5 w. in innings: 27
1st-Class 10 w. in match: 6
1st-Class catches: 161
One-Day 5 w. in innings: 2
Place in batting averages: 227th av. 15.40 (1999 184th av. 21.76)
Place in bowling averages: 119th av. 37.15 (1999 145th av. 51.13)
Strike rate: 102.38 (career 79.30)
Parents: Keith and Margaret

Wife and date of marriage: Anne, 20 September 1985
Children: Miles, 28 August 1987; Thomas, 20 April 1989
Family links with cricket: Father played Bradford League cricket
Education: Wrose Brow Middle; Salts Grammar School ('same school as the late Jim Laker')
Qualifications: 6 O-levels, advanced coaching award
Career outside cricket: 'None as yet'
Overseas tours: England A to Zimbabwe and Kenya 1989-90, to Pakistan and Sri Lanka 1990-91; England to New Zealand and Australia (World Cup) 1991-92, to South Africa 1995-96, to India and Pakistan (World Cup) 1995-96
Overseas teams played for: Natal 1988-89
Cricketers particularly admired: Ian Botham, Wasim Akram
Other sports played: Golf
Other sports followed: Football (Leeds United), rugby league (Bradford Bulls), rugby union (Worcester)
Injuries: Out for three and a half weeks with a pulled thigh muscle
Relaxations: 'Playing golf and watching Miles and Thomas in their sporting activities'
Extras: Took 11 for 108 on South African first-class debut for Natal B v Boland 1988. In 1991, v West Indies, became 11th person in history to take a wicket with first ball in Test cricket. Took a hat-trick in Sunday League v Sussex in 1993, the first Worcestershire player to take hat-trick in one-day cricket. Won 1993 Dick Lygon award for contribution to Worcestershire CCC. Has made three centuries as a nightwatchman. Released by Worcestershire at the end of the 2000 season and has joined Derbyshire for 2001
Opinions on cricket: 'I've been very fortunate to play this game for 19 years and enjoyed most of it. I hope everyone gets the same enjoyment as myself.'
Best batting: 120* Worcestershire v Warwickshire, Worcester 1987
Best bowling: 7-50 Worcestershire v Oxford University, The Parks 1985

2000 Season

	M	Inns	NO	Runs	HS	Avge	100s	50s	Ct	St	O	M	Runs	Wkts	Avge	Best	5wl	10wM
Test																		
All First	10	12	2	154	44*	15.40	-	-	5	-	221.5	72	483	13	37.15	3-34	-	-
1-day Int																		
NatWest	1	1	1	25	25*	-	-	-	1	-	10	0	43	3	14.33	3-43	-	
B & H	3	0	0	0	0	-	-	-	-	-	9.5	0	39	1	39.00	1-9	-	
1-day Lge	16	14	1	102	30	7.84	-	-	3	-	91.5	3	388	14	27.71	3-26	-	

Career Performances

	M	Inns	NO	Runs	HS	Avge	100s	50s	Ct	St	Balls	Runs	Wkts	Avge	Best	5wI	10wM
Test	9	14	7	128	28	18.28	-	-	5	-	1485	615	19	32.36	4-96	-	-
All First	371	427	121	6902	120 *	22.55	4	20	161	-	65108	25897	821	31.54	7-50	27	6
1-day Int	25	11	5	68	14	11.33	-	-	8	-	1501	1059	30	35.30	3-33	-	
NatWest	37	20	9	187	29 *	17.00	-	-	11	-	2179	1157	32	36.15	4-20	-	
B & H	61	29	16	260	36 *	20.00	-	-	13	-	2974	1709	55	31.07	4-27	-	
1-day Lge	227	108	49	735	31	12.45	-	-	52	-	8655	6204	264	23.50	5-24	2	

ILOTT, M. C. Essex

Name: <u>Mark</u> Christopher Ilott
Role: Left-hand bat, left-arm
fast-medium bowler
Born: 27 August 1970, Watford
Height: 6ft 1in **Weight:** 13st 9lbs
Nickname: Ramble, Chook
County debut: 1988
County cap: 1993
Test debut: 1993
Tests: 5
50 wickets in a season: 5
1st-Class 50s: 4
1st-Class 5 w. in innings: 26
1st-Class 10 w. in match: 3
1st-Class catches: 44
One-Day 5 w. in innings: 1
Place in batting averages: 243rd av. 13.22
(1999 222nd av. 18.12)
Place in bowling averages: 75th av. 27.84 (1999 50th av. 23.68)
Strike rate: 65.38 (career 55.04)
Parents: John and Glenys
Wife and date of marriage: Sandra Jane, 16 October 1994
Children: James Christopher Mark, 6 October 1996; Madeleine-Rose, 3 March 1999
Family links with cricket: 'Dad now umpires Minor Counties and continues to test me
about my knowledge of the rules – sorry, Dad – laws. Brother plays in Hertfordshire
premier league and has played for Hertfordshire. Mum's still watching'
Education: Kingsway Junior; Francis Combe Secondary Modern
Qualifications: 8 O-levels, 2 A-levels, first two coaching awards, diploma in Fitness
and Nutrition
Career outside cricket: 'Have my own hospitality business and am
consultant/publisher for rivals.net'

Off-season: 'Getting super fit; time with family; working on my business'
Overseas tours: England A to Sri Lanka 1990-91, to Australia 1992-93, to South Africa 1993-94, to India 1994-95; England to South Africa 1995-96
Overseas teams played for: East Torrens District, Adelaide 1989-91
Cricketers particularly admired: Malcolm Marshall, Graham Gooch, John Lever, Nasser Hussain
Young players to look out for: Andrew McGarry, Justin Bishop, Mark Pettini
Other sports played: Golf ('badly')
Other sports followed: Football (Liverpool and Watford)
Injuries: Out for four weeks with recurring hamstring injury
Relaxations: Guitar, children, gardening and going to the gym
Extras: Took his 450th wicket for Essex (Nick Knight) v Warwickshire at Chelmsford 1999
Opinions on cricket: 'Two divisional cricket has proved a success. Let's now insist the pitches are of a quality that is also conducive to good first-class cricket.'
Best batting: 60 England A v Warwickshire, Edgbaston 1995
Best bowling: 9-19 Essex v Northamptonshire, Luton 1995

2000 Season

	M	Inns	NO	Runs	HS	Avge	100s	50s	Ct	St	O	M	Runs	Wkts	Avge	Best	5wI	10wM
Test																		
All First	10	13	4	119	25	13.22	-	-	4	-	283.2	85	724	26	27.84	3-37	-	-
1-day Int																		
NatWest	2	2	1	6	6 *	6.00	-	-	1	-	18	2	65	4	16.25	3-20	-	
B & H	3	3	3	26	26 *	-	-	-	1	-	28	2	160	4	40.00	2-53	-	
1-day Lge	7	3	2	12	10	12.00	-	-	2	-	46	5	197	11	17.90	3-13	-	

Career Performances

	M	Inns	NO	Runs	HS	Avge	100s	50s	Ct	St	Balls	Runs	Wkts	Avge	Best	5wI	10wM
Test	5	6	2	28	15	7.00	-	-	-	-	1042	542	12	45.16	3-48	-	-
All First	176	228	48	2599	60	14.43	-	4	44	-	32474	15977	590	27.07	9-19	26	3
1-day Int																	
NatWest	23	13	6	125	54 *	17.85	-	1	6	-	1440	876	25	35.04	3-20	-	
B & H	36	14	4	107	26 *	10.70	-	-	4	-	1944	1205	56	21.51	5-21	1	
1-day Lge	118	72	25	517	56 *	11.00	-	1	19	-	4958	3703	144	25.71	4-15	-	

INGLIS, J. W.

Name: <u>John</u> William Inglis
Role: Right-hand bat
Born: 19 October 1979, Ripon,
North Yorkshire
Height: 6ft 2in **Weight:** 12st 7lbs
Nickname: Jingles
County debut: 2000
Parents: William and June
Marital status: Single
Family links with cricket: 'Father played
local amateur cricket, Markington/Ripon'
Education: St Wilfrid's RC, Ripon; Holy
Trinity Juniors, Ripon; Ripon Grammar
School; St Aidan's Sixth Form, Harrogate
Qualifications: 10 GCSEs
Off-season: 'Receiving coaching, working
hard at training, and improving my game for
the most important season of my life'

Overseas tours: Yorkshire to Perth 2000
Overseas teams played for: Marist Newman Old Boys, Perth 1997-98
Cricketers particularly admired: Hasan Raza
Young players to look out for: John Sadler, Chris Taylor, Michael Lumb
Other sports played: Rugby (captain of Ripon GS; captain of Harrogate U13)
Other sports followed: Rugby league (Hull FC Sharks)
Relaxations: Watching rugby league, relaxing with friends, playing on the computer
Extras: Wombwell Neil Lloyd Cricket Association winner (Bunbury Festival) 1995.
Daily Telegraph Batsman of the Year 1995. Yorkshire League Batsman Senior and
Junior winner (youngest ever) 1997. Played for England U15, U17, U18 and U19.
Played for England U19 v Pakistan U19 1998 and in first two 'One-Day
Internationals' v Australia U19 1999. Released by Yorkshire at the end of the 2000
season
Opinions on cricket: 'Annoyed at the lack of coaching and encouragement for the
younger players – they are the future of the game. Coaches help the senior players, but
get on and to grips with the juniors and young pros.'
Best batting: 2 Yorkshire v West Indians, Headingley 2000

2000 Season

	M	Inns	NO	Runs	HS	Avge	100s	50s	Ct	St	O	M	Runs	Wkts	Avge	Best	5wl	10wM
Test																		
All First	1	2	0	4	2	2.00	-	-	-	-								
1-day Int																		
NatWest																		
B & H																		
1-day Lge																		

Career Performances

	M	Inns	NO	Runs	HS	Avge	100s	50s	Ct	St	Balls	Runs	Wkts	Avge	Best	5wl	10wM
Test																	
All First	1	2	0	4	2	2.00	-	-	-	-							
1-day Int																	
NatWest																	
B & H																	
1-day Lge																	

INNES, K. J.   Northamptonshire

Name: <u>Kevin</u> John Innes
Role: Right-hand bat, right-arm medium bowler
Born: 24 September 1975, Wellingborough
Height: 5ft 10in **Weight:** 11st 5lbs
Nickname: KJ, Squirrel, Ernie
County debut: 1994
1st-Class 50s: 1
1st-Class catches: 9
Place in batting averages: (1999 128th av. 27.12)
Place in bowling averages: (1999 80th av. 28.60)
Strike rate: 22.16 (career 51.34)
Parents: Peter and Jane
Marital status: Engaged to Caroline Pinnock
Education: Boothville Middle School; Weston Favell Upper School, Northampton
Qualifications: 6 GCSEs, 4 O-levels, NCA coaching awards Levels 1 and 2
Off-season: 'Training to be an accountant, coaching age groups in Northampton, and getting fit for the coming season'
Overseas tours: England U18 to South Africa 1992-93, to Denmark 1993; England U19 to Sri Lanka 1993-94

Overseas teams played for: Karori, New Zealand 1995-97
Cricketers particularly admired: Glenn McGrath, Steve Waugh
Young players to look out for: Mark Powell
Other sports played: Golf, snooker, fishing
Injuries: Out for six to seven weeks with a stress fracture of the left foot
Relaxations: 'Spending time with my girlfriend; sleeping and eating out; music, reading books/magazines'
Extras: Played for England U19 in home series against India in 1994. Won the MCC Lord's Taverners Award U13 and U15. Became youngest player to play for Northants 2nd XI, aged 14 years 9 months. 2nd XI Championship Player of the Year 1998
Opinions on cricket: 'There are too many games/fixtures throughout the season, and players are therefore not able to get in as much quality practice. Play should also start at 10.30 all through the year, enabling the teams to have an hour for lunch and also for tea.'
Best batting: 63 Northamptonshire v Lancashire, Northampton 1996
Best bowling: 4-61 Northamptonshire v Lancashire, Northampton 1996

2000 Season

	M	Inns	NO	Runs	HS	Avge	100s	50s	Ct	St	O	M	Runs	Wkts	Avge	Best	5wI	10wM
Test																		
All First	2	4	1	66	32 *	22.00	-	-	-	-	22.1	4	82	6	13.66	3-23	-	-
1-day Int																		
NatWest	1	0	0	0	0	-	-	-	1	-								
B & H	2	1	0	19	19	19.00	-	-	-	-	14	0	101	1	101.00	1-38	-	
1-day Lge	12	9	2	181	55	25.85	-	1	2	-	73	5	327	16	20.43	4-36	-	

Career Performances

	M	Inns	NO	Runs	HS	Avge	100s	50s	Ct	St	Balls	Runs	Wkts	Avge	Best	5wI	10wM
Test																	
All First	17	25	5	436	63	21.80	-	1	9	-	1489	786	29	27.10	4-61	-	-
1-day Int																	
NatWest	5	3	2	33	25	33.00	-	-	2	-	123	114	5	22.80	3-26	-	
B & H	4	2	0	20	19	10.00	-	-	-	-	144	157	2	78.50	1-25	-	
1-day Lge	34	22	8	319	55	22.78	-	1	10	-	1008	922	33	27.93	4-36	-	

IRANI, R. C. Essex

Name: <u>Ronald</u> Charles Irani
Role: Right-hand bat, right-arm
medium bowler, county team captain
Born: 26 October 1971, Leigh, Lancashire
Height: 6ft 4in **Weight:** 13st 10lbs
Nickname: Reggie, Ledge
County debut: 1990 (Lancashire),
1994 (Essex)
County cap: 1994 (Essex)
Test debut: 1996
Tests: 3
One-Day Internationals: 10
1000 runs in a season: 5
50 wickets in a season: 1
1st-Class 50s: 43
1st-Class 100s: 14
1st-Class 5 w. in innings: 5
1st-Class catches: 60
One-Day 100s: 2
One-Day 5 w. in innings: 1
Place in batting averages: 11th av. 54.36 (1999 42nd av. 38.65)
Place in bowling averages: 50th av. 24.00 (1999 25th av. 21.25)
Strike rate: 58.21 (career 60.56)
Parents: Jimmy and Anne
Marital status: Single
Family links with cricket: 'Father played local league cricket in Bolton for 30 years;
mother did teas for many years!'
Education: Church Road Primary School; Smithills Comprehensive School
Qualifications: 9 GCSEs
Overseas tours: England YC to Australia 1989-90; England A to Pakistan 1995-96, to
Bangladesh and New Zealand 1999-2000; England to Zimbabwe and New Zealand
1996-97
Overseas teams played for: Technicol Natal, Durban 1992-93; Eden-Roskill,
Auckland 1993-94
Cricketers particularly admired: Mark Waugh, Javed Miandad, Wasim Akram, John
Crawley, Graham Gooch
Other sports followed: 'Most sports especially football'
Relaxations: Sleeping and watching football
Extras: Played for England U19 in home series v Australia 1991, scoring a century
and three 50s in six innings and being named Bull Man of the Series. Appointed vice-
captain of Essex in 1999. Achieved double of 1000 first-class runs and 50 first-class

wickets in 1999. Took over team captaincy of Essex at the start of the 2000 season, Nasser Hussain remaining as club captain. His career best innings of 168* v Glamorgan at Cardiff 2000 lasted nine hours and 20 minutes, during which time he received 479 balls. Scored 1196 first-class runs and took 42 first-class wickets in 2000. Has opened website: www.ronnieirani.com

Best batting: 168* Essex v Glamorgan, Cardiff 2000
Best bowling: 5-19 England A v Board XI, Karachi 1995-96

2000 Season

	M	Inns	NO	Runs	HS	Avge	100s	50s	Ct	St	O	M	Runs	Wkts	Avge	Best	5wI	10wM
Test																		
All First	17	29	7	1196	168 *	54.36	1	9	2	-	407.3	120	1008	42	24.00	5-79	1	-
1-day Int																		
NatWest	2	2	0	55	45	27.50	-	-	1	-	16	3	56	4	14.00	3-15	-	
B & H	3	3	0	93	50	31.00	-	1	-	-	24	4	89	3	29.66	2-23	-	
1-day Lge	15	15	1	329	52	23.50	-	1	4	-	106	18	354	14	25.28	3-10	-	

Career Performances

	M	Inns	NO	Runs	HS	Avge	100s	50s	Ct	St	Balls	Runs	Wkts	Avge	Best	5wI	10wM
Test	3	5	0	86	41	17.20	-	-	2	-	192	112	3	37.33	1-22	-	-
All First	144	237	30	7682	168 *	37.11	14	43	60	-	16293	8131	269	30.22	5-19	5	-
1-day Int	10	10	2	78	45 *	9.75	-	-	2	-	329	246	4	61.50	1-23	-	
NatWest	19	17	2	609	124	40.60	1	5	5	-	1142	750	27	27.77	4-41	-	
B & H	26	20	2	698	82 *	38.77	-	4	3	-	1224	925	32	28.90	4-30	-	
1-day Lge	113	107	15	2386	101 *	25.93	1	13	25	-	3931	2980	128	23.28	5-33	1	

43. Who captained England to series victories in 1977 and 1978-79?

JAMES, S. P. Glamorgan

Name: <u>Stephen</u> Peter James
Role: Right-hand opening bat, county
captain
Born: 7 September 1967, Lydney
Height: 6ft **Weight:** 13st
Nickname: Sid, Jamo
County debut: 1985
County cap: 1992
Test debut: 1998
Tests: 2
1000 runs in a season: 8
1st-Class 50s: 51
1st-Class 100s: 37
1st-Class 200s: 4
1st-Class 300s: 1
1st-Class catches: 160
One-Day 100s: 7

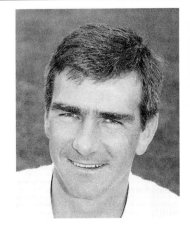

Place in batting averages: 35th av. 41.15
(1999 24th av. 42.37)
Parents: Peter and Margaret
Wife and date of marriage: Jane Louise, 26 September 1997
Children: Bethan Amy, 28 August 1998 ('during Test match!')
Family links with cricket: Father played for Gloucestershire 2nd XI. Distant relative
of Dominic Ostler
Education: Monmouth School; University College, Swansea; Cambridge University
Qualifications: BA (Hons) Wales – Classics; BA (Hons) Cantab – Land Economy
Off-season: 'Organising benefit; journalism – rugby reports for *Sunday Telegraph*;
coaching'
Overseas tours: Welsh Schools to Barbados 1984; Monmouth Schools to Sri Lanka
1985; Combined Universities to Barbados 1989; Glamorgan to Trinidad 1989-90, to
Zimbabwe 1990-91, to Cape Town 1993-94, to Pretoria 1995-96; England A to Kenya
and Sri Lanka 1997-98 (vice-captain)
Overseas teams played for: Bionics, Zimbabwe 1990-92; Universals Sports Club,
Zimbabwe 1992-96
Cricketers particularly admired: Michael Atherton, Graham Burgess
Young players to look out for: Ian Thomas, James Foster
Other sports played/followed: Rugby union (Cardiff RFC and Lydney RFC; 'played
for Lydney, Gloucestershire and Cambridge University and was on bench for Varsity
Match'), football (West Ham United)
Relaxations: Reading, *Telegraph* crosswords, videos, weight-training
Extras: Scored maiden century in only second first-class game. In 1995 broke

Matthew Maynard's club record for number of one-day runs in a season with 1263; in same season, also broke Hugh Morris's club record for number of Sunday League runs in a season with 815. First player to reach 1000 runs in 1997 and was voted the Cricketer of the Year by both the Wombwell Cricket Lovers' Society and the PCA. Appointed vice-captain of Glamorgan in 1999. Set record for highest post-war score by Glamorgan batsman, with 259* v Notts at Colwyn Bay 1999 (his fifth successive century v Notts), beating Matthew Maynard's 243 in 1991. Set record for highest individual score ever by a Glamorgan batsman, with 309* v Sussex at Colwyn Bay in 2000, setting in the process a new record first-wicket partnership for Glamorgan of 374 with Matthew Elliott (177); during his innings he also became the first Glamorgan batsman to record five scores of 200-plus. Appointed captain of Glamorgan for 2001. Granted a benefit for 2001

Opinions on cricket: 'The pitches this year have been dreadful.'

Best batting: 309* Glamorgan v Sussex, Colwyn Bay 2000

2000 Season

	M	Inns	NO	Runs	HS	Avge	100s	50s	Ct	St	O	M	Runs	Wkts	Avge	Best	5wI	10wM
Test										-								
All First	17	28	2	1070	309 *	41.15	3	2	5	-								
1-day Int																		
NatWest	3	3	1	56	27	28.00	-	-	3	-								
B & H	6	6	1	94	34	18.80	-	-	2	-								
1-day Lge	16	15	4	439	88 *	39.90	-	5	5	-								

Career Performances

	M	Inns	NO	Runs	HS	Avge	100s	50s	Ct	St	Balls	Runs	Wkts	Avge	Best	5wI	10wM
Test	2	4	0	71	36	17.75	-	-	-	-							
All First	221	385	29	14197	309 *	39.87	42	51	160	-	2	3	0	-		-	-	-
1-day Int																	
NatWest	27	26	3	1051	123	45.69	3	6	8	-							
B & H	39	39	3	1212	135	33.66	2	9	12	-							
1-day Lge	131	127	16	3777	107	34.02	2	27	31	-							

JARVIS, P. W.   Somerset

Name: <u>Paul</u> William Jarvis
Role: Right-hand bat, right-arm
fast-medium bowler
Born: 29 June 1965, Redcar, North Yorkshire
Height: 5ft 11in   **Weight:** 12st 7lbs
Nickname: Gnash, Jarv, Krusty
County debut: 1981 (Yorkshire),
1994 (Sussex), 1999 (Somerset)
County cap: 1986 (Yorkshire), 1994
(Sussex)
Test debut: 1987-88
Tests: 9
One-Day Internationals: 16
50 wickets in a season: 4
1st-Class 50s: 10
1st-Class 5 w. in innings: 22
1st-Class 10 w. in match: 3
1st-Class catches: 66
One-Day 5 w. in innings: 6

Place in batting averages: (1999 276th av. 9.12)
Place in bowling averages: (1999 107th av. 32.57)
Strike rate: 32.14 (career 54.31)
Parents: Malcolm and Marjorie
Marital status: Divorced
Children: Alexander Michael, 13 June 1989; Isabella Grace, 21 March 1993
Family links with cricket: Father still plays league cricket for Sudbrooke CC in
Gwent. Brother plays in Yorkshire (Selby Londesborough)
Education: Bydales Comprehensive School, Marske, Cleveland; 'studying for Sports
Science degree'
Qualifications: 4 O-levels, advanced cricket coach
Overseas tours: Yorkshire to St Lucia and Barbados 1987, to South Africa 1991;
England to India and Pakistan (World Cup) and Pakistan 1987-88, to Australia and
New Zealand 1987-88, to India and Sri Lanka 1992-93; unofficial England XI to
South Africa 1989-90
Overseas teams played for: Mosman Middle Harbour, Sydney 1984-85; Avendale,
Cape Town 1985-86; Manly-Warringah, Sydney 1987; Onslow, Wellington 1994-95
Cricketers particularly admired: Ian Botham, Malcolm Marshall
Young players to look out for: Matt Bulbeck
Other sports followed: Football
Relaxations: 'Walking my dogs, eating out, drinking real ale and good wine'
Extras: In 1981 became youngest player ever to play for Yorkshire in County

Championship (16 years, 2 months, 13 days). Became youngest player to take hat-trick in Sunday League, in 1982, and Championship, in 1985. Played for England YC v West Indies 1982 and Australia 1983. Banned from Test cricket for joining 1989-90 tour of South Africa; suspension remitted in 1992. Released by Sussex at end of 1998 season and joined Somerset for 1999. Retired at the end of the 2000 season

Best batting: 80 Yorkshire v Northamptonshire, Scarborough 1992
Best bowling: 7-55 Yorkshire v Surrey, Headingley 1986

2000 Season

	M	Inns	NO	Runs	HS	Avge	100s	50s	Ct	St	O	M	Runs	Wkts	Avge	Best	5wI	10wM
Test																		
All First	2	1	0	1	1	1.00	-	-	2	-	37.3	7	141	7	20.14	4-21	-	-
1-day Int																		
NatWest	1	1	1	2	2 *	-	-	-	-	-	9	1	43	2	21.50	2-43	-	
B & H	3	1	0	1	1	1.00	-	-	-	-	8	0	42	2	21.00	1-21	-	
1-day Lge	11	7	1	33	18	5.50	-	-	1	-	88.2	2	475	14	33.92	3-23	-	

Career Performances

	M	Inns	NO	Runs	HS	Avge	100s	50s	Ct	St	Balls	Runs	Wkts	Avge	Best	5wI	10wM
Test	9	15	2	132	29 *	10.15	-	-	2	-	1912	965	21	45.95	4-107	-	-
All First	215	268	67	3373	80	16.78	-	10	66	-	35525	18914	654	28.92	7-55	22	3
1-day Int	16	8	2	31	16 *	5.16	-	-	1	-	879	672	24	28.00	5-35	1	
NatWest	28	16	5	177	34 *	16.09	-	-	7	-	1706	1206	36	33.50	5-55	1	
B & H	50	27	9	353	63	19.61	-	1	4	-	2750	1709	78	21.91	4-34	-	
1-day Lge	163	96	32	693	43	10.82	-	-	35	-	6934	5349	231	23.15	6-27	4	

44. Which 38-year-old leg-spinner took 5-68 in England's second innings in Australia's victory at Lord's in 1985?

JEFFERSON, W. I.   Essex

Name: William (<u>Will</u>) Ingleby Jefferson
Role: Right-hand bat, right-arm
medium bowler
Born: 25 October 1979, Derby
Height: 6ft 9½in **Weight:** 14st 10lbs
Nickname: Jeffers, Jeffo, Ingles
County debut: 2000
1st-Class catches: 1
Parents: Richard and Pauline
Marital status: Single
Family links with cricket: Grandfather
Jefferson played for the Army and Combined
Services in the 1920s. Father, R. I. Jefferson,
played for Cambridge University 1961 and
Surrey 1961-66

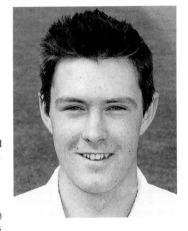

Education: Beeston Hall School, Norfolk;
Oundle School, Northants; Durham
University (reading Sport in the Community)
Qualifications: 9 GCSEs, 3 A-levels, Levels
1 and 2 cricket coaching awards
Career outside cricket: Student
Off-season: At Durham University
Overseas tours: Oundle School to South Africa 1995
Overseas teams played for: Young People's Club, Paarl, South Africa 1998-99
Cricketers particularly admired: Shaun Pollock, Jacques Kallis, Graeme Hick,
Stuart Law, Ricky Ponting, Nasser Hussain
Young players to look out for: Tim Phillips, Justin Ontong (South African)
Other sports played: Golf (12 handicap), tennis, squash, swimming
Other sports followed: Rugby union
Injuries: Out for three weeks with a lower back injury ('prevented me from bowling
all season')
Relaxations: Listening to music, reading cricket biographies, playing cards, watching
sport on television
Extras: Holmwoods School Cricketer of the Year 1998. Represented British
Universities 2000
Opinions on cricket: 'Levels of fitness have to keep improving if English cricket is
going to compete with the Australians and South Africans. We must use new
technologies in any ways we can to help assist improvements, especially in coaching.
Still far too much cricket when set against the miles that have to be travelled.'
Best batting: 41 British Universities v Zimbabweans, Fenner's 2000

2000 Season

	M	Inns	NO	Runs	HS	Avge	100s	50s	Ct	St	O	M	Runs	Wkts	Avge	Best	5wI	10wM
Test																		
All First	2	3	0	46	41	15.33	-	-	1	-								
1-day Int																		
NatWest																		
B & H																			
1-day Lge	3	3	0	117	65	39.00	-	2	1	-								

Career Performances

	M	Inns	NO	Runs	HS	Avge	100s	50s	Ct	St	Balls	Runs	Wkts	Avge	Best	5wI	10wM
Test																	
All First	2	3	0	46	41	15.33	-	-	1	-							
1-day Int																	
NatWest																	
B & H																	
1-day Lge	3	3	0	117	65	39.00	-	2	1	-							

JOHNSON, N. C. Hampshire

Name: Neil Clarkson Johnson
Role: Left-hand bat, right-arm fast-medium bowler
Born: 24 January 1970, Harare, Zimbabwe
County debut: 1997 (Leicestershire)
County cap: 1997 (Leicestershire)
Test debut: 1998-99
Tests: 13
One-Day Internationals: 48
1st-Class 50s: 27
1st-Class 100s: 6
1st-Class 5 w. in innings: 2
1st-Class catches: 105
One-Day 100s: 4
Place in batting averages: 68th av. 33.25
Place in bowling averages: 125th av. 38.46
Strike rate: 73.30 (career 61.47)
Education: Kingswood College, Grahamstown, South Africa
Overseas tours: South Africa A to Zimbabwe 1994-95; Zimbabwe to Pakistan 1998-99, to South Africa 1999-2000, to West Indies 1999-2000, to England 2000
Overseas teams played for: Natal 1992-93 – 1997-98; Western Province 2000-01

Extras: Moved from Zimbabwe to South Africa at the age of ten. Represented Eastern Province Schools, opening the bowling with Brett Schultz. Represented South African Schools 1988. Leicestershire's overseas player in 1997. Scored 76 and took 3-27 for Zimbabwe v South Africa and scored 132* v Australia in the 1999 World Cup, winning Man of the Match award on both occasions. Scored 95* in the NatWest Triangular Series international v West Indies at Bristol 2000, winning the Man of the Match award. Retired from international cricket after the NatWest Triangular Series v England and West Indies in 2000. Played for a World XI v an Asia XI in Dhaka and at The Oval 2000. Has joined Hampshire as overseas player for 2001
Best batting: 150 Leicestershire v Lancashire, Leicester 1997
Best bowling: 5-79 Natal v Boland, Stellenbosch 1993-94

2000 Season

	M	Inns	NO	Runs	HS	Avge	100s	50s	Ct	St	O	M	Runs	Wkts	Avge	Best	5wI	10wM
Test	2	3	0	74	51	24.66	-	1	2	-	54	14	159	3	53.00	2-41	-	-
All First	7	8	0	266	83	33.25	-	3	6	-	158.5	44	500	13	38.46	4-28	-	-
1-day Int	7	7	1	230	95 *	38.33	-	3	2	-	33	1	126	5	25.20	2-16	-	
NatWest																		
B & H																		
1-day Lge																		

Career Performances

	M	Inns	NO	Runs	HS	Avge	100s	50s	Ct	St	Balls	Runs	Wkts	Avge	Best	5wI	10wM
Test	13	23	1	532	107	24.18	1	4	13	-	1187	594	15	39.60	4-77	-	-
All First	99	151	18	4181	150	31.43	6	27	105	-	10134	5066	162	31.27	5-79	2	-
1-day Int	48	48	2	1679	132 *	36.50	4	11	19	-	1503	1220	35	34.85	4-42	-	
NatWest	2	2	0	19	15	9.50	-	-	1	-	18	19	0	-	-	-	-
B & H	8	8	1	130	58	18.57	-	2	1	-	318	307	8	38.37	2-38	-	
1-day Lge	11	11	1	300	80 *	30.00	-	2	6	-	284	325	14	23.21	3-37	-	

JOHNSON, P.   Nottinghamshire

Name: Paul Johnson
Role: Right-hand bat, right-arm 'occasional' bowler
Born: 24 April 1965, Newark, Notts
Height: 'Below average'   **Weight:** 'Above average'
Nickname: Johno, Midge
County debut: 1982
County cap: 1986
Benefit: 1995
1000 runs in a season: 8

1st-Class 50s: 112
1st-Class 100s: 38
1st-Class catches: 222
1st-Class stumpings: 1
One-Day 100s: 13
Place in batting averages: 170th av. 20.76
(1999 23rd av. 42.46)
Strike rate: (career 106.66)
Parents: Donald Edward and Joyce
Wife and date of marriage: Jackie,
24 December 1993
Children: Ruth, 28 September 1994;
Eve, 9 September 1996
Family links with cricket: Father played
local cricket and is a qualified coach
Education: Grove Comprehensive School,
Newark
Qualifications: 9 CSEs, NCA advanced
coach
Career outside cricket: Coaching
Off-season: 'i) Working for Lincs Cricket Board. ii) Sports and Therapeutic Massage
course. iii) Helping out at home! iv) Getting body back in one piece!'
Overseas tours: England A to Bermuda and West Indies 1991-92; Christians in Sport
to Zimbabwe 1997, 1998
Overseas teams played for: RAU Johannesburg 1985-86; Hutt District, Wellington,
New Zealand 1988-89
Cricketers particularly admired: Clive Rice and Mike Gatting
Young players to look out for: Samit Patel, Bilal Shafayat, Nige Malik, Gary Pratt
Other sports played: '"Royal Oak" pool team'
Other sports followed: Ice hockey (Nottingham Panthers), football
(Nottingham Forest and Notts County)
Injuries: Out for nine weeks with torn tricep
Relaxations: Listening to music, crosswords and reading autobiographies
Extras: Played for English Schools in 1980-81 and England YC 1982 and 1983.
Youngest player to join the Nottinghamshire staff. Made 235 for Nottinghamshire 2nd
XI, July 1982, aged 17. Won Man of the Match award in his first NatWest game (101*
v Staffordshire) in 1985, but missed the final owing to appendicitis. Sunday morning
soccer referee in Nottingham. Took over the Nottinghamshire captaincy from Tim
Robinson at the start of the 1996 season. Relinquished captaincy during 1998 season
Opinions on cricket: 'Who would take any notice?'
Best batting: 187 Nottinghamshire v Lancashire, Old Trafford 1993
Best bowling: 1-9 Nottinghamshire v Cambridge University, Trent Bridge 1984

2000 Season

	M	Inns	NO	Runs	HS	Avge	100s	50s	Ct	St	O	M	Runs	Wkts	Avge	Best	5wl	10wM
Test																		
All First	12	19	2	353	100	20.76	1	-	9	-								
1-day Int																		
NatWest																		
B & H	4	4	0	60	33	15.00	-	-	-	-								
1-day Lge	11	9	1	224	62	28.00	-	1	-	-								

Career Performances

	M	Inns	NO	Runs	HS	Avge	100s	50s	Ct	St	Balls	Runs	Wkts	Avge	Best	5wl	10wM
Test																		
All First	344	575	55	19188	187	36.90	38	112	222	1	640	605	6	100.83	1-9	-	-
1-day Int																		
NatWest	36	36	2	1048	146	30.82	3	3	12	-	18	20	0	-		-	-
B & H	62	58	11	1515	104 *	32.23	2	10	15	-							
1-day Lge	242	229	28	6690	167 *	33.28	8	39	75	-	1	1	0	-		-	-

JOHNSON, R. L.   Somerset

Name: <u>Richard</u> Leonard Johnson
Role: Right-hand bat, right-arm fast-medium
bowler, outfielder
Born: 29 December 1974, Chertsey, Surrey
Height: 6ft 2in **Weight:** 14st 2lbs
Nickname: Jono, Lenny
County debut: 1992 (Middlesex)
County cap: 1995 (Middlesex)
50 wickets in a season: 3
1st-Class 50s: 3
1st-Class 5 w. in innings: 7
1st-Class 10 w. in match: 2
1st-Class catches: 42
One-Day 5 w. in innings: 1
Place in batting averages: 171st av. 20.70
(1999 268th av. 10.75)
Place in bowling averages: 83rd av. 28.58
(1999 77th av. 28.31)
Strike rate: 56.76 (career 52.09)
Parents: Roger and Mary Anne
Marital status: Single
Family links with cricket: Father and grandfather played club cricket

Education: Sunbury Manor School; Spelthorne College
Qualifications: 9 GCSEs, A-level in Physical Education, NCA senior coaching award
Off-season: MCC tour to Canada; 'tour to West Indies as part of Mark Ramprakash's benefit year'
Overseas tours: England U18 to South Africa 1992-93; England U19 to Sri Lanka 1993-94; England A to India 1994-95; MCC to Bangladesh 1999-2000, to Canada 2000-01
Cricketers particularly admired: Ian Botham, Richard Hadlee and Angus Fraser 'for his quality bowling and his dedication to moaning'
Young players to look out for: Ed Joyce, David Nash
Other sports followed: Football (Tottenham), rugby (London Irish)
Relaxations: 'Quiet beer with mates'
Extras: Plays for Sunbury CC. Represented Middlesex at all levels from U11. Took 10 for 45 v Derbyshire in July 1994, becoming first person to take ten wickets in an innings since Ian Thomson (Sussex) in 1964; also most economical ten-wicket haul since Hedley Verity's 10 for 10 in 1932. Had to pull out of England's 1995-96 tour to South Africa due to a persistent back injury. Left Middlesex at the end of the 2000 season and has joined Somerset for 2001
Opinions on cricket: 'Two divisions has improved the competitiveness of the Championship – always something to play for, but still too much cricket.'
Best batting: 69 Middlesex v Essex, Chelmsford 2000
Best bowling: 10-45 Middlesex v Derbyshire, Derby 1994

2000 Season

	M	Inns	NO	Runs	HS	Avge	100s	50s	Ct	St	O	M	Runs	Wkts	Avge	Best	5wI	10wM
Test																		
All First	15	23	3	414	69	20.70	-	2	13	-	473	129	1429	50	28.58	6-71	2	-
1-day Int																		
NatWest	3	1	0	21	21	21.00	-	-	1	-	16	3	71	1	71.00	1-34	-	
B & H	1	1	0	2	2	2.00	-	-	-	-	10	1	29	0	-	-	-	-
1-day Lge	12	8	1	40	16	5.71	-	-	1	-	81.5	7	338	21	16.09	3-26	-	

Career Performances

	M	Inns	NO	Runs	HS	Avge	100s	50s	Ct	St	Balls	Runs	Wkts	Avge	Best	5wI	10wM
Test																	
All First	91	129	14	1747	69	15.19	-	3	42	-	14273	7668	274	27.98	10-45	7	2
1-day Int																	
NatWest	17	12	3	176	45 *	19.55	-	-	2	-	876	606	22	27.54	5-50	1	
B & H	15	12	0	119	26	9.91	-	-	2	-	816	638	18	35.44	3-33	-	
1-day Lge	81	55	15	435	29	10.87	-	-	9	-	3266	2787	84	33.17	4-45	-	

Name: <u>Geraint</u> Owen Jones
Role: Right-hand bat, wicket-keeper
Born: 14 July 1976, Kundiawa,
Papua New Guinea
Height: 5ft 10in **Weight:** 11st
Nickname: Jonesy, Oink
County debut: No first-team appearance
Parents: Emrys
Marital status: Single
Family links with cricket: 'Father was the
star off-spinner for Blaenau Ffestiniog School
side'
Education: Wilsonton Primary School,
Toowoomba, Queensland, Australia;
Harristown State High School, Toowoomba;
MacGregor State HS, Brisbane
Career outside cricket: 'Currently training
as a pharmacy technician'
Off-season: 'Working at H. Shackleton & Co
pharmacy, South Wales'
Overseas tours: Beenleigh-Logan U19 to New Zealand 1995
Overseas teams played for: Beenleigh-Logan, Brisbane 1995-98
Cricketers particularly admired: Ian Healy, Steve Waugh, Jack Russell
Young players to look out for: James Hockley, Mike Powell (Glamorgan),
Ben Powell (Abergavenny)
Other sports played: Rugby
Other sports followed: Rugby (Crickhowell RFC)
Relaxations: 'Reading Dick Francis novels; sleeping'
Opinions on cricket: 'Make all 2nd XI matches four-day games. Fewer 2nd XI
games, so emerging players can concentrate on skill development to prepare for first-
class cricket. Allow fans to have fun and make a bit of noise at the game. The more
they enjoy it, the better the chance they will return to watch more games, probably
bringing along a few more people as well.'

---

45. Which current Gloucestershire player struck a
118-ball 80 at Headingley in 1989?

JONES, I.   Somerset

Name: Ian Jones
Role: Right-hand bat, right-arm
fast bowler
Born: 11 March 1977, London
Height: 6ft 4in **Weight:** 17st
Nickname: Bubba, Jonah
County debut: 1999
Strike rate: (career 79.33)
Parents: Dianne and Ronnie
Marital status: Single
Family links with cricket: Brother plays in
Durham League for Kimblesworth CC
Education: Fyndoune Community College,
Sacriston, Durham
Qualifications: 9 GCSEs, City and Guilds
Diploma in Engineering, Level 1 coaching
award
Off-season: 'Working hard in the gym with
Shiney'

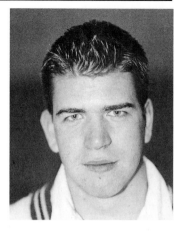

Overseas tours: Durham Academy to Sri Lanka 1996
Cricketers particularly admired: Glenn McGrath, Andrew Caddick, Allan Donald
Young players to look out for: Matt Bulbeck, Ian Blackwell, Ian Hunter
Other sports played: Football, shooting
Other sports followed: Football (Sunderland AFC)
Injuries: Missed all of 2000 season with ankle inversion (surgery twice on left ankle
during 2000)
Relaxations: 'Shooting, walking, listening to music, odd pint with Bully'
Extras: First player to sign on at Durham Cricket Academy
Opinions on cricket: 'More competition since two divisions have been brought in.
Should be more day/night matches. Televised games should be spread evenly between
counties instead of certain clubs being on all of the time.'
Best batting: 35 Somerset v Durham, Chester-le-Street 1999
Best bowling: 3-81 Somerset v New Zealanders, Taunton 1999

2000 Season (did not make any first-class or one-day appearances)

Career Performances

	M	Inns	NO	Runs	HS	Avge	100s	50s	Ct	St	Balls	Runs	Wkts	Avge	Best	5wI	10wM
Test																	
All First	3	4	1	78	35	26.00	-	-	-	-	476	341	6	56.83	3-81	-	-
1-day Int																	
NatWest																	
B & H																	
1-day Lge	1	1	1	5	5 *	-	-	-	-	-	43	53	1	53.00	1-53	-	

JONES, P. S.   Somerset

Name: Philip Steffan Jones
Role: Right-hand bat, right-arm
fast-medium bowler
Born: 9 February 1974, Llanelli
Height: 6ft 1in **Weight:** 14st
Nickname: Myfanwy, Elvis, Delilah, Jona
County debut: 1997
1st-Class 50s: 1
1st-Class 100s: 1
1st-Class 5 w. in innings: 2
1st-Class catches: 11
One-Day 5 w. in innings: 1
Place in batting averages: 271st av. 10.16
(1999 145th av. 25.54)
Place in bowling averages: 104th av. 32.35
(1999 135th av. 40.23)
Strike rate: 60.55 (career 64.20)
Parents: Lyndon and Ann
Marital status: Single
Family links with cricket: Father played cricket for Glamorgan 2nd XI and
Wales Schools; also played first-class rugby
Education: Llangennech Primary School; Ysgol Gyfun y Strade, Llanelli;
Loughborough University; Homerton College, Cambridge University
Qualifications: BSc Sports Science, PGCE in Physical Education
Career outside cricket: Teaching
Off-season: 'Training extremely hard to improve that bit extra from last year'
Overseas tours: Wales Minor Counties to Barbados 1996; Somerset CCC to South
Africa 1999, 2000
Cricketers particularly admired: 'Everyone who gives 100 per cent and does not
blame others!!'

Young players to look out for: Joe Tucker, Luke Sutton
Other sports played: Rugby union (Welsh Schools, Youth, U20, U21; Loughborough University, Cambridge University; Swansea, Bristol, Exeter and Moseley)
Other sports followed: Rugby union (New Zealand All Blacks), athletics
Injuries: Out for one week with an Achilles tendon problem and hamstring strain
Relaxations: 'Training in my own gym, dining out with my very supportive girlfriend Alex'
Extras: Schoolboy international from U13 to U19. Represented Wales Minor Counties. Took nine wickets in the Varsity match at Lord's in 1997. Man of the Match (5-23) in Sunday League game against Warwickshire 1998. Played first-class cricket and first-class rugby for two years ('last dual player, I think'). Recorded maiden Championship five-wicket return (5-41) v Surrey at Taunton 2000
Opinions on cricket: 'Good to see young so-called "unknowns" like "Banger" given the chance. Playing at the highest level is 60-70 per cent confidence, and if you believe in yourself, then other people's opinions mean nothing. As long as you can look at yourself in the mirror and say "I'm giving my all and I believe in myself and what I'm doing", then anything is possible. Too many players blame others, play at 50 per cent effort and play for external benefits (i.e. money). These players let themselves, their team-mates and the club down.'
Best batting: 105 Somerset v New Zealanders, Taunton 1999
Best bowling: 6-67 Cambridge University v Oxford University, Lord's 1997

2000 Season

	M	Inns	NO	Runs	HS	Avge	100s	50s	Ct	St	O	M	Runs	Wkts	Avge	Best	5wl	10wM
Test																		
All First	15	16	4	122	56 *	10.16	-	1	4	-	403.4	88	1294	40	32.35	5-41	1	-
1-day Int																		
NatWest	2	1	0	1	1	1.00	-	-	-	-	18	0	107	1	107.00	1-59	-	
B & H	3	1	0	0	0	0.00	-	-	-	-	13.1	1	60	1	60.00	1-20	-	
1-day Lge	16	10	6	54	27	13.50	-	-	1	-	127.4	11	620	28	22.14	4-32	-	

Career Performances

	M	Inns	NO	Runs	HS	Avge	100s	50s	Ct	St	Balls	Runs	Wkts	Avge	Best	5wl	10wM
Test																	
All First	38	48	13	576	105	16.45	1	1	11	-	5650	3123	88	35.48	6-67	2	-
1-day Int																	
NatWest	8	3	2	33	26 *	33.00	-	-	2	-	372	325	9	36.11	4-25	-	
B & H	8	4	2	26	12	13.00	-	-	2	-	337	248	6	41.33	2-51	-	
1-day Lge	45	23	11	89	27	7.41	-	-	9	-	1928	1647	72	22.87	5-23	1	

JONES, S. P.   Glamorgan

Name: <u>Simon</u> Philip Jones
Role: Left-hand bat, right-arm fast bowler
Born: 25 December 1978, Morriston
Hospital, Swansea
Height: 6ft 3in **Weight:** 13st 9lbs
Nickname: Racehorse, Raymond, Ray,
Ray Sauce
County debut: 1998
1st-Class 5 w. in innings: 1
1st-Class catches: 3
Place in batting averages: (1999 284th
av. 7.70)
Place in bowling averages: 120th av. 37.40
(1999 136th av. 40.84)
Strike rate: 62.40 (career 66.33)
Parents: Jeff and Irene
Marital status: Single
Family links with cricket: Father played for

Glamorgan and England (15 Tests)
Education: Halfway CP School; Coedcae Comprehensive School; Millfield School, Street, Somerset
Qualifications: 12 GCSEs, 1 A-level, Basic and Senior coaching awards
Off-season: 'Part-time job, training in the gym etc'
Overseas tours: Dyfed U15 to Zimbabwe 1994; Glamorgan to South Africa 1999
Cricketers particularly admired: Allan Donald, Michael Holding
Young players to look out for: Wayne Law, David Harrison
Other sports followed: Football (Manchester United)
Injuries: Out for half of the season with a stress fracture of the shin
Relaxations: Going out, relaxing with friends
Extras: His 4-47 v Warwickshire at Cardiff 2000 included a spell of 4-1 from 12 balls; among the spectators was his father, Jeff, who was attending a Glamorgan former players' reunion
Opinions on cricket: 'Too much cricket in the season. More rest in between games.'
Best batting: 19* Glamorgan v Oxford University, The Parks 1999
Best bowling: 5-31 Glamorgan v Sussex, Cardiff 1999

	M	Inns	NO	Runs	HS	Avge	100s	50s	Ct	St	O	M	Runs	Wkts	Avge	Best	5wI	10wM
Test																		
All First	5	3	0	13	13	4.33	-	-	-	-	104	12	374	10	37.40	4-47	-	-
1-day Int																		
NatWest																		
B & H	1	0	0	0	0	-	-	-	-	-	5	0	47	0	-		-	-
1-day Lge																		

Career Performances

	M	Inns	NO	Runs	HS	Avge	100s	50s	Ct	St	Balls	Runs	Wkts	Avge	Best	5wI	10wM
Test																	
All First	18	19	6	92	19 *	7.07	-	-	3	-	2388	1495	36	41.52	5-31	1	-
1-day Int																	
NatWest	1	0	0	0	0	-	-	-	-	-	30	30	0	-		-	-
B & H	1	0	0	0	0	-	-	-	-	-	30	47	0	-		-	-
1-day Lge	1	1	1	12	12 *	-	-	-	-	-	42	39	1	39.00	1-39	-	

JOYCE, E. C.   Middlesex

Name: <u>Edmund</u> Christopher Joyce
Role: Left-hand bat, right-arm medium bowler, gully fielder, occasional wicket-keeper
Born: 22 September 1978, Dublin
Height: 5ft 10in
County debut: 1999
1st-Class 50s: 1
1st-Class catches: 9
Place in batting averages: 113th av. 27.85
Parents: Maureen and Jimmy
Marital status: Single
Family links with cricket: Father was an occasional player; elder brother captains Merrion CC and has played for Ireland age group sides; younger brother represented Ireland U19 in Youth World Cup in Sri Lanka 1999-2000; two sisters (twins) are in Irish Ladies squad
Education: Presentation College, Bray, County Wicklow; Trinity College, Dublin
Qualifications: Irish Leaving Cert
Overseas tours: Ireland U19 to Bermuda (International Youth Tournament) 1997, to South Africa (Youth World Cup) 1997-98

Overseas teams played for: Coburg CC, Melbourne 1996-97
Cricketers particularly admired: Larry Gomes, Steve Waugh
Young players to look out for: Dominic Joyce (younger brother)
Other sports played: Rugby, soccer, golf
Relaxations: Music
Extras: Leinster U19 to Oxford Festival. Was only player to score a century at the International Youth Tournament, Bermuda 1997. Has represented Ireland senior side since 1997, including appearances in the Triple Crown tournament
Opinions on cricket: 'One competition less.'
Best batting: 51 Middlesex v Nottinghamshire, Trent Bridge 2000

2000 Season

	M	Inns	NO	Runs	HS	Avge	100s	50s	Ct	St	O	M	Runs	Wkts	Avge	Best	5wI	10wM
Test																		
All First	6	8	1	195	51	27.85	-	1	7	-	5	1	24	0	-	-	-	-
1-day Int																		
NatWest	1	1	0	29	29	29.00	-	-	-	-								
B & H																		
1-day Lge	5	5	3	110	40 *	55.00	-	-	1	-								

Career Performances

	M	Inns	NO	Runs	HS	Avge	100s	50s	Ct	St	Balls	Runs	Wkts	Avge	Best	5wI	10wM
Test																	
All First	9	13	1	286	51	23.83	-	1	9	-	114	102	0	-	-	-	-
1-day Int																	
NatWest	5	5	2	196	73	65.33	-	1	1	-							
B & H	3	3	0	76	42	25.33	-	-	1	-							
1-day Lge	6	6	3	130	40 *	43.33	-	-	1	-							

KATICH, S. M.   Durham

Name: <u>Simon</u> Mathew Katich
Role: Left-hand bat, left-arm spin bowler
Born: 21 August 1975, Midland, Western Australia
Height: 6ft **Weight:** 12st 8lbs
Nickname: Kat
County debut: 2000
County cap: 2000
1000 runs in a season: 1
1st-Class 50s: 16
1st-Class 100s: 8
1st-Class catches: 48

Place in batting averages: 27th av. 43.56
Strike rate: 141.20 (career 140.75)
Parents: Vince and Kerry
Marital status: Single
Education: Trinity College, Perth; University of Western Australia
Qualifications: Bachelor of Commerce degree
Off-season: Playing in Australia
Overseas tours: Australian Cricket Academy to South Africa 1996; Australia to Sri Lanka 1999-2000, to Zimbabwe 1999-2000
Overseas teams played for: Midland-Guildford, Western Australia; Western Australia 1996-97 –
Cricketers particularly admired: Steve Waugh, Shane Warne, Viv Richards
Young players to look out for: Brett Lee
Other sports followed: Australian Rules (Richmond), football (Newcastle United)
Relaxations: Golf, listening to music
Extras: Scored century (106) for Western Australia v England at Perth 1998-99; this was middle 100 of three centuries in successive first-class matches for Western Australia. Captained ACB Chairman's XI v England 1998-99. Scored 115 in Western Australia's first innings in their 1998-99 Sheffield Shield final victory. Second in Sheffield Shield averages 1998-99 with 909 runs at 56.81. *Wisden Australia*'s Sheffield Shield Cricketer of the Year 1998-99. Joined Durham as overseas player for 2000. Awarded ACB contract for 2000-01
Opinions on cricket: 'There is far too much cricket played in England, and the standard of wickets is not the same as it is in Australia. Far too many games finish within four days!'
Best batting: 154* Western Australia v Tasmania, Hobart 1998-99
Best bowling: 1-4 Western Australia v Victoria, Perth 1998-99
Stop press: Made One-Day International debut v Zimbabwe at Melbourne in the CUB Series 2000-01. Not returning to Durham in 2001

2000 Season

	M	Inns	NO	Runs	HS	Avge	100s	50s	Ct	St	O	M	Runs	Wkts	Avge	Best	5wI	10wM
Test																		
All First	16	28	3	1089	137*	43.56	3	5	21	-	117.4	14	342	5	68.40	1-10	-	-
1-day Int																		
NatWest	2	2	0	44	40	22.00	-	-	1	-								
B & H	6	6	0	116	62	19.33	-	2	5	-	1	0	8	0	-		-	-
1-day Lge	16	16	3	598	70*	46.00	-	6	8	-	17	1	94	2	47.00	1-25	-	

Career Performances

	M	Inns	NO	Runs	HS	Avge	100s	50s	Ct	St	Balls	Runs	Wkts	Avge	Best	5wI	10wM
Test																	
All First	45	81	13	3125	154 *	45.95	8	16	48	-	1126	610	8	76.25	1-4	-	-
1-day Int																	
NatWest	2	2	0	44	40	22.00	-	-	1	-							
B & H	6	6	0	116	62	19.33	-	2	5	-	6	8	0	-	-	-	
1-day Lge	16	16	3	598	70 *	46.00	-	6	8	-	102	94	2	47.00	1-25	-	

KEEDY, G. — Lancashire

Name: Gary Keedy
Role: Left-hand bat, slow left-arm bowler
Born: 27 November 1974, Wakefield
Height: 5ft 11in **Weight:** 12st 4lbs
Nickname: Keeds, Binbag
County debut: 1994 (Yorkshire), 1995 (Lancashire)
County cap: 2000 (Lancashire)
1st-Class 5 w. in innings: 4
1st-Class 10 w. in match: 2
1st-Class catches: 15
One-Day 5 w. in innings: 1
Place in batting averages: 253rd av. 12.00
Place in bowling averages: 70th av. 27.16 (1999 68th av. 27.34)
Strike rate: 77.51 (career 78.60)
Parents: Roy and Pat
Marital status: Engaged
Family links with cricket: Twin brother plays for Castleford in the Yorkshire League
Education: Garforth Comprehensive
Qualifications: 4 GCSEs, junior coaching award
Off-season: 'Full-time training with club on 12-month contract'
Overseas tours: England U18 to South Africa 1992-93, to Denmark 1994; England U19 to Sri Lanka 1993-94
Overseas teams played for: Frankston, Melbourne 1995-96
Cricketers particularly admired: Shane Warne, Graham Gooch
Young players to look out for: Jamie Haynes
Other sports followed: Football (Leeds United), rugby league (Leeds Rhinos)
Extras: Player of the Series for England U19 v West Indies U19 in 1993. Graduate of the Yorkshire Cricket Academy. Played for England U19 in the home series against India in 1994. His match return of 10-155 v Durham at Old Trafford 2000 included second innings figures of 6-56 from 50 overs. Awarded Lancashire cap 2000

Opinions on cricket: 'Left-armers bowling into the rough attacking a batsman should not be leg-side wided. If teams are battling not to lose, we spinners bowl this as an attacking option, trying to get the batsman out! It is *not* defensive!!! Please review this new rule.'

Best batting: 34 Lancashire v Surrey, Old Trafford 2000
Best bowling: 6-56 Lancashire v Durham, Old Trafford 2000

2000 Season

	M	Inns	NO	Runs	HS	Avge	100s	50s	Ct	St	O	M	Runs	Wkts	Avge	Best	5wI	10wM
Test																		
All First	13	15	3	144	34	12.00	-	-	2	-	478	142	1005	37	27.16	6-56	1	1
1-day Int																		
NatWest	1	0	0	0	0	-	-	-	-	-	10	0	40	1	40.00	1-40	-	
B & H																		
1-day Lge	6	2	1	1	1	1.00	-	-	1	-	33.3	0	149	9	16.55	5-30	1	

Career Performances

	M	Inns	NO	Runs	HS	Avge	100s	50s	Ct	St	Balls	Runs	Wkts	Avge	Best	5wI	10wM
Test																	
All First	65	74	41	363	34	11.00	-	-	15	-	13362	5982	170	35.18	6-56	4	2
1-day Int																	
NatWest	1	0	0	0	0	-	-	-	-	-	60	40	1	40.00	1-40	-	
B & H																	
1-day Lge	11	2	1	1	1	1.00	-	-	1	-	376	324	10	32.40	5-30	1	

46. Whose 8-38 in 1997 is the best Test analysis
returned by an Australian at Lord's?

KEEGAN, C. B.   Middlesex

Name: <u>Chad</u> Blake Keegan
Role: Right-hand bat, right-arm fast bowler
Born: 30 July 1979
Height: 6ft 1in **Weight:** 12st
County debut: No first-team appearance
Parents: Sharon and Blake
Marital status: Single
Education: Northlands Senior Primary,
Durban, South Africa; Durban High School
Overseas teams played for: Durban High
School Old Boys 1994-97; Crusaders, Durban
1998-99

Cricketers particularly admired:
Malcolm Marshall, Neil Johnson
Other sports played: Bodyboarding,
snowboarding, golf, wakeboarding
Other sports followed: Surfing, football
(Liverpool), skateboarding, BMX
Injuries: Out for one month with a pulled rib muscle
Relaxations: Music, guitar, art
Extras: Represented KwaZulu-Natal U13, KwaZulu-Natal Schools, KwaZulu-Natal
U19, KwaZulu-Natal Academy. Is an MCC Young Cricketer. Is not considered an
overseas player

KENDALL, W. S.   Hampshire

Name: <u>William</u> Salwey Kendall
Role: Right-hand bat, right-arm medium bowler, occasional wicket-keeper, county
vice-captain
Born: 18 December 1973, Wimbledon
Height: 5ft 10in **Weight:** 12st 7lbs
Nickname: Villy, Lemon, Baldy, Wiggy
County debut: 1996
County cap: 1999
1000 runs in a season: 3
1st-Class 50s: 24
1st-Class 100s: 8
1st-Class 200s: 1
1st-Class catches: 82
Place in batting averages: 34th av. 41.28 (1999 40th av. 39.53)

Strike rate: (career 68.90)
Parents: Tom and Sue
Marital status: Single
Family links with cricket: Father played club cricket with East Horsley, Hampshire Hogs and MCC. Older brother James played for Durham University. Younger brother, Ed, took new ball for Nottingham University
Education: Bradfield College, Berkshire; Keble College, Oxford University
Qualifications: 10 GCSEs, 3 A-levels, 1 AS-level, BA (Hons) Modern History
Career outside cricket: Journalism – weekly column in *Hampshire Chronicle* – and a little sports marketing
Off-season: 'Travelling with girlfriend, Emily, in India, Nepal and Australia, and trying to use my brain on return in December'
Overseas tours: Bradfield College to Barbados 1991; Troubadours to Argentina 1997; Hampshire CCC to Anguilla 1997
Overseas teams played for: Frankston Peninsular CC, Melbourne 1997-98
Cricketers particularly admired: Robin Smith, Graham Thorpe, Mark Ramprakash, Shane Warne, 'and anyone playing over 36'
Young players to look out for: Derek Kenway, Charlie van der Gucht, Lawrence Prittipaul, James Adams
Other sports played: Hockey (Oxford Blue), football (Independent Schools 1992; offered terms by Reading), squash, golf
Other sports followed: 'All sports'
Injuries: Out for one game with a hamstring pull
Relaxations: Playing or watching sport, socialising with friends, relaxing at home; 'hacking up golf courses, travelling and quiet days with girlfriend, Emily'
Extras: Surrey Young Cricketer of the Year 1992. Awarded Gray-Nicolls Trophy for Schoolboy Cricketer of the Year in memory of Len Newbery 1992. Made first-class debut for Oxford University in 1994. Hampshire Exiles Player of the Year for 1996. Appointed vice-captain of Hampshire for 2001
Opinions on cricket: 'The key must be to find a balance between giving county members enough cricket to watch and keeping players fresh enough to produce quality. The Championship, a one-day league (50 overs) and one knockout trophy is enough. Central contracts are an excellent idea so long as the right players are chosen and counties are adequately compensated. With this and the two divisional system, things are heading in the right direction. Consistency and patience are required by all. Good food at all grounds is vital.'
Best batting: 201 Hampshire v Sussex, Southampton 1999
Best bowling: 3-37 Oxford University v Derbyshire, The Parks 1995

2000 Season

	M	Inns	NO	Runs	HS	Avge	100s	50s	Ct	St	O	M	Runs	Wkts	Avge	Best	5wI	10wM
Test																		
All First	18	31	3	1156	161	41.28	3	5	17	-	1	0	1	0	-	-	-	-
1-day Int																		
NatWest	4	3	1	53	27	26.50	-	-	1	-								
B & H	2	2	1	2	2 *	2.00	-	-	1	-								
1-day Lge	13	13	5	388	85 *	48.50	-	3	3	-								

Career Performances

	M	Inns	NO	Runs	HS	Avge	100s	50s	Ct	St	Balls	Runs	Wkts	Avge	Best	5wI	10wM
Test																	
All First	89	142	19	4850	201	39.43	9	24	82	-	689	417	10	41.70	3-37	-	-
1-day Int																	
NatWest	8	7	2	112	39	22.40	-	-	3	-							
B & H	12	12	1	159	28	14.45	-	-	1	-							
1-day Lge	53	48	8	962	85 *	24.05	-	4	25	-	12	22	0	-	-	-	-

KENNIS, G. J. Somerset

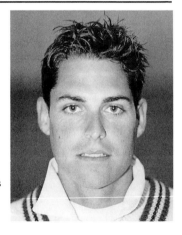

Name: <u>Gregor</u> John Kennis
Role: Right-hand bat, right-arm
off-spin bowler
Born: 9 March 1974, Yokohama, Japan
Height: 6ft 2in **Weight:** 13st
Nickname: G
County debut: 1994 (Surrey),
1998 (Somerset)
1st-Class 100s: 1
1st-Class catches: 13
Place in batting averages: (1999 52nd
av. 37.50)
Parents: Michael and Sally
Marital status: Single
Family links with cricket: 'Dad played for his
company side and is now a qualified coach'
Education: Tiffin Boys' School
Qualifications: 9 GCSEs, 1 A-level, senior
cricket coach
Overseas tours: Surrey U19 to Barbados 1991
Overseas teams played for: Claremont Nedlands, Perth 1995-96; Marist Newman
Old Boys CC, Perth 1996-99

Cricketers particularly admired: Steve Waugh, Andrew Howes
Other sports played: Golf
Other sports followed: Horse racing
Relaxations: Going racing, playing golf
Extras: Set a record for Surrey 2nd XI with his 258 against Leicestershire in 1995. Surrey 2nd XI Batsman of the Year 1995. Joined Somerset for 1998. Scored maiden first-class century (175) v New Zealanders at Taunton 1999. Played in one-day match for Somerset v Zimbabweans in 2000. Released by Somerset at the end of the 2000 season
Opinions on cricket: 'Twelve-month contracts should be brought in to make the sport in general more professional. How many other sportsmen at the top of their game have a six-month "close season"?'
Best batting: 175 Somerset v New Zealanders, Taunton 1999

2000 Season (did not make any first-class or one-day competition appearances)

Career Performances

	M	Inns	NO	Runs	HS	Avge	100s	50s	Ct	St	Balls	Runs	Wkts	Avge	Best	5wI	10wM
Test																	
All First	12	23	1	436	175	19.81	1	-	13	-	24	4	0	-	-	-	-
1-day Int																	
NatWest																	
B & H																	
1-day Lge	2	1	0	5	5	5.00	-	-	-	-							

47. At Trent Bridge in 1993, both of England's opening bowlers were winning their first caps. Who were they?

KENWAY, D. A.   Hampshire

Name: <u>Derek</u> Anthony Kenway
Role: Right-hand bat, occasional
wicket-keeper
Born: 12 June 1978, Fareham
Height: 5ft 10in **Weight:** 14st
Nickname: Kenners
County debut: 1997
1000 runs in a season: 1
1st-Class 50s: 11
1st-Class 100s: 2
1st-Class catches: 28
1st-Class stumpings: 1
Place in batting averages: 125th av. 26.34
(1999 26th av. 42.20)
Strike rate: (career 36.00)
Parents: Keith and Geraldine
Marital status: Single
Family links with cricket: Brother plays in
the Southern League

Education: Botley Primary School; St George's, Southampton; Barton Peveril College
Qualifications: 6 GCSEs, NCA coaching award, qualified snowboard instructor,
'Cypriot dancing'
Career outside cricket: 'Holidays'
Overseas tours: West of England U15 to West Indies 1993
Overseas teams played for: Beaumaris CC, Melbourne 1997-98
Cricketers particularly admired: Steve Soper, Robin Smith, Mark Waugh
Other sports played: Football, kickboxing, boxing, golf
Other sports followed: Football (Southampton FC)
Relaxations: Socialising, music
Extras: *Daily Telegraph* Batting Award (West) 1994. Southern League Young Player
of the Year in 1996. NBC Denis Compton Award 1999
Opinions on cricket: 'Longer lunch and tea breaks.'
Best batting: 136 Hampshire v Derbyshire, Derby 2000
Best bowling: 1-5 Hampshire v Warwickshire, Southampton 1997

2000 Season

	M	Inns	NO	Runs	HS	Avge	100s	50s	Ct	St	O	M	Runs	Wkts	Avge	Best	5wl	10wM
Test																		
All First	15	27	1	685	136	26.34	1	3	13	1								
1-day Int																		
NatWest																		
B & H	4	4	0	86	47	21.50	-	-	5	1								
1-day Lge	12	12	0	330	90	27.50	-	3	7	4								

Career Performances

	M	Inns	NO	Runs	HS	Avge	100s	50s	Ct	St	Balls	Runs	Wkts	Avge	Best	5wl	10wM
Test																	
All First	38	65	8	1880	136	32.98	2	11	28	1	72	76	2	38.00	1-5	-	-
1-day Int																	
NatWest	2	2	0	100	53	50.00	-	1	1	-							
B & H	5	5	0	95	47	19.00	-	-	5	1							
1-day Lge	31	27	0	676	90	25.03	-	5	12	4							

KERR, J. I. D. Somerset

Name: <u>Jason</u> Ian Douglas Kerr
Role: Right-hand bat, right-arm
fast-medium bowler, (wicket-keeper
'if required')
Born: 7 April 1974, Bolton, Lancashire
Height: 6ft 3in **Weight:** 12st 6lbs
Nickname: Junior B
County debut: 1993
1st-Class 50s: 5
1st-Class 5 w. in innings: 2
1st-Class catches: 15
Place in batting averages: (1999 192nd
av. 21.16)
Place in bowling averages: (1999 118th
av. 34.67)
Strike rate: 41.33 (career 58.36)
Parents: Len and Janet
Marital status: Single
Family links with cricket: 'Brother Andy is becoming a young legend'
Education: Withins High School; Bolton Met College
Qualifications: 5 GCSEs, BTEC National Diploma in Business Studies, cricket coach
Off-season: 'Yet again in rehabilitation! Helping "Pain et Vain's" profits go through

the roof. Jan-March in Perth, Australia, with Luke Sutton and Gregor Kennis'
Overseas tours: England U19 to India 1992-93; Lancashire U19 to Isle of Man
Overseas teams played for: Gordon Districts CC, Sydney, Australia 1994-95;
Taita CC, Wellington, New Zealand 1996-97; Subiaco-Floreat, Perth
Cricketers particularly admired: A.R. Caddick ('bowling machine')
Young players to look out for: Andy Kerr
Other sports followed: Football (Bolton 'The Great' Wanderers)
Injuries: Out for 80 per cent of the 2000 season with a herniated disc
Extras: His 7-23 v Leics at Taunton 1999 included a spell of 5-6 from 3.1 overs.
Completed hat-trick (Brian Lara, Nixon McLean, Corey Collymore) v West Indians at
Taunton 2000 in his first game of the 2000 season; Collymore was also his 100th first-
class wicket
Opinions on cricket: 'There's enough of those out there!'
Best batting: 80 Somerset v West Indians, Taunton 1995
Best bowling: 7-23 Somerset v Leicestershire, Taunton 1999

2000 Season

	M	Inns	NO	Runs	HS	Avge	100s	50s	Ct	St	O	M	Runs	Wkts	Avge	Best	5wI	10wM
Test																		
All First	4	5	1	116	34	29.00	-	-	-	-	62	13	248	9	27.55	4-18	-	-
1-day Int																		
NatWest																		
B & H																		
1-day Lge	3	3	2	14	13	14.00	-	-	1	-	17	0	97	3	32.33	2-53	-	

Career Performances

	M	Inns	NO	Runs	HS	Avge	100s	50s	Ct	St	Balls		Runs	Wkts	Avge	Best	5wI	10wM
Test																		
All First	50	71	11	1227	80	20.45	-	5	15	-	6070		3913	104	37.62	7-23	2	-
1-day Int																		
NatWest	9	7	2	32	21	6.40	-	-	2	-	342		297	8	37.12	3-32	-	
B & H	6	3	0	31	17	10.33	-	-	-	-	234		173	7	24.71	3-34	-	
1-day Lge	61	39	11	386	56	13.78	-	1	10	-	2215		2008	70	28.68	4-28	-	

---

48. Which 23-year-old took 7-50 to bowl England to victory
at The Oval in 1968 after the public had assisted the groundstaff
in mopping up the results of a deluge?

KEY, R. W. T.   Kent

Name: <u>Robert</u> William Trevor Key
Role: Right-hand bat
Born: 12 May 1979, Dulwich
Height: 6ft 1in **Weight:** 12st 7lbs
Nickname: Keysy
County debut: 1998
1st-Class 50s: 11
1st-Class 100s: 3
1st-Class catches: 37
Place in batting averages: 167th av. 20.85
(1999 130th av. 26.96)
Parents: Trevor and Lynn
Marital status: Single
Family links with cricket: Mother played
for Kent Ladies. Father played club cricket in
Derby. Sister Elizabeth played for her junior
school side
Education: Worsley Bridge Primary School;
Langley Park Boys' School
Qualifications: 10 GCSEs, NCA coaching award, GNVQ Business
Career outside cricket: 'Work in the futures market'
Overseas tours: Kent U13 to Holland; England U17 to Bermuda 1997; England U19
to South Africa (including Youth World Cup) 1997-98; England A to Zimbabwe and
South Africa 1998-99
Overseas teams played for: Green Point CC, Cape Town 1996-97
Cricketers particularly admired: Alan Wells, Steve Marsh, Graham Cowdrey,
'and all the Kent staff'
Other sports played: Hockey, football, snooker
Other sports followed: Football (Chelsea), basketball (Chicago Bulls)
Relaxations: Snooker, socialising with friends
Extras: Played for England U17 and England U19 Development XI. Also played for
South England U14 and U19. County tennis player. Played for England U19 against
Zimbabwe in 1997 and captained the England U17 side to victory in the International
Youth Tournament in Bermuda in July; played for the victorious England side in the
U19 World Cup in South Africa. Shared England U19 Man of the Series award with
Graeme Swann v Pakistan U19 1998
Best batting: 125 Kent v Somerset, Taunton 1999

2000 Season

	M	Inns	NO	Runs	HS	Avge	100s	50s	Ct	St	O	M	Runs	Wkts	Avge	Best	5wI	10wM
Test																		
All First	17	29	1	584	83	20.85	-	5	4	-	9.4	1	34	0	-	-	-	-
1-day Int																		
NatWest																		
B & H																		
1-day Lge	5	5	0	41	16	8.20	-	-	-	-								

Career Performances

	M	Inns	NO	Runs	HS	Avge	100s	50s	Ct	St	Balls	Runs	Wkts	Avge	Best	5wI	10wM
Test																	
All First	52	90	3	2084	125	23.95	3	11	37	-	64	35	0	-	-	-	-
1-day Int																	
NatWest	4	4	0	157	67	39.25	-	2	1	-							
B & H	1	1	0	4	4	4.00	-	-	-	-							
1-day Lge	26	23	3	596	76 *	29.80	-	5	1	-							

KHAN, A. Kent

Name: Amjad Khan
Role: Right-hand bat, right-arm fast bowler
Born: 14 October 1980, Copenhagen, Denmark
Height: 6ft **Weight:** 11st 7lbs
County debut: No first-team appearance
Parents: Aslam and Raisa
Marital status: Single
Education: Skolen på Duevej, Denmark; Falkonérgårdens Gymnasium
Overseas tours: Denmark U19 to Canada 1996, to Bermuda 1997, to South Africa and Wales 1998, to Ireland 1999; Denmark to Holland 1998, to Zimbabwe 1999
Overseas teams played for: Kjøbenhavns Boldklub, Denmark
Cricketers particularly admired: Wasim Akram, Sachin Tendulkar, Allan Donald

Young players to look out for: Baljit Singh, Andy Lambert
Other sports followed: Football (Denmark)
Relaxations: Working out, listening to music, sleeping
Extras: The youngest Danish international ever at age of 17. Played for Denmark in the NatWest Trophy 1999 and 2000

Opinions on cricket: 'Action should be taken to make the game more attractive and thereby remove all prejudices related to cricket. Coloured clothing and floodlights are a good start.'

2000 Season (did not make any first-class or one-day appearances)

Career Performances

	M	Inns	NO	Runs	HS	Avge	100s	50s	Ct	St	Balls	Runs	Wkts	Avge	Best	5wI	10wM
Test																	
All First																	
1-day Int																	
NatWest	2	2	0	2	2	1.00	-	-	-	-	105	93	3	31.00	2-38	-	
B & H																	
1-day Lge																	

KHAN, A. A. Leicestershire

Name: <u>Amer</u> Ali Khan
Role: Right-hand bat, leg-break bowler
Born: 5 November 1969, Lahore, Pakistan
Height: 5ft 9in **Weight:** 12st 7lbs
Nickname: Aga
County debut: 1995 (Middlesex), 1997 (Sussex), 1999 (Leics)
1st-Class 50s: 1
1st-Class 5 w. in innings: 1
1st-Class catches: 9
One-Day 5 w. in innings: 1
Strike rate: (career 82.60)
Parents: M. Hanif Khan and Shireen Hanif
Marital status: Single
Family links with cricket: 'Dad used to play club cricket; my cousin Sajid Hussain used to play for RDCA and PIA (first-class cricket); my cousin Amir Raza used to play for Islamabad (first-class cricket)'
Education: 25F Model Town; Muslim Model High School; MAO College (all Lahore)
Qualifications: Coaching
Overseas teams played for: Wakatu CC, Nelson, New Zealand 1995-96; Motueka CA, New Zealand 1997-98; Kuils River CC and Coronation CC, Cape Town 1998-99
Cricketers particularly admired: 'All of them who go out on the park and do the business'

Other sports played: Two-touch football, touch rugby
Other sports followed: Basketball (Chicago Bulls)
Relaxations: 'Going to the gym and cinema; chilling out; listening to music'
Extras: Released by Sussex at the end of the 1998 season and joined Leics for 1999. Released by Leicestershire at the end of the 2000 season
Best batting: 52 Sussex v Hampshire, Southampton 1997
Best bowling: 5-137 Sussex v Middlesex, Lord's 1997

2000 Season

	M	Inns	NO	Runs	HS	Avge	100s	50s	Ct	St	O	M	Runs	Wkts	Avge	Best	5wI	10wM
Test																		
All First																		
1-day Int																		
NatWest																		
B & H																		
1-day Lge	1	0	0	0	0	-	-	-	-	-	1.1	0	14	0	-		-	-

Career Performances

	M	Inns	NO	Runs	HS	Avge	100s	50s	Ct	St	Balls	Runs	Wkts	Avge	Best	5wI	10wM
Test																	
All First	23	29	5	337	52	14.04	-	1	9	-	3965	1991	48	41.47	5-137	1	-
1-day Int																	
NatWest	4	1	0	4	4	4.00	-	-	1	-	240	196	2	98.00	1-13	-	
B & H	5	3	0	15	8	5.00	-	-	2	-	294	217	8	27.12	3-31	-	
1-day Lge	14	9	3	48	22*	8.00	-	-	2	-	552	488	15	32.53	5-40	1	

49. According to legend, to whom did Colin Cowdrey politely introduce himself with the words, 'I'm Colin Cowdrey. We haven't met,' on arriving at the wicket at Perth in 1974-75?

KHAN, R. M. Derbyshire

Name: <u>Rawait</u> M. Khan
Role: Right-hand bat
Born: 5 March 1982, Birmingham
Height: 5ft 9in **Weight:** 9st 7lbs
Nickname: Ray
County debut: No first-team appearance
Parents: Hashim Khan and Barish Begum
Marital status: Single
Family links with cricket: Father played for
Warwickshire 2nd XI. Brother Zubair also
plays for Derbyshire
Education: Parkhill School; Moseley School;
Solihull College
Cricketers particularly admired: Steve
Waugh
Other sports played: Football, badminton
Relaxations: 'Socialising with friends'
Extras: Played for Derbyshire Board XI in
the NatWest 2000

2000 Season (did not make any first-class or one-day appearances)

Career Performances

	M	Inns	NO	Runs	HS	Avge	100s	50s	Ct	St	Balls	Runs	Wkts	Avge	Best	5wI	10wM
Test																	
All First																	
1-day Int																	
NatWest	1	1	0	29	29	29.00	-	-	-	-							
B & H																	
1-day Lge																	

50. What unenviable record did Alan Hurst set during the 1978-79 series?

KHAN, W. G. Sussex

Name: <u>Wasim</u> Gulzar Khan
Role: Left-hand bat, leg-break bowler
Born: 26 February 1971, Birmingham
Height: 6ft 1in **Weight:** 11st 11lbs
Nickname: Mowgli, Jai ('son of Tarzan')
County debut: 1992 (one-day, Warwicks),
1995 (first-class, Warwicks), 1998 (Sussex)
1st-Class 50s: 17
1st-Class 100s: 5
1st-Class catches: 36
Place in batting averages: 144th av. 23.83
(1999 217th av. 18.55)
Parents: Gulzar Ahmed (deceased) and
Zarina Begum
Marital status: Single
Education: Somerville; Small Heath
Comprehensive; Josiah Mason Sixth Form
College (all Birmingham)

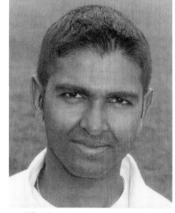

Qualifications: 6 O-levels, 1 A-level, coaching qualifications
Career outside cricket: Personal fitness training
Overseas tours: Warwickshire to Cape Town 1993, 1995
Overseas teams played for: Western Suburbs, Sydney 1990-91; North Perth 1991-93;
Albion, Melbourne 1993-95; Petone Riverside, Wellington, New Zealand 1996-97
Cricketers particularly admired: Dermot Reeve, Saeed Anwar, Graham Thorpe,
Michael DiVenuto
Young players to look out for: Paul Havell, Nick Wilton
Other sports played: Squash, football
Other sports followed: Football (Birmingham City FC)
Relaxations: Reading, listening to music, 'spending time on Brighton sea front!'
Extras: Most Promising Young Cricketer 1990. Scored four centuries in a row for
Warwickshire U19. Scored 171* v Northants in second trial game for Warwickshire
2nd XI. England Schools U19. Won Oxford/Cambridge U19 Festival 1989, 1990. Left
Warwickshire at the end of the 1997 season to join Sussex. Released by Sussex at the
end of the 2000 season
Best batting: 181 Warwickshire v Hampshire, Southampton 1995

2000 Season

	M	Inns	NO	Runs	HS	Avge	100s	50s	Ct	St	O	M	Runs	Wkts	Avge	Best	5wI	10wM
Test																		
All First	3	6	0	143	74	23.83	-	1	-	-	10	0	31	0	-	-	-	-
1-day Int																		
NatWest																		
B & H																		
1-day Lge																		

Career Performances

	M	Inns	NO	Runs	HS	Avge	100s	50s	Ct	St	Balls	Runs	Wkts	Avge	Best	5wI	10wM
Test																		
All First	57	101	8	2834	181	30.47	5	17	36	-	132	62	0	-	-	-	-
1-day Int																		
NatWest	1	1	0	2	2	2.00	-	-	1	-							
B & H	2	2	1	33	33	33.00	-	-	1	-							
1-day Lge	17	15	0	143	33	9.53	-	-	3	-							

KHAN, Z. M.   Derbyshire

Name: <u>Zubair</u> Mahmood Khan
Role: Left-hand bat, right-arm fast bowler
Born: 7 February 1983, Birmingham
Height: 6ft 1in **Weight:** 11st
Nickname: Zubs
County debut: 2000
Strike rate: 120.00 (career 120.00)
Parents: Hashim Khan
Marital status: Single
Family links with cricket: Father played cricket and coached cricket for a number of years. Brother Rawait also plays for Derbyshire
Education: Parkhill School; Moseley School; Solihull Sixth Form College
Cricketers particularly admired: Shaun Pollock
Young players to look out for: Zubair Khan, Rawait Khan
Other sports played: Football, snooker
Other sports followed: Football (Manchester United)
Relaxations: 'Socialising with mates or going to play snooker'

Extras: Represented West Midlands and England U16
Best bowling: 1-32 Derbyshire v Cambridge University, Fenner's 2000

2000 Season

	M	Inns	NO	Runs	HS	Avge	100s	50s	Ct	St	O	M	Runs	Wkts	Avge	Best	5wI	10wM
Test																		
All First	1	0	0	0	0	-	-	-	-	-	20	5	45	1	45.00	1-32	-	-
1-day Int																		
NatWest																		
B & H																		
1-day Lge																		

Career Performances

	M	Inns	NO	Runs	HS	Avge	100s	50s	Ct	St	Balls	Runs	Wkts	Avge	Best	5wI	10wM
Test																	
All First	1	0	0	0	0	-	-	-	-	-	120	45	1	45.00	1-32	-	-
1-day Int																	
NatWest																	
B & H																	
1-day Lge																	

KILLEEN, N. Durham

Name: Neil Killeen
Role: Right-hand bat, right-arm fast-medium bowler
Born: 17 October 1975, Shotley Bridge
Height: 6ft 2in **Weight:** 14st 12lbs
Nickname: Killer, Squeaky, Quinny
County debut: 1995
County cap: 1999
50 wickets in a season: 1
1st-Class 5 w. in innings: 6
1st-Class catches: 12
One-Day 5 w. in innings: 2
Place in batting averages: 270th av. 10.28
(1999 239th av. 15.68)
Place in bowling averages: 103rd av. 31.68
(1999 10th av. 18.44)
Strike rate: 78.68 (career 55.10)
Parents: Glen and Thora

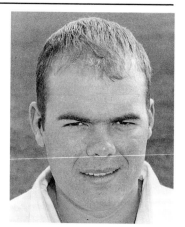

Marital status: Single
Education: Greencroft Comprehensive School; Derwentside College, University of Teesside
Qualifications: 8 GCSEs, 2 A-levels, advanced coaching award
Overseas tours: Durham CCC to Zimbabwe 1992; England U19 to West Indies 1994-95; MCC to Bangladesh 1999-2000
Cricketers particularly admired: Ian Botham, Curtly Ambrose
Young players to look out for: Melvyn Betts
Other sports played/followed: Athletics (English Schools javelin) and football
Relaxations: 'Spending time with friends and going out. Listening to music and watching television'
Extras: Was first Durham bowler to take five wickets in a Sunday League game (5-26 against Northamptonshire in 1995). Took three wickets in final over of National League game at Derby 2000, preventing Derbyshire scoring the six runs required for victory
Best batting: 48 Durham v Somerset, Chester-le-Street 1995
Best bowling: 7-85 Durham v Leicestershire, Leicester 1999

2000 Season

	M	Inns	NO	Runs	HS	Avge	100s	50s	Ct	St	O	M	Runs	Wkts	Avge	Best	5wI	10wM
Test																		
All First	10	15	1	144	38 *	10.28	-	-	1	-	288.3	84	697	22	31.68	3-14	-	-
1-day Int																		
NatWest	2	2	0	3	2	1.50	-	-	-	-	14	2	25	3	8.33	2-15	-	
B & H	6	3	1	14	11 *	7.00	-	-	2	-	44.5	8	160	8	20.00	2-13	-	
1-day Lge	13	5	2	60	21	20.00	-	-	3	-	104.5	8	415	29	14.31	6-31	1	

Career Performances

	M	Inns	NO	Runs	HS	Avge	100s	50s	Ct	St	Balls	Runs	Wkts	Avge	Best	5wI	10wM
Test																	
All First	40	60	11	623	48	12.71	-	-	12	-	7054	3522	128	27.51	7-85	6	-
1-day Int																	
NatWest	6	4	1	4	2	1.33	-	-	1	-	348	217	8	27.12	2-15	-	
B & H	22	13	4	60	24 *	6.66	-	-	4	-	1149	813	21	38.71	2-13	-	
1-day Lge	68	42	14	279	32	9.96	-	-	12	-	2959	2322	92	25.23	6-31	2	

KIRTLEY, R. J. Sussex

Name: Robert <u>James</u> Kirtley
Role: Right-hand bat, right-arm
fast-medium bowler
Born: 10 January 1975, Eastbourne
Height: 6ft **Weight:** 12st
Nickname: Ambi, Hurtler, Springer
County debut: 1995
County cap: 1998
50 wickets in a season: 3
1st-Class 50s: 1
1st-Class 5 w. in innings: 15
1st-Class 10 w. in match: 1
1st-Class catches: 21
One-Day 5 w. in innings: 1
Place in batting averages: 285th av. 8.11
(1999 267th av. 10.77)
Place in bowling averages: 54th av. 24.74
(1999 43rd av. 23.13)
Strike rate: 49.68 (career 49.00)
Parents: Bob and Pip
Marital status: Single

Family links with cricket: Brother plays league cricket
Education: St Andrews School, Eastbourne; Clifton College, Bristol
Qualifications: 9 GCSEs, 2 A-levels, NCA coaching first level
Career outside cricket: 'Still looking for ideas. Maybe teaching?'
Off-season: 'Resting my body, but I will probably find some cricket to play'
Overseas tours: Sussex YC to Barbados 1993, to Sri Lanka 1995; England A to
Bangladesh and New Zealand 1999-2000
Overseas teams played for: Mashonaland, Zimbabwe 1996-97; Namibian Cricket
Board/Wanderers, Windhoek, Namibia 1998-99
Cricketers particularly admired: Curtly Ambrose, Jim Andrew, Darren Gough
Other sports followed: Hockey, golf, football (Brighton & Hove Albion)
Relaxations: 'Inviting friends round for a braii (barbeque) and enjoying a cold beer
with them'
Extras: Played in the Mashonaland side which defeated England on their 1996-97 tour
of Zimbabwe, taking seven wickets in the match. Winner of an NBC Denis Compton
Award for promising cricketers. Vice-captain of Sussex for 2001
Opinions on cricket: 'There should be a guaranteed two weeks off during the middle
of the season in order to recharge, if we continue to play in the current set-up.'
Best batting: 59 Sussex v Durham, Eastbourne 1998
Best bowling: 7-21 Sussex v Hampshire, Southampton 1999

2000 Season

	M	Inns	NO	Runs	HS	Avge	100s	50s	Ct	St	O	M	Runs	Wkts	Avge	Best	5wI	10wM
Test																		
All First	16	22	4	146	26 *	8.11	-	-	5	-	521.4	138	1559	63	24.74	6-41	4	-
1-day Int																		
NatWest	2	1	1	7	7 *	-	-	-	1	-	20	1	74	2	37.00	2-45	-	
B & H	4	2	2	14	10 *	-	-	-	-	-	35	5	130	4	32.50	2-24	-	
1-day Lge	15	8	4	35	13 *	8.75	-	-	3	-	106	6	499	26	19.19	4-32	-	

Career Performances

	M	Inns	NO	Runs	HS	Avge	100s	50s	Ct	St	Balls	Runs	Wkts	Avge	Best	5wI	10wM
Test																	
All First	77	107	32	774	59	10.32	-	1	21	-	13477	7088	275	25.77	7-21	15	1
1-day Int																	
NatWest	7	2	1	13	7 *	13.00	-	-	1	-	438	307	15	20.46	5-39	1	
B & H	7	4	2	17	10 *	8.50	-	-	-	-	389	280	11	25.45	3-42	-	
1-day Lge	60	27	16	127	17 *	11.54	-	-	18	-	2397	1926	89	21.64	4-21	-	

KNIGHT, N. V.   Warwickshire

Name: <u>Nicholas</u> Verity Knight
Role: Left-hand bat, right-arm medium-fast
bowler, close fielder
Born: 28 November 1969, Watford
Height: 6ft 1in   **Weight:** 13st
Nickname: Stitch, Fungus
County debut: 1991 (Essex),
1995 (Warwickshire)
County cap: 1994 (Essex),
1995 (Warwickshire)
Test debut: 1995
Tests: 16
One-Day Internationals: 53
1000 runs in a season: 2
1st-Class 50s: 45
1st-Class 100s: 21
1st-Class 200s: 1
1st-Class catches: 214
One-Day 100s: 12
Place in batting averages: 41st av. 39.53 (1999 75th av. 34.23)
Strike rate: (career 159.00)
Parents: John and Rosemary

Wife and date of marriage: Trudie, 3 October 1998
Family links with cricket: Father played for Cambridgeshire. Brother Andy plays club cricket in local Cambridge leagues
Education: St John's School, Cambridge; Felsted Prep; Felsted School; Loughborough University
Qualifications: 9 O-levels, 3 A-levels, BSc (Hons) Sociology, coaching qualification
Overseas tours: Felsted School to Australia 1986-87; England A to India 1994-95, to Pakistan 1995-96, to Kenya and Sri Lanka 1997-98; England to Zimbabwe and New Zealand 1996-97, to Sharjah 1997-98, to West Indies 1997-98 (one-day series), to Bangladesh (Wills International Cup) 1998, to Australia 1998-99 (CUB Series), to Sharjah (Coca-Cola Cup) 1998-99, to South Africa and Zimbabwe 1999-2000 (one-day series), to Sri Lanka 2000-01 (one-day series)
Overseas teams played for: Northern Districts, Sydney 1991-92; East Torrens, Adelaide 1992-94
Cricketers particularly admired: David Gower, Graham Gooch
Other sports played: Rugby, hockey
Relaxations: Eating good food, painting
Extras: Captained English Schools 1987 and 1988, England YC v New Zealand 1989 and Combined Universities 1991. Played hockey for Essex and Young England. Played rugby for Eastern Counties. Won *Daily Telegraph* award 1988; voted Gray-Nicolls Cricketer of the Year 1988, Cricket Society Cricketer of the Year 1989, Essex Young Player of the Year 1991 and Essex U19 Player of the Year. Left Essex at the end of 1994 season to join Warwickshire. Scored successive centuries in the Texaco Trophy against Pakistan in 1996. Man of the Match after striking 96 off 117 balls in first Test v Zimbabwe at Bulawayo 1996-97 as England chased 205 for victory; he was run out off the last ball of the match while attempting the winning run and the match was drawn with the scores level (the first such Test result). Won successive one-day Man of the Match awards v West Indies 1997-98. Warwickshire vice-captain 1999. Member of England's 1999 World Cup squad. Scored maiden first-class 200 (233) v Glamorgan at Edgbaston 2000. With Anurag Singh, shared in record NatWest first-wicket stand for Warwickshire (185), v Hampshire at Edgbaston 2000
Best batting: 233 Warwickshire v Glamorgan, Edgbaston 2000
Best bowling: 1-61 Essex v Middlesex, Uxbridge 1994
Stop press: Forced to withdraw from England one-day squads to Kenya and Pakistan with knee problem

2000 Season

	M	Inns	NO	Runs	HS	Avge	100s	50s	Ct	St	O	M	Runs	Wkts	Avge	Best	5wI	10wM
Test	4	7	0	119	44	17.00	-	-	3	-								
All First	10	15	0	593	233	39.53	1	1	7	-								
1-day Int																		
NatWest	4	4	0	220	118	55.00	2	-	1	-								
B & H	3	2	0	47	30	23.50	-	-	-	-								
1-day Lge	9	9	1	378	82	47.25	-	4	2	-								

Career Performances

	M	Inns	NO	Runs	HS	Avge	100s	50s	Ct	St	Balls	Runs	Wkts	Avge	Best	5wI	10wM
Test	16	28	0	704	113	25.14	1	4	24	-							
All First	153	255	25	9265	233	40.28	22	45	214	-	159	191	1	191.00	1-61	-	-
1-day Int	53	53	5	1924	125 *	40.08	3	12	20	-							
NatWest	21	21	2	864	151	45.47	4	3	8	-							
B & H	35	31	3	886	104	31.64	1	4	10	-	6	4	0	-		-	-
1-day Lge	112	102	14	2835	134	32.21	4	12	48	-	84	85	2	42.50	1-14	-	

KRIKKEN, K. M.   Derbyshire

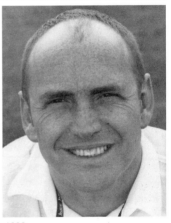

Name: <u>Karl</u> Matthew Krikken
Role: Right-hand bat, wicket-keeper,
occasional off-spin bowler
Born: 9 April 1969, Bolton
Height: 5ft 10in   **Weight:** 13st
Nickname: Krikk
County debut: 1987 (one-day),
1989 (first-class)
County cap: 1992
50 dismissals in a season: 5
1st-Class 50s: 22
1st-Class 100s: 1
1st-Class catches: 466
1st-Class stumpings: 30
Place in batting averages: 213th av. 17.00
(1999 160th av. 24.31)
Strike rate: (career 92.00)
Parents: Brian and Irene
Wife and date of marriage: Leesha, 3 October 1998
Children: Harry Evan, 20 December 1996; Chester, 19 December 1998
Family links with cricket: Father played for Lancashire and Worcestershire;
grandfather kept in local leagues
Education: Horwich Parish Church School; Rivington and Blackrod High School and
Sixth Form College
Qualifications: 6 O-levels, 3 A-levels, Level 3 coaching award
Off-season: 'Involved in cricket'
Overseas tours: Derbyshire to Bermuda 1993, to Malaga 1995, to Guernsey 1997, to
Portugal 1999
Overseas teams played for: CBC Old Boys, Kimberley, South Africa 1988-89;
Green Island, Dunedin, New Zealand 1990-91; United CC, Cape Town 1992-93;
Rivertonians, Cape Town 1993-94

Cricketers particularly admired: Derek Randall, Bob Taylor, Bruce French
Young players to look out for: 'A few in the ranks at Derby'
Other sports followed: Football (Wigan Athletic FC, Bolton Wanderers FC)
Injuries: Out for last eight weeks of the season with a broken left middle finger
Relaxations: Spending time with wife and family
Extras: Derbyshire Supporters' Player of the Year 1991 and 1996; Derbyshire Clubman of the Year 1993. Derbyshire vice-captain 1998-2000
Best batting: 104 Derbyshire v Lancashire, Old Trafford 1996
Best bowling: 1-54 Derbyshire v Hampshire, Derby 1999

2000 Season

	M	Inns	NO	Runs	HS	Avge	100s	50s	Ct	St	O	M	Runs	Wkts	Avge	Best	5wI	10wM
Test																		
All First	10	13	0	221	51	17.00	-	1	18	2								
1-day Int																		
NatWest	2	1	0	35	35	35.00	-	-	1	-								
B & H	5	1	0	13	13	13.00	-	-	5	1								
1-day Lge	9	9	1	76	34 *	9.50	-	-	7	5								

Career Performances

	M	Inns	NO	Runs	HS	Avge	100s	50s	Ct	St	Balls	Runs	Wkts	Avge	Best	5wI	10wM
Test																	
All First	190	280	54	5106	104	22.59	1	22	466	30	92	94	1	94.00	1-54	-	-
1-day Int																	
NatWest	20	12	5	201	55	28.71	-	1	15	1							
B & H	32	20	8	288	42 *	24.00	-	-	31	4							
1-day Lge	122	87	29	934	44 *	16.10	-	-	129	25							

KUMBLE, A.   Leicestershire

Name: Anil Kumble
Role: Right-hand bat, leg-spin bowler
Born: 17 December 1969, Bangalore
Height: 6ft 1in **Weight:** 12st 8lbs
Nickname: Apple, Kumbles
County debut: 1995 (Northants), 2000 (Leics)
County cap: 1995 (Northants), 2000 (Leics)
Test debut: 1990
Tests: 61
One-Day Internationals: 203
100 wickets in a season: 1
1st-Class 50s: 15

1st-Class 100s: 6
1st-Class 5 w. in innings: 49
1st-Class 10 w. in match: 13
1st-Class catches: 72
One-Day 5 w. in innings: 3
Place in batting averages: 261st av. 11.31
Place in bowling averages: 59th av. 25.17
Strike rate: 66.46 (career 58.07)
Parents: K.N. Krishnaswani and
Sarola Swami
Marital status: Single
Education: Holy Saint English School,
Bangalore; National High School, Bangalore;
National College and RV College of
Engineering, Bangalore
Overseas tours: India to England 1990, to
Australia 1991-92, to South Africa 1992-93,
to Zimbabwe 1992-93, to Sri Lanka 1993-94,

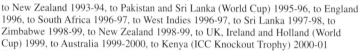

to New Zealand 1993-94, to Pakistan and Sri Lanka (World Cup) 1995-96, to England
1996, to South Africa 1996-97, to West Indies 1996-97, to Sri Lanka 1997-98, to
Zimbabwe 1998-99, to New Zealand 1998-99, to UK, Ireland and Holland (World
Cup) 1999, to Australia 1999-2000, to Kenya (ICC Knockout Trophy) 2000-01
Overseas teams played for: Karnataka, India 1989-90 –
Other sports followed: Tennis, football
Relaxations: Listening to music, watching television
Extras: Played for Northants 1995. Took 10-74 (14-159 in the match) v Pakistan in
the second Test at Delhi, February 1999, the first ten-wicket haul by a bowler in Tests
since Jim Laker's 10-53 v Australia at Old Trafford 1956. Represented India in the
1999 World Cup. Man of the Series, India v New Zealand 1999. In the first Test v
South Africa at Mumbai 1999-2000 he passed Bishen Bedi's total of 266 Test wickets
to move into second place behind Kapil Dev in the list of Indian Test wicket-takers.
Second in list of leading Test wicket-takers of 1999 with 54 (av. 27.06). Played for an
Asia XI v a World XI in Dhaka and at The Oval 2000. Joined Leicestershire for 2000
as overseas player; left Leicestershire at the end of the 2000 season
Best batting: 154* Karnataka v Kerala, Bijapur 1991-92
Best bowling: 10-74 India v Pakistan, Delhi 1998-99

2000 Season

	M	Inns	NO	Runs	HS	Avge	100s	50s	Ct	St	O	M	Runs	Wkts	Avge	Best	5wI	10wM
Test																		
All First	12	16	0	181	56	11.31	-	1	3	-	498.3	139	1133	45	25.17	6-44	2	1
1-day Int																		
NatWest	2	2	1	2	1 *	2.00	-	-	-	-	19.3	2	60	6	10.00	5-27	1	
B & H	4	3	0	11	9	3.66	-	-	-	-	30	5	96	9	10.66	4-28	-	
1-day Lge	12	7	1	31	13	5.16	-	-	6	-	99.5	11	346	16	21.62	3-26	-	

Career Performances

	M	Inns	NO	Runs	HS	Avge	100s	50s	Ct	St	Balls	Runs	Wkts	Avge	Best	5wI	10wM
Test	61	81	15	1192	88	18.06	-	3	29	-	19121	7733	276	28.01	10-74	16	3
All First	155	203	41	4012	154 *	24.76	6	15	72	-	41352	16855	712	23.67	10-74	49	13
1-day Int	203	99	34	693	26	10.66	-	-	72	-	10897	7634	267	28.59	6-12	2	
NatWest	7	4	2	10	6 *	5.00	-	-	1	-	474	263	17	15.47	5-27	1	
B & H	8	6	0	16	9	2.66	-	-	1	-	406	231	12	19.25	4-28	-	
1-day Lge	22	10	2	42	13	5.25	-	-	9	-	1013	693	32	21.65	3-25	-	

LACEY, S. J.   Derbyshire

Name: <u>Simon</u> James Lacey
Role: Right-hand bat, off-spin bowler
Born: 9 March 1975, Nottingham
Height: 5ft 11in **Weight:** 12st 11lbs
Nickname: Lace, Bone, Boneface, Spaceace, Junior Champ
County debut: 1997
1st-Class 50s: 2
1st-Class catches: 8
1st-Class stumpings: 1
Place in batting averages: 193rd av. 18.61 (1999 144th av. 25.66)
Place in bowling averages: 128th av. 39.12
Strike rate: 90.68 (career 100.96)
Parents: Phil and Anne
Wife and date of marriage: Keleigh, 26 October 1999
Family links with cricket: Brother plays league cricket for Langley Mill CC in Derbyshire County League
Education: Mundy Street School, Heanor; Aldercar Comprehensive School, Langley Mill; Mill Hill Sixth Form, Ripley
Qualifications: 6 GCSEs, senior coaching award

Career outside cricket: Police force or PE teacher
Cricketers particularly admired: Robin Smith, Phil Tufnell
Young players to look out for: Sam Patel, Ian Blackwell
Other sports played: Golf, volleyball (Nottingham Rockets)
Other sports followed: Football (Derby County, Ilkeston Town)
Relaxations: Golf, gardening, DIY
Extras: Was a member of the England Junior Volleyball squad in 1991. Captained the NAYC at U19 level against ESCA at Lord's in 1994. Released by Derbyshire at the end of the 2000 season
Opinions on cricket: 'All groundsmen should be contracted to the ECB to prevent clubs preparing sub-standard pitches to suit their own means. Points for a draw should be scrapped to try and provide more positive cricket.'
Best batting: 55* Derbyshire v Hampshire, Derby 2000
Best bowling: 4-84 Derbyshire v Hampshire, Derby 2000

2000 Season

	M	Inns	NO	Runs	HS	Avge	100s	50s	Ct	St	O	M	Runs	Wkts	Avge	Best	5wl	10wM
Test																		
All First	11	17	4	242	55 *	18.61	-	1	1	-	241.5	68	626	16	39.12	4-84	-	-
1-day Int																		
NatWest	2	1	0	0	0	0.00	-	-	-	-	19	3	87	1	87.00	1-62	-	
B & H																		
1-day Lge	11	9	0	60	40	6.66	-	-	3	-	60	2	309	3	103.00	2-32	-	

Career Performances

	M	Inns	NO	Runs	HS	Avge	100s	50s	Ct	St	Balls	Runs	Wkts	Avge	Best	5wl	10wM
Test																	
All First	26	36	10	553	55 *	21.26	-	2	8	1	3029	1429	30	47.63	4-84	-	-
1-day Int																	
NatWest	2	1	0	0	0	0.00	-	-	-	-	114	87	1	87.00	1-62	-	
B & H																	
1-day Lge	18	13	0	88	40	6.76	-	-	4	-	636	542	8	67.75	3-38	-	

LAMBERT, G. A. Yorkshire

Name: <u>Greg</u> Andrew Lambert
Role: Right-hand bat, right-arm medium-fast bowler
Born: 4 January 1980, Stoke-on-Trent
Height: 6ft 8in **Weight:** 16st
Nickname: Gonz, Sticks, Longdog, Bigbird, G-raffe
County debut: 2000
1st-Class catches: 1
Strike rate: 69.00 (career 69.00)
Parents: Steve and Louise
Marital status: Girlfriend Nicola
Family links with cricket: 'Grew up watching father playing for Bradshaw CC and Tadcaster CC'
Education: Riverside County Primary School; Tadcaster Grammar School
Qualifications: NVQ Sport and Rec, senior coaching award
Career outside cricket: Restaurant manager
Off-season: 'Training hard!'
Overseas tours: Yorkshire Cricket School to India 1999; Yorkshire CCC to Singapore and Perth 2000
Overseas teams played for: East Keilor, Melbourne 1998
Cricketers particularly admired: Glenn McGrath, Allan Donald, 'any player who makes it at pro sport'
Young players to look out for: Vic Craven, Joe Sayers, Michael Lumb
Other sports played: Football (York City Schoolboys U10 and U11), golf, 'anything'
Other sports followed: Rugby league (Halifax Blue Sox), football (Man Utd)
Relaxations: Music, socialising, walking the dog, watching Halifax Blue Sox
Extras: Played for Yorkshire Board XI in the NatWest 1999
Opinions on cricket: 'Two divisions a good idea to make the Championship more competitive; it can surely only improve players.'
Best batting: 3* Yorkshire v Kent, Canterbury 2000
Best bowling: 2-62 Yorkshire v Kent, Canterbury 2000

2000 Season

	M	Inns	NO	Runs	HS	Avge	100s	50s	Ct	St	O	M	Runs	Wkts	Avge	Best	5wI	10wM
Test																		
All First	2	3	2	6	3*	6.00	-	-	1	-	46	7	133	4	33.25	2-62	-	-
1-day Int																		
NatWest																			
B & H																			
1-day Lge																			

Career Performances

	M	Inns	NO	Runs	HS	Avge	100s	50s	Ct	St	Balls	Runs	Wkts	Avge	Best	5wI	10wM
Test																	
All First	2	3	2	6	3*	6.00	-	-	1	-	276	133	4	33.25	2-62	-	-
1-day Int																	
NatWest	1	1	0	0	0	0.00	-	-	-	-	18	22	2	11.00	2-22	-	
B & H																	
1-day Lge																	

LAMPITT, S. R.   Worcestershire

Name: <u>Stuart</u> Richard Lampitt
Role: Right-hand bat, right-arm
medium-fast bowler
Born: 29 July 1966, Wolverhampton
Height: 5ft 11in **Weight:** 14st
Nickname: Jed
County debut: 1985
County cap: 1989
Benefit: 2000
50 wickets in a season: 7
1st-Class 50s: 20
1st-Class 100s: 1
1st-Class 5 w. in innings: 19
1st-Class catches: 144
One-Day 5 w. in innings: 3
Place in batting averages: 206th av. 17.42
(1999 110th av. 29.50)
Place in bowling averages: 28th av. 20.94
(1999 40th av. 22.76)
Strike rate: 44.23 (career 53.42)
Parents: Joseph Charles and Muriel Ann
Marital status: Engaged to Clare

Education: Kingswinford Secondary School; Dudley College of Technology
Qualifications: 7 O-levels, Diploma in Business Studies, NCA advanced coach
Career outside cricket: 'Unknown as yet, but better start preparing!!'
Off-season: 'Completing benefit and coaching with WCB Youth Development'
Overseas tours: NCA U19 to Bermuda; Worcestershire to Bahamas 1990, to Zimbabwe 1990-91, to South Africa 1991-92, to Barbados 1996, to Portugal 2000
Overseas teams played for: Mangere, Auckland 1986-88; University CC, Perth 1991-93
Cricketers particularly admired: Ian Botham, Malcolm Marshall
Young players to look out for: 'The good ones'
Other sports played: Golf, fishing
Other sports followed: Football (Wolves FC)
Relaxations: Golf, fishing
Extras: Took five wickets and made 42 for Stourbridge in final of the William Younger Cup at Lord's in 1986. One of the Whittingdale Young Players of the Year 1990. 'Must be the only bowler to be hit for six first ball by Adrian Jones and Phil Tufnell (two master batsmen)'
Opinions on cricket: 'Great game!!'
Best batting: 122 Worcestershire v Middlesex, Lord's 1994
Best bowling: 7-45 Worcestershire v Warwickshire, Worcester 2000

2000 Season

	M	Inns	NO	Runs	HS	Avge	100s	50s	Ct	St	O	M	Runs	Wkts	Avge	Best	5wI	10wM
Test																		
All First	18	27	8	331	56 *	17.42	-	1	12	-	412.5	108	1173	56	20.94	7-45	2	-
1-day Int																		
NatWest	2	2	0	3	3	1.50	-	-	-	-	20	2	55	3	18.33	2-25	-	
B & H	3	0	0	0	0	-	-	-	1	-	13	0	32	3	10.66	2-16	-	
1-day Lge	16	14	1	128	39	9.84	-	-	5	-	114.1	17	426	13	32.76	3-32	-	

Career Performances

	M	Inns	NO	Runs	HS	Avge	100s	50s	Ct	St	Balls	Runs	Wkts	Avge	Best	5wI	10wM
Test																	
All First	226	298	69	5444	122	23.77	1	20	144	-	30829	16555	577	28.69	7-45	19	-
1-day Int																	
NatWest	27	20	4	223	54	13.93	-	1	7	-	1457	1008	41	24.58	5-22	1	
B & H	42	22	7	277	41	18.46	-	-	12	-	2134	1395	66	21.13	6-26	1	
1-day Lge	180	110	36	1349	41 *	18.22	-	-	54	-	6429	4984	198	25.17	5-67	1	

LANEY, J. S.   Hampshire

Name: <u>Jason</u> Scott Laney
Role: Right-hand bat, occasional off-spin
bowler
Born: 27 April 1973, Winchester
Height: 5ft 10in **Weight:** 13st 7lbs
Nickname: Chucky, Hurler, Crickethead,
Cricket Badger
County debut: 1993 (one-day),
1995 (first-class)
County cap: 1996
1000 runs in a season: 1
1st-Class 50s: 23
1st-Class 100s: 5
1st-Class catches: 57
One-Day 100s: 2
Place in batting averages: 175th av. 20.37
(1999 44th av. 38.38)
Strike rate: (career 192.00)

Parents: Geoff and Pam
Marital status: Single
Family links with cricket: Grandfather played good club cricket
Education: Pewsey Vale Comprehensive; St John's, Marlborough;
Leeds Metropolitan University
Qualifications: 8 GCSEs, 2 A-levels, BA (Hons) in Human Movement Studies
Career outside cricket: 'Plumber, dole casher'
Off-season: 'Attempting to find some kind of work'
Overseas tours: England U18 to Canada 1991
Overseas teams played for: Waikato, New Zealand 1994-95; Matabeleland and Old
Miltonians, Zimbabwe 1995-96; DHS Old Boys, South Africa 1996-97
Cricketers particularly admired: Rupert Cox, Ian Botham, Robin Smith, Malcolm
Marshall
Young players to look out for: Lawrence Prittipaul, Chris Tremlett, Jimmy Adams
Other sports played: Golf, cards, 'any other form of cricket'
Other sports followed: Football (Swindon Town FC)
Injuries: 'Bicknellitis; no time off cricket, just less time spent in the middle!'
Relaxations: 'Watching cricket videos, playing lots of cricket, scoring for my local
cricket team'
Extras: Hampshire Young Cricketer of the Year 1995. Became first Hampshire
cricketer to score a century before lunch on debut in the NatWest Trophy 1996
Opinions on cricket: 'Smashing game. The more I play, the more I want to play. I'm
a true cricket badger.'

Best batting: 112 Hampshire v Oxford University, The Parks 1996
Best bowling: 1-24 Hampshire v Northamptonshire, Northampton 1999

2000 Season

	M	Inns	NO	Runs	HS	Avge	100s	50s	Ct	St	O	M	Runs	Wkts	Avge	Best	5wI	10wM
Test																		
All First	14	25	1	489	81	20.37	-	2	12	-								
1-day Int																		
NatWest	4	3	1	75	43	37.50	-	-	1	-								
B & H	4	4	0	24	17	6.00	-	-	-	-								
1-day Lge	15	15	0	286	69	19.06	-	1	2	-								

Career Performances

	M	Inns	NO	Runs	HS	Avge	100s	50s	Ct	St	Balls	Runs	Wkts	Avge	Best	5wI	10wM
Test																	
All First	76	135	4	3988	112	30.44	5	23	57	-	384	224	2	112.00	1-24	-	-
1-day Int																	
NatWest	14	13	1	635	153	52.91	1	3	6	-							
B & H	17	17	0	245	41	14.41	-	-	3	-							
1-day Lge	64	64	1	1460	106 *	23.17	1	6	18	-	3	9	0	-	-	-	-

LANGER, J. L.   Middlesex

Name: <u>Justin</u> Lee Langer
Role: Left-hand bat, right-arm medium bowler
Born: 21 November 1970, Subiaco, Western Australia
Height: 5ft 8in   **Weight:** 12st 4lbs
Nickname: JL
County debut: 1998
County cap: 1998
Test debut: 1992-93
Tests: 33
One-Day Internationals: 8
1000 runs in a season: 3
1st-Class 50s: 56
1st-Class 100s: 37
1st-Class 200s: 9
1st-Class catches: 160
One-Day 100s: 2
Place in batting averages: 7th av. 61.33 (1999 3rd av. 58.22)

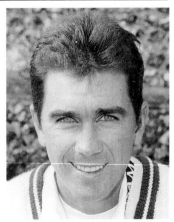

Strike rate: 36.00 (career 70.80)
Parents: Colin and Joy-Anne
Wife and date of marriage: Sue, 13 April 1996
Children: Jessica, 28 March 1997; Ali Rose 1998
Family links with cricket: Uncle, Robbie Langer, played Sheffield Shield cricket for Western Australia and World Series for Australia
Education: Liwara Catholic School; Aquinas College, Perth; University of Western Australia
Career outside cricket: Writing, stockbroking
Off-season: Playing in Australia
Overseas tours: Young Australia to England 1995; Australia to New Zealand 1992-93, to South Africa 1996-97, to England 1997, to Pakistan 1998-99, to West Indies 1998-99, to Sri Lanka and Zimbabwe 1999-2000, to New Zealand 1999-2000, to India 2000-01
Overseas teams played for: Western Australia 1991-92 –
Cricketers particularly admired: Graham Gooch, Mike Gatting, Graeme Hick, Allan Border, David Boon, Dennis Lillee
Young players to look out for: 'Ace' Shah, Jamie Hewitt
Other sports played: Tennis, golf, Aussie Rules, martial arts (has black belts in judo and taekwondo)
Other sports followed: Football (Man Utd), Aussie Rules (West Coast Eagles)
Relaxations: Family, writing
Extras: Scored 54 (Australia's only 50 of the match) in the second innings of his debut Test v West Indies at Adelaide 1992-93. Scored 233* on first-class debut for Middlesex at Lord's v Somerset 1998. With Mike Gatting, took part in an opening stand of 372 v Essex at Southgate in 1998, setting a new county record for the first wicket. His 241* for Middlesex v Kent at Lord's on 16 April 1999 was the earliest Championship double-century in an English first-class season and the highest score ever at Lord's in April. Appointed Middlesex vice-captain for 1999. Scored 179* and 52 in the third Test v England at Adelaide 1998-99, receiving Man of the Match award. Put on 238 for the sixth wicket with Adam Gilchrist in the fourth innings of Australia's victory v Pakistan at Hobart in November 1999; his 127 (coupled with 59 in the first innings) won him the Man of the Match award. His 223 at Sydney in the third Test v India, January 2000, was the highest Test score by an Australian v India. Scored 2013 first-class runs at 57.51 in the 1999-2000 season. Middlesex captain in 2000. Awarded ACB contract for 2000-01. Left Middlesex at the end of the 2000 season
Best batting: 274* Western Australia v South Australia, Perth 1996-97
Best bowling: 2-17 Australia A v South Africans, Brisbane 1997-98

2000 Season

	M	Inns	NO	Runs	HS	Avge	100s	50s	Ct	St	O	M	Runs	Wkts	Avge	Best	5wI	10wM
Test																		
All First	16	27	3	1472	213 *	61.33	5	7	25	-	6	1	35	1	35.00	1-29	-	-
1-day Int																		
NatWest	3	3	0	126	100	42.00	1	-	2	-								
B & H	1	1	1	66	66 *	-	-	-	1	1	-							
1-day Lge	15	15	1	374	93	26.71	-	3	11	-								

Career Performances

	M	Inns	NO	Runs	HS	Avge	100s	50s	Ct	St	Balls	Runs	Wkts	Avge	Best	5wI	10wM
Test	33	55	2	2213	223	41.75	7	10	23	-							
All First	178	313	35	14723	274 *	52.96	46	56	160	-	354	191	5	38.20	2-17	-	-
1-day Int	8	7	2	160	36	32.00	-	-	2	1							
NatWest	7	7	1	350	114 *	58.33	2	1	2	-	30	45	1	45.00	1-45	-	
B & H	6	6	1	202	71	40.40	-	2	4	-							
1-day Lge	38	37	2	1102	93	31.48	-	9	18	-	169	185	6	30.83	3-51	-	

LARAMAN, A. W.   Middlesex

Name: <u>Aaron</u> William Laraman
Role: Right-hand bat, right-arm fast bowler
Born: 10 January 1979, Enfield
Height: 6ft 5in **Weight:** 13st 5lbs
Nickname: Lazza
County debut: 1998 (one-day),
2000 (first-class)
1st-Class catches: 1
One-Day 5 w. in innings: 2
Strike rate: 31.50 (career 31.50)
Parents: William and Lynda
Marital status: Single
Education: St Paul's C of E School;
Enfield Grammar School
Qualifications: 8 GCSEs
Overseas tours: England U17 to Holland
1995; England U19 to South Africa 1997-98
Cricketers particularly admired:
Viv Richards, Ian Botham
Young players to look out for: Robert Key, Stephen Peters
Other sports followed: Football (Arsenal)
Relaxations: Working out at the gym, football, golf

Extras: Enfield Grammar School cap at the age of 13. Middlesex Colts county cap. Seaxe 2nd XI Player of the Year 1997. Took 4-39 on NatWest debut v Nottinghamshire at Lord's 2000
Best bowling: 4-33 Middlesex v Cambridge University, Fenner's 2000

2000 Season

	M	Inns	NO	Runs	HS	Avge	100s	50s	Ct	St	O	M	Runs	Wkts	Avge	Best	5wI	10wM
Test																		
All First	1	0	0	0	0	-	-	-	1	-	21	4	55	4	13.75	4-33	-	-
1-day Int																		
NatWest	3	1	0	2	2	2.00	-	-	1	-	23.3	3	66	8	8.25	4-39	-	
B & H																		
1-day Lge	8	7	4	30	11 *	10.00	-	-	2	-	63.1	4	275	17	16.17	6-42	2	

Career Performances

	M	Inns	NO	Runs	HS	Avge	100s	50s	Ct	St	Balls	Runs	Wkts	Avge	Best	5wI	10wM
Test																	
All First	2	0	0	0	0	-	-	-	1	-	126	55	4	13.75	4-33	-	-
1-day Int																	
NatWest	3	1	0	2	2	2.00	-	-	1	-	141	66	8	8.25	4-39	-	
B & H																	
1-day Lge	10	8	4	33	11 *	8.25	-	-	4	-	400	299	17	17.58	6-42	2	

51. Which of the 2000 season's overseas players was the first Australian to take six wickets in a Test innings at Edgbaston?

LATHWELL, M. N.   Somerset

Name: <u>Mark</u> Nicholas Lathwell
Role: Right-hand bat, right-arm
off-spin bowler
Born: 26 December 1971, Bletchley, Bucks
Height: 5ft 8in **Weight:** 12st
Nickname: Trough, Lathers
County debut: 1991
County cap: 1992
Test debut: 1993
Tests: 2
1000 runs in a season: 4
1st-Class 50s: 49
1st-Class 100s: 11
1st-Class 200s: 1
1st-Class catches: 96
One-Day 100s: 4
Place in batting averages: 181st av. 19.76
Strike rate: (career 84.76)

Parents: Derek Peter and Valerie
Wife and date of marriage: Lisa, October 1996
Children: Jason, 16 January 1995; Sam, 27 October 1997
Family links with cricket: Father and brother both club cricketers; father qualified
coach
Education: Overstone Primary, Wing, Bucks; Southmead School, Braunton, North
Devon; Braunton School and Community College
Qualifications: 5 GCSEs, cricket coaching certificate
Career outside cricket: Coaching
Overseas tours: England A to Australia 1992-93, to South Africa 1993-94
Cricketers particularly admired: Ian Botham, Graham Gooch
Other sports played: Darts
Other sports followed: Snooker
Relaxations: Cooking, eating, sleeping
Extras: Played for Devon. Spent one season on Lord's groundstaff. Played for
England U19 v Australia U19 1991. PCA Young Player of the Year and Somerset
Player of the Year 1992. Cricket Writers' Club Young Cricketer of the Year 1993
Opinions on cricket: 'Day/night cricket has brought another dimension to the one-day
game, but to keep these occasions special they must not be overplayed.'
Best batting: 206 Somerset v Surrey, Bath 1994
Best bowling: 2-21 Somerset v Sussex, Hove 1994

2000 Season

	M	Inns	NO	Runs	HS	Avge	100s	50s	Ct	St	O	M	Runs	Wkts	Avge	Best	5wI	10wM
Test																		
All First	9	14	1	257	54 *	19.76	-	1	4	-								
1-day Int																		
NatWest																			
B & H																			
1-day Lge	9	9	0	194	53	21.55	-	1	3	-								

Career Performances

	M	Inns	NO	Runs	HS	Avge	100s	50s	Ct	St	Balls	Runs	Wkts	Avge	Best	5wI	10wM
Test	2	4	0	78	33	19.50	-	-	-	-							
All First	143	251	10	8025	206	33.29	12	49	96	-	1102	684	13	52.61	2-21	-	-
1-day Int																	
NatWest	18	17	0	465	103	27.35	1	2	7	-	66	23	1	23.00	1-23	-	
B & H	21	21	0	821	121	39.09	2	6	7	-	25	50	0	-	-	-	-
1-day Lge	113	111	5	2839	117	26.78	1	17	28	-	102	85	0	-	-	-	-

LAW, D. R. Durham

Name: <u>Danny</u> Richard Law
Role: Right-hand bat, right-arm fast bowler
Born: 15 July 1975, London
Height: 6ft 5in **Weight:** 15st 7lbs
County debut: 1993 (Sussex), 1997 (Essex)
County cap: 1996 (Sussex)
1st-Class 50s: 11
1st-Class 100s: 1
1st-Class 5 w. in innings: 5
1st-Class catches: 42
Place in batting averages: 197th av. 18.00
Place in bowling averages: 111th av. 34.73
Strike rate: 58.33 (career 54.03)
Parents: Richard (deceased) and Claudette
Wife: Carly
Children: Sade
Education: Wolverstone Hall; Steyning Grammar School
Career outside cricket: 'Cricket coach, site investigation, labourer'
Off-season: Training and touring with Dulwich CC to Kenya and Uganda
Overseas tours: Sussex Schools U16 to Jersey 1991; England U18 to South Africa 1992-93, to Denmark 1993; England U19 to Sri Lanka 1993-94; Dulwich CC to Kenya and Uganda 2000-01

Overseas teams played for: Ashburton CC, Melbourne 1992-94; Essendon, Melbourne 1995-96
Cricketers particularly admired: Graham Gooch, Viv Richards, Michael Holding, Ian Botham
Young players to look out for: James Foster, Andy McGarry, Justin Bishop
Other sports played: Golf
Other sports followed: Football (Man Utd)
Relaxations: Cinema, music and family
Extras: Winner of Denis Compton award 1996. Left Sussex during the 1996 off-season and joined Essex for the 1997 season on a three-year contract. Took Championship hat-trick v Durham at Riverside 1998. Left Essex at the end of the 2000 season and has joined Durham for 2001
Opinions on cricket: 'Two divisions was a success. Anybody involved with a chance of being promoted will tell you how difficult it was playing at the end of the year with so much riding on every game.'
Best batting: 115 Sussex v Young Australia, Hove 1995
Best bowling: 5-33 Sussex v Durham, Hove 1996

2000 Season

	M	Inns	NO	Runs	HS	Avge	100s	50s	Ct	St	O	M	Runs	Wkts	Avge	Best	5wI	10wM
Test																		
All First	15	23	3	360	68 *	18.00	-	2	6	-	291.4	50	1042	30	34.73	5-78	1	-
1-day Int																		
NatWest	2	2	0	53	45	26.50	-	-	1	-	9	0	54	3	18.00	2-8	-	
B & H	3	3	0	62	34	20.66	-	-	-	-	11	0	61	0	-	-	-	
1-day Lge	15	13	2	193	37	17.54	-	-	4	-	95	4	442	18	24.55	3-41	-	

Career Performances

	M	Inns	NO	Runs	HS	Avge	100s	50s	Ct	St	Balls	Runs	Wkts	Avge	Best	5wI	10wM
Test																	
All First	80	124	5	2332	115	19.59	1	11	42	-	8213	5214	152	34.30	5-33	5	-
1-day Int																	
NatWest	14	10	1	188	47	20.88	-	-	4	-	153	149	4	37.25	2-8	-	
B & H	12	11	1	157	36 *	15.70	-	-	1	-	162	137	1	137.00	1-44	-	
1-day Lge	86	73	12	1415	82	23.19	-	5	19	-	1558	1393	48	29.02	3-26	-	

LAW, S. G. Essex

Name: <u>Stuart</u> Grant Law
Role: Right-hand bat, right-arm occasional bowler
Born: 18 October 1968, Herston, Brisbane, Australia
Height: 6ft 1in **Weight:** 13st 7lbs
Nickname: Judge, LA
County debut: 1996
County cap: 1996
Test debut: 1995-96
Tests: 1
One-Day Internationals: 54
1000 runs in a season: 5
1st-Class 50s: 72
1st-Class 100s: 46
1st-Class 200s: 2
1st-Class 5 w. in innings: 1
1st-Class catches: 235
One-Day 100s: 11
Place in batting averages: 10th av. 55.40 (1999 1st av. 73.32)
Strike rate: (career 97.20)
Parents: Grant and Pam
Wife and date of marriage: Debbie Lee, 31 December 1998
Family links with cricket: Grandfather and father played club cricket
Education: Stafford State School; Craigslea State High School
Off-season: Playing for Queensland
Overseas tours: Young Australia to England 1995; Australia to India and Pakistan (World Cup) 1995-96, to Sri Lanka (Singer World Series), India and South Africa 1996-97, to New Zealand (one-day series) 1997-98
Overseas teams played for: Queensland 1988-89 –
Cricketers particularly admired: Greg Chappell, Martin Crowe, Viv Richards
Young players to look out for: Ricky Anderson, Matt Windows
Other sports played: Golf ('very social'), 'try anything once', tennis
Other sports followed: Rugby league (Brisbane Broncos)
Relaxations: 'Spending days at the beach with my wife. Sports cars.'
Extras: Made his first-class debut for Queensland as a 19-year-old, scoring 179 in only his second appearance. Captained Queensland to their first Sheffield Shield title in 1994-95, to their second in 1996-97 and to the inaugural Pura Milk Cup title in 1999-2000. Made his Test debut for Australia against Sri Lanka at Perth in 1995-96 and scored an unbeaten 54. Played in all 17 One-Day Internationals for Australia in 1995-96. Man of the Match in the 1997 NatWest final at Lord's. One of *Wisden*'s Five

Cricketers of the Year 1998. Scored centuries (159 and 113*) in each innings v Yorkshire at Chelmsford 1999; Michael Vaughan scored two 100s for Yorks in the same match. Topped the first-class batting averages for 1999. Professional Cricketers' Association Player of the Year 1999. Man of the Match in inaugural Pura Milk Cup Final 1999-2000. Played for a World XI v an Asia XI at The Oval 2000

Opinions on cricket: 'Play too much.'

Best batting: 263 Essex v Somerset, Chelmsford 1999

Best bowling: 5-39 Queensland v Tasmania, Brisbane 1995-96

2000 Season

	M	Inns	NO	Runs	HS	Avge	100s	50s	Ct	St	O	M	Runs	Wkts	Avge	Best	5wI	10wM
Test																		
All First	16	27	2	1385	189	55.40	5	6	19	-	1	0	11	0	-	-	-	--
1-day Int																		
NatWest	2	2	0	31	27	15.50	-	-	2	-								
B & H	3	3	0	15	9	5.00	-	-	-	-	5	0	31	0	-	-	-	
1-day Lge	13	13	1	413	104 *	34.41	1	2	1	-	3	0	10	0	-	-	-	

Career Performances

	M	Inns	NO	Runs	HS	Avge	100s	50s	Ct	St	Balls	Runs	Wkts	Avge	Best	5wI	10wM
Test	1	1	1	54	54 *	-	-	1	1	-	18	9	0	-	-	-	-
All First	210	352	36	15465	263	48.93	48	72	235	-	7776	3781	80	47.26	5-39	1	-
1-day Int	54	51	5	1237	110	26.89	1	7	12	-	807	635	12	52.91	2-22	-	
NatWest	14	13	1	682	107	56.83	3	3	12	-	439	366	8	45.75	2-36	-	
B & H	19	18	0	560	116	31.11	1	2	10	-	384	351	9	39.00	2-13	-	
1-day Lge	71	70	4	2371	126	35.92	6	8	29	-	904	791	22	35.95	4-37	-	

LAW, W. L.   Glamorgan

Name: Wayne Lincoln Law
Role: Right-hand bat
Born: 4 September 1978, Swansea
Height: 5ft 10in **Weight:** 11st 5lbs
Nickname: Sods
County debut: 1997
1st-Class 50s: 5
1st-Class 100s: 1
1st-Class catches: 11
Place in batting averages: 221st av. 16.10 (1999 135th av. 26.66)
Strike rate: (career 46.33)
Parents: Lincoln and Barbara
Marital status: Single

Education: Pentip; Graig School, Llanelli
Qualifications: 1 GCSE, NCA senior and advanced coaching awards
Career outside cricket: Coaching
Overseas tours: Dyfed U15 to Zimbabwe 1994; Glamorgan to Cape Town 1998
Cricketers particularly admired: Robert Croft 'the hard man of county cricket'
Young players to look out for: David Harrison, Owen Parkin
Other sports played: Squash, running
Other sports followed: Rugby (Llanelli, Felinfoel)
Relaxations: Reading
Extras: Scored first-class century (131) v Lancashire at Colwyn Bay in 1998 in only his second Championship match. Released by Glamorgan at the end of the 2000 season

Best batting: 131 Glamorgan v Lancashire, Colwyn Bay 1998
Best bowling: 2-29 Glamorgan v Cambridge University, Fenner's 1998

2000 Season

	M	Inns	NO	Runs	HS	Avge	100s	50s	Ct	St	O	M	Runs	Wkts	Avge	Best	5wI	10wM
Test																		
All First	8	11	1	161	85	16.10	-	1	4	-								
1-day Int																		
NatWest																		
B & H																		
1-day Lge	1	1	0	0	0	0.00	-	-	-	-								

Career Performances

	M	Inns	NO	Runs	HS	Avge	100s	50s	Ct	St	Balls	Runs	Wkts	Avge	Best	5wI	10wM
Test																	
All First	23	35	4	883	131	28.48	1	5	11	-	139	89	3	29.66	2-29	-	-
1-day Int																	
NatWest	1	1	1	2	2 *	-	-	-	-	-							
B & H																	
1-day Lge	10	10	1	102	24	11.33	-	-	3	-	6	6	0	-	-	-	-

LAZENBURY, P. S.   Kent

Name: <u>Paul</u> Stuart Lazenbury
Role: Left-hand bat, leg-spin bowler
Born: 10 August 1978, Bath
Height: 6ft **Weight:** 12st 2lbs
Nickname: Lazers
County debut: No first-team appearance
Parents: Elizabeth and Stuart
Marital status: Single
Family links with cricket: Father played
local club cricket
Education: Malmesbury Church of England;
Malmesbury Comprehensive
Qualifications: 9 GCSEs, 1 GNVQ
Overseas tours: Gloucestershire Gypsies to
Cape Town 1997-98
Cricketers particularly admired:
Mike Atherton
Other sports played: Golf, 'I like to have a
go at most sports'

Other sports followed: Football (Bristol Rovers), 'I enjoy watching most sports'
Relaxations: Eating out, 'and having a few drinks with the lads'
Extras: Formerly with Gloucestershire; scored 1000 2nd XI runs in first full season
1998. Played for Gloucestershire Board XI in NatWest 1999. Played for Herefordshire
in 2000 and was in their ECB 38-County Cup winning side, scoring 118 in the final

---

2000 Season (did not make any first-class or one-day appearances)

Career Performances

	M	Inns	NO	Runs	HS	Avge	100s	50s	Ct	St	Balls	Runs	Wkts	Avge	Best	5wI	10wM
Test																	
All First																		
1-day Int																		
NatWest	1	1	0	3	3	3.00	-	-	-	-							
B & H																		
1-day Lge																		

LEATHERDALE, D. A.

Name: <u>David</u> Anthony Leatherdale
Role: Right-hand bat, right-arm medium bowler, cover fielder
Born: 26 November 1967, Bradford
Height: 5ft 10in **Weight:** 11st
Nickname: Lugsy, Spock
County debut: 1988
County cap: 1994
1000 runs in a season: 1
1st-Class 50s: 46
1st-Class 100s: 12
1st-Class 5 w. in innings: 2
1st-Class catches: 138
Place in batting averages: 44th av. 39.00 (1999 178th av. 22.35)
Place in bowling averages: 67th av. 26.73
Strike rate: 48.63 (career 52.48)
Parents: Paul and Rosalyn

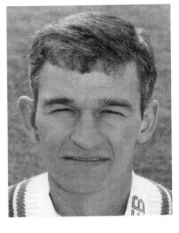

Wife: Vanessa
Children: Callum Edward, 6 July 1990; Christian Ellis, 5 years old
Family links with cricket: Father played local cricket; brother plays for East Bierley in Bradford League; brother-in-law played for England YC in 1979
Education: Bolton Royd Primary School; Pudsey Grangefield Secondary School
Qualifications: 8 O-levels, 2 A-levels; NCA coaching award (stage 1)
Overseas tours: England Indoor to Australia and New Zealand 1994-95
Overseas teams played for: Pretoria Police, South Africa 1987-88
Cricketers particularly admired: Mark Scott, George Batty, Peter Kippax
Other sports followed: Football, American football
Relaxations: Golf
Opinions on cricket: 'Changing the structure of cricket to make it more competitive is fine, but the amount of cricket played is still detrimental to the quality produced, due to the lack of time to rest, causing many players to play with injury and therefore not competing at their best.'
Best batting: 157 Worcestershire v Somerset, Worcester 1991
Best bowling: 5-20 Worcestershire v Gloucestershire, Worcester 1998

2000 Season

	M	Inns	NO	Runs	HS	Avge	100s	50s	Ct	St	O	M	Runs	Wkts	Avge	Best	5wI	10wM
Test																		
All First	17	30	5	975	132 *	39.00	2	7	9	-	154	34	508	19	26.73	3-17	-	-
1-day Int																		
NatWest	2	2	0	58	53	29.00	-	1	-	-	15	1	82	3	27.33	2-42	-	
B & H	3	1	1	17	17 *	-	-	-	1	-	12	1	43	2	21.50	2-23	-	
1-day Lge	16	15	0	314	43	20.93	-	-	6	-	71.2	2	345	13	26.53	3-30	-	

Career Performances

	M	Inns	NO	Runs	HS	Avge	100s	50s	Ct	St	Balls	Runs	Wkts	Avge	Best	5wI	10wM
Test																	
All First	179	289	34	8446	157	33.12	12	46	138	-	4986	2854	95	30.04	5-20	2	-
1-day Int																	
NatWest	24	21	1	421	53	21.05	-	1	8	-	268	234	6	39.00	3-14	-	
B & H	31	24	6	315	66	17.50	-	1	7	-	452	299	13	23.00	4-13	-	
1-day Lge	157	131	21	2145	70 *	19.50	-	8	74	-	1564	1352	66	20.48	4-19	-	

LEHMANN, D. S.   Yorkshire

Name: <u>Darren</u> Scott Lehmann
Role: Left-hand bat, slow left-arm bowler
Born: 5 February 1970, Gawler, Australia
Nickname: Boof
Height: 5ft 11in **Weight:** 14st 2lbs
County debut: 1997
County cap: 1997
Test debut: 1997-98
Tests: 5
One-Day Internationals: 60
1000 runs in a season: 2
1st-Class 50s: 69
1st-Class 100s: 43
1st-Class 200s: 5
1st-Class catches: 94
One-Day 100s: 5
Place in batting averages: 4th av. 67.13
Strike rate: 84.00 (career 95.09)
Off-season: Playing for South Australia
Overseas tours: Australia to Sri Lanka 1996-97, to New Zealand 1997-98, to Sharjah 1997-98, to India 1997-98, to Pakistan 1998-99, to Bangladesh 1998-99, to West Indies 1998-99 (one-day series), to UK, Ireland and Holland (World Cup) 1999, to Sri Lanka 1999-2000 (one-day series), to Zimbabwe 1999-2000 (one-day series)

Overseas teams played for: Salisbury District CC (now Northern Districts), Adelaide; South Australia 1987-88 – 1989-90; Victoria 1990-91 – 1992-93; South Australia 1993-94 –
Other sports followed: Australian Football League (Adelaide Crows)
Relaxations: Golf, watching sport
Extras: Represented South Australia at all age groups. Scored 1128 runs (av. 57.50) in his first full Sheffield Shield season. Man of the Match in CUB second final v England at Melbourne 1998-99. Played in Australia's 1999 World Cup winning side, striking the winning runs in the final v Pakistan. Released by Yorkshire at end of 1998 season. Scored 1142 runs at 63.44 (including seven centuries) in the 1999-2000 Australian season and was voted Interstate Cricketer of the Year 1999-2000 at the inaugural Allan Border Medal awards January 2000. Has scored 1000 runs in an Australian season five times. Returned to Yorkshire as overseas player in 2000. Won the EDS Walter Lawrence Trophy for the fastest first-class century of the 2000 season – 89 balls for Yorkshire v Kent at Canterbury. Top run-scorer in English first-class cricket 2000 with 1477 runs at an average of 67.13. Awarded ACB contract for 2000-01. Captain of South Australia since 1998-99
Best batting: 255 South Australia v Queensland, Adelaide 1996-97
Best bowling: 4-42 Yorkshire v Kent, Maidstone 1998

2000 Season

	M	Inns	NO	Runs	HS	Avge	100s	50s	Ct	St	O	M	Runs	Wkts	Avge	Best	5wI	10wM
Test																		
All First	16	23	1	1477	136	67.13	4	9	8	-	112	18	310	8	38.75	2-9	-	-
1-day Int																		
NatWest	2	2	1	55	48 *	55.00	-	-	1	-	6	0	26	3	8.66	3-26	-	
B & H	6	6	1	138	50	27.60	-	1	2	-	3	0	10	0	-		-	-
1-day Lge	16	16	3	564	89	43.38	-	4	3	-	41.4	1	178	6	29.66	2-13	-	

Career Performances

	M	Inns	NO	Runs	HS	Avge	100s	50s	Ct	St	Balls	Runs	Wkts	Avge	Best	5wI	10wM
Test	5	8	0	228	98	28.50	-	2	3	-	102	45	2	22.50	1-6	-	-
All First	169	288	18	14829	255	54.92	48	69	94	-	3138	1557	33	47.18	4-42	-	-
1-day Int	60	55	8	1527	110 *	32.48	2	8	9	-	466	417	11	37.90	2-4	-	
NatWest	7	6	1	188	105	37.60	1	-	2	-	84	45	4	11.25	3-26	-	
B & H	17	17	3	684	119	48.85	2	3	5	-	114	87	4	21.75	2-17	-	
1-day Lge	43	43	6	1662	99	44.91	-	14	10	-	476	388	13	29.84	3-43	-	

LEWIS, C. C.   Leicestershire

Name: <u>Christopher</u> Clairmonte Lewis
Role: Right-hand bat, right-arm
fast-medium bowler
Born: 14 February 1968,
Georgetown, Guyana
Height: 6ft 2in **Weight:** 13st
Nickname: Carl
County debut: 1987 (Leics), 1992 (Notts),
1996 (Surrey)
County cap: 1990 (Leics), 1994 (Notts),
1996 (Surrey)
Test debut: 1990
Tests: 32
One-Day Internationals: 53
50 wickets in a season: 2
1st-Class 50s: 34
1st-Class 100s: 7
1st-Class 200s: 2
1st-Class 5w. in innings: 20
1st-Class 10 w. in match: 3
1st-Class catches: 154

One-Day 100s: 1
One-Day 5 w. in innings: 2
Place in batting averages: 260th av. 11.42 (1999 14th av. 47.27)
Place in bowling averages: (1999 122nd av. 36.56)
Strike rate: 84.14 (career 58.93)
Parents: Philip and Patricia
Marital status: Single
Education: Willesden High School
Qualifications: 2 O-levels
Overseas tours: England YC to Australia (Youth World Cup) 1987-88; England A to
Kenya and Zimbabwe 1989-90; England to West Indies 1989-90, to Australia 1990-91,
to New Zealand 1991-92, to India and Sri Lanka 1992-93, to West Indies 1993-94,
to Australia 1994-95; England XI to New Zealand (Cricket Max) 1997
Cricketers particularly admired: Graham Gooch, Robin Smith
Other sports followed: Snooker, football, darts, American football, basketball
Injuries: Season disrupted by a long-standing hip injury
Relaxations: Music, sleeping
Extras: Suffers from Raynaud's disease, a problem of blood circulation. Left
Leicestershire at the end of 1991 season and signed for Nottinghamshire. Hit first Test
century v India at Madras on 1992-93 tour to India and Sri Lanka. Cornhill England

Player of the Year (jointly with Alec Stewart) 1992-93. His 247 v Durham at Chester-le-Street in 1993 is the highest score by a Nottinghamshire batsman since World War II. Left Nottinghamshire and joined Surrey for the 1996 season. Rejoined Leicestershire as vice-captain for the 1998 season and captained the club for much of the season in the absence through injury of James Whitaker. Scored 71* in 33 balls as Leicestershire made 204 in 19 overs and one ball to beat Northamptonshire at Grace Road in 1998. Retired during the 2000-01 off-season

Best batting: 247 Nottinghamshire v Durham, Chester-le-Street 1993
Best bowling: 6-22 Leicestershire v Oxford University, The Parks 1988

2000 Season

	M	Inns	NO	Runs	HS	Avge	100s	50s	Ct	St	O	M	Runs	Wkts	Avge	Best	5wI	10wM
Test																		
All First	5	7	0	80	24	11.42	-	-	6	-	98.1	12	302	7	43.14	2-33	-	-
1-day Int																		
NatWest	2	2	0	60	32	30.00	-	-	2	-	17	3	57	1	57.00	1-35	-	
B & H	3	3	1	34	29	17.00	-	-	-	-	24	5	79	4	19.75	2-6	-	
1-day Lge	10	9	2	77	26 *	11.00	-	-	4	-	76	13	238	13	18.30	4-34	-	

Career Performances

	M	Inns	NO	Runs	HS	Avge	100s	50s	Ct	St	Balls	Runs	Wkts	Avge	Best	5wI	10wM
Test	32	51	3	1105	117	23.02	1	4	25	-	6852	3490	93	37.52	6-111	3	-
All First	189	275	34	7406	247	30.73	9	34	154	-	32004	16225	543	29.88	6-22	20	3
1-day Int	53	40	14	374	33	14.38	-	-	20	-	2625	1942	66	29.42	4-30	-	
NatWest	26	21	2	452	89	23.78	-	2	16	-	1372	800	33	24.24	5-19	1	
B & H	46	33	13	583	55 *	29.15	-	1	18	-	2415	1613	69	23.37	5-46	1	
1-day Lge	130	114	26	2334	116 *	26.52	1	9	44	-	4966	3497	136	25.71	4-13	-	

52. Who scored two 50s, took five wickets and held two catches on his England Test debut at Old Trafford 1972?

LEWIS, J.   Gloucestershire

Name: Jonathan (Jon) Lewis
Role: Right-hand bat,
right-arm fast-medium bowler
Born: 26 August 1975, Aylesbury
Height: 6ft 2in **Weight:** 13st
Nickname: Lewy, JJ, Nugget
County debut: 1995
County cap: 1998
50 wickets in a season: 3
1st-Class 50s: 2
1st-Class 5 w. in innings: 12
1st-Class 10 w. in match: 1
1st-Class catches: 17
Place in batting averages: 286th av. 8.04
(1999 255th av. 13.30)
Place in bowling averages: 27th av. 20.91
(1999 90th av. 29.46)
Strike rate: 46.87 (career 51.80)
Parents: John and Jane
Marital status: Single
Education: Lawn Primary, Swindon; Churchfields Secondary, Swindon;
Swindon College
Qualifications: 9 GCSEs, BTEC in Leisure and Hospitality
Off-season: 'Training – on standby for England A to West Indies'
Overseas tours: Bath Schools to New South Wales, Australia 1993; England A to
West Indies 2000-01
Overseas teams played for: Marist, Christchurch, New Zealand 1994-95;
Richmond City, Melbourne 1995-96; Wanderers, Johannesburg; Techs CC, Cape Town
Cricketers particularly admired: Courtney Walsh, Jack Russell
Young players to look out for: Chris Taylor, Matt Windows
Other sports played: Golf, football (Bristol North West FC)
Other sports followed: Football (Swindon Town FC)
Relaxations: 'Chilling out'
Extras: Was on Northamptonshire staff in 1994 but made no first-team appearance.
Took Championship hat-trick (Gallian, Afzaal and Morris) v Nottinghamshire at Trent
Bridge 2000. Top first-class wicket-taker among English bowlers in 2000 with 72
wickets. Gloucestershire Player of the Year 2000
Opinions on cricket: 'You must always be looking to improve your game, at
whatever stage you are at. Keep learning every day. We are athletes and must treat
ourselves as athletes.'
Best batting: 62 Gloucestershire v Worcestershire, Cheltenham 1999

Best bowling: 8-95 Gloucestershire v Zimbabweans, Gloucester 2000
Stop press: Drafted into England A squad for tour of West Indies as replacement for the injured Steve Harmison

2000 Season

	M	Inns	NO	Runs	HS	Avge	100s	50s	Ct	St	O	M	Runs	Wkts	Avge	Best	5wI	10wM
Test																		
All First	17	23	2	169	38	8.04	-	-	4	-	562.3	169	1506	72	20.91	8-95	4	-
1-day Int																		
NatWest	1	1	1	4	4 *	-	-	-	2	-	9	1	30	1	30.00	1-30	-
B & H	4	1	1	15	15 *	-	-	-	1	-	29	1	126	3	42.00	2-32	-
1-day Lge	2	2	0	16	16	8.00	-	-	-	-	16	1	78	1	78.00	1-39	-

Career Performances

	M	Inns	NO	Runs	HS	Avge	100s	50s	Ct	St	Balls	Runs	Wkts	Avge	Best	5wI	10wM
Test																	
All First	77	115	17	1140	62	11.63	-	2	17	-	13677	6853	264	25.95	8-95	12	1
1-day Int																	
NatWest	7	5	3	14	6 *	7.00	-	-	5	-	380	222	9	24.66	3-27	-
B & H	14	7	3	64	33 *	16.00	-	-	1	-	702	595	19	31.31	3-31	-
1-day Lge	53	34	13	207	26 *	9.85	-	-	9	-	2110	1752	52	33.69	3-27	-

LEWIS, J. J. B.   Durham

Name: Jonathan (Jon) James Benjamin Lewis
Role: Right-hand bat, right-arm
slow-medium net bowler, county captain
Born: 21 May 1970, Isleworth, Middlesex
Height: 5ft 9in   **Weight:** 12st
Nickname: Judge, JJ, Miny-Me
County debut: 1990 (Essex), 1997 (Durham)
County cap: 1994 (Essex), 1998 (Durham)
1000 runs in a season: 2
1st-Class 50s: 41
1st-Class 100s: 9
1st-Class 200s: 1
1st-Class catches: 84
One-Day 100s: 1
Place in batting averages: 138th av. 24.80
(1999 30th av. 40.92)
Strike rate: (career 120.00)
Parents: Ted and Nina

Wife and date of marriage: Fiona, 6 July 1999
Family links with cricket: Father played county schools. Uncle is a lifelong Somerset supporter. Sister is right-arm medium-fast bowler for Cisco
Education: King Edward VI School, Chelmsford; Roehampton Institute of Higher Education
Qualifications: 5 O-levels, 3 A-levels, BSc (Hons) Sports Science, NCA Senior Coach
Career outside cricket: Precision engineer with Tees Precision
Off-season: Playing and coaching in Zululand, South Africa
Overseas teams played for: Old Hararians, Zimbabwe 1991-92; Taita District, New Zealand 1992-93; Eshowe and Zululand 1994-95; Richards Bay 1996-97; Empangeni, Natal 1997-98
Cricketers particularly admired: John Childs, Greg Matthews, Alan Walker, Shane Warne
Young players to look out for: Steve Harmison
Other sports followed: Soccer (West Ham United), rugby, basketball, 'most sports really'
Relaxations: Sleep
Extras: Hit century on first-class debut in Essex's final Championship match of the 1990 season. Joined Durham for the 1997 season – 'I am slowly learning the local dialect'. Scored a double century on his debut for Durham (210* v Oxford University), placing him in a small club, alongside Peter Bowler and Neil Taylor, of players who have scored centuries on debut for two different counties. Took over the captaincy of Durham towards the end of the 2000 season and has been appointed captain for 2001
Opinions on cricket: 'Central contracts appear to be working well.'
Best batting: 210* Durham v Oxford University, The Parks 1997
Best bowling: 1-73 Durham v Surrey, Riverside 1998

2000 Season

	M	Inns	NO	Runs	HS	Avge	100s	50s	Ct	St	O	M	Runs	Wkts	Avge	Best	5wI	10wM
Test																		
All First	16	28	2	645	115	24.80	1	4	8	-								
1-day Int																		
NatWest	2	2	0	11	10	5.50	-	-	-	-								
B & H	6	6	3	115	55 *	38.33	-	1	1	-								
1-day Lge	16	16	4	322	60	26.83	-	2	3	-								

Career Performances

	M	Inns	NO	Runs	HS	Avge	100s	50s	Ct	St	Balls	Runs	Wkts	Avge	Best	5wI	10wM
Test																	
All First	123	217	21	6624	210 *	33.79	10	41	84	-	120	121	1	121.00	1-73	-	-
1-day Int																	
NatWest	12	12	1	144	24 *	13.09	-	-	1	-							
B & H	20	20	4	454	67	28.37	-	2	4	-							
1-day Lge	103	90	20	1939	102	27.70	1	11	17	-	8	35	0	-		-	-

LEWRY, J. D.   Sussex

Name: <u>Jason</u> David Lewry
Role: Left-hand bat, left-arm fast-medium
bowler
Born: 2 April 1971, Worthing, West Sussex
Height: 6ft 3in **Weight:** 14st 7lbs
('depending on time of year!')
Nickname: Lewie, Urco
County debut: 1994
County cap: 1996
50 wickets in a season: 3
1st-Class 5 w. in innings: 17
1st-Class 10 w. in match: 2
1st-Class catches: 10
Place in batting averages: 289th av. 7.84
(1999 254th av. 13.58)
Place in bowling averages: 91st av. 29.60
(1999 51st av. 23.75)
Strike rate: 59.39 (career 47.88)
Parents: David and Veronica
Wife and date of marriage: Naomi Madeleine, 18 August 1997
Children: William Jason Joseph, 14 February 1998; Louis, 20 November 2000
Family links with cricket: Father coaches
Education: Thomas à Becket, Worthing; Durrington High School, Worthing; Worthing
Sixth Form College
Qualifications: 6 O-levels, 3 GCSEs, City & Guilds, NCA Award
Career outside cricket: 'Still looking, but with more urgency with each passing
year!'
Off-season: 'Spending time with my boys and the rattlesnake!'
Overseas tours: Goring CC to Isle of Wight 1992, 1993; England A to Zimbabwe and
South Africa 1998-99
Cricketers particularly admired: David Gower, Martin Andrews
Young players to look out for: 'Swing bowlers'
Other sports played: Golf, squash; darts, pool
Other sports followed: Football (West Ham United)
Relaxations: Golf, pub games, films, 'picking nose'
Best batting: 39 Sussex v Warwickshire, Hove 2000
Best bowling: 7-38 Sussex v Derbyshire, Derby 1999

2000 Season

	M	Inns	NO	Runs	HS	Avge	100s	50s	Ct	St	O	M	Runs	Wkts	Avge	Best	5wI	10wM
Test																		
All First	17	24	5	149	39	7.84	-	-	5	-	524.4	137	1569	53	29.60	6-66	3	-
1-day Int																		
NatWest	1	0	0	0	0	-	-	-	-	-	10	2	20	0	-	-	-	
B & H	4	3	0	28	10	9.33	-	-	-	-	33	3	125	4	31.25	2-32	-	
1-day Lge																		

Career Performances

	M	Inns	NO	Runs	HS	Avge	100s	50s	Ct	St	Balls	Runs	Wkts	Avge	Best	5wI	10wM
Test																	
All First	74	108	23	763	39	8.97	-	-	10	-	12978	6941	271	25.61	7-38	17	2
1-day Int																	
NatWest	6	4	3	19	9	19.00	-	-	-	-	384	244	11	22.18	4-42	-	
B & H	12	8	2	69	14 *	11.50	-	-	-	-	624	498	10	49.80	2-32	-	
1-day Lge	30	16	6	43	10 *	4.30	-	-	5	-	1222	994	42	23.66	4-29	-	

LIPTROT, C. G. — Worcestershire

Name: <u>Christopher</u> George Liptrot
Role: Left-hand bat, right-arm fast-medium bowler
Born: 13 December 1980, Wigan
Height: 6ft 2in **Weight:** 12st 6lbs
Nickname: Lippy
County debut: 1999
1st-Class 50s: 1
1st-Class 5 w. in innings: 2
1st-Class catches: 5
Place in batting averages: (1999 250th av. 14.20)
Place in bowling averages: (1999 112th av. 33.25)
Strike rate: 66.85 (career 60.48)
Parents: Brian and Susan
Marital status: Single
Family links with cricket: 'My father and brother play local cricket'

Education: St Matthews, Highfield, Wigan; The Deanery High School, Wigan
Qualifications: 9 GCSEs
Career outside cricket: 'I was formerly an electrician'

Overseas tours: Lancashire Leagues U19 Select XI to South Africa 1998
Overseas teams played for: Sunshine Coast, Brisbane 1999-2000
Cricketers particularly admired: Glenn McGrath, Darren Gough, Allan Donald, Graeme Hick
Young players to look out for: Vikram Solanki
Other sports played: Football, rugby
Other sports followed: Football (Everton FC), rugby league (Wigan Warriors)
Relaxations: Watching all sports; music
Extras: Represented England U19 in one-day and 'Test' series v Australia U19 1999. NBC Denis Compton Award 1999
Best batting: 61 Worcestershire v Warwickshire, Edgbaston 1999
Best bowling: 6-44 Worcestershire v Warwickshire, Worcester 2000

2000 Season

	M	Inns	NO	Runs	HS	Avge	100s	50s	Ct	St	O	M	Runs	Wkts	Avge	Best	5wI	10wM
Test																		
All First	4	3	1	1	1	0.50	-	-	5	-	78	11	324	7	46.28	6-44	1	-
1-day Int																		
NatWest																		
B & H																		
1-day Lge	4	3	3	18	15 *	-	-	-	-	-	17.1	0	117	5	23.40	3-44	-	

Career Performances

	M	Inns	NO	Runs	HS	Avge	100s	50s	Ct	St	Balls	Runs	Wkts	Avge	Best	5wI	10wM
Test																	
All First	15	19	7	143	61	11.91	-	1	5	-	1633	989	27	36.62	6-44	2	-
1-day Int																	
NatWest																	
B & H																	
1-day Lge	4	3	3	18	15 *	-	-	-	-	-	103	117	5	23.40	3-44	-	

53. Which former Kent and Gloucestershire bowler holds the record for the most wickets in a series for Australia v England?

LLOYD, G. D. — Lancashire

Name: <u>Graham</u> David Lloyd
Role: Right-hand bat, right-arm medium bowler
Born: 1 July 1969, Accrington
Height: 5ft 9in **Weight:** 12st 10lbs
Nickname: Bumble
County debut: 1988
County cap: 1992
One-Day Internationals: 5
1000 runs in a season: 5
1st-Class 50s: 59
1st-Class 100s: 21
1st-Class 200s: 3
1st-Class catches: 133
One-Day 100s: 3
Place in batting averages: 102nd av. 28.95
(1999 22nd av. 42.64)
Strike rate: (career 169.50)
Parents: David and Susan

Wife and date of marriage: Sharron, 11 October 1997
Children: Joseph, 20 December 1998
Family links with cricket: Father played for Lancashire and England
Education: Peel Park Primary; Hollins County High School, Accrington
Qualifications: 3 O-levels, NCA coaching certificate
Career outside cricket: Bookmaker
Overseas tours: England A to Australia 1992-93; Lancashire CCC to Guernsey 1995; England VI to Hong Kong 1997; England to Bangladesh (Wills International Cup) 1998
Overseas teams played for: Maroochydore CC, Queensland 1988-89 and 1991-95
Cricketers particularly admired: Steve Waugh
Young players to look out for: Andrew Flintoff, Chris Schofield
Other sports played: Football
Other sports followed: Football (Manchester United)
Relaxations: Horse racing
Extras: Won the EDS Walter Lawrence Trophy (for the fastest century of the year) two years running 1996, 1997. Scored 113 before lunch (having been 17* overnight; eventually out for 126) v Somerset at Old Trafford 2000. Granted a benefit for 2001
Best batting: 241 Lancashire v Essex, Chelmsford 1996
Best bowling: 1-4 Lancashire v Warwickshire, Edgbaston 1996

2000 Season

	M	Inns	NO	Runs	HS	Avge	100s	50s	Ct	St	O	M	Runs	Wkts	Avge	Best	5wl	10wM
Test																		
All First	16	22	1	608	126	28.95	1	2	20	-								
1-day Int																		
NatWest	3	1	1	2	2 *	-	-	-	2	-								
B & H	7	5	1	65	35 *	16.25	-	-	2	-								
1-day Lge	14	12	3	157	46	17.44	-	-	2	-								

Career Performances

	M	Inns	NO	Runs	HS	Avge	100s	50s	Ct	St	Balls	Runs	Wkts	Avge	Best	5wl	10wM
Test																	
All First	193	306	27	10811	241	38.74	24	59	133	-	339	440	2	220.00	1-4	-	-
1-day Int	5	4	1	39	22	13.00	-	-	2	-							
NatWest	27	22	3	591	96	31.10	-	3	7	-	30	35	1	35.00	1-23	-	
B & H	49	41	12	817	81 *	28.17	-	3	8	-	30	50	0	-		-	-
1-day Lge	169	154	27	3854	134	30.34	3	20	39	-	12	18	0	-		-	-

LOGAN, R. J.   Nottinghamshire

Name: Richard James Logan
Role: Right-hand bat, right-arm fast bowler
Born: 28 January 1980, Stone, Staffs
Height: 6ft 1in **Weight:** 13st 9lbs
Nickname: Gus, Logie
County debut: 1999 (Northants)
1st-Class 5 w. in innings: 1
1st-Class catches: 2
Place in batting averages: 294th av. 7.28
Place in bowling averages: 134th av. 41.18
Strike rate: 72.63 (career 60.36)
Marital status: Single
Family links with cricket: Father played for local club Cannock as batsman/wicket-keeper
Education: Walhouse C of E School, Cannock; Wolverhampton Grammar School
Qualifications: 11 GCSEs, 1 A-level, coaching awards (hockey and cricket)
Off-season: 'Living at home, relaxing, taking time out, playing hockey for Cannock'
Overseas tours: England U17 to Bermuda (International Youth Tournament) 1997; England U19 to South Africa (including Youth World Cup) 1997-98, to New Zealand 1998-99

Overseas teams played for: St George, Sydney 1999-2000
Cricketers particularly admired: Sir Richard Hadlee, Malcolm Marshall
Young players to look out for: Mark Powell
Other sports played: Hockey (Cannock – 'also played for Staffordshire from age 9 and for Midlands U14')
Other sports followed: Football (Wolverhampton Wanderers)
Relaxations: 'Spending time with my mates. Training'
Extras: Played for Staffordshire at every level from U11 to U19, and as captain from U13 to U17. Played for Midlands U14 and U15 (both as captain) and HMC Schools U15. 1995 *Daily Telegraph*/Lombard U15 Midlands Bowler and Batsman of the Year. Played for Northamptonshire U17 and U19 national champions in 1997. Has played for England U15, U17 and U19, including one-day and 'Test' series v Australia U19 1999. Recorded maiden first-class five-wicket return (5-61) v Middlesex at Northampton 2000; it included a spell of 4-5 in 27 balls. Left Northamptonshire in the 2000-01 off-season and has joined Nottinghamshire for 2001
Opinions on cricket: 'Two divisions have been good for the game. The season doesn't end until there is nothing to play for, which happens very seldom when there are two divisions. I still think there is too much cricket played, which means that the quality of cricket isn't as high as it could be.'
Best batting: 24 Northamptonshire v Essex, Ilford 2000
Best bowling: 5-61 Northamptonshire v Middlesex, Northampton 2000

2000 Season

	M	Inns	NO	Runs	HS	Avge	100s	50s	Ct	St	O	M	Runs	Wkts	Avge	Best	5wI	10wM
Test																		
All First	6	8	1	51	24	7.28	-	-	1	-	133.1	33	453	11	41.18	5-61	1	-
1-day Int																		
NatWest																		
B & H	2	1	0	1	1	1.00	-	-	-	-	17	0	101	3	33.66	3-52	-	
1-day Lge	2	2	0	17	17	8.50	-	-	-	-	9.5	0	82	0	-		-	-

Career Performances

	M	Inns	NO	Runs	HS	Avge	100s	50s	Ct	St	Balls	Runs	Wkts	Avge	Best	5wI	10wM
Test																	
All First	8	10	1	52	24	5.77	-	-	2	-	1147	631	19	33.21	5-61	1	-
1-day Int																	
NatWest																	
B & H	2	1	0	1	1	1.00	-	-	-	-	102	101	3	33.66	3-52	-	
1-day Lge	6	3	0	25	17	8.33	-	-	2	-	161	183	3	61.00	2-31	-	

LOYE, M. B.   Northamptonshire

Name: <u>Malachy</u> Bernard Loye
Role: Right-hand bat, off-spin bowler
Born: 27 September 1972, Northampton
Height: 6ft 2in   **Weight:** 13st 7lbs
Nickname: Mal, Chairman
County debut: 1991
County cap: 1994
1000 runs in a season: 1
1st-Class 50s: 30
1st-Class 100s: 12
1st-Class 200s: 1
1st-Class 300s: 1
1st-Class catches: 64
One-Day 100s: 2
Place in batting averages: 99th av. 29.64
(1999 172nd av. 22.78)
Parents: Patrick and Anne
Marital status: Single

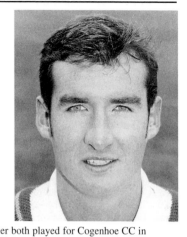

Family links with cricket: Father and brother both played for Cogenhoe CC in
Northampton
Education: Brixworth Primary School; Moulton Comprehensive School
Qualifications: GCSEs and senior coaching certificate
Overseas tours: England U18 to Canada 1991; England U19 to Pakistan 1991-92;
England A to South Africa 1993-94, to Zimbabwe and South Africa 1998-99;
Northamptonshire to Cape Town 1993, to Zimbabwe 1995, 1998, to Johannesburg 1996
Overseas teams played for: Riccarton, Christchurch, New Zealand 1992-95; Onslow,
Wellington, New Zealand 1995-96; North Perth, Australia 1997-98
Cricketers particularly admired: Wayne Larkins ('talent'), Gordon Greenidge
('power'), Curtly Ambrose ('ultimate cricketer')
Young players to look out for: Monty Panesar
Other sports played: Swimming, boxing
Other sports followed: Football (Northampton Town and Liverpool FC), rugby union
(Ireland), boxing
Relaxations: 'Playing the guitar, going out to bars, swimming and sleeping'
Extras: Played for England U19 in the home series against Australia U19 in 1991 and
against Sri Lanka U19 1992. Voted Professional Cricketers' Association's Young
Player of the Year 1993 and Whittingdale Young Player of the Year 1993. Shared a
county record opening stand of 372 with Richard Montgomerie versus Yorkshire in
1996. His 322* v Glamorgan in 1998 is the highest individual first-class score for the
county; the highest to that point was Raman Subba Row's 300. During his innings,
Loye put on 401 for the fifth wicket with David Ripley, setting a new fifth wicket
record for first-class cricket in England. Voted the PCA's Player of the Year in 1998

Opinions on cricket: 'Great game; just not enough "great" people running it.'
Best batting: 322* Northamptonshire v Glamorgan, Northampton 1998

2000 Season

	M	Inns	NO	Runs	HS	Avge	100s	50s	Ct	St		O	M	Runs	Wkts	Avge	Best	5wl	10wM
Test																			
All First	12	18	1	504	93	29.64	-	3	1	-									
1-day Int																			
NatWest	3	3	0	62	24	20.66	-	-	-	-									
B & H	2	2	0	76	57	38.00	-	1	1	-									
1-day Lge	14	14	0	371	75	26.50	-	4	1	-									

Career Performances

	M	Inns	NO	Runs	HS	Avge	100s	50s	Ct	St	Balls		Runs	Wkts	Avge	Best	5wl	10wM
Test																		
All First	126	200	19	6578	322 *	36.34	14	30	64	-	13		43	0	-	-	-	-
1-day Int																		
NatWest	17	16	3	329	65	25.30	-	1	4	-								
B & H	23	23	5	551	68 *	30.61	-	3	8	-								
1-day Lge	99	95	7	2685	122	30.51	2	17	19	-								

LUCAS, D. S.   Nottinghamshire

Name: David Scott Lucas
Role: Right-hand bat, left-arm medium-fast bowler
Born: 19 August 1978, Nottingham
Height: 6ft 3in **Weight:** 13st
Nickname: Muke, Lukey
County debut: 1999
1st-Class 5 w. in innings: 1
1st-Class catches: 3
Place in batting averages: 127th av. 26.28
Place in bowling averages: 106th av. 32.88
(1999 65th av. 26.26)
Strike rate: 60.40 (career 53.66)
Parents: Mary and Terry
Marital status: Single
Education: Horsendale Primary School; Djanogly City Technology College, Nottingham

Qualifications: 6 GCSEs, pass in Computer-Aided Design
Off-season: 'Playing indoor cricket for Nottingham Bulldogs'
Overseas tours: England (Indoor) to Australia (Indoor Cricket World Cup) 1998
Overseas teams played for: Bankstown Canterbury Bulldogs, Sydney 1996-97
Cricketers particularly admired: Wasim Akram, Stuart Law, Steve Waugh, Darren Gough
Young players to look out for: Usman Afzaal, Paul Franks, Chris Read, Matthew Hoggard, 'Clive Rice'
Other sports played: Indoor cricket, football
Other sports followed: Football (Arsenal), rugby league (Wigan Warriors)
Injuries: Out for one month with a back spasm
Relaxations: Food, 'spending valuable time with my girlfriend Donna'
Extras: Won Yorkshire League with Rotherham in 1996. Was selected to represent England at Indoor Cricket World Cup in Australia in October 1998. His 4-61 v Essex at Chelmsford 2000 included a burst of 4-3 in 13 balls
Opinions on cricket: 'Too much cricket. Second XI cricket should become four-day and be played on first-class grounds to give the players a chance of impressing in first-class surroundings. The season should run from May to October because of change in climate.'
Best batting: 46* Nottinghamshire v Middlesex, Trent Bridge 2000
Best bowling: 5-104 Nottinghamshire v Essex, Trent Bridge 1999

2000 Season

	M	Inns	NO	Runs	HS	Avge	100s	50s	Ct	St	O	M	Runs	Wkts	Avge	Best	5wI	10wM
Test																		
All First	10	12	5	184	46 *	26.28	-	-	3	-	271.5	57	888	27	32.88	4-61	-	-
1-day Int																		
NatWest																			
B & H	2	0	0	0	0	-	-	-	-	-	9	0	61	1	61.00	1-33	-	
1-day Lge	11	4	0	9	5	2.25	-	-	1	-	90.3	3	475	15	31.66	4-27	-	

Career Performances

	M	Inns	NO	Runs	HS	Avge	100s	50s	Ct	St	Balls	Runs	Wkts	Avge	Best	5wI	10wM
Test																	
All First	16	19	8	242	46 *	22.00	-	-	3	-	2254	1282	42	30.52	5-104	1	-
1-day Int																	
NatWest	1	1	1	14	14 *	-	-	-	-	-	36	40	0	-	-	-	
B & H	2	0	0	0	0	-	-	-	-	-	54	61	1	61.00	1-33	-	
1-day Lge	15	5	1	28	19 *	7.00	-	-	2	-	657	592	19	31.15	4-27	-	

LUMB, M. J. Yorkshire

Name: <u>Michael</u> John Lumb
Role: Left-hand bat, right-arm medium bowler
Born: 12 February 1980, Johannesburg
Height: 6ft **Weight:** 13st
Nickname: Bird Doo, Lugpuss
County debut: 2000
1st-Class 50s: 1
Parents: Richard and Susan
Marital status: Single
Family links with cricket: Father played for Yorkshire. Uncle played for Natal
Education: Montrose Primary School; St Stithians College
Qualifications: Matriculation
Off-season: Playing cricket in South Africa
Overseas tours: Transvaal U19 to Barbados
Overseas teams played for: Pirates CC, Johannesburg; Wanderers CC, Johannesburg
Cricketers particularly admired: 'My father', Graham Thorpe, Darren Gough, Craig White, Jacques Kallis
Young players to look out for: Grant Elliott, Matthew Hoggard, Joe Sayers
Other sports played: Rugby ('1st team at school'), golf, football
Other sports followed: Rugby union (Super-12)
Relaxations: Surfing, reading, socialising with friends
Extras: Has Yorkshire 2nd XI cap. Scored 66* on first-class debut v Zimbabweans at Headingley 2000
Opinions on cricket: 'Splitting the Championship has proved to be exciting and I think it's a good idea. Changes must be made to make the game more appealing to spectators, to get bigger crowds in.'
Best batting: 66* Yorkshire v Zimbabweans, Headingley 2000

2000 Season

	M	Inns	NO	Runs	HS	Avge	100s	50s	Ct	St	O	M	Runs	Wkts	Avge	Best	5wI	10wM
Test																		
All First	1	2	1	68	66 *	68.00	-	1	-	-								
1-day Int																		
NatWest																		
B & H																		
1-day Lge																		

Career Performances

	M	Inns	NO	Runs	HS	Avge	100s	50s	Ct	St	Balls	Runs	Wkts	Avge	Best	5wl	10wM
Test																	
All First	1	2	1	68	66 *	68.00	-	1	-	-							
1-day Int																	
NatWest																	
B & H																	
1-day Lge																	

LUNGLEY, T.   Derbyshire

Name: Tom Lungley
Role: Left-hand bat, right-arm medium bowler
Born: 25 July 1979, Derbyshire
Height: 6ft 2in   **Weight:** 13st
Nickname: Lungo
County debut: 2000
Strike rate: 23.33 (career 23.33)
Parents: Richard and Christina
Marital status: Single
Family links with cricket: 'Dad was captain of Derby Road CC. Grandad was bat maker in younger days'
Education: Risley Lower Grammar School; Saint John Houghton School; South East Derbyshire College
Qualifications: 9 GCSEs, Sport and Recreation Levels 1 and 2, pool lifeguard qualification, coaching qualifications in cricket, tennis, basketball, football and volleyball
Off-season: 'Playing cricket in Bloemfontein'
Overseas teams played for: Delacombe Park, Melbourne 1999-2000
Cricketers particularly admired: Ian Botham, Dennis Lillee, Courtney Walsh, Curtly Ambrose, Brian Lara, Richard Hadlee, Glenn McGrath
Young players to look out for: Matt Moss, Ian Darlington 'and the General "Pattern"!!'
Other sports played: 'Enjoy playing most sports, mainly football and basketball'
Other sports followed: Football (Derby County), basketball (Derby Storm)
Injuries: Out for three weeks with shin splints
Relaxations: 'Shopping, watching videos, having a laugh with mates'
Extras: First homegrown cricketer to become professional from Ockbrook and

Borrowash CC. Scored 109 in Derbyshire Cup final 2000, gaining Man of the Match award

Opinions on cricket: 'Think two divisions is a good idea, and wish the wages in cricket were the same as in football.'

Best bowling: 3-10 Derbyshire v Cambridge University, Fenner's 2000

2000 Season

	M	Inns	NO	Runs	HS	Avge	100s	50s	Ct	St	O	M	Runs	Wkts	Avge	Best	5wI	10wM
Test																		
All First	1	0	0	0	0	-	-	-	-	-	23.2	11	41	6	6.83	3-10	-	-
1-day Int																		
NatWest	1	1	0	3	3	3.00	-	-	-	-	4	0	24	0	-		-	-
B & H																		
1-day Lge	3	3	0	45	15	15.00	-	-	-	-	26	1	104	5	20.80	2-26	-	

Career Performances

	M	Inns	NO	Runs	HS	Avge	100s	50s	Ct	St	Balls	Runs	Wkts	Avge	Best	5wI	10wM
Test																	
All First	1	0	0	0	0	-	-	-	-	-	140	41	6	6.83	3-10	-	-
1-day Int																	
NatWest	1	1	0	3	3	3.00	-	-	-	-	24	24	0	-		-	-
B & H																	
1-day Lge	3	3	0	45	15	15.00	-	-	-	-	156	104	5	20.80	2-26	-	

MADDY, D. L.   Leicestershire

Name: Darren Lee Maddy
Role: Right-hand opening bat, right-arm medium bowler
Born: 23 May 1974, Leicester
Height: 5ft 9in **Weight:** 11st
Nickname: Roaster, Dazza, Fire Starter
County debut: 1993 (one-day), 1994 (first-class)
County cap: 1996
Test debut: 1999
Tests: 3
One-Day Internationals: 8
1000 runs in a season: 2
1st-Class 50s: 25
1st-Class 100s: 12
1st-Class 200s: 1
1st-Class catches: 119
One-Day 100s: 5

Place in batting averages: 128th av. 26.25 (1999 47th av. 37.85)
Place in bowling averages: (1999 28th av. 21.66)
Strike rate: 72.85 (career 77.33)
Parents: William Arthur and Hilary Jean
Wife and date of marriage: Justine Marie, 7 October 2000
Family links with cricket: Father and younger brother, Greg, play club cricket
Education: Herrick Junior School, Leicester; Roundhills, Thurmaston; Wreake Valley, Syston
Qualifications: 8 GCSEs
Career outside cricket: 'Undecided'
Off-season: 'Enjoying married life with Justine. Keeping fit and watching Leicester Tigers. Watching England on Sky. Learning to play the drums'

Overseas tours: Leicestershire to Bloemfontein 1995, to Western Transvaal 1996, to Durban 1997, to Barbados 1998; England A to Kenya and Sri Lanka 1997-98, to Zimbabwe and South Africa 1998-99; England to South Africa and Zimbabwe 1999-2000
Overseas teams played for: Wanderers, Johannesburg 1992-93; Northern Free State, South Africa 1993-95; Rhodes University, South Africa 1995-97
Cricketers particularly admired: Brian Lara, Michael Atherton, Richard Hadlee, Viv Richards, 'Babe Ruth' Dakin, Paul Nixon
Young players to look out for: Ashley Wright, Mike Sutliff
Other sports played: 5-a-side football, golf, squash
Other sports followed: Rugby (Leicester Tigers), football (Leicester City), baseball, golf, boxing – 'most sports really except for horse racing and motor racing'
Relaxations: 'Going to the gym, playing sport, spending time with my wife, Justine; listening to music, watching TV, going on holiday, scuba diving, bungee jumping, playing the drums'
Extras: Set a new 2nd XI Championship run aggregate record (1498) beating the previous one which had stood since 1961. Rapid Cricketline 2nd XI Championship Player of the Year 1994. Scored his maiden first-class 200 against Kenya at Nairobi on England A's 1997-98 tour and was leading run-scorer on the tour with 687 runs at 68.7. Set a new record for the number of runs scored in the B&H competition in one season, previously held by Graham Gooch. Also set a record for the most B&H Gold Awards won in one season (five in 1998). Carried his bat (158*) for Leicestershire v Yorkshire at Leicester 1999. Won Vodafone Man of the Match award for his 110 for First Class Counties Select XI v Sri Lanka A in one-day match at Chester-le-Street 1999
Opinions on cricket: 'Day/night cricket is a great idea to introduce cricket to the

younger generation. Two divisions has proved to be a great idea in both competitions, as this has helped to make each game more competitive through the season. We must play on better pitches, which will then produce better cricketers. To stop home teams preparing wickets to suit their strengths, the opposing captain should have first choice of whether to bat or bowl, without the toss of a coin. Abolish bonus points; only give out points for first innings lead and then for a draw or win.'

Best batting: 202 England A v Kenya, Nairobi 1997-98
Best bowling: 3-5 Leicestershire v Gloucestershire, Leicester 1999

2000 Season

	M	Inns	NO	Runs	HS	Avge	100s	50s	Ct	St	O	M	Runs	Wkts	Avge	Best	5wI	10wM
Test																		
All First	17	25	1	630	102	26.25	1	4	16	-	85	17	277	7	39.57	2-10	-	-
1-day Int																		
NatWest	2	2	0	90	72	45.00	-	1	-	-								
B & H	4	4	0	11	8	2.75	-	-	1	-	6.5	0	34	0	-		-	-
1-day Lge	16	15	3	393	87 *	32.75	-	2	4	-	47.3	2	203	13	15.61	4-16	-	

Career Performances

	M	Inns	NO	Runs	HS	Avge	100s	50s	Ct	St	Balls	Runs	Wkts	Avge	Best	5wI	10wM
Test	3	4	0	46	24	11.50	-	-	4	-	84	40	0	-	-	-	-
All First	121	189	10	5757	202	32.16	13	25	119	-	2088	1085	27	40.18	3-5	-	-
1-day Int	8	6	0	113	53	18.83	-	1	1	-							
NatWest	13	12	0	278	89	23.16	-	2	6	-	201	166	7	23.71	2-38	-	
B & H	27	27	4	1221	151	53.08	4	6	8	-	227	206	6	34.33	3-32	-	
1-day Lge	103	93	9	2289	106 *	27.25	1	16	37	-	1241	1137	44	25.84	4-16	-	

---

54. Who ground out his first – and so far only – Ashes century
in 424 minutes at Sydney in 1990-91?

MAHER, J. P.   Glamorgan

Name: James (<u>Jimmy</u>) Patrick Maher
Role: Left-hand bat, right-arm medium
bowler
Born: 27 February 1974, Innisfail,
Queensland, Australia
Nickname: Mahbo, Marzo, Rock
County debut: No first-team appearance
One-Day Internationals: 2
1st-Class 50s: 24
1st-Class 100s: 5
1st Class 200s: 1
1st-Class catches: 77
Family links with cricket: Father, Warren,
played for Queensland Country
Education: St Augustine's College, Cairns
Career outside cricket: Broadcasts for a
radio station in Brisbane
Overseas teams played for: Easts-Redlands,
Brisbane; Queensland 1993-94 –
Other sports followed: Rugby league (Canterbury Bulldogs)
Extras: Represented Australia U17 and U19. Attended Australian Cricket Academy
1993. Represented Australia v New Zealand and South Africa in the CUB Series
1997-98. Scored 102 v Western Australia in the final of the Mercantile Mutual Cup
1999-2000 at Perth. Can throw both left and right handed. Has joined Glamorgan for
2001 as overseas player
Best batting: 208* Queensland v South Australia, Adelaide 1998-99
Best bowling: 3-11 Queensland v Western Australia, Perth 1995-96

2000 Season (did not make any first-class or one-day appearances)

Career Performances

	M	Inns	NO	Runs	HS	Avge	100s	50s	Ct	St	Balls	Runs	Wkts	Avge	Best	5wl	10wM
Test																	
All First	80	141	19	4347	208 *	35.63	6	24	77	-	714	412	10	41.20	3-11	-	-
1-day Int	2	2	0	21	13	10.50	-	-	-	-							
NatWest																	
B & H																	
1-day Lge																	

MALCOLM, D. E.   Leicestershire

Name: <u>Devon</u> Eugene Malcolm
Role: Right-hand bat, right-arm fast bowler
Born: 22 February 1963, Kingston, Jamaica
Height: 6ft 2in **Weight:** 15st 8lbs
Nickname: Dude
County debut: 1984 (Derbyshire),
1998 (Northamptonshire)
County cap: 1989 (Derbyshire),
1999 (Northamptonshire)
Benefit: 1997 (Derbyshire)
Test debut: 1989
Tests: 40
One-Day Internationals: 10
50 wickets in a season: 7
1st-Class 50s: 1
1st-Class 5 w. in innings: 37
1st-Class 10 w. in match: 7
1st-Class catches: 40
One-Day 5 w. in innings: 2
Place in batting averages: 306th av. 2.66 (1999 300th av. 3.20)
Place in bowling averages: 82nd av. 28.47 (1999 82nd av. 28.76)
Strike rate: 58.15 (career 51.07)
Parents: Albert and Brendalee (deceased)
Wife and date of marriage: Jennifer, October 1989
Children: Erica Cian, 11 June 1991; Natile Jade, 25 June 1993;
Stephany, 11 July 1995
Education: St Elizabeth Technical High School; Richmond College;
Derby College of Higher Education
Qualifications: O-levels, Diploma in Business Administration, Level II coaching
certificate
Off-season: 'Working for telecommunications company; distributing free cricket
equipment and running coaching clinics in townships in South Africa; cricket tour to
Barbados'
Overseas tours: England to West Indies 1989-90, to Australia 1990-91, to India and
Sri Lanka 1992-93, to West Indies 1993-94, to Australia 1994-95, to South Africa
1995-96; England A to Bermuda and West Indies 1991-92
Overseas teams played for: Ellerslie, Auckland 1985-87
Cricketers particularly admired: Michael Holding, Sir Richard Hadlee, Sir Viv
Richards, Steve Waugh
Young players to look out for: David Sales, Ian Blackwell, Mudhsuden Panesar
Other sports played: Football, table tennis

Other sports followed: Football (Man United), boxing

Relaxations: 'Movies, music, eating, debating with Jenny (wife)'

Extras: Played league cricket for Sheffield Works and Sheffield United; he once took six wickets for no runs off 15 deliveries. Became eligible to play for England in 1987. Took 10 for 137 v West Indies in Port-of-Spain Test, 1989-90. Took 9-57 v South Africa at The Oval in 1994; received the 'Century of Bottles' Award for this best performance against the touring South Africans. Was one of *Wisden*'s Five Cricketers of the Year 1995. Joined Northamptonshire for 1998. Took part in the Christians in Sport millennium tour to South Africa, the aims of which included distributing cricket kit to disadvantaged youngsters, coaching and playing matches against teams in the townships. Left Northants at the end of the 2000 season and has joined Leicestershire for 2001

Opinions on cricket: 'Two divisions have kept both Championship and National League closely contested to the very last games of the season. Competition like this can only develop more competitive cricketers for the national team. Central contracts have already produced much-rested and enthusiastic cricketers (bowlers) for the national team. That's the way to go.'

Best batting: 51 Derbyshire v Surrey, Derby 1989

Best bowling: 9-57 England v South Africa, The Oval 1994

2000 Season

	M	Inns	NO	Runs	HS	Avge	100s	50s	Ct	St	O	M	Runs	Wkts	Avge	Best	5wI	10wM
Test																		
All First	7	10	1	24	8	2.66	-	-	-	-	184.1	46	541	19	28.47	5-45	1	-
1-day Int																		
NatWest	2	1	0	0	0	0.00	-	-	-	-	19	2	56	2	28.00	1-25	-	
B & H	2	1	0	6	6	6.00	-	-	1	-	20	2	78	1	78.00	1-45	-	
1-day Lge	8	6	1	16	6	3.20	-	-	1	-	51	4	243	4	60.75	1-12	-	

Career Performances

	M	Inns	NO	Runs	HS	Avge	100s	50s	Ct	St	Balls	Runs	Wkts	Avge	Best	5wI	10wM
Test	40	58	19	236	29	6.05	-	-	7	-	8480	4748	128	37.09	9-57	5	2
All First	268	319	98	1694	51	7.66	-	1	40	-	46581	27845	912	30.53	9-57	37	7
1-day Int	10	5	2	9	4	3.00	-	-	1	-	526	404	16	25.25	3-40	-	
NatWest	27	13	1	31	10*	2.58	-	-	1	-	1607	1035	38	27.23	7-35	1	
B & H	38	21	6	110	16	7.33	-	-	5	-	2159	1547	55	28.12	5-27	1	
1-day Lge	86	36	12	153	42	6.37	-	-	10	-	3697	3096	111	27.89	4-21	-	

MALIK, M. N.
Nottinghamshire

Name: Muhammad Nadeem Malik
Role: Right-hand bat, right-arm fast-medium bowler
Born: 6 October 1982, Nottingham
Height: 6ft 5in **Weight:** 13st 8lbs
County debut: No first-team appearance
Parents: Abdul Malik and Arshad Begum
Marital status: Single
Education: Meadows Primary School; Wilford Meadows Secondary School; Bilborough College
Qualifications: 8 GCSEs
Off-season: England U19 tour to India
Overseas tours: ZRK tour to Pakistan 2000; England U19 to India 2000-01
Cricketers particularly admired: Wasim Akram, Curtly Ambrose, Glenn McGrath
Other sports played: Football
Other sports followed: Football
Injuries: Out for two weeks with sore shins
Relaxations: Music, games consoles
Extras: Took 15 wickets at an average of 19.40 for Nottinghamshire 2nd XI 2000. Played for Nottinghamshire Board XI in the NatWest 2000

2000 Season (did not make any first-class or one-day appearances)

Career Performances

	M	Inns	NO	Runs	HS	Avge	100s	50s	Ct	St	Balls	Runs	Wkts	Avge	Best	5wI	10wM
Test																	
All First																	
1-day Int																	
NatWest	1	1	1	1	1*	-	-	-	-	-	36	20	0	-		-	-
B & H																	
1-day Lge																	

MARSH, A. J.   Derbyshire

Name: <u>Adrian</u> John Marsh
Role: Left-hand bat, right-arm medium 'net bowler'
Born: 4 November 1978, Nottingham
Height: 5ft 8in **Weight:** 11st
Nickname: AJ, Chicken Man, Swampy, Bone
County debut: No first-team appearance
Parents: Pam
Marital status: Single
Family links with cricket: 'All the family played for Langley Mill in Derbyshire County League'
Education: Mundy C of E Junior School, Heanor; Grace Dieu Prep School; Abbotsholme School (A-levels)
Career outside cricket: Accountant
Off-season: Working for Beechdale Motor Group

Overseas teams played for: Ellerslie CC, Auckland; Durban Crusaders
Cricketers particularly admired: David Gower, Mark Taylor
Young players to look out for: Samit Patel
Other sports followed: Football (Nottingham Forest)
Relaxations: Socialising, football
Extras: Played for ESCA U19. Played for Derbyshire Board XI in the NatWest 1999 and 2000
Opinions on cricket: 'Second XI cricket to be always played over four days.'

2000 Season (did not make any first-class or one-day appearances)

Career Performances

	M	Inns	NO	Runs	HS	Avge	100s	50s	Ct	St	Balls	Runs	Wkts	Avge	Best	5wI	10wM
Test																	
All First																		
1-day Int																		
NatWest	3	3	0	60	53	20.00	-	1	1	-							
B & H																		
1-day Lge																		

MARSH, D. J.   Leicestershire

Name: <u>Daniel</u> James Marsh
Role: Right-hand bat, slow left-arm bowler;
all-rounder
Born: 14 June 1973, Subiaco, Western
Australia
Nickname: Marshy
County debut: No first-team appearance
1st-Class 50s: 10
1st-Class 100s: 5
1st-Class 5 w. in innings: 1
1st-Class catches: 42
Strike rate: (career 87.86)
Family links with cricket: Father, Rodney,
played for Western Australia and Australia
Overseas teams played for: South Australia
1993-94 – 1995-96; Tasmania 1996-97 –
Extras: Attended Australian Cricket
Academy 1994. Has played league cricket in

England. Scored 437 runs and took 24 wickets in the 1997-98 Sheffield Shield. Man of
the Match in Prime Minister's XI v England one-day game on England's 1998-99 tour
of Australia. Scored maiden Sheffield Shield century (123) v Western Australia at
Hobart 1998-99. Took 4-6 from 7.4 overs v Western Australia 1999-2000. Tasmania's
Player of the Year 1999-2000. Represented Australia A v Pakistanis in a one-day match
at Adelaide 1999-2000. Has joined Leicestershire as overseas player for 2001
Best batting: 157 Tasmania v India, Hobart 1999-2000
Best bowling: 7-57 Tasmania v New South Wales, Sydney 1997-98

2000 Season (did not make any first-class or one-day appearances)

Career Performances

	M	Inns	NO	Runs	HS	Avge	100s	50s	Ct	St	Balls	Runs	Wkts	Avge	Best	5wl	10wM
Test																	
All First	48	77	14	2350	157	37.30	5	10	42	-	8171	3844	93	41.33	7-57	1	-
1-day Int																	
NatWest																	
B & H																	
1-day Lge																	

MARSH, S. A.　　　　　　　　　　　　　Kent

Name: <u>Steven</u> Andrew Marsh
Role: Right-hand bat, wicket-keeper
Born: 27 January 1961, Westminster
Height: 5ft 11in **Weight:** 13st 7lbs
Nickname: Marshy
County debut: 1982
County cap: 1986
Benefit: 1995
50 dismissals in a season: 8
1st-Class 50s: 55
1st-Class 100s: 9
1st-Class catches: 688
1st-Class stumpings: 61
Place in batting averages: (1999 171st av. 23.30)
Strike rate: (career 101.00)
Parents: Melvyn Graham and Valerie Ann
Wife and date of marriage:
Julie, 27 September 1986
Children: Hayley Ann, 15 May 1987; Christian James Robert, 20 November 1990
Family links with cricket: Father played local cricket for Lordswood. Father-in-law, Bob Wilson, played for Kent 1954-66
Education: Walderslade Secondary School for Boys; Mid-Kent College of Higher and Further Education
Qualifications: 6 O-levels, 2 A-levels, OND in Business Studies, 'Cycling proficiency'
Overseas tours: Fred Rumsey XI to Barbados 1986-87
Overseas teams played for: Avendale CC, Cape Town 1985-86
Cricketers particularly admired: Robin Smith, Graham Cowdrey, Ian Botham, Colin Johns, Mark Bradley
Young players to look out for: Robert Key, Ben Phillips
Other sports followed: Golf, football (Chelsea FC)
Extras: Appointed Kent vice-captain in 1991. In the match v Middlesex at Lord's in 1991 he equalled the world record of eight catches in an innings and scored 108*. Represented England A in two one-day matches v Sri Lanka at Old Trafford 1991. Took over as Kent captain during 1995 season after injury to Mark Benson and held post until end of 1998 season. Won Man of the Match award in National League match v Worcestershire Royals at Worcester 2000, his last match before retiring from county cricket. Retired at the end of the 2000 season and has joined PCA Management as Commercial Executive
Opinions on cricket: 'Much better now we have two divisions in both one- and four-day cricket.'

Best batting: 142 Kent v Sussex, Horsham 1997
Best bowling: 2-20 Kent v Warwickshire, Edgbaston 1990

2000 Season

	M	Inns	NO	Runs	HS	Avge	100s	50s	Ct	St	O	M	Runs	Wkts	Avge	Best	5wl	10wM
Test																		
All First																		
1-day Int																		
NatWest	1	1	0	23	23	23.00	-	-	1	-								
B & H																		
1-day Lge	8	7	0	78	38	11.14	-	-	3	-								

Career Performances

	M	Inns	NO	Runs	HS	Avge	100s	50s	Ct	St	Balls	Runs	Wkts	Avge	Best	5wl	10wM
Test																	
All First	291	429	69	10098	142	28.05	9	55	688	61	202	240	2	120.00	2-20	-	-
1-day Int																	
NatWest	27	19	3	237	55	14.81	-	1	36	5	9	14	1	14.00	1-3	-	
B & H	64	48	14	641	71	18.85	-	1	78	6							
1-day Lge	217	154	45	2017	59	18.50	-	4	200	23							

MARTIN, P. J. Lancashire

Name: Peter James Martin
Role: Right-hand bat, right-arm
fast-medium bowler
Born: 15 November 1968, Accrington
Height: 6ft 5in **Weight:** 15st 4lbs
Nickname: Digger, Long John
County debut: 1989
County cap: 1994
Test debut: 1995
Tests: 8
One-Day Internationals: 19
50 wickets in a season: 2
1st-Class 50s: 5
1st-Class 100s: 1
1st-Class 5 w. in innings: 14
1st-Class 10 w. in match: 1
1st-Class catches: 40
One-Day 5 w. in innings: 5

Place in batting averages: 214th av. 16.75 (1999 238th av. 15.71)
Place in bowling averages: 7th av. 15.46 (1999 21st av. 20.56)
Strike rate: 47.26 (career 61.33)
Parents: Keith and Catherine Lina
Marital status: Single
Education: Danum School, Doncaster
Qualifications: 6 O-levels, 2 A-levels
Overseas tours: England YC to Australia (Youth World Cup) 1987-88, 'and various other tours with English Schools and NAYC'; England to South Africa 1995-96, to India and Pakistan (World Cup) 1995-96, to Sharjah (Champions Trophy) 1997-98, to Bangladesh (Wills International Cup) 1998-99
Overseas teams played for: Southern Districts, Queensland 1988-89; South Launceston, Tasmania 1989-90; South Canberra, ACT 1990-92
Cricketers particularly admired: 'Too many to mention'
Other sports followed: Football (Manchester United), rugby league (St Helens), golf
Injuries: Out for six weeks with a broken thumb
Relaxations: Music, painting, golf, cooking, walking, rugby league
Extras: Plays district football and basketball for Doncaster. Played for England A v Sri Lankans 1991
Best batting: 133 Lancashire v Durham, Gateshead Fell 1992
Best bowling: 8-32 Lancashire v Middlesex, Uxbridge 1997

2000 Season

	M	Inns	NO	Runs	HS	Avge	100s	50s	Ct	St	O	M	Runs	Wkts	Avge	Best	5wI	10wM
Test																		
All First	9	11	3	134	40	16.75	-	-	2	-	236.2	83	464	30	15.46	7-67	3	-
1-day Int																		
NatWest	1	1	0	18	18	18.00	-	-	-	-	10	0	44	3	14.66	3-44	-	
B & H	7	1	0	0	0	0.00	-	-	4	-	53.5	6	223	10	22.30	2-6	-	
1-day Lge	4	0	0	0	0	-	-	-	-	-	30	4	113	3	37.66	1-19	-	

Career Performances

	M	Inns	NO	Runs	HS	Avge	100s	50s	Ct	St	Balls	Runs	Wkts	Avge	Best	5wI	10wM
Test	8	13	0	115	29	8.84	-	-	6	-	1452	580	17	34.11	4-60	-	-
All First	171	199	51	2824	133	19.08	1	5	40	-	28765	12968	469	27.65	8-32	14	1
1-day Int	19	13	7	38	6	6.33	-	-	1	-	1000	751	27	27.81	4-44	-	
NatWest	23	9	6	94	31 *	31.33	-	-	1	-	1376	805	43	18.72	5-30	1	
B & H	33	10	7	43	11 *	14.33	-	-	12	-	1772	1245	46	27.06	3-31	-	
1-day Lge	113	32	17	177	35 *	11.80	-	-	22	-	4472	3191	143	22.31	5-21	4	

MARTIN-JENKINS, R. S. C. Sussex

Name: <u>Robin</u> Simon Christopher
Martin-Jenkins
Role: Right-hand bat, right-arm
medium-fast bowler
Born: 28 October 1975, Guildford
Height: 6ft 5in **Weight:** 14st
Nickname: Tucker
County debut: 1995
County cap: 2000
1st-Class 50s: 7
1st-Class 5 w. in innings: 2
1st-Class catches: 11
Place in batting averages: 152nd av. 22.68
(1999 213th av. 18.77)
Place in bowling averages: 115th av. 36.42
(1999 62nd av. 25.57)
Strike rate: 65.48 (career 57.68)
Parents: Christopher and Judy
Wife and date of marriage: Flora, 19 February 2000
Family links with cricket: Father is *The Times* chief cricket correspondent and *TMS* commentator. Brother captains the Radley Rangers
Education: Cranleigh Prep School, Surrey; Radley College, Oxon; Durham University
Qualifications: 10 GCSEs, 3 A-levels, 1 AS-level, Grade 3 bassoon, BA (Hons) Social Sciences
Career outside cricket: Weekly columnist for *Brighton Evening Argus*
Off-season: Playing in Cape Town
Overseas tours: Radley College to Barbados 1992; Sussex U19 to Sri Lanka 1995; Durham University to Vienna 1995; MCC to Kenya 1998-99
Overseas teams played for: Lima CC, Peru 1994
Cricketers particularly admired: Angus Fraser, Robin Smith
Young players to look out for: Matt Prior, Kabir Ali
Other sports played: Hockey, fives
Other sports followed: Tennis, skiing, football (Liverpool FC)
Injuries: Out for two weeks with tendonitis of the left shin; for one week with a side strain
Relaxations: Food, drink, television
Extras: European Player of the Year, Vienna 1995. Played for ESCA from U15 to U19. *Daily Telegraph* Bowling Award 1994. Best Performance Award for Sussex 1998. NBC Denis Compton Award 1999. Awarded Sussex cap June 2000
Opinions on cricket: 'Two divisions are fine, but we still do not have enough practice days during the season. The England team should be number one priority – success for them means a healthier game all round (packed Oval in September).'

Best batting: 86 Sussex v Essex, Arundel 2000
Best bowling: 7-54 Sussex v Glamorgan, Hove 1998

2000 Season

	M	Inns	NO	Runs	HS	Avge	100s	50s	Ct	St	O	M	Runs	Wkts	Avge	Best	5wI	10wM
Test																		
All First	15	23	1	499	86	22.68	-	2	4	-	360.1	75	1202	33	36.42	5-94	1	-
1-day Int																		
NatWest	1	1	0	16	16	16.00	-	-	-	-	10	1	28	2	14.00	2-28	-	
B & H	4	3	0	52	45	17.33	-	-	2	-	35	9	101	6	16.83	2-24	-	
1-day Lge	14	10	0	43	20	4.30	-	-	5	-	102	7	438	16	27.37	2-30	-	

Career Performances

	M	Inns	NO	Runs	HS	Avge	100s	50s	Ct	St	Balls	Runs	Wkts	Avge	Best	5wI	10wM
Test																	
All First	44	69	6	1412	86	22.41	-	7	11	-	5942	3066	103	29.76	7-54	2	-
1-day Int																	
NatWest	2	1	0	16	16	16.00	-	-	-	-	120	52	4	13.00	2-24	-	
B & H	16	13	0	154	45	11.84	-	-	2	-	819	600	23	26.08	4-57	-	
1-day Lge	47	31	1	250	44	8.33	-	-	13	-	1944	1332	39	34.15	3-27	-	

MASCARENHAS, A. D.   Hampshire

Name: Adrian Dimitri Mascarenhas
Role: Right-hand bat, right-arm medium bowler
Born: 30 October 1977, Chiswick, London
Height: 6ft 2in **Weight:** 11st 7lbs
Nickname: Dimmie, Genii, Gibson
County debut: 1996
County cap: 1998
1st-Class 50s: 10
1st-Class 100s: 1
1st-Class 5 w. in innings: 2
1st-Class catches: 18
Place in batting averages: 172nd av. 20.56 (1999 142nd av. 25.83)
Place in bowling averages: 81st av. 28.42 (1999 144th av. 51.05)
Strike rate: 67.25 (career 67.95)
Parents: Malik and Pauline
Marital status: Single

Family links with cricket: Uncle played in Sri Lanka and brothers both play for Melville CC in Perth, WA
Education: Our Lady's Primary, Melbourne; Trinity College, Perth
Overseas teams played for: Melville CC, Perth 1991-97
Cricketers particularly admired: Viv Richards, Malcolm Marshall, the Waugh twins
Other sports followed: Aussie Rules (Collingwood)
Relaxations: Aussie Rules, tennis, golf, 'occasional scenario'
Extras: Played for Western Australia at U17 and U19 level as captain. Won NatWest Man of the Match awards in semi-final v Lancashire 1998 (3-28 and 73) and in quarter-final v Middlesex 2000 (4-25). Scored maiden first-class century (100) v Derbyshire at Derby 2000. Put on 90 for the tenth wicket with Simon Francis v Surrey at The Oval 2000, the pair falling just two runs short of pulling off a remarkable Championship victory
Best batting: 100 Hampshire v Derbyshire, Derby 2000
Best bowling: 6-88 Hampshire v Glamorgan, Southampton 1996

2000 Season

	M	Inns	NO	Runs	HS	Avge	100s	50s	Ct	St	O	M	Runs	Wkts	Avge	Best	5wI	10wM
Test																		
All First	16	24	1	473	100	20.56	1	2	3	-	313.5	88	796	28	28.42	4-52	-	-
1-day Int																		
NatWest	4	3	1	82	67 *	41.00	-	1	-	-	40	9	92	10	9.20	4-25	-	
B & H	4	4	1	34	21 *	11.33	-	-	-	-	32	4	124	4	31.00	2-41	-	
1-day Lge	15	12	1	166	33	15.09	-	-	4	-	120	14	540	21	25.71	3-21	-	

Career Performances

	M	Inns	NO	Runs	HS	Avge	100s	50s	Ct	St	Balls	Runs	Wkts	Avge	Best	5wI	10wM
Test																	
All First	55	79	6	1657	100	22.69	1	10	18	-	6728	3378	99	34.12	6-88	2	-
1-day Int																	
NatWest	10	9	3	252	73	42.00	-	2	2	-	498	262	18	14.55	4-25	-	
B & H	12	12	2	203	53	20.30	-	2	-	-	480	338	8	42.25	4-28	-	
1-day Lge	53	45	5	754	79	18.85	-	5	17	-	1829	1460	57	25.61	3-9	-	

55. Who was selected to play for Australia at Sydney
in 1986-87 having played in only six first-class matches and took
6-78 in England's first innings?

MASON, T. J.   Essex

Name: <u>Timothy</u> James Mason
Role: Right-hand middle-order bat,
off-spin bowler
Born: 12 April 1975, Leicester
Height: 5ft 9in **Weight:** 10st 8lbs
Nickname: Biffa, Perry, Stone
County debut: 1994 (Leicestershire),
2000 (Essex)
1st-Class 50s: 1
1st-Class catches: 8
Place in batting averages: 257th av. 11.66
Place in bowling averages: 142nd av. 50.71
Strike rate: 102.64 (career 103.37)
Parents: Phillip John and Anthea Jane
Marital status: Single
Family links with cricket: Father plays club
cricket and is manager of Leicestershire
Schools U11
Education: Brookvale High School, Leicester; Denstone College
Qualifications: 9 GCSEs, 3 A-levels
Overseas tours: Denstone College to South Africa 1993; England U19 to Sri Lanka
1993-94; Westgold CC to Northern Transvaal 1996; Leicestershire to Sri Lanka 1999
Overseas teams played for: Eastern Freestate, South Africa 1994-95; Westgold CC,
Western Transvaal 1995-97
Cricketers particularly admired: Allan Lamb, Malcolm Marshall, Jon Dakin,
Darren 'Roasting' Maddy
Other sports followed: Rugby union (Leicester Tigers), football (Leicester City)
Relaxations: 'Going out with girlfriend Nicole and friends; listening to most types of
music; watching virtually all sports'
Extras: Captained Leicestershire Schools at all age levels. 1992 *Daily Telegraph* U19
Midlands Bowler of the Year; 1993 *Daily Telegraph* U19 National Bowler of the Year;
1993 Gray-Nicolls Outstanding Schoolboy Player of the Year. Dislocated shoulder
prevented him from going on England U18 tour to South Africa 1992-93. Played in the
winning Bain Hogg team in 1996. Left Leicestershire at end of 1999 season and joined
Essex for 2000
Best batting: 52* Essex v Glamorgan, Cardiff 2000
Best bowling: 3-32 Leicestershire v Worcestershire, Worcester 1999

2000 Season

	M	Inns	NO	Runs	HS	Avge	100s	50s	Ct	St	O	M	Runs	Wkts	Avge	Best	5wI	10wM
Test																		
All First	10	14	2	140	52 *	11.66	-	1	4	-	239.3	55	710	14	50.71	3-38	-	-
1-day Int																		
NatWest	2	2	0	9	6	4.50	-	-	-	-	7	0	27	0	-		-	-
B & H																		
1-day Lge	14	10	4	51	12	8.50	-	-	9	-	77.1	0	390	6	65.00	2-14	-	

Career Performances

	M	Inns	NO	Runs	HS	Avge	100s	50s	Ct	St	Balls	Runs	Wkts	Avge	Best	5wI	10wM
Test																	
All First	17	20	3	226	52 *	13.29	-	1	8	-	2481	1154	24	48.08	3-32	-	-
1-day Int																	
NatWest	7	5	0	80	36	16.00	-	-	3	-	330	191	3	63.66	3-29	-	
B & H	8	4	2	61	30	30.50	-	-	2	-	378	271	10	27.10	3-41	-	
1-day Lge	55	36	14	188	21 *	8.54	-	-	16	-	1698	1491	33	45.18	4-12	-	

MASTERS, D. D.   Kent

Name: <u>David</u> Daniel Masters
Role: Right-hand bat, right-arm medium-fast bowler
Born: 22 April 1978, Chatham
Height: 6ft 4ins   **Weight:** 12st 5lbs
Nickname: Hod, Race Horse, Hoddy
County debut: 2000
1st-Class 5 w. in innings: 3
1st-Class catches: 4
Place in batting averages: 299th av. 5.46
Place in bowling averages: 51st av. 24.18
Strike rate: 54.41 (career 54.41)
Parents: Kevin and Tracey
Marital status: Single
Family links with cricket:
'Dad was on staff at Kent 1983-86'
Education: Luton Junior School; Fort Luton High School; Mid-Kent College
Qualifications: 8 GCSEs, GNVQ in Leisure and Tourism, qualified coach in cricket, football and athletics, bricklayer and plasterer
Career outside cricket: Builder
Off-season: 'On building site and working hard at my game'

Overseas teams played for: Double View, Perth 1998-99
Cricketers particularly admired: Ian Botham
Young players to look out for: 'My brother Daniel Masters', James Hockley
Other sports played: Football, boxing 'and most other sports'
Other sports followed: Football (Manchester United)
Relaxations: 'Going out with mates'
Extras: Recorded maiden first-class five-wicket return (5-37) v Zimbabweans at Canterbury 2000. His 6-27 v Durham at Tunbridge Wells 2000 included a final spell of 4-9 from 10.2 overs. Joint Kent Player of the Year 2000 (with Martin Saggers)
Opinions on cricket: 'Great game.'
Best batting: 21 Kent v Hampshire, Canterbury 2000
Best bowling: 6-27 Kent v Durham, Tunbridge Wells 2000

2000 Season

	M	Inns	NO	Runs	HS	Avge	100s	50s	Ct	St	O	M	Runs	Wkts	Avge	Best	5wI	10wM
Test																		
All First	16	20	7	71	21	5.46	-	-	4	-	435.2	104	1161	48	24.18	6-27	3	-
1-day Int																		
NatWest	2	1	0	1	1	1.00	-	-	-	-	18.1	0	59	1	59.00	1-23	-	
B & H	2	1	1	12	12 *	-	-	-	1	-	10	2	31	1	31.00	1-19	-	
1-day Lge	14	9	2	33	10 *	4.71	-	-	2	-	99.1	8	433	9	48.11	2-10	-	

Career Performances

	M	Inns	NO	Runs	HS	Avge	100s	50s	Ct	St	Balls	Runs	Wkts	Avge	Best	5wI	10wM
Test																	
All First	16	20	7	71	21	5.46	-	-	4	-	2612	1161	48	24.18	6-27	3	-
1-day Int																	
NatWest	2	1	0	1	1	1.00	-	-	-	-	109	59	1	59.00	1-23	-	
B & H	2	1	1	12	12 *	-	-	-	1	-	60	31	1	31.00	1-19	-	
1-day Lge	14	9	2	33	10 *	4.71	-	-	2	-	595	433	9	48.11	2-10	-	

56. Who opened the bowling for Australia with Merv Hughes
at Lord's in 1993 when Craig McDermott fell ill?

MAUNDERS, J. K. Middlesex

Name: <u>John</u> Kenneth Maunders
Role: Left-hand bat, right-arm medium bowler
Born: 4 April 1981, Ashford, Middlesex
Height: 5ft 10in **Weight:** 12st 7lbs
Nickname: Chop
County debut: 1999
1st-Class catches: 1
Parents: Kenneth and Lynn
Marital status: Single
Family links with cricket: Grandfather and two uncles played club cricket
Education: Ashford Park Primary School; Ashford High School; Spelthorne College of Further Education
Qualifications: 10 GCSEs, Duke of Edinburgh Awards (Bronze and Silver)
Career outside cricket: Student
Off-season: Playing in Australia
Overseas tours: England U19 to New Zealand 1998-99, to Malaysia and (Youth World Cup) Sri Lanka 1999-2000
Cricketers particularly admired: Justin Langer
Young players to look out for: Ian Bell, Mark Wallace
Other sports played: Hockey
Other sports followed: Football (Liverpool)
Injuries: Out for five weeks with a broken finger
Relaxations: Spending time with girlfriend, listening to music, sleeping, keeping fit
Extras: Awarded junior county cap at the age of 12. Has been Seaxe Player of Year. Represented England U17 and U19. NBC Denis Compton Award 1999
Best batting: 9 Middlesex v Cambridge University, Fenner's 1999

2000 Season (did not make any first-class or one-day appearances)

Career Performances

	M	Inns	NO	Runs	HS	Avge	100s	50s	Ct	St	Balls	Runs	Wkts	Avge	Best	5wI	10wM
Test																	
All First	1	2	0	13	9	6.50	-	-	1	-							
1-day Int																	
NatWest																	
B & H																	
1-day Lge																	

MAYNARD, M. P. Glamorgan

Name: <u>Matthew</u> Peter Maynard
Role: Right-hand bat, right-arm medium
bowler, occasional wicket-keeper
Born: 21 March 1966, Oldham, Lancashire
Height: 5ft 11in **Weight:** 13st
Nickname: Ollie
County debut: 1985
County cap: 1987
Benefit: 1996
Test debut: 1988
Tests: 4
One-Day Internationals: 14
1000 runs in a season: 10
1st-Class 50s: 114
1st-Class 100s: 44
1st-Class 200s: 3
1st-Class catches: 326
1st-Class stumpings: 7
One-Day 100s: 12
Place in batting averages: 65th av. 34.09 (1999 35th av. 40.29)
Strike rate: (career 184.16)
Parents: Ken (deceased) and Pat
Wife and date of marriage: Susan, 27 September 1986
Children: Tom, 25 March 1989; Ceri Lloyd, 5 August 1993
Family links with cricket: Father played for many years for Duckinfield. Brother
Charles plays for St Fagans. Son Tom plays for Cardiff County and the Vale U11 and
Wales U12
Education: Ysgol David Hughes, Menai Bridge, Anglesey
Qualifications: Cricket coach
Career outside cricket: 'Ice cream taster'
Off-season: 'Working for Thomas, Carroll Ltd in PR'
Overseas tours: North Wales XI to Barbados 1982; Glamorgan to Barbados 1982, to
South Africa 1993; unofficial England XI to South Africa 1989-90; HKCC (Australia)
to Bangkok and Hong Kong 1990; England VI to Hong Kong Sixes 1992, 1994;
England to West Indies 1993-94; England XI to New Zealand (Cricket Max) 1997
(captain)
Overseas teams played for: St Joseph's, Whakatane, New Zealand 1986-88;
Gosnells, Perth, Western Australia 1988-89; Papakura and Northern Districts, New
Zealand 1990-92; Morrinsville College and Northern Districts 1991-92; Otago, New
Zealand 1996-97
Cricketers particularly admired: Ian Botham, Viv Richards, David Gower

Young players to look out for: Tom Maynard
Other sports played: Golf
Other sports followed: Football (Manchester City), golf and squash
Relaxations: 'Spending time with my wife and family and relaxing'
Extras: Scored century on first-class debut v Yorkshire at Swansea in 1985, reaching his 100 with three successive straight sixes and becoming the youngest centurion for Glamorgan; he scored 1000 runs in his first full season. In 1987 set record for fastest 50 for Glamorgan (14 mins) v Yorkshire and became youngest player to be awarded Glamorgan cap. Voted Young Cricketer of the Year 1988 by the Cricket Writers' Club. Banned from Test cricket for five years for joining 1989-90 tour of South Africa; ban remitted 1992. Scored 987 runs in July 1991, including a century in each innings v Gloucestershire at Cheltenham. Captained Glamorgan for most of 1992 in Alan Butcher's absence. Appointed Glamorgan captain 1996. Voted Wombwell Cricket Lovers' Society captain of the year for 1997. Was one of *Wisden*'s Five Cricketers of the Year 1998. Appointed honorary fellow of University of Wales, Bangor. Set new Glamorgan one-day record stand for third wicket (204) with Jacques Kallis in National League match v Surrey at Pontypridd 1999. Passed 20,000 first-class runs during his 186 in Glamorgan's first innings v Yorkshire at Headingley 1999. Won Gold Award in the B&H Cup Final 2000 for his 104 from 118 balls, having also won the award in the semi-final v Surrey for his 109 from 115 balls. Stood down as Glamorgan captain at the end of the 2000 season
Opinions on cricket: 'Two divisions have been a big success this year, but beware!'
Best batting: 243 Glamorgan v Hampshire, Southampton 1991
Best bowling: 3-21 Glamorgan v Oxford University, The Parks 1987

2000 Season

	M	Inns	NO	Runs	HS	Avge	100s	50s	Ct	St	O	M	Runs	Wkts	Avge	Best	5wI	10wM
Test																		
All First	15	22	1	716	119 *	34.09	2	5	17	2	15.3	5	32	0	-		-	-	-
1-day Int	4	2	0	3	3	1.50	-	-	1	-								
NatWest	3	2	0	36	36	18.00	-	-	2	-								
B & H	6	6	0	319	109	53.16	2	-	-	-								
1-day Lge	14	14	2	501	88 *	41.75	-	4	10	1								

Career Performances

	M	Inns	NO	Runs	HS	Avge	100s	50s	Ct	St	Balls	Runs	Wkts	Avge	Best	5wI	10wM
Test	4	8	0	87	35	10.87	-	-	3	-							
All First	337	549	56	20897	243	42.38	47	114	326	7	1105	861	6	143.50	3-21	-	-
1-day Int	14	12	1	156	41	14.18	-	-	3	-							
NatWest	42	40	3	1559	151 *	42.13	2	12	20	-	18	8	0	-	-	-	-
B & H	54	54	6	2121	151 *	44.18	6	9	17	-	30	38	0	-	-	-	-
1-day Lge	211	203	16	5941	132	31.77	4	39	88	2	64	64	1	64.00	1-13	-

McCAGUE, M. J. Kent

Name: <u>Martin</u> John McCague
Role: Right-hand bat, right-arm fast bowler
Born: 24 May 1969, Larne, Northern Ireland
Height: 6ft 5in **Weight:** 17st 2lbs
Nickname: Munga, Macca
County debut: 1991
County cap: 1992
Test debut: 1993
Tests: 3
50 wickets in a season: 4
1st-Class 50s: 6
1st-Class 5 w. in innings: 25
1st-Class 10 w. in match: 2
1st-Class catches: 75
One-Day 5 w. in innings: 3
Place in batting averages: 207th av. 17.36
(1999 155th av. 24.72)
Place in bowling averages: 90th av. 29.42
(1999 121st av. 35.90)
Strike rate: 55.57 (career 50.13)
Parents: Mal and Mary
Wife and date of marriage: Leigh-Anne, 8 February 1997
Children: Monte Frederick, 15 September 1998
Education: Hedland Senior High School
Qualifications: Electrician
Off-season: 'Time with family, working and a bit of golf'
Overseas tours: England A to South Africa 1993-94; England to Australia 1994-95;
Kent Cricket Board XI to West Indies 1998-99
Overseas teams played for: Western Australia 1990-91
Cricketers particularly admired: Paul Strang, Courtney Walsh
Young players to look out for: Lawrence Prittipaul, Geraint Jones
Other sports played: Golf, snooker
Other sports followed: Football (Crystal Palace FC), American football
Injuries: Out for eight weeks with two ankle operations
Relaxations: Playing golf
Extras: Kent Player of the Year in 1996. Struck 20-ball 50 v Leicestershire Foxes in
National League at Canterbury 2000
Opinions on cricket: 'Two divisions has raised standards. Central contracts have
proved a huge success for the performance of Test players. Game is moving in the
right direction.'
Best batting: 72 Kent v Yorkshire, Canterbury 2000
Best bowling: 9-86 Kent v Derbyshire, Derby 1994

2000 Season

	M	Inns	NO	Runs	HS	Avge	100s	50s	Ct	St	O	M	Runs	Wkts	Avge	Best	5wI	10wM
Test																		
All First	7	11	0	191	72	17.36	-	1	2	-	129.4	20	412	14	29.42	5-52	1	-
1-day Int																		
NatWest																		
B & H																		
1-day Lge	7	5	1	120	56	30.00	-	1	1	-	46.2	4	206	11	18.72	3-29	-	

Career Performances

	M	Inns	NO	Runs	HS	Avge	100s	50s	Ct	St	Balls	Runs	Wkts	Avge	Best	5wI	10wM
Test	3	5	0	21	11	4.20	-	-	1	-	593	390	6	65.00	4-121	-	-
All First	133	185	45	2320	72	16.57	-	6	75	-	22762	12293	454	27.07	9-86	25	2
1-day Int																	
NatWest	16	12	7	126	31 *	25.20	-	-	4	-	882	592	22	26.90	5-26	1	
B & H	30	19	8	169	30	15.36	-	-	7	-	1532	1186	39	30.41	5-43	1	
1-day Lge	102	56	16	427	56	10.67	-	1	17	-	3873	3331	134	24.85	5-40	1	

McGARRY, A. C. Essex

Name: <u>Andrew</u> Charles McGarry
Role: Right-hand bat, right-arm
fast-medium bowler
Born: 8 November 1981, Basildon, Essex
Height: 6ft 5in **Weight:** 12st 7lbs
Nickname: Rodders
County debut: 1999
Strike rate: 57.00 (career 58.20)
Parents: Christine and George
Marital status: Single
Family links with cricket: Father played,
and eldest brother plays recreational cricket
Education: Widford Lodge Preparatory
School, Chelmsford; King Edward VI GS,
Chelmsford; South East Essex College of
Arts and Technology, Southend
Qualifications: 9 GCSEs, Level 1 and 2
ECB coaching awards
Career outside cricket: Student
Off-season: Studying. England U19 tour of India
Overseas tours: England U19 to India 2000-01
Cricketers particularly admired: Ian Botham, Allan Donald

Young players to look out for: Justin Bishop, Monty Panesar, Mark Pettini
Other sports played: Basketball, volleyball, football
Other sports followed: Football (Aston Villa)
Relaxations: Going out, listening to music
Extras: First Brian Johnston Scholarship winner 1996
Opinions on cricket: 'Two division cricket has created a much more competitive season, as shown by the last game promotion race between six sides in division two, meaning nearly all games have importance in the last round of matches.'
Best batting: 1 Essex v Worcestershire, Chelmsford 2000
Best bowling: 3-29 Essex v Worcestershire, Chelmsford 2000

2000 Season

	M	Inns	NO	Runs	HS	Avge	100s	50s	Ct	St	O	M	Runs	Wkts	Avge	Best	5wI	10wM
Test																		
All First	3	3	2	1	1	1.00	-	-	-	-	57	10	227	6	37.83	3-29	-	-
1-day Int																		
NatWest																		
B & H																		
1-day Lge	4	1	1	0	0 *	-	-	-	-	-	17	2	63	2	31.50	2-20	-	

Career Performances

	M	Inns	NO	Runs	HS	Avge	100s	50s	Ct	St	Balls	Runs	Wkts	Avge	Best	5wI	10wM
Test																	
All First	4	4	3	1	1	1.00	-	-	-	-	582	376	10	37.60	3-29	-	-
1-day Int																	
NatWest																	
B & H																	
1-day Lge	4	1	1	0	0 *	-	-	-	-	-	102	63	2	31.50	2-20	-	

57. Who became the world's then top wicket-taker in Tests when he passed Alec Bedser's total of 236 wickets at Adelaide in 1962-63?

McGRATH, A. Yorkshire

Name: Anthony McGrath
Role: Right-hand bat, right-arm
medium bowler
Born: 6 October 1975, Bradford
Height: 6ft 1in **Weight:** 14st
Nickname: Gripper, Mags
County debut: 1995
County cap: 1999
1st-Class 50s: 19
1st-Class 100s: 7
1st-Class catches: 57
One-Day 100s: 1
Place in batting averages: 104th av. 28.84
(1999 107th av. 29.67)
Strike rate: (career 69.35)
Parents: Terry and Kathleen
Marital status: Single
Family links with cricket: Brother Dermot

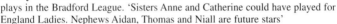

plays in the Bradford League. 'Sisters Anne and Catherine could have played for
England Ladies. Nephews Aidan, Thomas and Niall are future stars'
Education: St Winefrides; St Blaize; Yorkshire Martyrs Collegiate School
Qualifications: 9 GCSEs, BTEC National Diploma in Leisure Studies, senior
coaching award
Overseas tours: England U19 to West Indies 1994-95; England A to Pakistan
1995-96, to Australia 1996-97; MCC to Bangladesh 1999-2000
Overseas teams played for: Deep Dene, Melbourne 1998-99
Cricketers particularly admired: Darren Lehmann, Nasser Hussain, Ronnie Irani,
Robin Smith
Other sports played: Football (Green Man FC)
Other sports followed: Football (Manchester United)
Relaxations: Watching football. Music. Socialising with friends
Extras: Captained Yorkshire Schools U13, U14, U15 and U16; captained English
Schools U17. Bradford League Young Cricketer of the Year 1992 and 1993. Played for
England U17, and for England U19 in home series against India 1994. Appeared as
12th man for England in the first Test against West Indies at Headingley in 1995
Best batting: 142* Yorkshire v Middlesex, Headingley 1999
Best bowling: 3-18 Yorkshire v Surrey, The Oval 1999

2000 Season

	M	Inns	NO	Runs	HS	Avge	100s	50s	Ct	St	O	M	Runs	Wkts	Avge	Best	5wl	10wM
Test																		
All First	10	14	1	375	133	28.84	1	1	8	-								
1-day Int																		
NatWest	1	1	0	64	64	64.00	-	1	-	-	4	0	23	0	-		-	-
B & H																		
1-day Lge	10	9	4	224	85 *	44.80	-	1	6	-								

Career Performances

	M	Inns	NO	Runs	HS	Avge	100s	50s	Ct	St	Balls	Runs	Wkts	Avge	Best	5wl	10wM
Test																	
All First	92	156	10	4254	142 *	29.13	7	19	57	-	971	492	14	35.14	3-18	-	-
1-day Int																	
NatWest	14	13	1	420	84	35.00	-	4	5	-	42	37	0	-		-	-
B & H	22	20	1	511	109 *	26.89	1	1	8	-	12	10	2	5.00	2-10	-	
1-day Lge	70	63	13	1564	85 *	31.28	-	11	22	-	270	187	7	26.71	2-20	-	

McGRATH, G. D. Worcestershire

Name: <u>Glenn</u> Donald McGrath
Role: Right-hand bat, right-arm fast bowler
Born: 9 February 1970, Dubbo,
New South Wales
Height: 6ft 6in **Weight:** 14st
Nickname: Pigeon
County debut: 2000
County cap: 2000
Test debut: 1993-94
Tests: 62
One-Day Internationals: 121
50 wickets in a season: 1
1st-Class 50s: 1
1st-Class 5 w. in innings: 28
1st-Class 10 w. in match: 6
1st-Class catches: 32
One-Day 5 w. in innings: 4
Place in batting averages: 276th av. 9.33
Place in bowling averages: 3rd av. 13.21
Strike rate: 31.17 (career 48.68)
Parents: Kevin and Bev
Wife and date of marriage: Jane, 17 July 1999

Children: James, 20 January 2000
Education: Narromine High School
Off-season: Playing cricket in Australia
Overseas tours: Australia to South Africa 1993-94, to Pakistan 1994-95, to West Indies 1994-95, to India 1995-96, to India, Pakistan and Sri Lanka (World Cup) 1995-96, to South Africa 1996-97, to England 1997, to Pakistan 1998-99, to West Indies 1998-99, to UK, Ireland and Holland (World Cup) 1999, to Sri Lanka and Zimbabwe 1999-2000, to New Zealand 1999-2000, to Kenya (ICC Knockout Trophy) 2000-01, to India 2000-01
Overseas teams played for: New South Wales 1992-93 –
Cricketers particularly admired: Dennis Lillee, Rod Marsh
Young players to look out for: Don Nash
Other sports played: Golf
Other sports followed: Rugby league (Cronulla Sharks)
Relaxations: 'Going to my property in outback NSW'
Extras: One of *Wisden*'s Five Cricketers of the Year 1998. Became the tenth Australian to take 200 Test wickets when he dismissed Alec Stewart in England's first innings in the fifth Test at Sydney, January 1999. Broke John Snow's and Bruce Taylor's record of 27 wickets by a visiting bowler in a Caribbean Test series, taking 30 wickets in Australia's 1998-99 tour. *Wisden Australia*'s Cricketer of the Year 1998-99. Played in Australia's 1999 World Cup winning side. Was leading Test wicket-taker of 1999 with 67 (av. 21.27). Winner of the inaugural Allan Border Medal 2000. Joined Worcestershire as overseas player for 2000. FICA International Cricketer of the Year 2000. Took 30 National League wickets at an average of 8.13 in 2000, recording in the process the lowest runs-per-over ratio (2.16) in a Sunday/National League season. Top wicket-taker in English first-class cricket 2000 with 80 wickets at an average of 13.21. Named Player of the Year in 2000 by Worcestershire's supporters' club. Awarded ACB contract for 2000-01. Left Worcestershire at the end of the 2000 season
Opinions on cricket: 'As the game is becoming more and more professional, to succeed you need to be as dedicated to fitness and developing a positive attitude as you are to the skills of the game.'
Best batting: 55 Worcestershire v Nottinghamshire, Worcester 2000
Best bowling: 8-38 Australia v England, Lord's 1997
Stop press: Returned match figures of 10-27 from 33 overs in the first Test v West Indies at Brisbane, winning the Man of the Match award and moving into third place in the list of Australian Test wicket-takers behind Dennis Lillee and Shane Warne. Took 300th Test wicket (Brian Lara) in the middle of his maiden first-class hat-trick (Campbell, Lara, Adams) v West Indies in the second Test at Perth 2000-01

2000 Season

	M	Inns	NO	Runs	HS	Avge	100s	50s	Ct	St	O	M	Runs	Wkts	Avge	Best	5wI	10wM
Test																		
All First	14	15	3	112	55	9.33	-	1	3	-	415.4	132	1057	80	13.21	8-41	6	3
1-day Int																		
NatWest	2	1	1	1	1*	-	-	-	1	-	20	4	46	4	11.50	4-23	-	
B & H	1	0	0	0	0	-	-	-	-	-	2	0	21	0	-	-	-	
1-day Lge	14	7	3	1	1	0.25	-	-	1	-	112.4	30	244	30	8.13	4-9	-	

Career Performances

	M	Inns	NO	Runs	HS	Avge	100s	50s	Ct	St	Balls	Runs	Wkts	Avge	Best	5wI	10wM
Test	62	76	23	316	39	5.96	-	-	19	-	14863	6458	288	22.42	8-38	17	2
All First	114	120	38	518	55	6.31	-	1	32	-	25024	10797	514	21.00	8-38	28	6
1-day Int	121	37	21	63	11	3.93	-	-	13	-	6473	4266	183	23.31	5-14	4	
NatWest	2	1	1	1	1*	-	-	-	1	-	120	46	4	11.50	4-23	-	
B & H	1	0	0	0	0	-	-	-	-	-	12	21	0	-	-	-	
1-day Lge	14	7	3	1	1	0.25	-	-	1	-	676	244	30	8.13	4-9	-	

McKEOWN, P. C.   Lancashire

Name: <u>Patrick</u> Christopher McKeown
Role: Right-hand bat
Born: 1 June 1976, Liverpool
Height: 6ft 3in **Weight:** 13st
Nickname: Paddy
County debut: 1996
1st-Class 50s: 3
1st-Class catches: 14
Place in batting averages: (1999 100th av. 30.85)
Parents: Paddy and Cathy
Marital status: Single
Education: St Mary's College, Crosby; Rossall School (Blackpool)
Qualifications: 7 GCSEs, 3 A-levels
Overseas tours: Rossall School to Australia 1994-95
Overseas teams played for: Subiaco-Floreat, Perth, Australia 1995-96
Cricketers particularly admired: Graeme Hick and Neil Fairbrother
Other sports followed: Football (Liverpool)
Relaxations: 'Playing most sports, especially football and rugby. I enjoy spending time on the golf course'

Extras: Represented England Schools U19, and U18 versus India. Played for Development of Excellence U19, National Cricket Association U19, Headmasters' Conference U19. Awarded 2nd XI cap in 1996. Scored 307 in less than a day for Lancashire 2nd XI v Gloucestershire 2nd XI at Bristol in 1998, setting a record for the highest individual score made for Lancashire 2nd XI. Released by Lancashire at the end of the 2000 season

Best batting: 75 Lancashire v Cambridge University, Fenner's 1999

2000 Season

	M	Inns	NO	Runs	HS	Avge	100s	50s	Ct	St	O	M	Runs	Wkts	Avge	Best	5wI	10wM
Test																		
All First	3	4	0	69	33	17.25	-	-	1	-								
1-day Int																		
NatWest																		
B & H																		
1-day Lge	1	1	0	1	1	1.00	-	-	-	-	0.2	0	4	0	-		-	-

Career Performances

	M	Inns	NO	Runs	HS	Avge	100s	50s	Ct	St	Balls	Runs	Wkts	Avge	Best	5wI	10wM
Test																	
All First	19	27	1	679	75	26.11	-	3	14	-							
1-day Int																	
NatWest	1	1	0	42	42	42.00	-	-	-	-	60	51	0	-		-	-
B & H	1	1	0	10	10	10.00	-	-	-	-							
1-day Lge	18	18	0	264	69	14.66	-	1	5	-	2	4	0	-		-	-

58. At Edgbaston in 1985, David Gower caught Wayne Phillips at silly mid-off under unusual circumstances. What happened?

McLEAN, R. A.   Northamptonshire

Name: <u>Ross</u> Alexander McLean
Role: Right-hand bat, right-arm fast-medium
bowler
Born: 16 March 1981, Northampton
Height: 6ft 3in   **Weight:** 14st
Nickname: Gibbon
County debut: No first-team appearance
Parents: Valerie and Peter
Marital status: Single
Education: Hopping Hill Lower School,
Duston C of E Lower School; Reylands
Middle School; Duston Upper School;
University of Leeds
Qualifications: 3 A-levels, ECB Level 1
cricket coach, hockey and basketball awards
Career outside cricket: Student
Overseas tours: Northamptonshire U19 to
South Africa

Cricketers particularly admired: Alec Swann, Learie Constantine, Douglas Jardine,
Mike Atherton, Curtly Ambrose
Young players to look out for: Mark Powell, Richard Kafman
Other sports played: Hockey
Other sports followed: Football (Northampton Town), rugby (Northampton Saints)
Relaxations: Reading, fishing, computers
Extras: Played for Northamptonshire Board XI in NatWest 2000
Opinions on cricket: 'General tardy response to developments and new ideas. Over-
romanticising of the game.'

2000 Season (did not make any first-class or one-day appearances)

Career Performances

	M	Inns	NO	Runs	HS	Avge	100s	50s	Ct	St	Balls	Runs	Wkts	Avge	Best	5wI	10wM
Test																	
All First																	
1-day Int																	
NatWest	1	1	1	10	10*	-	-	-	-	-	60	21	1	21.00	1-21	-	
B & H																	
1-day Lge																	

MIDDLEBROOK, J. D. — Yorkshire

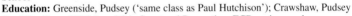

Name: <u>James</u> Daniel Middlebrook
Role: Right-hand bat, off-spin bowler
Born: 13 May 1977, Leeds
Height: 6ft 1in **Weight:** 13st
Nickname: Midi, Midders, Midhouse
County debut: 1998
1st-Class 5 w. in innings: 1
1st-Class 10 w. in match: 1
1st-Class catches: 12
Place in batting averages: 241st av. 13.40
Place in bowling averages: 55th av. 24.87
Strike rate: 54.41 (career 60.72)
Parents: Ralph and Mavis
Marital status: Single
Family links with cricket: 'Dad is a senior staff coach/Cricket Development Officer for Leeds and Manager, Yorkshire Cricket School'
Education: Greenside, Pudsey ('same class as Paul Hutchison'); Crawshaw, Pudsey
Qualifications: NVQ Level 2 in Sport and Recreation, ECB senior coach
Overseas tours: Yorkshire CCC to Guernsey
Overseas teams played for: Stokes Valley CC, New Zealand; Gold Coast Dolphins, Brisbane; Surfers Paradise CC, Brisbane
Cricketers particularly admired: John Emburey, Ian Botham
Young players to look out for: Matthew Wood, Matthew Hoggard, 'Me!'
Other sports played: Golf, tennis, squash, badminton
Other sports followed: Football (Leeds United), athletics
Relaxations: 'Any music – MTV – sleeping, socialising, catching up with old friends'
Extras: Played for Pudsey Congs since age of seven. Played for Yorkshire at all age levels U11 to 1st XI. Awarded Yorkshire 2nd XI cap 1998. His maiden first-class five-wicket return (6-82) v Hampshire at Southampton 2000 included a spell of four wickets in five balls; finished with match figures of 10-170
Best batting: 45 Yorkshire v Derbyshire, Derby 2000
Best bowling: 6-82 Yorkshire v Hampshire, Southampton 2000

> 59. At Perth in 1982-83, which Middlesex pace bowler
> became the 500th man to play for England?

2000 Season

	M	Inns	NO	Runs	HS	Avge	100s	50s	Ct	St	O	M	Runs	Wkts	Avge	Best	5wI	10wM
Test																		
All First	11	15	0	201	45	13.40	-	-	5	-	281.1	68	771	31	24.87	6-82	1	1
1-day Int																		
NatWest	2	1	1	6	6*	-	-	-	3	-	8	1	38	0	-	-	-	-
B & H																		
1-day Lge	10	6	1	30	15*	6.00	-	-	-	-	73	0	320	11	29.09	3-16	-	

Career Performances

	M	Inns	NO	Runs	HS	Avge	100s	50s	Ct	St	Balls	Runs	Wkts	Avge	Best	5wI	10wM
Test																	
All First	19	27	2	340	45	13.60	-	-	12	-	2672	1193	44	27.11	6-82	1	1
1-day Int																	
NatWest	2	1	1	6	6*	-	-	-	3	-	48	38	0	-	-	-	-
B & H																	
1-day Lge	11	7	1	35	15*	5.83	-	-	-	-	450	339	11	30.81	3-16	-	

MILLNS, D. J.   Nottinghamshire

Name: <u>David</u> James Millns
Role: Left-hand bat, right-arm
fast-medium swing bowler
Born: 27 February 1965,
Mansfield, Nottinghamshire
Height: 6ft 3in **Weight:** 14st 7lbs
Nickname: Rocket Man
County debut: 1988 (Nottinghamshire),
1990 (Leicestershire)
County cap: 1991 (Leicestershire),
2000 (Nottinghamshire – see **Extras**)
Benefit: 1999 (Leicestershire)
50 wickets in a season: 4
1st-Class 50s: 8
1st-Class 100s: 3
1st-Class 5 w. in innings: 23
1st-Class 10 w. in match: 4
1st-Class catches: 75
Place in batting averages: 112th av. 27.85 (1999 174th av. 22.66)
Place in bowling averages: 89th av. 29.33 (1999 5th av. 16.17)
Strike rate: 45.23 (career 47.86)
Parents: Bernard and Brenda

Wife and date of marriage: Wanda Marie, 25 September 1993
Children: Dylan, 17 April 1998
Family links with cricket: Andy Pick, former Notts CCC player, is brother-in-law.
Brother Paul and his son Matthew play for Clipstone MWCC
Education: Samuel Barlow Junior; Garibaldi Comprehensive; North Notts College of
Further Education; Nottingham Trent Polytechnic
Qualifications: Advanced coach
Career outside cricket: 'Undecided'
Off-season: 'Having a second child with my wife'
Overseas tours: England A to Australia 1992-93; Leicestershire to South Africa 1994,
1995, to Holland 1994, 1996, to Barbados 1998
Overseas teams played for: Uitenhage, Port Elizabeth, South Africa 1988-89;
Birkenhead, Auckland 1989-91; Tasmania, Australia 1994-95; Boland, South Africa
1996-97
Cricketers particularly admired: Darren Gough, Glenn McGrath
Young players to look out for: Paul Franks, Usman Afzaal, David Lucas, Chris Read
Other sports followed/played: Football (Leicester City), rugby union (Leicester
Tigers), golf ('taking money off J.J. Whitaker on the golf course gives me great
pleasure')
Injuries: Out for three months with torn hamstring and torn cartilage
Relaxations: Computers and property development
Extras: Harold Larwood Bowling Award 1984. Asked to be released by
Nottinghamshire at the end of 1989 season and joined Leicestershire in 1990. Finished
third in national bowling averages in 1990. Britannic Assurance Player of the Month in
August 1991 after taking 9-37 v Derbyshire, the best Leicestershire figures since
George Geary's 10-18 v Glamorgan in 1929. Was players' representative on
Cricketers' Association Executive for Leicestershire. Leicestershire Cricketer of the
Year 1992. Leicestershire Bowling Award 1990, 1991, 1992 and 1994. Left
Leicestershire at end of 1999 season and rejoined Nottinghamshire for 2000, taking
5-58 v Northamptonshire at Trent Bridge in his first match. Awarded Notts cap 2000
Opinions on cricket: 'Congratulations to the ECB for the new format.
Congratulations to the England cricket team on beating West Indies.'
Best batting: 121 Leicestershire v Northamptonshire, Northampton 1997
Best bowling: 9-37 Leicestershire v Derbyshire, Derby 1991

2000 Season

	M	Inns	NO	Runs	HS	Avge	100s	50s	Ct	St	O	M	Runs	Wkts	Avge	Best	5wI	10wM
Test																		
All First	8	11	4	195	50 *	27.85	-	1	2	-	226.1	42	880	30	29.33	5-58	1	-
1-day Int																		
NatWest																		
B & H	3	2	1	6	6 *	6.00	-	-	1	-	15.5	2	105	3	35.00	3-35	-	
1-day Lge	4	3	2	25	13	25.00	-	-	1	-	33	2	185	4	46.25	2-46	-	

Career Performances

	M	Inns	NO	Runs	HS	Avge	100s	50s	Ct	St	Balls	Runs	Wkts	Avge	Best	5wI	10wM
Test																	
All First	170	201	62	3075	121	22.12	3	8	75	-	26420	15042	552	27.25	9-37	23	4
1-day Int																	
NatWest	11	5	3	49	29 *	24.50	-	-	2	-	648	423	12	35.25	3-22	-	
B & H	30	16	9	109	39 *	15.57	-	-	6	-	1339	1013	32	31.65	4-26	-	
1-day Lge	47	25	13	157	20 *	13.08	-	-	10	-	1812	1585	37	42.83	2-11	-	

MOHAMMED, I. Gloucestershire

Name: Imraan Mohammed
Role: Right-hand opening bat,
right-arm off-spin bowler
Born: 31 December 1976, Solihull
Height: 5ft 9in **Weight:** 11st
Nickname: Immy
County debut: 2000
1st-Class 50s: 2
1st-Class 100s: 1
1st-Class catches: 1
Place in batting averages: 256th av. 11.83
(1999 57th av. 37.14)
Strike rate: (career 107.66)
Parents: Sadiq and Nighat
Marital status: Single
Family links with cricket: Father Sadiq
played for Pakistan and Gloucestershire.
Uncles Hanif, Mushtaq and Wazir also played
for Pakistan
Education: Crossways School, Thornbury; St Patricks High School, Karachi; Karachi
Grammar School; Joseph Chamberlain College, Birmingham; Cambridge University
Qualifications: BA (Hons) Economics
Overseas tours: Cambridge University CC to Pakistan 1999
Overseas teams played for: Pakistan Customs, Pakistan 1999-2000
Cricketers particularly admired: Sachin Tendulkar, Steve Waugh, Imran Khan,
Javed Miandad, Hanif Mohammed, Martin Crowe, Wasim Akram, Ricky Ponting
Young players to look out for: Anurag Singh, Ed Smith, Owais Shah
Other sports played: Table tennis, tennis, badminton, football (all recreational)
Other sports followed: Tennis, boxing and football
Relaxations: Reading fiction and autobiographies, going to the movies, 'my music'
Extras: A member of the Mohammed family that has produced five Test cricketers so

far and holds the record for producing the most first-class cricketers from a single family. Achieved two Blues while at Cambridge. Played for Cambridge University and British Universities in 1999. Released by Gloucestershire at the end of the 2000 season **Opinions on cricket:** 'The game has become far more competitive, testing, aggressive, and demanding of endurance and fitness. The price of some of the above may have been that it has lost some of its old world charm and the spirit which cricket advocates, not to mention some of the old colourful "characters". It has certainly become more exciting and spectator-friendly, which is probably the most important thing.'
Best batting: 136 Cambridge University v Yorkshire, Headingley 1998
Best bowling: 1-13 Cambridge University v Yorkshire, Headingley 1998

2000 Season

	M	Inns	NO	Runs	HS	Avge	100s	50s	Ct	St	O	M	Runs	Wkts	Avge	Best	5wI	10wM
Test																		
All First	4	6	0	71	24	11.83	-	-	1	-								
1-day Int																		
NatWest	2	2	0	53	53	26.50	-	1	1	-	7	1	38	1	38.00	1-38	-	
B & H																		
1-day Lge																		

Career Performances

	M	Inns	NO	Runs	HS	Avge	100s	50s	Ct	St	Balls	Runs	Wkts	Avge	Best	5wI	10wM
Test																	
All First	20	30	3	840	136	31.11	2	2	2	-	323	186	3	62.00	1-13	-	-
1-day Int																	
NatWest	2	2	0	53	53	26.50	-	1	1	-	42	38	1	38.00	1-38	-	
B & H																	
1-day Lge																	

MONTGOMERIE, R. R.   Sussex

Name: Richard Robert Montgomerie
Role: Right-hand opening bat
Born: 3 July 1971, Rugby
Height: 5ft 10in **Weight:** 13st
Nickname: Monty
County debut: 1991 (Northamptonshire), 1999 (Sussex)
County cap: 1995 (Northamptonshire), 1999 (Sussex)
1000 runs in a season: 2
1st-Class 50s: 37
1st-Class 100s: 13

1st-Class catches: 120
One-Day 100s: 1
Place in batting averages: 76th av. 32.10
(1999 58th av. 37.00)
Parents: Robert and Gillian
Marital status: Single
Family links with cricket: Father captained
Oxfordshire
Education: Bilton Grange; Rugby School;
Worcester College, Oxford University
Qualifications: 12 O-levels, 4 A-levels,
BA (Hons) Chemistry, Level II coaching
Off-season: Teaching/coaching at Brighton
College
Overseas tours: Oxford University to
Namibia 1991; Northamptonshire to
Zimbabwe and Johannesburg; Christians in
Sport to South Africa 2000
Overseas teams played for: Sydney University CC 1995-96
Cricketers particularly admired: 'Many'
Young players to look out for: Matt Prior
Other sports followed: Golf, rackets, real tennis and many others
Relaxations: Any sport, good television, reading and 'occasionally testing my brain'
Extras: Scored unbeaten 50 in each innings of 1991 Varsity match and was Oxford
captain in 1994. Oxford rackets Blue 1990. Captained Combined Universities 1994.
Released by Northants at the end of the 1998 season and joined Sussex for 1999.
Scored his first 100 for Sussex (113*) against Northants, his former county, at Hove
1999. Took part in the Christians in Sport millennium tour to South Africa, the aims of
which included distributing cricket kit to disadvantaged youngsters, coaching and
playing matches against teams in the townships. Scored 133 and 95 v Nottinghamshire
at Hove 2000
Opinions on cricket: 'The new two league system is having the desired effect of
making every match matter. Central contracts seem to be working too – keeping the
quick bowlers fit is key to our international success.'
Best batting: 192 Northamptonshire v Kent, Canterbury 1995

2000 Season

	M	Inns	NO	Runs	HS	Avge	100s	50s	Ct	St	O	M	Runs	Wkts	Avge	Best	5wI	10wM
Test																		
All First	17	30	2	899	133	32.10	2	4	17	-								
1-day Int																		
NatWest	2	2	1	121	68 *	121.00	-	2	-	-								
B & H	4	4	0	82	36	20.50	-	-	1	-								
1-day Lge	15	15	1	419	89	29.92	-	2	5	-								

Career Performances

	M	Inns	NO	Runs	HS	Avge	100s	50s	Ct	St	Balls	Runs	Wkts	Avge	Best	5wI	10wM
Test																	
All First	130	227	22	6804	192	33.19	13	37	120	-	108	72	0	-		-	-	-
1-day Int																	
NatWest	10	10	3	477	109	68.14	1	5	3	-							
B & H	21	19	2	503	75	29.58	-	2	3	-	6	0	0	-		-	-	-
1-day Lge	65	64	4	1870	89	31.16	-	15	18	-							

MORRIS, A. C.   Hampshire

Name: <u>Alexander</u> Corfield Morris
Role: Left-hand bat, right-arm medium-fast bowler
Born: 4 October 1976, Barnsley
Height: 6ft 6in **Weight:** 'Off-season 18st; season hopefully 14st 7lbs'
County debut: 1995 (Yorkshire), 1998 (Hampshire)
50 wickets in a season: 1
1st-Class 50s: 4
1st-Class 5 w. in innings: 3
1st-Class 10 w. in match: 1
1st-Class catches: 22
Place in batting averages: 237th av. 14.00
Place in bowling averages: 98th av. 31.22 (1999 8th av. 17.75)
Strike rate: 61.05 (career 46.29)
Parents: Chris and Janet
Marital status: Single

Family links with cricket: Brother Zac plays for Hampshire
Education: Wilthorpe Primary School; Holgate School, Barnsley; Barnsley College
Qualifications: 4 GCSEs, BTEC National Diploma in Sports Science, senior cricket coach
Overseas tours: England U19 to West Indies 1994-95, to Zimbabwe 1995-96; England VI to Hong Kong 1996; Michael Vaughan XI to Tenerife 1996; Craig Dudley XI to Cyprus 1997; Anthony McGrath XI to Gran Canaria 1998; Alex Morris XI to Cyprus 1999
Cricketers particularly admired: 'Everyone I've ever been on an overseas tour with'
Other sports followed: Football (Barnsley FC)
Relaxations: 'Feeding the horse; enjoying a quiet drink with the Judge'

Extras: Played for Yorkshire U11-U19; made debut for 2nd XI at age 16. Played for England U15 against Barbados and in 1994 for both England U17 and U19 against India. Played junior football with both Barnsley and Rotherham and had trials for Nottingham Forest and Leeds. Left Yorkshire and signed for Hampshire along with his brother Zac for the 1998 season

Best batting: 60 Yorkshire v Lancashire, Old Trafford 1996

60 Hampshire v Leicestershire, Southampton 2000

Best bowling: 5-52 Hampshire v Worcestershire, Southampton 1999

2000 Season

	M	Inns	NO	Runs	HS	Avge	100s	50s	Ct	St	O	M	Runs	Wkts	Avge	Best	5wI	10wM
Test																		
All First	8	12	1	154	60	14.00	-	1	4	-	183.1	43	562	18	31.22	3-48	-	-
1-day Int																		
NatWest	1	1	1	3	3 *	-	-	-	-	-	8	0	45	1	45.00	1-45	-	
B & H																		
1-day Lge	5	2	1	16	16 *	16.00	-	-	1	-	42	2	223	7	31.85	3-59	-	

Career Performances

	M	Inns	NO	Runs	HS	Avge	100s	50s	Ct	St	Balls	Runs	Wkts	Avge	Best	5wI	10wM
Test																	
All First	42	57	10	866	60	18.42	-	4	22	-	4861	2579	105	24.56	5-52	3	1
1-day Int																	
NatWest	2	2	2	4	3 *	-	-	-	-	-	96	88	2	44.00	1-43	-	
B & H	1	0	0	0	0	-	-	-	1	-	6	4	0	-	-	-	
1-day Lge	32	19	5	232	48 *	16.57	-	-	6	-	792	708	26	27.23	4-49	-	

60. At which ground did Shane Warne deliver his 'ball of the century' or 'ball from hell' to dismiss Mike Gatting in 1993?

MORRIS, J. E.   Nottinghamshire

Name: <u>John</u> Edward Morris
Role: Right-hand bat, right-arm medium bowler
Born: 1 April 1964, Crewe
Height: 5ft 10in **Weight:** 13st 6lbs
Nickname: Animal
County debut: 1982 (Derbyshire), 1994 (Durham), 2000 (Notts)
County cap: 1986 (Derbyshire), 1998 (Durham), 2000 (Notts)
Benefit: 1999 (Durham)
Test debut: 1990
Tests: 3
One-Day Internationals: 8
1000 runs in a season: 11
1st-Class 50s: 100
1st-Class 100s: 48
1st-Class 200s: 2
1st-Class catches: 153
One-Day 100s: 9

Place in batting averages: 95th av. 30.05 (1999 94th av. 31.68)
Strike rate: 16.00 (career 126.75)
Parents: George (Eddie) and Jean
Wife and date of marriage: Sally, 30 September 1990
Children: Thomas Edward, 27 June 1991
Family links with cricket: Father played for Crewe for many years as an opening bowler
Education: Shavington Comprehensive School; Dane Bank College of Further Education
Qualifications: O-levels
Overseas tours: England to Australia 1990-91; Romany to South Africa 1993; MCC to Bahrain 1994-95
Overseas teams played for: Umbilo, Durban, South Africa 1982-84; Alex Old Boys, Pietermaritzburg, South Africa 1984-85; Subiaco-Floreat, Western Australia 1986-87; Griqualand West, South Africa 1988-89, 1993-94; Protea, Johannesburg, South Africa 1993
Other sports followed: Golf, football (Derby County)
Relaxations: The golf course and home life
Extras: In 1984 became youngest player to score a Sunday League century. Was the first batsman to pass 5000 runs for Durham. Passed 20,000 first-class runs during Durham's first innings v Derbyshire, his former county, at Chester-le-Street 1999. Left Durham at end of 1999 season and joined Nottinghamshire for 2000. Has set up a

sports management agency with Somerset's Peter Bowler. Passed 5000 Sunday/National League career runs in 2000, against his former club Durham at Trent Bridge. Scored 50th first-class century (115) v Sussex at Hove 2000. Awarded Notts cap 2000

Best batting: 229 Derbyshire v Gloucestershire, Cheltenham 1993
Best bowling: 1-6 Derbyshire v Cambridge University, Fenner's 1993

2000 Season

	M	Inns	NO	Runs	HS	Avge	100s	50s	Ct	St	O	M	Runs	Wkts	Avge	Best	5wI	10wM
Test																		
All First	13	20	0	601	115	30.05	1	3	7	-	2.4	0	26	1	26.00	1-26	-	-
1-day Int																		
NatWest	1	1	0	18	18	18.00	-	-	-	-								
B & H	4	4	0	46	39	11.50	-	-	-	-								
1-day Lge	13	12	0	323	73	26.91	-	3	3	-								

Career Performances

	M	Inns	NO	Runs	HS	Avge	100s	50s	Ct	St	Balls	Runs	Wkts	Avge	Best	5wI	10wM
Test	3	5	2	71	32	23.66	-	-	3	-							
All First	354	596	33	20899	229	37.12	50	100	153	-	1014	939	8	117.37	1-6	-	-
1-day Int	8	8	1	167	63 *	23.85	-	1	2	-							
NatWest	31	30	3	874	109	32.37	1	5	9	-							
B & H	62	58	6	1527	145	29.36	3	7	13	-	24	14	0	-	-	-	
1-day Lge	229	218	12	5288	134	25.66	5	24	51	-	9	8	0	-	-	-	

61. Who was left high and dry on 99* after a run-out closed his side's innings at Perth in 1994-95?

MORRIS, Z. C. Hampshire

Name: <u>Zachary</u> Clegg Morris
Role: Right-hand bat, left-arm fast bowler
Born: 4 September 1978, Barnsley
Height: 6ft 2in **Weight:** 14st
Nickname: Cleggy, Z-man, Big Dog,
Badger, Ted
County debut: 1998
Parents: Lance and Janet
Marital status: 'Passionate'
Family links with cricket: Brother also
plays for Hampshire
Education: Wilthorpe Primary School;
Holgate Secondary School; '"The
Commercial", Summer Lane, Barnsley'
Qualifications: Level 1 coaching award,
'labourer, truck driver, baker, barman, cement
renderer'

Career outside cricket: 'World traveller'
Off-season: 'Improving my game on and off the field somewhere warm'
Overseas tours: Sheffield Cricket Lovers to Holland 1990, to Magaluf 1992; England
U15 to South Africa 1993; England U19 to Pakistan 1996-97
Overseas teams played for: Strathfield CC, Sydney 1998-99; Melville CC, Perth
2000-01
Cricketers particularly admired: Peter Hartley
Young players to look out for: Lawrence Prittipaul
Other sports played: Football (Barnsley Schools age groups 11 to 16; represented
Barnsley 15 age group v London at Wembley)
Other sports followed: Football (Southampton FC)
Injuries: Out for three weeks with tear in left quad; also had ligament strain in right
knee
Relaxations: Swimming, training, novels, parties, daytime sleeping
Extras: 'Pretty useful groundsman!' Moved to Hampshire in the 1997-98 close season
along with his brother, Alex. Represented England U19 v Pakistan U19 1998.
'Switched from bowling slow left-arm to left-arm seam at beginning of 2000 season
due to an incurable case of yips caught while drinking a shandy!'
Opinions on cricket: 'Pay should be somehow based on performance – i.e. larger win
bonuses (team and personal); bowlers paid more than batsmen; all-rounders paid
double.'
Best batting: 10 Hampshire v Gloucestershire, Southampton 1998

2000 Season (did not make any first-class or one-day appearances)

Career Performances

	M	Inns	NO	Runs	HS	Avge	100s	50s	Ct	St	Balls	Runs	Wkts	Avge	Best	5wl	10wM
Test																	
All First	2	4	0	11	10	2.75	-	-	-	-	205	99	0	-	-	-	-
1-day Int																	
NatWest																		
B & H																		
1-day Lge																		

MULLALLY, A. D. Hampshire

Name: <u>Alan</u> David Mullally
Role: Right-hand bat, left-arm fast bowler
Born: 12 July 1969, Southend
Height: 6ft 5in **Weight:** 14st
Nickname: Bob, Bryan, Eric, Spider,
'too many to mention'
County debut: 1988 (Hampshire),
1990 (Leicestershire)
County cap: 1993 (Leicestershire),
2000 (Hampshire – see **Extras**)
Test debut: 1996
Tests: 18
One-Day Internationals: 41
50 wickets in a season: 4
1st-Class 50s: 2
1st-Class 5 w. in innings: 23
1st-Class 10 w. in match: 4
1st-Class catches: 36
One-Day 5 w. in innings: 2
Place in batting averages: 297th av. 6.00 (1999 289th av. 6.25)
Place in bowling averages: 10th av. 16.97 (1999 70th av. 27.53)
Strike rate: 42.10 (career 62.43)
Parents: Michael and Ann
Marital status: Single
Education: Cannington High School and Primary, Perth, Australia; Wembley and
Carlisle Technical College
Qualifications: 'This and that'
Career outside cricket: Musician
Off-season: England one-day squad to Sri Lanka

Overseas tours: Western Australia to India; Leicestershire to Jamaica 1992-93; England to Zimbabwe and New Zealand 1996-97, to Australia 1998-99, to Sharjah (Coca-Cola Cup) 1998-99, to South Africa and Zimbabwe 1999-2000, to Sri Lanka 2000-01 (one-day series)
Overseas teams played for: Western Australia 1987-90; Victoria 1990-91
Cricketers particularly admired: Geoff Marsh, Dermot Reeve
Other sports followed: Australian Rules football, basketball, most sports
Relaxations: Music
Injuries: Season disrupted by rib injury originally incurred on tour of South Africa 1999-2000
Extras: English-qualified as he was born in Southend, he made his first-class debut for Western Australia in the 1987-88 Sheffield Shield final, and played for Australian YC 1988-89. Played one match for Hampshire in 1988 before joining Leicestershire. Represented England in the 1999 World Cup. Left Leicestershire at end of 1999 season and rejoined Hampshire for 2000. Played for a World XI v an Asia XI at The Oval 2000. Took 28 wickets in five innings in August 2000, including 9-93 (14-188 in the match) v Derbyshire at Derby
Best batting: 75 Leicestershire v Middlesex, Leicester 1996
Best bowling: 9-93 Hampshire v Derbyshire, Derby 2000
Stop press: Forced to withdraw from England one-day squads to Kenya and Pakistan 2000-01 with recurrence of rib injury

2000 Season

	M	Inns	NO	Runs	HS	Avge	100s	50s	Ct	St	O	M	Runs	Wkts	Avge	Best	5wI	10wM
Test																		
All First	8	12	2	60	12	6.00	-	-	-	-	343.5	105	832	49	16.97	9-93	5	1
1-day Int	7	2	0	0	0	0.00	-	-	-	-	56.2	7	171	8	21.37	3-27	-	
NatWest	4	0	0	0	0	-	-	-	1	-	38	7	127	5	25.40	2-8	-	
B & H	4	2	1	15	13	15.00	-	-	1	-	31.2	7	133	2	66.50	1-28	-	
1-day Lge	11	7	2	21	7	4.20	-	-	1	-	93	11	341	17	20.05	4-30	-	

Career Performances

	M	Inns	NO	Runs	HS	Avge	100s	50s	Ct	St	Balls	Runs	Wkts	Avge	Best	5wI	10wM
Test	18	26	4	127	24	5.77	-	-	6	-	4342	1713	56	30.58	5-105	1	-
All First	185	209	52	1374	75	8.75	-	2	36	-	35150	16238	563	28.84	9-93	23	4
1-day Int	41	17	7	65	20	6.50	-	-	7	-	2218	1369	53	25.83	4-18	-	
NatWest	24	10	5	58	19 *	11.60	-	-	3	-	1482	787	40	19.67	5-18	1	
B & H	45	18	6	51	13	4.25	-	-	2	-	2454	1561	43	36.30	3-33	-	
1-day Lge	105	48	21	219	38	8.11	-	-	18	-	4647	3300	116	28.44	5-15	1	

MUNTON, T. A. Derbyshire

Name: <u>Timothy</u> Alan Munton
Role: Right-hand bat, right-arm
fast-medium bowler, county vice-captain
Born: 30 July 1965, Melton Mowbray
Height: 6ft 6in **Weight:** 15st 7lbs
Nickname: Harry, Captain Sensible
County debut: 1985 (Warwicks),
2000 (Derbys)
County cap: 1990 (Warwicks),
2000 (Derbys)
Benefit: 1998 (Warwicks)
Test debut: 1991
Tests: 2
50 wickets in a season: 6
1st-Class 50s: 3
1st-Class 5 w. in innings: 34
1st-Class 10 w. in match: 6
1st-Class catches: 80
One-Day 5 w. in innings: 2
Place in batting averages: 246th av. 12.73 (1999 295th av. 5.00)
Place in bowling averages: 99th av. 31.22 (1999 16th av. 19.76)
Strike rate: 75.34 (career 59.08)
Parents: Alan and Brenda
Wife and date of marriage: Helen, 20 September 1986
Children: Camilla Dallas, 13 August 1988; Harrison George Samuel, 17 February 1992
Family links with cricket: Father played for Buckminster CC
Education: Sarson High School; King Edward VII Upper School, Melton Mowbray
Qualifications: CSE grade 1, 9 O-levels, 1 A-level
Overseas tours: England A to Pakistan 1990-91, to Bermuda and West Indies
1991-92, to Pakistan 1995-96
Overseas teams played for: Victoria University, Wellington, New Zealand 1985-86;
Witwatersrand University, Johannesburg, South Africa 1986-87
Cricketers particularly admired: Richard Hadlee, David Gower
Other sports followed: Basketball, soccer, golf
Relaxations: 'Playing golf, spending time with my family'
Extras: Appeared for Leicestershire 2nd XI 1982-84. Second highest wicket-taker in
1990 with 78. Was voted Warwickshire Player of the Season 1990, 1991 and 1994.
Was one of *Wisden*'s Five Cricketers of the Year 1995. Assumed the Warwickshire
captaincy after the retirement of Dermot Reeve in 1996 but was replaced by Brian
Lara for the 1998 season after missing the whole of the 1997 season through injury.
Took Championship hat-trick v Kent at Maidstone 1999. Left Warwickshire in 1999-

2000 off-season and joined Derbyshire for 2000 on a two-year contract. Awarded Derbyshire cap 2000. Appointed vice-captain of Derbyshire for 2001
Best batting: 54* Warwickshire v Worcestershire, Worcester 1992
Best bowling: 8-89 Warwickshire v Middlesex, Edgbaston 1991

2000 Season

	M	Inns	NO	Runs	HS	Avge	100s	50s	Ct	St	O	M	Runs	Wkts	Avge	Best	5wI	10wM
Test																		
All First	16	22	7	191	52	12.73	-	1	7	-	439.3	122	1093	35	31.22	7-34	2	-
1-day Int																		
NatWest	2	1	0	2	2	2.00	-	-	-	-	15	6	22	2	11.00	2-4	-	
B & H	5	1	1	8	8*	-	-	-	-	-	46	7	129	8	16.12	2-15	-	
1-day Lge	15	12	3	54	18	6.00	-	-	3	-	133	16	446	12	37.16	3-24	-	

Career Performances

	M	Inns	NO	Runs	HS	Avge	100s	50s	Ct	St	Balls	Runs	Wkts	Avge	Best	5wI	10wM
Test	2	2	1	25	25*	25.00	-	-	-	-	405	200	4	50.00	2-22	-	-
All First	243	259	97	1682	54*	10.38	-	3	80	-	42420	18406	718	25.63	8-89	34	6
1-day Int																	
NatWest	37	12	6	30	17	5.00	-	-	6	-	2230	1107	39	28.38	3-36	-	
B & H	38	16	10	68	13	11.33	-	-	6	-	2290	1309	44	29.75	4-35	-	
1-day Lge	170	53	31	196	18	8.90	-	-	35	-	7463	4833	166	29.11	5-23	2	

MURALITHARAN, M.   Lancashire

Name: Muttiah Muralitharan
Role: Right-hand bat, off-spin bowler
Born: 17 April 1972, Kandy, Sri Lanka
Height: 5ft 5in
Nickname: Murali
County debut: 1999
County cap: 1999
Test debut: 1992-93
Tests: 57
One-Day Internationals: 141
50 wickets in a season: 1
1st-Class 5 w. in innings: 50
1st-Class 10 w. in match: 13
1st-Class catches: 63
One-Day 5 w. in innings: 3
Place in batting averages: (1999 298th av. 3.75)
Place in bowling averages: (1999 2nd av. 11.77)

Strike rate: (career 50.29)

Education: St Anthony's College, Kandy

Overseas tours: Sri Lanka to England 1991, to India 1993-94, to Zimbabwe 1994-95, to New Zealand 1994-95, 1996-97, to South Africa 1994-95 (Mandela Cup), to Sharjah (one-day tournaments) 1994-95, 1995-96, 1996-97, 1998-99, to Pakistan 1995-96, to India and Pakistan (World Cup) 1995-96, to Singapore (Singer Cup) 1995-96, to Australia 1995-96, to West Indies 1996-97, to Kenya (KCA Centenary Tournament) 1996-97, to India (Independence Cup) 1996-97, to India 1997-98, to South Africa 1997-98, to Pakistan (Independence Cup) 1997-98, to England 1998, to Bangladesh 1998-99 (Wills International Cup), to Australia (CUB series) 1998-99, to UK, Ireland and Holland (World  Cup) 1999, to Zimbabwe 1999-2000, to Pakistan 1999-2000, to Kenya (ICC Knockout Trophy) 2000-01, to South Africa 2000-01

Overseas teams played for: Tamil Union Cricket and Athletic Club 1991-92 –

Extras: Took 16-220 from 113.5 overs v England at The Oval 1998, the fifth best bowling analysis in Test cricket; it included 9-65 in England's second innings, in which he took his 200th Test victim (Dominic Cork) in 42 Tests. His bowling action has attracted controversy – including calls for throwing – but was studied by the ICC in 1996 and cleared. One of *Wisden*'s Five Cricketers of the Year 1999. Represented Sri Lanka in the 1999 World Cup. Was Lancashire's overseas player in 1999, taking an astonishing 66 wickets in the 12 Championship innings in which he bowled; his haul included eight returns of five or more wickets in an innings (including five returns of seven) and he had five match returns of ten or more wickets. Played for an Asia XI v a World XI in Dhaka 2000. Took 13-171 at Galle in 2000, winning the Man of the Match award in Sri Lanka's first Test win over South Africa

Best batting: 39 Sri Lanka v India, Colombo 1997-98

Best bowling: 9-65 Sri Lanka v England, The Oval 1998

Stop press: Took 7-30 v India in the Champions Trophy in Sharjah 2000, the best return in One-Day International history. Took 300th Test wicket (Shaun Pollock) v South Africa 2000-01 in his 58th Test; only Dennis Lillee (55 Tests) has reached this mark in fewer matches

2000 Season (did not make any first-class or one-day appearances)

Career Performances

	M	Inns	NO	Runs	HS	Avge	100s	50s	Ct	St	Balls	Runs	Wkts	Avge	Best	5wI	10wM
Test	57	75	31	576	39	13.09	-	-	26	-	18212	7442	291	25.57	9-65	22	4
All First	117	141	48	1045	39	11.23	-	-	63	-	30577	12242	608	20.13	9-65	50	13
1-day Int	141	66	29	186	18	5.02	-	-	63	-	7675	5266	194	27.14	5-23	3	
NatWest	3	2	0	15	15	7.50	-	-	-	-	168	141	1	141.00	1-43	-	
B & H	1	0	0	0	0	-	-	-	-	-	60	14	1	14.00	1-14	-	
1-day Lge	7	1	1	13	13 *	-	-	-	4	-	338	188	10	18.80	3-12	-	

MURTAGH, T. J. Surrey

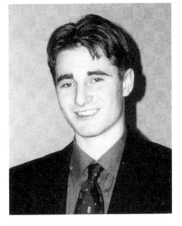

Name: <u>Timothy</u> James Murtagh
Role: Left-hand bat, right-arm
fast-medium bowler
Born: 2 August 1981, Lambeth, London
Height: 6ft **Weight:** 12st
Nickname: Murts
County debut: 2000 (one-day)
Strike rate: 12.00 (career 12.00)
Parents: Dominic and Elizabeth
Marital status: Single
Family links with cricket: 'Chris, younger
brother, plays in Surrey age-group cricket and
is in their Development of Excellence
Programme; Uncle Andy (A. J. Murtagh)
played for Hampshire'
Education: Regina Coeli, Purley, Surrey;
John Fisher, Purley, Surrey; St Mary's
University, Twickenham
Qualifications: 10 GCSEs, 2 A-levels
Career outside cricket: Student (Sports Science and Media Studies)
Overseas tours: Surrey U17 to South Africa 1997; England U19 to Malaysia and
(Youth World Cup) Sri Lanka 1999-2000
Cricketers particularly admired: Darren Gough, Glenn McGrath
Young players to look out for: Michael Carberry, Ian Bell
Other sports played: Rugby (was captain of John Fisher 2nd XV), skiing ('in the past')
Other sports followed: Football (Liverpool FC), rugby
Relaxations: Playing golf, watching sport, films, reading
Extras: Represented British Universities 2000. Represented England U19 in one-day
and 'Test' series v Sri Lanka U19 2000; named Player of the Series

Best batting: 12* British Universities v Zimbabweans, Fenner's 2000
Best bowling: 1-6 British Universities v Zimbabweans, Fenner's 2000

2000 Season

	M	Inns	NO	Runs	HS	Avge	100s	50s	Ct	St	O	M	Runs	Wkts	Avge	Best	5wI	10wM
Test																		
All First	1	1	1	12	12 *	-	-	-	-	-	2	0	6	1	6.00	1-6	-	-
1-day Int																		
NatWest																		
B & H																		
1-day Lge	2	1	0	0	0	0.00	-	-	-	-	17	1	102	1	102.00	1-50	-	

Career Performances

	M	Inns	NO	Runs	HS	Avge	100s	50s	Ct	St	Balls	Runs	Wkts	Avge	Best	5wI	10wM
Test																	
All First	1	1	1	12	12 *	-	-	-	-	-	12	6	1	6.00	1-6	-	-
1-day Int																	
NatWest																	
B & H																	
1-day Lge	2	1	0	0	0	0.00	-	-	-	-	102	102	1	102.00	1-50	-	

NAPIER, G. R.   Essex

Name: <u>Graham</u> Richard Napier
Role: Right-hand bat, right-arm
medium bowler
Born: 6 January 1980, Colchester
Height: 5ft 10in **Weight:** 12st 7lbs
Nickname: Plank, Napes
County debut: 1997
1st-Class catches: 6
Strike rate: (career 54.00)
Parents: Roger and Carol
Marital status: Single
Family links with cricket: Father played for
Palmers Boys School 1st XI (1965-68), Essex
Police divisional teams, and Harwich
Immigration CC. 'Now makes guest
appearances on Walton beach'
Education: Myland School, Colchester;
Gilberd School, Colchester
Qualifications: NCA coaching award

Career outside cricket: 'Still deciding'
Off-season: 'Playing cricket for Campbell Town CC in Sydney and spending as many days as I can on the beach'
Overseas tours: England U17 to Bermuda; England U19 to South Africa (including Youth World Cup) 1997-98
Overseas teams played for: Campbell Town CC, Sydney 2000-01
Cricketers particularly admired: Stuart Law, Peter Such
Young players to look out for: James Foster, Will Jefferson, Chris Taylor
Other sports followed: Football (Ipswich Town FC)
Injuries: Out for whole of winter 1999 to March 2000 after operation for stress fracture of the back
Relaxations: 'Studying nuclear physics and authority of the Dead Sea Scrolls'
Extras: Represented England U19 in one-day and 'Test' series v Australia U19 1999
Opinions on cricket: 'Two divisional cricket is an obvious success. The introduction of an England U23 side to play against first-class teams to help develop former England U19 players in their early first-class careers.'
Best batting: 35* Essex v Nottinghamshire, Worksop 1997
Best bowling: 2-25 Essex v Cambridge University, Fenner's 1997

2000 Season

	M	Inns	NO	Runs	HS	Avge	100s	50s	Ct	St	O	M	Runs	Wkts	Avge	Best	5wI	10wM
Test																		
All First	1	2	0	26	21	13.00	-	-	4	-	8	2	28	0	-	-	-	-
1-day Int																		
NatWest	2	2	0	96	79	48.00	-	1	-	-	7	0	37	1	37.00	1-37	-	
B & H																		
1-day Lge	11	10	0	212	78	21.20	-	2	4	-	12	0	58	1	58.00	1-32	-	

Career Performances

	M	Inns	NO	Runs	HS	Avge	100s	50s	Ct	St	Balls	Runs	Wkts	Avge	Best	5wI	10wM
Test																	
All First	6	8	2	107	35 *	17.83	-	-	6	-	270	185	5	37.00	2-25	-	-
1-day Int																	
NatWest	2	2	0	96	79	48.00	-	1	-	-	42	37	1	37.00	1-37	-	
B & H	2	0	0	0	0	-	-	-	-	-	54	62	0	-	-	-	
1-day Lge	24	18	0	300	78	16.66	-	2	6	-	210	186	7	26.57	3-22	-	

62. Who scored 103 in Australia's second innings at
The Oval in 1981 on his Test debut?

NASH, D. C. Middlesex

Name: <u>David</u> Charles Nash
Role: Right-hand bat, wicket-keeper
Born: 19 January 1978, Chertsey, Surrey
Height: 5ft 8in **Weight:** 11st 3lbs
Nickname: Nashy, Knocker
County debut: 1995 (one-day), 1997 (first-class)
County cap: 1999
50 dismissals in a season: 1
1st-Class 50s: 7
1st-Class 100s: 2
1st-Class catches: 96
1st-Class stumpings: 9
Place in batting averages: 178th av. 20.22
(1999 59th av. 36.63)
Strike rate: (career 19.00)
Parents: David and Christine
Marital status: Single
Family links with cricket: 'Father played
club cricket, and brother Glen is a very talented left-hand bat and off-spinner'
Education: Chennestone County Middle; Sunbury Manor; Malvern College, Worcs
Qualifications: 10 GCSEs, 1 A-level, NCA coaching award, qualified football referee
Off-season: 'Playing club cricket in Perth for Fremantle; working hard on fitness and game; and improving my golf swing'
Overseas tours: England U15 to South Africa 1993; British Airways Youth Team to West Indies 1993-94; England U19 to Zimbabwe 1995-96, to Pakistan 1996-97; England A to Kenya and Sri Lanka 1997-98
Overseas teams played for: Fremantle, Perth 2000-01
Cricketers particularly admired: George Simons and Gareth Rees 'for their big hearts', 'the whole victorious Sunbury CC squad', and Angus Fraser 'for always smiling and enjoying his cricket, however unlucky he is!'
Young players to look out for: David Sales, Owais Shah, Andrew Strauss
Other sports played: Football ('played for Millwall U15s and my district side') rugby, snooker ('always getting beaten by Richard Johnson')
Other sports followed: Football (Brentford), rugby union (London Irish)
Injuries: 'Earache from listening to the drivel spoken by Messrs Johnson, Fraser and Dutch'
Relaxations: 'I enjoy playing golf, listening to music, going out with my mates, and visiting friends at uni in Leeds and Nottingham'
Extras: Represented Middlesex at all ages. Played for England U14, U15, U17 and U19. Once took six wickets in six balls when aged 11 – 'when I could bowl!' *Daily Telegraph* Southern England Batting Award 1993. Seaxe Young Player of the Year 1993

441

Opinions on cricket: 'Pitches still need to improve – they are far too bowler friendly. The two divisional structure has worked well because it has sustained interest throughout, but I feel the points structure for winning and drawing a game causes negative cricket, i.e. teams taking safe option of a draw. I feel central contracts are a good idea, especially for seamers.'

Best batting: 114 Middlesex v Somerset, Lord's 1998
Best bowling: 1-8 Middlesex v Essex, Chelmsford 1997

2000 Season

	M	Inns	NO	Runs	HS	Avge	100s	50s	Ct	St	O	M	Runs	Wkts	Avge	Best	5wI	10wM
Test																		
All First	17	24	2	445	75 *	20.22	-	1	32	4								
1-day Int																		
NatWest	1	0	0	0	0	-			-	-								
B & H	1	1	0	1	1	1.00	-	-	2	1								
1-day Lge	4	1	1	25	25 *	-	-	-	2	2								

Career Performances

	M	Inns	NO	Runs	HS	Avge	100s	50s	Ct	St	Balls	Runs	Wkts	Avge	Best	5wI	10wM
Test																	
All First	56	81	12	1898	114	27.50	2	7	96	9	19	19	1	19.00	1-8	-	-
1-day Int																	
NatWest	2	1	0	3	3	3.00	-	-	1	-							
B & H	5	3	2	11	9 *	11.00	-	-	4	1							
1-day Lge	39	28	5	452	43	19.65	-	-	34	7							

NEWELL, K. Glamorgan

Name: Keith Newell
Role: Right-hand bat, occasional right-arm medium bowler
Born: 25 March 1972, Crawley
Height: 6ft **Weight:** 13st
Nickname: Nightstalker, Greavsie
County debut: 1993 (one-day, Sussex),
1995 (first-class, Sussex), 1999 (Glamorgan)
1st-Class 50s: 10
1st-Class 100s: 4
1st-Class catches: 20
One-Day 100s: 1
One-Day 5 w. in innings: 1
Place in batting averages: 201st av. 17.80 (1999 186th av. 21.72)
Strike rate: 61.20 (career 82.20)

Parents: Peter Charles and Julie Anne
Marital status: Single
Family links with cricket: Brother Mark played for Sussex and Derbyshire. Brother Jonathan plays for Sussex U17 and U19
Education: Gossops Green Junior School; Ifield Community College
Qualifications: 'A few GCSEs', coaching certificate
Career outside cricket: Cricket coach
Overseas teams played for: Zimbabwe Universals 1989-90; Bulawayo Athletic Club 1991-92, 1995-96; Riverside CC, Wellington 1992-93; Randwick CC, Sydney 1998-99
Cricketers particularly admired: Ian Botham
Young players to look out for: Mike Powell
Other sports played: Table tennis, golf, football (Henfield FC)
Other sports followed: Football (Spurs)
Relaxations: Going to the cinema
Extras: Released by Sussex at end of 1998 season and joined Glamorgan
Opinions on cricket: 'Still, as always, a long season.'
Best batting: 135 Sussex v West Indians, Hove 1995
Best bowling: 4-61 Sussex v Kent, Horsham 1997

2000 Season

	M	Inns	NO	Runs	HS	Avge	100s	50s	Ct	St	O	M	Runs	Wkts	Avge	Best	5wI	10wM
Test																		
All First	13	21	1	356	64	17.80	-	1	5	-	51	23	100	5	20.00	2-18	-	-
1-day Int																		
NatWest	3	3	1	226	129	113.00	1	1	-	-	9	0	57	1	57.00	1-31	-	
B & H	6	6	0	93	49	15.50	-	-	2	-	7.2	0	45	2	22.50	2-6	-	
1-day Lge	16	14	0	317	78	22.64	-	2	2	-	45.5	3	222	10	22.20	3-32	-	

Career Performances

	M	Inns	NO	Runs	HS	Avge	100s	50s	Ct	St	Balls	Runs	Wkts	Avge	Best	5wI	10wM
Test																	
All First	65	112	12	2634	135	26.34	4	10	20	-	1973	975	24	40.62	4-61	-	-
1-day Int																	
NatWest	9	7	2	378	129	75.60	1	2	1	-	264	205	3	68.33	1-31	-	
B & H	16	14	1	286	62 *	22.00	-	1	3	-	249	227	4	56.75	2-6	-	
1-day Lge	70	61	4	1161	97	20.36	-	4	14	-	1115	924	28	33.00	5-33	1	

NEWELL, M.   Nottinghamshire

Name: Michael Newell
Role: Right-hand opening bat, leg-break bowler, occasional wicket-keeper
Born: 25 February 1965, Blackburn
Height: 5ft 9in **Weight:** 11st 4lbs
Nickname: Mugly, Tricky, Animal
County debut: 1984
County cap: 1987
Benefit: 1999
1000 runs in a season: 1
1st-Class 50s: 24
1st-Class 100s: 5
1st-Class 200s: 1
1st-Class catches: 93
1st-Class stumpings: 1
One-Day 100s: 1
Strike rate: (career 51.86)
Parents: Barry and Janet
Wife and date of marriage: Jayne, 23 September 1989
Children: Elizabeth Rose, 1 September 1993
Family links with cricket: Father chairman of Notts Unity CC and brother, Paul, is the captain
Education: West Bridgford Comprehensive
Qualifications: 8 O-levels, 3 A-levels, NCA advanced coach
Cricketers particularly admired: Mathew Dowman, Dominic Cork, James Hindson
Young players to look out for: Paul Franks, Mathew Dowman
Other sports followed: Rugby union, football, darts
Relaxations: Football, studying, being at home
Opinions on cricket: 'Too many pros – maximum of 20 per club. Four-day cricket is a must at 2nd XI.'
Best batting: 203* Nottinghamshire v Derbyshire, Derby 1987
Best bowling: 2-38 Nottinghamshire v Sri Lankans, Trent Bridge 1988

---

63. Which England batsman scored a double hundred and two scores of 150-plus in the 1985 series?

Career Performances

	M	Inns	NO	Runs	HS	Avge	100s	50s	Ct	St	Balls	Runs	Wkts	Avge	Best	5wl	10wM
Test																	
All First	102	178	26	4636	203 *	30.50	6	24	93	1	363	282	7	40.28	2-38	-	-
1-day Int																	
NatWest	5	5	0	136	60	27.20	-	1	3	-	6	10	0	-		-	-
B & H	10	10	1	205	39	22.77	-	-	2	-							
1-day Lge	24	21	4	611	109 *	35.94	1	3	8	-							

NIXON, P. A.   Kent

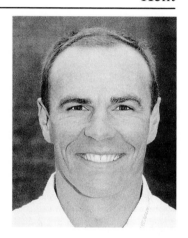

Name: <u>Paul</u> Andrew Nixon
Role: Left-hand bat, wicket-keeper
Born: 21 October 1970, Carlisle
Height: 6ft **Weight:** 12st 10lbs
Nickname: Badger
County debut: 1989 (Leicestershire), 2000 (Kent)
County cap: 1984 (Leicestershire)
1000 runs in a season: 1
50 dismissals in a season: 5
1st-Class 50s: 26
1st-Class 100s: 12
1st-Class catches: 516
1st-Class stumpings: 42
Place in batting averages: 75th av. 32.11 (1999 102nd av. 30.66)
Parents: Brian and Sylvia
Wife and date of marriage: Jen, 9 October 1999
Family links with cricket: 'Grandad and father played local league cricket. Mum made the teas for Edenhall CC, Penrith'
Education: Langwathby Primary; Ullswater High
Qualifications: 2 O-levels, 6 GCSEs, coaching certificates
Career outside cricket: 'Used to be farming. Father sold up'
Off-season: England tour to Pakistan and Sri Lanka
Overseas tours: Cumbria Schools U15 to Denmark 1985; Leicestershire to Barbados, Jamaica, Holland, Johannesburg, Bloemfontein; MCC to Bangladesh 1999-2000; England A to India and Bangladesh 1994-95; England to Pakistan and Sri Lanka 2000-01

Overseas teams played for: Melville, Western Australia; North Fremantle, Western Australia; Mitchells Plain, Cape Town 1993; Primrose CC, Cape Town 1995-96
Cricketers particularly admired: David Gower, Ian Botham, Ian Healy, Viv Richards
Young players to look out for: Darren Stevens
Other sports played: Golf, training with Leicester Tigers rugby team
Other sports followed: Football (Leicester City, Carlisle United, Liverpool), rugby (Leicester Tigers)
Relaxations: Team-building; winning books and tapes; health hydros
Extras: County captain of Cumbria at football, cricket and rugby. Youngest person to score a century against Yorkshire (at U15). Played for England U15. Played in Minor Counties Championship for Cumberland at 16. MCC Young Pro in 1988. Took eight catches in debut match v Warwickshire at Hinckley in 1989. Played for Carlisle United. Leicester Young Player of the Year two years running. Only second Leicester wicket-keeper to score 1000 runs in a season. Voted Cumbria Sports Personality of the Year 1994-95. Was part of Leicestershire's County Championship winning side in 1996 and 1998. Left Leicestershire at end of 1999 season and joined Kent for 2000. Captained First-Class Counties Select XI v New Zealand A at Milton Keynes 2000
Opinions on cricket: '1. 25-over day/night league. 2. "Premier Division" rather than "Division One". 3. Regional cricket against tourists. 4. Start season four weeks later so we go on into October. 5. Bats should have any company's name on them. 6. All kids under 16 should only pay £10 per year membership.'
Best batting: 134* Kent v Hampshire, Canterbury 2000

2000 Season

	M	Inns	NO	Runs	HS	Avge	100s	50s	Ct	St	O	M	Runs	Wkts	Avge	Best	5wI	10wM
Test																		
All First	18	25	7	578	134 *	32.11	1	3	47	2	3	1	10	0	-		-	-	-
1-day Int																		
NatWest	2	1	1	38	38 *	-	-	-	3	2								
B & H	2	2	1	56	37	56.00	-	-	6	-								
1-day Lge	14	11	2	170	30 *	18.88	-	-	22	4								

Career Performances

	M	Inns	NO	Runs	HS	Avge	100s	50s	Ct	St	Balls	Runs	Wkts	Avge	Best	5wI	10wM
Test									SIS								
All First	199	281	61	6847	134 *	31.12	12	26	516	42	30	14	0	-		-	-	-
1-day Int																	
NatWest	24	20	8	342	51	28.50	-	1	31	7							
B & H	29	23	6	376	53	22.11	-	1	36	6							
1-day Lge	154	131	24	2317	96 *	21.65	-	10	147	29							

NOON, W. M.   Nottinghamshire

Name: <u>Wayne</u> Michael Noon
Role: Right-hand bat, wicket-keeper
Born: 5 February 1971, Grimsby
Height: 5ft 9in **Weight:** 11st 7lbs
Nickname: Noonie, Spain Boon
County debut: 1988 (one-day, Northants),
1989 (first-class, Northants), 1994 (Notts)
County cap: 1995 (Notts)
1st-Class 50s: 12
1st-Class catches: 187
1st-Class stumpings: 20
Parents: Trafford and Rosemary
Marital status: Engaged
Education: Caistor Grammar School
Qualifications: 5 O-levels
Career outside cricket:
Manager of G. Atkins (bookmakers)
Overseas tours: Lincolnshire U15 to
Pakistan 1984; England YC to Australia 1989-90; Rutland tourists to South Africa
1988; Northamptonshire to Durban 1992, to Cape Town 1993
Overseas teams played for: Burnside West, Christchurch, New Zealand 1989-90 and
1993-96; Rivertonians, Cape Town 1993-94; Canterbury, Christchurch 1994-95
Cricketers particularly admired: Ian Botham
Other sports followed: Football (Lincoln City), horse racing (flat)
Relaxations: Having a bet. Eating out and having a pint
Extras: Played for England YC v New Zealand YC 1989; captain v Australian YC
1989-90 and Pakistan YC 1990. Was the 1000th player to appear in the Sunday League
competition. Broke the Northants record for most 2nd XI hundreds in one season in 1993.
Took seven catches for Notts in Kent's first innings at Trent Bridge 1999, breaking Bruce
French's county record of six
Best batting: 83 Nottinghamshire v Northamptonshire, Northampton 1997

2000 Season

	M	Inns	NO	Runs	HS	Avge	100s	50s	Ct	St	O	M	Runs	Wkts	Avge	Best	5wI	10wM
Test																		
All First	1	2	0	7	7	3.50	-	-	1	-								
1-day Int																		
NatWest																		
B & H																		
1-day Lge																		

Career Performances

	M	Inns	NO	Runs	HS	Avge	100s	50s	Ct	St		Balls	Runs	Wkts	Avge		Best	5wl	10wM
Test																			
All First	89	140	22	2474	83	20.96	-	12	187	20		30	34	0	-		-	-	-
1-day Int																			
NatWest	7	4	1	73	34	24.33	-	-	4	2									
B & H	18	11	3	152	46	19.00	-	-	9	4									
1-day Lge	80	51	14	460	38	12.43	-	-	60	14									

ORMOND, J. Leicestershire

Name: James Ormond
Role: Right-hand bat, right-arm fast-'ish' bowler
Born: 20 August 1977, Walsgrave, Coventry
Height: 6ft 3in **Weight:** 15st
Nickname: Horse
County debut: 1995
County cap: 1999
50 wickets in a season: 1
1st-Class 50s: 1
1st-Class 5 w. in innings: 11
1st-Class catches: 10
Place in batting averages: 254th av. 11.87 (1999 257th av. 13.07)
Place in bowling averages: 62nd av. 25.36 (1999 56th av. 24.67)
Strike rate: 51.88 (career 47.34)
Parents: Richard and Margaret
Marital status: Single
Family links with cricket: 'Dad played years of cricket in Warwickshire'
Education: St Anthony's, Bedworth; St Thomas More, Nuneaton; North Warwickshire College of Further Education
Qualifications: 6 GCSEs
Off-season: 'At home in Coventry'
Overseas tours: England U19 to Zimbabwe 1995-96; England A to Kenya and Sri Lanka 1997-98
Overseas teams played for: Sydney University CC 1996, 1998, 1999
Cricketers particularly admired: Curtly Ambrose, Courtney Walsh, Allan Donald, Sachin Tendulkar, Brian Lara, Steve Griffin
Young players to look out for: Darren Stevens, Carl Crowe
Other sports played: Football, mountain biking, 'anything'

Other sports followed: Football (Coventry City)

Injuries: Out for two weeks with a back injury; for three and a half weeks with a hamstring injury

Relaxations: Spending time with friends and family

Extras: Played for the Development of Excellence side and England U19 against South Africa U19 in 1995. Played for England U19 against New Zealand U19 in 1996. Won Leicestershire's 2nd XI bowling award. NBC Denis Compton Award 1999. His 6-50 v Derbyshire at Leicester 2000 included a burst of four wickets in six balls. Also bowls off-spin. 'Jon Dakin is the biggest cricketer in the world'

Opinions on cricket: 'I think we should play less cricket; it would improve the standard – more time to prepare. It would also make games more competitive.'

Best batting: 50* Leicestershire v Warwickshire, Leicester 1999

Best bowling: 6-33 Leicestershire v Somerset, Leicester 1998

2000 Season

	M	Inns	NO	Runs	HS	Avge	100s	50s	Ct	St	O	M	Runs	Wkts	Avge	Best	5wI	10wM
Test																		
All First	12	15	7	95	30 *	11.87	-	-	1	-	380.3	75	1116	44	25.36	6-50	3	-
1-day Int																		
NatWest	2	2	2	1	1 *	-	-	-	-	-	17	2	74	3	24.66	2-52	-	
B & H	4	3	1	15	14 *	7.50	-	-	1	-	34	7	100	6	16.66	4-27	-	
1-day Lge	12	8	5	19	5 *	6.33	-	-	4	-	96.3	11	384	15	25.60	3-43	-	

Career Performances

	M	Inns	NO	Runs	HS	Avge	100s	50s	Ct	St	Balls	Runs	Wkts	Avge	Best	5wI	10wM
Test																	
All First	50	53	12	486	50 *	11.85	-	1	10	-	8332	4310	176	24.48	6-33	11	-
1-day Int																	
NatWest	4	3	2	11	10	11.00	-	-	1	-	222	166	5	33.20	2-52	-	
B & H	7	4	1	15	14 *	5.00	-	-	1	-	366	236	12	19.66	4-27	-	
1-day Lge	38	25	15	131	18	13.10	-	-	9	-	1581	1091	53	20.58	4-12	-	

64. Which former Lancashire coach bowled Australia to victory at Sydney in 1986-87 with 5-72 in England's second innings?

OSTLER, D. P. Warwickshire

Name: <u>Dominic</u> Piers Ostler
Role: Right-hand bat, right-arm
medium bowler
Born: 15 July 1970, Solihull
Height: 6ft 2in **Weight:** 13st 7lbs
Nickname: Ossie
County debut: 1990
County cap: 1991
Benefit: 2000
1000 runs in a season: 5
1st-Class 50s: 59
1st-Class 100s: 11
1st-Class 200s: 1
1st-Class catches: 210
One-Day 100s: 1
Place in batting averages: 14th av. 49.81
(1999 173rd av. 22.72)
Strike rate: 30.00 (career 233.00)

Parents: Mike and Ann
Marital status: Engaged to Karen
Family links with cricket: Brother used to play for Knowle and Dorridge CC
Education: Our Lady of the Wayside; Princethorpe College; Solihull College of
Technology
Qualifications: 4 O-levels, A-levels, City and Guilds Recreation Course
Career outside cricket: 'In business'
Overseas tours: Gladstone Small's Benefit Tour to Barbados 1991; England A to
Pakistan 1995-96; England Cricket Max Tour to New Zealand 1997; Andy Moles'
Benefit Tour to Barbados 1997
Overseas teams played for: Avendale CC, Cape Town 1991-92
Cricketers particularly admired: Jason Ratcliffe, Simon Millington, Graeme Welch
Young players to look out for: Ian Bell, Nick Warren
Other sports played: Golf, snooker
Other sports followed: Football (Birmingham City FC)
Relaxations: 'Spending time with fiancée, Karen; snooker and golf'
Extras: Played club cricket for Moseley in the Birmingham League. Made his
Warwickshire 2nd XI debut in 1989 and was a member of Warwickshire U19 side that
won Esso U19 County Festivals in 1988 and 1989. Has collected winner's medals for
B&H Cup, County Championship, NatWest Trophy and Sunday League. Played for an
England XI in the Cricket Max tournament in New Zealand in 1997. Scored 1000 runs
in his benefit season in 2000
Opinions on cricket: 'Wickets need to improve dramatically.'

Best batting: 208 Warwickshire v Surrey, Edgbaston 1995
Best bowling: 1-46 Warwickshire v Middlesex, Edgbaston 2000

2000 Season

	M	Inns	NO	Runs	HS	Avge	100s	50s	Ct	St	O	M	Runs	Wkts	Avge	Best	5wI	10wM
Test																		
All First	16	24	2	1096	145	49.81	2	7	19	-	5	0	46	1	46.00	1-46	-	-
1-day Int																		
NatWest	5	5	0	150	63	30.00	-	1	1	-								
B & H	3	2	1	27	16 *	27.00	-	-	1	-								
1-day Lge	16	16	3	385	79 *	29.61	-	2	7	-								

Career Performances

	M	Inns	NO	Runs	HS	Avge	100s	50s	Ct	St	Balls	Runs	Wkts	Avge	Best	5wI	10wM
Test																	
All First	176	291	23	9178	208	34.24	12	59	210	-	233	249	1	249.00	1-46	-	-
1-day Int																	
NatWest	38	37	3	1039	104	30.55	1	7	17	-	15	10	1	10.00	1-4	-	
B & H	34	32	5	1082	87	40.07	-	9	17	-							
1-day Lge	153	143	20	3780	91 *	30.73	-	27	42	-	6	4	0	-	-	-	-

PANESAR, M. S. Northamptonshire

Name: <u>Mudhsuden</u> Singh Panesar
Role: Left-hand bat, slow left-arm bowler
Born: 25 April 1982, Luton
Height: 6ft **Weight:** 12st
Nickname: Monty
County debut: No first-team appearance
Parents: Paramjit and Gursharan
Marital status: Single
Education: St Matthew's Junior School;
Stopsley High School; Bedford Modern
School; Loughborough University (from
September 2001)
Qualifications: 10 GCSEs, 3 A-levels
Off-season: England U19 tour of India
Overseas tours: Bedford Modern School to
Barbados 1999; England U19 to India
2000-01
Cricketers particularly admired: Bishen
Bedi, Sachin Tendulkar, Phil Tufnell
Other sports played: Tennis, badminton

Other sports followed: Football (Arsenal, India)
Relaxations: Sleeping, music, eating
Extras: Represented England U19 v Sri Lanka U19 in one-day and 'Test' series 2000
Opinions on cricket: 'Everything is good.'

PARKIN, O. T. Glamorgan

Name: <u>Owen</u> Thomas Parkin
Role: Right-hand bat, right-arm medium-fast swing bowler
Born: 24 August 1972, Coventry
Height: 6ft 3in **Weight:** 12st 7lbs
Nickname: Parky, Longterm, Parallel, Calamari
County debut: 1994
1st-Class 5 w. in innings: 2
1st-Class catches: 9
One-Day 5 w. in innings: 1
Place in batting averages: (1999 299th av. 3.50)
Place in bowling averages: 11th av. 17.11 (1999 44th av. 23.38)
Strike rate: 38.11 (career 54.80)
Parents: Vernon Cyrus and Sarah Patricia
Marital status: Single
Family links with cricket: Younger brother Morgan plays for Glamorgan at U17 and U19 level
Education: Bournemouth Grammar School; Bath University
Qualifications: 9 GCSEs, 4 A-levels, 1 S-level, BSc (Hons) Mathematics
Career outside cricket: Maths teacher
Off-season: In Queensland coaching and playing
Overseas tours: Dorset Youth to Denmark
Overseas teams played for: Kew, Melbourne 1992-93; North Balwyn, Melbourne 1994-95; Balmain, Sydney 1997-99; ATW Clubites, Bundaberg, Queensland 1999-2000
Cricketers particularly admired: Malcolm Marshall, Richard Hadlee
Young players to look out for: Michael Powell, Wayne Law
Other sports played: 'Most sports socially'
Other sports followed: Rugby, football (Nottingham Forest), golf
Relaxations: '*Telegraph* crossword'
Extras: Played for Dorset in the NatWest Trophy 1992 and 1993. ASW Young Player of the Month July 1994. Took 5 for 28 on debut in Sunday League at Hove – a club record

Best batting: 24* Glamorgan v Essex, Chelmsford 1998
Best bowling: 5-24 Glamorgan v Somerset, Cardiff, 1998

2000 Season

	M	Inns	NO	Runs	HS	Avge	100s	50s	Ct	St	O	M	Runs	Wkts	Avge	Best	5wI	10wM
Test																		
All First	5	6	3	30	13 *	10.00	-	-	-	-	108	30	291	17	17.11	4-14	-	-
1-day Int																		
NatWest	3	1	0	0	0	0.00	-	-	1	-	29.4	2	115	6	19.16	3-37	-	
B & H	4	3	3	1	1 *	-	-	-	1	-	32	5	161	9	17.88	4-60	-	
1-day Lge	16	8	4	20	5 *	5.00	-	-	6	-	126	10	636	20	31.80	3-39	-	

Career Performances

	M	Inns	NO	Runs	HS	Avge	100s	50s	Ct	St	Balls	Runs	Wkts	Avge	Best	5wI	10wM
Test																	
All First	36	43	20	203	24 *	8.82	-	-	9	-	5261	2569	96	26.76	5-24	2	-
1-day Int																	
NatWest	10	5	2	3	2	1.00	-	-	5	-	496	333	10	33.30	3-23	-	
B & H	8	5	3	16	8	8.00	-	-	2	-	384	310	14	22.14	4-60	-	
1-day Lge	55	22	9	41	6	3.15	-	-	11	-	2421	1855	78	23.78	5-28	1	

PARSONS, K. A. Somerset

Name: <u>Keith</u> Alan Parsons
Role: Right-hand bat, right-arm medium bowler
Born: 2 May 1973, Taunton
Height: 6ft 1in **Weight:** 14st
Nickname: Pilot, Pars, Orv
County debut: 1992
County cap: 1999
1st-Class 50s: 19
1st-Class 100s: 4
1st-Class 5 w. in innings: 2
1st-Class catches: 77
Place in batting averages: 48th av. 37.25 (1999 124th av. 27.72)
Place in bowling averages: 131st av. 40.27 (1999 89th av. 29.39)
Strike rate: 82.18 (career 76.66)
Parents: Alan and Lynne
Marital status: Single; girlfriend Sharon

Family links with cricket: Identical twin brother, Kevin, was on the Somerset staff 1992-94 and now captains the Somerset Board XI. Father played six seasons for Somerset 2nd XI and captained National Civil Service XI

Education: Bishop Henderson Primary School; The Castle School, Taunton; Richard Huish Sixth Form College, Taunton

Qualifications: 8 GCSEs, 3 A-levels, NCA senior coach

Off-season: 'Working for Set Square Recruitment Agency in Taunton'

Overseas tours: Castle School to Barbados 1989; Somerset CCC to Cape Town 1999, 2000

Overseas teams played for: Kapiti Old Boys, Horowhenu, New Zealand 1992-93; Taita District, Wellington, New Zealand 1993-96; Wembley Downs CC, Perth 1998

Cricketers particularly admired: Andy Caddick, Marcus Trescothick, Glenn McGrath, Saqlain Mushtaq

Other sports followed: Rugby union (Bath RFC), football (Nottingham Forest FC), golf, horse racing

Relaxations: Playing golf, watching movies, listening to music 'and the odd social pint of beer'

Extras: Captained two National Cup winning sides – Taunton St Andrews in National U15 Club Championship and Richard Huish College in National U17 School Championship. Represented English Schools at U15 and U19 level. Somerset Young Player of the Year 1993. Took 5-13 from 7.5 overs v Lancashire at Taunton 2000. Scored maiden Championship century (108*) v Yorkshire at Taunton 2000

Opinions on cricket: 'Really enjoyed the two divisional structure last year – kept the leagues very competitive until the end of the season. However, I'm somewhat disappointed at missing out in 2001 on the tremendous lunches served at Derby.'

Best batting: 193* Somerset v West Indians, Taunton 2000

Best bowling: 5-13 Somerset v Lancashire, Taunton 2000

2000 Season

	M	Inns	NO	Runs	HS	Avge	100s	50s	Ct	St	O	M	Runs	Wkts	Avge	Best	5wI	10wM
Test																		
All First	15	22	2	745	193 *	37.25	2	1	17	-	150.4	41	443	11	40.27	5-13	1	-
1-day Int																		
NatWest	2	2	1	61	37 *	61.00	-	-	-	-	20	2	63	2	31.50	2-33	-	
B & H	3	2	0	21	15	10.50	-	-	1	-	12	0	75	1	75.00	1-32	-	
1-day Lge	16	15	2	436	69	33.53	-	3	1	-	46	1	249	7	35.57	2-25	-	

Career Performances

	M	Inns	NO	Runs	HS	Avge	100s	50s	Ct	St	Balls	Runs	Wkts	Avge	Best	5wl	10wM
Test																	
All First	87	140	14	3450	193 *	27.38	4	19	77	-	4753	2529	62	40.79	5-13	2	-
1-day Int																	
NatWest	17	15	5	353	51	35.30	-	1	3	-	680	473	17	27.82	4-43	-	
B & H	13	11	4	140	33 *	20.00	-	-	6	-	240	290	4	72.50	2-60	-	
1-day Lge	91	74	14	1503	69	25.05	-	7	36	-	2100	1717	47	36.53	3-21	-	

PATEL, D. Worcestershire

Name: Depesh Patel
Role: Right-hand bat, right-arm fast-medium
bowler
Born: 23 September 1981, Wolverhampton
Height: 6ft 4in **Weight:** 13st
Nickname: Dip, Dippy, Dipster
County debut: No first-team appearance
Parents: Balvant and Mena
Marital status: Single
Family links with cricket: 'Dad played for
Thompson's CC for 18 years. Brother Vijay
plays for Wolverhampton CC'
Education: Wilkinson Primary School;
Moseley Park Grammar School; Bilston
Community College

Qualifications: GCSEs, Level 1 coaching
award
Career outside cricket: 'Studying IT skills'
Off-season: 'Keeping fit, watching TV, coaching'
Cricketers particularly admired: Allan Donald, Glenn McGrath, Sachin Tendulkar
Young players to look out for: Ryan Driver, Kadeer Ali
Other sports followed: Football (Wolverhampton Wanderers)
Relaxations: 'Listening to music, playing pool, chilling with friends'
Extras: Scored 120 aged 15 against Cheshire playing for Staffordshire. Has best
bowling of 7 for 1 playing against Glamorgan U11 for Staffordshire U11. Played for
Worcestershire Board XI in the 1999 NatWest
Opinions on cricket: 'One-day cricket is played at a faster pace than five years ago.'

2000 Season (did not make any first-class or one-day appearances)

Career Performances

	M	Inns	NO	Runs	HS	Avge	100s	50s	Ct	St	Balls	Runs	Wkts	Avge	Best	5wI	10wM
Test																	
All First																	
1-day Int																	
NatWest	1	1	1	19	19 *	-	-	-	-	-	42	36	1	36.00	1-36	-	
B & H																	
1-day Lge																	

PATEL, M. M. Kent

Name: <u>Minal</u> Mahesh Patel
Role: Right-hand bat, slow left-arm bowler
Born: 7 July 1970, Bombay, India
Height: 5ft 8in **Weight:** 10st
Nickname: Spin, Geez, Diamond, Ho-Chi
County debut: 1989
County cap: 1994
Test debut: 1996
Tests: 2
50 wickets in a season: 3
1st-Class 50s: 6
1st-Class 5 w. in innings: 21
1st-Class 10 w. in match: 8
1st-Class catches: 69
Place in batting averages: 198th av. 17.93
(1999 251st av. 13.80)
Place in bowling averages: 58th av. 25.15
(1999 58th av. 24.88)
Strike rate: 74.41 (career 71.68)
Parents: Mahesh and Aruna
Wife and date of marriage: Karuna, 8 October 1995
Family links with cricket: Father played good club cricket in Africa, India and
England
Education: Maypole CP; Dartford Grammar School; Erith College of Technology;
Manchester Polytechnic
Qualifications: 6 O-levels, 3 A-levels, BA (Hons) Economics
Career outside cricket: Writes for *Racing Post*
Off-season: MCC tour to Argentina and Chile in February 2001
Overseas tours: Dartford GS to Barbados 1988; England A to India and Bangladesh

1994-95; MCC to Malta 1997, 1999, to Fiji, Sydney and Hong Kong 1998, to East and Central Africa 1999, to Bangladesh 1999-2000 (captain), to Argentina and Chile 2001
Overseas teams played for: St Augustine's, Cape Town 1993-94; Alberton, Johannesburg 1997-98
Cricketers particularly admired: Derek Underwood, Aravinda De Silva
Young players to look out for: Bobby Key
Other sports followed: Football (Tottenham Hotspur), snooker 'and most American sports'
Injuries: Out for four weeks with impingement on left shoulder
Relaxations: Spread betting, DJ-ing, golf
Extras: Played for English Schools 1988, 1989 and NCA England South 1989. Was voted Kent League Young Player of the Year 1987 while playing for Blackheath. First six overs in NatWest Trophy were all maidens. Whittingdale Young Player of the Year 1994
Opinions on cricket: 'At this early stage, the two division format has made a positive impact as far as players and their efforts for the *entire* season are concerned.'
Best batting: 67 Kent v Gloucestershire, Canterbury 1999
Best bowling: 8-96 Kent v Lancashire, Canterbury 1994

2000 Season

	M	Inns	NO	Runs	HS	Avge	100s	50s	Ct	St	O	M	Runs	Wkts	Avge	Best	5wI	10wM
Test																		
All First	14	16	1	269	60	17.93	-	1	13	-	570.3	202	1157	46	25.15	6-77	2	-
1-day Int																		
NatWest	2	1	0	7	7	7.00	-	-	-	-	10	1	36	2	18.00	2-36	-	
B & H	2	1	1	8	8 *	-	-	-	-	-	5	0	27	0	-	-	-	
1-day Lge	8	5	1	18	14 *	4.50	-	-	2	-	65	8	282	12	23.50	2-13	-	

Career Performances

	M	Inns	NO	Runs	HS	Avge	100s	50s	Ct	St	Balls	Runs	Wkts	Avge	Best	5wI	10wM
Test	2	2	0	45	27	22.50	-	-	2	-	276	180	1	180.00	1-101	-	-
All First	126	174	34	2093	67	14.95	-	6	69	-	28172	11966	393	30.44	8-96	21	8
1-day Int																	
NatWest	11	4	1	18	7	6.00	-	-	5	-	608	344	11	31.27	2-29	-	
B & H	15	8	6	54	18 *	27.00	-	-	4	-	606	464	9	51.55	2-29	-	
1-day Lge	25	13	4	51	14 *	5.66	-	-	5	-	1052	797	31	25.70	3-22	-	

PATTERSON, A. D.   Sussex

Name: <u>Andrew</u> David Patterson
Role: Right-hand bat, wicket-keeper, 'filthy' leg-spin bowler
Born: 4 September 1975, Belfast
Height: 5ft 10in **Weight:** 12st
Nickname: Irish, Baby, Baby Patto, Patto, Patsy, Semtex, Drew, Dingle Butt
County debut: 2000
1st-Class catches: 18
Place in batting averages: 295th av. 6.70
Parents: Phyllis and Billy
Marital status: 'Slightly whipped!! by Sarah'
Family links with cricket: 'Dad played club cricket in Belfast. Brother Mark plays for Surrey (when not injured!!). Mum played for Belfast Ladies'

Education: Carnmoney Primary School; Belfast Royal Academy; University of Ulster at Jordanstown
Qualifications: 3 A-levels, second-class honours degree in Sport and Leisure Studies, PGCE (PE), qualified coach of cricket, football, rugby, hockey, tennis, basketball, volleyball and swimming, qualified fitness instructor
Career outside cricket: Teacher (PE), personal trainer
Off-season: Overseas tour to South Africa with Ireland for three weeks in March
Overseas tours: Ireland to Denmark (European Championships) 1996, to Malaysia (ICC Trophy) 1997, to South Africa 2000-01; Northern Ireland to Malaysia (Commonwealth Games) 1998
Overseas teams played for: Mount Maunganui CC, Bay of Plenty, New Zealand 1996-97; Western Province, South Africa 1999-2000
Cricketers particularly admired: Ian Healy, John Solanki ('my first club coach'), Michael 'The Turk' Turkington
Young players to look out for: 'Mark Robinson, Tony Cottey,' Davy 'Froggy' Hamilton, Samuel Perkins, Gavin Weir
Other sports played: Football, hockey (Mossley HC and Irish Universities), golf
Other sports followed: Football (Linfield FC and Liverpool FC)
Injuries: Out for six weeks with groin injury; 'for last month of season with "lack of run-itis"'
Relaxations: 'Practising the art of being ubiquitous. Playing the harpsichord. Public speaking competitions. Writing jingles for adverts and verses for assorted cards. Gambling poorly against my dad and brother'
Extras: Represented Ireland at all age-groups U15-U21 to full international. 'To my

knowledge the only county cricketer with 11 fingers and toes.' 'My brother has one of the best strike rates in county cricket whenever his Zimmer frame is at The Oval!'
Released by Sussex at the end of the 2000 season
Opinions on cricket: 'Great game.'
Best batting: 31 Ireland v Scotland, Dublin 1997

2000 Season

	M	Inns	NO	Runs	HS	Avge	100s	50s	Ct	St	O	M	Runs	Wkts	Avge	Best	5wI	10wM
Test																		
All First	8	10	1	67	20 *	6.70	-	-	17	-								
1-day Int																		
NatWest	2	1	0	1	1	1.00	-	-	2	-								
B & H																			
1-day Lge	5	2	0	32	20	16.00	-	-	4	1								

Career Performances

	M	Inns	NO	Runs	HS	Avge	100s	50s	Ct	St	Balls	Runs	Wkts	Avge	Best	5wI	10wM
Test																	
All First	10	15	1	155	31	11.07	-	-	18	-							
1-day Int																	
NatWest	8	7	0	59	30	8.42	-	-	6	1							
B & H	6	6	1	116	50	23.20	-	1	5	2							
1-day Lge	5	2	0	32	20	16.00	-	-	4	1							

65. Which player went into the third Test at Trent Bridge in 1993 with more Test runs and Test wickets than the rest of the team combined?

Name: <u>Mark</u> William Patterson
Role: Right-hand bat, right-arm
fast-medium bowler
Born: 2 February 1974, Belfast
Height: 6ft **Weight:** 13st 7lbs ('but
increasing!')
Nickname: Patto, Paddy, Tripod
County debut: 1996
1st-Class 5 w. in innings: 1
Strike rate: (career 23.57)
Parents: Billy and Phyllis
Marital status: Engaged to Shavarne – 'what
a lucky girl!'
Family links with cricket: 'Father played
club cricket. Brother Andy played first-class
cricket for Sussex 2000. Mum played for
Belfast Ladies'
Education: Carnmoney Primary School;
Belfast Royal Academy; University of Ulster
Qualifications: 9 GCSEs, 3 A-levels, BA (Hons) Sport and Leisure Studies. Qualified
coach in soccer, cricket, rugby, hockey, basketball, swimming and squash. 'Now also a
football referee for Surrey FA – hoping to pursue much further'
Career outside cricket: 'Aspiring football referee'
Off-season: 'Teaching PE at Chesham Park College. Refereeing local football matches
to be the next David Elleray'
Overseas tours: Ireland U19 to Denmark (International Youth Tournament) 1993;
Ireland to Denmark (European Championships) 1996, to Malaysia (ICC Trophy) 1997;
Northern Ireland to Malaysia (Commonwealth Games) 1998; 'Surrey pre-season to
Royal Marines, Exmouth 1999'
Overseas teams played for: Mount Maunganui, Bay of Plenty, New Zealand 1994-
95; Marist Newman, Perth 1999-2000
Cricketers particularly admired: John Solanky and Raman Lamba ('my first club's
professionals'), Michael Turkington, 'my bro and particularly my father, William'
Young players to look out for: Ian Latham, Samuel Perkins ('age 2'), Ed Joyce 'and
those Pattersons waiting to be conceived'
Other sports followed: Football (Linfield FC and Northern Ireland – 'the British
champions!')
Injuries: Out for the whole season after a patellar tendonitis operation in April 2000
Relaxations: 'Eating, yoga and trying to be at one with myself and those around me.
DIY, plastering and using my power tools'
Extras: 1993 Irish Young Cricketer of the Year. In 1996 took 6 for 80 against South
Africa A – the best ever figures by a Surrey bowler on debut

Opinions on cricket: 'The two divisional system has begun very well, although there should be even more incentives to get into division one. Wickets still need to be improved, although new penalties for poor wickets are a good start. More central contracts for England players – 16 minimum.'
Best batting: 4 Surrey v South Africa A, The Oval 1996
Best bowling: 6-80 Surrey v South Africa A, The Oval 1996

2000 Season (did not make any first-class or one-day appearances)

Career Performances

	M	Inns	NO	Runs	HS	Avge	100s	50s	Ct	St	Balls	Runs	Wkts	Avge	Best	5wI	10wM
Test																	
All First	2	3	0	6	4	2.00	-	-	-	-	243	163	10	16.30	6-80	1	-
1-day Int																	
NatWest	2	1	0	1	1	1.00	-	-	-	-	138	154	4	38.50	3-66	-	
B & H	7	5	1	23	9	5.75	-	-	-	-	342	330	10	33.00	3-48	-	
1-day Lge																	

PATTISON, I. Durham

Name: Ian Pattison
Role: Right-hand bat, right-arm medium bowler
Born: 5 May 1982, Sunderland
Height: 5ft 11in **Weight:** 12st
Nickname: Patto, Patta
County debut: No first-team appearance
Parents: Stewart and Janice
Marital status: Single
Family links with cricket: Dad and brother play in local leagues
Education: New Seaham Primary School; Seaham Comprehensive
Qualifications: 6 GCSEs, Level 1 coaching badge
Off-season: England U19 tour to India
Overseas tours: England U19 to Malaysia and (Youth World Cup) Sri Lanka 1999-2000, to India 2000-01

Cricketers particularly admired: Jacques Kallis, Simon Katich, Steve Waugh
Young players to look out for: Ian Bell, Nicky Peng, Mark Wallace
Other sports followed: Football (Sunderland AFC)

Injuries: 'Plagued all summer' by patellar tendonitis
Relaxations: Golf, watching Sunderland AFC, horse racing
Extras: Played for Durham Board XI in NatWest 2000

2000 Season (did not make any first-class or one-day appearances)

Career Performances

	M	Inns	NO	Runs	HS	Avge	100s	50s	Ct	St	Balls	Runs	Wkts	Avge	Best	5wl	10wM
Test																	
All First																	
1-day Int																	
NatWest	3	3	2	56	48 *	56.00	-	-	1	-	60	56	2	28.00	1-25	-	
B & H																	
1-day Lge																	

PAYNTER, D. E. Northamptonshire

Name: <u>David</u> Edward Paynter
Role: Right-hand bat, right-arm off-spin bowler
Born: 25 January 1981, Truro, Cornwall
Height: 6ft 2½in **Weight:** 12st 7lbs
Nickname: Paints
County debut: No first-team appearance
Parents: Mark and Carole
Marital status: Single
Family links with cricket: Great-grandfather (Eddie Paynter) played for Lancashire (1926-1945) and England and was on the Bodyline tour
Education: Larchmont First School; Clayton Middle School
Qualifications: 9 GCSEs, Level I, II and III coaching awards
Off-season: Playing in New Zealand for Grafton, Auckland
Overseas tours: Yorkshire U19 to India 1998-99
Overseas teams played for: Grafton, Auckland 1999-2001
Cricketers particularly admired: Mark Waugh, Ricky Ponting
Young players to look out for: John Sadler, Daren Drake, Craig Mowatt
Other sports played: Table tennis (Yorkshire U14), rugby (Queensbury RFC)
Other sports followed: Football (Bradford City), rugby league (Bradford Bulls)

Relaxations: Gym work, listening to music, socialising with friends
Extras: Bradford League Young Player of the Year 2000
Opinions on cricket: 'All good. Need more coverage of the county game on TV. Need to play more day/night games – they attract more families and have a great atmosphere.'

PEIRCE, M. T. E. Sussex

Name: Michael <u>Toby</u> Edward Peirce
Role: Left-hand bat, slow left-arm bowler
Born: 14 June 1973, Maidenhead
Height: 5ft 10in **Weight:** 12st
Nickname: Carrot, Juice
County debut: 1994 (one-day), 1995 (first-class)
1st-Class 50s: 17
1st-Class 100s: 2
1st-Class catches: 30
Place in batting averages: 185th av. 19.39 (1999 108th av. 29.64)
Strike rate: 66.00 (career 178.33)
Parents: Mike and Kate
Wife and date of marriage: Natasha, February 2000
Education: Ardingly College; Durham University
Qualifications: 11 GCSEs, 3 A-levels, BA (Hons) Dunelm
Career outside cricket: 'Open to offers'
Overseas tours: Ardingly College to India 1988-89; Sussex Schools U14 to Barbados 1986; Sussex Schools U19 to India 1990-91; MCC to New Zealand 1999
Overseas teams played for: Kilbirnie CC, Wellington, New Zealand 1991-92; Van der Stel CC, Stellenbosch, South Africa 1996-99; Somerset West, South Africa 1999-2000
Cricketers particularly admired: David Smith, David Gower
Young players to look out for: Steve Harmison, Nick Wilton
Other sports played: Golf, touch rugby
Other sports followed: Football (Brighton & Hove Albion), 'most sports'
Relaxations: 'Golf, good food and drink; Natasha'
Extras: Released by Sussex at the end of the 2000 season
Best batting: 123 Sussex v Glamorgan, Cardiff 1999
Best bowling: 1-16 Sussex v Warwickshire, Hove 1998
1-16 Sussex v Northamptonshire, Hove 1999

2000 Season

	M	Inns	NO	Runs	HS	Avge	100s	50s	Ct	St	O	M	Runs	Wkts	Avge	Best	5wI	10wM
Test																		
All First	14	24	1	446	86	19.39	-	2	3	-	11	3	37	1	37.00	1-37	-	-
1-day Int																		
NatWest																		
B & H																		
1-day Lge																		

Career Performances

	M	Inns	NO	Runs	HS	Avge	100s	50s	Ct	St	Balls	Runs	Wkts	Avge	Best	5wI	10wM
Test																	
All First	69	122	2	2928	123	24.40	2	17	30	-	535	272	3	90.66	1-16	-	-
1-day Int																	
NatWest	1	1	0	1	1	1.00	-	-	-	-							
B & H	6	6	0	150	44	25.00	-	-	2	-							
1-day Lge	9	9	1	94	29	11.75	-	-	2	-							

PENBERTHY, A. L.   Northamptonshire

Name: <u>Anthony</u> Leonard Penberthy
Role: Left-hand bat, right-arm medium bowler, county vice-captain
Born: 1 September 1969, Troon, Cornwall
Height: 6ft 1in **Weight:** 12st
Nickname: Berth, Penbers, Sir Leonard, Denzil
County debut: 1989
County cap: 1994
1st-Class 50s: 30
1st-Class 100s: 5
1st-Class 5 w. in innings: 4
1st-Class catches: 88
One-Day 5 w. in innings: 4
Place in batting averages: 33rd av. 41.31 (1999 97th av. 31.21)
Place in bowling averages: 35th av. 22.37 (1999 127th av. 38.68)
Strike rate: 49.12 (career 70.39)
Parents: Gerald (deceased) and Wendy
Wife and date of marriage: Rebecca, 9 November 1996
Children: Georgia Lily, 4 March 1998

Family links with cricket: Father played in local leagues in Cornwall and became a qualified umpire instructor
Education: Troon County Primary; Camborne Comprehensive
Qualifications: 3 O-levels, 3 CSEs, Levels 1 and 2 coaching certificates
Career outside cricket: Coaching
Off-season: Coaching
Overseas tours: Druids to Zimbabwe 1988; Northants to Durban 1992, to Cape Town 1993, to Zimbabwe 1995, 1998, to Johannesburg 1996, to Grenada 2000
Cricketers particularly admired: Ian Botham, David Gower, Dennis Lillee, Viv Richards, Eldine Baptiste
Young players to look out for: Graeme Swann, David Sales, Mark Powell
Other sports played: Football, golf
Other sports followed: Football (West Ham United), rugby (Northampton Saints)
Relaxations: Listening to music, watching films and comedy programmes, 'walking my Irish setter'
Extras: Had football trials for Plymouth Argyle but came to Northampton for cricket trials instead. Took wicket with first ball in first-class cricket – Mark Taylor caught behind, June 1989. Played for England YC v New Zealand YC 1989. Took only the second Sunday/National League hat-trick in Northants history v Somerset at Northampton in 1999. Appointed vice-captain of Northamptonshire for 2001
Opinions on cricket: 'Two divisional system has led to more competitive cricket. Wickets must improve, and the pitch liaison officers should be more consistent with their findings.'
Best batting: 128 Northamptonshire v Warwickshire, Northampton 1998
Best bowling: 5-37 Northamptonshire v Glamorgan, Swansea 1993

2000 Season

	M	Inns	NO	Runs	HS	Avge	100s	50s	Ct	St	O	M	Runs	Wkts	Avge	Best	5wI	10wM
Test																		
All First	15	21	2	785	116	41.31	1	5	10	-	131	30	358	16	22.37	5-54	1	-
1-day Int																		
NatWest	3	2	0	65	54	32.50	-	1	1	-	28	2	119	4	29.75	3-44	-	
B & H	2	2	1	46	28 *	46.00	-	-	-	-	20	0	70	1	70.00	1-24	-	
1-day Lge	15	13	3	197	39 *	19.70	-	-	6	-	110	8	437	22	19.86	5-29	1	

Career Performances

	M	Inns	NO	Runs	HS	Avge	100s	50s	Ct	St	Balls	Runs	Wkts	Avge	Best	5wI	10wM
Test																	
All First	148	218	25	5268	128	27.29	5	30	88	-	13304	7145	189	37.80	5-37	4	-
1-day Int																	
NatWest	26	18	2	423	79	26.43	-	4	9	-	1165	835	23	36.30	5-56	1	
B & H	31	25	6	575	62	30.26	-	2	7	-	1370	960	26	36.92	3-22	-	
1-day Lge	139	114	24	2153	81 *	23.92	-	10	35	-	4797	3979	146	27.25	5-29	3	

PENG, N. Durham

Name: Nicky Peng
Role: Right-hand bat
Born: 18 September 1982, Newcastle
Height: 6ft 3in
Nickname: Pengy, King
County debut: 2000
1st-Class 50s: 1
1st-Class catches: 1
Place in batting averages: 217th av. 16.50
Parents: Linda and Wilf
Marital status: Single
Education: Royal Grammar School,
Newcastle-upon-Tyne
Qualifications: 10 GCSEs
Off-season: England U19 tour of India
Overseas tours: England U19 to India
2000-01

Cricketers particularly admired:
Steve Waugh, Jacques Kallis, Mike Atherton, Alec Stewart
Young players to look out for: Gordon Muchall, Ian Bell, Mark Wallace, Kabir Ali
Other sports followed: Football, rugby (Newcastle, especially England)
Injuries: Damaged ankle ligaments
Relaxations: Socialising with friends from school; relaxing with girlfriend
Extras: Full name Nicky Peng Gillender. Has represented England at U14, U15, U17
and U19 levels. Represented Minor Counties at age 15. Scored 98 on his
Championship debut v Surrey at Riverside 2000. Represented England U19 v Sri
Lanka U19 in one-day and 'Test' series 2000, scoring 123 in second 'Test' at
Northampton
Opinions on cricket: 'Everything seems to be moving in the right direction, with
young players being given more opportunities. The standard of pitches in county
cricket must improve.'
Best batting: 98 Durham v Surrey, Riverside 2000
Stop press: Scored 132 in England's first innings in the second U19 'Test' at Chennai
(Madras) 2000-01

2000 Season

	M	Inns	NO	Runs	HS	Avge	100s	50s	Ct	St	O	M	Runs	Wkts	Avge	Best	5wI	10wM
Test																		
All First	8	14	0	231	98	16.50	-	1	1	-								
1-day Int																		
NatWest																		
B & H	5	4	0	30	14	7.50	-	-	-	-								
1-day Lge	4	4	0	46	36	11.50	-	-	-	-								

Career Performances

	M	Inns	NO	Runs	HS	Avge	100s	50s	Ct	St	Balls	Runs	Wkts	Avge	Best	5wI	10wM
Test																	
All First	8	14	0	231	98	16.50	-	1	1	-							
1-day Int																	
NatWest																	
B & H	5	4	0	30	14	7.50	-	-	-	-							
1-day Lge	4	4	0	46	36	11.50	-	-	-	-							

PENNEY, T. L.   Warwickshire

Name: <u>Trevor</u> Lionel Penney
Role: Right-hand bat, leg-break bowler
Born: 12 June 1968, Harare, Zimbabwe
Height: 6ft **Weight:** 11st 2lbs
Nickname: TP, Blondie
County debut: 1992
County cap: 1994
1000 runs in a season: 2
1st-Class 50s: 36
1st-Class 100s: 15
1st-Class catches: 88
1st-Class stumpings: 2
Place in batting averages: 37th av. 40.64
(1999 158th av. 24.61)
Strike rate: (career 43.16)
Parents: George and Bets
Wife and date of marriage: Deborah-Anne, 19 December 1992
Children: Samantha Anne, 20 August 1995; Kevin, 7 June 1998
Family links with cricket: Father played club cricket. Brother Stephen captained Zimbabwe Schools
Education: Blakiston Junior School; Prince Edward Boys High School, Zimbabwe

Qualifications: 3 O-levels
Career outside cricket: Tobacco buyer. Zimbabwe Board XI player/coach
Off-season: Coaching Zimbabwe Board XI
Overseas tours: Zimbabwe U24 to England 1984; Zimbabwe to Sri Lanka 1987;
ICC Associates team to Australia (Youth World Cup) 1987-88 (captain)
Overseas teams played for: Old Hararians, Zimbabwe 1983-89 and 1992-98;
Scarborough, Perth 1989-90; Avendale, South Africa 1990-91; Boland, South Africa
1991-92
Cricketers particularly admired: Colin Bland, Ian Botham, Allan Donald,
Steve Waugh
Other sports played: Hockey (Zimbabwe and Africa), squash, tennis, golf and white
water rafting
Other sports followed: Basketball (Chicago Bulls), American football (San Francisco
49ers), Formula One motor racing
Relaxations: 'Playing golf and drinking cold Castles on Lake Kariba. Spending time
with my family'
Extras: Played for Zimbabwe against Sri Lanka in 1987. Played hockey for
Zimbabwe from 1984-87 and also made the African team who played Asia in 1987.
Qualified to play for England in 1992. Captained Old Hararians to victory in three
Zimbabwe domestic trophies 1998-99
Best batting: 151 Warwickshire v Middlesex, Lord's 1992
Best bowling: 3-18 Mashonaland v Mashonaland U24, Harare 1993-94

2000 Season

	M	Inns	NO	Runs	HS	Avge	100s	50s	Ct	St	O	M	Runs	Wkts	Avge	Best	5wI	10wM
Test																		
All First	13	18	4	569	100 *	40.64	1	2	8	-								
1-day Int																		
NatWest	5	5	2	170	45 *	56.66	-	-	2	-								
B & H	3	1	0	25	25	25.00	-	-	3	-								
1-day Lge	15	14	4	291	51	29.10	-	1	8	-								

Career Performances

	M	Inns	NO	Runs	HS	Avge	100s	50s	Ct	St	Balls		Runs	Wkts	Avge	Best	5wI	10wM
Test																		
All First	154	244	45	7952	151	39.95	15	36	88	2	259		184	6	30.66	3-18	-	-
1-day Int																		
NatWest	34	32	8	709	90	29.54	-	2	18	-	13		16	1	16.00	1-8	-	
B & H	33	28	6	635	57 *	28.86	-	3	14	1								
1-day Lge	131	115	38	2164	83 *	28.10	-	9	49	-	6		2	0	-		-	-

PETERS, S. D.   Essex

Name: <u>Stephen</u> David Peters
Role: Right-hand bat, leg-break bowler
Born: 10 December 1978, Harold Wood
Height: 5ft 11in **Weight:** 11st
Nickname: Geezer
County debut: 1996
1st-Class 50s: 9
1st-Class 100s: 2
1st-Class catches: 40
Place in batting averages: 118th av. 27.36
(1999 114th av. 28.76)
Strike rate: (career 23.00)
Parents: Brian and Lesley
Marital status: Single
Family links with cricket: 'All family is
linked with Upminster CC. The best bar in
Upminster!!'
Education: Upminster Junior School;
Coopers Coborn and Company School

Qualifications: 9 GCSEs
Career outside cricket: 'Making sure all bars in Romford sell Budweiser!'
Overseas tours: Essex U14 to Barbados; Essex U15 to Hong Kong; England U19 to
Pakistan 1996-97, to South Africa (including Youth World Cup) 1997-98
Cricketers particularly admired: 'Anyone who plays at the top level'
Young players to look out for: Tim Phillips, Barry Hyam, Michael Davies
Other sports played: Football, golf
Other sports followed: Football (West Ham United)
Injuries: Back injury, but no time off needed
Relaxations: 'My sofa; keeping in touch with my mates'
Extras: The Sir John Hobbs Jubilee Memorial Prize 1994; a *Daily Telegraph* regional
batting award 1994. Represented England at U14, U15, U17 and U19. Scored century
(110) on county debut v Cambridge University at Fenner's 1996. Essex Young Player
of the Year 1996. Scored a century (107) and was Man of the Match in the U19 World
Cup final in South Africa 1997-98
Opinions on cricket: 'Day/night cricket is the way forward.'
Best batting: 110 Essex v Cambridge University, Fenner's 1996
Best bowling: 1-19 Essex v Oxford University, Chelmsford 1999

2000 Season

	M	Inns	NO	Runs	HS	Avge	100s	50s	Ct	St	O	M	Runs	Wkts	Avge	Best	5wI	10wM
Test																		
All First	16	28	6	602	77 *	27.36	-	4	12	-								
1-day Int																		
NatWest	2	2	0	64	58	32.00	-	1	2	-								
B & H	3	3	0	106	43	35.33	-	-	-	-								
1-day Lge	15	15	1	340	73 *	24.28	-	2	3	-								

Career Performances

	M	Inns	NO	Runs	HS	Avge	100s	50s	Ct	St	Balls	Runs	Wkts	Avge	Best	5wI	10wM
Test																	
All First	47	76	12	1737	110	27.14	2	9	40	-	23	19	1	19.00	1-19	-	-
1-day Int																	
NatWest	3	3	0	70	58	23.33	-	1	3	-							
B & H	10	8	1	192	58 *	27.42	-	1	2	-							
1-day Lge	43	37	2	554	73 *	15.82	-	3	11	-							

PETTINI, M. L. Essex

Name: <u>Mark</u> Lewis Pettini
Role: Right-hand bat, right-arm
medium bowler
Born: 7 August 1983, Brighton, East Sussex
Height: 5ft 11in **Weight:** 10st 12lbs
Nickname: Swampy
County debut: No first-team appearance
Parents: Pauline and Max
Marital status: Single
Family links with cricket: 'Brother Tom
currently captains Cambridgeshire U14
county side. Mum and Dad are very keen
supporters while Grandad plays a demon
game of beach cricket'
Education: Avalon Primary School, Sydney,
Australia; Meridian Primary School;
Comberton Village College and Hills Road
Sixth Form College, Cambridge
Qualifications: 10 GCSEs, Level 1 cricket coaching award
Off-season: Studying for A-levels
Cricketers particularly admired: Brian Lara, Sachin Tendulkar, Steve Waugh
Young players to look out for: 'Brother Tom'

Other sports played: Tennis, swimming ('keeping fit'), table tennis
Other sports followed: Tennis, basketball
Injuries: Out for one week with quad strain
Relaxations: Fishing, watching sport, sleeping
Extras: Captained Cambridgeshire county sides from U11-U16. Took hat-trick against Bedfordshire U12. Highest score of 173* v Hampshire U16 1999
Opinions on cricket: 'The best game there is, the best game there was, and the best game there ever will be.'

PHILLIPS, B. J.   Kent

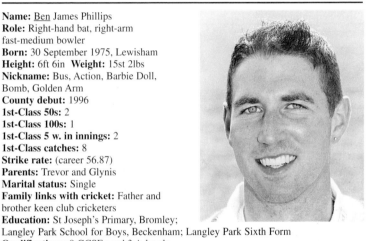

Name: <u>Ben</u> James Phillips
Role: Right-hand bat, right-arm fast-medium bowler
Born: 30 September 1975, Lewisham
Height: 6ft 6in **Weight:** 15st 2lbs
Nickname: Bus, Action, Barbie Doll, Bomb, Golden Arm
County debut: 1996
1st-Class 50s: 2
1st-Class 100s: 1
1st-Class 5 w. in innings: 2
1st-Class catches: 8
Strike rate: (career 56.87)
Parents: Trevor and Glynis
Marital status: Single
Family links with cricket: Father and brother keen club cricketers
Education: St Joseph's Primary, Bromley; Langley Park School for Boys, Beckenham; Langley Park Sixth Form
Qualifications: 9 GCSEs and 3 A-levels
Overseas teams played for: University of Queensland, Australia 1993-94; Cape Technikon Greenpoint, Cape Town, South Africa 1994-95, 1996-98; University of Western Australia, Perth 1998-99
Cricketers particularly admired: Carl Hooper, Courtney Walsh, Dennis Lillee
Young players to look out for: Rob Key
Other sports followed: Football (West Ham United) and basketball (Chicago Bulls)
Injuries: Out for most of 2000 season with a stress fracture of the back
Relaxations: 'Enjoy watching a decent film or listening to music. Slothing it on a beach somewhere sunny in the off-season'
Extras: Represented England U19 Schools in 1993-94. Set Langley Park School record for the fastest half century, off 11 balls

Best batting: 100* Kent v Lancashire, Old Trafford 1997
Best bowling: 5-47 Kent v Sussex, Horsham 1997

2000 Season

	M	Inns	NO	Runs	HS	Avge	100s	50s	Ct	St	O	M	Runs	Wkts	Avge	Best	5wl	10wM
Test																		
All First																		
1-day Int																		
NatWest																		
B & H	2	1	0	0	0	0.00	-	-	-	-	15	1	53	4	13.25	2-25	-	
1-day Lge	1	0	0	0	0	-	-	-	-	-	7	0	25	4	6.25	4-25	-	

Career Performances

	M	Inns	NO	Runs	HS	Avge	100s	50s	Ct	St	Balls	Runs	Wkts	Avge	Best	5wl	10wM
Test																	
All First	27	39	4	584	100*	16.68	1	2	8	-	3697	1914	65	29.44	5-47	2	-
1-day Int																	
NatWest	2	1	1	9	9*	-	-	-	1	-	90	67	3	22.33	3-14	-	
B & H	6	3	1	1	1*	0.50	-	-	1	-	242	156	10	15.60	3-13	-	
1-day Lge	18	8	2	49	29	8.16	-	-	7	-	562	443	20	22.15	4-25	-	

PHILLIPS, N. C.   Durham

Name: <u>Nicholas</u> Charles Phillips
Role: Right-hand bat, off-spin bowler
Born: 10 May 1974, Pembury, Kent
Height: 6ft **Weight:** 12st 5lbs
Nickname: Jenks, Dr W
County debut: 1994 (Sussex),
1998 (Durham)
1st-Class 50s: 3
1st-Class 5 w. in innings: 3
1st-Class 10 w. in match: 1
1st-Class catches: 25
Place in batting averages: 282nd av. 8.44
(1999 263rd av. 11.66)
Place in bowling averages: (1999 124th
av. 37.61)
Strike rate: 134.42 (career 95.87)
Parents: Robert and Joan
Marital status: Single
Family links with cricket: Father plays club cricket for Hastings. Represents Sussex

Over 50s and has represented Kent 2nd XI, Kent League XI and has scored over 100 club 100s
Education: Hilden Grange School, Tonbridge; St Thomas's School, Winchelsea; William Parker School, Hastings
Qualifications: 8 GCSEs, NCA coaching award
Overseas tours: Sussex U18 to India 1990-91
Overseas teams played for: Maris CC, Auckland 1996-97; Taita Districts, Wellington, New Zealand 1998-99
Cricketers particularly admired: Norman Gifford
Other sports followed: Hockey, football
Relaxations: Spending time with friends and girlfriend. Listening to music. Eating out and socialising with fellow players
Extras: Represented England U19 in home series against West Indies U19 in 1993. Has played hockey for Sussex U14 and U16. Released by Sussex at the end of the 1997 season and joined Durham. Returned the best figures for a Durham spinner since the county attained first-class status with his 12-268 v Glamorgan at Cardiff 1999
Best batting: 53 Sussex v Young Australia, Hove 1995
Best bowling: 6-97 Durham v Glamorgan, Cardiff 1999

2000 Season

	M	Inns	NO	Runs	HS	Avge	100s	50s	Ct	St	O	M	Runs	Wkts	Avge	Best	5wI	10wM
Test																		
All First	5	9	0	76	29	8.44	-	-	3	-	156.5	36	415	7	59.28	3-53	-	-
1-day Int																		
NatWest	1	1	0	5	5	5.00	-	-	-	-	1.5	0	6	1	6.00	1-6	-	
B & H	1	1	0	16	16	16.00	-	-	2	-	8.4	2	17	3	5.66	3-17	-	
1-day Lge	16	10	3	90	29 *	12.85	-	-	5	-	119.3	6	517	24	21.54	4-30	-	

Career Performances

	M	Inns	NO	Runs	HS	Avge	100s	50s	Ct	St	Balls	Runs	Wkts	Avge	Best	5wI	10wM
Test																	
All First	47	69	12	858	53	15.05	-	3	25	-	7670	3951	80	49.38	6-97	3	1
1-day Int																	
NatWest	5	4	0	42	21	10.50	-	-	-	-	209	100	4	25.00	2-16	-	
B & H	8	7	1	50	16	8.33	-	-	4	-	347	274	10	27.40	3-17	-	
1-day Lge	63	45	10	374	38 *	10.68	-	-	16	-	2401	1961	64	30.64	4-13	-	

PHILLIPS, T. J.   Essex

Name: <u>Timothy</u> James Phillips
Role: Left-hand bat, slow left-arm bowler
Born: 13 March 1981, Cambridge
Height: 6ft 1in **Weight:** 11st 5lbs
Nickname: TP
County debut: 1999
1st-Class catches: 1
Strike rate: (career 57.00)
Parents: Martin (deceased) and Carolyn
Marital status: Single
Family links with cricket: Father played in
Lancashire League. Brother Nick plays local
village cricket
Education: Felsted Preparatory School;
Felsted School; Durham University
Qualifications: 10 GCSEs, 3 A-levels
Overseas tours: Felsted School to Australia
1995-96; England U19 to Malaysia and (Youth
World Cup) Sri Lanka 1999-2000
Cricketers particularly admired: David Gower, Phil Tufnell
Young players to look out for: Mark Pettini
Other sports played: Hockey (Essex Schools U14, U15; East of England U21 trials),
squash, golf
Other sports followed: Football (Cambridge United FC)
Relaxations: 'Spending time with friends at the local pub; cinema, travelling'
Extras: Winner of *Daily Telegraph* U14 National Bowling Award 1995. Holmwoods
School Cricketer of the Year runner-up 1997 and 1998. Broke Felsted School record
for runs scored in a season. NBC Denis Compton Award 1999
Opinions on cricket: 'More games should be played spanning the weekend. National
League should have more day/night games.'
Best batting: 16 Essex v Sri Lanka A, Chelmsford 1999
Best bowling: 4-42 Essex v Sri Lanka A, Chelmsford 1999

---

66. Which batsman scored a century for Australia in
each innings at Old Trafford in 1997?

2000 Season (did not make any first-class or one-day appearances)

Career Performances

	M	Inns	NO	Runs	HS	Avge	100s	50s	Ct	St	Balls	Runs	Wkts	Avge	Best	5wl	10wM
Test																	
All First	3	4	0	27	16	6.75	-	-	1	-	456	278	8	34.75	4-42	-	-
1-day Int																	
NatWest																	
B & H																	
1-day Lge	1	1	0	0	0	0.00	-	-	1	-	48	56	2	28.00	2-56	-	

PIERSON, A. R. K. Derbyshire

Name: <u>Adrian</u> Roger Kirshaw Pierson
Role: Right-hand bat, off-spin bowler
Born: 21 July 1963, Enfield, Middlesex
Height: 6ft 4in **Weight:** 12st
Nickname: Skirlog, Stick, Bunny, Logga
County debut: 1985 (Warwickshire),
1993 (Leicestershire), 1998 (Somerset)
County cap: 1995 (Leicestershire)
50 wickets in a season: 1
1st-Class 50s: 5
1st-Class 100s: 1
1st-Class 5 w. in innings: 14
1st-Class catches: 86
One-Day 5 w. in innings: 1
Place in batting averages: 166th av. 21.00
(1999 259th av. 12.90)
Place in bowling averages: (1999 147th
av. 60.69)
Strike rate: 110.57 (career 75.10)
Parents: Patrick and Patricia
Wife and date of marriage: Helen Majella, 28 September 1990
Children: Eleanor, 7 February 1997
Education: Lochinver House, Potters Bar, Herts; Kent College, Canterbury;
Hatfield Polytechnic
Qualifications: 8 O-levels, 2 A-levels, ECB advanced coach, private pilot's licence
Overseas tours: Warwickshire to Barbados, St Lucia, Trinidad; Leicestershire to
Jamaica, Bloemfontein, Durban
Overseas teams played for: Walmer CC, Port Elizabeth 1985-90; Manicaland,
Zimbabwe 1990-91

Cricketers particularly admired: Tony Greig, Phil Edmonds, John Emburey
Other sports played: Golf – 'won the County Cricketers' Golf Society Silver Salver with my mate Colin Metson and won the *Daily Mail* "Mijas" trophy with Chris Balderstone in 1996'
Other sports followed: 'Any sport except horse racing, but especially Formula One motor racing'
Relaxations: Flying, driving, reading, chess 'and playing with my daughter'
Extras: On Lord's groundstaff 1984-85 and on Warwickshire staff from 1985-91. First Championship wicket was Viv Richards. Won two Gold Awards in the Benson and Hedges. Released by Leicestershire at the end of the 1997 season and joined Somerset. Left Somerset at the end of the 2000 season and has joined Derbyshire for 2001 as assistant coach
Opinions on cricket: 'I believe counties will soon be playing one-day cricket only, with the longer game being played by regional sides picked from these teams in order to select a Test side. As time goes on there is more interest in one-day cricket publicly and so market forces will push the game this way. PS: Off-spinners (at least "orthodox" ones) are becoming an endangered species. Change the lbw rule – pads are for protecting the legs!!'
Best batting: 108* Somerset v Sussex, Hove 1998
Best bowling: 8-42 Leicestershire v Warwickshire, Edgbaston 1994

2000 Season

	M	Inns	NO	Runs	HS	Avge	100s	50s	Ct	St	O	M	Runs	Wkts	Avge	Best	5wI	10wM
Test																		
All First	6	9	3	126	48	21.00	-	-	3	-	129	37	313	7	44.71	3-41	-	-
1-day Int																		
NatWest																		
B & H																		
1-day Lge	2	2	1	39	31*	39.00	-	-	1	-	18	0	84	3	28.00	2-50	-	

Career Performances

	M	Inns	NO	Runs	HS	Avge	100s	50s	Ct	St	Balls	Runs	Wkts	Avge	Best	5wI	10wM
Test																	
All First	179	222	69	2641	108*	17.26	1	5	86	-	27264	13759	363	37.90	8-42	14	-
1-day Int																	
NatWest	14	7	2	42	20*	8.40	-	-	2	-	854	448	13	34.46	3-20	-	
B & H	20	14	10	57	11	14.25	-	-	6	-	950	584	14	41.71	3-34	-	
1-day Lge	78	42	17	258	31*	10.32	-	-	35	-	2811	2306	68	33.91	5-36	1	

PIETERSEN, K. P.   Nottinghamshire

Name: <u>Kevin</u> Peter Pietersen
Role: Right-hand bat, right-arm off-spin
bowler; all-rounder
Born: 27 June 1980, Pietermaritzburg, South
Africa
Height: 6ft 4in **Weight:** 14st 2lbs
Nickname: Piety, KP
County debut: No first-team appearance
Strike rate: (career 73.34)
Parents: Jannie and Penny
Marital status: Single
Education: Merchiston Prep School;
Pietermaritzburg College; University of South
Africa (studying BComm)
Career outside cricket: 'Heading towards
computer business'
Off-season: 'Relaxing with friends and
family under the *sunny* South African skies'
Overseas tours: KwaZulu-Natal to Zimbabwe, to Australia
Overseas teams played for: KwaZulu-Natal 1997-2000
Cricketers particularly admired: Shaun Pollock, Steve Waugh, Errol Stewart
Other sports played: Rugby (Provincial at school)
Other sports followed: Rugby (Natal Sharks), Formula One (Ferrari)
Relaxations: 'Going to the beach in Durban and visiting game reserves'
Extras: Played for South African Schools B 1997. Merit award for cricket from Natal
1997. Scored 61* and had figures of 4-141 from 56 overs for KwaZulu-Natal v
England on their 1999-2000 tour of South Africa. Had trial for Warwickshire 2nd XI v
Surrey 2nd XI. Is not considered an overseas player
Opinions on cricket: 'Have not played first-class cricket in England yet – only a trial
for Warwickshire 2nds against Surrey 2nds; standard seems good and pitches looked
all right.'
Best batting: 61* KwaZulu-Natal v England, Durban 1999-2000
Best bowling: 4-141 KwaZulu-Natal v England, Durban 1999-2000

2000 Season (did not make any first-class or one-day appearances)

Career Performances

	M	Inns	NO	Runs	HS	Avge	100s	50s	Ct	St	Balls	Runs	Wkts	Avge	Best	5wI	10wM
Test																	
All First	10	13	2	253	61 *	23.00	-	2	10	-	1687	762	23	33.13	4-141	-	-
1-day Int																	
NatWest																	
B & H																	
1-day Lge																	

PIPE, D. J. Worcestershire

Name: David James Pipe
Role: Right-hand bat, wicket-keeper
Born: 16 December 1977, Bradford
Height: 5ft 10in **Weight:** 11st 7lbs
Nickname: Pipes, Pipey, Pip
County debut: 1998
1st-Class 50s: 1
1st-Class catches: 2
1st-Class stumpings: 1
Parents: David and Dorothy
Marital status: Single
Family links with cricket: 'My dad and
uncle played in the local league'
Education: Stocks Lane Primary School;
Hainsworth Moor Middle School;
Queensbury School; BICC
Qualifications: 8 GCSEs, BTEC National in
Business and Finance, HND Leisure Studies,
senior coaching award

Career outside cricket: Coaching and studying
Off-season: Playing for Manly, Sydney
Overseas teams played for: Leeming Spartans CC and South Metropolitan Cricket
Association, Perth 1998-99; Manly CC, Australia 1999-2000, 2000-01
Cricketers particularly admired: 'Any player that consistently puts in 100 per cent
effort for both their preparation and participation in the game of cricket'
Young players to look out for: 'All the up-and-coming young players at
Worcestershire'
Other sports followed: Rugby league (Bradford Bulls, Northern Eagles), football
(Bradford City), boxing ('all British fighters'), AFL (West Coast Eagles)

Relaxations: Watching sport, watching films, playing golf, socialising with friends, listening to music
Extras: MCC School of Merit Wilf Slack Memorial Trophy winner 1995. Awarded 2nd XI cap 1999. Played for Worcestershire Board XI in 2000 NatWest. Scored 54 on Championship debut v Warwickshire at Worcester 2000
Opinions on cricket: 'Wickets must be improved and all 2nd XI Championship games should be played over four days.'
Best batting: 54 Worcestershire v Warwickshire, Worcester 2000

2000 Season

	M	Inns	NO	Runs	HS	Avge	100s	50s	Ct	St	O	M	Runs	Wkts	Avge	Best	5wI	10wM
Test																		
All First	3	5	0	107	54	21.40	-	1	-	-								
1-day Int																		
NatWest	1	1	0	56	56	56.00	-	1	1	-								
B & H																		
1-day Lge	6	5	0	106	45	21.20	-	-	-	-								

Career Performances

	M	Inns	NO	Runs	HS	Avge	100s	50s	Ct	St	Balls	Runs	Wkts	Avge	Best	5wI	10wM
Test																	
All First	5	7	0	128	54	18.28	-	1	2	1							
1-day Int																	
NatWest	1	1	0	56	56	56.00	-	1	1	-							
B & H																	
1-day Lge	6	5	0	106	45	21.20	-	-	-	-							

67. Who dismissed Allan Border at Old Trafford in 1993
to claim his first Test wicket?

PIPER, K. J. Warwickshire

Name: <u>Keith</u> John Piper
Role: Right-hand bat, wicket-keeper
Born: 18 December 1969, Leicester
Height: 5ft 7in **Weight:** 10st 8lbs
Nickname: Tubbsy, Garden Boy
County debut: 1989
County cap: 1992
50 dismissals in a season: 2
1st-Class 50s: 11
1st-Class 100s: 2
1st-Class catches: 437
1st-Class stumpings: 31
Place in batting averages: 208th av. 17.33
(1999 187th av. 21.71)
Strike rate: (career 28.00)
Parents: John and Charlotte
Marital status: Single
Family links with cricket: Father plays club
cricket in Leicester
Education: Seven Sisters Junior; Somerset Senior
Qualifications: Senior coaching award, basketball coaching award, volleyball
coaching award
Overseas tours: Haringey Cricket College to Barbados 1986, to Trinidad 1987, to
Jamaica 1988; Warwickshire to La Manga 1989, to St Lucia 1990; England A to India
1994-95, to Pakistan 1995-96
Overseas teams played for: Desmond Haynes's XI, Barbados v Haringey Cricket College
Cricketers particularly admired: Jack Russell, Alec Stewart, Dermot Reeve,
Colin Metson
Other sports followed: Snooker, football, tennis
Relaxations: Music, eating
Extras: London Young Cricketer of the Year 1989 and in the last five 1992. Played for
England YC 1989. Was batting partner (116*) to Brian Lara when he reached his 501*,
v Durham, Edgbaston 1994. Granted a benefit for 2001
Best batting: 116* Warwickshire v Durham, Edgbaston 1994
Best bowling: 1-57 Warwickshire v Nottinghamshire, Edgbaston 1992

2000 Season

	M	Inns	NO	Runs	HS	Avge	100s	50s	Ct	St	O	M	Runs	Wkts	Avge	Best	5wl	10wM
Test																		
All First	16	18	3	260	69	17.33	-	1	28	3								
1-day Int																		
NatWest	5	3	3	16	8 *	-	-	-	1	2								
B & H	3	1	0	0	0	0.00	-	-	2	-								
1-day Lge	15	7	6	44	12 *	44.00	-	-	15	7								

Career Performances

	M	Inns	NO	Runs	HS	Avge	100s	50s	Ct	St	Balls		Runs	Wkts	Avge	Best	5wl	10wM
Test																		
All First	172	239	37	3892	116 *	19.26	2	11	437	31	28		57	1	57.00	1-57	-	-
1-day Int																		
NatWest	34	17	9	154	19	19.25	-	-	43	5								
B & H	28	18	6	128	29	10.66	-	-	37	5								
1-day Lge	109	57	31	445	38 *	17.11	-	-	106	28								

POLLARD, P. R. Worcestershire

Name: <u>Paul</u> Raymond Pollard
Role: Left-hand opening bat, right-arm medium bowler
Born: 24 September 1968, Carlton, Nottinghamshire
Height: 5ft 11in **Weight:** 12st
Nickname: Polly, Sugar Ray
County debut: 1987 (Nottinghamshire), 1999 (Worcestershire)
County cap: 1992 (Nottinghamshire)
1000 runs in a season: 3
1st-Class 50s: 48
1st-Class 100s: 14
1st-Class catches: 153
One-Day 100s: 5
Place in batting averages: 109th av. 28.34 (1999 203rd av. 19.84)
Strike rate: (career 68.75)
Parents: Eric (deceased) and Mary
Wife and date of marriage: Kate, 14 March 1992
Education: Gedling Comprehensive
Overseas teams played for: Southern Districts, Brisbane 1988; North Perth 1990

Cricketers particularly admired: David Gower, Derek Randall, Ian Botham, Graham Gooch

Other sports followed: Football, golf, ice hockey

Relaxations: Watching videos, playing golf and music

Extras: Made debut for Nottinghamshire 2nd XI in 1985. Worked in Nottinghamshire CCC office on a Youth Training Scheme. Shared stands of 222 and 282 with Tim Robinson in the same game v Kent 1989. Was youngest player to reach 1000 runs for Nottinghamshire. Released by Nottinghamshire at end of 1998 season and joined Worcestershire for 1999

Best batting: 180 Nottinghamshire v Derbyshire, Trent Bridge 1993

Best bowling: 2-79 Nottinghamshire v Gloucestershire, Bristol 1993

2000 Season

	M	Inns	NO	Runs	HS	Avge	100s	50s	Ct	St	O	M	Runs	Wkts	Avge	Best	5wI	10wM
Test																		
All First	14	24	1	652	123 *	28.34	1	5	3	-	0.1	0	4	0	-	-	-	-
1-day Int																		
NatWest	2	2	0	67	55	33.50	-	1	3	-								
B & H	3	2	1	84	54 *	84.00	-	1	-	-								
1-day Lge	13	12	0	353	89	29.41	-	2	-	-								

Career Performances

	M	Inns	NO	Runs	HS	Avge	100s	50s	Ct	St	Balls	Runs	Wkts	Avge	Best	5wI	10wM
Test																	
All First	182	320	23	9376	180	31.56	14	48	153	-	275	272	4	68.00	2-79	-	-
1-day Int																	
NatWest	17	17	2	498	96	33.20	-	3	7	-	18	9	0	-	-	-	-
B & H	35	33	3	947	104	31.56	1	8	11	-							
1-day Lge	120	109	10	3349	132 *	33.82	4	18	42	-							

PORTER, J. J.   Surrey

Name: Joseph (Joe) James Porter

Role: Left-hand bat

Born: 5 May 1980

Height: 5ft 11in **Weight:** 12st

Nickame: JP

County debut: No first-team appearance

1st-Class 50s: 4

Place in batting averages: 97th av. 29.70

Parents: Bob and Judy

Marital status: Single

Education: Rokeby; St John's, Leatherhead; Oxford Brookes University
Qualifications: 7 GCSEs, 3 A-levels
Career outside cricket: Second year at Oxford Brookes University, reading Business Studies and Leisure Management
Off-season: Studying
Overseas tours: Surrey Cricket Board to Barbados 1999; Surrey U19 to Barbados 1999-2000; Oxford Universities to Pakistan 2000
Overseas teams played for: Havelock North, Hawkes Bay, New Zealand 1998-99
Cricketers particularly admired: Alec Stewart, Jimmy Adams, Brian Lara
Young players to look out for: Andrew Hollingsworth, Tim Murtagh
Other sports played: Rugby (Sutton and Epsom Rugby Club)
Other sports followed: Rugby (London Wasps)
Relaxations: Watching films
Extras: The Cricket Society's Wetherell Award for the leading all-rounder in schools cricket 1998. Played for Oxford Universities and British Universities in 2000
Best batting: 93 British Universities v Zimbabweans, Fenner's 2000

2000 Season (did not make any first-class or one-day appearances)

Career Performances

	M	Inns	NO	Runs	HS	Avge	100s	50s	Ct	St	Balls	Runs	Wkts	Avge	Best	5wI	10wM
Test																	
All First	6	10	0	297	93	29.70	-	4	-	-	36	50	0	-	-	-	-
1-day Int																	
NatWest																	
B & H																	
1-day Lge																	

68. What feat did Ian and Greg Chappell achieve at The Oval in 1972?

POWELL, M. J.   Northamptonshire

Name: <u>Mark</u> John Powell
Role: Right-hand bat, off-spin bowler
Born: 4 November 1980, Northampton
Height: 5ft 11in **Weight:** 11st 6lbs
Nickname: Powelly, Piggy, Perfect
County debut: 2000
Parents: David and Philippa
Marital status: Single
Education: Flore School, Northants;
Campion School, Bugbrooke, Northants;
Loughborough University
Qualifications: 10 GCSEs, 3 A-levels
Career outside cricket: Student
Off-season: Second year at Loughborough
University studying Information Management
and Business Studies
Overseas tours: Northants U19 to South
Africa 2000
Cricketers particularly admired: Adam Gilchrist, Mike Atherton, Curtly Ambrose
Young players to look out for: Monty Panesar
Other sports played: Golf
Other sports followed: Football (Tottenham Hotspur), rugby union (Northampton
Saints)
Relaxations: TV, cinema, music
Extras: Played for England U15 in inaugural Youth World Cup 1996; knocked out in
semi-finals by Pakistan at Headingley. Played for Midlands U19 v Australia U19 1999.
Scored 50 in Loughborough University's BUSA Final win at Fenner's 2000
Opinions on cricket: 'No opinions that have not already been stated by others.'
Best batting: 1 Northamptonshire v Worcestershire, Worcester 2000

2000 Season

	M	Inns	NO	Runs	HS	Avge	100s	50s	Ct	St	O	M	Runs	Wkts	Avge	Best	5wI	10wM
Test																		
All First	1	2	0	2	1	1.00	-	-	-	-								
1-day Int																		
NatWest																		
B & H																		
1-day Lge																		

Career Performances

	M	Inns	NO	Runs	HS	Avge	100s	50s	Ct	St	Balls	Runs	Wkts	Avge	Best	5wl	10wM
Test																	
All First	1	2	0	2	1	1.00	-	-	-	-							
1-day Int																	
NatWest																	
B & H																	
1-day Lge																	

POWELL, M. J.   Warwickshire

Name: <u>Michael</u> James Powell
Role: Right-hand opening bat, right-arm
medium bowler, county captain
Born: 5 April 1975, Bolton
Height: 5ft 10in **Weight:** 11st
Nickname: Arthur, Powelly
County debut: 1996
County cap: 1999
1000 runs in a season: 1
1st-Class 50s: 12
1st-Class 100s: 5
1st-Class catches: 32
Place in batting averages: 26th av. 43.58
(1999 68th av. 35.28)
Strike rate: 72.00 (career 82.80)
Parents: Terry and Pat
Wife and date of marriage:
Sarah, 26 October 1996

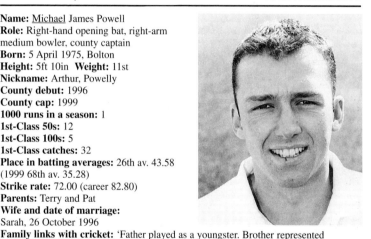

Family links with cricket: 'Father played as a youngster. Brother represented
Warwickshire youth teams'
Education: Horwich Parish C of E School; Rivington and Blackrod High School,
Horwich; Lawrence Sheriff Boys Grammar School, Rugby
Qualifications: 6 GCSEs, 2 A-levels, Levels I-III coaching awards
Career outside cricket: PE teacher
Off-season: 'Cape Town, South Africa'
Overseas tours: England U18 to South Africa 1992-93 (captain), to Denmark 1993
(captain); England U19 to Sri Lanka 1993-94; England A to West Indies 2000-01
Overseas teams played for: Avendale CC, Cape Town 1994-95, 1996-97, 2000-01
Cricketers particularly admired: Ian Botham, Dermot Reeve, Roger Twose
Young players to look out for: Graham Wagg, Ian Bell
Other sports played: Rugby (Warwickshire U16-U18), golf

Other sports followed: Football (Manchester United – 'who else?')

Relaxations: Golf, snooker, 'spending time with my wife Sarah, my dog Winston and cats Brian and Graeme'

Extras: Captained Warwickshire age-group sides U14-U19. Captained England U17 and U18. 2nd XI Player of the Month June 1996. Scored a career-best 210 against Somerset 2nd XI in July 1996. Became first uncapped Warwickshire player for 49 years to carry his bat, against Nottinghamshire at Edgbaston, June 1998. With Mark Wagh, shared in record first-wicket stand for Warwickshire in matches v Essex (230) at Chelmsford 2000. Appointed captain of Warwickshire for 2001

Opinions on cricket: 'Improvement of pitches around the circuit desperately needed!! A new ball must be due at 80 overs, not 100!! A replacement for the benefit system needed that still rewards county players for great service but prevents hangers-on and thus provides more opportunities for younger players to blossom.'

Best batting: 145 Warwickshire v Northamptonshire, Northampton 2000

Best bowling: 2-16 Warwickshire v Oxford University, The Parks 1998

Stop press: Drafted into the England A squad for the West Indies tour as replacement for the injured David Sales. Shared in record opening stand for England A (224) with Ian Ward v Barbados at Bridgetown 2000-01, scoring 96

2000 Season

	M	Inns	NO	Runs	HS	Avge	100s	50s	Ct	St	O	M	Runs	Wkts	Avge	Best	5wI	10wM
Test																		
All First	17	26	2	1046	145	43.58	2	8	10	-	24	6	80	2	40.00	1-0	-	-
1-day Int																		
NatWest	5	5	0	71	25	14.20	-	-	6	-								
B & H																		
1-day Lge	12	11	1	181	41	18.10	-	-	3	-	27	0	124	6	20.66	2-13	-	

Career Performances

	M	Inns	NO	Runs	HS	Avge	100s	50s	Ct	St	Balls	Runs	Wkts	Avge	Best	5wI	10wM
Test																	
All First	44	71	3	2253	145	33.13	5	12	32	-	414	200	5	40.00	2-16	-	-
1-day Int																	
NatWest	5	5	0	71	25	14.20	-	-	6	-							
B & H																	
1-day Lge	19	16	3	338	51	26.00	-	1	4	-	180	147	6	24.50	2-13	-	

POWELL, M. J.   Glamorgan

Name: <u>Michael</u> John Powell
Role: Right-hand bat
Born: 3 February 1977, Abergavenny, South Wales
Height: 6ft 1in **Weight:** 14st 7lbs
Nickname: Powelly, Ape Man, Clyde
County debut: 1997
County cap: 2000
1000 runs in a season: 1
1st-Class 50s: 14
1st-Class 100s: 5
1st-Class 200s: 1
1st-Class catches: 27
Place in batting averages: 94th av. 30.10 (1999 13th av. 48.18)
Strike rate: (career 64.00)
Parents: John and Linda
Marital status: Single
Family links with cricket: 'My dad played for Abergavenny CC and my uncle played for Glamorgan 2nd XI'
Education: Crickhowell Primary School; Crickhowell Secondary School; Pontypool College
Qualifications: 5 GCSEs, BTEC National Sports Science, NCA coaching award
Off-season: Training; playing rugby
Overseas teams played for: Western Suburbs, Brisbane 1996-97; Cornwall CC, Auckland 1998-99, 2000-01
Cricketers particularly admired: Stuart Law, Mark Waugh
Young players to look out for: Matthew Sneade, Leighton James, Ben Powell
Other sports played: Rugby (Crickhowell RFC)
Relaxations: Eating and sleeping
Extras: Scored 200 not out on his first-class debut. Scored 1210 runs at 75.63 in the 1997 2nd XI Championship, the second-highest ever total behind Alan Brazier's 1212 for Surrey 2nd XI in 1948. 2nd XI Championship Player of the Year 1997. Awarded Glamorgan cap 2000
Best batting: 200* Glamorgan v Oxford University, The Parks 1997
Best bowling: 2-39 Glamorgan v Oxford University, The Parks 1999

2000 Season

	M	Inns	NO	Runs	HS	Avge	100s	50s	Ct	St	O	M	Runs	Wkts	Avge	Best	5wI	10wM
Test																		
All First	18	28	0	843	128	30.10	2	4	11	-								
1-day Int																		
NatWest	2	2	0	4	3	2.00	-	-	2	-								
B & H	6	6	0	186	67	31.00	-	1	1	-								
1-day Lge	16	16	3	396	86	30.46	-	2	1	-								

Career Performances

	M	Inns	NO	Runs	HS	Avge	100s	50s	Ct	St	Balls	Runs	Wkts	Avge	Best	5wI	10wM
Test																	
All First	55	89	10	3029	200 *	38.34	6	14	27	-	128	111	2	55.50	2-39	-	-
1-day Int																	
NatWest	5	5	0	20	11	4.00	-	-	2	-							
B & H	6	6	0	186	67	31.00	-	1	1	-							
1-day Lge	47	45	6	931	86	23.87	-	3	10	-							

PRATT, A.   Durham

Name: Andrew Pratt
Role: Left-hand bat, wicket-keeper
Born: 4 March 1975, Bishop Auckland
Height: 6ft **Weight:** 12st
Nickname: Pratty (Inzamam)
County debut: 1997
1st-Class catches: 11
Place in batting averages: 165th av. 21.22
Parents: Gordon and Brenda
Marital status: Engaged
Family links with cricket: Brother was with
MCC Young Cricketers for four years.
Younger brother Gary plays for Durham and
England U19. Father played in local leagues
Education: Willington Junior School;
Willington Parkside Comprehensive School;
Durham New College
Qualifications: 9 GCSEs, Advanced
Diploma in Information Technology, cricket coaching certificate
Off-season: 'Playing golf'
Overseas teams played for: Hallam, Melbourne 1997-98
Cricketers particularly admired: Alan Knott, Jack Russell

Young players to look out for: Jimmy Daley
Other sports played: Golf
Other sports followed: Football (Middlesbrough FC)
Injuries: Long-term finger injury
Relaxations: Sleeping
Extras: Played for Durham County Schools at all levels and for the North of England U15. Played for MCC Young Cricketers for three years. He and brother Gary became the first brothers to play in a Championship match for Durham, against Lancashire at Old Trafford 2000
Best batting: 38 Durham v Somerset, Taunton 2000

2000 Season

	M	Inns	NO	Runs	HS	Avge	100s	50s	Ct	St	O	M	Runs	Wkts	Avge	Best	5wI	10wM
Test																		
All First	7	10	1	191	38	21.22	-	-	7	-								
1-day Int																		
NatWest																		
B & H																		
1-day Lge	7	6	2	17	10	4.25	-	-	2	2								

Career Performances

	M	Inns	NO	Runs	HS	Avge	100s	50s	Ct	St	Balls	Runs	Wkts	Avge	Best	5wI	10wM
Test																	
All First	10	13	1	231	38	19.25	-	-	11	-							
1-day Int																	
NatWest																	
B & H																	
1-day Lge	10	9	3	51	26	8.50	-	-	5	2							

69. How many balls did it take Ian Botham to reach his century at Headingley in 1981? Was it a) 87; b) 94; c) 110?

PRATT, G. J.   Durham

Name: <u>Gary</u> Joseph Pratt
Role: Left-hand top-order bat
Born: 22 December 1981, Bishop Auckland
Height: 5ft 10in
Nickname: Pratty, Gazza
County debut: 2000
1st-Class catches: 1
Parents: Gordon and Brenda
Marital status: Single
Family links with cricket: Father played
local cricket for Crook and Durham City.
Brother Andrew plays for Durham; brother
Neil plays for Darlington CC
Education: Crook; Willington Parkside
Qualifications: 8 GCSEs
Off-season: England U19 tour to India
Overseas tours: England U19 to Malaysia
and (Youth World Cup) Sri Lanka 1999-2000,
to India 2000-01
Cricketers particularly admired: Michael Atherton, Mark Waugh
Young players to look out for: Ian Bell, Nicky Peng
Other sports played: Football
Relaxations: Listening to music, socialising with friends
Extras: NBC Denis Compton Award 1999. On his first-class debut against Lancashire
at Old Trafford 2000, he and brother Andrew became the first brothers to play in a
Championship match for Durham. Represented England U19 v Sri Lanka U19 in one-
day and 'Test' series 2000
Opinions on cricket: 'Tea could be a bit longer.'
Best batting: 23 Durham v Kent, Riverside 2000

2000 Season

	M	Inns	NO	Runs	HS	Avge	100s	50s	Ct	St	O	M	Runs	Wkts	Avge	Best	5wI	10wM
Test																		
All First	2	3	0	39	23	13.00	-	-	1	-								
1-day Int																		
NatWest																		
B & H																		
1-day Lge																		

	M	Inns	NO	Runs	HS	Avge	100s	50s	Ct	St	Balls	Runs	Wkts	Avge	Best	5wI	10wM
Test																	
All First	2	3	0	39	23	13.00	-	-	1	-							
1-day Int																	
NatWest																	
B & H																	
1-day Lge																	

PRICHARD, P. J.   Essex

Name: <u>Paul</u> John Prichard
Role: Right-hand bat,
cover/mid-wicket fielder
Born: 7 January 1965, Brentwood, Essex
Height: 5ft 10in **Weight:** 13st
Nickname: Pablo
County debut: 1984
County cap: 1986
Benefit: 1996
1000 runs in a season: 8
1st-Class 50s: 97
1st-Class 100s: 28
1st-Class 200s: 3
1st-Class catches: 201
One-Day 100s: 6
Place in batting averages: 116th av. 27.67
(1999 83rd av. 32.76)
Strike rate: (career 144.50)
Parents: John and Margaret

Wife and date of marriage: Kate, 28 December 2000
Children: Danielle Jade, 23 April 1993; Alexander James, 16 August 1995
Family links with cricket: Father played club cricket in Essex
Education: Warley Primary School; Brentwood County High School
Qualifications: Advanced cricket coaching certificate
Career outside cricket: Sales and marketing with Ridley's Brewery
Off-season: Fitness training and practising
Overseas tours: England A to Australia 1992-93
Overseas teams played for: VOB Cavaliers, Cape Town 1981-82; Sutherland,
Sydney 1984-87; Waverley, Sydney 1987-92
Cricketers particularly admired: Malcolm Marshall, Allan Border, David Gower,
Mark Waugh, Greg Matthews

Young players to look out for: Steve Harmison, Paul Franks
Other sports played: Golf, football (Essex cricketers' team), tennis, badminton
Other sports followed: Football (West Ham United), rugby union
Relaxations: 'Watching football and rugby live, live concerts, good food and restaurants – all with the Mrs!'
Extras: Shared county record first-wicket partnership of 316 v Kent in 1994 and county record second-wicket partnership of 403 v Leicestershire in 1990, both with Graham Gooch at Chelmsford. Britannic Assurance Cricketer of the Year 1992. Essex joint Player of the Year 1993. Appointed Essex captain for 1995. Won the B&H Gold Award for his 92 from 113 balls v Leicestershire in the 1998 final at Lord's. Resigned as Essex captain at end of 1998 season
Opinions on cricket: 'Two divisions fantastic. Quality of cricket was better up to last session of last game. Congratulations to Test team for a great summer and for creating much more interest amongst youth and future sponsors of the game, as well as TV coverage.'
Best batting: 245 Essex v Leicestershire, Chelmsford 1990
Best bowling: 1-28 Essex v Hampshire, Chelmsford 1991

2000 Season

	M	Inns	NO	Runs	HS	Avge	100s	50s	Ct	St	O	M	Runs	Wkts	Avge	Best	5wl	10wM
Test																		
All First	17	31	3	775	96	27.67	-	5	10	-								
1-day Int																		
NatWest	2	2	0	26	26	13.00	-	-	-	-								
B & H	3	3	0	62	34	20.66	-	-	-	-								
1-day Lge	9	9	0	113	24	12.55	-	-	1	-								

Career Performances

	M	Inns	NO	Runs	HS	Avge	100s	50s	Ct	St	Balls	Runs	Wkts	Avge	Best	5wl	10wM
Test																	
All First	323	529	49	16633	245	34.65	31	97	201	-	289	497	2	248.50	1-28	-	-
1-day Int																	
NatWest	36	35	5	1138	94	37.93	-	9	14	-							
B & H	59	56	8	1542	114	32.12	2	8	14	-							
1-day Lge	196	177	10	4315	107	25.83	4	19	53	-							

70. Which future Australia captain scored 219 in Australia's first innings at Trent Bridge in 1989?

PRIOR, M. J.   Sussex

Name: <u>Matthew</u> James Prior
Role: Right-hand bat, wicket-keeper
Born: 26 February 1982, Johannesburg
Height: 5ft 11in **Weight:** 12st
Nickname: Aldrich, MP
County debut: No first-team appearance
Parents: Mike and Terri
Marital status: Single
Education: King Edward VII Prep School,
Johannesburg; Brighton College, East Sussex
Qualifications: 9 GCSEs, 3 A-levels
Off-season: 'Relaxing until Christmas, then
may go to Australia for a couple of months'
Overseas tours: Sussex Academy to Cape
Town 1999
Cricketers particularly admired: Steve
Waugh, Mark Boucher, Allan Donald
Young players to look out for: Krishana

Singh, Mike Yardy, Nicky Peng, 'all Sussex Academy players'
Other sports played: Hockey (Brighton & Hove HC), golf, squash
Other sports followed: Rugby (London Wasps, 'any team playing in the Super-12')
Relaxations: Listening to music, surfing, going out with friends
Extras: Has played for Sussex since U12. Has played for England since U14,
captaining England U17. Reserve for England U19 tour to India 2000-01. Played for
Sussex Board XI in NatWest 2000
Opinions on cricket: 'Too much playing, too little preparation and practice.'

2000 Season (did not make any first-class or one-day appearances)

Career Performances

	M	Inns	NO	Runs	HS	Avge	100s	50s	Ct	St	Balls	Runs	Wkts	Avge	Best	5wI	10wM
Test																	
All First																	
1-day Int																	
NatWest	1	1	0	3	3	3.00	-	-	-	-							
B & H																	
1-day Lge																	

PRITTIPAUL, L. R. — Hampshire

Name: <u>Lawrence</u> Roland Prittipaul
Role: Right-hand bat, right-arm
medium/occasional off-spin bowler
Born: 19 October 1979, Portsmouth
Height: 6ft **Weight:** 13st
Nickname: Lawrie, Throat, Toy Boy, Lozzer
County debut: 1999 (one-day),
2000 (first-class)
1st-Class 50s: 1
1st-Class 100s: 1
1st-Class catches: 1
Place in batting averages: 15th av. 49.66
Parents: Roland and Christine
Marital status: Single
Family links with cricket: 'Cousin
Shivnarine Chanderpaul plays for West
Indies. Father plays for Southsea. Mother
washes whites and sister played Hampshire
Juniors'

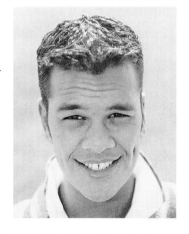

Education: Meon First and Middle School, Portsmouth; St John's College, Southsea;
Portsmouth College
Qualifications: 7 GCSEs, GNVQs, coaching awards, first aid
Career outside cricket: Writing for the *Evening News*
Off-season: 'Going back to sunny Cape Town to play for Milnerton CC'
Overseas teams played for: Milnerton, Cape Town 1999-2001
Cricketers particularly admired: 'My father', Carl Hooper
Young players to look out for: 'Deano' Wilson
Other sports played: Tennis
Other sports followed: Football (Portsmouth)
Relaxations: 'Spending time with girlfriend Kim. Listening to music – not hers
though'
Extras: Scored first century at age 13 for St John's College. Played for Hants Colts
from age 11 to 18; took 29 wickets and broke bowling record aged 11. Represented
England U17. Scored 185 for Hants U19 in 1998. Won Player of the Year award in
Southern League 1998. Has played for Hants 2nd XI since age 18; scored over 1000
runs for Hants 2nd XI in 1999. Scored 52 in first-class debut innings v Kent at
Canterbury, following up with maiden first-class century (152) v Derbyshire on home
debut at Southampton 2000
Opinions on cricket: 'Playing with Shane Warne this year – when he bowls for us the
lbw law should change, so you can be out if the ball pitches outside leg stump. Also,
only when the opposition bats, one hand/one bounce should come into it.'
Best batting: 152 Hampshire v Derbyshire, Southampton 2000

2000 Season

	M	Inns	NO	Runs	HS	Avge	100s	50s	Ct	St	O	M	Runs	Wkts	Avge	Best	5wI	10wM
Test																		
All First	4	6	0	298	152	49.66	1	1	1	-								
1-day Int																		
NatWest																		
B & H																		
1-day Lge	6	4	1	87	61	29.00	-	1	1	-	1	0	14	0	-		-	-

Career Performances

	M	Inns	NO	Runs	HS	Avge	100s	50s	Ct	St	Balls	Runs	Wkts	Avge	Best	5wI	10wM
Test																	
All First	4	6	0	298	152	49.66	1	1	1	-							
1-day Int																	
NatWest	3	3	0	66	30	22.00	-	-	3	-	156	125	4	31.25	2-53	-	
B & H																	
1-day Lge	8	4	1	87	61	29.00	-	1	2	-	6	14	0	-	-	-	

PYEMONT, J. P.   Derbyshire

Name: <u>James</u> Patrick Pyemont
Role: Right-hand top-order bat,
off-spin bowler
Born: 10 April 1978, Eastbourne
Height: 6ft **Weight:** 11st 7lbs
Nickname: Pumper, Pyeko, Pye, Pyemo,
Piggy, Pykethon
County debut: 1997 (Sussex),
1999 (Derbyshire)
1st-Class 50s: 4
1st-Class 100s: 1
1st-Class catches: 16
Place in batting averages: 157th av. 22.35
(1999 169th av. 23.41)
Strike rate: 325.00 (career 337.00)
Parents: Christopher and Christina
Marital status: Single
Family links with cricket: Father played for
Cambridge University and Sussex 2nd XI
Education: St Bede's School, Eastbourne; Tonbridge School, Kent; Trinity Hall,
Cambridge University
Qualifications: 9 GCSEs, 3 A-levels, BA (Hons) (Cantab), NCA qualified coach

Career outside cricket: Teaching
Off-season: Studying
Overseas tours: Sussex U19 to Barbados 1993; Cambridge University to Pakistan 1999; British Universities to South Africa 1999
Cricketers particularly admired: David Gower
Young players to look out for: Stephen Stubbings
Other sports played: 'Anything'
Other sports followed: Football (Brighton & Hove Albion)
Relaxations: Reading, films
Extras: Joined Derbyshire in 1999 from Sussex. 'Bagged a king pair on Championship debut on television.' Cambridge Blue 1998-2000 (captain 2000). Played in the Old Tonbridgians side that won *The Cricketer* Cup 1998-99. Represented British Universities 2000. Scored maiden first-class century (124) in the Varsity match at Lord's 2000
Opinions on cricket: 'Wickets should be prepared to ensure that the best possible cricket should be on offer both for the players and the crowd. Central contracts are an excellent idea.'
Best batting: 124 Cambridge University v Oxford Universities, Lord's 2000
Best bowling: 1-26 Cambridge University v Derbyshire, Fenner's 2000

2000 Season

	M	Inns	NO	Runs	HS	Avge	100s	50s	Ct	St	O	M	Runs	Wkts	Avge	Best	5wI	10wM
Test																		
All First	11	15	1	313	124	22.35	1	-	5	-	54.1	18	141	1	141.00	1-26	-	-
1-day Int																		
NatWest																		
B & H																		
1-day Lge	8	8	0	163	50	20.37	-	1	5	-								

Career Performances

	M	Inns	NO	Runs	HS	Avge	100s	50s	Ct	St	Balls	Runs	Wkts	Avge	Best	5wI	10wM
Test																	
All First	29	42	3	838	124	21.48	1	4	16	-	337	161	1	161.00	1-26	-	-
1-day Int																	
NatWest																	
B & H	5	5	0	74	25	14.80	-	-	3	-							
1-day Lge	16	16	1	218	50	14.53	-	1	7	-							

RAMPRAKASH, M. R. Surrey

Name: <u>Mark</u> Ravindra Ramprakash
Role: Right-hand bat, right arm off-spin
bowler
Born: 5 September 1969, Bushey, Herts
Height: 5ft 10in **Weight:** 12st 4lbs
Nickname: Ramps, Bloodaxe
County debut: 1987 (Middlesex)
County cap: 1990 (Middlesex)
Benefit: 2000 (Middlesex)
Test debut: 1991
Tests: 38
One-Day Internationals: 13
1000 runs in a season: 10
1st-Class 50s: 97
1st-Class 100s: 46
1st-Class 200s: 5
1st-Class catches: 170
One-Day 100s: 7
One-Day 5 w. in innings: 1

Place in batting averages: 16th av. 49.29 (1999 25th av. 42.24)
Strike rate: 408.00 (career 109.34)
Parents: Deonarine and Jennifer
Date of marriage: 24 September 1993
Family links with cricket: Father played club cricket in Guyana
Education: Gayton High School; Harrow Weald Sixth Form College
Qualifications: 6 O-levels, 2 A-levels
Career outside cricket: 'Any ideas welcome'
Overseas tours: England YC to Sri Lanka 1986-87, to Australia (Youth World Cup)
1987-88; England A to Pakistan 1990-91, to West Indies 1991-92, to India 1994-95
(vice-captain); Lion Cubs to Barbados 1993; England to New Zealand 1991-92,
to West Indies 1993-94, to Australia 1994-95, to South Africa 1995-96, to West Indies
1997-98, to Australia 1998-99, to South Africa 1999-2000
Overseas teams played for: Nairobi Jafferys, Kenya 1988; North Melbourne 1989
Cricketers particularly admired: 'All the great all-rounders'
Other sports followed: Snooker, football
Relaxations: 'Being at home with the family, going to movies, eating out'
Extras: Did not begin to play cricket until he was nine years old; played for
Bessborough CC at age 13, played for Middlesex 2nd XI aged 16 and made first-team
debut for Middlesex aged 17. Scored 204* in NCA Guernsey Festival Tournament and
in 1987 made 186* on his debut for Stanmore CC. Voted Best U15 Schoolboy of 1985
by Cricket Society, Best Young Cricketer of 1986 and Most Promising Player of the

Year in 1988. Man of the Match in Middlesex's NatWest Trophy final win in 1988, on his debut in the competition. Played for England YC v New Zealand YC in 1989. Won Cricket Writers' Young Cricketer of the Year award 1991. Finished top of the Whyte and Mackay batting ratings in 1995 and again in 1997. Appointed Middlesex captain during 1997 season after Mike Gatting stood down. Scored maiden Test 100 (154) v West Indies at Bridgetown 1997-98, sharing in a record sixth-wicket partnership for England in Tests v West Indies (205) with Graham Thorpe and receiving Man of the Match award. Achieved feat of scoring a century against all other first-class counties with his 128* v Glamorgan in 1998. Became the first player to score three 200s v Surrey with his 209* at Lord's 1999. Stood down as Middlesex captain at end of 1999 season. Leading run-scorer in the single-division four-day era of the County Championship with 8392 runs (av. 56.32) 1993-99. Scored two centuries in the match v Sussex at Southgate 2000 to become the first Middlesex player to record 100s in each innings of a game on four occasions; his 112 in the second innings was his 50th first-class century. Left Middlesex in the 2000-01 off-season and has joined Surrey for 2001

Best batting: 235 Middlesex v Yorkshire, Headingley 1995
Best bowling: 3-32 Middlesex v Glamorgan, Lord's 1998

2000 Season

	M	Inns	NO	Runs	HS	Avge	100s	50s	Ct	St	O	M	Runs	Wkts	Avge	Best	5wI	10wM
Test	4	7	0	95	56	13.57	-	1	6	-	1	0	1	0	-	-	-	-
All First	17	28	4	1183	120 *	49.29	4	7	15	-	68	18	148	1	148.00	1-11	-	-
1-day Int																		
NatWest	3	3	0	55	42	18.33	-	-	6	-								
B & H	1	1	0	6	6	6.00	-	-	-	-								
1-day Lge	12	12	2	408	61 *	40.80	-	3	5	-	17	2	56	0	-		-	-

Career Performances

	M	Inns	NO	Runs	HS	Avge	100s	50s	Ct	St	Balls	Runs	Wkts	Avge	Best	5wI	10wM
Test	42	74	6	1796	154	26.41	1	11	34	-	847	446	4	111.50	1-2	-	-
All First	287	473	62	19048	235	46.34	51	97	170	-	3499	1926	32	60.18	3-32	-	-
1-day Int	13	13	3	265	51	26.50	-	1	6	-	12	14	0	-	-	-	
NatWest	31	30	1	869	104	29.96	1	3	16	-	360	217	9	24.11	2-15	-	
B & H	41	40	8	1296	119 *	40.50	2	7	17	-	240	166	9	18.44	3-35	-	
1-day Lge	161	153	27	5120	147 *	40.63	4	36	52	-	481	425	15	28.33	5-38	1	

RAMSDEN, G.   Yorkshire

Name: Gary Ramsden
Role: Right-hand bat, right-arm fast bowler
Born: 2 March 1983, Dewsbury
Height: 5ft 10in **Weight:** 11st 7lbs
Nickname: Rambo
County debut: 2000
Strike rate: 72.00 (career 72.00)
Parents: Peter and Angela
Marital status: Single
Family links with cricket: Father plays for
local club, Moorlands CC
Education: Crowlees Junior School;
Castle Hall
Qualifications: 5 GCSEs, CSCA (leadership
award)
Off-season: Keeping fit, relaxing
Overseas tours: Yorkshire CCC to Singapore
and Perth 2000

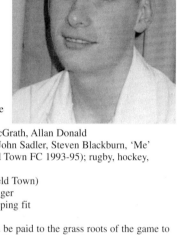

Cricketers particularly admired: Glenn McGrath, Allan Donald
Young players to look out for: Joe Sayers, John Sadler, Steven Blackburn, 'Me'
Other sports played: Football (Huddersfield Town FC 1993-95); rugby, hockey,
tennis, rounders, basketball – all at school
Other sports followed: Football (Huddersfield Town)
Injuries: Out for one week with a broken finger
Relaxations: Music, movies, socialising, keeping fit
Extras: Is a Yorkshire Academy player
Opinions on cricket: 'More attention should be paid to the grass roots of the game to
ensure that success can be obtained more regularly in the future.'
Best bowling: 1-32 Yorkshire v Derbyshire, Derby 2000

2000 Season

	M	Inns	NO	Runs	HS	Avge	100s	50s	Ct	St	O	M	Runs	Wkts	Avge	Best	5wI	10wM
Test																		
All First	1	1	1	0	0*	-	-	-	-	-	12	1	68	1	68.00	1-32	-	-
1-day Int																		
NatWest																		
B & H																		
1-day Lge	1	0	0	0	0	-	-	-	-	-	4	0	26	2	13.00	2-26	-	

Career Performances

	M	Inns	NO	Runs	HS	Avge	100s	50s	Ct	St	Balls	Runs	Wkts	Avge	Best	5wI	10wM
Test																	
All First	1	1	1	0	0*	-	-	-	-	-	72	68	1	68.00	1-32	-	-
1-day Int																	
NatWest																	
B & H																	
1-day Lge	1	0	0	0	0	-	-	-	-	-	24	26	2	13.00	2-26	-	

RANDALL, S. J. Nottinghamshire

Name: Stephen John Randall
Role: Right-hand bat, right-arm off-spin bowler
Born: 9 June 1980, Nottingham
Height: 5ft 10in **Weight:** 11st
Nickname: Rags, Raggio, Shag, Rago
County debut: 1999
1st-Class catches: 3
Strike rate: 132.00 (career 594.00)
Parents: Rob and Glenda
Marital status: Single
Family links with cricket: 'Dad played in local bucket bangers league'
Education: Heyman; The West Bridgford School; 'the year 2000 summer with my mates Bert and 80s Wayne'
Qualifications: 9 GCSEs
Career outside cricket: 'Any ideas welcome'
Off-season: 'Training hard; practising hard'
Overseas tours: England U17 to Bermuda 1997; Nottinghamshire to South Africa 1998, 1999, 2000
Cricketers particularly admired: Paul Franks, Eddie Hemmings, Mark Bowen, Tim Robinson
Young players to look out for: AJ Harris, Bilal Shifayat, Matt Whiley
Other sports played: Golf
Other sports followed: Football (Notts County FC)
Relaxations: 'Alexandra!'
Extras: Took part in the Christians in Sport millennium tour to South Africa, the aims of which included distributing cricket kit to disadvantaged youngsters, coaching and playing matches against teams in the townships

Opinions on cricket: 'Pitches should be good enough to make a four-day game last four days.'
Best batting: 20 Nottinghamshire v Glamorgan, Colwyn Bay 1999
Best bowling: 1-109 Nottinghamshire v Essex, Trent Bridge 2000

2000 Season

	M	Inns	NO	Runs	HS	Avge	100s	50s	Ct	St	O	M	Runs	Wkts	Avge	Best	5wI	10wM
Test																		
All First	1	0	0	0	0	-	-	-	-	-	22	2	109	1	109.00	1-109	-	-
1-day Int																		
NatWest																		
B & H																			
1-day Lge																			

Career Performances

	M	Inns	NO	Runs	HS	Avge	100s	50s	Ct	St	Balls	Runs	Wkts	Avge	Best	5wI	10wM
Test																	
All First	4	5	1	30	20	7.50	-	-	3	-	594	346	1	346.00	1-109	-	-
1-day Int																	
NatWest	1	1	0	1	1	1.00	-	-	-	-	60	43	0	-	-	-	-
B & H																	
1-day Lge																	

71. Who captained England in the first Test at Brisbane in 1990-91 in place of the injured Graham Gooch?

RASHID, U. B. A.　　　　　　　　　Sussex

Name: <u>Umer</u> Bin Abdul Rashid
Role: Left-hand bat, slow left-arm bowler
Born: 6 February 1976, Southampton
Height: 6ft 3in **Weight:** 12st 7lbs
Nickname: Umie, Looney, Bin
County debut: 1995 (one-day, Middlesex),
1996 (first-class, Middlesex), 1999 (Sussex)
1st-Class 50s: 7
1st-Class 100s: 1
1st-Class 5 w. in innings: 1
1st-Class catches: 11
One-Day 5 w. in innings: 1
Place in batting averages: 87th av. 30.78
(1999 106th av. 30.26)
Place in bowling averages: 135th av. 43.21
(1999 139th av. 44.26)
Strike rate: 89.69 (career 89.73)
Parents: Mirza and Sebea
Marital status: Single
Education: Southfield Combined First and Middle School; Ealing Green High; Ealing
Tertiary College; South Bank University
Qualifications: 7 GCSEs, 2 A-levels
Cricketers particularly admired: Carl Hooper, Aamir Sohail
Young players to look out for: Vikram Solanki, Owais Shah, David Nash,
David Sales, Anurag Singh
Other sports followed: Football (Southampton FC), Formula One motor racing
Relaxations: 'Chilling out with family and friends, playing Nintendo and computer
games. A keen reader of books by John Grisham'
Extras: Lord's Taverners' Cricketer of the Year 1994-95. Played England U19 against
South Africa in 1995. Played for the Combined Universities side in the B&H Cup.
Released by Middlesex at end of 1998 season and joined Sussex for the 1999 season.
Recorded maiden first-class five-wicket return (5-103) v Northamptonshire at
Northampton 2000. Scored maiden first-class century (110) v Glamorgan at Colwyn
Bay 2000
Best batting: 110 Sussex v Glamorgan, Colwyn Bay 2000
Best bowling: 5-103 Sussex v Northamptonshire, Northampton 2000

2000 Season

	M	Inns	NO	Runs	HS	Avge	100s	50s	Ct	St	O	M	Runs	Wkts	Avge	Best	5wI	10wM
Test																		
All First	15	22	3	585	110	30.78	1	4	6	-	343.5	84	994	23	43.21	5-103	1	-
1-day Int																		
NatWest	2	1	0	5	5	5.00	-	-	-	-	15	2	57	3	19.00	3-32	-	
B & H	4	3	0	12	6	4.00	-	-	2	-	27	5	121	2	60.50	2-25	-	
1-day Lge	15	12	1	147	34	13.36	-	-	6	-	94	2	446	15	29.73	3-38	-	

Career Performances

	M	Inns	NO	Runs	HS	Avge	100s	50s	Ct	St	Balls	Runs	Wkts	Avge	Best	5wI	10wM
Test																	
All First	27	42	6	1054	110	29.27	1	7	11	-	3410	1675	38	44.07	5-103	1	-
1-day Int																	
NatWest	4	2	1	29	24 *	29.00	-	-	-	-	192	144	4	36.00	3-32	-	
B & H	18	16	3	272	82	20.92	-	1	5	-	897	715	13	55.00	2-25	-	
1-day Lge	38	22	2	200	34	10.00	-	-	17	-	1540	1173	50	23.46	5-24	1	

RATCLIFFE, J. D.   Surrey

Name: Jason David Ratcliffe
Role: Right-hand bat, right-arm medium/off-spin bowler, slip fielder; all-rounder
Born: 19 June 1969, Solihull
Height: 6ft 4in **Weight:** 14st 7lbs
Nickname: Ratters, Fridge
County debut: 1988 (Warwickshire), 1995 (Surrey)
County cap: 1998 (Surrey)
1st-Class 50s: 38
1st-Class 100s: 5
1st-Class 5 w. in innings: 1
1st-Class catches: 68
One-Day 100s: 1
Place in batting averages: (1999 193rd av. 21.15)
Place in bowling averages: (1999 9th av. 17.93)
Strike rate: 59.00 (career 61.84)
Parents: David and Sheila
Wife and date of marriage: Andrea, 7 January 1995
Family links with cricket: Father (D.P. Ratcliffe) played for Warwickshire 1956-62

Education: Meadow Green Primary School; Sharmans Cross Secondary School; Solihull Sixth Form College
Qualifications: 6 O-levels, 3 A-levels, NCA staff coach
Career outside cricket: Sports PR and marketing
Off-season: Working for PCA management in London
Overseas tours: NCA (South) to Ireland 1988; Warwickshire to South Africa 1991-92
Overseas teams played for: West End, Kimberley, South Africa 1987-88; Belmont, Newcastle, NSW 1990-91; Penrith, Sydney 1992-94; Parramatta, Sydney 1999-2000
Cricketers particularly admired: 'Too many to name'
Young players to look out for: Joe Porter, Tim Murtagh
Other sports followed: Football (Birmingham City FC)
Relaxations: Music, reading, eating out
Extras: Has won three Championship winner's medals (Warwickshire and Surrey), a NatWest winner's medal (Warwicks), a Sunday League winner's medal (Surrey) and a B&H winner's medal (Surrey). Is treasurer of the Professional Cricketers' Association
Best batting: 135 Surrey v Worcestershire, Worcester 1997
Best bowling: 6-48 Surrey v Sri Lanka A, The Oval 1999

2000 Season

	M	Inns	NO	Runs	HS	Avge	100s	50s	Ct	St	O	M	Runs	Wkts	Avge	Best	5wI	10wM
Test																		
All First	2	4	0	28	26	7.00	-	-	2	-	9.5	2	46	1	46.00	1-21	-	-
1-day Int																		
NatWest	3	1	0	13	13	13.00	-	-	-	-	12	1	61	1	61.00	1-17	-	
B & H	4	3	2	45	24	45.00	-	-	-	-	22.5	3	79	6	13.16	3-15	-	
1-day Lge	13	9	4	107	42 *	21.40	-	-	5	-	89	3	354	10	35.40	3-39	-	

Career Performances

	M	Inns	NO	Runs	HS	Avge	100s	50s	Ct	St	Balls	Runs	Wkts	Avge	Best	5wI	10wM
Test																	
All First	135	242	13	6545	135	28.58	5	38	68	-	1608	897	26	34.50	6-48	1	-
1-day Int																	
NatWest	18	16	1	492	105	32.80	1	3	1	-	120	102	1	102.00	1-17	-	
B & H	16	13	3	170	41	17.00	-	-	6	-	185	121	8	15.12	3-15	-	
1-day Lge	70	60	8	1031	82	19.82	-	5	21	-	1102	842	22	38.27	3-39	-	

72. At Melbourne in 1998-99 Australia's second innings
lasted four hours. What was unusual about those four hours?

RAWNSLEY, M. J.   Worcestershire

Name: <u>Matthew</u> James Rawnsley
Role: Right-hand bat, slow left-arm bowler
Born: 8 June 1976, Birmingham
Height: 6ft 3in **Weight:** 12st 8lbs
Nickname: Scrawny, Dog
County debut: 1996
1st-Class 5 w. in innings: 3
1st-Class 10 w. in match: 1
1st-Class catches: 14
One-Day 5 w. in innings: 1
Place in batting averages: 288th av. 7.84
Strike rate: 136.00 (career 86.48)
Parents: Christopher (deceased) and June
Marital status: Single
Family links with cricket: 'Brother
sometimes turns out for Old Griffinians
RFC's cricket section's 3rd XI Sunday
irregulars'

Education: Northfield Manor Primary School, Birmingham; Bourneville Secondary
School, Birmingham; Brynteg Comprehensive, Bridgend
Qualifications: 9 GCSEs and 4 A-levels, NCA coaching award, qualified canoe
instructor
Overseas tours: Worcestershire CCC to Zimbabwe 1997
Overseas teams played for: Kumeu, Auckland 1995-96; Sunrise Sports Club, Harare,
Zimbabwe 1996-97
Cricketers particularly admired: Richard Illingworth, Dave Houghton
Young players to look out for: Vikram Solanki
Other sports played: Rugby (Old Griffinians RFC)
Other sports followed: Rugby
Relaxations: TV, eating
Extras: Set record for the most wickets at the Oxford Festival (27). Warwickshire U19
Player of the Year in 1995. Took ten wickets and scored 133 not out against
Gloucestershire 2nd XI in 1997. Recorded maiden Championship five-wicket return
(5-125) v Middlesex at Southgate 2000
Best batting: 26 Worcestershire v Essex, Chelmsford 1997
Best bowling: 6-44 Worcestershire v Oxford University, The Parks 1998

2000 Season

	M	Inns	NO	Runs	HS	Avge	100s	50s	Ct	St	O	M	Runs	Wkts	Avge	Best	5wI	10wM
Test																		
All First	9	13	0	102	18	7.84	-	-	5	-	204	55	573	9	63.66	5-125	1	-
1-day Int																		
NatWest	1	1	0	5	5	5.00	-	-	-	-	10	0	26	0	-		-	-
B & H																		
1-day Lge	3	3	2	13	5 *	13.00	-	-	1	-	21.5	2	90	5	18.00	3-31	-	

Career Performances

	M	Inns	NO	Runs	HS	Avge	100s	50s	Ct	St	Balls	Runs	Wkts	Avge	Best	5wI	10wM
Test																	
All First	27	33	4	299	26	10.31	-	-	14	-	3892	1798	45	39.95	6-44	3	1
1-day Int																	
NatWest	4	3	1	7	5	3.50	-	-	1	-	210	131	4	32.75	2-36	-	
B & H																	
1-day Lge	24	13	3	38	7	3.80	-	-	7	-	781	600	22	27.27	5-26	1	

READ, C. M. W.   Nottinghamshire

Name: <u>Christopher</u> Mark Wells Read
Role: Right-hand bat, wicket-keeper
Born: 10 August 1978, Paignton, Devon
Height: 5ft 8in **Weight:** 11st
Nickname: Readie, Little Eddie, Lambchops, Wells Road, Bouch
County debut: 1997 (one-day, Glos), 1998 (Notts)
County cap: 1999 (Notts)
Test debut: 1999
Tests: 3
One-Day Internationals: 9
50 dismissals in a season: 1
1st-Class 50s: 6
1st-Class 100s: 1
1st-Class catches: 163
1st-Class stumpings: 6
Place in batting averages: 143rd av. 23.95 (1999 183rd av. 21.76)
Parents: Geoffrey and Carolyn
Marital status: Single
Family links with cricket: Father played local club cricket and is an avid fan

Education: Roselands Primary School; Torquay Boys' Grammar School;
University of Bath
Qualifications: 9 GCSEs, 4 A-levels, senior coaching award
Career outside cricket: 'Unsure'
Off-season: England A tour to West Indies
Overseas tours: West of England U13 to Holland 1991; West of England U15 to West
Indies 1992-93; England U17 to Holland (ICC Youth tournament) 1995; England U19
to Pakistan 1996-97; England A to Kenya and Sri Lanka 1997-98, to Zimbabwe and
South Africa 1998-99, to West Indies 2000-01; England to South Africa and Zimbabwe
1999-2000
Cricketers particularly admired: Alan Knott, Bob Taylor, Jack Russell, Keith Piper,
Graham Thorpe
Other sports played: Hockey, table tennis
Other sports followed: Football (Torquay United)
Relaxations: Reading, listening to music, keeping fit and going out with friends
Extras: Represented Devon in Minor Counties Championship and NatWest in 1995,
1996 and 1997, the county winning the Minor Counties Championship three years
running. Played for England U18 against New Zealand U19 in 1996. Has also played
hockey for Devon U18 and U21 and for West of England U17. Played for England
U19 in the series against Zimbabwe U19. He was selected for the England A tour to
Kenya and Sri Lanka aged 18 and without having played a first-class game. Joined
Nottinghamshire for 1998 season. His 160 (his maiden first-class century) v
Warwickshire at Trent Bridge 1999 was the highest score by a Notts wicket-keeper for
more than 30 years. Recorded eight dismissals on Test debut in the first Test v New
Zealand at Edgbaston 1999. Made One-Day International debut v South Africa at
Bloemfontein, January 2000
Opinions on cricket: 'All One-Day International cricket is played over 50 overs with
a white ball, so why do we play two 50-over cup competitions with the red ball? Also,
in Test match cricket a new ball is taken every 80 overs. Why in our domestic county
game is it 100 overs?'
Best batting: 160 Nottinghamshire v Warwickshire, Trent Bridge 1999

2000 Season

	M	Inns	NO	Runs	HS	Avge	100s	50s	Ct	St	O	M	Runs	Wkts	Avge	Best	5wI	10wM
Test																		
All First	16	23	3	479	56 *	23.95	-	3	40	-								
1-day Int																		
NatWest	1	1	0	13	13	13.00	-	-	-	1								
B & H	4	4	0	39	15	9.75	-	-	2	-								
1-day Lge	16	13	3	124	29 *	12.40	-	-	25	2								

Career Performances

	M	Inns	NO	Runs	HS	Avge	100s	50s	Ct	St	Balls	Runs	Wkts	Avge	Best	5wl	10wM
Test	3	4	0	38	37	9.50	-	-	10	1							
All First	60	89	13	1777	160	23.38	1	6	163	6							
1-day Int	9	6	2	70	26 *	17.50	-	-	11	2							
NatWest	9	8	2	116	37	19.33	-	-	8	3							
B & H	4	4	0	39	15	9.75	-	-	2	-							
1-day Lge	42	34	6	565	62	20.17	-	1	53	5							

REIFFEL, P. R. Nottinghamshire

Name: <u>Paul</u> Ronald Reiffel
Role: Right-hand bat, right-arm fast-medium bowler
Born: 19 April 1966, Box Hill, Victoria, Australia
Height: 6ft 2in
Nickname: Pistol
County debut: 2000
Test debut: 1991-92
Tests: 35
One-Day Internationals: 92
1st-Class 50s: 15
1st-Class 5 w. in innings: 16
1st-Class 10 w. in match: 2
1st-Class catches: 71
Place in bowling averages: 76th av. 27.90
Strike rate: 66.71 (career 59.83)
Education: Jordanville Technical School
Overseas tours: Australia U19 to India and Sri Lanka 1984-85; Australia XI to Zimbabwe 1991-92; Australia to New Zealand 1992-93, to England 1993, to South Africa 1993-94, to Sharjah 1993-94, to West Indies 1994-95, to India and Pakistan (World Cup) 1995-96, to India 1996-97, to South Africa 1996-97, to England 1997, to India 1997-98
Overseas teams played for: Victoria 1987-88 –
Extras: Represented Victoria U16 and U19. Played league cricket in Lancashire for East Lancashire. Took 49 wickets in Victoria's Sheffield Shield winning season 1990-91. Prevented by injury from taking up his post as Northamptonshire's overseas player in 1998. Took his 200th wicket for Victoria v Western Australia at Perth 1998-99. Played in Australia's World Cup winning side 1999. Retired from international cricket in July 1999. Appointed captain of Victoria 1999. Returned match figures of 9-130 in the 1999-2000 Pura Milk Cup final. *Wisden Australia*'s Pura Milk Cricketer of the

Year 1999-2000. Joined Nottinghamshire as overseas player for 2000 as replacement for the injured Shoaib Akhtar; left Nottinghamshire at the end of the 2000 season
Best batting: 86 Victoria v Tasmania, St Kilda 1990-91
Best bowling: 6-57 Victoria v Tasmania, St Kilda 1990-91

2000 Season

	M	Inns	NO	Runs	HS	Avge	100s	50s	Ct	St	O	M	Runs	Wkts	Avge	Best	5wI	10wM
Test																		
All First	7	8	4	275	74	68.75	-	3	-	-	233.3	60	586	21	27.90	5-62	1	-
1-day Int																		
NatWest	1	1	0	19	19	19.00	-	-	1	-	10	0	52	0	-	-	-	-
B & H																		
1-day Lge	8	4	1	41	18	13.66	-	-	1	-	59	11	223	8	27.87	3-8	-	

Career Performances

	M	Inns	NO	Runs	HS	Avge	100s	50s	Ct	St	Balls	Runs	Wkts	Avge	Best	5wI	10wM
Test	35	50	14	955	79 *	26.52	-	6	15	-	6403	2804	104	26.96	6-71	5	-
All First	152	185	54	3231	86	24.66	-	15	71	-	30218	13288	505	26.31	6-57	16	2
1-day Int	92	57	21	503	58	13.97	-	1	25	-	4732	3096	106	29.20	4-13	-	
NatWest	1	1	0	19	19	19.00	-	-	1	-	60	52	0	-	-	-	-
B & H																		
1-day Lge	8	4	1	41	18	13.66	-	-	1	-	354	223	8	27.87	3-8	-	

73. Who made 56 batting with Ian Botham in England's second innings at Headingley in 1981?

RENSHAW, S. J.   Hampshire

Name: <u>Simon</u> John Renshaw
Role: Right-hand bat, right-arm
fast-medium bowler
Born: 6 March 1974, Bebington, Wirral
Height: 6ft 3in **Weight:** 14st 4lbs
Nickname: Rennie Arnoux, Toady
County debut: 1996
1st-Class 50s: 1
1st-Class 5 w. in innings: 1
1st-Class catches: 14
One-Day 5 w. in innings: 1
Place in batting averages: 258th av. 11.50
(1999 247th av. 14.42)
Place in bowling averages: (1999 123rd
av. 37.50)
Strike rate: 70.42 (career 69.93)
Parents: Michael and Barbara
Wife and date of marriage: Tracy,
26 September 1998

Family links with cricket: Father and brother play in local league competitions
Education: Birkenhead Prep School; Birkenhead; Leeds University
Qualifications: 9 GCSEs, 4 A-levels, BSc Microbiology, Grade 1 coach
Career outside cricket: Coaching
Overseas teams played for: Mulgrave, Melbourne 1995-96; Ashwood, Melbourne
1996-97
Cricketers particularly admired: Ian Botham, Viv Richards
Other sports followed: Football (Everton FC)
Relaxations: 'Away trips'
Extras: His 6-25 against Surrey in 1997 is the best bowling by a Hampshire bowler in
the Benson and Hedges Cup. Released by Hampshire at the end of the 2000 season
Opinions on cricket: 'Pitches around the country need to be better. From 2nd XI
one-day to 1st XI four-day, at out-grounds or Test grounds, there are too many sub-
standard pitches.'
Best batting: 56 Hampshire v Surrey, Guildford 1997
Best bowling: 5-110 Hampshire v Derbyshire, Chesterfield 1997

2000 Season

	M	Inns	NO	Runs	HS	Avge	100s	50s	Ct	St	O	M	Runs	Wkts	Avge	Best	5wI	10wM
Test																		
All First	4	7	1	69	26	11.50	-	-	1	-	82.1	22	219	7	31.28	3-23	-	-
1-day Int																		
NatWest																		
B & H																		
1-day Lge	3	2	0	1	1	0.50	-	-	-	-	17	1	75	2	37.50	1-19	-	

Career Performances

	M	Inns	NO	Runs	HS	Avge	100s	50s	Ct	St	Balls	Runs	Wkts	Avge	Best	5wI	10wM
Test																	
All First	39	48	20	459	56	16.39	-	1	14	-	6504	3580	93	38.49	5-110	1	-
1-day Int																	
NatWest	4	2	0	5	4	2.50	-	-	1	-	186	133	4	33.25	2-20	-	
B & H	12	8	3	28	23	5.60	-	-	2	-	708	532	21	25.33	6-25	1	
1-day Lge	39	22	14	178	27 *	22.25	-	-	2	-	1506	1291	44	29.34	4-40	-	

RHODES, S. J.   Worcestershire

Name: Steven (<u>Steve</u>) John Rhodes
Role: Right-hand bat, wicket-keeper
Born: 17 June 1964, Bradford, West Yorkshire
Height: 5ft 8in **Weight:** 12st 4lbs
Nickname: Bumpy, Wilf
County debut: 1981 (Yorkshire), 1985 (Worcestershire)
County cap: 1986 (Worcestershire)
Benefit: 1996
Test debut: 1994
Tests: 11
One-Day Internationals: 9
1000 runs in a season: 2
50 dismissals in a season: 12
1st-Class 50s: 65
1st-Class 100s: 11
1st-Class catches: 968
1st-Class stumpings: 113
Place in batting averages: 121st av. 26.86 (1999 167th av. 23.64)
Parents: William Ernest and Norma Kathleen
Wife and date of marriage: Judy Ann, 6 March 1993

Children: Holly Jade, 20 August 1985; George Harry, 26 October 1993; Lily Amber, 3 March 1995

Family links with cricket: Father played for Nottinghamshire 1959-64

Education: Bradford Moor Junior School; Lapage St Middle; Carlton-Bolling Comprehensive, Bradford

Qualifications: 4 O-levels, advanced coach, 'attended Bradford Management Centre for ECB – Coaching and Management Skills course'

Career outside cricket: Marketing department at Worcestershire CCC

Off-season: Marketing department at Worcestershire CCC. Blade tour to Barbados

Overseas tours: England A to Sri Lanka 1986, to Zimbabwe and Kenya 1989-90, to Pakistan 1990-91, to West Indies 1991-92, to South Africa 1993-94; England to Australia 1994-95; MCC to Kenya 1999; Blade Group to Barbados 2000-01

Overseas teams played for: Past Bros, Bundaberg, Queensland; Avis Vogeltown, New Plymouth, New Zealand; Melville, Perth, Australia

Cricketers particularly admired: Graeme Hick, Richard Hadlee, Courtney Walsh, Glenn McGrath

Young players to look out for: Paul Franks

Other sports followed: Horse racing and golf

Injuries: 'Niggles'

Relaxations: Horse racing

Extras: Played for England YC v Australia YC in 1983 and set record for most victims in an innings for England YC. Youngest wicket-keeper to play for Yorkshire. Released by Yorkshire to join Worcestershire at end of 1984 season. Set one-day record of four stumpings in an innings v Warwickshire in Sunday League at Edgbaston 1986. Was one of four players put on stand-by as reserves for 1992 World Cup squad. Writes a weekly cricket column for a Birmingham newspaper. One of *Wisden*'s Five Cricketers of the Year 1995. Overtook David Bairstow as the wicket-keeper with the most dismissals in the Sunday League. Made 1000th first-class dismissal of his career when he caught Graeme Swann off Alamgir Sheriyar v Northants at Northampton 1999. Equalled his own Worcestershire record for the most catches in a match with nine v Gloucestershire at Worcester 2000. Made the equal highest number of first-class wicket-keeping dismissals in the 2000 season (55 with Barry Hyam)

Opinions on cricket: 'Two division structure seems to be working. Central contracts: right idea and we can see the benefit – we all want England to be the best team in the world, but I do think that the England management have to be brave enough in saying "this guy rests and this guy needs to play" rather than deciding all play or all rest. They have to be sensible about central contracts, and I do not think they have been this in the 2000 season.'

Best batting: 122* Worcestershire v Young Australia, Worcester 1995

2000 Season

	M	Inns	NO	Runs	HS	Avge	100s	50s	Ct	St	O	M	Runs	Wkts	Avge	Best	5wI	10wM
Test																		
All First	18	28	6	591	103	26.86	1	1	54	1								
1-day Int																		
NatWest	2	2	0	43	43	21.50	-	-	2	1								
B & H	3	0	0	0	0	-	-	-	-	-								
1-day Lge	16	15	4	300	48 *	27.27	-	-	18	5								

Career Performances

	M	Inns	NO	Runs	HS	Avge	100s	50s	Ct	St	Balls	Runs	Wkts	Avge	Best	5wI	10wM
Test	11	17	5	294	65 *	24.50	-	1	46	3							
All First	382	541	142	13019	122 *	32.62	11	65	968	113	6	30	0	-	-	-	-
1-day Int	9	8	2	107	56	17.83	-	1	9	2							
NatWest	44	35	12	462	61	20.08	-	2	54	8	6	1	0	-	-	-	
B & H	69	47	8	575	51 *	14.74	-	1	90	10							
1-day Lge	245	155	43	2101	48 *	18.75	-	-	259	77							

RICHARDSON, A.　　　　　Warwickshire

Name: Alan Richardson
Role: Right-hand middle-order bat, right-arm 'windmill-like trundler'
Born: 6 May 1975, Newcastle-under-Lyme, Staffs
Height: 6ft 2in **Weight:** 13st
Nickname: Richo
County debut: 1995 (Derbyshire), 1999 (Warwickshire)
1st-Class 5 w. in innings: 1
1st-Class 10 w. in match: 1
1st-Class catches: 4
Place in bowling averages: 126th av. 38.51 (1999 45th av. 23.43)
Strike rate: 81.85 (career 65.41)
Parents: Roy and Sandra
Marital status: Single
Family links with cricket: 'Dad captained Little Stoke 3rd XI'
Education: Manor Hill First School; Walton Priory Middle School; Alleynes High School, Stone; Stafford College of Further Education
Qualifications: 8 GCSEs, 2 A-levels, 2 AS-levels, qualified senior cricket coach

Career outside cricket: 'Cutting grass'
Off-season: 'Holidaying in Australia, to include groomsman's duties for Chris
Feltham's marriage to Suzie. New Year in Cape Town in preparation for new season'
Overseas tours: Derbyshire to La Manga 1995; Warwickshire to Bloemfontein 2000
Overseas teams played for: Northern Natal, South Africa 1994-96; Hawkesbury CC,
Sydney 1997-99; Northern Districts, Sydney 1999-2000
Cricketers particularly admired: Angus Fraser, Jack Whelan, Andrew Power ('still
as dedicated as ever')
Young players to look out for: Jim Troughton, Mark Higgs, Brad Haddin, 'anyone
from Staffordshire'
Other sports played: Golf ('of sorts')
Other sports followed: Football ('a nutty, bordering on obsessional, Stoke City fan')
Injuries: 'Battled through gamely suffering in September' with ligament damage in
hip
Relaxations: 'Socialising, travelling (especially to Australia) and going to the gym
(honest!)'
Extras: *The Cricketer*/Slazenger Cricketer of the Month June 1991. *Cricket World*
award for best bowling performance in Oxford U19 Festival (8-60 v Devon). Topped
Minor Counties bowling averages with Staffordshire 1998 and won Minor Counties
bowling award. Most Improved 2nd XI Player 1999. Outstanding Performance of the
Year 1999 for his 8-51 v Gloucestershire on home debut; besides being the season's
best analysis, it was the best return by a Warwickshire player on debut at Edgbaston
Opinions on cricket: 'After complaining about wickets being too "sporty" we seem to
have gone too far the other way. Where's the fun if the wicket hasn't got inconsistent
bounce and extravagant sideways movement?! Let's get more results with the help of
seamers. Still far better than cutting grass, though.'
Best batting: 17* Warwickshire v Northamptonshire, Northampton 2000
Best bowling: 8-51 Warwickshire v Gloucestershire, Edgbaston 1999

2000 Season

	M	Inns	NO	Runs	HS	Avge	100s	50s	Ct	St	O	M	Runs	Wkts	Avge	Best	5wI	10wM
Test																		
All First	13	9	7	43	17 *	21.50	-	-	3	-	368.2	96	1040	27	38.51	4-69	-	-
1-day Int																		
NatWest																			
B & H																			
1-day Lge	3	1	0	0	0	0.00	-	-	-	-	23.2	1	109	4	27.25	2-34	-	

Career Performances

	M	Inns	NO	Runs	HS	Avge	100s	50s	Ct	St	Balls	Runs	Wkts	Avge	Best	5wI	10wM
Test																	
All First	20	18	10	56	17 *	7.00	-	-	4	-	3467	1639	53	30.92	8-51	1	1
1-day Int																	
NatWest	3	3	0	3	3	1.00	-	-	-	-	168	116	1	116.00	1-48	-	
B & H	3	2	1	2	1 *	2.00	-	-	-	-	72	48	1	48.00	1-16	-	
1-day Lge	6	2	1	11	11 *	11.00	-	-	-	-	249	194	7	27.71	2-16	-	

RICHARDSON, S. A. Yorkshire

Name: <u>Scott</u> Andrew Richardson
Role: Right-hand bat, right-arm medium bowler
Born: 5 September 1977, Oldham
Height: 6ft 2in **Weight:** 13st 9lbs
Nickname: Richo, Tickle
County debut: 2000
Parents: Mike and Anne
Marital status: Single
Family links with cricket: 'Dad is an ex-professional in local leagues. He owns Romida Sports (specialist cricket shop)'
Education: Hulme Grammar School, Oldham; Manchester Grammar School
Qualifications: 11 GCSEs, 2 A-levels
Career outside cricket: 'Work for Romida Sports'
Off-season: 'Working for Romida Sports'
Overseas tours: Manchester GS to Barbados 1993, to Cape Town 1995; MCC to Philadelphia 2000
Overseas teams played for: Easts-Redlands, Brisbane 1996-98; Redbank Plains, Queensland 1998-99
Cricketers particularly admired: Michael Atherton, Robin Smith
Young players to look out for: Michael Lumb
Other sports played: Golf, football
Other sports followed: Football (Manchester United), rugby league (Oldham)
Relaxations: Watching Man Utd and Oldham rugby league side; movies; playing golf
Opinions on cricket: 'I believe that 2nd XI cricket should remain because the step up from Board/league cricket to first-class cricket is far too big.'
Best batting: 11 Yorkshire v West Indians, Headingley 2000

2000 Season

	M	Inns	NO	Runs	HS	Avge	100s	50s	Ct	St	O	M	Runs	Wkts	Avge	Best	5wI	10wM
Test																		
All First	1	2	0	14	11	7.00	-	-	-	-								
1-day Int																		
NatWest																		
B & H																		
1-day Lge																		

Career Performances

	M	Inns	NO	Runs	HS	Avge	100s	50s	Ct	St	Balls	Runs	Wkts	Avge	Best	5wI	10wM
Test																	
All First	1	2	0	14	11	7.00	-	-	-	-							
1-day Int																	
NatWest																	
B & H																	
1-day Lge																	

RIPLEY, D.   Northamptonshire

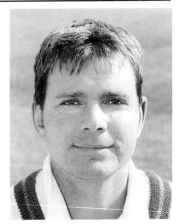

Name: David Ripley
Role: Right-hand bat, wicket-keeper, county captain
Born: 13 September 1966, Leeds
Height: 5ft 11in **Weight:** 12st
Nickname: Spud, Rips, Austin
County debut: 1984
County cap: 1987
50 dismissals in a season: 4
1st-Class 50s: 32
1st-Class 100s: 8
1st-Class 200s: 1
1st-Class catches: 634
1st-Class stumpings: 81
Place in batting averages: 81st av. 31.66
(1999 21st av. 42.68)
Strike rate: (career 30.00)
Parents: Arthur and Brenda
Wife and date of marriage: Jackie, 24 September 1988
Children: Joe David, 11 October 1989; George William, 5 March 1994; Charlie John, 10 March 2000
Education: Woodlesford Primary; Royds High, Leeds

Qualifications: 5 O-levels, staff coach, 'attending ECB Level 3 coaching this winter'
Career outside cricket: Cricket development officer for Northampton
Off-season: Working in Northampton as cricket development officer
Overseas tours: England YC to West Indies 1984-85; Northants to Durban 1991-92, to Cape Town 1992-93, to Zimbabwe 1994-95, 1998, to Johannesburg 1996, to Grenada 2000
Overseas teams played for: Marists and Poverty Bay, New Zealand 1985-87
Cricketers particularly admired: Alan Knott, Bob Taylor, Jack Russell 'and many other keepers', Clive Radley, Ian Botham, Dennis Lillee
Young players to look out for: 'Sales, Swann', James Foster, Monty Panesar
Other sports played: Football (locally), golf
Other sports followed: Football (Leeds United), rugby league (Castleford), golf, WWF wrestling ('admire The Rock'), 'local sports teams'
Injuries: Out for one week with a twisted ankle
Relaxations: 'Eating out, spending time with the family, improving my knowledge of Guinness and red wine'
Extras: Finished top of wicket-keepers' dismissals list for 1988 and 1992 and was voted Wombwell Cricket Lovers' Society Best Wicket-keeper 1992. Played for England YC v Sri Lanka 1986. Northamptonshire Player of the Year in 1988, 1997 and 1999. Put on 401 for the fifth wicket with Mal Loye v Glamorgan 1998, setting a new fifth-wicket partnership record for first-class cricket in England and registering a career best 209. Put on 293 for the seventh wicket with David Sales v Essex 1999, setting a new seventh-wicket partnership record for the county. Also shared in county record partnership for the eighth wicket, 164 v Lancashire in 1987 with Nick Cook. Lies second, behind K. V. Andrew, in Northants wicket-keeping dismissals list. Vice-captain of Northants 1999-2000. Appointed county captain for 2001
Opinions on cricket: 'Enjoyed the season with extra competitive edge. Wickets still not good enough for four days but getting better. England have a good team; get behind them.'
Best batting: 209 Northamptonshire v Glamorgan, Northampton 1998
Best bowling: 2-89 Northamptonshire v Essex, Ilford 1987

2000 Season

	M	Inns	NO	Runs	HS	Avge	100s	50s	Ct	St	O	M	Runs	Wkts	Avge	Best	5wI	10wM
Test																		
All First	13	18	3	475	56	31.66	-	3	38	4								
1-day Int																		
NatWest	3	2	0	6	4	3.00	-	-	4	1								
B & H	2	1	1	9	9 *	-	-	-	4	-								
1-day Lge	15	12	3	126	30	14.00	-	-	6	4								

Career Performances

	M	Inns	NO	Runs	HS	Avge	100s	50s	Ct	St	Balls	Runs	Wkts	Avge	Best	5wI	10wM
Test																	
All First	292	385	98	8212	209	28.61	9	32	634	81	60	103	2	51.50	2-89	-	-
1-day Int																	
NatWest	41	23	9	149	27 *	10.64	-	-	44	4							
B & H	49	32	13	392	36 *	20.63	-	-	55	6							
1-day Lge	167	103	43	1092	52 *	18.20	-	1	114	19							

ROBERTS, T. W. Lancashire

Name: <u>Timothy</u> William Roberts
Role: Right-hand bat, right-arm off-spin
bowler
Born: 4 March 1978, Kettering,
Northamptonshire
Height: 5ft 7in **Weight:** 10st 9lbs
County debut: No first-team appearance
Parents: David and Shirley
Marital status: Single
Family links with cricket: 'Brother Andy
was a leg-spinner at Northants for 10 years.
Dad Dave had trials for Northants'
Education: Our Lady's Convent, Kettering;
Bishop Stopford School, Kettering; Durham
University
Qualifications: 2.1 degree in Geology,
Level 2 cricket coach
Off-season: Training
Overseas tours: England U17 to Holland 1995
Overseas teams played for: Eastern Suburbs, Wellington, New Zealand 1999-2000
Cricketers particularly admired: Michael Slater, Ricky Ponting, Andy Roberts,
David Young
Other sports played: Golf, badminton, squash
Other sports followed: Football (Rushden & Diamonds FC)
Relaxations: 'A quiet beer with friends'
Extras: Played for British Universities v New Zealanders at The Parks 1999
Best batting: 49 British Universities v New Zealanders, The Parks 1999

Career Performances

	M	Inns	NO	Runs	HS	Avge	100s	50s	Ct	St	Balls	Runs	Wkts	Avge	Best	5wI	10wM
Test																	
All First	1	2	0	88	49	44.00	-	-	-	-							
1-day Int																	
NatWest																	
B & H																	
1-day Lge																	

ROBINSON, D. D. J. Essex

Name: <u>Darren</u> David John Robinson
Role: Right-hand opening bat, right-arm medium-fast bowler
Born: 2 March 1973, Braintree, Essex
Height: 5ft 11in **Weight:** 14st
Nickname: Pie Shop
County debut: 1993
County cap: 1997
1st-Class 50s: 19
1st-Class 100s: 6
1st-Class 200s: 1
1st-Class catches: 76
One-Day 100s: 3
Place in batting averages: 58th av. 35.06
(1999 120th av. 28.07)
Parents: David and Dorothy
Marital status: Engaged
Children: Kalli, 20 July 1998; Cameron, 20 May 2000
Family links with cricket: Father plays club cricket for Halstead
Education: Tabor High School, Braintree; Chelmsford College of Further Education
Qualifications: 5 GCSEs, BTEC National Diploma in Building and Construction
Career outside cricket: Site investigation and surveying
Off-season: 'Drinking beer with my mates'
Overseas tours: England U18 to Canada 1991; England U19 to Pakistan 1991-92
Overseas teams played for: Waverley, Sydney 1992-94; Eden Roskill CC, Auckland 1995-96
Cricketers particularly admired: Graham Gooch, Stuart Law
Young players to look out for: James Foster

Other sports followed: Golf, football, rugby, swimming
Injuries: Out for two and a half weeks with a broken finger; for seven weeks with a broken thumb
Relaxations: Reading crime novels, music, eating out, pubs
Extras: *Daily Telegraph* batting award 1988 and International Youth Tournament in Canada batting award 1991
Opinions on cricket: 'Two divisions has been a revelation for the game.'
Best batting: 200 Essex v New Zealanders, Chelmsford 1999

2000 Season

	M	Inns	NO	Runs	HS	Avge	100s	50s	Ct	St	O	M	Runs	Wkts	Avge	Best	5wI	10wM
Test																		
All First	12	19	3	561	93 *	35.06	-	4	5	-	0.3	0	8	0	-	-	-	-
1-day Int																		
NatWest																			
B & H																			
1-day Lge	5	5	0	101	51	20.20	-	1	2	-								

Career Performances

	M	Inns	NO	Runs	HS	Avge	100s	50s	Ct	St	Balls	Runs	Wkts	Avge	Best	5wI	10wM
Test																	
All First	89	155	7	4128	200	27.89	7	19	76	-	51	45	0	-	-	-	-
1-day Int																	
NatWest	14	12	1	247	62	22.45	-	2	5	-							
B & H	17	15	3	451	137 *	37.58	2	-	2	-							
1-day Lge	72	71	8	1685	129 *	26.74	1	8	22	-	17	26	1	26.00	1-7	-

ROBINSON, M. A.   Sussex

Name: Mark Andrew Robinson
Role: Right-hand bat, right-arm
fast-medium bowler
Born: 23 November 1966, Hull
Height: 6ft 3in **Weight:** 13st
Nickname: Jessy, Coddy, Scoope, Tiger, Stormy, Storm
County debut: 1987 (Northamptonshire), 1991 (Yorkshire), 1996 (Sussex)
County cap: 1990 (Northamptonshire), 1992 (Yorkshire), 1997 (Sussex)
1st-Class 5 w. in innings: 10
1st-Class 10 w. in match: 2
1st-Class catches: 40
Place in batting averages: (1999 296th av. 4.84)
Place in bowling averages: 110th av. 33.56 (1999 95th av. 29.95)

Strike rate: 85.50 (career 66.83)
Parents: Malcolm and Joan
Wife and date of marriage: Julia, 8 October 1994
Children: Samuel Lewis, 11 January 1996; Eleanor Grace, 20 July 2000
Family links with cricket: Grandfather a prominent local cricketer and 'father was hostile bowler in the back garden'
Education: Fifth Avenue Primary; Endike Junior High; Hull Grammar School
Qualifications: 6 O-levels, 2 A-levels, advanced cricket coach, badminton coach, rugby union coach
Career outside cricket: Self-employed cricket coach
Off-season: 'Coaching in Hull; spending time with my family'
Overseas tours: England U19 North to Bermuda; Yorkshire to Cape Town 1991-92, 1992-93, to West Indies 1993-94
Overseas teams played for: East Shirley, Canterbury, New Zealand 1987-89; Canterbury, New Zealand 1989-98
Cricketers particularly admired: Peter Moores, Keith Greenfield, Tony Cottey 'and any other player who lives for the game'
Young players to look out for: David Barrick, Steve Patterson, Matt Prior, Nick Wilton, Nick Hatch
Injuries: 'None – Osbourne just gets better'
Extras: Took hat-trick with first three balls of innings in Yorkshire League playing for Hull v Doncaster. First player to win Yorkshire U19 Bowler of the Season in two successive years, 1984 and 1985. Northamptonshire Uncapped Player of the Year in 1989. Endured a world record 12 innings without scoring a run in 1990. Sussex Clubman of the Year 1997 and 1998. Scored 500th first-class run on the same day as he took 500th first-class wicket v Surrey at Hove 1999. Was not out in ten successive innings during 1999-2000, equalling the record for county cricket
Opinions on cricket: 'Don't let the wolf in again.'
Best batting: 27 Sussex v Lancashire, Old Trafford 1997
Best bowling: 9-37 Yorkshire v Northamptonshire, Harrogate 1993

2000 Season

	M	Inns	NO	Runs	HS	Avge	100s	50s	Ct	St	O	M	Runs	Wkts	Avge	Best	5wI	10wM
Test																		
All First	9	11	8	19	8 *	6.33	-	-	3	-	228	77	537	16	33.56	3-88	-	-
1-day Int																		
NatWest	2	1	1	8	8 *	-	-	-	-	-	20	0	59	1	59.00	1-26	-	
B & H	1	1	0	5	5	5.00	-	-	-	-	5	0	9	0	-	-	-	
1-day Lge	15	6	3	16	15 *	5.33	-	-	1	-	116	7	460	18	25.55	4-23	-	

Career Performances

	M	Inns	NO	Runs	HS	Avge	100s	50s	Ct	St	Balls	Runs	Wkts	Avge	Best	5wI	10wM
Test																	
All First	214	242	104	548	27	3.97	-	-	40	-	34955	16586	523	31.71	9-37	10	2
1-day Int																	
NatWest	27	10	7	19	8 *	6.33	-	-	3	-	1800	982	36	27.27	4-32	-	
B & H	30	14	7	11	5	1.57	-	-	5	-	1666	986	35	28.17	4-53	-	
1-day Lge	156	58	25	104	15 *	3.15	-	-	15	-	6821	4871	146	33.36	4-23	-	

ROBINSON, R.   Durham

Name: Ryan Robinson
Role: Right-hand bat, right-arm
medium bowler
Born: 19 October 1976, Huddersfield,
West Yorkshire
Height: 6ft 1in **Weight:** 13st
Nickname: Robbo
County debut: 1999 (one-day)
Parents: Peter and Jennifer
Marital status: Single
Family links with cricket: 'Cousin coaches
local Stiffs CC'
Education: Emley First; Kirkburton Middle;
Shelley High and Sixth Form
Qualifications: 9 GCSEs
Overseas teams played for: Darling,
Cape Town 1994-95
Cricketers particularly admired:
Jacques Kallis
Young players to look out for: Nicky Peng
Other sports played: Football (Emley FC – Unibond Premier)
Other sports followed: Rugby league (Thornhill RLFC)

Relaxations: Golf and fishing
Extras: Released by Durham at the end of the 2000 season

2000 Season

	M	Inns	NO	Runs	HS	Avge	100s	50s	Ct	St	O	M	Runs	Wkts	Avge	Best	5wI	10wM
Test																		
All First																		
1-day Int																		
NatWest																		
B & H	3	3	0	97	68	32.33	-	1	-	-								
1-day Lge	4	4	0	10	7	2.50	-	-	1	-	6.1	0	30	1	30.00	1-17	-	

Career Performances

	M	Inns	NO	Runs	HS	Avge	100s	50s	Ct	St	Balls	Runs	Wkts	Avge	Best	5wI	10wM
Test																	
All First																	
1-day Int																	
NatWest																	
B & H	3	3	0	97	68	32.33	-	1	-	-							
1-day Lge	13	12	0	62	33	5.16	-	-	3	-	289	244	5	48.80	2-22	-	

ROLLINS, A. S. Northamptonshire

Name: <u>Adrian</u> Stewart Rollins
Role: Right-hand bat, right-arm medium bowler, occasional wicket-keeper
Born: 8 February 1972, Barking, Essex
Height: 6ft 5in **Weight:** 16st 10lbs
Nickname: Rollie, Blah-Blah, Unit, Eclipse
County debut: 1993 (Derbyshire), 2000 (Northants)
County cap: 1995 (Derbyshire)
1000 runs in a season: 3
1st-Class 50s: 37
1st-Class 100s: 11
1st-Class 200s: 1
1st-Class catches: 100
1st-Class stumpings: 1
One-Day 100s: 1
Place in batting averages: 123rd av. 26.50 (1999 43rd av. 38.60)

Strike rate: (career 90.00)
Parents: Marva
Marital status: 'Living in sin'
Children: Stepdaughter Gemma, 6 yrs; son, Jared Terrell, 1 June 1999
Family links with cricket: 'Brother [Robert] played for Essex 1991-99. Brother Gary should be playing. Uncles played in Essex League'
Education: Avenue Primary, Manor Park, London; Little Ilford Comprehensive, Manor Park, London
Qualifications: 10 GCSEs, 4 A-levels, NCA coaching award, Diploma in Sports Psychology, 'I am also doing a course in business management at present'
Career outside cricket: 'Living off the missus'
Off-season: Captaining Taranaki in New Zealand
Overseas tours: London Federation of Boys Clubs to Barbados 1987; Northants to Grenada 2000
Overseas teams played for: Kaponga, New Zealand 1993-94; Taranaki, New Zealand 2000-01 (captain)
Cricketers particularly admired: Phillip DeFreitas, Malcolm Marshall, David Gower, Viv Richards, Gordon Greenidge, Desmond Haynes, Michael Holding
Young players to look out for: Jared Rollins, Carl and Ryan Hurst, Mark Powell, Monty Panesar
Other sports played: Basketball, badminton (played for New Ham Schools), football, 'racketball master'
Other sports followed: Football (West Ham United), basketball
Relaxations/interests: 'Cuzza and Cookie are quite interesting'
Extras: Made Championship debut on same day as brother. Became 500th first-class player for Derbyshire, for whom he was named Young Player of the Year 1993. Was the 100th Derbyshire player to score a hundred. In 1995 set record for the highest score by a Derbyshire opener to carry his bat, and his 200 not out against Gloucestershire was the longest innings by a Derbyshire player. He became the youngest English-qualified Derbyshire double centurion. Voted Derbyshire Player of the Year for 1995. Took part in record third-wicket partnership for Derbyshire (316*) with Kim Barnett against Leicestershire 1997. Scored century before lunch against Glamorgan at Chesterfield August 1997. Left Derbyshire at end of 1999 season and joined Northamptonshire for 2000. Scored 100 and 96 v Middlesex 2000, failing by just four runs to become the first player since Graham Gooch in 1990 to score a century in both innings at Lord's
Opinions on cricket: 'Two divisions has worked. Great game. Team first every time.'
Best batting: 210 Derbyshire v Hampshire, Chesterfield 1997
Best bowling: 1-19 Derbyshire v Essex, Chelmsford 1995

2000 Season

	M	Inns	NO	Runs	HS	Avge	100s	50s	Ct	St	O	M	Runs	Wkts	Avge	Best	5wI	10wM
Test																		
All First	16	24	0	636	100	26.50	1	4	19	-								
1-day Int																		
NatWest	1	1	0	20	20	20.00	-	-	-	-								
B & H	1	1	0	1	1	1.00	-	-	-	-								
1-day Lge	6	6	0	71	28	11.83	-	-	3	-								

Career Performances

	M	Inns	NO	Runs	HS	Avge	100s	50s	Ct	St	Balls	Runs	Wkts	Avge	Best	5wI	10wM
Test																	
All First	117	211	18	6657	210	34.49	12	37	100	1	90	122	1	122.00	1-19	-	-
1-day Int																	
NatWest	12	12	0	298	80	24.83	-	3	8	-							
B & H	12	12	1	263	70 *	23.90	-	2	2	-							
1-day Lge	70	64	5	1084	126 *	18.37	1	1	29	-	12	15	0	-	-	-	-

ROSE, G. D. Somerset

Name: <u>Graham</u> David Rose
Role: Right-hand bat, right-arm
fast-medium bowler, first slip
Born: 12 April 1964, Tottenham
Height: 6ft 4in **Weight:** 15st 7lbs
Nickname: Rosie, Hagar, Yid
County debut: 1985 (Middlesex),
1987 (Somerset)
County cap: 1988 (Somerset)
Benefit: 1997 (£91,500)
1000 runs in a season: 1
50 wickets in a season: 5
1st-Class 50s: 41
1st-Class 100s: 11
1st-Class 5 w. in innings: 15
1st-Class 10 w. in match: 1
1st-Class catches: 116
One-Day 100s: 2
Place in batting averages: 43rd av. 39.23 (1999 46th av. 38.00)
Place in bowling averages: 101st av. 31.31 (1999 126th av. 38.64)
Strike rate: 68.79 (career 56.33)
Parents: William and Edna

Wife and date of marriage: Teresa Julie, 19 September 1987
Children: Georgina Charlotte, 6 December 1990; Felix William Michael, 11 August 1997
Family links with cricket: Father and brothers have played club cricket
Education: Northumberland Park School, Tottenham
Qualifications: 6 O-levels, 4 A-levels, NCA coaching certificate
Off-season: Working for Rowan Dartington Stockbrokers in Bristol and Taunton
Overseas teams played for: Carey Park, Bunbury, Western Australia 1984-85; Fremantle, Perth 1986-87; Paarl, Cape Town 1988-89
Cricketers particularly admired: Andrew Caddick, Jimmy Cook, Richard Hadlee, Malcolm Marshall, Mushtaq Ahmed
Young players to look out for: Matthew Bulbeck, Peter Trego
Other sports followed: Football, rugby, golf
Injuries: Out for two weeks with injury to left hamstring
Relaxations: Wine, golf, 'Georgina and Felix'
Extras: Played for England YC v Australia YC 1983. Took 6-41 on Middlesex debut in 1985, then scored 95 on debut for Somerset in 1987. Completed double of 1000 runs and 50 wickets in first-class cricket in 1990 and set records for fastest recorded centuries in NatWest Trophy (36 balls v Devon) and Sunday League (46 balls v Glamorgan; since bettered). Cricket Society's All-rounder of the Year 1997
Opinions on cricket: 'It will be interesting, to say the least, to see how the new over-rate penalties will affect Championship cricket and how games are approached and played. After all, promotion and relegation may well be decided by over rates as much as scoring runs and taking wickets.'
Best batting: 191 Somerset v Sussex, Taunton 1997
Best bowling: 7-47 Somerset v Nottinghamshire, Taunton 1996

2000 Season

	M	Inns	NO	Runs	HS	Avge	100s	50s	Ct	St	O	M	Runs	Wkts	Avge	Best	5wI	10wM
Test																		
All First	15	18	5	510	124	39.23	2	1	4	-	332.3	79	908	29	31.31	5-74	1	-
1-day Int																		
NatWest																		
B & H	2	1	1	15	15*	-	-	-	-	-	6	2	18	1	18.00	1-18	-	
1-day Lge	13	12	2	89	20	8.90	-	-	3	-	100	13	397	9	44.11	2-18	-	

Career Performances

	M	Inns	NO	Runs	HS	Avge	100s	50s	Ct	St	Balls	Runs	Wkts	Avge	Best	5wI	10wM
Test																	
All First	245	339	63	8628	191	31.26	11	41	116	-	33858	17713	601	29.47	7-47	15	1
1-day Int																	
NatWest	25	21	3	372	110	20.66	1	1	4	-	1366	889	29	30.65	3-11	-	
B & H	56	49	5	926	79	21.04	-	4	12	-	2968	1968	68	28.94	4-21	-	
1-day Lge	204	176	34	3624	148	25.52	1	18	51	-	8054	5934	198	29.96	4-26	-	

ROSEBERRY, M. A. Middlesex

Name: <u>Michael</u> Anthony Roseberry
Role: Right-hand opening bat, right-arm
medium bowler
Born: 28 November 1966,
Sunderland
Height: 6ft 2in **Weight:** 14st 10lbs
Nickname: Micky
County debut: 1985 (Middlesex),
1995 (Durham)
County cap: 1990 (Middlesex),
1998 (Durham)
1000 runs in a season: 4
1st-Class 50s: 56
1st-Class 100s: 21
1st-Class catches: 156
One-Day 100s: 6
Place in batting averages: 72nd av. 32.29
(1999 161st av. 24.15)
Strike rate: (career 127.75)
Parents: Matthew and Jean
Wife and date of marriage: Helen Louise, 22 February 1991
Children: Jordan Louise, 29 May 1992; Lauren Ella, 19 February 1994
Family links with cricket: Brother Andrew played for Glamorgan and Leicestershire
Education: Tonstall Preparatory School, Sunderland; Durham School
Qualifications: 5 O-levels, 1 A-level, Level 3 coaching
Career outside cricket: Director in family business
Off-season: Working in business; getting fit
Overseas tours: England YC to West Indies 1984-85; England A to Australia 1992-93;
England XI and Lord's Taverners to Hong Kong 'on numerous occasions'; MCC
to West Africa 1993-94; Durham CCC to South Africa 1994-95
Overseas teams played for: Fremantle, Western Australia 1986; Melville, Perth 1988;
Alberton, Johannesburg 1994-96
Cricketers particularly admired: 'Desmond Haynes for the obvious and his
generosity on the golf course'
Other sports played: 'Played rugby union at a good level when at school,
representing Durham County at all levels except the senior side'
Other sports followed: 'Follow golf and very loyal supporter of Sunderland FC'
Relaxations: 'Eating out and spending time with my family, which is limited during
the summer'
Extras: Won Lord's Taverners/MCC Cricketer of the Year 1983, Cricket Society
award for Best Young Cricketer of the Year 1984 and twice won Cricket Society award

for best all-rounder in schools cricket. Played in Durham League as a professional while still at school. At age 16, playing for Durham School v St Bees, he hit 216 in 160 minutes. In 1992 scored 2044 runs – joint highest in first-class cricket with Peter Bowler – and was named Middlesex Player of the Year and Lucozade Player of the Year. Left Middlesex at end of 1994 to return to his native Durham as captain for the 1995 season but relinquished the captaincy during the 1996 season. Rejoined Middlesex for 1999 season. Passed 3000 Sunday/National League runs v Glamorgan at Lord's 2000

Best batting: 185 Middlesex v Leicestershire, Lord's 1993
Best bowling: 1-1 Middlesex v Sussex, Hove 1988

2000 Season

	M	Inns	NO	Runs	HS	Avge	100s	50s	Ct	St	O	M	Runs	Wkts	Avge	Best	5wI	10wM
Test																		
All First	11	20	3	549	139 *	32.29	1	2	3	-								
1-day Int																		
NatWest	2	2	1	24	21 *	24.00	-	-	-	-								
B & H	1	1	0	3	3	3.00	-	-	1	-								
1-day Lge	6	6	0	193	72	32.16	-	2	2	-								

Career Performances

	M	Inns	NO	Runs	HS	Avge	100s	50s	Ct	St	Balls	Runs	Wkts	Avge	Best	5wI	10wM
Test																	
All First	225	384	41	11530	185	33.61	21	56	156	-	511	406	4	101.50	1-1	-	-
1-day Int																	
NatWest	20	20	2	727	121	40.38	3	1	7	-	36	42	1	42.00	1-22	-	
B & H	34	32	3	710	84	24.48	-	6	8	-	6	2	0	-	-	-	
1-day Lge	145	139	17	3933	119 *	32.23	3	30	52	-	4	7	0	-	-	-	

RUSSELL, R. C. Gloucestershire

Name: Robert Charles Russell
Role: Left-hand bat, wicket-keeper
Born: 15 August 1963, Stroud
Height: 5ft 8¼in **Weight:** 9st 9lbs
Nickname: Jack
County debut: 1981
County cap: 1985
Benefit: 1994
Test debut: 1988
Tests: 54
One-Day Internationals: 39

1000 runs in a season: 1
50 dismissals in a season: 15
1st-Class 50s: 79
1st-Class 100s: 8
1st-Class catches: 1078
1st-Class stumpings: 119
One-Day 100s: 2
Place in batting averages: 98th av. 29.65
(1999 82nd av. 32.91)
Strike rate: (career 56.00)
Parents: John and Jennifer
Wife and date of marriage: Aileen Ann,
6 March 1985
Children: Stepson, Marcus Anthony, 1980;
Elizabeth Ann, March 1988;
Victoria, 1989; Charles David, 1991;
Katherine Jane, 1996
Education: Uplands County Primary School;
Archway Comprehensive School; Bristol Polytechnic ('walked out after two months of accountancy course. Couldn't understand the sociology and economics – wanted to play cricket instead')
Qualifications: 7 O-levels, 2 A-levels
Career outside cricket: Professional artist
Off-season: Painting
Overseas tours: England A to Australia 1992-93 (vice-captain); England to Pakistan 1987-88, to India and West Indies 1989-90, to Australia 1990-91, to New Zealand 1991-92, to West Indies 1993-94, to Australia 1994-95, to South Africa 1995-96, to Pakistan and India (World Cup) 1995-96, to Zimbabwe and New Zealand 1996-97, to West Indies 1997-98, to Bangladesh (Wills International Cup) 1998-99
Cricketers particularly admired: Alan Knott, Bob Taylor, Ian Botham, Rodney Marsh 'and other greats'
Young players to look out for: Chris Taylor
Other sports followed: Football (Tottenham Hotspur), rugby (England), snooker, 'anything competitive'
Relaxations: Playing cricket and painting pictures. 'I love comedians and comedies. Life is too short, you need to laugh as much as you can'
Extras: Spotted at age nine by Gloucestershire coach, Graham Wiltshire. Became youngest Gloucestershire wicket-keeper (17 years 307 days) and set record for most dismissals in a match on first-class debut: 8 (7 caught, 1 stumped) for Gloucestershire v Sri Lankans at Bristol, 1981. Hat-trick of catches v Surrey at The Oval 1986. Represented England YC v West Indies YC in 1982. Was chosen as England's Man of the Test Series, England v Australia 1989 and was one of *Wisden*'s Five Cricketers of the Year 1990. Opened Jack Russell Gallery in Chipping Sodbury, South Gloucestershire, in 1995; his paintings are sold and displayed in museums and private collections all around the world. Books of his that have been published include *A*

Cricketer's Art – Sketches by Jack Russell (1988), *Sketches of a Season – illustrated by Jack Russell* (1989), *Jack Russell's Sketch Book* (1996) and *Jack Russell – Unleashed*, an autobiography which made the top ten bestsellers in 1997. He also has his own website: http://www.jackrussell.co.uk. Commissioned by Dean of Gloucester to do a drawing of Gloucester Cathedral to raise funds for 900th Anniversary. Still turns out for his original club, Stroud CC, whenever he can. Captain of Gloucestershire and Player of the Year 1995. Broke Bob Taylor's long-standing world record for the number of dismissals in a Test match with 11 (all caught) in the second Test v South Africa at Johannesburg 1995-96; his 27 Test dismissals in the series is a record for England. Awarded MBE in 1996 for services to cricket. Was the Whyte and Mackay wicket-keeper/batsman of the year 1995, 1996, 1997. Announced his retirement from international cricket in October 1998 after the Wills International Cup in Bangladesh. Became seventh wicket-keeper to take 1000 first-class catches when he caught Tim Robinson v Notts at Bristol 1999. Set a new NatWest dismissals record by claiming his 67th victim (Adrian Rollins) v Derbyshire at Bristol 1999. Man of the Match in Gloucestershire's NatWest final victory over Somerset 1999. Leading wicket-keeper in the single-division four-day County Championship era with 356 victims (335 caught/21 stumped) 1993-99
Best batting: 129* England v Boland, Paarl 1995-96
Best bowling: 1-4 Gloucestershire v West Indians, Bristol 1991

2000 Season

	M	Inns	NO	Runs	HS	Avge	100s	50s	Ct	St	O	M	Runs	Wkts	Avge	Best	5wI	10wM
Test																		
All First	16	23	3	593	110*	29.65	1	2	50	4								
1-day Int																		
NatWest	6	6	1	180	84	36.00	-	2	6	2								
B & H	7	4	3	19	12	19.00	-	-	6	2								
1-day Lge	16	15	6	310	55*	34.44	-	1	17	8								

Career Performances

	M	Inns	NO	Runs	HS	Avge	100s	50s	Ct	St	Balls	Runs	Wkts	Avge	Best	5wI	10wM
Test	54	86	16	1897	128*	27.10	2	6	153	12							
All First	425	632	132	15031	129*	30.06	8	79	1078	119	56	68	1	68.00	1-4	-	-
1-day Int	39	30	7	404	50	17.56	-	1	41	6							
NatWest	51	39	11	819	84	29.25	-	3	70	13							
B & H	76	56	21	1107	119*	31.62	1	4	76	15							
1-day Lge	241	190	44	3516	108	24.08	1	15	199	45							

SAGGERS, M. J.   Kent

Name: <u>Martin</u> John Saggers
Role: Right-hand bat, right-arm
fast-medium bowler
Born: 23 May 1972, King's Lynn
Height: 6ft 2in **Weight:** 13st 10lbs
Nickname: Saggs, Saggsy, Saggy Bits, Bits
from Hell, Sagaloo, Pony, Bruv, Wibs, Jerry,
Nazi, Hitler's Dream Child, Tank Driver
County debut: 1996 (Durham), 1999 (Kent)
50 wickets in a season: 1
1st-Class 5 w. in innings: 4
1st-Class catches: 6
Place in batting averages: 291st av. 7.58
Place in bowling averages: 22nd av. 20.14
(1999 3rd av. 16.00)
Strike rate: 44.77 (career 44.28)
Parents: Brian and Edna
Marital status: Single
Family links with cricket: Grandfather played in the Essex League
Education: Roseberry Avenue Primary School; Springwood High School;
University of Huddersfield
Qualifications: BA (Hons) Architectural Studies International
Career outside cricket: Architectural technician/consultant
Off-season: 'Lazing in the jacuzzi at Eastwell Manor all day, every day, with
occasional visits to the sauna and steam room'
Overseas teams played for: Randburg CC, Johannesburg 1996-98; Southern Suburbs,
Johannesburg 1998-99
Cricketers particularly admired: Allan Donald, Neil Foster, Darren Gough,
Terry Gammons
Young players to look out for: Robert Ferley, James Hockley, Darren Jordan
Other sports played: Golf ('improving slowly')
Other sports followed: Football (Tottenham Hotspur), British Touring Car
Championship, Formula One
Injuries: Out for three weeks in total with a sprained ankle (twice)
Relaxations: 'Going to the "Bat and Ball" for dinner. Beating Hockers and Kriss at
golf on the PlayStation. Annoying my housemates by listening to loud music'
Extras: Released by Durham at end of 1998 season and joined Kent. Took career best
7-79 against his old county, Durham, at Riverside 2000. Joint Kent Player of the Year
2000 (with David Masters)
Opinions on cricket: 'Best game in the world. The new two division system creates
competitive matches right through to the last game of the season.'

Best batting: 24 Kent v Derbyshire, Derby 2000
Best bowling: 7-79 Kent v Durham, Riverside 2000

2000 Season

	M	Inns	NO	Runs	HS	Avge	100s	50s	Ct	St	O	M	Runs	Wkts	Avge	Best	5wl	10wM
Test																		
All First	14	17	5	91	24	7.58	-	-	3	-	425.2	99	1148	57	20.14	7-79	2	-
1-day Int																		
NatWest																		
B & H																		
1-day Lge	6	4	3	13	10 *	13.00	-	-	2	-	46.4	3	187	13	14.38	3-22	-	

Career Performances

	M	Inns	NO	Runs	HS	Avge	100s	50s	Ct	St	Balls	Runs	Wkts	Avge	Best	5wl	10wM
Test																	
All First	26	35	10	219	24	8.76	-	-	6	-	4251	2109	96	21.96	7-79	4	-
1-day Int																	
NatWest	2	1	0	0	0	0.00	-	-	-	-	118	98	2	49.00	2-42	-	
B & H	5	5	3	58	34 *	29.00	-	-	2	-	246	247	5	49.40	2-49	-	
1-day Lge	19	10	7	44	13	14.66	-	-	5	-	802	554	30	18.46	4-35	-	

SALES, D. J. G.   Northamptonshire

Name: <u>David</u> John Grimwood Sales
Role: Right-hand bat, right-arm
occasional bowler
Born: 3 December 1977, Carshalton, Surrey
Height: 6ft **Weight:** 14st 7lbs
Nickname: Jumble, Grimmers, Johnny
Hartson, Peanut
County debut: 1994 (one-day),
1996 (first-class)
County cap: 1999
1000 runs in a season: 1
1st-Class 50s: 15
1st-Class 100s: 5
1st-Class 200s: 2
1st-Class 300s: 1
1st-Class catches: 53
Place in batting averages: 53rd av. 35.65
(1999 8th av. 51.64)
Strike rate: (career 33.66)

Parents: John and Daphne
Marital status: Single
Family links with cricket: Father played club cricket
Education: Cumnor House Prep School, Croydon; Caterham Boys' School
Qualifications: 7 GCSEs, cricket coach
Career outside cricket: 'Burning up golf courses!'
Off-season: Training, golf and fishing
Overseas tours: England U15 to South Africa 1993; England U19 to West Indies 1994-95, to Zimbabwe 1995-96, to Pakistan 1996-97; England A to Kenya and Sri Lanka 1997-98, to Bangladesh and New Zealand 1999-2000; Northants to Grenada 2000
Cricketers particularly admired: Graham Gooch, Darren Cousins
Young players to look out for: Jason Brown, Mark Powell
Other sports followed: Football (Crystal Palace), golf
Injuries: Injuries to knee and left thigh
Relaxations: Golf and fishing
Extras: In 1994, became youngest batsman (16 years 289 days) to score a 50 in the Sunday League with his 56-ball 70* v Essex at Chelmsford. Scored 210* v Worcs 1996 to become first Englishman to score a double century on his Championship debut and the youngest ever to score a double century. Became the youngest Englishman to score a first-class 300 (303*) v Essex at Northampton 1999 aged 21 years 240 days (and became the first Englishman to 1000 runs for 1999 in the process). PCA/CGU Young Player of the Year 1999. Scored 276 off 375 balls v Nottinghamshire at Northampton 2000. Took over temporarily as wicket-keeper from the injured David Ripley v Glamorgan at Cardiff 2000
Best batting: 303* Northamptonshire v Essex, Northampton 1999
Best bowling: 4-25 Northamptonshire v Sri Lanka A, Northampton 1999
Stop press: Was selected for the England A tour of West Indies but was flown home at the start of the tour with a serious knee injury

2000 Season

	M	Inns	NO	Runs	HS	Avge	100s	50s	Ct	St	O	M	Runs	Wkts	Avge	Best	5wl	10wM
Test																		
All First	13	20	0	713	276	35.65	1	5	9	-								
1-day Int																		
NatWest	3	3	1	101	65	50.50	-	1	2	-	2	0	13	0	-		-	-
B & H	2	2	1	64	64 *	64.00	-	1	-	-								
1-day Lge	15	15	5	547	84 *	54.70	-	5	5	-	4	0	17	0	-		-	-

Career Performances

	M	Inns	NO	Runs	HS	Avge	100s	50s	Ct	St	Balls	Runs	Wkts	Avge	Best	5wI	10wM
Test																	
All First	74	115	10	3710	303 *	35.33	8	15	53	-	303	163	9	18.11	4-25	-	-
1-day Int																	
NatWest	9	9	1	288	65	36.00	-	3	5	-	12	13	0	-	-	-	-
B & H	7	7	1	131	64 *	21.83	-	1	2	-					-	-	-
1-day Lge	62	58	10	1350	84 *	28.12	-	7	21	-	24	17	0	-	-	-	-

SALISBURY, I. D. K.   Surrey

Name: Ian David Kenneth Salisbury
Role: Right-hand bat, leg-break bowler
Born: 21 January 1970, Moulton,
Northampton
Height: 5ft 11in **Weight:** 12st 7lbs
Nickname: Solly, Dingle, Sals
County debut: 1989 (Sussex), 1997 (Surrey)
County cap: 1991 (Sussex), 1998 (Surrey)
Test debut: 1992
Tests: 12
One-Day Internationals: 4
50 wickets in a season: 6
1st-Class 50s: 16
1st-Class 100s: 1
1st-Class 5 w. in innings: 33
1st-Class 10 w. in match: 6
1st-Class catches: 150
One-Day 5 w. in innings: 1
Place in batting averages: 142nd av. 24.07 (1999 197th av. 20.76)
Place in bowling averages: 17th av. 18.92 (1999 32nd av. 21.91)
Strike rate: 43.90 (career 62.07)
Parents: Dave and Margaret
Wife and date of marriage: Emma Louise, 25 September 1993
Family links with cricket: 'Dad is vice-president of my first club, Brixworth. He also
re-lays cricket squares (e.g. Lord's, Northampton, Leicester)'
Education: Moulton Primary; Moulton Comprehensive (both Northampton)
Qualifications: 7 O-levels, NCA coaching certificate, 'life'
Off-season: England tour to Pakistan
Overseas tours: England A to Pakistan 1990-91, to Bermuda and West Indies
1991-92, to India 1994-95, to Pakistan 1995-96; England to India and Sri Lanka
1992-93, to West Indies 1993-94, to Pakistan 2000-01; World Masters XI v Indian
Masters XI November 1996 ('Masters aged 26?')

Overseas teams played for: University of New South Wales, Sydney 1997-2000
Cricketers particularly admired: 'Any that keep performing day in, day out, for both country and county (e.g. Saqlain, Martin Bicknell, Andrew Caddick, Steve Waugh)'
Young players to look out for: Ben Hollioake, Owais Shah, Alex Tudor, David Sales, Paul Franks, Steve Harmison, Luke Sutton
Other sports played: 'Most sports'
Other sports followed: Football (Southampton FC, Northampton Town FC), rugby union (Northampton Saints), 'any England team'
Relaxations: 'Spending time with wife, Emma; meeting friends and relaxing with them and eating out with good wine. Also, Sydney has its moments!!'
Extras: Picked to play two Tests for England against Pakistan in 1992, 'proudest moments of my career'. Originally selected for England A tour to Australia 1992-93 but was asked to stay on in India and played in the first two Tests of the series. In 1992 was named Young Player of the Year by both the Wombwell Cricket Lovers and the Cricket Writers. One of *Wisden*'s Five Cricketers of the Year 1993. Left Sussex during the 1996-97 off-season to join Surrey. Won the Bill O'Reilly Medal for Sydney first-grade player of the year 1999-2000, taking 36 wickets at 10.31 and averaging 40 with the bat playing for University of New South Wales
Opinions on cricket: 'Improve the standard of cricket pitches (e.g. ECB-contract groundsmen, so no doctoring of pitches).'
Best batting: 100* Surrey v Somerset, The Oval 1999
Best bowling: 8-60 Surrey v Somerset, The Oval 2000

2000 Season

	M	Inns	NO	Runs	HS	Avge	100s	50s	Ct	St	O	M	Runs	Wkts	Avge	Best	5wI	10wM
Test																		
All First	16	19	6	313	57 *	24.07	-	2	6	-	380.3	101	984	52	18.92	8-60	3	2
1-day Int																		
NatWest	3	1	1	21	21 *	-	-	-	-	-	26	1	91	1	91.00	1-30	-	
B & H	2	1	1	0	0 *	-	-	-	1	-	12	0	44	0	-	-	-	
1-day Lge	6	4	1	23	13	7.66	-	-	6	-	36.4	2	141	11	12.81	4-32	-	

Career Performances

	M	Inns	NO	Runs	HS	Avge	100s	50s	Ct	St	Balls	Runs	Wkts	Avge	Best	5wI	10wM
Test	12	22	2	284	50	14.20	-	1	5	-	2078	1346	19	70.84	4-163	-	-
All First	226	290	60	4315	100 *	18.76	1	16	150	-	40843	20542	658	31.21	8-60	33	6
1-day Int	4	2	1	7		7.00	-	-	1	-	186	177	5	35.40	3-41	-	
NatWest	28	17	5	164	34 *	13.66	-	-	5	-	1685	966	33	29.27	3-28	-	
B & H	36	21	8	169	19	13.00	-	-	14	-	1917	1355	43	31.51	4-53	-	
1-day Lge	128	85	22	790	48 *	12.53	-	-	45	-	4752	3942	116	33.98	5-30	1	

SAMPSON, P. J. Surrey

Name: <u>Philip</u> James Sampson
Role: Right-hand bat, right-arm fast-medium
bowler
Born: 6 September 1980, Manchester,
England
Height: 6ft 1in **Weight:** 14st
Nickname: Sammo, Boss Hogg
County debut: 2000 (one-day)
Parents: Les and Kay
Marital status: Single
Family links with cricket: Father played
league cricket and was chairman of the
Harlequins club, Pretoria. Brother was
captain of Northern Transvaal (Northerns) at
Youth level
Education: Waterkloof House Preparatory
School, Pretoria; Pretoria Boys High School
Qualifications: Matriculation (A-level
equivalent)

Career outside cricket: 'Haven't thought about that one yet!!'
Off-season: 'Playing club cricket in South Africa and working hard on my fitness'
Overseas teams played for: Harlequins, Pretoria 1999, 2000, 2001
Cricketers particularly admired: Allan Donald, Alec Stewart, Steve Waugh, Sachin
Tendulkar
Young players to look out for: Carl Greenidge
Other sports played: Golf, social football
Other sports followed: Football (Manchester United), Formula One motor racing
Injuries: Out for four to five weeks overall with side strain and torn tendons in ankle
Relaxations: Going to the theatre and movies, socialising with friends, listening to
music
Extras: Captain of school 1st XI 1998. Trophy for best all-round cricketer at school.
Represented Northerns at U15, U18, U19. Played for Buckinghamshire in the Minor
Counties 1999. Played for Surrey Board XI in the NatWest 2000
Opinions on cricket: 'Changing.'

---

74. Which Australian batsman finished his career with a
Test average at Lord's of 100.60?

2000 Season

	M	Inns	NO	Runs	HS	Avge	100s	50s	Ct	St	O	M	Runs	Wkts	Avge	Best	5wI	10wM
Test																		
All First																		
1-day Int																		
NatWest	1	1	1	4	4 *	-	-	-	1	-	10	2	26	0	-		-	-
B & H																		
1-day Lge	2	1	0	4	4	4.00	-	-	-	-	12	0	67	0	-		-	-

Career Performances

	M	Inns	NO	Runs	HS	Avge	100s	50s	Ct	St	Balls	Runs	Wkts	Avge	Best	5wI	10wM
Test																	
All First																	
1-day Int																	
NatWest	1	1	1	4	4 *	-	-	-	1	-	60	26	0	-		-	-
B & H																	
1-day Lge	2	1	0	4	4	4.00	-	-	-	-	72	67	0	-		-	-

SAQLAIN MUSHTAQ　　　　　　Surrey

Name: Saqlain Mushtaq
Role: Right-hand bat, off-spin bowler
Born: 29 December 1976, Lahore, Pakistan
Height: 5ft 9in **Weight:** 11st 4lbs
Nickname: Saqi, Baba
County debut: 1997
County cap: 1998
Test debut: 1995-96
Tests: 28
One-Day Internationals: 124
50 wickets in a season: 3
1st-Class 50s: 6
1st-Class 5 w. in innings: 40
1st-Class 10 w. in match: 12
1st-Class catches: 45
One-Day 5 w. in innings: 5
Place in batting averages: 196th av. 18.08
Place in bowling averages: 5th av. 15.39
(1999 1st av. 11.37)
Strike rate: 41.03 (career 49.78)
Parents: Nasim Akhtar and Mushtaq Ahmed
Wife and date of marriage: Sana ('Sunny') Saqlain, 11 April 2000

Education: Lahore MAO College

Career outside cricket: 'Looking after the wife'

Off-season: 'In October Pakistan are touring Kenya for the ICC Knockout Trophy tournament, then England are coming to Pakistan'

Overseas tours: Pakistan to Australia 1995-96, to Sharjah 1995-96, 1996-97, 1997-98, to Singapore 1995-96, to England 1996, to Sri Lanka 1996-97, to Toronto and Nairobi 1996-97, to Australia 1996-97, to India 1996-97, to South Africa 1997-98, to Zimbabwe 1997-98, to Sri Lanka 1997-98, to Toronto 1997-98, 1998-99, to Bangladesh 1998-99, to India 1998-99, to UK, Ireland and Holland (World Cup) 1999, to Australia 1999-2000, to West Indies 1999-2000, to Kenya (ICC Knockout Trophy) 2000-01

Overseas teams played for: PIA, Islamabad 1994-1998

Cricketers particularly admired: Imran Khan, Wasim Akram, Waqar Younis

Young players to look out for: Younis Khan, Shoaib Malik

Other sports played: Squash

Other sports followed: Hockey (Pakistan), football (Manchester United and Arsenal)

Injuries: Knee injury; 'no time off for the wicked'

Relaxations: 'I would like to go on a month's holiday to America with my wife. I like listening to music when free or travelling'

Extras: Won Man of the Series award in 1998-99 Test series v India. Took only the second hat-trick in World Cup cricket, v Zimbabwe at The Oval 1999; his victims were Olonga, Huckle and Mbangwa; it was his second hat-trick in One-Day Internationals v Zimbabwe. Took the fifth hat-trick of his career, for Surrey v Sussex at Hove 1999. Topped the first-class bowling averages in 1999, taking 58 wickets at an astonishing average of 11.37 in the seven games he played for Surrey. One of *Wisden*'s Five Cricketers of the Year 2000. Played for an Asia XI v a World XI at The Oval 2000. Took 7-11 from 9.3 overs (including a spell of 7-5 in 34 balls) v Derbyshire at The Oval 2000

Opinions on cricket: 'The cricket nowadays is a lot more modernised than it was two years ago. It has become a very fast, quick and active game. It really has changed what with things such as five points being deducted if the umpire thinks there is cheating going on or if you misbehave towards the umpire. Also there are free hits (different).'

Best batting: 79 Pakistan v Zimbabwe, Sheikhupura 1996-97

Best bowling: 8-65 Surrey v Derbyshire, The Oval 1998

Stop press: Returned his best One-Day International figures (5-20) in the third One-Day International v England at Rawalpindi 2000-01, winning the Man of the Match award. Took 8-164 (all eight wickets to fall) from 74 overs in England's first innings in the first Test at Lahore 2000-01, winning the Man of the Match award

75. Which fast-bowling legend took his 200th Test wicket at Edgbaston in 1985?

2000 Season

	M	Inns	NO	Runs	HS	Avge	100s	50s	Ct	St	O	M	Runs	Wkts	Avge	Best	5wI	10wM
Test																		
All First	12	14	2	217	66	18.08	-	2	8	-	451.2	127	1016	66	15.39	7-11	6	2
1-day Int																		
NatWest	3	0	0	0	0	-	-	-	1	-	27	1	96	3	32.00	2-36	-	
B & H																		
1-day Lge	9	4	3	15	7 *	15.00	-	-	2	-	77	10	260	18	14.44	3-12	-	

Career Performances

	M	Inns	NO	Runs	HS	Avge	100s	50s	Ct	St	Balls	Runs	Wkts	Avge	Best	5wI	10wM
Test	28	45	10	479	79	13.68	-	2	11	-	8122	3530	116	30.43	6-46	10	2
All First	100	142	39	1535	79	14.90	-	6	45	-	23451	9738	471	20.67	8-65	40	12
1-day Int	124	74	26	611	37 *	12.72	-	-	32	-	6491	4614	227	20.32	5-29	5	
NatWest	11	3	2	15	6 *	15.00	-	-	1	-	655	353	25	14.12	4-17	-	
B & H	7	3	1	18	11	9.00	-	-	2	-	382	247	10	24.70	4-46	-	
1-day Lge	27	15	6	99	29 *	11.00	-	-	6	-	1168	782	39	20.05	3-12	-	

SAVIDENT, L.   Hampshire

Name: Lee Savident
Role: Right-hand bat, right-arm
medium bowler
Born: 22 October 1976, Guernsey
Height: 6ft 5in **Weight:** 15st 10lbs
Nickname: Sav, Frenchman
County debut: 1997
1st-Class catches: 2
Strike rate: (career 96.00)
Parents: Nev and Sue
Marital status: Single ('occupied')
Education: Castel Primary School; Grammar
School, Guernsey; Guernsey College of
Further Education
Qualifications: 5 GCSEs and 1 A-level
Overseas teams played for: Glenwood Old
Boys, Durban, South Africa 1997-99
Cricketers particularly admired:
Malcolm Marshall, Darren Gough
Young players to look out for: Si Francis, James Adams
Other sports played: Football, golf
Other sports followed: Football (Tottenham Hotspur)

Relaxations: Playing golf; watching football
Extras: First person from the Channel Islands to play first-class cricket. Retired at the end of the 2000 season
Opinions on cricket: 'Changing.'
Best batting: 10* Hampshire v Zimbabweans, Southampton 2000
Best bowling: 2-86 Hampshire v Yorkshire, Portsmouth 1997

2000 Season

	M	Inns	NO	Runs	HS	Avge	100s	50s	Ct	St	O	M	Runs	Wkts	Avge	Best	5wl	10wM
Test																		
All First	1	2	1	17	10 *	17.00	-	-	1	-	8	0	39	0	-		-	-
1-day Int																		
NatWest																		
B & H																		
1-day Lge	3	3	0	34	25	11.33	-	-	-	-	7	1	20	0	-		-	-

Career Performances

	M	Inns	NO	Runs	HS	Avge	100s	50s	Ct	St	Balls	Runs	Wkts	Avge	Best	5wl	10wM
Test																	
All First	4	6	2	32	10 *	8.00	-	-	2	-	384	286	4	71.50	2-86	-	-
1-day Int																	
NatWest																	
B & H																	
1-day Lge	8	7	2	94	39	18.80	-	-	1	-	157	124	6	20.66	3-41	-	

SAXELBY, M.   Derbyshire

Name: Mark Saxelby
Role: Left-hand bat, right-arm medium bowler
Born: 4 January 1969, Newark
Height: 6ft 4in **Weight:** 16st 7lbs
Nickname: Sax
County debut: 1989 (Nottinghamshire), 1994 (Durham), 2000 (Derbyshire)
1000 runs in a season: 1
1st-Class 50s: 17
1st-Class 100s: 2
1st-Class catches: 18
One-Day 100s: 1
Strike rate: (career 119.27)
Parents: Ken and Margaret
Family links with cricket: Brother Kevin played for Notts; father played local cricket
Education: Nottingham High School; Nottingham University

Qualifications: 7 O-levels, 2 A-levels
Overseas teams played for: Hutt CC,
New Zealand 1989-91
Cricketers particularly admired:
Derek Randall
Other sports followed: Most sports,
especially rugby
Relaxations: Cinema, pubs, walking
Extras: Released by Durham at the end of
the 1995 season. Was club professional with
Heanor Town in the Derbyshire Premier
League, scoring 2600 runs in his two seasons
with the club at an average of more than 60;
his seven centuries included a 93-ball 145 v
Ilkeston. Played for Nottinghamshire Board
XI in the NatWest 2000. Played one County
Championship match for Derbyshire v
Lancashire in 2000
Best batting: 181 Durham v Derbyshire, Chesterfield 1994
Best bowling: 3-41 Nottinghamshire v Derbyshire, Derby 1991
Note: Mark Saxelby died on 12 October 2000

2000 Season

	M	Inns	NO	Runs	HS	Avge	100s	50s	Ct	St	O	M	Runs	Wkts	Avge	Best	5wI	10wM
Test																		
All First	1	2	0	23	17	11.50	-	-	-	-								
1-day Int																		
NatWest	1	1	0	23	23	23.00	-	-	-	-								
B & H																		
1-day Lge																		

Career Performances

	M	Inns	NO	Runs	HS	Avge	100s	50s	Ct	St	Balls	Runs	Wkts	Avge	Best	5wI	10wM
Test																	
All First	61	106	7	2916	181	29.45	2	17	18	-	1312	903	11	82.09	3-41	-	-
1-day Int																	
NatWest	9	9	1	163	41	20.37	-	-	2	-	220	176	5	35.20	2-42	-	
B & H	10	8	1	151	80 *	21.57	-	1	-	-	198	146	1	146.00	1-36	-	
1-day Lge	58	48	7	1118	100 *	27.26	1	5	11	-	1014	878	25	35.12	4-29	-	

SCHOFIELD, C. P.   Lancashire

Name: <u>Chris</u> Paul Schofield
Role: Left-hand bat, leg-break bowler
Born: 6 October 1978, Birch Hill,
Wardle, Rochdale
Height: 6ft 1in **Weight:** 11st 5lbs
Nickname: Scoey, Junior, Scoffer
County debut: 1998
Test debut: 2000
Tests: 2
1st-Class 50s: 7
1st-Class 5 w. in innings: 4
1st-Class catches: 17
Place in batting averages: 124th av. 26.40
(1999 198th av. 20.50)
Place in bowling averages: 80th av. 28.25
(1999 109th av. 32.79)
Strike rate: 57.53 (career 58.56)
Parents: David and Judith
Marital status: Single

Family links with cricket: Father played with local club team Whittles and brother
plays with local team Littleborough
Education: St John's; Wardle High School
Qualifications: 4 GCSEs, NVQ Levels 2 and 3 in Information Technology
Off-season: Touring West Indies with England A
Overseas tours: England U17 to Bermuda 1997; England U19 to South Africa
(including Youth World Cup) 1997-98; England A to Bangladesh and New Zealand
1999-2000, to West Indies 2000-01
Cricketers particularly admired: Shane Warne, Stuart Law
Young players to look out for: Graeme Swann, Robert Key
Other sports played: Football (Littleborough FC, Whittles FC), snooker (Wardle Con
Club – handicap of four)
Other sports followed: Football ('like watching Liverpool FC')
Relaxations: Listening to music, playing snooker, socialising
Extras: Was part of England U19 World Cup winning squad 1997-98. Won double
twice in two years with Littleborough CC (Wood Cup and Lancashire Cup 1997;
League and Wood Cup 1998). Awarded 2nd XI cap 1998. Won Sir Ron
Brierley/Crusaders Scholarship 1998. NBC Denis Compton Award 1999. Was the only
uncapped player to be contracted to England in 2000. Made Test debut in first Test v
Zimbabwe at Lord's 2000 but did not get a bowl as Gough, Caddick and Giddins
bowled the opposition out twice

Best batting: 74 England A v Central Districts, Palmerston North 1999-2000
Best bowling: 6-120 England A v Bangladesh, Chittagong 1999-2000

2000 Season

	M	Inns	NO	Runs	HS	Avge	100s	50s	Ct	St	O	M	Runs	Wkts	Avge	Best	5wI	10wM
Test	2	3	0	67	57	22.33	-	1	-	-	18	2	73	0	-	-	-	-
All First	17	22	2	528	70 *	26.40	-	4	6	-	374	80	1102	39	28.25	5-48	1	-
1-day Int																		
NatWest	4	1	0	1	1	1.00	-	-	2	-	37	1	166	11	15.09	4-34	-	
B & H	3	3	0	42	23	14.00	-	-	-	-	27	2	104	7	14.85	4-34	-	
1-day Lge	12	9	2	125	34	17.85	-	-	1	-	89.5	2	439	11	39.90	2-37	-	

Career Performances

	M	Inns	NO	Runs	HS	Avge	100s	50s	Ct	St	Balls	Runs	Wkts	Avge	Best	5wI	10wM
Test	2	3	0	67	57	22.33	-	1	-	-	108	73	0	-	-	-	-
All First	35	47	8	1074	74	27.53	-	7	17	-	5915	2960	101	29.30	6-120	4	-
1-day Int																	
NatWest	4	1	0	1	1	1.00	-	-	2	-	222	166	11	15.09	4-34	-	
B & H	3	3	0	42	23	14.00	-	-	-	-	162	104	7	14.85	4-34	-	
1-day Lge	14	11	2	158	34	17.55	-	-	1	-	593	471	13	36.23	2-32	-	

SCOTT, B. J. M. Surrey

Name: Benjamin (Ben) James Matthew Scott
Role: Right-hand bat, wicket-keeper
Born: 4 August 1981, Isleworth, Middlesex
Height: 5ft 8in **Weight:** 11st 3lbs
Nickname: Scotty, Head
County debut: No first-team appearance
Parents: Terry and Edna
Marital status: Single
Family links with cricket: Father and brother played club cricket
Education: Chatsworth School, Hounslow; Whitton School, Richmond; Richmond College
Qualifications: 9 GCSEs, 3 A-levels, ECB Level 1, YMCA Fitness Instructor's Award
Off-season: 'Overseas'
Overseas tours: MCC YC to South Africa 2000

Overseas teams played for: Portland CC, Victoria, Australia 1999-2000
Cricketers particularly admired: Alec Stewart, Alan Knott, Steve Waugh, Justin Langer
Young players to look out for: Alan Colman, Chad Keegan, Nick Compton
Other sports played: Football, squash, swimming
Other sports followed: Football (Man Utd)
Relaxations: Music, piano/guitar, socialising
Extras: Middlesex YC cap. Finchley CC Player of the Season 2000. Represented ESCA U14 and U15. Played for Development of Excellence XI v Australia U19 1999. Played for Middlesex Board XI in the NatWest 1999
Opinions on cricket: 'The skill level in cricket has reached such a level that the only dividing factor between sides and cricketers is their mental toughness.'

2000 Season (did not make any first-class or one-day appearances)

Career Performances

	M	Inns	NO	Runs	HS	Avge	100s	50s	Ct	St	Balls	Runs	Wkts	Avge	Best	5wI	10wM
Test																	
All First																		
1-day Int																		
NatWest	1	1	0	11	11	11.00	-	-	-	-							
B & H																		
1-day Lge																		

SCOTT, D. A.   Kent

Name: <u>Darren</u> Anthony Scott
Role: Left-hand bat, off-spin bowler
Born: 26 August 1973, Canterbury
Height: 6ft 2in **Weight:** 13st
Nickname: Stavros, Bubble
County debut: 1998
1st-Class catches: 3
Strike rate: 85.50 (career 92.46)
Parents: Linda and Tony
Marital status: Engaged to Julia Skeet
Education: St Stephens Primary School, Canterbury; Chaucer Technology School, Canterbury; Canterbury Christ Church University College, Canterbury
Qualifications: 7 GCSEs, A-levels, BSc (Hons) Business Studies and Sports Science (2:1), AAT, Level 2 cricket coach
Career outside cricket: Accountant/sports trader
Overseas teams played for: Fish Hoek CC, Cape Town 1991-92

Cricketers particularly admired: David Gower, Graeme Fowler
Young players to look out for: Rob Key, James Hockley, Chris Schofield
Other sports played: Badminton, football
Other sports followed: Football (Nottingham Forest), American football (San Francisco 49ers)
Relaxations: Reading, watching sport, gardening
Extras: Represented the ECB in the Triple Crown and European Championships 1998. Awarded 2nd XI cap 1998. Retired at the end of the 2000 season
Opinions on cricket: 'Wickets need drastically improving to ensure players are prepared for Test cricket.'
Best batting: 17* Kent v Oxford University, Canterbury 1998
Best bowling: 4-151 Kent v New Zealanders, Canterbury 1999

2000 Season

	M	Inns	NO	Runs	HS	Avge	100s	50s	Ct	St	O	M	Runs	Wkts	Avge	Best	5wI	10wM
Test																		
All First	3	3	2	8	4 *	8.00	-	-	2	-	57	18	157	4	39.25	2-40	-	-
1-day Int																		
NatWest																			
B & H																			
1-day Lge	2	1	0	27	27	27.00	-	-	1	-	14	0	61	5	12.20	3-21	-	

Career Performances

	M	Inns	NO	Runs	HS	Avge	100s	50s	Ct	St	Balls	Runs	Wkts	Avge	Best	5wI	10wM
Test																	
All First	8	10	8	46	17 *	23.00	-	-	3	-	1202	613	13	47.15	4-151	-	-
1-day Int																	
NatWest																		
B & H																		
1-day Lge	4	1	0	27	27	27.00	-	-	1	-	138	118	5	23.60	3-21	-	

SCUDERI, J. C.   Lancashire

Name: <u>Joseph</u> Charles Scuderi
Role: Right-hand bat, right-arm
medium bowler
Born: 24 December 1968, Ingham,
Queensland, Australia
Height: 5ft 11in **Weight:** 11st 7lbs
Nickname: Scud
County debut: 2000
1st-Class 50s: 14
1st-Class 100s: 3
1st-Class 5 w. in innings: 8
1st-Class 10 w. in match: 1
1st-Class catches: 24
Place in batting averages: 145th av. 23.72
Place in bowling averages: 47th av. 23.78
Strike rate: 51.42 (career 73.50)
Parents: Enrico and Nalda
Marital status: Single
Education: Macknade State Primary; Ingham State High (both Queensland)
Off-season: Preparing for the next season
Overseas tours: Australia U19 to New Zealand 1987
Overseas teams played for: South Australia 1988-89 – 1998-99
Cricketers particularly admired: Jeff Thomson, Ian Botham, Mike Atherton
Young players to look out for: Kyle Hogg, James Anderson
Other sports followed: Rugby league (Sydney City), football (Manchester United)
Injuries: Out for six weeks overall with knee, shoulder and back injuries
Relaxations: Listening to and playing music
Extras: South Australia Player of the Year 1991-92. Was in Australia squad of 20 for
World Cup 1992. Played for Prime Minister's XI v Pakistan and England. Has played
for Italy since 1998. Has played Lancashire League cricket. Is not considered an
overseas player
Opinions on cricket: 'Fitness is becoming more important, sometimes at the expense
of the skills.'
Best batting: 125* South Australia v Western Australia, Adelaide 1991-92
Best bowling: 7-79 South Australia v New South Wales, Adelaide 1991-92

2000 Season

	M	Inns	NO	Runs	HS	Avge	100s	50s	Ct	St	O	M	Runs	Wkts	Avge	Best	5wI	10wM
Test																		
All First	9	13	2	261	51	23.72	-	1	-	-	120	28	333	14	23.78	4-58	-	-
1-day Int																		
NatWest	2	1	0	7	7	7.00	-	-	1	-	7	1	31	0	-		-	-
B & H	2	1	0	42	42	42.00	-	-	-	-	3	0	13	0	-		-	-
1-day Lge	6	4	1	30	14	10.00	-	-	1	-	30	2	165	4	41.25	1-30	-	

Career Performances

	M	Inns	NO	Runs	HS	Avge	100s	50s	Ct	St	Balls	Runs	Wkts	Avge	Best	5wI	10wM
Test																	
All First	70	113	16	2928	125 *	30.18	3	14	24	-	12496	5755	170	33.85	7-79	8	1
1-day Int																	
NatWest	2	1	0	7	7	7.00	-	-	1	-	42	31	0	-		-	-
B & H	2	1	0	42	42	42.00	-	-	-	-	18	13	0	-		-	-
1-day Lge	6	4	1	30	14	10.00	-	-	1	-	180	165	4	41.25	1-30	-	

SEXTON, A. J.   Hampshire

Name: <u>Andrew</u> John Sexton
Role: Left-hand top-order bat, right-arm off-spin bowler
Born: 23 July 1979, Southampton
Height: 5ft 11in **Weight:** 12st
Nickname: Sexy, Seko, Fred
County debut: 2000
1st-Class catches: 3
Place in batting averages: 272nd av. 10.14
Parents: Brian and Christine
Marital status: Single
Family links with cricket: Father played representative cricket for New Forest Cricket Association and Southern League; represents Dorset Over 50s. Brother Neil plays for Dorset 2nd XI and U23
Education: Broadstone; Corfe Hills; Westminster College
Qualifications: GCSEs, GNVQ Business Studies and Leisure and Tourism, ECB coaching Level 1
Off-season: Playing club cricket in South Africa
Overseas tours: MCC Young Cricketers to Cape Town 2000

Overseas teams played for: Bassendean CC, Perth 1999-2000
Cricketers particularly admired: Robin Smith, Graham Thorpe
Young players to look out for: Chris Tremlett, Derek Kenway
Other sports played: Football, badminton
Other sports followed: Football (Liverpool FC, Bournemouth AFC)
Relaxations: Socialising
Extras: Scored 196 for Dorset v Cumberland in the 1999 Minor Counties final, the highest individual score in a Minor Counties final (but was on losing side)
Opinions on cricket: 'Second XIs to play in the same league format as first teams, with reverse fixtures so that second team players have better facilities in which to improve.'
Best batting: 36 Hampshire v Durham, Basingstoke 2000

2000 Season

	M	Inns	NO	Runs	HS	Avge	100s	50s	Ct	St	O	M	Runs	Wkts	Avge	Best	5wI	10wM
Test																		
All First	4	7	0	71	36	10.14	-	-	3	-								
1-day Int																		
NatWest	2	2	0	35	34	17.50	-	-	1	-								
B & H																			
1-day Lge																			

Career Performances

	M	Inns	NO	Runs	HS	Avge	100s	50s	Ct	St	Balls	Runs	Wkts	Avge	Best	5wI	10wM
Test																	
All First	4	7	0	71	36	10.14	-	-	3	-							
1-day Int																	
NatWest	2	2	0	35	34	17.50	-	-	1	-							
B & H																		
1-day Lge																		

SHAH, I. H.   Hampshire

Name: <u>Irfan</u> Hussain Shah
Role: Right-hand bat, off-spin bowler
Born: 20 June 1979, Barking, Essex
Height: 5ft 11in **Weight:** 11st
Nickname: Irf, Shah, Saqqi
County debut: No first-team appearance
Parents: Ajaib and Nisa
Marital status: Single
Education: Cleveland Junior School, Ilford, Essex; Loxford High School, Ilford,

Essex; London Cricket College, Haringey; City of Westminster College

Qualifications: IT Level II, GNVQ (Advanced) Leisure and Tourism, NCA senior coach

Career outside cricket: 'Coaching/working with young people at sports centres'

Off-season: 'Playing in Pakistan to develop my spin bowling'

Cricketers particularly admired: Saqlain Mushtaq, Steve Waugh, 'Hainault and Clayhall CC players A. Ahmed, D. McEwan, I. Patel, Y. Patel, R. Rollins, G. Rollins'

Young players to look out for: Will Kendall, Dimitri Mascarenhas, U. Shah, M. and K. Ismail, G. Kandola, R. Boppara, Z. Sharif, R. Anderson, C. Greenidge, K. and K. Ali, S. Khan, C. Adams

Other sports played: Badminton, snooker

Other sports followed: Snooker (Ronnie O'Sullivan), football (West Ham Utd)

Relaxations: 'Praying, worshipping; going out – club, cinema, snooker club; spending time with family and friends; and just chilling'

Extras: Played for Northumberland in the NatWest 1999

Opinions on cricket: 'Not been involved that long to comment. I would like to say too many good players don't get opportunities and without that opportunity you can't see the potential.'

2000 Season (did not make any first-class or one-day appearances)

Career Performances

	M	Inns	NO	Runs	HS	Avge	100s	50s	Ct	St	Balls	Runs	Wkts	Avge	Best	5wI	10wM
Test																	
All First																	
1-day Int																	
NatWest	1	0	0	0	0	-	-	-	1	-	60	64	1	64.00	1-64	-	
B & H																	
1-day Lge																	

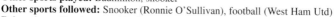

76. Who reached 200 dismissals in Test cricket when he caught Ian Chappell off Derek Underwood in Australia's first innings at Adelaide in 1974-75?

SHAH, K. Z. — Derbyshire

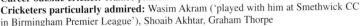

Name: <u>Kasir</u> Zamir Shah
Role: Left-hand bat, left-arm fast bowler
Born: 15 June 1978, Jhelum, Punjab, Pakistan
Height: 6ft **Weight:** 12st
Nickname: The Cap
County debut: 1999 (one-day), 2000 (first-class)
Strike rate: 84.00 (career 84.00)
Parents: Zamir Shah and Zabeda Bibi
Marital status: Single
Education: Anderton Park School; Wheelers Lane Secondary School, Birmingham; Cadbury College, King's Norton, Birmingham; University of Manchester
Qualifications: 11 GCSEs, 3 A-levels, BSc Pharmacology (2.1)
Career outside cricket: Trainee pharmacist
Cricketers particularly admired: Wasim Akram ('played with him at Smethwick CC in Birmingham Premier League'), Shoaib Akhtar, Graham Thorpe
Young players to look out for: 'My little brother Qasim'
Other sports played: Football (Acock Green FC, Central Warwickshire League; also won college football championship with 1st XI)
Other sports followed: Football (Manchester United – 'winning team')
Relaxations: 'Spending time with my friends'
Extras: Played for Warwickshire U19 and 2nd XI. Took hat-trick v Notts in U19 competition. Was in Warwickshire's U19 Festival winning side at Fenner's. 'Scored 42* for Smethwick CC v Pakistan in 1999 World Cup warm-up match ("most enjoyable innings").' Took wicket (John Crawley) with second ball in first-class cricket v Lancashire at Derby 2000. Released by Derbyshire at the end of the 2000 season
Opinions on cricket: 'Not enough natural talent; too many average players.'
Best batting: 38* Derbyshire v Kent, Derby 2000
Best bowling: 2-24 Derbyshire v Lancashire, Derby 2000

---

77. Who were Darren Gough's hat-trick victims at Sydney in 1998-99?

2000 Season

	M	Inns	NO	Runs	HS	Avge	100s	50s	Ct	St	O	M	Runs	Wkts	Avge	Best	5wI	10wM
Test																		
All First	4	6	2	102	38 *	25.50	-	-	-	-	56	8	260	4	65.00	2-24	-	-
1-day Int																		
NatWest	1	1	1	1	1 *	-	-	-	-	-	8	0	46	2	23.00	2-46	-	
B & H																		
1-day Lge	4	4	0	32	20	8.00	-	-	1	-	32	1	145	2	72.50	1-36	-	

Career Performances

	M	Inns	NO	Runs	HS	Avge	100s	50s	Ct	St	Balls	Runs	Wkts	Avge	Best	5wI	10wM
Test																	
All First	4	6	2	102	38 *	25.50	-	-	-	-	336	260	4	65.00	2-24	-	-
1-day Int																	
NatWest	1	1	1	1	1 *	-	-	-	-	-	48	46	2	23.00	2-46	-	
B & H																	
1-day Lge	7	5	1	32	20	8.00	-	-	2	-	300	258	5	51.60	2-36	-	

SHAH, O. A. — Middlesex

Name: <u>Owais</u> Alam Shah
Role: Right-hand bat, off-spin bowler
Born: 22 October 1978, Karachi, Pakistan
Height: 6ft 1in **Weight:** 12st
Nickname: Ace
County debut: 1995 (one-day),
1996 (first-class)
County cap: 1999
1st-Class 50s: 14
1st-Class 100s: 6
1st-Class catches: 42
One-Day 100s: 2
Place in batting averages: 140th av. 24.45
(1999 125th av. 27.63)
Place in bowling averages: (1999 92nd
av. 29.63)
Strike rate: 52.50 (career 56.11)
Parents: Jamshed and Mehjabeen
Marital status: Single
Family links with cricket: Father played for his college side
Education: Berkley's Junior School; Isleworth and Syon School; Lampton School;
Westminster University, Harrow

Qualifications: 7 GCSEs, 2 A-levels
Overseas tours: England U19 to Zimbabwe 1995-96, to South Africa 1997-98; England A to Australia 1996-97, to Kenya and Sri Lanka 1997-98
Cricketers particularly admired: Viv Richards, Wasim Akram
Young players to look out for: Stephen Peters, Paul Franks, Robert Key, Matthew Wood, Graeme Swann
Other sports played: Snooker
Other sports followed: Football (Manchester United)
Relaxations: 'Spend time with friends. Gym. Music'
Extras: Middlesex Sports Federation Award winner. Man of the Series in U17 'Test' series against India 1994. Played for Middlesex U13, Ken Barrington Trophy (national champions) winners, and Middlesex U15, county competition winners, as captain. Scored record 232 for England U15 against England U16. Awarded 2nd XI cap in 1996. Captained the England U19 side to success in the 1997-98 U19 World Cup in South Africa, scoring 54 not out in the final. Captain of England U19 against Pakistan U19 (one-day and 'Test' matches) 1998
Best batting: 140 Middlesex v Yorkshire, Lord's 1998
Best bowling: 3-33 Middlesex v Gloucestershire, Bristol 1999

2000 Season

	M	Inns	NO	Runs	HS	Avge	100s	50s	Ct	St	O	M	Runs	Wkts	Avge	Best	5wI	10wM
Test																		
All First	12	20	0	489	76	24.45	-	3	7	-	35	8	126	4	31.50	1-11	-	-
1-day Int																		
NatWest	1	1	0	49	49	49.00	-	-	-	-								
B & H	1	1	0	0	0	0.00	-	-	-	-	7	0	35	2	17.50	2-35	-	
1-day Lge	9	9	0	174	39	19.33	-	-	-	-	8	0	54	1	54.00	1-21	-	

Career Performances

	M	Inns	NO	Runs	HS	Avge	100s	50s	Ct	St	Balls	Runs	Wkts	Avge	Best	5wI	10wM
Test																	
All First	63	105	8	2951	140	30.42	6	14	42	-	954	574	17	33.76	3-33	-	-
1-day Int																	
NatWest	9	9	1	186	49	23.25	-	-	2	-							
B & H	9	8	1	126	43	18.00	-	-	5	-	50	37	4	9.25	2-2	-	
1-day Lge	61	57	7	1415	134	28.30	2	6	13	-	151	176	3	58.66	1-4	-	

SHAHID, N.   Surrey

Name: Nadeem Shahid
Role: Right-hand bat, leg-spin bowler
Born: 23 April 1969, Karachi
Height: 6ft **Weight:** 12st
Nickname: Nad, Gonads etc
'too many to mention'
County debut: 1989 (Essex), 1995 (Surrey)
County cap: 1998 (Surrey)
1000 runs in a season: 1
1st-Class 50s: 29
1st-Class 100s: 7
1st-Class catches: 117
One-Day 100s: 2
Place in batting averages: 52nd av. 36.16
Strike rate: (career 70.13)
Parents: Ahmed and Salma
Marital status: Single
Family links with cricket: Brother plays
cricket in Suffolk

Education: Stoke High; Northgate High; Ipswich School; Plymouth Polytechnic
Qualifications: 6 O-levels, 1 A-level, coaching certificate
Overseas tours: Ipswich School to Barbados (Sir Garfield Sobers Trophy) 1987;
England (South) to N Ireland (Youth World Tournament) 1988
Overseas teams played for: Gosnells, Perth, Western Australia 1989-91;
Fairfield, Sydney 1992-93
Cricketers particularly admired: Ian Botham, Shane Warne, Graham Thorpe and
Nasser Hussain
Young players to look out for: 'Every one'
Other sports followed: Golf, tennis, badminton, squash, 'most ball sports'
Extras: Youngest Suffolk player, aged 17. Played for HMC, MCC Schools, ESCA
U19, NCA Young Cricketers (Lord's and International Youth tournament in Belfast),
England U25 and at every level for Suffolk. TSB Young Player of the Year 1987,
winner of the *Daily Telegraph* Bowling Award 1987 and 1988, Cricket Society's
All-rounder of the Year 1988 and Laidlaw Young Player of the Year for Essex 1993.
Essex Society Player of the Year 1993. Released by Essex at end of 1994 season and
signed for Surrey. Member of the Surrey Sunday League winning side of 1996.
Member of Surrey County Championship winning squad of 1999 and 2000
Best batting: 139 Surrey v Yorkshire, The Oval 1995
Best bowling: 3-91 Essex v Surrey, The Oval 1990

2000 Season

	M	Inns	NO	Runs	HS	Avge	100s	50s	Ct	St	O	M	Runs	Wkts	Avge	Best	5wI	10wM
Test																		
All First	9	12	0	434	80	36.16	-	3	13	-	1	0	6	0	-	-	-	-
1-day Int																		
NatWest																		
B & H																		
1-day Lge	7	7	2	239	109 *	47.80	1	1	6	-								

Career Performances

	M	Inns	NO	Runs	HS	Avge	100s	50s	Ct	St	Balls	Runs	Wkts	Avge	Best	5wI	10wM
Test																	
All First	121	191	25	5348	139	32.21	7	29	117	-	3016	1999	43	46.48	3-91	-	-
1-day Int																	
NatWest	9	7	1	163	85 *	27.16	-	1	5	-	72	30	4	7.50	3-30	-	
B & H	22	15	5	271	65 *	27.10	-	2	3	-	150	131	1	131.00	1-59	-	
1-day Lge	98	85	14	1796	109 *	25.29	2	5	34	-	66	72	0	-	-	-	

SHARIF, Z.   Essex

Name: Zoheb Sharif
Role: Left-hand bat, leg-spin bowler
Born: 22 February 1983, Leytonstone
Height: 5ft 10in **Weight:** 11st
Nickname: Omar
County debut: No first-team appearance
Parents: Khalid and Robina
Marital status: Single
Education: Henry Maynard Junior School;
Chigwell School; Warwick School; Coopers
Coburn School
Qualifications: 9 GCSEs
Career outside cricket: A-level student
Off-season: Studying for three A-levels
Overseas tours: Essex U13 to Holland 1995
Overseas teams played for: PNT CC,
Pakistan 1996
Cricketers particularly admired:
Saeed Anwar, Rahul Dravid, Brian Lara, Sachin Tendulkar, Imran Khan
Young players to look out for: Gurdeep Kandola, Irfan Shah, James Foster, Will
Jefferson, Mark Pettini, Nicky Peng, Kadeer Ali, Tony Palladino
Other sports followed: Football (Manchester United)

Relaxations: Listening to music, watching TV
Extras: MCC Young Player of the Year at U13, U15 and U17 level. Was in England U17 squad v Scotland 2000. Had contract with MCC Young Cricketers
Opinions on cricket: 'I do not feel I have enough experience to comment on the game today.'

SHAW, A. D. Glamorgan

Name: <u>Adrian</u> David Shaw
Role: Right-hand bat, wicket-keeper, off-spin bowler
Born: 17 February 1972, Neath
Height: 5ft 11in **Weight:** 12st 12lbs
Nickname: Shawsy, Spinkster, Bernard, Strong Dance, The Groin, Gilmore, Catalogue Boy, Hairy Palms, Wigster
County debut: 1992 (one-day), 1994 (first-class)
County cap: 1999
50 dismissals in a season: 1
1st-Class 50s: 8
1st-Class 100s: 1
1st-Class catches: 169
1st-Class stumpings: 14
Place in batting averages: 54th av. 35.53 (1999 196th av. 20.80)
Parents: David Colin and Christina
Marital status: Single
Family links with cricket: 'Grandfather once lived in a house next door to Ynysygerwn Cricket Club'
Education: Catwg Primary; Llangatwg Comprehensive; Neath Tertiary College
Qualifications: 9 O-levels, 3 A-levels, various coaching badges
Career outside cricket: 'Professional sponger, layabout and general good-for-nothing'
Off-season: 'My average week will consist of training very hard from Monday thru Friday and then occupying the bottom of a bottle of Budweiser for two days. A healthy mix, I think you'll agree!!'
Overseas tours: Welsh Schools U17 to Barbados 1987; England YC to New Zealand 1990-91; Glamorgan pre-season tours, including to Cape Town 1999
Overseas teams played for: Welkom Police, Free State 1995-96
Cricketers particularly admired: Michael Powell
Other sports played: Rugby (formerly centre with Neath RFC; Welsh U19 and U21 squad member)

Other sports followed: Rugby (Neath RFC)
Injuries: Out for two months after an operation for a groin injury
Relaxations: 'I spend a lot of my time working as an adult video tester for my local video store, a most fulfilling hobby'
Extras: One of youngest players (18 years 7 days) to play first-class rugby for Neath. Played for Neath against Swansea six days after playing cricket against Zimbabwe for Glamorgan, and had the 'pleasure' of marking Scott Gibbs. Neath RFC Back of the Year 1993-94. Voted Glamorgan 2nd XI Player of the Year and Glamorgan Young Player of the Year in 1995. 2nd XI Player of the Month, June 1996. Claimed 12 victims in 2nd XI game v Gloucestershire at Usk in 1998, a record for 2nd XI cricket. Awarded county Young Player of the Month for August 1999 'at the geriatric age of 27'. 'Voted "the biggest idiot in the game" by fellow Glamorgan players for my contribution over the last 10 years'
Opinions on cricket: 'The greatest game in the world, apart from rugby, tennis, football, darts, hockey, squash, marbles, ping pong etc, etc.'
Best batting: 140 Glamorgan v Oxford University, The Parks 1999

2000 Season

	M	Inns	NO	Runs	HS	Avge	100s	50s	Ct	St	O	M	Runs	Wkts	Avge	Best	5wI	10wM
Test																		
All First	12	18	5	462	88 *	35.53	-	3	29	4								
1-day Int																		
NatWest	3	2	1	39	32	39.00	-	-	5	-								
B & H	6	5	1	12	8	3.00	-	-	6	2								
1-day Lge	9	6	0	55	24	9.16	-	-	5	1								

Career Performances

	M	Inns	NO	Runs	HS	Avge	100s	50s	Ct	St	Balls	Runs	Wkts	Avge	Best	5wI	10wM
Test																	
All First	71	96	15	1730	140	21.35	1	8	169	14	6	7	0	-	-	-	-
1-day Int																	
NatWest	9	8	2	151	47	25.16	-	-	13	-							
B & H	14	12	2	76	25	7.60	-	-	15	6							
1-day Lge	52	36	8	421	48	15.03	-	-	29	8							

SHEIKH, M. A.   Warwickshire

Name: <u>Mohammed</u> Avez Sheikh
Role: Left-hand bat, right-arm
medium bowler
Born: 2 July 1973, Birmingham
Height: 6ft
Nickname: Sheikhy
Education: Broadway School
County debut: 1997
1st-Class 50s: 1
Strike rate: 138.00 (career 64.14)
Overseas teams played for:
Western Province CC 1997-98
Extras: Has also played for Warwickshire
U19 and played for both Worcestershire and
Essex 2nd XIs in 1995
Best batting: 58* Warwickshire v
Northamptonshire, Northampton 2000
Best bowling: 2-14 Warwickshire v
Middlesex, Edgbaston 1997

2000 Season

	M	Inns	NO	Runs	HS	Avge	100s	50s	Ct	St	O	M	Runs	Wkts	Avge	Best	5wI	10wM
Test																		
All First	1	1	1	58	58*	-	-	1	-	-	23	7	68	1	68.00	1-36	-	-
1-day Int																		
NatWest																		
B & H	2	1	0	7	7	7.00	-	-	-	-	11.1	3	29	3	9.66	2-20	-	
1-day Lge	9	5	2	72	36	24.00	-	-	1	-	70.3	4	280	8	35.00	2-24	-	

Career Performances

	M	Inns	NO	Runs	HS	Avge	100s	50s	Ct	St	Balls	Runs	Wkts	Avge	Best	5wI	10wM
Test																	
All First	5	7	2	157	58*	31.40	-	1	-	-	449	187	7	26.71	2-14	-	-
1-day Int																	
NatWest	2	2	1	17	12*	17.00	-	-	2	-	108	56	2	28.00	2-18	-	
B & H	4	1	0	7	7	7.00	-	-	-	-	181	98	5	19.60	2-20	-	
1-day Lge	19	11	3	86	36	10.75	-	-	5	-	777	514	24	21.41	3-28	-	

SHERIYAR, A.   Worcestershire

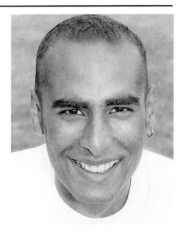

Name: Alamgir Sheriyar
Role: Right-hand bat, left-arm fast bowler
Born: 15 November 1973, Birmingham
Height: 6ft 1in **Weight:** 13st
Nickname: Sheri
County debut: 1993 (one-day, Leics),
1994 (first-class, Leics), 1996 (Worcs)
County cap: 1997 (Worcs)
50 wickets in a season: 2
1st-Class 5 w. in innings: 13
1st-Class 10 w. in match: 3
1st-Class catches: 15
Place in batting averages: 281st av. 8.62
(1999 285th av. 7.16)
Place in bowling averages: 121st av. 37.42
(1999 57th av. 24.70)
Strike rate: 59.64 (career 49.75)
Parents: Mohammed Zaman (deceased) and
Safia Sultana
Marital status: Single
Family links with cricket: Brothers play a bit
Education: George Dixon Secondary School, Birmingham; Joseph Chamberlain Sixth
Form College, Birmingham; Oxford Brookes University
Qualifications: 6 O-levels
Overseas tours: Leicestershire to South Africa 1995; Worcestershire to
Barbados 1996; England A to Bangladesh and New Zealand 1999-2000
Cricketers particularly admired: Wasim Akram
Other sports followed: Football, basketball
Relaxations: Time at home, music
Extras: Played for English Schools U17 and has also played in the Indoor National
League. Became only the second player to take a hat-trick on his first-class debut.
Asked to be released by Leicestershire at the end of the 1995 season and joined
Worcestershire for 1996. First bowler to reach 50 first-class wickets in 1999 and ended
season as leading wicket-taker with 92. Took second first-class hat-trick of his career v
Kent at Worcester 1999
Opinions on cricket: 'It's a batsman's game.'
Best batting: 21 Worcestershire v Nottinghamshire, Trent Bridge 1997
            21 Worcestershire v Pakistan A, Worcester 1997
Best bowling: 7-130 Worcestershire v Hampshire, Southampton 1999

2000 Season

	M	Inns	NO	Runs	HS	Avge	100s	50s	Ct	St	O	M	Runs	Wkts	Avge	Best	5wI	10wM
Test																		
All First	11	11	3	69	17	8.62	-	-	-	-	278.2	59	1048	28	37.42	4-51	-	-
1-day Int																		
NatWest																		
B & H	2	0	0	0	0	-	-	-	1	-	14	0	60	3	20.00	2-44	-	
1-day Lge	3	2	2	2	1*	-	-	-	-	-	20	2	98	1	98.00	1-37	-	

Career Performances

	M	Inns	NO	Runs	HS	Avge	100s	50s	Ct	St	Balls	Runs	Wkts	Avge	Best	5wI	10wM
Test																	
All First	93	95	33	505	21	8.14	-	-	15	-	15176	9175	305	30.08	7-130	13	3
1-day Int																	
NatWest	5	3	1	10	10	5.00	-	-	-	-	221	194	4	48.50	2-52	-	
B & H	10	4	2	28	15	14.00	-	-	1	-	439	335	11	30.45	3-40	-	
1-day Lge	54	17	11	54	19	9.00	-	-	5	-	1728	1529	57	26.82	4-18	-	

SIDEBOTTOM, R. J.   Yorkshire

Name: Ryan Jay Sidebottom
Role: Left-hand bat, left-arm
fast bowler
Born: 15 January 1978, Huddersfield
Height: 6ft 4in **Weight:** 14st 7lbs
Nickname: Siddy, Sexual, Jazz
County debut: 1997
County cap: 2000
1st-Class 50s: 1
1st-Class 5 w. in innings: 4
1st-Class 10 w. in match: 1
1st-Class catches: 11
One-Day 5 w. in innings: 1
Place in batting averages: (1999 275th
av. 9.73)
Place in bowling averages: 2nd av. 12.50
(1999 111th av. 32.87)
Strike rate: 33.58 (career 54.55)
Parents: Arnie and Gillian
Marital status: Single
Family links with cricket: Father played cricket for Yorkshire and England and
football for Manchester United and Huddersfield Town

Education: Almondbury Primary, Huddersfield; Lepton Middle; King James Grammar School, Almondbury
Qualifications: 5 GCSEs
Off-season: 'Training hard; getting fitter and stronger.' England A tour to West Indies
Overseas tours: England U17 to Holland 1995; MCC to Bangladesh 1999-2000; England A to West Indies 2000-01
Overseas teams played for: Ringwood, Melbourne 1998
Cricketers particularly admired: Darren Gough, Chris Silverwood, Glenn McGrath
Young players to look out for: Joe Sayers, Scott Richardson
Other sports played: Football (once with Sheffield United), 'all sports'
Other sports followed: 'Love rugby league (any team)', football (Man Utd)
Injuries: Out for 'too long for my liking' with groin injury
Relaxations: 'Music (R&B), films, clubbing, going out with my team-mates'
Extras: NBC Denis Compton Award 1999. Recorded maiden first-class five-wicket return (5-27) v Kent at Headingley 2000, following up with 6-16 in second innings for maiden ten-wicket match. Top English bowler in first-class averages in 2000 (second overall) with 24 wickets at 12.50. Awarded Yorkshire cap 2000
Opinions on cricket: 'More advertising of the game to heighten its profile. Needs better marketing for players because they work very hard.'
Best batting: 54 Yorkshire v Glamorgan, Cardiff 1998
Best bowling: 6-16 Yorkshire v Kent, Headingley 2000
Stop press: Took 5-31 (8-65 in the match) in the Busta Cup for England A v Jamaica at Kingston 2000-01, winning the Man of the Match award

2000 Season

	M	Inns	NO	Runs	HS	Avge	100s	50s	Ct	St	O	M	Runs	Wkts	Avge	Best	5wI	10wM
Test																		
All First	6	7	2	15	6 *	3.00	-	-	2	-	134.2	46	300	24	12.50	6-16	4	1
1-day Int																		
NatWest	1	0	0	0	0	-	-	-	-	-	4	2	9	1	9.00	1-9	-	
B & H	6	1	0	8	8	8.00	-	-	2	-	38	7	171	1	171.00	1-54	-	
1-day Lge	7	6	2	36	21	9.00	-	-	-	-	43	4	183	2	91.50	1-23	-	

Career Performances

	M	Inns	NO	Runs	HS	Avge	100s	50s	Ct	St	Balls	Runs	Wkts	Avge	Best	5wI	10wM
Test																	
All First	24	32	10	247	54	11.22	-	1	11	-	3273	1550	60	25.83	6-16	4	1
1-day Int																	
NatWest	6	1	1	7	7 *	-	-	-	1	-	240	167	7	23.85	3-15	-	
B & H	10	4	1	13	8	4.33	-	-	3	-	454	326	6	54.33	2-26	-	
1-day Lge	37	17	7	79	24 *	7.90	-	-	3	-	1552	1135	37	30.67	6-40	1	

SIERRA, R. E.   Warwickshire

Name: <u>Ryan</u> Edward Sierra
Role: Left-hand bat (No. 3), left-arm medium
bowler, cover fielder
Born: 8 September 1980, Petersburg,
South Africa
Height: 5ft 9in **Weight:** 12st 7lbs
Nickname: Teddy
County debut: No first-team appearance
Parents: John and Margaret
Marital status: Single
Family links with cricket: 'Both my father
and grandfather played representative cricket
and are passionate about the game'
Education: St John's College, Johannesburg;
Wits University, Johannesburg (studying
BComm degree)
Overseas tours: South Africa U15 to
England (U15 World Cup) 1996

Cricketers particularly admired: Daryll Cullinan
Other sports played: Rugby (1st team at St John's College)
Other sports followed: International rugby
Relaxations: Listening to music
Extras: Played for Gauteng Colts 1996-99, South Africa Schools U19 1997 and South
Africa Schools Colts 1999. Played against touring Nottinghamshire side 1998-99,
scoring 86. Is not considered an overseas player

---

78. Who took 16-137 for Australia v England at Lord's
in 1972 on his Test debut?

SILVERWOOD, C. E. W.   Yorkshire

Name: <u>Christopher</u> Eric Wilfred Silverwood
Role: Right-hand bat, right-arm
fast-medium bowler
Born: 5 March 1975, Pontefract
Height: 6ft 1in **Weight:** 12st 9lbs
Nickname: Spoons, Silvers, Chubby
County debut: 1993
County cap: 1996
Test debut: 1996-97
Tests: 5
One-Day Internationals: 6
50 wickets in a season: 1
1st-Class 50s: 4
1st-Class 5 w. in innings: 15
1st-Class 10 w. in match: 1
1st-Class catches: 22
One-Day 5 w. in innings: 1
Place in batting averages: 209th av. 17.30
(1999 249th av. 14.38)
Place in bowling averages: 88th av. 29.30 (1999 19th av. 20.40)
Strike rate: 67.50 (career 51.38)
Parents: Brenda
Wife and date of marriage: Emma, 3 October 1997
Family links with cricket: 'Dad played a bit'
Education: Gibson Lane School, Kippax; Garforth Comprehensive
Qualifications: 8 GCSEs, City and Guilds in Leisure and Recreation
Off-season: To West Indies with England A tour
Overseas tours: England A to Kenya and Sri Lanka 1997-98, to Bangladesh and New Zealand 1999-2000, to West Indies 2000-01; England to Zimbabwe and New Zealand 1996-97, to West Indies 1997-98, to Bangladesh (Wills International Cup) 1998-99, to South Africa 1999-2000
Overseas teams played for: Wellington, Cape Town 1993-94, 1995-96
Cricketers particularly admired: Ian Botham, Allan Donald
Other sports played: Karate
Other sports followed: Rugby league (Castleford)
Relaxations: Listening to music, watching videos, 'riding my motorbike'
Extras: Black belt in karate. Attended the Yorkshire Cricket Academy. Represented Yorkshire at athletics. Played for England U19 in the home series against India in 1994. Called up from England A tour of Bangladesh and New Zealand to England tour of South Africa 1999-2000 as injury cover. Took his first five-wicket haul in Test cricket (5-91) in South Africa's only innings in the fourth Test at Cape Town, January 2000

Best batting: 58 Yorkshire v Lancashire, Old Trafford 1997
Best bowling: 7-93 Yorkshire v Kent, Headingley 1997
Stop press: Took 4-45 from 32 overs for England A in Trinidad and Tobago's first innings in the Busta Cup match at Port of Spain 2000-01

2000 Season

	M	Inns	NO	Runs	HS	Avge	100s	50s	Ct	St	O	M	Runs	Wkts	Avge	Best	5wI	10wM
Test																		
All First	9	11	1	173	48	17.30	-	-	1	-	292.3	80	762	26	29.30	4-60	-	-
1-day Int																		
NatWest	2	1	0	2	2	2.00	-	-	-	-	17	1	65	0	-		-	-
B & H	1	1	0	4	4	4.00	-	-	-	-	8	0	42	2	21.00	2-42	-	
1-day Lge	8	5	0	26	12	5.20	-	-	-	-	51.5	7	194	12	16.16	4-11	-	

Career Performances

	M	Inns	NO	Runs	HS	Avge	100s	50s	Ct	St	Balls	Runs	Wkts	Avge	Best	5wI	10wM
Test	5	6	3	19	7 *	6.33	-	-	3	-	804	415	11	37.72	5-91	1	-
All First	97	128	28	1519	58	15.19	-	4	22	-	16032	8502	312	27.25	7-93	15	1
1-day Int	6	4	0	17	12	4.25	-	-	-	-	252	201	3	67.00	2-27	-	
NatWest	14	5	3	25	12 *	12.50	-	-	4	-	737	446	12	37.16	3-24	-	
B & H	21	8	0	33	8	4.12	-	-	4	-	1042	771	37	20.83	5-28	1	
1-day Lge	78	42	21	180	14 *	8.57	-	-	6	-	3205	2281	106	21.51	4-11	-	

---

79. Who was the first wicket-keeper to
score a Test century for Australia against England?

SINGH, A.   Worcestershire

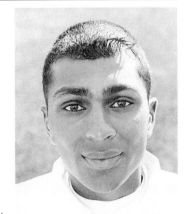

Name: Anurag Singh
Role: Right-hand bat, right-arm 'all sorts'
Born: 9 September 1975, Kanpur, India
Height: 5ft 11½in **Weight:** 11st
Nickname: Ragi
County debut: 1995 (Warwickshire)
1st-Class 50s: 7
1st-Class 100s: 4
1st-Class catches: 15
One-Day 100s: 1
Place in batting averages: 158th av. 22.28
(1999 242nd av. 15.40)
Parents: Vijay and Rajul
Marital status: Single
Education: Sacred Heart,
Roehampton/Bishop Gilpin,
Wimbledon/Mayfield Prep, Walsall; King
Edward's School, Birmingham; Gonville and
Caius College, Cambridge; College of Law, London
Qualifications: 12 GCSEs, 1 AO-level, 4 A-levels, passed Law School exams
Career outside cricket: Solicitor at Wragge & Co in Birmingham
Off-season: 'Working for Wragge & Co if not selected for any tours'
Overseas tours: England U19 to West Indies 1994-95; Warwickshire U21 to
South Africa; Warwickshire CCC to South Africa
Overseas teams played for: Gordon CC, Sydney; Avendale CC, Cape Town
Cricketers particularly admired: Steve Waugh, Sachin Tendulkar, Michael Atherton
Young players to look out for: Nick Warren, Kabir Ali
Other sports played: Hockey ('college and school'), football ('college and firm')
Other sports followed: Football (Aston Villa FC)
Relaxations: Reading, socialising with friends
Extras: Broke school record for number of runs in a season (1102). *Daily Telegraph*
regional award for batting (twice) and bowling (once). Tiger Smith Memorial Award
for Warwickshire Most Promising Young Cricketer 1994, Coney Edmonds Trophy for
Warwickshire Best U19 Cricketer 1994, Lord's Taverners' Trophy for Best Young
Cricketer 1994, Gray-Nicolls Len Newbery Award for ESCA U19 Best Player 1994.
Scored two centuries for England U19 against India U19 in 1994. Scored one century
against West Indies U20 and was Man of the Series 1994-95. Awarded 2nd XI cap in
1995. Cambridge Blue 1996-98; captain of Cambridge University 1997-98. With Nick
Knight, shared in record NatWest first-wicket stand for Warwickshire (185), v
Hampshire at Edgbaston 2000. Left Warwickshire at the end of the 2000 season and
has joined Worcestershire for 2001

Opinions on cricket: 'Two divisional cricket has definitely helped improve the intensity and competitiveness of every game. Should be more day/night cricket, as this makes cricket more attractive and accessible to the masses. Pitches and practice facilities must continue to improve.'

Best batting: 157 Cambridge University v Sussex, Hove 1996

2000 Season

	M	Inns	NO	Runs	HS	Avge	100s	50s	Ct	St	O	M	Runs	Wkts	Avge	Best	5wI	10wM
Test																		
All First	5	7	0	156	79	22.28	-	1	1	-	6.5	0	66	0	-	-	-	-
1-day Int																		
NatWest	2	2	0	95	85	47.50	-	1	-	-								
B & H																			
1-day Lge	8	8	0	195	74	24.37	-	1	3	-								

Career Performances

	M	Inns	NO	Runs	HS	Avge	100s	50s	Ct	St	Balls	Runs	Wkts	Avge	Best	5wI	10wM
Test																	
All First	43	67	3	1829	157	28.57	4	7	15	-	95	111	0	-	-	-	-
1-day Int																	
NatWest	4	4	0	146	85	36.50	-	1	-	-							
B & H	17	17	1	446	123	27.87	1	3	4	-							
1-day Lge	24	24	1	524	86	22.78	-	4	7	-							

---

80. Which Kent pace bowler had match figures of 10-104
on his Ashes debut at Edgbaston in 1985?

SMETHURST, M. P.   Lancashire

Name: Michael (<u>Mike</u>) Paul Smethurst
Role: Right-hand bat, right-arm
fast bowler
Born: 11 October 1976, Oldham
Height: 6ft 5in **Weight:** 14st 6lbs
County debut: 1999
50 wickets in a season: 1
1st-Class 50s: 1
1st-Class 5 w. in innings: 3
1st-Class catches: 4
Place in batting averages: 199th av. 17.88
Place in bowling averages: 25th av. 20.73
(1999 85th av. 29.00)
Strike rate: 40.51 (career 43.85)
Parents: Julie Martin ('Mum')
Marital status: Single
Education: Middleton Parish Primary
School; Hulme Grammar School, Oldham;
University of Salford
Qualifications: 9 GCSEs, 4 A-levels, BA (Hons) Leisure Management
Off-season: 12-month contract with Lancashire
Overseas tours: Lancashire to Cape Town 1999, 2000
Other sports followed: Football (Manchester United)
Extras: Recorded maiden first-class five-wicket return (7-50) v Durham at Riverside
2000
Best batting: 66 Lancashire v Surrey, Old Trafford 2000
Best bowling: 7-37 Lancashire v New Zealand A, Liverpool 2000

2000 Season

	M	Inns	NO	Runs	HS	Avge	100s	50s	Ct	St	O	M	Runs	Wkts	Avge	Best	5wI	10wM
Test																		
All First	16	19	10	161	66	17.88	-	1	3	-	378.1	90	1161	56	20.73	7-37	3	-
1-day Int																		
NatWest	2	0	0	0	0	-	-	-	1	-	16.3	0	63	3	21.00	2-30	-	
B & H	2	1	1	10	10 *	-	-	-	-	-	16	0	77	3	25.66	2-34	-	
1-day Lge	8	3	1	6	3 *	3.00	-	-	2	-	48	1	238	2	119.00	1-35	-	

Career Performances

	M	Inns	NO	Runs	HS	Avge	100s	50s	Ct	St	Balls	Runs	Wkts	Avge	Best	5wI	10wM
Test																	
All First	21	23	10	166	66	12.76	-	1	4	-	3026	1538	69	22.28	7-37	3	-
1-day Int																	
NatWest	3	1	1	4	4 *	-	-	-	1	-	159	109	7	15.57	4-46	-	
B & H	2	1	1	10	10 *	-	-	-	-	-	96	77	3	25.66	2-34	-	
1-day Lge	12	5	1	7	3 *	1.75	-	-	2	-	404	349	7	49.85	2-13	-	

SMITH, A. M. Gloucestershire

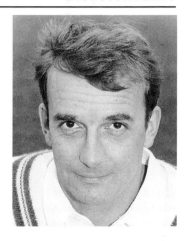

Name: Andrew Michael Smith
Role: Right-hand bat, left-arm fast-medium swing bowler
Born: 1 October 1967, Dewsbury, West Yorks
Height: 5ft 9in **Weight:** 12st 3lbs
Nickname: Smudge
County debut: 1991
County cap: 1995
Test debut: 1997
Tests: 1
50 wickets in a season: 5
1st-Class 50s: 4
1st-Class 5 w. in innings: 20
1st-Class 10 w. in match: 5
1st-Class catches: 25
One-Day 5 w. in innings: 1
Place in batting averages: (1999 287th av. 6.75)
Place in bowling averages: 26th av. 20.76 (1999 20th av. 20.49)
Strike rate: 50.13 (career 49.22)
Parents: Hugh and Margaret
Wife and date of marriage: Sarah, 2 October 1993
Children: William James, 9 October 1994; Amelia Lucy, 14 June 1997
Family links with cricket: Father (Birstall club) and brother (East Ardsley club) local league cricketers in Yorkshire
Education: Queen Elizabeth Grammar School, Wakefield; Exeter University; University of the West of England, Bristol
Qualifications: 9 O-levels, 4 A-levels, BA (Hons) French and German, PGDip Law
Career outside cricket: Studying to be a lawyer
Off-season: 'Organising my benefit season, staying fit, painting the windows'

Overseas tours: Queen Elizabeth Grammar School to Holland 1985; Bradford Junior Cricket League to Barbados 1986; Exeter University to Barbados 1987; Gloucestershire to Kenya 1990, to Sri Lanka 1992-93, to Zimbabwe 1996, to Cape Town 2000; England A to Pakistan 1995-96; MCC to New Zealand 1999

Overseas teams played for: Waimea, New Zealand 1990; WTTU, New Zealand 1991

Cricketers particularly admired: Richard Hadlee, Allan Donald, Jonty Rhodes, Sanath Jayasuriya, Wasim Akram, Courtney Walsh, Martin Bicknell

Young players to look out for: Owais Shah, Michael Gough

Other sports played: Football, golf

Other sports followed: Football (Leeds United)

Injuries: Out for 'the odd game' with a groin injury, 'but I normally bite the bullet'

Relaxations: Looking after the kids ('hardly relaxing!'). Crosswords. Computers

Extras: Played for Yorkshire age groups. Played for English Schools U19, NAYC and represented Combined Universities in the B&H Cup in 1988 and 1990. Finished the 1997 season as leading first-class wicket-taker with 83 wickets. Gloucestershire Player of the Year 1997. Took 400th first-class wicket when Jack Russell caught Keith Parsons v Somerset at Bath 1999. Granted a benefit for 2001

Opinions on cricket: 'Well done to the England team last summer. Central contracts have helped to keep Goughy and Caddick fresh. What does Jon Lewis (GCCC) have to do to get on an A tour by rights? When a no-ball is bowled in the NCL the field should not change for the free hit. What about blindfolding the bowler too? Or tying his legs together?'

Best batting: 61 Gloucestershire v Yorkshire, Gloucester 1998

Best bowling: 8-73 Gloucestershire v Middlesex, Lord's 1996

2000 Season

	M	Inns	NO	Runs	HS	Avge	100s	50s	Ct	St	O	M	Runs	Wkts	Avge	Best	5wI	10wM
Test																		
All First	9	10	6	54	14	13.50	-	-	1	-	250.4	70	623	30	20.76	5-52	1	-
1-day Int																		
NatWest	6	1	1	2	2 *	-	-	-	1	-	60	12	156	9	17.33	3-18	-	
B & H	7	0	0	0	0	-	-	-	2	-	49.4	8	163	6	27.16	4-27	-	
1-day Lge	16	10	6	15	3 *	3.75	-	-	1	-	133	24	370	18	20.55	3-20	-	

Career Performances

	M	Inns	NO	Runs	HS	Avge	100s	50s	Ct	St	Balls	Runs	Wkts	Avge	Best	5wI	10wM
Test	1	2	1	4	4 *	4.00	-	-	-	-	138	89	0	-	-	-	-
All First	133	176	48	1590	61	12.42	-	4	25	-	22346	11147	454	24.55	8-73	20	5
1-day Int																	
NatWest	26	10	6	53	13	13.25	-	-	6	-	1501	800	38	21.05	4-46	-	
B & H	45	22	12	91	15 *	9.10	-	-	10	-	2472	1634	55	29.70	6-39	1	
1-day Lge	137	70	42	317	26 *	11.32	-	-	21	-	5640	4032	142	28.39	4-29	-	

SMITH, B. F.   Leicestershire

Name: Benjamin (<u>Ben</u>) Francis Smith
Role: Right-hand bat, right-arm
medium bowler, county vice-captain
Born: 3 April 1972, Corby
Height: 5ft 9in **Weight:** 11st
Nickname: Smudge, Ferret, Gadget
County debut: 1990
County cap: 1995
1000 runs in a season: 2
1st-Class 50s: 31
1st-Class 100s: 14
1st-Class 200s: 1
1st-Class catches: 74
One-Day 100s: 1
Place in batting averages: 71st av. 32.66
(1999 72nd av. 34.85)
Strike rate: (career 139.50)
Parents: Keith and Janet
Wife and date of marriage: Lisa, 10 October 1998
Family links with cricket: 'Dad, grandad and both uncles played club, colts and
England U15s'
Education: Tugby C of E; Kibworth High; Robert Smyth, Market Harborough
Qualifications: 5 O-levels, NCA coaching certificate
Off-season: Playing for Central Districts, New Zealand
Overseas tours: England YC to New Zealand 1990-91; Rutland Tourists to South
Africa 1992; MCC to Bangladesh 1999-2000
Overseas teams played for: Alexandria, Zimbabwe 1990; Bankstown-Canterbury,
Sydney 1993-96; Central Hawke's Bay CC, New Zealand 1997-98
Cricketers particularly admired: David Gower, Viv Richards
Young players to look out for: Michael Jones
Other sports played: Tennis, golf 'and pre-match football!'
Other sports followed: Football (Leicester City), rugby union (Leicester Tigers)
Relaxations: 'Nights out and in, good music, food and golf; team meals and end-of-
season parties!'
Extras: Played tennis for Leicestershire aged 12. Cricket Society Young Player of the
Year 1991. Took part in Leicestershire record fifth-wicket partnership (322) with Phil
Simmons v Notts at Worksop 1998. 'Two Championship medals so far!' Appointed
vice-captain of Leicestershire for 2001
Opinions on cricket: 'An even amount of teams in each division to play
Championship games starting on the same day, to eliminate *some* weather and
selection problems.'

Best batting: 204 Leicestershire v Surrey, The Oval 1998
Best bowling: 1-5 Leicestershire v Essex, Ilford 1991

2000 Season

	M	Inns	NO	Runs	HS	Avge	100s	50s	Ct	St	O	M	Runs	Wkts	Avge	Best	5wl	10wM
Test																		
All First	17	23	2	686	111 *	32.66	2	2	10	-	3	1	6	0	-	-	-	-
1-day Int																		
NatWest	2	2	0	15	9	7.50	-	-	1	-								
B & H	4	4	1	102	64 *	34.00	-	1	2	-								
1-day Lge	16	15	2	508	90	39.07	-	4	2	-								

Career Performances

	M	Inns	NO	Runs	HS	Avge	100s	50s	Ct	St	Balls	Runs	Wkts	Avge	Best	5wl	10wM
Test																	
All First	159	235	31	7384	204	36.19	15	31	74	-	279	211	2	105.50	1-5	-	-
1-day Int																	
NatWest	17	16	1	359	63 *	23.93	-	2	8	-							
B & H	32	30	2	768	90	27.42	-	6	15	-							
1-day Lge	140	137	15	3515	115	28.81	1	18	34	-	18	15	0	-	-	-	

SMITH, E. T.   Kent

Name: <u>Edward</u> Thomas Smith
Role: Right-hand bat
Born: 19 July 1977, Pembury, Kent
Height: 6ft 2in **Weight:** 12st 10lbs
Nickname: Smudger, Hughie
County debut: 1996
1000 runs in a season: 1
1st-Class 50s: 17
1st-Class 100s: 6
1st-Class catches: 17
Place in batting averages: 150th av. 23.05
(1999 34th av. 40.47)
Parents: Jonathan and Gillie
Marital status: Single
Family links with cricket: Father wrote
Good Enough? with Chris Cowdrey
Education: Tonbridge School; Peterhouse,
Cambridge University

Qualifications: 11 GCSEs, 3 A-levels, degree in History
Career outside cricket: Journalist
Off-season: Cricketing visit to Bombay at end of January 2001
Cricketers particularly admired: Martin Crowe, Greg Chappell
Young players to look out for: Andrew Symonds, Robert Key, James Hockley, Matt Banes
Other sports followed: Football (Arsenal FC)
Relaxations: Reading, socialising, listening to music
Extras: Scored a century (101) on his first-class debut against Glamorgan in 1996 and in doing so became the youngest player to score a century on debut for Cambridge University. He was also the first person to score 50 or more in each of his first five first-class games. Cambridge Blue in 1996. Played for England U19 against New Zealand U19 in 1996
Opinions on cricket: 'Everyone knows we should play less, practise with more intensity and in better facilities, and play on much better wickets. So why don't we do it?'
Best batting: 190 Cambridge University v Leicestershire, Fenner's 1997

2000 Season

	M	Inns	NO	Runs	HS	Avge	100s	50s	Ct	St	O	M	Runs	Wkts	Avge	Best	5wI	10wM
Test																		
All First	11	18	0	415	175	23.05	1	-	6	-	6	0	20	0	-	-	-	-
1-day Int																		
NatWest																		
B & H	1	1	0	18	18	18.00	-	-	-	-								
1-day Lge	1	1	0	14	14	14.00	-	-	-	-								

Career Performances

	M	Inns	NO	Runs	HS	Avge	100s	50s	Ct	St	Balls	Runs	Wkts	Avge	Best	5wI	10wM
Test																	
All First	61	103	6	3507	190	36.15	6	17	17	-	54	45	0	-	-	-	-
1-day Int																	
NatWest	3	3	0	33	19	11.00	-	-	-	-							
B & H	5	5	0	79	43	15.80	-	-	3	-							
1-day Lge	18	15	2	301	72 *	23.15	-	2	2	-							

SMITH, G. J.   Nottinghamshire

Name: Gregory (<u>Greg</u>) James Smith
Role: Right-hand bat, left-arm fast-medium
bowler
Born: 30 October 1971, Pretoria
Height: 6ft 3in
Nickname: G
County debut: No first-class appearance
1st-Class 50s: 2
1st-Class 5 w. in innings: 5
1st-Class catches: 9
Strike rate: (career 56.98)
Education: Pretoria BHS; Pretoria Technikon
Overseas tours: South Africa A to England
1996
Overseas teams played for: Villagers CC,
South Africa; Northerns 1993-94 –

Extras: Attended national academy in South
Africa. Made first-class debut for Northern
Transvaal B v Transvaal B at Johannesburg 1993-94. Is not considered an overseas
player
Best batting: 68 Northerns v Western Province, Centurion 1995-96
Best bowling: 6-35 Northerns v Western Province, Centurion 1997-98

2000 Season (did not make any first-class or one-day appearances)

Career Performances

	M	Inns	NO	Runs	HS	Avge	100s	50s	Ct	St	Balls	Runs	Wkts	Avge	Best	5wI	10wM
Test																	
All First	57	72	27	580	68	12.88	-	2	9	-	9745	4827	171	28.22	6-35	5	-
1-day Int																	
NatWest																	
B & H																	
1-day Lge																	

SMITH, N. M. K.   Warwickshire

Name: <u>Neil</u> Michael Knight Smith
Role: Right-hand bat, off-spin bowler
Born: 27 July 1967, Solihull
Height: 6ft **Weight:** 14st 3lbs
Nickname: Gert
County debut: 1987
County cap: 1993
One-Day Internationals: 7
1000 runs in a season: 1
1st-Class 50s: 31
1st-Class 100s: 4
1st-Class 5 w. in innings: 17
1st-Class catches: 62
One-Day 100s: 2
One-Day 5 w. in innings: 3
Place in batting averages: 132nd av. 25.77
(1999 164th av. 24.00)
Place in bowling averages: 100th av. 31.25
(1999 114th av. 33.75)
Strike rate: 66.57 (career 74.82)
Parents: Mike (M.J.K.) and Diana
Wife and date of marriage: Rachel, 4 December 1993
Family links with cricket: Father (M.J.K.) captained Warwickshire and England
Education: Warwick School
Qualifications: 3 O-levels, cricket coach Grade 1
Career outside cricket: 'Six winters sport coaching at Oratory School, Oxford, and Warwick School'
Off-season: Hosting for ITC Sports at ICC tournament in Kenya; 'walking the dogs and getting fit again for the bleep test'
Overseas tours: England to South Africa 1995-96, to India and Pakistan (World Cup) 1995-96; England XI to New Zealand (Cricket Max) 1997-98
Overseas teams played for: Phoenix, Perth, Western Australia 1989-90
Cricketers particularly admired: David Gower, Ian Botham, Allan Donald
Young players to look out for: Ian Bell, Tony Frost, Alan Richardson
Other sports played: Golf
Other sports followed: Rugby union, football
Relaxations: Sport
Extras: Followed in his father's footsteps when he led the Warwickshire side out against Northamptonshire in the Sunday League 1997 – the first time both father and son have captained Warwickshire. Reached 100 v Durham at Edgbaston at 4.09pm on 17 April 1998, thereby scoring the then earliest century in County Championship

history. His 147 v Somerset at Taunton 1998 is the highest score by a Warwickshire No. 9. Warwickshire captain 1999-2000

Opinions on cricket: 'Pitches are the main fault in English cricket. Two divisions will work if the game is played hard but true and fair.'

Best batting: 161 Warwickshire v Yorkshire, Headingley 1989

Best bowling: 7-42 Warwickshire v Lancashire, Edgbaston 1994

2000 Season

	M	Inns	NO	Runs	HS	Avge	100s	50s	Ct	St	O	M	Runs	Wkts	Avge	Best	5wI	10wM
Test																		
All First	17	20	2	464	87	25.77	-	4	8	-	310.4	70	875	28	31.25	5-66	1	-
1-day Int																		
NatWest	5	4	2	61	28 *	30.50	-	-	2	-	34	0	140	6	23.33	3-37	-	
B & H	3	2	1	7	4	7.00	-	-	-	-	1	0	10	1	10.00	1-10	-	
1-day Lge	16	14	2	171	75 *	14.25	-	1	9	-	83.3	3	345	18	19.16	3-10	-	

Career Performances

	M	Inns	NO	Runs	HS	Avge	100s	50s	Ct	St	Balls	Runs	Wkts	Avge	Best	5wI	10wM
Test																	
All First	177	252	32	6054	161	27.51	4	31	62	-	24917	12336	333	37.04	7-42	17	
1-day Int	7	6	1	100	31	20.00	-	-	1	-	261	190	6	31.66	3-29	-	
NatWest	41	36	8	621	72	22.17	-	4	13	-	1678	1051	45	23.35	5-17	1	
B & H	39	32	3	596	125	20.55	1	3	5	-	1343	1024	35	29.25	3-29	-	
1-day Lge	184	155	20	3085	111 *	22.85	1	18	70	-	5859	4473	172	26.00	6-33	2	

---

81. The sixth Test at The Oval in 1993 was the final Test for one of cricket's best-loved commentators. Who was he?

SMITH, R. A.   Hampshire

Name: <u>Robin</u> Arnold Smith
Role: Right-hand bat, slip fielder,
county captain
Born: 13 September 1963,
Durban, South Africa
Height: 6ft **Weight:** 15st
Nickname: The Judge
County debut: 1982
County cap: 1985
Benefit: 1996
Test debut: 1988
Tests: 62
One-Day Internationals: 71
1000 runs in a season: 11
1st-Class 50s: 122
1st-Class 100s: 55
1st-Class 200s: 1
1st-Class catches: 214
One-Day 100s: 27
Place in batting averages: 173rd av. 20.51 (1999 20th av. 42.69)
Strike rate: (career 78.50)
Parents: John and Joy
Wife and date of marriage: Katherine, 21 September 1988
Children: Harrison Arnold, 4 December 1991; Margaux Elizabeth, 28 July 1994
Family links with cricket: Grandfather played for Natal in Currie Cup. Brother Chris played for Natal, Hampshire and England
Education: Northlands Boys High, Durban
Qualifications: Matriculation, '62 England caps'
Career outside cricket: Director of Judge Tours. Set up Masuri Helmets and Chase Bats with former county cricketer Jon Hardy. Is partner in a chain of sports theme bars
Overseas tours: England to India and West Indies 1989-90, to Australia 1990-91, to Australia and New Zealand (World Cup) 1991-92, to India and Sri Lanka 1992-93, to West Indies 1993-94, to South Africa 1995-96, to India and Pakistan (World Cup) 1995-96; England XI to New Zealand (Cricket Max) 1997-98
Overseas teams played for: Natal 1980-84; Perth, Australia 1984-85 (grade cricket)
Cricketers particularly admired: Malcolm Marshall, Brian Lara, Graeme Hick, Graham Gooch, Allan Lamb
Other sports followed: Soccer, athletics, rugby, golf, racing
Relaxations: 'Reading (Leslie Thomas in particular), trout fishing, assembling a good wine cellar, keeping fit and spending as much time as possible with my lovely wife Katherine and my children'

Extras: Played rugby for Natal Schools and for Romsey RFC as a full-back. Held 19 school athletics records and two South African schools records in shot putt and 100-metre hurdles. One of *Wisden's* Five Cricketers of the Year 1990. Cornhill England Player of the Year 1991-92. Passed 6000 runs in Sunday/National League v Gloucestershire at Southampton 1999. Hampshire captain since 1998
Best batting: 209* Hampshire v Essex, Southend 1987
Best bowling: 2-11 Hampshire v Surrey, Southampton 1985

2000 Season

	M	Inns	NO	Runs	HS	Avge	100s	50s	Ct	St	O	M	Runs	Wkts	Avge	Best	5wI	10wM
Test																		
All First	17	29	0	595	61	20.51	-	3	3	-	2	0	26	0	-		-	-	-
1-day Int																		
NatWest	4	3	2	104	61	104.00	-	1	1	-								
B & H	4	4	0	71	56	17.75	-	1	-	-								
1-day Lge	15	15	2	464	88 *	35.69	-	4	2	-								

Career Performances

	M	Inns	NO	Runs	HS	Avge	100s	50s	Ct	St	Balls	Runs	Wkts	Avge	Best	5wI	10wM
Test	62	112	15	4236	175	43.67	9	28	39	-	24	6	0	-	-	-	-
All First	385	651	83	24203	209 *	42.61	56	122	214	-	1099	993	14	70.92	2-11	-	-
1-day Int	71	70	8	2419	167 *	39.01	4	15	26	-							
NatWest	44	43	13	2309	158	76.96	8	10	22	-	17	13	2	6.50	2-13	-	-
B & H	62	59	8	2270	155 *	44.50	5	10	22	-	6	2	0	-	-	-	-
1-day Lge	198	191	22	6522	131	38.59	10	40	73	-	2	0	1	0.00	1-0	-

---

82. Who succeeded Graham Gooch as captain
after England's innings defeat at Headingley in 1993?

SMITH, T. M.   Derbyshire

Name: <u>Trevor</u> Mark Smith
Role: Left-hand bat, right-arm
fast-medium bowler
Born: 18 January 1977, Derby
Height: 6ft 3in **Weight:** 14st
Nickname: Tricky
County debut: 1997
1st-Class 50s: 1
1st-Class 5 w. in innings: 5
1st-Class 10 w. in match: 1
1st-Class catches: 7
Place in batting averages: 239th av. 13.81
Place in bowling averages: (1999 22nd
av. 20.83)
Strike rate: 99.33 (career 48.50)
Parents: Graham and Marilyn
Marital status: Single
Family links with cricket: Three brothers all
play for Sandiacre Town CC; father umpires in local league

Education: Cloudside Junior School, Sandiacre; Friesland Comprehensive School,
Sandiacre; Broxtowe College of Further Education, Chilwell, Notts
Qualifications: 9 GCSEs, BTEC National Diploma in Business and Finance,
Level II coach
Career outside cricket: '*Still* working on it'
Off-season: 'Recovering from ankle operation, coaching and some educational
courses'
Overseas teams played for: Alma Marist CC, Cape Town 1999-2000; 'Gran Canaria
Town June 1999; Ayia Napa Select XI September 2000'
Cricketers particularly admired: Allan Donald, Ian Botham, Phillip DeFreitas,
Curtly Ambrose, Courtney Walsh
Young players to look out for: Ben Spendlove
Other sports played: Football, golf ('very poorly')
Other sports followed: Football (Derby County; Blue Eagles – 'brother's team')
Injuries: Out for two weeks mid-season and last six weeks of the season with an ankle
injury
Relaxations: 'Playing golf and doing nothing; music; spending time with girlfriend'
Extras: Had three Championship five-wicket hauls in four innings in September 1999
Opinions on cricket: 'The two divisions have made for more "interesting" cricket
(i.e. no meaningless end-of-season games). All we need now is good summers so we
can play!!'
Best batting: 53* Derbyshire v Lancashire, Derby 2000
Best bowling: 6-32 Derbyshire v Essex, Derby 1998

2000 Season

	M	Inns	NO	Runs	HS	Avge	100s	50s	Ct	St	O	M	Runs	Wkts	Avge	Best	5wI	10wM
Test																		
All First	10	13	2	152	53 *	13.81	-	1	4	-	149	24	571	9	63.44	3-51	-	-
1-day Int																		
NatWest	1	0	0	0	0	-	-	-	-	-	10	1	25	1	25.00	1-25	-	
B & H	5	1	0	0	0	0.00	-	-	1	-	31	2	118	3	39.33	3-14	-	
1-day Lge	3	3	0	19	12	6.33	-	-	-	-	21	2	119	5	23.80	3-45	-	

Career Performances

	M	Inns	NO	Runs	HS	Avge	100s	50s	Ct	St	Balls	Runs	Wkts	Avge	Best	5wI	10wM
Test																	
All First	26	32	9	298	53 *	12.95	-	1	7	-	3007	1752	62	28.25	6-32	5	1
1-day Int																	
NatWest	1	0	0	0	0	-	-	-	-	-	60	25	1	25.00	1-25	-	
B & H	5	1	0	0	0	0.00	-	-	1	-	186	118	3	39.33	3-14	-	
1-day Lge	10	9	4	38	12	7.60	-	-	3	-	399	409	16	25.56	4-38	-	

SNAPE, J. N.　　　　　　　　　Gloucestershire

Name: <u>Jeremy</u> Nicholas Snape
Role: Right-hand bat, off-spin bowler;
all-rounder
Born: 27 April 1973, Stoke-on-Trent,
Staffordshire
Height: 5ft 8in **Weight:** 12st
Nickname: Snapey, Coot, Jez, Snapper
County debut: 1992 (Northamptonshire),
1999 (Gloucestershire)
County cap: 1999 (Gloucestershire)
1st-Class 50s: 14
1st-Class 5 w. in innings: 1
1st-Class catches: 50
One-Day 5 w. in innings: 1
Place in batting averages: 56th av. 35.17
(1999 177th av. 22.52)
Place in bowling averages: 48th av. 23.90
(1999 150th av. 67.00)
Strike rate: 68.10 (career 90.13)
Parents: Keith and Barbara
Marital status: Single
Family links with cricket: 'Brother Jonathan plays league cricket for Rode Park CC
in Cheshire. Dad loves cricket now, and Mum hates the sweep shot!'

Education: Denstone College, Staffordshire; Durham University
Qualifications: 8 GCSEs, 3 A-levels, BSc Natural Science
Career outside cricket: Director of Capetours – tailor-made holidays to Southern Africa (www.capetours.co.uk)
Off-season: 'Working for Capetours; several trips to South Africa; big family Christmas; and intensive training and coaching programme from the New Year with John Bracewell'
Overseas tours: England U18 to Canada 1991 (captain); England U19 to Pakistan 1991-92; Durham University to South Africa 1993, to Vienna (European Indoor Championships) 1994; Northamptonshire to Cape Town 1993; Christians in Sport to Zimbabwe 1994-95; Troubadours to South Africa 1997; Gloucestershire to Kimberley, South Africa 1999
Overseas teams played for: Petone, Wellington, New Zealand 1994-95; Wainuiomata, Wellington, New Zealand 1995-96; Techs CC, Cape Town 1996-99
Cricketers particularly admired: Allan Lamb, Anil Kumble, Jack Russell
Young players to look out for: George Hancock ('Tim's nipper')
Relaxations: Travelling, music, cooking, good food and wine
Extras: Sir Jack Hobbs award (U15 Schoolboy 1988). B&H Gold Award winner for Combined Universities v Worcestershire 1992 (3-34) at The Parks. Player of the Tournament at European Indoor 6-a-side Championships in 1994. Left Northants at end of 1998 season and joined Gloucestershire for 1999
Opinions on cricket: 'Delighted to move to Gloucestershire where the lads display a great work ethic. We are all keen for improvement and to build on the successes of the last couple of years. In general, I hope that the England side continue to do well and that our domestic game can keep pace with the world's insatiable appetite for one-day excitement!'
Best batting: 98* Gloucestershire v Essex, Gloucester 1999
Best bowling: 5-65 Northamptonshire v Durham, Northampton 1995

2000 Season

	M	Inns	NO	Runs	HS	Avge	100s	50s	Ct	St	O	M	Runs	Wkts	Avge	Best	5wI	10wM
Test																		
All First	15	20	3	598	69	35.17	-	4	8	-	113.3	44	239	10	23.90	3-70	-	-
1-day Int																		
NatWest	6	5	0	46	13	9.20	-	-	2	-	14	0	71	1	71.00	1-35	-	
B & H	7	3	0	35	26	11.66	-	-	2	-	22	0	110	3	36.66	2-48	-	
1-day Lge	16	15	1	265	71	18.92	-	1	5	-	48	2	228	5	45.60	1-19	-	

Career Performances

	M	Inns	NO	Runs	HS	Avge	100s	50s	Ct	St	Balls	Runs	Wkts	Avge	Best	5wI	10wM
Test																	
All First	71	105	20	2255	98 *	26.52	-	14	50	-	7842	3974	87	45.67	5-65	1	-
1-day Int																	
NatWest	19	16	4	243	54	20.25	-	1	7	-	535	381	10	38.10	2-19	-	
B & H	30	22	4	352	52	19.55	-	2	12	-	1248	876	27	32.44	5-32	1	
1-day Lge	86	65	18	1005	77 *	21.38	-	3	29	-	2511	1986	76	26.13	4-27	-	

SOLANKI, V. S. Worcestershire

Name: <u>Vikram</u> Singh Solanki
Role: Right-hand bat, off-spin bowler
Born: 1 April 1976, Udaipur, India
Height: 6ft 1in **Weight:** 12st
Nickname: Mowgli, Vik
County debut: 1993 (one-day),
1995 (first-class)
County cap: 1998
One-Day Internationals: 8
1000 runs in a season: 2
1st-Class 50s: 34
1st-Class 100s: 9
1st-Class 5 w. in innings: 3
1st-Class 10 w. in match: 1
1st-Class catches: 119
One-Day 100s: 1
Place in batting averages: 25th av. 43.76
(1999 33rd av. 40.57)
Place in bowling averages: (1999 97th av. 30.23)
Strike rate: 55.00 (career 69.24)
Parents: Vijay Singh and Florabell
Marital status: Single
Family links with cricket: 'Father played in India. Brother Vishal (11 yrs) is keen cricketer'
Education: St Luke's, Udaipur; Merridale, Wolverhampton; Regis School, Wolverhampton
Qualifications: 9 GCSEs, 3 A-levels
Off-season: England A tour to West Indies
Overseas tours: England U18 to South Africa 1992-93, to Denmark (ICC Youth Tournament) 1994; England U19 to West Indies 1994-95; Worcestershire CCC to Barbados 1996, to Zimbabwe 1997; England A to Zimbabwe and South Africa

1998-99, to Bangladesh and New Zealand 1999-2000, to West Indies 2000-01; England to South Africa and Zimbabwe 1999-2000 (one-day series), to Kenya (ICC Knockout Trophy) 2000-01, to Pakistan 2000-01 (one-day series)
Overseas teams played for: Midland-Guildford, Perth, Western Australia
Cricketers particularly admired: Sachin Tendulkar, Graeme Hick, Tom Moody
Other sports played: 'Enjoy playing most sports'
Relaxations: 'Spending time with friends and family'
Extras: Scored more first-class runs in 1999 season than any other English player. Topped batting averages with 597 first-class runs (av. 59.70) on England A tour of Bangladesh and New Zealand 1999-2000. Made One-Day International debut v South Africa at Bloemfontein, January 2000
Best batting: 185 England A v Bangladesh, Chittagong 1999-2000
Best bowling: 5-69 Worcestershire v Middlesex, Lord's 1996
Stop press: Drafted into England one-day squad for Kenya and Pakistan 2000-01 as replacement for the injured Nick Knight

2000 Season

	M	Inns	NO	Runs	HS	Avge	100s	50s	Ct	St	O	M	Runs	Wkts	Avge	Best	5wI	10wM
Test																		
All First	16	28	2	1138	161 *	43.76	2	8	23	-	82.3	9	270	9	30.00	3-80	-	-
1-day Int																		
NatWest	2	2	0	7	7	3.50	-	-	-	-								
B & H	3	1	0	1	1	1.00	-	-	1	-								
1-day Lge	16	15	1	226	59 *	16.14	-	1	1	-	3	0	14	0	-		-	-

Career Performances

	M	Inns	NO	Runs	HS	Avge	100s	50s	Ct	St	Balls	Runs	Wkts	Avge	Best	5wI	10wM
Test																	
All First	101	170	12	5799	185	36.70	9	34	119	-	4778	2887	69	41.84	5-69	3	1
1-day Int	8	7	1	96	24	16.00	-	-	2	-							
NatWest	10	9	0	135	50	15.00	-	1	1	-	195	149	2	74.50	1-48	-	
B & H	12	10	0	132	25	13.20	-	-	5	-	18	17	1	17.00	1-17	-	
1-day Lge	87	72	10	1473	120 *	23.75	1	6	25	-	150	155	4	38.75	1-9	-	

SPEAK, N. J.   Durham

Name: <u>Nicholas</u> Jason Speak
Role: Right-hand bat,
leg-spin bowler
Born: 21 November 1966, Manchester
Height: 6ft **Weight:** 12st 4lbs
Nickname: Speaky
County debut: 1986-87 (Lancashire),
1997 (Durham)
County cap: 1992 (Lancashire),
1998 (Durham)
1000 runs in a season: 3
1st-Class 50s: 56
1st-Class 100s: 14
1st-Class 200s: 1
1st-Class catches: 108
One-Day 100s: 1
Place in batting averages: 101st av. 29.05
(1999 55th av. 37.40)

Strike rate: (career 90.50)
Parents: John and Irene
Wife and date of marriage: Michele Frances, 29 March 1993
Children: Kenneth John, 24 September 1995; Ella Frances, 13 July 1997
Family links with cricket: Father and uncle were league professionals in Lancashire and Yorkshire
Education: Broad Oak, Didsbury; Parrs Wood High School, Manchester; Sixth Form College, Didsbury, Manchester
Qualifications: 5 O-levels, Levels 1 and 2 coaching
Off-season: Playing for Dandenong CC, Melbourne
Overseas tours: Lancashire to Jamaica 1986-87, 1993, to Zimbabwe 1989, to Tasmania 1990, to Perth 1991, to Johannesburg 1992
Overseas teams played for: Maroochydore, Queensland 1988-89; South Canberra 1989-90; North Canberra 1990-91, 1992-93; Hawthorn, Melbourne 1994-96; Dandenong, Melbourne 1997-98, 2000-01
Cricketers particularly admired: Mark Waugh, Shane Warne, Sachin Tendulkar
Young players to look out for: Chris Schofield, Stephen Harmison
Other sports played: Golf, football, lacrosse
Other sports followed: Football (Manchester City FC)
Relaxations: Golf (Brancepeth Castle GC)
Extras: Scored century for Australian Capital Territories v England A at Canberra 1992-93. Released by Lancashire at the end of the 1996 season and joined Durham for 1997. Appointed Durham vice-captain for 1999. Succeeded David Boon as Durham captain for 2000 but was relieved of captaincy at the end of August

Opinions on cricket: 'Hopefully things are heading in the right direction.'
Best batting: 232 Lancashire v Leicestershire, Leicester 1992
Best bowling: 1-0 Lancashire v Warwickshire, Edgbaston 1991

2000 Season

	M	Inns	NO	Runs	HS	Avge	100s	50s	Ct	St	O	M	Runs	Wkts	Avge	Best	5wI	10wM
Test																		
All First	14	24	5	552	89 *	29.05	-	4	3	-								
1-day Int																		
NatWest	2	2	2	48	33 *	-	-	-	1	-								
B & H	6	6	0	190	72	31.66	-	1	2	-								
1-day Lge	12	12	1	212	53 *	19.27	-	1	1	-								

Career Performances

	M	Inns	NO	Runs	HS	Avge	100s	50s	Ct	St	Balls	Runs	Wkts	Avge	Best	5wI	10wM
Test																	
All First	174	303	33	9597	232	35.54	15	56	108	-	181	191	2	95.50	1-0	-	-
1-day Int																	
NatWest	13	13	3	402	83	40.20	-	4	4	-	24	31	0	-	-	-	
B & H	31	29	2	777	82	28.77	-	5	3	-							
1-day Lge	106	98	11	2281	102 *	26.21	1	10	21	-							

---

83. Who injured a shoulder tackling
a pitch invader during the first Test at Perth in 1982-83 and took
no further part in the series?

Name: <u>Martin</u> Peter Speight
Role: Right-hand bat, 'right-arm pies',
wicket-keeper
Born: 24 October 1967, Walsall
Height: 5ft 10in **Weight:** 12st 7lbs
Nickname: Sprog, Badger, Eco Warrior
County debut: 1986 (Sussex),
1997 (Durham)
County cap: 1991 (Sussex), 1998 (Durham)
1000 runs in a season: 2
50 dismissals in a season: 3
1st-Class 50s: 47
1st-Class 100s: 13
1st-Class catches: 289
1st-Class stumpings: 5
One-Day 100s: 3
Place in batting averages: 168th av. 20.82
(1999 143rd av. 25.72)
Strike rate: (career 10.50)
Parents: Peter John and Val
Marital status: 'Married but in middle of divorce'
Education: The Windmills School, Hassocks; Hurstpierpoint College Junior and
Senior Schools; Durham University (St Chad's College)
Qualifications: 13 O-levels, 3 A-levels, BA (Hons) Ancient History/Archaeology
Career outside cricket: Artist
Off-season: 'Painting various commissions; promoting Martin Speight Ltd; coaching;
a bit of golf; PCA trip to Malta (October); six weeks in India (January/February)'
Overseas tours: NCA U19 to Bermuda 1985; Hurstpierpoint College to India 1985-
86; England YC to Sri Lanka 1986-87
Overseas teams played for: Karori, Wellington, New Zealand 1989-90; University
CC, Wellington 1990-93; North City, Wellington 1995-96; Wellington CA 1989-90,
1992-93, 1995-96
Cricketers particularly admired: Viv Richards
Young players to look out for: Jo Wood
Other sports played: Squash
Other sports followed: 'Most sports, particularly rugby'
Relaxations: 'Art, red and white wine, good food, painting, most music'
Extras: Member of Durham University UAU winning side 1987. Played for
Combined Universities in B&H Cup 1987 and 1988. Member of Durham University's
men's hockey team to Barbados 1988. Sussex Most Promising Player 1989. Walter
Lawrence Trophy for fastest first-class 100 of 1992 – 62 balls v Lancashire at Hove.
Scored 47-ball Sunday League 100 v Somerset at Taunton 1993, the fastest 100 in the

50-over Sunday League. Has won two Gold Awards in the Benson and Hedges competition. Created an oil painting of the maiden first-class game at Arundel Castle between Sussex and Hampshire which was later auctioned to raise £1200 for the Sussex YC tour to India 1990-91, and of which a limited edition has also been printed and sold. Book of his paintings, *A Cricketer's View*, a collection of 54 paintings and commentary, published in 1995. Various commissions and a print of Abergavenny CC published in 1997. His paintings have also been reproduced on greetings cards and mugs, and as wooden jigsaws. Joined Durham from Sussex for the 1997 season. Oil painting of the Lord's Pavilion exhibited in the Lord's Museum 2000

Opinions on cricket: 'Pitches still poor. Until they improve, English cricket will struggle.'

Best batting: 184 Sussex v Nottinghamshire, Eastbourne 1993
Best bowling: 1-2 Sussex v Middlesex, Hove 1988

2000 Season

	M	Inns	NO	Runs	HS	Avge	100s	50s	Ct	St	O	M	Runs	Wkts	Avge	Best	5wI	10wM
Test																		
All First	11	18	1	354	55	20.82	-	1	29	-								
1-day Int																		
NatWest	2	2	0	11	10	5.50	-	-	1	-								
B & H	6	6	0	95	41	15.83	-	-	8	-								
1-day Lge	12	11	0	144	55	13.09	-	1	12	3								

Career Performances

	M	Inns	NO	Runs	HS	Avge	100s	50s	Ct	St	Balls	Runs	Wkts	Avge	Best	5wI	10wM
Test																	
All First	185	308	28	8921	184	31.86	13	47	289	5	21	32	2	16.00	1-2	-	-
1-day Int																	
NatWest	22	20	1	462	60	24.31	-	2	11	1							
B & H	46	43	1	915	83	21.78	-	4	39	2							
1-day Lge	152	140	7	3549	126	26.68	3	17	72	14							

SPENDLOVE, B. L. Derbyshire

Name: Benjamin (<u>Ben</u>) Lee Spendlove
Role: Right-hand bat, right-arm spin bowler
Born: 4 November 1978, Derby
Height: 6ft **Weight:** 13st
Nickname: Silky
County debut: 1997
1st-Class 50s: 2
1st-Class catches: 10
Place in batting averages: (1999 189th
av. 21.46)
Parents: Lee and Christine
Marital status: Engaged to Beckie
Children: Zack Benjamin,
8 September 1999
Family links with cricket: Father played
local leagues and was coach of Trent College
first team

Education: Harrington Junior School, Long
Eaton; Trent College, Long Eaton; 'School of Life'
Qualifications: 9 GCSEs, coaching Level 1
Career outside cricket: 'Dad'
Off-season: 'Looking after my son with my fianceé; keeping fit and relaxing'
Overseas tours: England U17 to Holland (International Youth Tournament) 1995
Overseas teams played for: Gold Coast CC, Queensland, Australia 1995-96
Cricketers particularly admired: Alec Stewart, Chris Adams
Young players to look out for: Ian Blackwell
Other sports played: Hockey (Derbyshire U15), rugby (Midlands U16)
Other sports followed: Football (Derby County)
Injuries: Out for eight weeks with a shoulder injury
Relaxations: Golf, music, eating out
Extras: Represented England at U15, U17 and U19. Fielded as 12th man for England
in Test match v South Africa at Edgbaston 1998, taking two catches (Gerry Liebenberg
and Hansie Cronje) off bowling of Dominic Cork. Played in a Lord's final aged 19
Opinions on cricket: 'It is good to see England competing with other nations once
again.'
Best batting: 63 Derbyshire v Warwickshire, Edgbaston 1999

2000 Season

	M	Inns	NO	Runs	HS	Avge	100s	50s	Ct	St	O	M	Runs	Wkts	Avge	Best	5wI	10wM
Test																		
All First	1	1	0	0	0	0.00	-	-	2	-								
1-day Int																		
NatWest																		
B & H																		
1-day Lge	1	1	0	4	4	4.00	-	-	-	-								

Career Performances

	M	Inns	NO	Runs	HS	Avge	100s	50s	Ct	St	Balls	Runs	Wkts	Avge	Best	5wI	10wM
Test																	
All First	20	36	2	656	63	19.29	-	2	10	-							
1-day Int																	
NatWest	6	5	0	142	58	28.40	-	1	1	-							
B & H	2	2	0	16	11	8.00	-	-	1	-							
1-day Lge	13	12	0	132	26	11.00	-	-	3	-							

SPIRES, J. A.   Warwickshire

Name: James (<u>Jamie</u>) Ashley Spires
Role: Right-hand bat, left-arm spinner
Born: 12 November 1979, Solihull
Height: 6ft **Weight:** 12st 12lbs
Nickname: Spiro, Guff
County debut: No first-team appearance
Parents: Stuart and Carol
Marital status: Single
Family links with cricket: 'Dad used to play for King Edward's Camp Hill with the likes of Gladstone Small and Trevor Penney'
Education: Eversfield School; Solihull School
Qualifications: 10 GCSEs, 4 A-levels
Off-season: 'Playing PlayStation 2 and catching up with university mates'
Overseas tours: Warwickshire U19 to Cape Town 1998
Overseas teams played for: SA Police, Bloemfontein 1999
Cricketers particularly admired: Gary Sobers
Young players to look out for: Ian Bell
Other sports played: Football

Other sports followed: Football ('big Nottingham Forest fan; season ticket holder for 15 seasons')
Relaxations: Playing PlayStation 2; listening to music
Extras: Warwickshire U19 Player of the Year 1999. Played for ECB U19 v Pakistan U19 1999
Opinions on cricket: 'Not enough time to recover during the season.'

SPIRING, K. R. Worcestershire

Name: Karl Reuben Spiring
Role: Right-hand middle-order bat
Born: 13 November 1974, Southport
Height: 5ft 11in **Weight:** 13st
Nickname: Spud, Ginga
County debut: 1993 (one-day), 1994 (first-class)
County cap: 1997
1000 runs in a season: 1
1st-Class 50s: 13
1st-Class 100s: 4
1st-Class catches: 22
Place in batting averages: (1999 286th av. 6.90)
Parents: Pete and June
Marital status: Engaged to Jess Hybert
Education: St Paul's, Hereford; Bishops of Bluecoat, Hereford/Monmouth School; Durham University
Qualifications: 9 GCSEs, 3 A-levels, NCA Senior Coach, UK CAA PPL(H), Australian CASA PPL(H), studying/training for FAA Commercial Pilot's Licence (Helicopters)
Career outside cricket: 'Working in the helicopter industry. Also running my own business, RSH, an independent helicopter charter consultancy service'
Off-season: 'Looking for job in helicopter industry. Any offers?'
Overseas tours: Worcestershire to Barbados 1996
Overseas teams played for: Fremantle-Mosman Park Pirates, Perth, Western Australia 1995-97
Cricketers particularly admired: Peter Carlstein
Young players to look out for: Vikram 'Solankipose', Chris 'Liprot'
Injuries: Out 'for an annoying amount of time' with 'every knee injury possible'
Relaxations: 'Taking people up for helicopter pleasure flights'
Extras: Father was a professional footballer. Rapid Cricketline 2nd XI Player of the Month June 1994. Worcestershire Uncapped Player of the Year 1994

Opinions on cricket: 'Far too much played. Players' opinions on the game are completely disregarded by the people in charge.'
Best batting: 150 Worcestershire v Essex, Chelmsford 1997

2000 Season

	M	Inns	NO	Runs	HS	Avge	100s	50s	Ct	St	O	M	Runs	Wkts	Avge	Best	5wI	10wM
Test																		
All First	3	4	1	96	38	32.00	-	-	-	-								
1-day Int																		
NatWest																		
B & H	3	2	0	27	17	13.50	-	-	-	-								
1-day Lge	4	4	0	135	71	33.75	-	1	3	-								

Career Performances

	M	Inns	NO	Runs	HS	Avge	100s	50s	Ct	St	Balls	Runs	Wkts	Avge	Best	5wI	10wM
Test																	
All First	45	78	10	2237	150	32.89	4	13	22	-	12	10	0	-	-	-	-
1-day Int																	
NatWest	5	5	0	198	57	39.60	-	2	2	-							
B & H	15	12	1	229	35	20.81	-	-	4	-							
1-day Lge	37	33	10	774	71	33.65	-	3	13	-							

STEAD, R. A.   Yorkshire

Name: Roger Alexander Stead
Role: Right-hand bat, right-arm medium bowler
Born: 18 April 1980, Dewsbury
Height: 6ft 1in **Weight:** 13st
Nickname: Zani, Steady
County debut: No first-team appearance
Parents: Roger and Linda
Marital status: Single
Education: Lightcliffe Church of England School; Hipperholme and Lightcliffe High School; University of Durham
Qualifications: 10 GCSEs, 4 A-levels
Career outside cricket: Student at University of Durham
Cricketers particularly admired: Jacques Kallis, Steve Waugh
Young players to look out for: John Sadler

Other sports played: Football (Calderdale district and local team), athletics (200m – Calderdale district)
Other sports followed: Football ('mad Leeds United supporter since early age')
Extras: Scored 88* on 2nd XI debut v Warwicks at Edgbaston 1998. Took 4-29 first time he bowled for 2nd XI, v Notts at Trent Bridge 1999

STELLING, W. F. Leicestershire

Name: <u>William</u> Frederik Stelling
Role: Right-hand bat, right-arm medium-fast bowler
Born: 30 June 1969, Johannesburg
Height: 6ft 4in **Weight:** 13st 6lbs
Nickname: Bomber, Stealth, Will
County debut: 2000
1st-Class 50s: 1
1st-Class 5 w. in innings: 1
1st-Class catches: 8
Strike rate: 30.00 (career 71.30)
Parents: Kathy and William
Wife and date of marriage: Kerrie Anne, 11 March 2000
Education: St Peters Preparatory School; Michaelhouse; St Stithians College; University of Cape Town

Career outside cricket: Sports journalism
Off-season: 'Backpacking in Mexico and South America or playing cricket and golf in New Zealand'
Overseas tours: Leicestershire to Anguilla 2000
Overseas teams played for: Western Province B and Western Province 1991-92, 1993-94; Boland 1994-96; Lesotho (invitational)
Cricketers particularly admired: Steve Waugh, Kepler Wessels, Hylton Ackerman (Snr)
Young players to look out for: Lawrence Prittipaul
Other sports played: Golf
Other sports followed: 'All major sports, especially rugby (Canterbury Crusaders)'
Injuries: Out for most of 2000 with groin strains, injury to right index finger and patellar tendonitis
Relaxations: Internet surfing, golf, beach bats, gym, running
Extras: Made highest score of 162* in 25-over game when ten years old. Played for Transvaal Schools 1986-87. Played rugby for Transvaal U20. Made first-class cricket debut for Western Province B v Natal B at Pietermaritzburg in 1991-92. Played for Holland in 1995 NatWest Trophy. Played for East Lancs in the Lancashire League.

Played for the Berkshire club Finchampstead. Won Thames Valley League Batting Award 1998. Represented Berkshire in the NatWest Trophy in 1999 and also played for them against Bangladesh in a World Cup warm-up match, taking 7-32. Scored 412 runs (av. 68.70) for Leics 2nd XI 1999 with a top score of 130 v Yorks. Joined Leicestershire for 2000 on a two-year contract; is not considered an overseas player. AON Trophy winner's medal 2000. Recorded maiden first-class five-wicket return (5-49) on Championship debut v Kent at Leicester 2000

Opinions on cricket: 'Too much cricket. Too many first-class teams. Too many contracted players. Strength versus strength is needed. Ten first-class counties, with promotion and relegation to division two and division three incorporating Minor Counties. Half as many four-day games to ensure 100 per cent effort, but no change to one-day games. A final in Championship and NCL could help.'

Best batting: 53 Western Province B v KwaZulu-Natal B, Pietermaritzburg 1991-92
Best bowling: 5-49 Leicestershire v Kent, Leicester 2000

2000 Season

	M	Inns	NO	Runs	HS	Avge	100s	50s	Ct	St	O	M	Runs	Wkts	Avge	Best	5wI	10wM
Test																		
All First	1	0	0	0	0	-	-	-	-	-	25	8	49	5	9.80	5-49	1	-
1-day Int																		
NatWest																		
B & H	1	1	1	50	50 *	-	-	-	1	-	6	0	46	0	-		-	
1-day Lge	1	1	1	10	10 *	-	-	-	-	-	9	2	35	3	11.66	3-35	-	

Career Performances

	M	Inns	NO	Runs	HS	Avge	100s	50s	Ct	St	Balls	Runs	Wkts	Avge	Best	5wI	10wM
Test																	
All First	18	28	2	475	53	18.26	-	1	8	-	2353	1029	33	31.18	5-49	1	-
1-day Int																	
NatWest	3	3	2	85	76 *	85.00	-	1	-	-	162	87	3	29.00	3-18	-	
B & H	1	1	1	50	50 *	-	-	-	1	-	36	46	0	-		-	
1-day Lge	1	1	1	10	10 *	-	-	-	-	-	54	35	3	11.66	3-35	-	

STEMP, R. D.   Nottinghamshire

Name: <u>Richard</u> David Stemp
Role: Right-hand bat, slow left-arm bowler
Born: 11 December 1967, Erdington,
Birmingham
Height: 6ft **Weight:** 12st 4lbs
Nickname: Stempy, Sheriff, Badger
County debut: 1990 (Worcestershire),
1993 (Yorkshire), 1999 (Nottinghamshire)
County cap: 1996 (Yorkshire),
2000 (Nottinghamshire)
1st-Class 50s: 2
1st-Class 5 w. in innings: 14
1st-Class 10 w. in match: 1
1st-Class catches: 67
Place in batting averages: 292nd av. 7.50
(1999 290th av. 6.16)
Place in bowling averages: 84th av. 28.66
(1999 148th av. 60.87)

Strike rate: 72.42 (career 81.23)
Parents: Arnold and Rita Homer
Marital status: Single
Family links with cricket: Father played Birmingham League cricket for Old Hill
Education: Britannia High School, Rowley Regis
Qualifications: NCA coaching award
Overseas tours: England A to India 1994-95, to Pakistan 1995-96
Overseas teams played for: Pretoria Technikon 1988-89
Cricketers particularly admired: Ian Botham, Phil Tufnell
Other sports followed: Indoor cricket, American football (New England Patriots)
Relaxations: Ornithology, music, driving
Extras: Played for England indoor cricket team v Australia in ManuLife 'Test' series
1990. Moved to Yorkshire at end of 1992 season (first English non-Yorkshireman to be
signed for the county). Included in England Test squad against New Zealand in 1994.
Left Yorkshire at the end of the 1998 season and joined Notts for 1999. Awarded
Nottinghamshire cap 2000
Best batting: 65 Yorkshire v Durham, Chester-le-Street 1996
Best bowling: 6-37 Yorkshire v Durham, Durham University 1994

2000 Season

	M	Inns	NO	Runs	HS	Avge	100s	50s	Ct	St	O	M	Runs	Wkts	Avge	Best	5wI	10wM
Test																		
All First	11	11	5	45	11	7.50	-	-	7	-	398.2	140	946	33	28.66	5-123	1	-
1-day Int																		
NatWest	1	1	0	0	0	0.00	-	-	-	-	10	0	47	1	47.00	1-47	-	
B & H	4	1	0	2	2	2.00	-	-	-	-	22.3	2	105	3	35.00	1-23	-	
1-day Lge	13	2	1	9	5	9.00	-	-	2	-	99	3	404	14	28.85	4-36	-	

Career Performances

	M	Inns	NO	Runs	HS	Avge	100s	50s	Ct	St	Balls	Runs	Wkts	Avge	Best	5wI	10wM
Test																	
All First	160	189	63	1544	65	12.25	-	2	67	-	29893	12788	368	34.75	6-37	14	1
1-day Int																	
NatWest	14	5	2	13	12	4.33	-	-	1	-	846	533	18	29.61	4-45	-	
B & H	23	5	1	5	2	1.25	-	-	-	-	1197	784	22	35.63	3-22	-	
1-day Lge	96	30	12	176	29 *	9.77	-	-	22	-	3909	3084	100	30.84	4-25	-	

STEPHENSON, J. P.   Hampshire

Name: <u>John</u> Patrick Stephenson
Role: Right-hand bat, right-arm medium bowler
Born: 14 March 1965, Stebbing, Essex
Height: 6ft 1in   **Weight:** 12st 7lbs
Nickname: Stan
County debut: 1985 (Essex), 1995 (Hants)
County cap: 1989 (Essex), 1995 (Hants)
Test debut: 1989
Tests: 1
1000 runs in a season: 5
1st-Class 50s: 71
1st-Class 100s: 23
1st-Class 200s: 1
1st-Class 5 w. in innings: 10
1st-Class catches: 173
One-Day 100s: 7

One-Day 5 w. in innings: 3
Place in batting averages: 296th av. 6.40 (1999 209th av. 19.31)
Place in bowling averages: 136th av. 43.53 (1999 88th av. 29.35)
Strike rate: 79.46 (career 61.87)
Parents: Pat and Eve

Wife and date of marriage: Fiona Maria, 24 September 1994
Children: Emma-Lydia, 19 May 1997; Camilla, 30 April 2000
Family links with cricket: Father was member of Rugby Meteors *Cricketer* Cup
winning side in 1973. Three brothers played in Felsted 1st XI; Guy played for Essex
2nd XI and now plays for Teddington
Education: Felsted Prep School; Felsted Senior School; Durham University
Qualifications: 7 O-levels, 3 A-levels, BA General Arts, Level 3 coaching award,
SFA registered representative
Career outside cricket: Stockbroker at Durlachers
Off-season: 'Planning my benefit and stockbroking'
Overseas tours: English Schools U19 to Zimbabwe 1982-83; England A to Kenya and
Zimbabwe 1989-90, to Bermuda and West Indies 1991-92; MCC to Kenya 1999
Overseas teams played for: Fitzroy, Melbourne 1982-83, 1987-88; Boland, South
Africa 1988-89; Gold Coast Dolphins and Bond University, Australia 1990-91;
St George's, Argentina 1994-95; Belgrano, Argentina 1994-95; Victoria CC, South
Africa 1995-96
Cricketers particularly admired: Brian Hardie
Young players to look out for: Matthew Wood
Relaxations: Watching cricket, reading (*Sunday Telegraph*, *Wisden*, *The Cricketer*),
alternative music
Extras: Awarded 2nd XI cap in 1984 when leading run-scorer with Essex 2nd XI.
Essex Young Player of the Year 1985. Captained Durham University to victory in
UAU Championship 1986 and was captain of Combined Universities team 1987 in the
first year that it was drawn from all universities. Was leading wicket-taker on England
A tour to Bermuda and West Indies 1991-92. Scored two not out centuries v Somerset
at Taunton in 1992 and was on the field for the whole game (the first Essex player to
achieve this). First Essex player to achieve 500 runs and 20 wickets in Sunday League
season 1993. Took over the captaincy of Hampshire in 1996, but relinquished it at the
end of the 1997 season. Founded the One Test Wonder Club in 1996. Scored 83* v
Durham 2000, becoming the first opening batsman to carry his bat five times in the
Sunday/National League. Granted a benefit for 2001
Opinions on cricket: 'Let's have more day/night cricket. Identify the class players in
ability and attitude and stick with them.'
Best batting: 202* Essex v Somerset, Bath 1990
Best bowling: 7-51 Hampshire v Middlesex, Lord's 1995

2000 Season

	M	Inns	NO	Runs	HS	Avge	100s	50s	Ct	St	O	M	Runs	Wkts	Avge	Best	5wI	10wM
Test																		
All First	10	15	0	96	19	6.40	-	-	7	-	172.1	33	566	13	43.53	4-68	-	-
1-day Int																		
NatWest	4	4	0	110	40	27.50	-	-	5	-	17	4	65	2	32.50	2-31	-	
B & H	4	4	1	27	17	9.00	-	-	3	-	5	0	22	0	-		-	-
1-day Lge	10	10	2	228	83*	28.50	-	1	2	-	42.4	1	185	6	30.83	4-40	-	

Career Performances

	M	Inns	NO	Runs	HS	Avge	100s	50s	Ct	St	Balls	Runs	Wkts	Avge	Best	5wI	10wM
Test	1	2	0	36	25	18.00	-	-	-	-							
All First	278	468	44	13719	202 *	32.35	24	71	173	-	20295	11193	328	34.12	7-51	10	-
1-day Int																	
NatWest	33	31	1	930	107	31.00	1	7	16	-	1195	920	29	31.72	5-34	1	
B & H	50	45	7	1537	142	40.44	2	11	14	-	1558	1111	42	26.45	3-22	-	
1-day Lge	184	166	23	4134	110 *	28.90	4	19	74	-	5387	4233	166	25.50	6-33	2	

STEVENS, D. I. Leicestershire

Name: <u>Darren</u> Ian Stevens
Role: Right-hand bat, right-arm medium bowler
Born: 30 April 1976, Leicester
Height: 5ft 11in **Weight:** 12st
Nickname: Stevo
County debut: 1997
1st-Class 50s: 5
1st-Class 100s: 1
1st-Class catches: 19
One-Day 100s: 1
Place in batting averages: 169th av. 20.77 (1999 119th av. 28.10)
Strike rate: (career 55.00)
Parents: Maddy and Robert
Marital status: Single
Family links with cricket: Father played local club cricket
Education: Richmond Primary School; Mount Grace High School; John Cleveland College, Hinckley; Hinckley Tech; Charles Klein College
Qualifications: 5 GCSEs, BTEC National in Sports Studies
Off-season: Six months in New Zealand
Overseas tours: Leicestershire U19 to South Africa 1994-95
Overseas teams played for: Wanderers CC, Johannesburg, South Africa 1995-97; Rhodes University, Grahamstown, South Africa 1997-98; Fairfield CC, Sydney; Hawthorn-Waverley, Melbourne
Cricketers particularly admired: Ian Botham, Viv Richards, Curtly Ambrose
Young players to look out for: Steve Adshead, Ashley Wright, Mike Sutliff ('next Gower')
Other sports played: Golf, squash, football
Other sports followed: Football (Leicester City), rugby union (Leicester Tigers)

Relaxations: 'Relaxing with friends, chilling to music'
Extras: Scored maiden first-class 100 (130) in fourth Championship match, v Sussex at Arundel 1999. Won Sir Ron Brierley/Crusaders Scholarship 1999
Opinions on cricket: 'What a great game.'
Best batting: 130 Leicestershire v Sussex, Arundel 1999
Best bowling: 1-5 Leicestershire v Sussex, Eastbourne 1997

2000 Season

	M	Inns	NO	Runs	HS	Avge	100s	50s	Ct	St	O	M	Runs	Wkts	Avge	Best	5wI	10wM
Test																		
All First	15	22	0	457	78	20.77	-	2	6	-	6	2	14	0	-		-	-
1-day Int																		
NatWest	2	2	0	188	133	94.00	1	1	-	-								
B & H	1	1	0	2	2	2.00	-	-	-	-								
1-day Lge	12	11	2	121	32	13.44	-	-	4	-								

Career Performances

	M	Inns	NO	Runs	HS	Avge	100s	50s	Ct	St	Balls	Runs	Wkts	Avge	Best	5wI	10wM
Test																	
All First	29	46	0	1057	130	22.97	1	5	19	-	55	25	1	25.00	1-5	-	-
1-day Int																	
NatWest	4	4	0	225	133	56.25	1	1	-	-							
B & H	2	2	0	18	16	9.00	-	-	-	-							
1-day Lge	28	27	3	437	82	18.20	-	2	7	-							

STEWART, A. J.   Surrey

Name: <u>Alec</u> James Stewart
Role: Right-hand bat, wicket-keeper, honorary club captain
Born: 8 April 1963, Merton, London
Height: 5ft 11in **Weight:** 13st 2lbs
Nickname: Stewie, Ming
County debut: 1981
County cap: 1985
Benefit: 1994 (£202,187)
Test debut: 1989-90
Tests: 102
One-Day Internationals: 132
1000 runs in a season: 8
50 dismissals in a season: 1
1st-Class 50s: 129
1st-Class 100s: 44

1st-Class 200s: 2
1st-Class catches: 580
1st-Class stumpings: 21
One-Day 100s: 18
Place in batting averages: 73rd av. 32.21
(1999 117th av. 28.38)
Strike rate: (career 160.33)
Parents: Michael and Sheila
Wife and date of marriage: Lynn,
28 September 1991
Children: Andrew James, 21 May 1993;
Emily Elizabeth, 6 September 1996
Family links with cricket: Father (Micky)
played for England (1962-64), Surrey (1954-
72) and Malden Wanderers and was team
manager of England (1987-1992). Brother
Neil captains Malden Wanderers
Education: Tiffin Boys School
Qualifications: 'Streetwise'

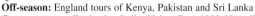

Off-season: England tours of Kenya, Pakistan and Sri Lanka
Overseas tours: England to India (Nehru Cup) 1989-90, to West Indies 1989-90, to
Australia 1990-91, to Australia and New Zealand (World Cup) 1991-92, to India and
Sri Lanka 1992-93, to West Indies 1993-94, to Australia 1994-95, to South Africa
1995-96, to Pakistan and India (World Cup) 1995-96, to Zimbabwe and New Zealand
1996-97, to Sharjah (Champions Trophy) 1997-98, to West Indies 1997-98, to
Australia 1998-99 (captain), to Sharjah (Coca-Cola Cup) 1998-99, to South Africa
1999-2000, to Kenya (ICC Knockout Trophy) 2000-01, to Pakistan and Sri Lanka
2000-01
Overseas teams played for: Midland-Guildford, Perth, Western Australia 1981-89
Cricketers particularly admired: Graham Monkhouse, Graham Gooch, Alan Knott,
Geoff Arnold, K. Gartrell
Young players to look out for: Tim Murtagh
Other sports followed: Football (Chelsea)
Relaxations: 'Spending as much time with my family as possible'
Extras: Cornhill England Player of the Year (jointly with Chris Lewis) 1992-93. One
of *Wisden*'s Five Cricketers of the Year 1993. Shared in a record fifth-wicket
partnership for England in Tests v West Indies (150) with Graham Thorpe at
Bridgetown 1993-94, becoming in that match the first Englishman to score a century
in each innings against West Indies. He was the leading scorer in Test cricket in the
1996 calendar year (with 793 runs). Cornhill England Player of the Year (for the
second time) 1996-97. Appointed captain of England 1998 (though had captained
England in a Test match for the first time v India at Madras 1992-93). Awarded MBE
in HM The Queen's birthday honours list 1998. His 164 in England's second innings v
South Africa at Old Trafford in 1998 was a record by a captain/wicket-keeper in Tests.
Captained England in the 1999 World Cup; stood down as captain afterwards. Leading

run-scorer in world Test cricket in the 1990s with 6407 runs (av. 40.81). Captained a World XI v an Asia XI at The Oval 2000. Captained England v West Indies in the 100th Test played at Lord's in June 2000 (his own 99th Test appearance) in place of the injured Nasser Hussain. Made 126th One-Day International appearance v Zimbabwe at The Oval 2000, breaking Graham Gooch's England record of 125 ODIs. NatWest Man of the Series v Zimbabwe and West Indies 2000; during the tournament he became the second wicket-keeper (after Adam Gilchrist) to record six dismissals in a One-Day International (v Zimbabwe at Old Trafford) and recorded scores of 74*, 101, 100 and 97 in successive ODIs. Scored century (105) on his 100th Test appearance in the third Test v West Indies 2000, in the process taking part (with Marcus Trescothick) in a record England partnership for any wicket v West Indies at Old Trafford (179); his century won him the Man of the Match award and, taking place as it did on The Queen Mother's 100th birthday, also won him the Slazenger 'Sheer Instinct' award for 2000

Opinions on cricket: 'Until the standard of pitches and practice pitches improves, the quality of cricket and cricketers won't.'

Best batting: 271* Surrey v Yorkshire, The Oval 1997

Best bowling: 1-7 Surrey v Lancashire, Old Trafford 1989

2000 Season

	M	Inns	NO	Runs	HS	Avge	100s	50s	Ct	St	O	M	Runs	Wkts	Avge	Best	5wl	10wM
Test	7	11	1	343	124 *	34.30	2	-	17	1								
All First	10	15	1	451	124 *	32.21	2	-	24	1								
1-day Int	7	7	2	408	101	81.60	2	2	12	-								
NatWest	3	3	1	150	70 *	75.00	-	1	2	-								
B & H	4	4	2	199	97 *	99.50	-	2	3	-								
1-day Lge	5	5	1	164	72 *	41.00	-	1	3	1								

Career Performances

	M	Inns	NO	Runs	HS	Avge	100s	50s	Ct	St	Balls	Runs	Wkts	Avge	Best	5wl	10wM
Test	102	183	13	6868	190	40.40	14	35	189	9	20	13	0	-	-	-	-
All First	395	654	70	23357	271 *	39.99	46	129	580	21	481	423	3	141.00	1-7	-	-
1-day Int	132	127	10	3786	116	32.35	4	21	123	11							
NatWest	46	43	7	1818	125 *	50.50	3	13	54	5							
B & H	70	70	12	2814	167 *	48.51	4	20	51	11							
1-day Lge	181	165	17	4606	125	31.12	7	26	139	13	4	8	0	-	-	-

STRAUSS, A. J.   Middlesex

Name: <u>Andrew</u> John Strauss
Role: Left-hand bat, left-arm medium bowler
Born: 2 March 1977, Johannesburg,
South Africa
Height: 5ft 11in **Weight:** 13st
Nickname: Straussy, Johann, Levi, Mareman,
Muppet
County debut: 1997 (one-day),
1998 (first-class)
1st-Class 50s: 8
1st-Class 100s: 1
1st-Class catches: 12
Place in batting averages: 69th av. 33.15
(1999 104th av. 30.50)
Parents: David and Dawn
Marital status: Single
Education: Caldicott Prep School;
Radley College; Durham University
Qualifications: 4 A-levels, BA (Hons) Economics
Career outside cricket: 'Not sure yet'
Off-season: Playing for Mosman CC in Sydney
Overseas tours: Durham University to Zimbabwe 1997-98; Middlesex to South
Africa 2000
Overseas teams played for: Sydney University 1998-99; Mosman, Sydney 1999-
2001
Cricketers particularly admired: Allan Donald, Brian Lara, Saqlain Mushtaq
Young players to look out for: Ed 'Team Drunk' Joyce
Other sports played: Golf (Durham University 1998), rugby (Durham University
1996-97)
Other sports followed: 'Anything with a ball'
Injuries: 'Depression from listening to David Nash's sob stories about why his runs
had dried up'
Relaxations: 'Any new economic theory books, especially on how chaos theory can
influence accepted non-linear market forecasting models'
Extras: Opened the batting for Radley with Ben Hutton, with whom he has also
opened at Middlesex. Scored maiden first-class century (111*) v Northamptonshire at
Lord's 2000
Opinions on cricket: 'We are heading in the right direction. There is plenty still to
do.'
Best batting: 111* Middlesex v Northamptonshire, Lord's 2000

2000 Season

	M	Inns	NO	Runs	HS	Avge	100s	50s	Ct	St	O	M	Runs	Wkts	Avge	Best	5wI	10wM
Test																		
All First	17	28	2	862	111 *	33.15	1	3	6	-	1	0	13	0	-	-	-	-
1-day Int																		
NatWest	3	3	0	110	56	36.66	-	1	-	-								
B & H																		
1-day Lge	12	12	0	263	90	21.91	-	1	3	-								

Career Performances

	M	Inns	NO	Runs	HS	Avge	100s	50s	Ct	St	Balls	Runs	Wkts	Avge	Best	5wI	10wM
Test																	
All First	29	51	3	1496	111 *	31.16	1	8	12	-	6	13	0	-	-	-	-
1-day Int																	
NatWest	3	3	0	110	56	36.66	-	1	-	-							
B & H	3	3	1	48	29	24.00	-	-	-	-							
1-day Lge	23	22	2	327	90	16.35	-	1	6	-							

STRONG, M. R. Northamptonshire

Name: <u>Michael</u> Richard Strong
Role: Left-hand bat, right-arm
fast-medium bowler
Born: 28 June 1974, Cuckfield, West Sussex
Height: 6ft 1in **Weight:** 12st 10lbs
Nickname: Strongy, Strongbow, Lager
County debut: 1997 (one-day, Sussex),
1998 (first-class, Sussex), 2000
(Northamptonshire)
1st-Class catches: 2
Place in bowling averages: 37th av. 22.41
Strike rate: 42.16 (career 63.16)
Parents: David and Gillian
Marital status: Single
Family links with cricket: Father and
brother both played club cricket in Sussex
Education: St Peter's School, Burgess Hill;
Brighton College; Brunel University College
(formerly West London Institute)
Qualifications: 9 GCSEs, 3 A-levels, BA/BSc (QTS) PE and Geography, various
coaching awards
Career outside cricket: 'PE teacher and lager drinker'

Off-season: 'Teaching and coaching in a school; playing football; helping out on my dad's farm'
Overseas tours: Brighton College to India 1991-92; Northamptonshire to Grenada 2000
Overseas teams played for: Umbilo CC, Durban 1992-93, 1997-2000
Cricketers particularly admired: 'WG', Ranjitsinhji
Young players to look out for: William Lewry, Mark Powell, 'Devon Malcolm'
Other sports played: Football (Ardingly FC, 'promoted as champions three years in succession')
Other sports followed: Football (Chelsea and Brighton, 'also keeping an eye on Man City as I've got a wager on them finishing above Leicester!')
Injuries: Out for four weeks with hamstring problems
Relaxations: Cooking, travelling, golf, seeing friends
Extras: 'Would like to thank the master in charge of cricket at Brighton College, John Spencer, for all the time he spent coaching me from the age of ten.' Most Improved Sussex Player 1998. Left Sussex in 1999-2000 off-season and joined Northants. NatWest Man of the Match v Yorkshire 2000
Opinions on cricket: 'Two divisions has given games a more competitive edge throughout the whole season. Standard of pitches needs to be addressed. Prize monies need to be increased for us poor cricketers!?'
Best batting: 35* Sussex v Leicestershire, Arundel 1999
Best bowling: 4-46 Northamptonshire v Oxford Universities, The Parks 2000

2000 Season

	M	Inns	NO	Runs	HS	Avge	100s	50s	Ct	St	O	M	Runs	Wkts	Avge	Best	5wI	10wM
Test																		
All First	4	7	2	72	27 *	14.40	-	-	1	-	84.2	15	269	12	22.41	4-46	-	-
1-day Int																		
NatWest	2	2	0	22	21	11.00	-	-	-	-	17	3	72	5	14.40	3-10	-	
B & H																		
1-day Lge	4	3	1	2	1 *	1.00	-	-	1	-	27.4	1	138	4	34.50	2-38	-	

Career Performances

	M	Inns	NO	Runs	HS	Avge	100s	50s	Ct	St	Balls	Runs	Wkts	Avge	Best	5wI	10wM
Test																	
All First	6	10	4	125	35 *	20.83	-	-	2	-	758	434	12	36.16	4-46	-	-
1-day Int																	
NatWest	2	2	0	22	21	11.00	-	-	-	-	102	72	5	14.40	3-10	-	
B & H																	
1-day Lge	7	6	2	6	2 *	1.50	-	-	1	-	258	235	4	58.75	2-38	-	

STUBBINGS, S. D.   Derbyshire

Name: <u>Stephen</u> David Stubbings
Role: Left-hand opening bat, 'right-arm express bowler'
Born: 31 March 1978, Huddersfield
Height: 6ft 3in   **Weight:** 15st 4lbs
Nickname: Stubbo
County debut: 1997
1000 runs in a season: 1
1st-Class 50s: 4
1st-Class 100s: 1
1st-Class catches: 7
Place in batting averages: 80th av. 31.75 (1999 190th av. 21.30)
Parents: David and Marie
Marital status: Single
Family links with cricket: 'My younger brother Jonathan is also an emerging fast-bowling all-rounder with Delacombe Park

CC. My father has also played for the club, and Mum has driven me to enough games and training sessions for her to know more than she probably wants to about the game'
Education: Belvedere Park Primary; Frankston High School, Victoria, Australia; Swinburne University, Australia
Qualifications: Victorian Certificate of Education (VCE)
Off-season: Playing cricket in Tasmania for the Kingborough Knights
Overseas tours: Derbyshire to Portugal 2000
Overseas teams played for: Delacombe Park CC , Melbourne 1990-94; Frankston Peninsula CC, Victoria 1994-2000; Kingborough CC, Tasmania 2000-01
Cricketers particularly admired: Mark Taylor, Michael Atherton, Steve Waugh, Matthew Mott, Ricky Ponting
Young players to look out for: James Pyemont, Will Kendall, Gary Keedy, Sam Patel
Other sports followed: Aussie Rules (Essendon Bombers)
Injuries: Rested for one National League game with a hip strain
Relaxations: 'Fishing, golf, eating out, drinking with friends, sleeping, listening to music, watching sport'
Extras: Represented Victoria at U17, U19 and Colts levels. Won two-year scholarship at the Victorian Institute of Sport. Scored maiden first-class century (135*) v Kent at Canterbury 2000, taking part in an unbroken opening partnership of 293 with Steve Titchard (141*); it was the first occasion on which Derbyshire had batted all day without losing a wicket
Opinions on cricket: 'At the moment I think the game is very healthy from an international perspective, but here in England the game is ill. Too many matches, too

many teams and too little quality practice time means county cricket is struggling to produce consistent world-class performers. I also believe for the long-term good of the game England need to become a power once again, or interest in the game itself could eventually die out.'

Best batting: 135* Derbyshire v Kent, Canterbury 2000

2000 Season

	M	Inns	NO	Runs	HS	Avge	100s	50s	Ct	St	O	M	Runs	Wkts	Avge	Best	5wI	10wM
Test																		
All First	18	32	4	889	135 *	31.75	1	4	4	-								
1-day Int																		
NatWest	2	1	0	16	16	16.00	-	-	-	-								
B & H	5	3	1	14	14	7.00	-	-	-	-								
1-day Lge	15	14	1	284	59	21.84	-	1	-	-								

Career Performances

	M	Inns	NO	Runs	HS	Avge	100s	50s	Ct	St	Balls	Runs	Wkts	Avge	Best	5wI	10wM
Test																	
All First	24	44	4	1129	135 *	28.22	1	4	7	-	30	41	0	-	-	-	-
1-day Int																	
NatWest	2	1	0	16	16	16.00	-	-	-	-							
B & H	7	5	1	22	14	5.50	-	-	-	-							
1-day Lge	22	21	1	386	59	19.30	-	1	1	-							

---

84. Who scored 71 in Australia's first innings and took 5-69
in England's second at Perth in 1986-87?

SUCH, P. M.　　　　　　　　　　　　　　　Essex

Name: <u>Peter</u> Mark Such
Role: Right-hand bat, off-spin bowler
Born: 12 June 1964, Helensburgh, Scotland
Height: 6ft **Weight:** 11st 7lbs
Nickname: Sushi, Suchy
County debut: 1982 (Nottinghamshire),
1987 (Leicestershire), 1990 (Essex)
County cap: 1991 (Essex)
Test debut: 1993
Tests: 11
50 wickets in a season: 6
1st-Class 50s: 2
1st-Class 5 w. in innings: 47
1st-Class 10 w. in match: 9
1st-Class catches: 112
One-Day 5 w. in innings: 3
Place in batting averages: 298th av. 5.88
(1999 271st av. 10.30)
Place in bowling averages: 87th av. 29.30 (1999 100th av. 31.09)
Strike rate: 70.44 (career 67.69)
Parents: John and Margaret
Wife and date of marriage: Nicola Jane, 25 September 1999
Family links with cricket: Father and brother both village cricketers
Education: Lantern Lane Primary; Harry Carlton Comprehensive, East Leake, Notts
Qualifications: 9 O-levels, 3 A-levels, advanced cricket coach, three Pitman computer
training courses/diplomas
Off-season: Staying at home preparing for a benefit year
Overseas tours: England A to Australia 1992-93, 1996-97, to South Africa 1993-94;
England to Australia 1998-99
Overseas teams played for: Kempton Park, South Africa 1982-83; Bathurst, Australia
1985-86; Matabeleland, Zimbabwe 1989-92
Cricketers particularly admired: Bob White, Eddie Hemmings, Graham Gooch,
John Childs
Young players to look out for: James Foster, Matthew Wood, Michael Powell,
Jason Brown
Other sports played: Golf
Other sports followed: Rugby union
Relaxations: 'Music, playing golf, socialising with mates, reading'
Extras: Played for England YC v Australian YC 1983 and for TCCB XI v New
Zealand 1985. Left Nottinghamshire at end of 1986 season; joined Leicestershire in
1987 and was released at end of 1989; signed by Essex for 1990. Played in one-day

games for England A v Sri Lanka 1991. Joint winner with J.H. Childs of the Essex Player of the Year Award 1992 and shared the award again in 1993. Took 6-67 on Test debut v Australia 1993 – best figures by an England Test debutant since John Lever in India 1976-77. Set record for the most overs bowled in a County Championship innings – 86 overs against Leicestershire in August 1997; he ended up with figures of 4 for 96. Set the unenviable record of having scored the longest duck in English Test history with his 72-minute innings in the third Test v New Zealand at Old Trafford 1999. Completed the set of five-wicket returns against all the first-class counties when he took 5-51 v Middlesex at Chelmsford 2000. Is vice-chairman of the Professional Cricketers' Association. Granted a benefit for 2001

Opinions on cricket: 'Two divisional format has added life to what would have been dead games. Everything matters throughout the season. Pitch Liaison Officers have been a success, but clubs should have no right of appeal for poor pitches. Need to keep the pressure on clubs over pitches. Central England contracts a good idea. County cricket now needs to look after itself by playing the sort of cricket people want to see, when they want to see it. It needs a better structure/format, in which spectators' and sponsors' interests are paramount.'

Best batting: 54 Essex v Worcestershire, Chelmsford 1993
54 Essex v Nottinghamshire, Chelmsford 1996
Best bowling: 8-93 Essex v Hampshire, Colchester 1995

2000 Season

	M	Inns	NO	Runs	HS	Avge	100s	50s	Ct	St	O	M	Runs	Wkts	Avge	Best	5wI	10wM
Test																		
All First	12	13	4	53	14	5.88	-	-	3	-	422.4	101	1055	36	29.30	7-167	3	1
1-day Int																		
NatWest																		
B & H																		
1-day Lge																		

Career Performances

	M	Inns	NO	Runs	HS	Avge	100s	50s	Ct	St	Balls	Runs	Wkts	Avge	Best	5wI	10wM
Test	11	16	5	67	14 *	6.09	-	-	4	-	3124	1242	37	33.56	6-67	2	-
All First	291	307	116	1528	54	8.00	-	2	112	-	55850	24574	825	29.78	8-93	47	9
1-day Int																	
NatWest	25	9	5	21	8 *	5.25	-	-	4	-	1554	872	25	34.88	3-56	-	
B & H	38	14	8	46	10 *	7.66	-	-	7	-	1947	1207	32	37.71	4-43	-	
1-day Lge	139	58	34	208	19 *	8.66	-	-	37	-	5507	4240	144	29.44	5-29	3	

SUTCLIFFE, I. J.   Leicestershire

Name: Iain John Sutcliffe
Role: Left-hand bat, leg-spin bowler
Born: 20 December 1974, Leeds
Height: 6ft 1in **Weight:** 12st
Nickname: Sooty, Bertie, Ripper
County debut: 1995
County cap: 1997
1st-Class 50s: 19
1st-Class 100s: 5
1st-Class catches: 49
One-Day 100s: 2
Place in batting averages: 179th av. 19.93
(1999 181st av. 21.85)
Strike rate: (career 53.40)
Parents: John and Valerie
Marital status: Single
Education: Leeds Grammar School;
Oxford University
Qualifications: 10 GCSEs, 4 A-levels, 2.1
PPE degree
Overseas tours: Leeds GS to Kenya
Cricketers particularly admired: David Gower, Brian Lara, Saeed Anwar
Other sports followed: Boxing (Mike Tyson), football (Liverpool)
Relaxations: Listening to music, eating out
Extras: Played NCA England U14 and NCA Development Team U18/U19. Oxford
boxing Blue 1994 and 1995, British Universities Light-middleweight Champion 1993.
In 1995, took part (with C. Gupte) in record partnership for Oxford University against
a first-class county (283 v Hampshire at The Parks), in which he scored 163*
Best batting: 167 Leicestershire v Middlesex, Leicester 1998
Best bowling: 2-21 Oxford University v Cambridge University, Lord's 1996

2000 Season

	M	Inns	NO	Runs	HS	Avge	100s	50s	Ct	St	O	M	Runs	Wkts	Avge	Best	5wI	10wM
Test																		
All First	12	17	1	319	53	19.93	-	2	11	-	1.3	0	12	0	-	-	-	-
1-day Int																		
NatWest																		
B & H																		
1-day Lge	3	2	0	71	53	35.50	-	1	2	-								

Career Performances

	M	Inns	NO	Runs	HS	Avge	100s	50s	Ct	St	Balls	Runs	Wkts	Avge	Best	5wI	10wM
Test																	
All First	88	132	12	3643	167	30.35	5	19	49	-	267	212	5	42.40	2-21	-	-
1-day Int																	
NatWest	8	8	2	377	103 *	62.83	1	2	2	-							
B & H	15	15	1	425	105 *	30.35	1	3	2	-							
1-day Lge	24	23	1	414	96	18.81	-	2	7	-							

SUTLIFF, M. D. R.   Gloucestershire

Name: Michael David Richard Sutliff
Role: Left-hand bat
Born: 8 November 1975, Melton Mowbray, Leicestershire
Height: 6ft 1in **Weight:** 13st
Nickname: Sutty, Blur
County debut: No first-team appearance
Parents: David and Nancye
Marital status: Single
Family links with cricket: Father is a keen cricketer; brother Martin played for Leicestershire Schools
Education: Merton County Primary; Roundhill Community College; Wreake Valley Community College; Wyggeston & Queen Elizabeth I Sixth Form College; University of Northumbria at Newcastle upon Tyne
Qualifications: 3 A-levels, BA (Hons) Sports Studies
Career outside cricket: Fitness instructor, coach
Overseas tours: Leicestershire Colts to South Africa 1994
Overseas teams played for: Claremont, Cape Town 1998-99; Brunswick, Melbourne 1999-2000; Old Collegians, Christchurch, New Zealand 2000-01
Cricketers particularly admired: David Gower, Steve Waugh
Young players to look out for: Darren Stevens, Sam Vesty (cricket and rugby)
Other sports played: Squash, golf
Other sports followed: Athletics ('Girlfriend Helen Frost went to Olympics in Sydney with Team GB'), football (Leicester City FC), rugby (Leicester Tigers)
Relaxations: 'All sport, a good film or CD, catching up with friends, talking, shark diving'
Extras: Played for Leicestershire Board XI in the NatWest 1999 and 2000

Opinions on cricket: 'Clubs and ECB should concentrate time, energy and resources into producing the best possible wickets. There are enough talented players in England to compete with the best in the world if they are given the best facilities to develop their skills.'

2000 Season (did not make any first-class or one-day appearances)

Career Performances

	M	Inns	NO	Runs	HS	Avge	100s	50s	Ct	St		Balls		Runs	Wkts	Avge		Best	5wI	10wM
Test																				
All First																				
1-day Int																				
NatWest	2	2	0	6	5	3.00	-	-	-	-										
B & H																				
1-day Lge																				

SUTTON, L. D.   Derbyshire

Name: <u>Luke</u> David Sutton
Role: Right-hand bat, wicket-keeper
Born: 4 October 1976, Keynsham
Height: 5ft 11in **Weight:** 12st 7lbs
Nickname: Sutts
County debut: 1997 (Somerset),
2000 (Derbyshire)
1st-Class 50s: 2
1st-Class catches: 30
1st-Class stumpings: 1
Place in batting averages: 120th av. 27.13
Parents: David and Molly
Marital status: Single
Education: Edgarley Hall, Glastonbury,
Somerset; Millfield School, Street, Somerset;
Durham University
Qualifications: 9 GCSEs, 4 A-levels,
2.1 degree in Economics, various cricket
coaching awards
Career outside cricket: 'None yet'
Off-season: Playing club cricket in Perth, Australia
Overseas tours: Various Somerset Schools tours to Holland; West of England U15
to West Indies 1991; Millfield School to Zimbabwe 1993, to Sri Lanka 1994; Durham
University to Zimbabwe 1997

Overseas teams played for: UNSW, Sydney 1998-99; Northville, Port Elizabeth, South Africa 1999-2000

Cricketers particularly admired: Ian Healy, Steve Waugh, Adrian Pierson, Alec Stewart, Paul Nixon, Ian Salisbury, Anthony Wilcox, Marcus Trescothick

Young players to look out for: Lawrence Prittipaul, Lian Wharton ('Tetley')

Other sports played: Golf, football

Other sports followed: Football (Newcastle United), rugby (Bath)

Relaxations: 'Spending time with my girlfriend Emma; keeping fit, going to the beach'

Extras: Captain of the England U15 side that played against South Africa and also played for England U18 and U19. Won John Hobbs Award for the U16 Cricketer of the Year in 1992 and the Gray Nicolls Award for the English Schools Cricketer of the Year in 1995. Left Somerset at the end of the 1999 season and joined Derbyshire for 2000

Opinions on cricket: 'The two division system has made a huge difference, as have central contracts. We just need to concentrate on continuing to improve the standard of pitches. Otherwise it is a fantastic game that is moving in the right direction all the time.'

Best batting: 79 Derbyshire v Hampshire, Derby 2000

2000 Season

	M	Inns	NO	Runs	HS	Avge	100s	50s	Ct	St	O	M	Runs	Wkts	Avge	Best	5wI	10wM
Test																		
All First	10	16	1	407	79	27.13	-	2	20	1								
1-day Int																		
NatWest	2	2	0	66	45	33.00	-	-	1	-								
B & H	1	1	0	0	0	0.00	-	-	-	-								
1-day Lge	10	9	1	133	53 *	16.62	-	1	8	2								

Career Performances

	M	Inns	NO	Runs	HS	Avge	100s	50s	Ct	St	Balls	Runs	Wkts	Avge	Best	5wI	10wM
Test																		
All First	13	22	4	448	79	24.88	-	2	30	1							
1-day Int																		
NatWest	2	2	0	66	45	33.00	-	-	1	-							
B & H	5	5	1	105	60	26.25	-	1	-	-							
1-day Lge	10	9	1	133	53 *	16.62	-	1	8	2							

SWANN, A. J.   Northamptonshire

Name: <u>Alec</u> James Swann
Role: Right-hand bat,
off-spin bowler, occasional wicket-keeper
Born: 26 October 1976, Northampton
Height: 6ft 2in **Weight:** 12st 8lbs
Nickname: Ron
County debut: 1996
1st-Class 50s: 5
1st-Class 100s: 4
1st-Class catches: 19
Place in batting averages: (1999 91st
av. 31.83)
Strike rate: 56.00 (career 89.25)
Parents: Ray and Mavis
Marital status: Single
Family links with cricket: Dad played for
Northumberland, Bedfordshire, Northants II
and England Amateurs. Still plays local

league cricket. Brother Graeme plays for Northants and toured South Africa and
Zimbabwe with England 1999-2000
Education: Sponne School, Towcester
Qualifications: 9 GCSEs, 4 A-levels, NCA coaching award
Off-season: 'Playing golf and perhaps football'
Overseas tours: Northants to Zimbabwe 1998, to Grenada 2000
Overseas teams played for: Wallsend, NSW, Australia 1995-96, 1997-98;
Montrose CC, Cape Town 1998-99
Cricketers particularly admired: Mark and Steve Waugh, Robin Smith,
Russell Warren
Young players to look out for: Mark Powell, Graeme Swann
Other sports played: Golf, snooker, occasionally football
Other sports followed: Football (Newcastle United)
Injuries: Out for four weeks with damaged Achilles tendon
Relaxations: Reading, watching films, golf
Extras: Played for England Schools U15 and U19. Opened batting for Bedfordshire
(with father in Minor Counties game). *Daily Telegraph* U15 Young Cricketer of the
Year 1992. Midlands Club Cricket Conference Young Cricketer of the Year 1992.
Played for England U19 against New Zealand in 1996
Best batting: 154 Northamptonshire v Nottinghamshire, Northampton 1999
Best bowling: 2-30 Northamptonshire v Gloucestershire, Northampton 2000

2000 Season

	M	Inns	NO	Runs	HS	Avge	100s	50s	Ct	St	O	M	Runs	Wkts	Avge	Best	5wI	10wM
Test																		
All First	3	5	1	201	108	50.25	1	1	1	-	28	13	42	3	14.00	2-30	-	-
1-day Int																		
NatWest	1	1	0	40	40	40.00	-	-	-	-	3	0	16	0	-		-	-
B & H																		
1-day Lge																		

Career Performances

	M	Inns	NO	Runs	HS	Avge	100s	50s	Ct	St	Balls	Runs	Wkts	Avge	Best	5wI	10wM
Test																	
All First	31	48	2	1286	154	27.95	4	5	19	-	357	196	4	49.00	2-30	-	-
1-day Int																	
NatWest	3	3	0	149	74	49.66	-	1	1	-	18	16	0	-		-	-
B & H																	
1-day Lge	8	8	0	180	60	22.50	-	1	2	-							

SWANN, G. P.   Northamptonshire

Name: <u>Graeme</u> Peter Swann
Role: Right-hand bat, off-spin bowler
Born: 24 March 1979, Northampton
Height: 6ft **Weight:** 11st 7lbs
Nickname: G-spot, Swanny
County debut: 1997 (one-day),
1998 (first-class)
County cap: 1999
One-Day Internationals: 1
50 wickets in a season: 1
1st-Class 50s: 9
1st-Class 100s: 2
1st-Class 5 w. in innings: 6
1st-Class 10 w. in match: 1
1st-Class catches: 36
One-Day 5 w. in innings: 1
Place in batting averages: 136th av. 24.87
(1999 95th av. 31.60)
Place in bowling averages: 107th av. 33.31 (1999 83rd av. 28.78)
Strike rate: 68.41 (career 62.61)
Parents: Raymond and Mavis
Marital status: Single

Family links with cricket: Dad has played Minor Counties cricket for Bedfordshire and Northumberland and also for England Amateurs. Brother is contracted to Northants. 'Cat is named after Gus Logie'
Education: Abington Vale Lower School; Sponne School, Towcester
Qualifications: 10 GCSEs, 4 A-levels, NCA coaching award
Career outside cricket: 'A bit of freelance sports journalism'
Off-season: 'Lowering my golf handicap; wasting money'
Overseas tours: England U19 to South Africa (including Youth World Cup) 1997-98; England A to Zimbabwe and South Africa 1998-99; England to South Africa 1999-2000
Cricketers particularly admired: Don Bradman, Devon Malcolm, Neil Foster, Shane Warne, the Waugh brothers
Young players to look out for: Tim Roberts, Mark Powell, Richard Logan, Alec Swann, 'David Capel'
Other sports played: Golf, rugby (Northants county schools), football, tennis
Other sports followed: Football (Newcastle United, Northampton Town), rugby (Northampton Saints)
Injuries: Out for two days with a shattered finger
Relaxations: 'Socialising, playing with puppies, feeding horses, reading classic literature and Meg and Mog books'
Extras: Played for England U14, U15, U17 and U19. *Daily Telegraph* regional bowling award winner in 1994. Gray-Nicolls Len Newbery Schools Cricketer of the Year in 1996. Took 8-118 for England U19 in second 'Test' v Pakistan U19 1998, the best ever figures in an U19 'Test'. Scored 92 and 111 in Championship match v Leicestershire at Grace Road in 1998. Drafted into England 13 for the fourth Test v New Zealand 1999. Completed Championship double of 500 runs and 50 wickets 1999. Made One-Day International debut v South Africa at Bloemfontein, January 2000
Opinions on cricket: 'Two divisions definitely works. Every game in the last two months seems to be a "must win", which is great. Pitches are still poor, and not judged uniformly. No one seemingly cares if wickets seam all over the place on the first day, but if they dare to spin…!!!'
Best batting: 130* Northamptonshire v Sri Lanka A, Northampton 1999
Best bowling: 6-41 Northamptonshire v Leicestershire, Northampton 1999
Stop press: Drafted into England A squad in West Indies 2000-01 as replacement for Jason Brown who was promoted to the senior tour of Sri Lanka. Had match figures of 9-62 and scored 49 runs v Windward Islands in St Lucia in the Busta Cup, winning the Man of the Match award

2000 Season

	M	Inns	NO	Runs	HS	Avge	100s	50s	Ct	St	O	M	Runs	Wkts	Avge	Best	5wI	10wM
Test																		
All First	16	24	0	597	72	24.87	-	3	8	-	467.3	92	1366	41	33.31	6-118	2	-
1-day Int																		
NatWest	3	2	0	35	18	17.50	-	-	4	-	27.5	1	125	4	31.25	2-25	-	
B & H	2	1	0	28	28	28.00	-	-	-	-	11	0	60	2	30.00	2-31	-	
1-day Lge	16	13	0	201	57	15.46	-	1	4	-	69.5	1	345	14	24.64	4-14	-	

Career Performances

	M	Inns	NO	Runs	HS	Avge	100s	50s	Ct	St	Balls	Runs	Wkts	Avge	Best	5wI	10wM
Test																	
All First	55	79	7	2061	130 *	28.62	2	9	36	-	8891	4421	142	31.13	6-41	6	1
1-day Int	1	0	0	0	0	-	-	-	-	-	30	24	0	-	-	-	
NatWest	6	5	0	140	42	28.00	-	-	5	-	280	216	7	30.85	2-25	-	
B & H	3	1	0	28	28	28.00	-	-	-	-	102	74	3	24.66	2-31	-	
1-day Lge	40	30	3	512	63	18.96	-	3	8	-	1256	1032	41	25.17	5-35	1	

SYMINGTON, M. J. Durham

Name: <u>Marc</u> Joseph Symington
Role: Right-hand bat, right-arm
medium bowler
Born: 10 January 1980,
Newcastle upon Tyne
Height: 5ft 9in **Weight:** 10st 8lbs
Nickname: Simo
County debut: 1998
1st-Class catches: 1
Strike rate: 102.00 (career 45.71)
Parents: Keith and Sheila
Marital status: Single
Family links with cricket: Grandfather
(Ron Symington) played 24 years in
Northumberland League, then umpired in
same league for 21 years. Father currently
plays for Norton CC in North East Premier
League. Brother (Craig) plays for Norton CC
and Durham U19. Mother is club committee member
Education: St Joseph's, Norton, Stockton-on-Tees; St Michael's, Billingham,
Stockton-on-Tees; Stockton Sixth Form College

Qualifications: 5 GCSEs, BTEC in Sports Science, Level I coach
Off-season: Playing cricket and attending cricket academy in Western Australia
Overseas tours: Durham U21 to Sri Lanka 1996; England U19 to New Zealand 1998-99
Overseas teams played for: Claremont Nedlands, Perth 2000-01
Cricketers particularly admired: Graham Thorpe, Darren Gough, Adam Gilchrist
Young players to look out for: Ian Hunter, Gary Pratt, James Foster
Other sports played: Football ('played for Middlesbrough U16'), golf, hockey, snooker
Other sports followed: Football (Middlesbrough FC)
Injuries: Out for two games with shin splints
Relaxations: Playing golf and snooker and socialising with friends
Extras: Contracted player for Norton CC in 2000, scoring 466 runs (av. 42.36) and taking 25 wickets (av. 16.20)
Opinions on cricket: 'Third umpire is beginning to be used too much. Most decisions should be left to the umpires in the middle and the players' honesty.'
Best batting: 36 Durham v Yorkshire, Riverside 2000
Best bowling: 3-55 Durham v Derbyshire, Derby 1998

2000 Season

	M	Inns	NO	Runs	HS	Avge	100s	50s	Ct	St	O	M	Runs	Wkts	Avge	Best	5wI	10wM
Test																		
All First	1	2	1	44	36	44.00	-	-	-	-	17	2	67	1	67.00	1-61	-	-
1-day Int																		
NatWest																		
B & H																		
1-day Lge	5	5	0	23	16	4.60	-	-	3	-	13	0	68	1	68.00	1-15	-	

Career Performances

	M	Inns	NO	Runs	HS	Avge	100s	50s	Ct	St	Balls	Runs	Wkts	Avge	Best	5wI	10wM
Test																	
All First	3	3	2	52	36	52.00	-	-	1	-	320	215	7	30.71	3-55	-	-
1-day Int																	
NatWest																	
B & H																	
1-day Lge	10	8	0	43	16	5.37	-	-	4	-	276	282	4	70.50	1-15	-	

TAHIR, N. — Warwickshire

Name: Naqaash Tahir
Role: Right-hand bat, right-arm fast bowler
Born: 14 November 1983, Birmingham
Height: 5ft 10in
Nickname: Naq
County debut: No first-team appearance
Parents: Mohammed Amin and
Ishrat Nasreen
Marital status: Single
Family links with cricket: Father and
brother both cricketers
Education: Nelson Mandela; Moseley
School; Spring Hill College
Qualifications: Level 1 coaching
Off-season: 'I'm intending to go to Pakistan
on tour'
Overseas tours: Warwickshire U15 to South
Africa 1999

Cricketers particularly admired: Wasim Akram, Waqar Younis, Darren Gough,
Alec Stewart, Nick Knight, Saeed Anwar
Other sports followed: Football (Manchester United)
Relaxations: Fitness work
Extras: Has been Moseley Ashfield U15 Player of the Year, Warwickshire U15 Youth
Player of the Year and top wicket-taker for Warwickshire U16
Opinions on cricket: 'Cricket is a very interesting, very highly professional game. It's
a game in which you depend on yourself and must perform to the best of your ability.'

---

85. Who had gone a record 119 Test innings without
a duck before he was caught by Allan Border off Greg Matthews
in England's second innings at Melbourne in 1990-91?

TAYLOR, B. V. Sussex

Name: <u>Billy</u> Victor Taylor
Role: Left-hand bat, right-arm medium-fast bowler
Born: 11 January 1977, Southampton
Height: 6ft 3in **Weight:** 13st 7lbs
Nickname: Howzat, Crusty
County debut: 1999
1st-Class catches: 1
Strike rate: 118.00 (career 107.25)
Parents: Victor and Jackie
Marital status: Engaged to Barbara
Family links with cricket: Both older brothers, Martin and James, play club cricket in Hampshire; James has played Minor Counties cricket for Wiltshire
Education: Townhill Park; Bitterne Park; So Tec College
Qualifications: 5 GCSEs, NVQ Level 2 Carpentry and Joinery
Career outside cricket: Carpenter
Off-season: 'Playing cricket in New Zealand; working on fitness and playing a lot of golf'
Overseas tours: Sussex/Hampshire to Cyprus 1999
Overseas teams played for: Central Hawke's Bay, New Zealand 1996-97; Manawatu Foxton CC/Horowhenu Reps, New Zealand 1998-99, 2000-01
Cricketers particularly admired: Martin and James Taylor, Malcolm Marshall, David Gower
Other sports played: Golf
Other sports followed: Football (Havant & Waterlooville FC, 'my brother James plays for them')
Relaxations: 'Golf, swimming, falconry and going for walks in the country'
Extras: Played Minor Counties cricket for Wiltshire 1996-98 and has played club cricket for Winchester KS since 1993. Took 98 wickets in New Zealand club cricket in 1998-99. Sussex 2nd XI Player of the Year 1999, 2000
Opinions on cricket: 'Should have the same length breaks for lunch and tea. Should have the new ball at 80 overs. Keep the league system the same, but in the four-day league only play each other once, not twice, as we play too much cricket in this country.'
Best batting: 14 Sussex v Derbyshire, Derby 1999
Best bowling: 3-27 Sussex v Worcestershire, Worcester 2000

2000 Season

	M	Inns	NO	Runs	HS	Avge	100s	50s	Ct	St	O	M	Runs	Wkts	Avge	Best	5wI	10wM
Test																		
All First	5	6	4	9	6	4.50	-	-	-	-	118	28	405	6	67.50	3-27	-	-
1-day Int																		
NatWest	2	1	0	1	1	1.00	-	-	1	-	15	2	49	5	9.80	4-26	-	
B & H																		
1-day Lge	11	5	2	9	5	3.00	-	-	1	-	73	4	340	13	26.15	2-30	-	

Career Performances

	M	Inns	NO	Runs	HS	Avge	100s	50s	Ct	St	Balls	Runs	Wkts	Avge	Best	5wI	10wM
Test																	
All First	6	8	4	23	14	5.75	-	-	1	-	858	513	8	64.12	3-27	-	-
1-day Int																	
NatWest	3	1	0	1	1	1.00	-	-	1	-	150	92	5	18.40	4-26	-	
B & H																	
1-day Lge	20	7	4	31	21 *	10.33	-	-	2	-	804	652	24	27.16	3-22	-	

TAYLOR, C. G. — Gloucestershire

Name: Christopher (<u>Chris</u>) Glyn Taylor
Role: Right-hand bat, right-arm
off-spin bowler
Born: 27 September 1976, Bristol
Height: 5ft 8in **Weight:** 10st
Nickname: Tales, Tootsie
County debut: 2000
1st-Class 100s: 1
1st-Class catches: 8
Place in batting averages: 130th av. 25.89
Strike rate: 55.00 (career 55.00)
Parents: Chris and Maggie
Marital status: Girlfriend Sarah
Family links with cricket: Father and
grandfather both played local club cricket
Education: Brentry Primary School;
Colston's Collegiate School
Qualifications: GCSEs and A-levels
Career outside cricket: Teaching
Off-season: 'Couple of holidays'
Overseas teams played for: Harbord CC, Manly, Australia 2000
Cricketers particularly admired: Jonty Rhodes, Mark Waugh

Other sports played: Rugby, hockey (both county level); squash, tennis
Other sports followed: Rugby
Injuries: Out for two weeks with injury to left shoulder
Relaxations: Fishing
Extras: Represented England Schools U18. In 1995-96 won the Cricket Society's
A. A. Thomson Fielding Prize and Wetherell Award. Set school record of 278* v
Hutton Grammar School. Made his highest score of 300* for Gloucestershire 2nd XI
v Somerset 1999. Scored maiden first-class century (104) in the Championship match
v Middlesex 2000, becoming the first player from any county to score a century at
Lord's on Championship debut; also the first player to score a century for
Gloucestershire in match that was both first-class and Championship debut
Opinions on cricket: 'Fitness is a key factor for players to produce their best
performances through the long season.'
Best batting: 104 Gloucestershire v Middlesex, Lord's 2000
Best bowling: 3-126 Gloucestershire v Northamptonshire, Cheltenham 2000

2000 Season

	M	Inns	NO	Runs	HS	Avge	100s	50s	Ct	St	O	M	Runs	Wkts	Avge	Best	5wI	10wM
Test																		
All First	12	22	3	492	104	25.89	1	-	8	-	27.3	5	136	3	45.33	3-126	-	-
1-day Int																		
NatWest	6	5	2	57	41	19.00	-	-	4	-								
B & H	5	2	1	32	23 *	32.00	-	-	-	-								
1-day Lge	13	8	1	75	37 *	10.71	-	-	4	-								

Career Performances

	M	Inns	NO	Runs	HS	Avge	100s	50s	Ct	St	Balls	Runs	Wkts	Avge	Best	5wI	10wM
Test																	
All First	12	22	3	492	104	25.89	1	-	8	-	165	136	3	45.33	3-126	-	-
1-day Int																	
NatWest	7	6	2	57	41	14.25	-	-	5	-							
B & H	5	2	1	32	23 *	32.00	-	-	-	-							
1-day Lge	13	8	1	75	37 *	10.71	-	-	4	-							

86. Which brothers made their Test debuts at Trent Bridge in 1997?

TAYLOR, C. R. Yorkshire

Name: Christopher (<u>Chris</u>) Robert Taylor
Role: Right-hand opening bat
Born: 21 February 1981, Pudsey, West Yorkshire
Height: 6ft 3in **Weight:** 14st
Nickname: CT
County debut: No first-team appearance
Parents: Phil and Elaine
Marital status: Single
Education: Waterloo Infant and Junior School, Pudsey; Benton Park High School, Leeds
Qualifications: 9 GCSEs, 4 A-levels
Off-season: Playing for Western Suburbs CC, Sydney ('the Magpies')
Overseas teams played for: Western Suburbs CC, Sydney 1999-2001
Cricketers particularly admired:
Geoffrey Boycott, Michael Atherton, Michael Vaughan, Courtney Walsh
Young players to look out for: Michael Clarke (NSW), Michael Lumb
Other sports played: Rugby, football, tennis, basketball (all for Benton Park HS 1st teams)
Other sports followed: Football (Everton – 'since I was four years old'), 'enjoy watching all sports'
Relaxations: Watching cricket, listening to music (Oasis), going to the beach ('in Australia!'), being with friends and family
Extras: Represented Yorkshire Schools U10-U15. Represented North of England at Bunbury Festival 1996 and was awarded Neil Lloyd Trophy for top run-scorer in festival. Selected for England U15 team for Lombard World Cup 1996. Has also represented England U17 and U19. Yorkshire CCC Supporters' Club Young Player of the Year 1999. Junior pro contract with Yorkshire 2000
Opinions on cricket: 'Progress is being made as England are developing once again as a world force in cricket. This improvement will be maintained, providing county clubs continue to develop and foster talented youngsters – YCCC Academy and Durham CCC are testimony to this. The benefits of this approach are starting to be realised at both county and international levels.'

TAYLOR, J. P.   Northamptonshire

Name: Jonathan <u>Paul</u> Taylor
Role: Left-hand bat, left-arm
fast-medium bowler, occasional left-arm spin
bowler
Born: 8 August 1964, Ashby-de-la-Zouch,
Leicestershire
Height: 6ft 2in   **Weight:** 14st
Nickname: Roadie, PT
County debut: 1984 (Derbyshire),
1991 (Northamptonshire)
County cap: 1992 (Northamptonshire)
Benefit: 2000
Test debut: 1992-93
Tests: 2
One-Day Internationals: 1
50 wickets in a season: 6
1st-Class 50s: 8
1st-Class 5 w. in innings: 18
1st-Class 10 w. in match: 4
1st-Class catches: 58
One-Day 5 w. in innings: 1
Place in batting averages: 267th av. 10.66 (1999 232nd av. 16.63)
Place in bowling averages: 38th av. 22.50 (1999 93rd av. 29.72)
Strike rate: 53.12 (career 56.15)
Parents: Derek (deceased) and Janet
Wife and date of marriage: Elaine Mary, 30 July 1993
Children: Christopher Paul, 8 July 1994; Danny Michael, 6 February 1997
Family links with cricket: Father and brother played local league cricket
Education: Pingle School, Swadlincote, Derbyshire
Qualifications: 6 O-levels, NCA senior coach
Off-season: 'Finishing off my benefit year, then in the Marketing Department at the club'
Overseas tours: Midland Club Cricket Conference to Australia 1990-91; England to India and Sri Lanka 1992-93; England A to South Africa 1993-94; Northamptonshire to Natal 1993, to Zimbabwe 1995, 1998, to Johannesburg 1996, to Grenada 2000
Overseas teams played for: Papakura, New Zealand 1984-85; Napier High School Old Boys, New Zealand 1985-86; North Kalgoorlie, Western Australia 1990-91; Great Boulder, Western Australia 1991-92; Montrose CC, Cape Town 1998-99
Cricketers particularly admired: Dennis Lillee, Courtney Walsh, Curtly Ambrose
Young players to look out for: Jason Brown, Michael Davies, Graeme Swann, Richard Logan

Other sports followed: Soccer, rugby, basketball

Injuries: Out for three months with right knee injury that required arthroscopy

Relaxations: 'Looking after two hyperactive little lads. Relaxing ... I think not; enjoyable ... definitely!!!'

Extras: Spent four seasons on the staff at Derbyshire 1984-87 and played Minor Counties cricket for Staffordshire 1989-90. Won Man of the Match in the Bain Clarkson Final in 1987 for Derbyshire, after being released. Played first game at Lord's in NatWest Trophy final 1992. Was voted Northamptonshire's Player of the Year in 1992. Selected for England Indoor World Cup squad 1995

Opinions on cricket: 'Two divisions has proved how much more competitive every game of cricket can be. Right down to the last round of both the leagues there were still lots of issues to be decided. Players are being asked to play under pressure all the time, which I believe will enhance the performance of the player when he makes the England team.'

Best batting: 86 Northamptonshire v Durham, Northampton 1995

Best bowling: 7-23 Northamptonshire v Hampshire, Bournemouth 1992

2000 Season

	M	Inns	NO	Runs	HS	Avge	100s	50s	Ct	St	O	M	Runs	Wkts	Avge	Best	5wI	10wM
Test																		
All First	7	10	1	96	27	10.66	-	-	3	-	212.3	50	540	24	22.50	6-27	1	1
1-day Int																		
NatWest																		
B & H																		
1-day Lge	6	3	0	14	11	4.66	-	-	2	-	43	2	164	6	27.33	2-32	-	

Career Performances

	M	Inns	NO	Runs	HS	Avge	100s	50s	Ct	St	Balls	Runs	Wkts	Avge	Best	5wI	10wM
Test	2	4	2	34	17 *	17.00	-	-	-	-	288	156	3	52.00	1-18	-	-
All First	171	196	62	1980	86	14.77	-	8	58	-	29762	15273	530	28.81	7-23	18	4
1-day Int	1	1	0	1	1	1.00	-	-	-	-	18	20	0	-	-	-	
NatWest	30	12	6	40	9	6.66	-	-	6	-	1767	1182	39	30.30	4-34	-	
B & H	32	14	7	62	14	8.85	-	-	6	-	1797	1101	42	26.21	5-45	1	
1-day Lge	127	45	21	243	24	10.12	-	-	29	-	5453	4182	142	29.45	4-41	-	

THOMAS, I. J. Glamorgan

Name: <u>Ian</u> James Thomas
Role: Left-hand bat, right-arm off-spin bowler
Born: 9 May 1979, Newport, Gwent
Height: 5ft 11in **Weight:** 13st 7lbs
Nickname: Bolts, Action Man
County debut: 2000
1st-Class 50s: 1
1st-Class catches: 3
Parents: Alun and Amanda
Marital status: Single
Family links with cricket: Father club stalwart of Machen CC
Education: Machen Primary School; Bedwas Comprehensive; Bassaleg Comprehensive; University of Wales Institute, Cardiff (UWIC)
Qualifications: 9 GCSEs, 2 A-levels
Career outside cricket: Marketing and management of sport and events
Off-season: 'Finishing my third year at university and hopefully getting a BSc degree in Sports Development at UWIC. Training hard at Glamorgan's new indoor cricket centre'
Overseas tours: British Universities to South Africa 1999
Cricketers particularly admired: Adrian Dale, Steve James, Marcus Trescothick
Young players to look out for: Mark Wallace, David Harrison, Chris Taylor, Rhys Thomas
Other sports played: Golf, rugby (Machen RFC)
Other sports followed: Rugby (Newport RFC)
Relaxations: Walking, training, music
Extras: Glamorgan Young Player of the Month June, July, August and September 2000. Scored 82 on Championship debut v Essex at Southend 2000
Opinions on cricket: 'Not yet gained enough experience to comment.'
Best batting: 82 Glamorgan v Essex, Southend 2000

	M	Inns	NO	Runs	HS	Avge	100s	50s	Ct	St	O	M	Runs	Wkts	Avge	Best	5wI	10wM
Test																		
All First	3	5	1	177	82	44.25	-	1	3	-								
1-day Int																		
NatWest																		
B & H																		
1-day Lge	4	4	0	100	36	25.00	-	-	2	-								

Career Performances

	M	Inns	NO	Runs	HS	Avge	100s	50s	Ct	St	Balls	Runs	Wkts	Avge	Best	5wI	10wM
Test																	
All First	4	6	2	186	82	46.50	-	1	5	-							
1-day Int																	
NatWest																	
B & H																	
1-day Lge	4	4	0	100	36	25.00	-	-	2	-							

THOMAS, S. D.   Glamorgan

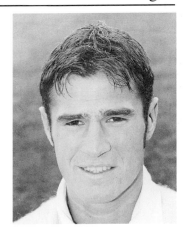

Name: Stuart <u>Darren</u> Thomas
Role: Left-hand middle-order bat, right-arm fast-medium bowler
Born: 25 January 1975, Morriston
Height: 6ft **Weight:** 12st
Nickname: Tedster, Thommo
County debut: 1992
County cap: 1997
50 wickets in a season: 4
1st-Class 50s: 9
1st-Class 5 w. in innings: 15
1st-Class catches: 38
One-Day 5 w. in innings: 3
Place in batting averages: 131st av. 25.84 (1999 245th av. 14.66)
Place in bowling averages: 85th av. 28.78 (1999 55th av. 24.26)
Strike rate: 52.28 (career 49.70)
Parents: Stu and Anne
Wife and date of marriage: Claire, 30 September 2000
Family links with cricket: 'Old man used to bowl a heavy ball or two'
Education: Old Road; Graig Comprehensive; Neath Tertiary College

Qualifications: 4 GCSEs, BTEC National Diploma in Sports Science, advanced cricket coach
Career outside cricket: 'DIY on my self-build project'
Off-season: 'Building and decorating my pad'
Overseas tours: Glamorgan to South Africa 1992-93, 1996, 1998, to Portugal 1995, to Zimbabwe 1996; England U18 to South Africa 1992-93; England U19 to Sri Lanka 1993-94; England A to Zimbabwe and South Africa 1998-99, to Bangladesh and New Zealand 1999-2000
Overseas teams played for: Rovers CC, Welkom, Free State 1995
Cricketers particularly admired: Steve Barwick and Keith Newell 'for their preparation for the next day's play'
Young players to look out for: Mark Wallace, James Foster, 'Ronnie Irani'
Other sports played: Rugby (New Dock Stars)
Relaxations: 'Listening to and participating in our schoolboy-like dressing room banter'
Extras: Became youngest player (17 years 217 days) to take five wickets on debut, v Derbyshire in 1992, and finished eighth in national bowling averages. BBC Welsh Young Sports Personality 1992. Played last U19 'Test' against India at Edgbaston 1994. Broke Alan Wilkins' (Glamorgan) best Benson and Hedges bowling record on his debut in the competition with 6 for 20 in 1995. Took 7-16 v Surrey in the Sunday League in 1998, the best analysis by a Glamorgan bowler in the competition. Glamorgan Player of the Year 1998. Took 8-50 for England A v Zimbabwe A at Harare on 1998-99 tour – the first eight-wicket haul by an England A tourist
Opinions on cricket: 'Need a day's rest in between four-day cricket and one-day cricket. Body needs time to recover. Please!'
Best batting: 78* Glamorgan v Gloucestershire, Abergavenny 1995
Best bowling: 8-50 England A v Zimbabwe A, Harare 1998-99

2000 Season

	M	Inns	NO	Runs	HS	Avge	100s	50s	Ct	St	O	M	Runs	Wkts	Avge	Best	5wI	10wM
Test																		
All First	17	20	7	336	52	25.84	-	1	2	-	488	93	1612	56	28.78	5-43	2	-
1-day Int																		
NatWest	2	2	0	14	11	7.00	-	-	-	-	17	1	73	5	14.60	4-27	-	
B & H	3	3	1	18	7	9.00	-	-	-	-	20	0	99	4	24.75	3-49	-	
1-day Lge	12	7	0	72	21	10.28	-	-	2	-	93.4	4	438	18	24.33	4-42	-	

Career Performances

	M	Inns	NO	Runs	HS	Avge	100s	50s	Ct	St	Balls	Runs	Wkts	Avge	Best	5wI	10wM
Test																	
All First	112	150	33	2222	78 *	18.99	-	9	38	-	18043	10562	363	29.09	8-50	15	-
1-day Int																	
NatWest	12	10	1	134	40	14.88	-	-	2	-	717	559	23	24.30	5-74	1	
B & H	16	11	4	113	29	16.14	-	-	5	-	680	601	24	25.04	6-20	1	
1-day Lge	57	43	6	425	38 *	11.48	-	-	8	-	2117	1788	73	24.49	7-16	1	

THOMPSON, D. J. Essex

Name: <u>David</u> James Thompson
Role: Right-hand bat, right-arm fast bowler
Born: 11 March 1976, Wandsworth, London
Height: 6ft 3in
Nickname: Thommo
County debut: 1994 (Surrey), 1999 (Essex)
1st-Class catches: 1
Place in batting averages: (1999 292nd av. 5.50)
Place in bowling averages: (1999 78th av. 28.54)
Strike rate: 109.50 (career 51.20)
Marital status: Single
Education: Ernest Bevin School, Wandsworth; Westminster School
Overseas tours: England U19 to West Indies 1994-95
Cricketers particularly admired: Michael Holding
Young players to look out for: Tim Phillips
Other sports played: Football
Other sports followed: Football (Liverpool)
Relaxations: Music, socialising

Extras: Left Surrey after 1994 season and joined Lancashire. Joined Essex for 1999; released by Essex at the end of the 2000 season
Best batting: 22 Essex v Northamptonshire, Northampton 1999
Best bowling: 4-46 Essex v Somerset, Chelmsford 1999

2000 Season

	M	Inns	NO	Runs	HS	Avge	100s	50s	Ct	St	O	M	Runs	Wkts	Avge	Best	5wl	10wM
Test																		
All First	2	1	0	15	15	15.00	-	-	-	-	36.3	12	106	2	53.00	2-76	-	-
1-day Int																		
NatWest																		
B & H																		
1-day Lge																		

Career Performances

	M	Inns	NO	Runs	HS	Avge	100s	50s	Ct	St	Balls	Runs	Wkts	Avge	Best	5wl	10wM
Test																	
All First	11	13	0	109	22	8.38	-	-	1	-	1485	914	29	31.51	4-46	-	-
1-day Int																	
NatWest																	
B & H																	
1-day Lge	3	2	1	2	1 *	2.00	-	-	-	-	81	67	2	33.50	2-34	-

THORPE, G. P. Surrey

Name: <u>Graham</u> Paul Thorpe
Role: Left-hand bat, occasional
right-arm medium bowler
Born: 1 August 1969, Farnham
Height: 5ft 10in **Weight:** 12st 9lbs
Nickname: Chalky
County debut: 1988
County cap: 1991
Benefit: 2000
Test debut: 1993
Tests: 60
One-Day Internationals: 60
1000 runs in a season: 8
1st-Class 50s: 92
1st-Class 100s: 33
1st-Class 200s: 3
1st-Class catches: 217
One-Day 100s: 7
Place in batting averages: 146th av. 23.50 (1999 27th av. 41.64)
Strike rate: (career 92.36)
Parents: 'Mr and Mrs Thorpe'

Wife: Nicola
Children: Henry and Amelia
Family links with cricket: Both brothers play for Farnham, father also plays cricket and mother is 'professional scorer'
Education: Weydon Comprehensive; Farnham College
Qualifications: 7 O-levels, PE Diploma
Off-season: England tours to Kenya, Pakistan and Sri Lanka
Overseas tours: England A to Zimbabwe and Kenya 1989-90, to Pakistan 1990-91, to Bermuda and West Indies 1991-92, to Australia 1992-93; England to West Indies 1993-94, to Australia 1994-95, to South Africa 1995-96, to India and Pakistan (World Cup) 1995-96, to Zimbabwe and New Zealand 1996-97, to Sharjah (Champions Trophy) 1997-98, to West Indies 1997-98, to Australia 1998-99, to Sharjah (Coca-Cola Cup) 1998-99, to Kenya (ICC Knockout Trophy) 2000-01, to Pakistan and Sri Lanka 2000-01
Cricketers particularly admired: Grahame Clinton, Waqar Younis, Ian Botham, Viv Richards
Young players to look out for: Ian Ward, Ben Hollioake
Other sports followed: Football (Chelsea FC), golf
Relaxations: Sleeping
Extras: Played for English Schools cricket U15 and U19 and England Schools football U18. Scored a century against Australia on his Test debut at Trent Bridge 1993. Shared in a record fifth-wicket partnership for England in Tests v West Indies (150) with Alec Stewart at Bridgetown 1993-94. Shared in a record fourth-wicket partnership for England in Tests v Australia (288) with Nasser Hussain at Edgbaston 1997. England's Player of the Series and leading run-scorer in the 1997 Ashes campaign with 453 runs at an average of 50.33. Shared in a record sixth-wicket partnership for England in Tests v West Indies (205) with Mark Ramprakash at Bridgetown 1997-98. Cornhill England Player of the Year 1997-98. One of *Wisden*'s Five Cricketers of the Year 1998. Represented England in the 1999 World Cup. Played for a World XI v an Asia XI at The Oval 2000
Best batting: 223* England v South Australia, Adelaide 1998-99
Best bowling: 4-40 Surrey v Australians, The Oval 1993
Stop press: Reached 2000 One-Day International runs in third ODI v Pakistan at Rawalpindi 2000-01. With Craig White, shared in a new record sixth-wicket partnership for England in Tests v Pakistan (166) in the first Test at Lahore 2000-01; his century was the first in Test history to contain only one boundary (he added a second four before being out for 118). Scored match-winning 64* in third Test at Karachi 2000-01 to steer England to a series victory v Pakistan

2000 Season

	M	Inns	NO	Runs	HS	Avge	100s	50s	Ct	St	O	M	Runs	Wkts	Avge	Best	5wl	10wM
Test	3	4	0	96	46	24.00	-	-	3	-								
All First	11	16	0	376	115	23.50	1	1	9	-								
1-day Int	7	5	1	102	42	25.50	-	-	1	-								
NatWest	2	2	1	101	55	101.00	-	1	1	-								
B & H	4	3	0	37	21	12.33	-	-	-	-								
1-day Lge	8	8	3	344	126 *	68.80	1	2	7	-								

Career Performances

	M	Inns	NO	Runs	HS	Avge	100s	50s	Ct	St	Balls	Runs	Wkts	Avge	Best	5wl	10wM
Test	60	109	13	3695	138	38.48	6	24	56	-	138	37	0	-	-	-	-
All First	261	435	61	16487	223 *	44.08	36	92	217	-	2309	1290	25	51.60	4-40	-	-
1-day Int	60	57	9	1888	89	39.33	-	17	33	-	120	97	2	48.50	2-15	-	
NatWest	30	29	8	1159	145 *	55.19	1	9	18	-	13	12	0	-	-	-	
B & H	48	46	4	1653	103	39.35	1	12	20	-	168	131	4	32.75	3-35	-	
1-day Lge	129	119	17	3831	126 *	37.55	5	26	51	-	318	307	8	38.37	3-21	-	

TITCHARD, S. P.   Derbyshire

Name: Stephen Paul Titchard
Role: Right-hand bat, right-arm
medium bowler
Born: 17 December 1967,
Warrington, Cheshire
Height: 6ft 3in   **Weight:** 15st
Nickname: Titch, Stainy, Tyrone
County debut: 1990 (Lancs), 1999 (Derbys)
1st-Class 50s: 30
1st-Class 100s: 6
1st-Class catches: 54
Place in batting averages: 85th av. 31.17
(1999 122nd av. 27.85)
Strike rate: (career 97.50)
Parents: Alan and Margaret
Marital status: Single
Family links with cricket: Father, uncle and
two brothers have played for Grappenhall 1st
XI in the Manchester Association League. Father also represented the Army
Education: Lymm County High School; Priestley College
Qualifications: 3 O-levels, NCA senior coaching award
Career outside cricket: Coach

Overseas tours: Lancashire to Tasmania and Western Australia 1990, to Western Australia 1991, to Johannesburg 1992
Overseas teams played for: South Canberra, Australia 1991-92
Cricketers particularly admired: Graham Gooch, Malcolm Marshall
Other sports followed: Football (Manchester City) and rugby league (Warrington)
Relaxations: Snooker, golf, 'most sports'
Extras: Played for England U19. Made record scores for Manchester Association U18 (200*) and Cheshire Schools U19 (203*). Released by Lancashire at end of 1998 season and joined Derbyshire. Took part in an unbroken opening partnership of 293 with Steve Stubbings (135*) v Kent at Canterbury 2000, scoring 141*; it was the first occasion on which Derbyshire had batted all day without losing a wicket
Best batting: 163 Lancashire v Essex, Chelmsford 1996
Best bowling: 1-11 Lancashire v Northamptonshire, Old Trafford 1997
              1-11 Lancashire v Kent, Old Trafford 1997

2000 Season

	M	Inns	NO	Runs	HS	Avge	100s	50s	Ct	St	O	M	Runs	Wkts	Avge	Best	5wI	10wM
Test																		
All First	11	19	2	530	141 *	31.17	1	3	-	-	5	2	5	0	-	-	-	-
1-day Int																		
NatWest	1	1	0	13	13	13.00	-	-	-	-								
B & H	5	1	0	7	7	7.00	-	-	1	-								
1-day Lge	4	4	0	57	33	14.25	-	-	-	-								

Career Performances

	M	Inns	NO	Runs	HS	Avge	100s	50s	Ct	St	Balls	Runs	Wkts	Avge	Best	5wI	10wM
Test																	
All First	104	181	14	5227	163	31.29	6	30	54	-	390	195	4	48.75	1-11	-	-
1-day Int																	
NatWest	6	6	1	142	92	28.40	-	1	1	-							
B & H	8	4	0	108	82	27.00	-	1	2	-							
1-day Lge	47	46	4	1002	96	23.85	-	3	5	-	54	48	1	48.00	1-19	-	

TOLLEY, C. M.   Nottinghamshire

Name: Christopher (<u>Chris</u>) Mark Tolley
Role: Right-hand bat, left-arm
medium bowler
Born: 30 December 1967, Kidderminster
Height: 5ft 9in **Weight:** 11st 7lbs
Nickname: Red Dog, Warrior
County debut: 1989 (Worcestershire),
1996 (Nottinghamshire)
County cap: 1993 (Worcestershire),
1997 (Nottinghamshire)
1st-Class 50s: 13
1st-Class 5 w. in innings: 5
1st-Class catches: 42
One-Day 5 w. in innings: 1
Place in batting averages: 111th av. 27.87
(1999 256th av. 13.25)
Strike rate: 78.00 (career 72.39)
Parents: Ray and Liz
Wife and date of marriage: Simone, 12 December 1998
Family links with cricket: Brother (Richard) plays for Blossomfield CC
Education: Oldswinford C of E; Redhill Comprehensive School; King Edward VI
College, Stourbridge; Loughborough University
Qualifications: 9 O-levels, 3 A-levels, BSc (Hons) PE, Sports Science & Recreation
Management, QTS, SMT Dip, advanced cricket coach and Level II hockey coach
Career outside cricket: PE teacher
Overseas tours: British Universities Sports Federation to Barbados, October 1989;
Worcestershire to Zimbabwe and South Africa; Nottinghamshire to South Africa
Overseas teams played for: Lancaster Park, Christchurch, New Zealand 1996-97
Cricketers particularly admired: Ian Botham, Graeme Hick
Young players to look out for: Ed Joyce
Other sports played: Hockey (South Notts HC – 'promotion and cup runners-up last
season!')
Injuries: Side strain and injury to hip flexor
Relaxations: 'Food, wine and now gardening (I must be getting old)'
Extras: Played for English Schools U19 in 1986 and for the Combined Universities in
B&H Cup. Asked to be released by Worcestershire at the end of the 1995 season and
joined Nottinghamshire for the 1996 season. Took first-class hat-trick against
Leicestershire in 1997. Appointed as a Cricket Development Officer at
Nottinghamshire in autumn 2000 but remains registered as a player
Opinions on cricket: 'Two divisions seems to be working – more to play for over a
longer period.'

Best batting: 84 Worcestershire v Derbyshire, Derby 1994
Best bowling: 7-45 Nottinghamshire v Worcestershire, Kidderminster 1998

2000 Season

	M	Inns	NO	Runs	HS	Avge	100s	50s	Ct	St	O	M	Runs	Wkts	Avge	Best	5wI	10wM
Test																		
All First	6	9	1	223	60	27.87	-	2	2	-	52	22	107	4	26.75	3-22	-	-
1-day Int																		
NatWest	1	1	0	20	20	20.00	-	-	-	-	10	0	38	1	38.00	1-38	-	
B & H	3	3	1	59	49 *	29.50	-	-	-	-	17	1	58	0	-		-	-
1-day Lge	13	10	2	134	38	16.75	-	-	3	-	88.1	3	352	9	39.11	2-27	-	

Career Performances

	M	Inns	NO	Runs	HS	Avge	100s	50s	Ct	St	Balls	Runs	Wkts	Avge	Best	5wI	10wM
Test																	
All First	106	148	31	2666	84	22.78	-	13	42	-	13682	6623	189	35.04	7-45	5	-
1-day Int																	
NatWest	14	11	3	202	77	25.25	-	1	1	-	768	465	17	27.35	3-21	-	
B & H	23	20	3	414	77	24.35	-	3	3	-	1080	691	9	76.77	1-12	-	
1-day Lge	94	61	14	783	44	16.65	-	-	27	-	3257	2537	95	26.70	5-16	1	

TREGO, P. D.   Somerset

Name: <u>Peter</u> David Trego
Role: Right-hand bat, right-arm
'quickish' bowler
Born: 12 June 1981, Weston-super-Mare
Height: 6ft **Weight:** 12st 7lbs
Nickname: Tregs 'and many more'
County debut: 2000
1st-Class 50s: 1
1st-Class catches: 3
Place in batting averages: 189th av. 19.14
Place in bowling averages: 109th av. 33.50
Strike rate: 55.05 (career 55.05)
Parents: Carol and Paul
Marital status: Single
Family links with cricket: 'Brother Sam
played for Somerset; Dad plays for Uphill
Castle – both strong batsmen'
Education: St Martins, Weston-super-Mare;
Wyvern Comprehensive

Qualifications: Lifeguard (at Hutton Moor Leisure Centre)

Off-season: Making components for loft conversions

Cricketers particularly admired: Ian Botham and Graham Rose – 'they have both been huge inspirations to me'

Young players to look out for: Mathew Gitcham, Michael Coles (Somerset), Ian Flanagan, James Adams

Other sports played: Football ('I had a winter contract with Weston-super-Mare; now playing for Torrington FC')

Other sports followed: Football (Man Utd), darts, golf

Relaxations: Golf, snooker, music, socialising with friends, shopping

Extras: Won Best Batsman award at U16 – averaged 137 in nine games. Scored century for Somerset 2nd XI v Glos 1999. Attended Lilleshall with England U17. Represented England U19 v Sri Lanka U19 in one-day and 'Test' series 2000, scoring 53* and taking 3-41 in the second 'One-Day International' at Cardiff

Opinions on cricket: 'Cricket today in my opinion has to be taken very seriously to achieve even an average standard of play. The great thing about cricket for me is that there is always a challenge around the corner. You can never relax or lose concentration; you must always strive to better your game.'

Best batting: 62 Somerset v Yorkshire, Taunton 2000

Best bowling: 4-84 Somerset v Yorkshire, Scarborough 2000

2000 Season

	M	Inns	NO	Runs	HS	Avge	100s	50s	Ct	St	O	M	Runs	Wkts	Avge	Best	5wI	10wM
Test																		
All First	7	8	1	134	62	19.14	-	1	3	-	165.1	34	603	18	33.50	4-84	-	-
1-day Int																		
NatWest	1	0	0	0	0	-	-	-	-	-	6	0	30	2	15.00	2-30	-	
B & H																		
1-day Lge	3	2	0	14	14	7.00	-	-	1	-	20	0	95	0	-		-	-

Career Performances

	M	Inns	NO	Runs	HS	Avge	100s	50s	Ct	St	Balls	Runs	Wkts	Avge	Best	5wI	10wM
Test																	
All First	7	8	1	134	62	19.14	-	1	3	-	991	603	18	33.50	4-84	-	-
1-day Int																	
NatWest	2	1	0	0	0	0.00	-	-	-	-	78	72	4	18.00	2-30	-	
B & H																	
1-day Lge	3	2	0	14	14	7.00	-	-	1	-	120	95	0	-		-	-

TREMLETT, C. T.   Hampshire

Name: <u>Christopher</u> Timothy Tremlett
Role: Right-hand bat, right-arm medium-fast bowler
Born: 2 September 1981, Southampton
Height: 6ft 7in **Weight:** 14st 7lbs
Nickname: Twiggy, Doorsnake
County debut: 2000
Strike rate: 37.00 (career 37.00)
Parents: Timothy and Carolyn
Marital status: Single
Family links with cricket: 'Grandfather [Maurice] played county cricket for Somerset and three Tests for England. Dad played for Hants and England A'
Education: Otterbourne Primary, Chandlers Ford; Thornden School, Chandlers Ford; Taunton's College, Southampton
Qualifications: 8 GCSEs, BTEC Sports Science

Career outside cricket: Student
Off-season: 'Hopefully going on tour to India with England U19; finishing education at college'
Overseas tours: West of England U15 to West Indies; Hampshire U16 to Jersey; England U19 to India 2000-01
Cricketers particularly admired: Glenn McGrath, Mark Waugh, Ben Smyth, Rory Miller
Young players to look out for: Jimmy Adams, Chris Benham, Ben Smyth
Other sports played: Basketball, volleyball, golf, badminton, tennis
Other sports followed: Football (Arsenal)
Relaxations: Music, shopping, sports
Extras: Took wicket (Mark Richardson) with first ball in first-class cricket v New Zealand A at Portsmouth 2000; finished with debut match figures of 6-91. Hit 30 not out off 15 balls on National League debut. Represented England U19 v Sri Lanka U19 in 'Test' series 2000
Opinions on cricket: 'I think having the two divisions in both leagues is a good idea, but I think only two teams should go down and not three.'
Best batting: 17 Hampshire v New Zealand A, Portsmouth 2000
Best bowling: 4-16 Hampshire v New Zealand A, Portsmouth 2000

2000 Season

	M	Inns	NO	Runs	HS	Avge	100s	50s	Ct	St	O	M	Runs	Wkts	Avge	Best	5wI	10wM
Test																		
All First	1	2	0	33	17	16.50	-	-	-	-	37	14	91	6	15.16	4-16	-	-
1-day Int																		
NatWest	1	1	0	10	10	10.00	-	-	-	-	8	0	35	2	17.50	2-35	-	
B & H																		
1-day Lge	5	2	1	30	30 *	30.00	-	-	1	-	41	0	185	4	46.25	1-20	-	

Career Performances

	M	Inns	NO	Runs	HS	Avge	100s	50s	Ct	St	Balls		Runs	Wkts	Avge	Best	5wI	10wM
Test																		
All First	1	2	0	33	17	16.50	-	-	-	-	222		91	6	15.16	4-16	-	-
1-day Int																		
NatWest	1	1	0	10	10	10.00	-	-	-	-	48		35	2	17.50	2-35	-	
B & H																		
1-day Lge	5	2	1	30	30 *	30.00	-	-	1	-	246		185	4	46.25	1-20	-	

TRESCOTHICK, M. E. Somerset

Name: Marcus Edward Trescothick
Role: Left-hand bat, right-arm swing bowler, reserve wicket-keeper
Born: 25 December 1975, Keynsham, Bristol
Height: 6ft 3in **Weight:** 14st 7lbs
Nickname: Banger
County debut: 1993
County cap: 1999
Test debut: 2000
Tests: 3
One-Day Internationals: 7
1st-Class 50s: 29
1st-Class 100s: 7
1st-Class catches: 114
One-Day 100s: 3
Place in batting averages: 28th av. 43.41
(1999 54th av. 37.41)
Strike rate: 124.00 (career 72.48)
Parents: Martyn and Lin
Marital status: Single
Family links with cricket: Father played for Somerset 2nd XI; uncle played club cricket; girlfriend plays for Taunton Ladies and Somerset Ladies CC

Education: Sir Bernard Lovell School
Qualifications: 7 GCSEs
Career outside cricket: Playing abroad
Off-season: Touring with England
Overseas tours: England U18 to South Africa 1992-93; England U19 to Sri Lanka 1993-94, to West Indies 1994-95 (captain); England A to Bangladesh and New Zealand 1999-2000; England to Kenya (ICC Knockout Trophy) 2000-01, to Pakistan and Sri Lanka 2000-01
Overseas teams played for: Melville CC, Perth 1997-99
Cricketers particularly admired: Andrew Caddick
Young players to look out for: Joe Tucker, Pete Trego, Matthew Wood
Other sports followed: Golf, football (Bristol City FC)
Relaxations: 'Spending time at home (it's such a rare thing), playing golf'
Extras: Member of England U19 squad for home series against West Indies 1993. Man of the Series against India U19 in 1994, scoring most runs in the series. Whittingdale Young Player of the Month, August 1994. Captained England U19 v South Africa 1995. Took a hat-trick for Somerset against Young Australia in 1995. Scored more than 1000 runs for England U19. Scored 322 in the second innings of a 2nd XI game against Warwickshire in 1997 – Somerset were chasing a target of 612 and Trescothick was the last man out with the score on 605! Vice-captain of Somerset 1999-2000. Made One-Day International debut v Zimbabwe in NatWest Series at The Oval 2000, scoring 79; scored 87 in same series v West Indies at Riverside 2000, winning Man of the Match award. Made Test debut in third Test v West Indies at Old Trafford 2000, scoring 66 and 38*; in first innings took part with Alec Stewart in record England partnership for any wicket in Tests v West Indies at Old Trafford (179). Scored 78 in England's first innings of the fifth Test 2000, sharing in a new record first-wicket stand for England in Tests v West Indies at The Oval (159) with Michael Atherton. PCA Player of the Year 2000
Opinions on cricket: 'Central contracts and two divisions have been great for our season. I'm sure things are looking up.'
Best batting: 190 Somerset v Middlesex, Taunton 1999
Best bowling: 4-36 Somerset v Young Australia, Taunton 1995
Stop press: Scored maiden Test century (122) v Sri Lanka at Galle 2000-01, in the process batting throughout the third day in temperatures that topped 105 degrees Fahrenheit

2000 Season

	M	Inns	NO	Runs	HS	Avge	100s	50s	Ct	St	O	M	Runs	Wkts	Avge	Best	5wI	10wM
Test	3	5	1	190	78	47.50	-	2	3	-	1	0	2	0	-	-	-	-
All First	12	19	2	738	105	43.41	1	5	11	-	62	13	207	3	69.00	1-18	-	-
1-day Int	7	7	1	288	87*	48.00	-	2	1	-	3.4	0	20	2	10.00	2-7	-	
NatWest	2	2	0	88	87	44.00	-	1	-	-	9	0	36	2	18.00	2-23	-	
B & H	3	3	1	55	29*	27.50	-	-	-	-	1	0	7	0	-	-	-	
1-day Lge	11	11	1	464	92*	46.40	-	5	3	-	68	2	329	16	20.56	4-50	-	

Career Performances

	M	Inns	NO	Runs	HS	Avge	100s	50s	Ct	St	Balls	Runs	Wkts	Avge	Best	5wl	10wM
Test	3	5	1	190	78	47.50	-	2	3	-	6	2	0	-	-	-	-
All First	104	173	7	5147	190	31.00	7	29	114	-	2247	1330	31	42.90	4-36	-	-
1-day Int	7	7	1	288	87 *	48.00	-	2	1	-	22	20	2	10.00	2-7	-	
NatWest	11	10	0	369	116	36.90	1	1	2	-	162	128	4	32.00	2-23	-	
B & H	14	14	3	405	122	36.81	1	2	7	-	186	141	8	17.62	3-46	-	
1-day Lge	81	72	10	1681	110	27.11	1	8	26	-	978	823	31	26.54	4-50	-	

TROTT, B. J.   Kent

Name: <u>Benjamin</u> James Trott
Role: Right-hand bat, right-arm medium-fast bowler
Born: 14 March 1975, Wellington, Somerset
Height: 6ft 5in **Weight:** 13st 10lbs
Nickname: Trotsky
County debut: 1997 (Somerset), 2000 (Kent)
1st-Class catches: 2
Strike rate: 63.00 (career 46.90)
Parents: Alan Robert and Jane Elizabeth
Marital status: Single
Family links with cricket: Younger brother Thomas plays for Somerset U16
Education: Wellesley Park Primary School, Wellington; Court Fields Community School, Wellington; The Richard Huish College, Taunton; The College of St Mark and St John, Plymouth
Qualifications: 8 GCSEs, 3 A-levels, BEd (Hons) Physical Education and Information Technology; sports coaching – cricket, rugby, football, hockey
Career outside cricket: Teacher (primary)
Off-season: 'Teaching, other work, and most importantly working on physical strength for next season'
Overseas teams played for: Claremont Nedlands, Perth 1998-99
Cricketers particularly admired: Glenn McGrath, Darren Gough, Andrew Caddick
Young players to look out for: 'My younger brother Thomas', Arul Suppiah, Tom Webley
Other sports played: Football, golf
Other sports followed: Football (Manchester United)
Injuries: Out for two weeks with a hamstring injury
Relaxations: Music, golf

Extras: Wellington Young Player of the Year in 1993. Wellington Players' Player of the Year in 1996. Played for Somerset 1997-99; joined Kent in 2000

Opinions on cricket: 'I feel that with the two divisions, in both the National League and the Championship, the competitions have the chance of increased tension until the end of the season and that crowds will remain throughout due to this. I feel that the way forward is an increased number of floodlit one-day games where there is increased interest from children, who are the future of English cricket.'

Best batting: 1* Somerset v Glamorgan, Taunton 1997
Best bowling: 3-74 Somerset v Glamorgan, Taunton 1997

2000 Season

	M	Inns	NO	Runs	HS	Avge	100s	50s	Ct	St	O	M	Runs	Wkts	Avge	Best	5wI	10wM
Test																		
All First	2	2	2	0	0*	-	-	-	1	-	42	9	133	4	33.25	2-44	-	-
1-day Int																		
NatWest																		
B & H																		
1-day Lge																		

Career Performances

	M	Inns	NO	Runs	HS	Avge	100s	50s	Ct	St	Balls	Runs	Wkts	Avge	Best	5wI	10wM
Test																	
All First	5	4	3	1	1*	1.00	-	-	2	-	516	317	11	28.81	3-74	-	-
1-day Int																	
NatWest																	
B & H																	
1-day Lge	1	0	0	0	0	-	-	-	-	-	24	29	1	29.00	1-29	-	

---

87. Who scored 311 in Australia's first innings at Old Trafford in 1964 and who scored 256 for England in reply?

TROUGHTON, J. O. Warwickshire

Name: <u>Jim</u> Oliver Troughton
Role: Left-hand bat, slow left-arm bowler
Born: 2 March 1979, London
Height: 5ft 11in **Weight:** 12st 12lbs
Nickname: Troughts, JT
County debut: No first-team appearance
Parents: Ali and David
Marital status: Engaged to Naomi
Family links with cricket: Father was a
Middlesex Colt. Great-grandfather Henry
Crichton played for Warwickshire
Education: Bridgetown School, Stratford-
upon-Avon; Trinity School, Leamington Spa;
Birmingham University
Qualifications: 8 GCSEs, 3 A-levels,
BSc Sport & Exercise Science
Career outside cricket: 'Coaching/acting'
Off-season: 'Exchange trip to Free State to
train with Free State A squad October-December 2000. MCC tour to Australia and
Singapore February 2001'
Overseas tours: Warwickshire Development of Excellence squad to Cape Town 1998;
MCC to Australia and Singapore 2001
Overseas teams played for: Harvinia CC, Free State, South Africa 2000
Cricketers particularly admired: Graham Thorpe, Steve Waugh, Allan Donald,
Ashley Giles
Young players to look out for: Ian Bell, Andrew Gait
Other sports played: Football (Stoke City youth player)
Other sports followed: 'Hooked on Manchester United since going to their soccer
school aged five'
Relaxations: 'Music, films, playing my guitar, spending time with Naomi, going
abroad'
Extras: County colours U12-U19. Has represented England U15, U16 and U17.
Represented ECB Midlands U19 v Pakistan U19 1998. Has won the Alec Hastilow
Trophy and the Coney Edmonds Trophy (Warwickshire awards). Played for
Warwickshire Board XI in the NatWest 1999 and 2000
Opinions on cricket: 'Tight cricketing schedule sometimes overshadows the
importance of improving techniques in the nets. Good to see a higher emphasis placed
on fitness; you need to be an athlete in today's game.'

Career Performances

	M	Inns	NO	Runs	HS	Avge	100s	50s	Ct	St	Balls	Runs	Wkts	Avge	Best	5wI	10wM
Test																	
All First																	
1-day Int																	
NatWest	2	2	0	56	38	28.00	-	-	2	-	60	34	3	11.33	3-34	-	
B & H																	
1-day Lge																	

TUCKER, J. P.   Somerset

Name: <u>Joseph</u> Peter Tucker
Role: Right-hand bat, right-arm fast-medium
bowler, occasional wicket-keeper
Born: 14 September 1979, Bath
Height: 6ft 3in **Weight:** 13st 7lbs
Nickname: Tucks, My Boy, Skid, Cheeky,
Seth, Cyrus the Virus
County debut: 2000
1st-Class catches: 1
Strike rate: 66.00 (career 66.00)
Parents: Geoff and Chris
Marital status: 'Taken'
Family links with cricket: 'Dad's been
playing for too long (got Viv Richards out).
Brothers try to hit it too hard'
Education: Camely; Pensford Primary
School, Bristol; Chew Valley; Colston's
Collegiate School, Bristol; Richard Huish
Sixth Form College, Taunton
Qualifications: 10 GCSEs, 3 A-levels, senior coaching award
Career outside cricket: 'Motocross – busting bigger than anyone'
Off-season: 'Training on a 12-week programme with Steffan Jones (legend), then
training in Perth for two months. Eating and resting well. Spending time on my 426
Yamaha'
Overseas tours: Avon to Barbados 1994; West of England U15 to West Indies 1996;
England U17 to Bermuda (International Youth Tournament) 1997; England U19 to
South Africa (including Youth World Cup) 1997-98, to New Zealand 1998-99
Cricketers particularly admired: Allan Donald, Michael Holding, Curtly Ambrose,
Shoaib Akhtar, Michael Atherton

Young players to look out for: Marcus Trescothick, 'Me', 'My son', Steffan Jones
Other sports played: 'Ride motocross with my cousin Martyn'
Other sports followed: Football (Clevedon Town, Bristol City, Man Utd), motocross ('my cousin Martyn riding for Bud Yamaha')
Injuries: Out for half of 2000 with stress fracture of the back, glandular fever 'and lots more'
Relaxations: 'Going to the gym, watching movies, seeing mates and girlfriend and family, also drinking tea with "Chunks"'
Extras: Made his 2nd XI debut for Somerset at the age of 15. Took 4 for 31 against Holland for England U17 in the International Youth Tournament in Bermuda in 1997, which England U17 won. Was part of the England U19 squad that won the Youth World Cup in South Africa 1997-98. Took 7-60 for ECB South U19 v Pakistan U19 1998. Took 5-35 for England U19 in second 'Test' v New Zealand U19 1998-99. Has attended Dennis Lillee coaching school, Chennai (Madras). Missed entire 1999 season with stress fracture of the back and missed 13 weeks at start of 2000 season due to glandular fever, liver and kidney failure, jaundice, tonsillitis 'and more – just about recovered, I think'. Made county debut v West Indies 2000, taking wicket of Brian Lara with his second ball
Opinions on cricket: 'I do have an opinion on the game, but there is no point expressing it because no one listens or does anything about it.'
Best batting: 14 Somerset v West Indians, Taunton 2000
Best bowling: 1-28 Somerset v West Indians, Taunton 2000

2000 Season

	M	Inns	NO	Runs	HS	Avge	100s	50s	Ct	St	O	M	Runs	Wkts	Avge	Best	5wl	10wM
Test																		
All First	1	1	0	14	14	14.00	-	-	1	-	11	3	47	1	47.00	1-28	-	-
1-day Int																		
NatWest																		
B & H																		
1-day Lge																		

Career Performances

	M	Inns	NO	Runs	HS	Avge	100s	50s	Ct	St	Balls	Runs	Wkts	Avge	Best	5wl	10wM
Test																	
All First	1	1	0	14	14	14.00	-	-	1	-	66	47	1	47.00	1-28	-	-
1-day Int																	
NatWest																	
B & H																	
1-day Lge																	

TUDOR, A. J.   Surrey

Name: <u>Alexander</u> Jeremy Tudor
Role: Right-hand bat, right-arm fast bowler
Born: 23 October 1977,
West Brompton, London
Height: 6ft 4in **Weight:** 13st 7lbs
Nickname: Big Al, Bambi, Tudes
County debut: 1995
County cap: 1999
Test debut: 1998-99
Tests: 3
1st-Class 50s: 3
1st-Class 5 w. in innings: 9
1st-Class catches: 13
Place in batting averages: 110th av. 28.30
(1999 157th av. 24.66)
Place in bowling averages: 39th av. 22.78
(1999 37th av. 22.37)
Strike rate: 38.87 (career 44.38)
Parents: Daryll and Jennifer
Marital status: Single
Family links with cricket: Brother was on the staff at The Oval
Education: Wandle Primary, Earlsfield; St Mark's C of E, Fulham; City of
Westminster College
Off-season: England A tour of West Indies
Overseas tours: England U15 to South Africa 1992-93; England U19 to Zimbabwe
1995-96, to Pakistan 1996-97; England to Australia 1998-99, to South Africa 1999-2000,
to Pakistan 2000-01; England A to West Indies 2000-01
Cricketers particularly admired: Curtly Ambrose, Brian Lara
Other sports followed: Basketball, football (QPR)
Relaxations: Listening to music
Extras: Played for London Schools at all ages from U8. Played for England U17
against India in 1994. MCC Young Cricketer. Took 4-89 in Australia's first innings on
Test debut at Perth 1998-99; his victims included both Waugh twins. Scored 99* in
second innings of first Test v New Zealand at Edgbaston 1999, bettering the highest
score by a nightwatchman for England (Harold Larwood's 98 v Australia at Sydney
1932-33) and winning the Man of the Match award; in total he scored 131 unbeaten
runs in the match
Best batting: 99* England v New Zealand, Edgbaston 1999
Best bowling: 7-48 Surrey v Lancashire, The Oval 2000
Stop press: Drafted temporarily into England Test squad for tour of Pakistan 2000-01
as replacement for the injured Andrew Flintoff. Took 5-37 for England A v West Indies
B at Grenada in the Busta Cup 2000-01

2000 Season

	M	Inns	NO	Runs	HS	Avge	100s	50s	Ct	St	O	M	Runs	Wkts	Avge	Best	5wI	10wM
Test																		
All First	14	16	6	283	64 *	28.30	-	1	5	-	304.3	71	1071	47	22.78	7-48	3	-
1-day Int																		
NatWest	2	1	1	10	10 *	-	-	-	1	-	18	1	84	3	28.00	2-48	-	
B & H	4	1	0	0	0	0.00	-	-	1	-	32	5	125	8	15.62	2-12	-	
1-day Lge	10	6	2	22	7	5.50	-	-	1	-	68	10	281	14	20.07	4-26	-	

Career Performances

	M	Inns	NO	Runs	HS	Avge	100s	50s	Ct	St	Balls	Runs	Wkts	Avge	Best	5wI	10wM
Test	3	6	3	166	99 *	55.33	-	1	-	-	350	239	8	29.87	4-89	-	-
All First	57	72	22	1048	99 *	20.96	-	3	13	-	7456	4435	168	26.39	7-48	9	-
1-day Int																	
NatWest	5	2	1	11	10 *	11.00	-	-	1	-	285	184	9	20.44	4-39	-	
B & H	5	2	0	0	0	0.00	-	-	1	-	246	166	10	16.60	2-12	-	
1-day Lge	24	17	4	125	29 *	9.61	-	-	6	-	878	712	31	22.96	4-26	-	

TUFNELL, P. C. R.   Middlesex

Name: <u>Philip</u> Clive Roderick Tufnell
Role: Right-hand bat, slow left-arm spinner
Born: 29 April 1966, Barnet, Hertfordshire
Height: 6ft **Weight:** 12st
Nickname: Cat, Tuffers
County debut: 1986
County cap: 1990
Benefit: 1999
Test debut: 1990-91
Tests: 41
One-Day Internationals: 20
50 wickets in a season: 8
1st-Class 50s: 1
1st-Class 5 w. in innings: 46
1st-Class 10 w. in match: 5
1st-Class catches: 103
One-Day 5 w. in innings: 1
Place in batting averages: 283rd av. 8.33
(1999 265th av. 11.64)
Place in bowling averages: 41st av. 23.07 (1999 61st av. 25.47)
Strike rate: 68.16 (career 73.27)
Parents: Sylvia and Alan

Wife: Lisa
Children: Poppy and Ellie
Education: Highgate School; Southgate School
Qualifications: O-level in Art
Off-season: 'Media work and Tufnell's Tours'
Overseas tours: England YC to West Indies 1984-85; England to Australia 1990-91, to New Zealand and Australia (World Cup) 1991-92, to India and Sri Lanka 1992-93, to West Indies 1993-94, to Australia 1994-95, to Zimbabwe and New Zealand 1996-97, to West Indies 1997-98, to South Africa 1999-2000
Overseas teams played for: Queensland University, Australia
Young players to look out for: Andrew Flintoff
Other sports played: Fives
Other sports followed: Football (Arsenal)
Injuries: Out for one month with a burst appendix
Relaxations: Sleeping, eating out
Extras: MCC Young Cricketer of the Year 1984 and Middlesex Uncapped Bowler of the Year 1987. Had match figures of 11 for 93 in the final Test against Australia at The Oval in 1997, winning the Man of the Match award. Played for a World XI v an Asia XI in Dhaka 2000. Took 900th first-class wicket (Guy Welton) v Nottinghamshire at Lord's 2000. Middlesex Player of the Season 2000
Opinions on cricket: 'Cricket administration should be held more accountable.'
Best batting: 67* Middlesex v Worcestershire, Lord's 1996
Best bowling: 8-29 Middlesex v Glamorgan, Cardiff 1993

2000 Season

	M	Inns	NO	Runs	HS	Avge	100s	50s	Ct	St	O	M	Runs	Wkts	Avge	Best	5wI	10wM
Test																		
All First	16	21	9	100	19	8.33	-	-	4	-	738.3	255	1500	65	23.07	6-48	3	-
1-day Int																		
NatWest																		
B & H	1	1	0	6	6	6.00	-	-	-	-	10	1	38	2	19.00	2-38	-	
1-day Lge																		

Career Performances

	M	Inns	NO	Runs	HS	Avge	100s	50s	Ct	St	Balls	Runs	Wkts	Avge	Best	5wI	10wM
Test	41	57	28	146	22*	5.03	-	-	12	-	11054	4386	120	36.55	7-47	5	2
All First	285	314	120	1925	67*	9.92	-	1	103	-	69758	27915	952	29.32	8-29	46	5
1-day Int	20	10	9	15	5*	15.00	-	-	4	-	1020	699	19	36.78	4-22	-	
NatWest	8	1	0	8	8	8.00	-	-	4	-	570	323	10	32.30	3-29	-	
B & H	16	9	4	62	18	12.40	-	-	2	-	869	629	17	37.00	3-32	-	
1-day Lge	37	13	7	36	13*	6.00	-	-	5	-	1548	1192	45	26.48	5-28	1	

TURNER, R. J.   Somerset

Name: Robert (Rob) Julian Turner
Role: Right-hand middle-order bat,
wicket-keeper
Born: 25 November 1967, Malvern,
Worcestershire
Height: 6ft 2in   **Weight:** 14st
Nickname: Noddy, Turns, Ledge
County debut: 1991
County cap: 1994
1000 runs in a season: 2
50 dismissals in a season: 5
1st-Class 50s: 35
1st-Class 100s: 8
1st-Class catches: 446
1st-Class stumpings: 39
Place in batting averages: 174th av. 20.50
(1999 6th av. 52.91)
Parents: Derek Edward and Doris Lilian
Wife and date of marriage: Lucy, 25 September 1999
Children: 'First due on 26 March 2001'
Family links with cricket: 'Father and both brothers (Richard and Simon) are closely
associated with Weston-super-Mare CC. Simon played for Somerset in 1984, also as a
wicket-keeper. My wife, Lucy, plays for MCC Ladies and Somerset Ladies (also as a
wicket-keeper!)'
Education: Uphill Primary School, Weston-super-Mare; Broadoak Comprehensive,
Weston-super-Mare; Millfield School, Street; Magdalene College, Cambridge
University
Qualifications: BEng (Hons) Engineering, Diploma in Computer Science,
NCA coaching award, SFA securities representative of the London Stock Exchange
Career outside cricket: Rowan Dartington Stockbrokers
Off-season: 'Working for Rowan Dartington Stockbrokers and preparing for
fatherhood!'
Overseas tours: Millfield School to Barbados 1985; Combined Universities to
Barbados 1989; Qantas Airlines Tournament, Kuala Lumpur, Malaysia 1992-93;
English Lions to New Zealand (Cricket Max) 1997; MCC to New Zealand 1999, to
Canada 2000; England A to Bangladesh and New Zealand 1999-2000 (vice-captain)
Overseas teams played for: Claremont-Nedlands, Perth, Western Australia 1991-93
Cricketers particularly admired: Jack Russell
Young players to look out for: Marcus Trescothick, Ian Ward, Paul Franks
Other sports followed: Football ('The Villa')
Relaxations: 'Reading, sleeping, beer and curry; the piano'

Extras: Captain of Cambridge University (Blue 1988-91) and Combined Universities 1991. Equalled Somerset records of six catches in an innings and eight dismissals in a match v West Indians 1995; also had eight dismissals in a match v Durham in the same season. Wombwell Cricket Lovers' Society Wicket-keeper of the Year 1999. Highest-placed Englishman in the 1999 batting averages. Sheffield Cricket Lovers' Society Allrounder of the Year 1999. Was on stand-by for England tours of West Indies 1997-98 and South Africa and Zimbabwe 1999-2000

Opinions on cricket: 'Two-divisional status has been a great success in terms of exciting cricket for both players and spectators. End-of-season jostling for position to gain promotion or avoid relegation adds a new dimension in both competitions.'

Best batting: 144 Somerset v Kent, Taunton 1997

2000 Season

	M	Inns	NO	Runs	HS	Avge	100s	50s	Ct	St	O	M	Runs	Wkts	Avge	Best	5wI	10wM
Test																		
All First	18	26	2	492	75	20.50	-	2	39	-								
1-day Int																		
NatWest	2	2	1	18	16 *	18.00	-	-	3	-								
B & H	3	2	0	41	29	20.50	-	-	2	-								
1-day Lge	15	14	4	210	44	21.00	-	-	14	3								

Career Performances

	M	Inns	NO	Runs	HS	Avge	100s	50s	Ct	St	Balls	Runs	Wkts	Avge	Best	5wI	10wM
Test																	
All First	176	270	48	6803	144	30.64	8	35	446	39	19	29	0	-	-	-	-
1-day Int																	
NatWest	17	14	4	248	52	24.80	-	2	30	2							
B & H	28	25	9	557	70	34.81	-	1	26	1							
1-day Lge	107	92	26	1449	67	21.95	-	4	101	14							

---

88. Which England captain's 100 at Adelaide in 1986-87 was the 100th century for England in Tests in Australia?

UDAL, S. D. Hampshire

Name: <u>Shaun</u> David Udal
Role: Right-hand bat, off-spin bowler
Born: 18 March 1969, Farnborough, Hants
Height: 6ft 2in **Weight:** 14st
Nickname: Shaggy
County debut: 1989
County cap: 1992
One-Day Internationals: 10
50 wickets in a season: 5
1st-Class 50s: 18
1st-Class 100s: 1
1st-Class 5 w. in innings: 24
1st-Class 10 w. in match: 4
1st-Class catches: 78
One-Day 5 w. in innings: 1
Place in batting averages: 188th av. 19.22
(1999 231st av. 17.40)
Place in bowling averages: 71st av. 27.26
(1999 66th av. 26.72)

Strike rate: 70.10 (career 70.95)
Parents: Robin Francis and Mary Elizabeth
Wife and date of marriage: Emma Jane, 5 October 1991
Children: Katherine Mary, 26 August 1992; Rebecca Jane, 17 November 1995
Family links with cricket: Father played for Camberley CC for 42 years, and also for Surrey Colts; brother is Camberley 1st XI captain. Grandfather played for Leicestershire and Middlesex
Education: Tower Hill Primary; Cove Comprehensive
Qualifications: 8 CSEs, qualified print finisher, company director
Career outside cricket: '7 Corners Printing Group – sales and marketing'
Off-season: 'Golfing holiday, family holiday, working for 7 Corners and at the Dummer Cricket Centre for Major Ron Ferguson'
Overseas tours: England to Australia 1994-95; England A to Pakistan 1995-96; England XI to New Zealand (Cricket Max) 1997
Overseas teams played for: Hamilton Wickham, Newcastle, NSW 1990-91
Cricketers particularly admired: Robin Smith, Ian Botham, Shane Warne
Young players to look out for: Dimi Mascarenhas, Michael Powell
Other sports played: Football, snooker, golf (handicap of 14)
Other sports followed: Football (West Ham Utd, Aldershot)
Injuries: Ankle injury; no time off required
Relaxations: 'Good nights out!'
Extras: Has taken two hat-tricks in club cricket. Has scored a double hundred (202) in

a 40-over club game. Man of the Match on NatWest debut against Berkshire 1991. Took 8-50 v Sussex in the first game of 1992 season, his seventh Championship match. Named Hampshire Cricket Association Player of the Year 1993. Vice-captain of Hampshire 1998-2000

Opinions on cricket: 'Two divisions definitely working. Keep supporting the game. It is always easier to criticise rather than praise.'

Best batting: 117* Hampshire v Warwickshire, Southampton 1997

Best bowling: 8-50 Hampshire v Sussex, Southampton 1992

2000 Season

	M	Inns	NO	Runs	HS	Avge	100s	50s	Ct	St	O	M	Runs	Wkts	Avge	Best	5wI	10wM
Test																		
All First	12	21	3	346	85	19.22	-	1	8	-	350.3	104	818	30	27.26	5-58	1	-
1-day Int																		
NatWest	4	1	0	8	8	8.00	-	-	-	-	24	2	82	3	27.33	2-24	-	
B & H	4	3	0	34	19	11.33	-	-	3	-	27	0	111	2	55.50	2-27	-	
1-day Lge	16	11	4	97	51 *	13.85	-	1	6	-	122.2	3	500	14	35.71	2-18	-	

Career Performances

	M	Inns	NO	Runs	HS	Avge	100s	50s	Ct	St	Balls	Runs	Wkts	Avge	Best	5wI	10wM
Test																	
All First	167	240	44	4363	117 *	22.26	1	18	78	-	32072	15637	452	34.59	8-50	24	4
1-day Int	10	6	4	35	11 *	17.50	-	-	1	-	570	371	8	46.37	2-37	-	
NatWest	27	12	5	136	39 *	19.42	-	-	12	-	1521	872	36	24.22	4-20	-	
B & H	40	24	5	239	34	12.57	-	-	13	-	2280	1492	44	33.90	4-40	-	
1-day Lge	159	105	30	1107	78	14.76	-	6	51	-	6662	5376	177	30.37	5-43	1	

89. What record did Rod Marsh set in the 1982-83 series?

VAN DER GUCHT, C. G. Hampshire

Name: <u>Charlie</u> Graham van der Gucht
Role: Left-hand bat, left-arm spin bowler
Born: 14 January 1980, London
Height: 6ft **Weight:** 12st 1lb
Nickname: Gucht, Chilli
County debut: 2000
Strike rate: 44.00 (career 44.00)
Parents: Nicola and Mike
Marital status: Single
Family links with cricket: Grandfather
played/kept wicket for Gloucestershire and
Bengal in the 1930s
Education: Cothill House; Radley College;
Durham University
Qualifications: 10 GCSEs, 3 A-levels
Off-season: 'Studying at Durham; getting
work experience'
Overseas tours: West of England to West
Indies 1995; British Universities to Port Elizabeth 1999; Durham University to Cape
Town 2000
Overseas teams played for: Gordon DCC, Sydney 1998-99
Cricketers particularly admired: Phil Tufnell, Muttiah Muralitharan, Gary Sobers,
Henry Fitz
Young players to look out for: Iain Brunnschweiler, Lawrence Prittipaul, Matthew
Banes, Irfan Shah
Other sports played: Rackets
Other sports followed: Football (Southampton)
Injuries: Out for two weeks with a shoulder injury
Relaxations: Keeping fit, playing golf, reading, 'going to "Klute"'
Extras: Leading wicket-taker at Gordon club in Sydney 1998-99. Played for
Hampshire Board XI in 1999 NatWest, winning Man of the Match award in fourth
round v Glamorgan at Southampton
Opinions on cricket: 'Good game.'
Best bowling: 3-75 Hampshire v Zimbabweans, Southampton 2000

2000 Season

	M	Inns	NO	Runs	HS	Avge	100s	50s	Ct	St	O	M	Runs	Wkts	Avge	Best	5wI	10wM
Test																		
All First	1	1	1	0	0 *	-	-	-	-	-	22	7	75	3	25.00	3-75	-	-
1-day Int																		
NatWest																			
B & H																			
1-day Lge																			

Career Performances

	M	Inns	NO	Runs	HS	Avge	100s	50s	Ct	St	Balls	Runs	Wkts	Avge	Best	5wI	10wM
Test																	
All First	1	1	1	0	0 *	-	-	-	-	-	132	75	3	25.00	3-75	-	-
1-day Int																	
NatWest	3	2	0	4	3	2.00	-	-	-	-	144	95	5	19.00	3-35	-
B & H																	
1-day Lge																	

VAUGHAN, M. P. Yorkshire

Name: Michael Paul Vaughan
Role: Right-hand bat, off-spin bowler
Born: 29 October 1974, Eccles, Manchester
Height: 6ft 2in **Weight:** 11st 7lbs
Nickname: Virgil, Frankie, Chippo
County debut: 1993
County cap: 1995
Test debut: 1999-2000
Tests: 8
1000 runs in a season: 4
1st-Class 50s: 38
1st-Class 100s: 18
1st-Class catches: 59
Place in batting averages: 29th av. 43.30
(1999 129th av. 27.12)
Place in bowling averages: (1999 137th
av. 42.40)
Strike rate: 59.83 (career 83.69)
Parents: Graham John and Dee
Marital status: Single
Family links with cricket: Father played league cricket for Worsley CC. Brother plays for Sheffield Collegiate. Mother is related to the famous Tyldesley family (Lancashire and England)

Education: St Marks, Worsley, Manchester; Dore Juniors, Sheffield; Silverdale Comprehensive, Sheffield
Qualifications: 7 GCSEs
Off-season: Touring Pakistan and Sri Lanka with England
Overseas tours: Yorkshire to West Indies 1994, to South Africa 1995, to Zimbabwe 1996; England U19 to India 1992-93, to Sri Lanka 1993-94 (captain); England A to India 1994-95, to Australia 1996-97, to Zimbabwe and South Africa 1998-99 (captain); England to South Africa 1999-2000, to Pakistan and Sri Lanka 2000-01
Cricketers particularly admired: Glenn Chapple, Graham Lloyd, 'all the present Yorkshire team'
Young players to look out for: Matthew Wood, Matthew Hoggard
Other sports played: Football (Baslow FC), golf
Other sports followed: Football (Sheffield Wednesday), all golf
Relaxations: Most sports. 'Enjoy a good meal with friends'
Extras: Played club cricket for Sheffield Collegiate in the Yorkshire League. *Daily Telegraph* U15 Batsman of the Year, 1990. Maurice Leyland Batting Award 1990. Rapid Cricketline Player of the Month, June 1993. The Cricket Society's Most Promising Young Cricketer 1993. A. A. Thompson Memorial Trophy – The Roses Cricketer of the Year 1993. Whittingdale Cricketer of the Month, July 1994. Scored 1066 runs in first full season of first-class cricket in 1994. Captained England U19 in home series against India 1994. Scored two 100s (100 and 151) v Essex at Chelmsford 1999; Stuart Law scored two 100s for Essex in the same match. Struck 69 in England's only innings of the rain-shortened fifth Test at Centurion, January 2000, a match-winning maiden Test 50 that earned him the Man of the Match award. Man of the Match for his 76 in England's only innings in the fourth Test v West Indies at his home ground of Headingley 2000
Best batting: 183 Yorkshire v Glamorgan, Cardiff 1996
Best bowling: 4-39 Yorkshire v Oxford University, The Parks 1994

2000 Season

	M	Inns	NO	Runs	HS	Avge	100s	50s	Ct	St	O	M	Runs	Wkts	Avge	Best	5wI	10wM
Test	4	6	0	169	76	28.16	-	1	-	-	8	3	25	0	-	-	-	-
All First	13	21	1	866	155 *	43.30	2	4	2	-	59.5	15	152	6	25.33	2-32	-	-
1-day Int																		
NatWest	2	2	0	86	70	43.00	-	1	-	-	2	0	4	1	4.00	1-4	-	
B & H	5	4	1	37	15 *	12.33	-	-	3	-	12	1	35	1	35.00	1-18	-	
1-day Lge	9	9	2	108	39	15.42	-	-	4	-	14.5	1	70	5	14.00	4-27	-	

Career Performances

	M	Inns	NO	Runs	HS	Avge	100s	50s	Ct	St	Balls	Runs	Wkts	Avge	Best	5wI	10wM
Test	8	13	0	373	76	28.69	-	2	6	-	156	98	0	-	-	-	-
All First	144	255	13	8372	183	34.59	18	38	59	-	7867	4443	94	47.26	4-39	-	-
1-day Int																	
NatWest	19	19	1	483	85	26.83	-	4	4	-	270	156	5	31.20	1-4	-	
B & H	30	28	2	812	88	31.23	-	6	8	-	549	354	11	32.18	2-28	-	
1-day Lge	86	84	6	1836	72	23.53	-	8	27	-	998	813	31	26.22	4-27	-	

WADE, J. Northamptonshire

Name: James Wade
Role: Right-hand top-order bat, slip fielder
Born: 7 May 1981, Bedford
Height: 5ft 11in **Weight:** 11st 8lbs
Nickname: Wadey
County debut: No first-team appearance
Parents: Nigel and Joanna
Marital status: Single
Family links with cricket: 'Dad played club
cricket'
Education: Bedford Modern School;
Loughborough University
Qualifications: 9 GCSEs, 3 A-levels
Career outside cricket: Student
Off-season: At university
Overseas tours: Bedford Modern School to
Caribbean 1997, 1999; Northamptonshire
U19 to South Africa 2000
Overseas teams played for: South Sydney 1999-2000
Cricketers particularly admired: Mark Waugh, Michael Slater, Shane Warne
Other sports played: Football (Watford School of Excellence 1994-95), golf
Relaxations: Socialising with friends, golf, snooker
Opinions on cricket: 'Split over games in leagues should be abolished for win-lose
games'

WAGG, G. G. Warwickshire

Name: <u>Graham</u> Grant Wagg
Role: Right-hand middle-order bat, left-arm fast-medium bowler
Born: 28 April 1983, Rugby
Height: 6ft **Weight:** 12st 2lbs
Nickname: Stiggy
County debut: No first-team appearance
Parents: John and Dawn
Marital status: Single
Family links with cricket: Father is qualified coach and played for Warwickshire junior sides and 2nd XI
Education: Roughton-Leigh Primary, Rugby; Ashlawn School, Rugby
Qualifications: Level 1 cricket coach
Off-season: In South Africa playing cricket
Overseas tours: Warwickshire CCC Development tour to South Africa 1998
Overseas teams played for: Hams Tech, East London, South Africa 1999
Cricketers particularly admired: Ian Botham, Courtney Walsh, Glenn McGrath
Young players to look out for: Ian Bell, Kyle Hogg
Other sports played: Fishing, football
Other sports followed: Football (Man United)
Relaxations: Clubbing, music
Extras: Represented England U16 and U17. Played for Warwickshire Board XI in the NatWest 2000

2000 Season (did not make any first-class or one-day appearances)

Career Performances

	M	Inns	NO	Runs	HS	Avge	100s	50s	Ct	St	Balls	Runs	Wkts	Avge	Best	5wl	10wM
Test																	
All First																	
1-day Int																	
NatWest	1	1	0	0	0	0.00	-	-	-	-	30	17	0	-	-	-	-
B & H																	
1-day Lge																	

WAGH, M. A.   Warwickshire

Name: <u>Mark</u> Anant Wagh
Role: Right-hand bat, off-spin bowler
Born: 20 October 1976, Birmingham
Height: 6ft 2in **Weight:** 13st
Nickname: Waggy
County debut: 1997
County cap: 2000
1st-Class 50s: 12
1st-Class 100s: 8
1st-Class 200s: 1
1st-Class catches: 31
Place in batting averages: 21st av. 45.53
(1999 88th av. 32.15)
Strike rate: (career 105.53)
Parents: Mohan and Rita
Marital status: Single
Education: Harborne Junior School;
King Edward's School, Birmingham;
Keble College, Oxford
Qualifications: 12 GCSEs, 4 A-levels, BA degree, basic coaching
Career outside cricket: Stockbroker
Off-season: Working for Williams De Broë
Overseas tours: Warwickshire U19 to South Africa 1992
Cricketers particularly admired: Andy Flower
Other sports followed: Hockey, snooker, football
Relaxations: Snooker and going out with friends
Extras: Oxford Blue 1996-98; Oxford University captain 1997. With Michael Powell, shared in record first-wicket stand for Warwickshire in matches v Essex (230) at Chelmsford 2000. Awarded Warwickshire cap 2000
Best batting: 216* Warwickshire v Oxford University, The Parks 1999
Best bowling: 4-11 Warwickshire v Middlesex, Lord's 1998

2000 Season

	M	Inns	NO	Runs	HS	Avge	100s	50s	Ct	St	O	M	Runs	Wkts	Avge	Best	5wI	10wM
Test																		
All First	9	16	3	592	137	45.53	2	3	4	-	25	9	55	0	-		-	-
1-day Int																		
NatWest																		
B & H																		
1-day Lge	3	3	0	58	31	19.33	-	-	-	-	4	0	15	0	-		-	-

Career Performances

	M	Inns	NO	Runs	HS	Avge	100s	50s	Ct	St	Balls	Runs	Wkts	Avge	Best	5wI	10wM
Test																	
All First	65	104	11	3275	216 *	35.21	9	12	31	-	3166	1694	30	56.46	4-11	-	-
1-day Int																	
NatWest																		
B & H	3	3	1	36	23	18.00	-	-	-	-	174	119	3	39.66	1-39	-	
1-day Lge	6	6	0	96	31	16.00	-	-	-	-	24	15	0	-		-	-

WALKER, M. J. Kent

Name: Matthew Jonathan Walker
Role: Left-hand bat, right-arm
medium bowler
Born: 2 January 1974, Gravesend, Kent
Height: 5ft 6in **Weight:** 13st 3lbs
Nickname: Walks, Walkdog,
Pumba, Sweetie Pud, Cheeky Monkey, Dicky
Neurerker, Merse
County debut: 1992-93
County cap: 2000
1st-Class 50s: 11
1st-Class 100s: 2
1st-Class 200s: 1
1st-Class catches: 47
One-Day 100s: 1
Place in batting averages: 133rd av. 25.52
(1999 139th av. 26.33)
Strike rate: 74.00 (career 106.16)
Parents: Richard and June
Wife and date of marriage: Claudia, 25 September 1999
Family links with cricket: Grandfather Jack played one game for Kent as a wicket-keeper. Father played for Kent and Middlesex 2nd XIs and was on Lord's groundstaff. Mother coached ex-England Ladies captain Megan Lear
Education: Shorne C of E Primary School; King's School, Rochester
Qualifications: 9 GCSEs, 2 A-levels, advanced coaching award
Career outside cricket: 'Possibly in media/journalism'
Off-season: 'Training, holidaying and a bit of work on the side'
Overseas tours: Kent U17 to New Zealand 1990-91; England U19 to Pakistan 1991-92, to India 1992-93 (captain); Kent to Zimbabwe 1992-93
Cricketers particularly admired: Aravinda De Silva, Sachin Tendulkar, Darren Lehmann

Young players to look out for: James Hockley, Bob Key

Other sports played: Hockey (England U14-U21 [captain U15-U17], Kent U14-U21, South East U16-U18), rugby (Kent U18), football (trials for Chelsea and Gillingham), athletics (Kent U15 javelin champion)

Other sports followed: Football (Charlton Athletic), rugby (Gravesend RFC), hockey (Canterbury HC)

Relaxations: Music and films ('avid collector of both'). 'Any good restaurant with a cheeky little bottle of white'

Extras: Captained England U16 cricket team and England U16 hockey team in same year. Captained England U19 v West Indies in 1993 home series. Received Sir Jack Hobbs award for best young cricketer 1989, and *Daily Telegraph* U15 batting award 1989. Woolwich Kent League's Young Cricketer of the Year 1994. Scored 275 not out against Somerset in 1996 – the highest ever individual score by a Kent batsman at Canterbury – and was on the pitch for the whole game. Became an Eminent Roffensian in 1995. Awarded Kent cap 2000

Opinions on cricket: 'Better wickets should be encouraged if the standard is to improve. Pitch inspectors should be stricter.'

Best batting: 275* Kent v Somerset, Canterbury 1996

Best bowling: 1-3 First-Class Counties XI v New Zealand A, Milton Keynes 2000

2000 Season

	M	Inns	NO	Runs	HS	Avge	100s	50s	Ct	St	O	M	Runs	Wkts	Avge	Best	5wI	10wM
Test																		
All First	15	25	4	536	61	25.52	-	1	12	-	74	12	187	6	31.16	1-3	-	-
1-day Int																		
NatWest	2	2	1	21	15 *	21.00	-	-	-	-	2	1	3	0	-		-	-
B & H	2	2	0	17	17	8.50	-	-	-	-								
1-day Lge	14	13	0	224	63	17.23	-	1	5	-	33	1	178	6	29.66	2-27	-	-

Career Performances

	M	Inns	NO	Runs	HS	Avge	100s	50s	Ct	St	Balls	Runs	Wkts	Avge	Best	5wI	10wM
Test																	
All First	70	117	12	2845	275 *	27.09	3	11	47	-	637	321	6	53.50	1-3	-	-
1-day Int																	
NatWest	7	7	2	212	73	42.40	-	2	-	-	72	36	1	36.00	1-33	-	
B & H	24	23	3	726	117	36.30	1	5	9	-							
1-day Lge	85	79	8	1421	80	20.01	-	7	21	-	234	204	6	34.00	2-27	-	

WALLACE, M. A. Glamorgan

Name: <u>Mark</u> Alex Wallace
Role: Left-hand bat, wicket-keeper
Born: 19 November 1981, Abergavenny,
Gwent
Height: 5ft 10in **Weight:** 12st
Nickname: Wally, Grom, Marcellus
County debut: 1999
1st-Class 50s: 2
1st-Class catches: 22
Parents: Ryland and Alvine
Marital status: Single
Family links with cricket: Father plays
league cricket for Abergavenny
Education: Crickhowell Primary School;
Crickhowell High School
Qualifications: 10 GCSEs, 3 A-levels
Off-season: 'England U19 tour to India.
Watching "the Martyrs" – sadly without Dean

Cosker's natural flair this season; he will be sadly missed'
Overseas tours: Gwent U15 to South Africa 1996; Wales U16 to Jersey 1996, 1997;
England U17 to Ireland (International Youth Tournament) 1999; England U19 to New
Zealand 1998-99, to Malaysia and (Youth World Cup) Sri Lanka 1999-2000, to India
2000-01
Cricketers particularly admired: Chris Read, Keith Piper, Adrian Shaw, Steve
James, Adam Gilchrist
Young players to look out for: Mike Powell, Ian Bell, John Maunders, Graeme
Bridge, David Harrison, Nicky Peng, Ian 'the Body' Thomas
Other sports played: Football, touch rugby ('badly'), golf
Other sports followed: Football (Merthyr Tydfil FC – 'missing Dean Cosker on the
left flank')
Injuries: Out for two weeks with a dislocated finger; for three weeks with a broken
thumb
Relaxations: Sleep, golf, 'the Tydfil', cinema
Extras: Represented England U19 in home series against Pakistan 1998, Australia
1999 and Sri Lanka (as captain for second 'Test') 2000, although missed the one-day
series v Sri Lanka due to injury. Made first-class debut v Somerset 1999 aged 17 years
287 days – youngest ever Glamorgan wicket-keeper. NBC Denis Compton Award
1999
Opinions on cricket: 'Thirty minutes for tea break. Pick England A team on merit or
it will lose its credibility.'
Best batting: 64* Glamorgan v Yorkshire, Headingley 1999

2000 Season

	M	Inns	NO	Runs	HS	Avge	100s	50s	Ct	St	O	M	Runs	Wkts	Avge	Best	5wl	10wM
Test																		
All First	3	5	1	116	59 *	29.00	-	1	10	-								
1-day Int																		
NatWest																		
B & H																		
1-day Lge	4	3	1	15	8 *	7.50	-	-	3	1								

Career Performances

	M	Inns	NO	Runs	HS	Avge	100s	50s	Ct	St	Balls	Runs	Wkts	Avge	Best	5wl	10wM
Test																	
All First	6	9	2	214	64 *	30.57	-	2	22	-							
1-day Int																	
NatWest																	
B & H																	
1-day Lge	7	5	1	18	8 *	4.50	-	-	7	3							

WARD, I. J. Surrey

Name: <u>Ian</u> James Ward
Role: Left-hand bat, right-arm 'very low' bowler
Born: 30 September 1973, Plymouth
Height: 5ft 8in ('taller than G. Thorpe')
Weight: 13st
Nickname: Wardy, Cocker, Son of Baboon, Dwarf, Stumpy, Pig in a Passage, Warley ('courtesy of Henry Thorpe')
County debut: 1996
County cap: 2000
1000 runs in a season: 1
1st-Class 50s: 21
1st-Class 100s: 4
1st-Class catches: 34
Place in batting averages: 38th av. 40.63 (1999 51st av. 37.70)
Parents: Tony and Mary
Wife and date of marriage: Joanne, 15 February 1998
Children: Robert, 21 September; Lennox, 10 April
Family links with cricket: Grandfather and father played for Devon
Education: Valley End; Millfield School; 'Ben Hollioake's house'

Qualifications: 8 GCSEs, 3 A-levels, NCA coaching award
Career outside cricket: 'Marketing sport in some way. John Wayne impersonator'
Off-season: 'In Perth and on tour in West Indies with England A'
Overseas tours: Surrey U19 to Barbados 1990; Millfield to Jamaica 1991, to Australia; Malden Wanderers to Jersey 1994; England A to Bangladesh and New Zealand 1999-2000, to West Indies 2000-01
Overseas teams played for: North Perth CC, Western Australia 1996-97; Perth CC, Western Australia; Marist Newman Old Boys CC
Cricketers particularly admired: Graham Thorpe, Mark Wasley (North Perth CC), Ali Brown, Justin Langer, Martin Bicknell
Young players to look out for: Tim Murtagh, Mike Johnson (North Perth CC)
Other sports played: Golf and 'Vortex'
Other sports followed: Football (Liverpool), beach volleyball, Formula One motor racing
Injuries: Back injury; no time off required
Relaxations: 'Spending time with my wife, walking dog, running; and letting Ben Hollioake tell me all I need to know'
Extras: Released by Surrey at 18 and missed four years of cricket, returning to the county in 1996. Surrey 2nd XI cap at the age of 23. Awarded Surrey cap 2000
Opinions on cricket: 'Still play too much. More time needed to practise, train and prepare. Wickets and practice wickets *must improve* or our players will not learn how to play on good overseas pitches. Groundsmen should be contracted to ECB. ECB contracts for England players have worked well. Two divisions excellent, but points for wins in Championship cricket should be higher or points for winning on first innings awarded.'
Best batting: 158* Surrey v Kent, Canterbury 2000
Stop press: Scored centuries in three successive Busta Cup matches for England A in West Indies 2000-01; during his 135 v Barbados at Bridgetown, he shared in record opening stand for England A (224) with Michael Powell

2000 Season

	M	Inns	NO	Runs	HS	Avge	100s	50s	Ct	St	O	M	Runs	Wkts	Avge	Best	5wI	10wM
Test																		
All First	16	25	3	894	158 *	40.63	3	3	4	-	5	2	10	0	-	-	-	-
1-day Int																		
NatWest	3	2	0	57	29	28.50	-	-	-	-								
B & H	4	2	0	11	9	5.50	-	-	1	-								
1-day Lge	14	13	1	429	90 *	35.75	-	3	3	-								

90. Whose 200* at Headingley in 1993 was the last of
his eight centuries against England?

Career Performances

	M	Inns	NO	Runs	HS	Avge	100s	50s	Ct	St	Balls	Runs	Wkts	Avge	Best	5wl	10wM
Test																	
All First	56	93	9	2849	158 *	33.91	4	21	34	-	156	102	0	-	-	-	-
1-day Int																	
NatWest	11	9	1	177	29	22.12	-	-	-	-							
B & H	5	3	0	12	9	4.00	-	-	1	-							
1-day Lge	54	51	8	1195	91	27.79	-	7	11	-	53	84	0	-	-	-	

WARD, T. R. Leicestershire

Name: <u>Trevor</u> Robert Ward
Role: Right-hand bat, occasional
off-spin bowler
Born: 18 January 1968, Farningham, Kent
Height: 5ft 11in **Weight:** 13st
Nickname: Wardy, Chikka
County debut: 1986 (Kent),
2000 (Leicestershire)
County cap: 1989 (Kent)
Benefit: 1999 (Kent)
1000 runs in a season: 6
1st-Class 50s: 70
1st-Class 100s: 23
1st-Class 200s: 1
1st-Class catches: 205
One-Day 100s: 7
Place in batting averages: 250th av. 12.22
(1999 218th av. 18.46)
Strike rate: (career 135.37)
Parents: Robert Henry and Hazel Ann
Wife and date of marriage: Sarah Ann, 29 September 1990
Children: Holly Ann, 23 October 1995; Samuel Joseph, 25 April 1998
Family links with cricket: Father played club cricket
Education: Anthony Roper County Primary; Hextable Comprehensive
Qualifications: 7 O-levels, NCA coaching award
Overseas tours: NCA to Bermuda 1985; England YC to Sri Lanka 1986-87,
to Australia (Youth World Cup) 1987-88
Overseas teams played for: Scarborough, Perth, Western Australia 1985;
Gosnells, Perth 1993
Cricketers particularly admired: Ian Botham, Graham Gooch, Robin Smith
Other sports followed: Most sports

Relaxations: Fishing, watching television, golf
Extras: Was awarded £1000 for becoming the first player to score 400 runs in the Benson and Hedges Cup in 1995. Released by Kent at end of 1999 season and joined Leicestershire for 2000 on a three-year contract
Best batting: 235* Kent v Middlesex, Canterbury 1991
Best bowling: 2-10 Kent v Yorkshire, Canterbury 1996

2000 Season

	M	Inns	NO	Runs	HS	Avge	100s	50s	Ct	St	O	M	Runs	Wkts	Avge	Best	5wI	10wM
Test																		
All First	7	10	1	110	39	12.22	-	-	8	-								
1-day Int																		
NatWest																		
B & H	4	4	0	83	34	20.75	-	-	-	-								
1-day Lge	14	13	0	219	61	16.84	-	2	4	-								

Career Performances

	M	Inns	NO	Runs	HS	Avge	100s	50s	Ct	St	Balls	Runs	Wkts	Avge	Best	5wI	10wM
Test																	
All First	213	365	20	12007	235 *	34.80	24	70	205	-	1083	647	8	80.87	2-10	-	-
1-day Int																	
NatWest	24	24	1	934	120	40.60	1	8	4	-	174	154	4	38.50	2-25	-	
B & H	54	54	3	1730	125	33.92	2	12	11	-	12	10	0	-	-	-	
1-day Lge	185	179	6	5057	131	29.23	4	32	41	-	228	187	6	31.16	3-20	-	

WARNE, S. K.   Hampshire

Name: <u>Shane</u> Keith Warne
Role: Right-hand bat, leg-spin bowler
Born: 13 September 1969, Upper Ferntree Gully, Victoria
Height: 6ft **Weight:** 13st 7lbs
Nickname: Suicide, Window Sill, Warney, Trueman
County debut: 2000
County cap: 2000
Test debut: 1991-92
Tests: 84
One-Day Internationals: 149
50 wickets in a season: 1
1st-Class 50s: 9
1st-Class 5 w. in innings: 31
1st-Class 10 w. in match: 4
1st-Class catches: 123

One-Day 5 w. in innings: 1
Place in batting averages: 163rd av. 21.55
Place in bowling averages: 43rd av. 23.14
Strike rate: 54.82 (career 61.73)
Parents: Keith and Brigitte
Wife and date of marriage: Simone,
1 September 1995
Children: Brooke and Jackson
Education: Hampton High School; Mentone
Grammar School
Overseas tours: Australia to Sri Lanka 1992-
93, to New Zealand 1992-93, to England
1993, to South Africa 1993-94, to Pakistan
1994-95, to West Indies 1994-95, to India,
Pakistan and Sri Lanka (World Cup) 1995-96,
to South Africa 1996-97, to England 1997, to
India 1997-98, to West Indies 1998-99, to
UK, Ireland and Holland (World Cup) 1999,

to Sri Lanka and Zimbabwe 1999-2000, to New Zealand 1999-2000, to India 2000-01
Overseas teams played for: St Kilda, Victoria; Victoria 1990-91 –
Cricketers particularly admired: Ian Chappell, Allan Border, Peter Hartley
Players to look out for: Will Kendall, Giles White's leg spin, Lawrence Prittipaul
Other sports played: Golf (14 handicap)
Other sports followed: Football (Chelsea), Australian Rules (St Kilda)
Extras: One of *Wisden*'s Five Cricketers of the Year 1993. Has captained Australia in
One-Day Internationals. Took Test hat-trick v England at Melbourne 1994-95. Took
300th Test wicket (Jacques Kallis) v South Africa at Sydney 1998. Man of the Match
in 1999 World Cup semi-final v South Africa and final v Pakistan. Shares record (with
Geoff Allott of New Zealand) for the number of wickets in a World Cup tournament
(20 in 1999). Was leading wicket-taker in world Test cricket in the 1990s with 351
wickets (av. 25.67). Voted one of *Wisden*'s Five Cricketers of the Century. Voted
Carlton and United One-Day International Player of the Year at the inaugural Allan
Border Medal awards January 2000. Tops the list of Australian Test wicket-takers,
having passed Dennis Lillee's record of 355 by dismissing Paul Wiseman of New
Zealand in the first Test at Auckland 2000. Played for Hampshire in 2000 as overseas
player. Featured on a limited-edition Australian stamp issued in 2000. Awarded
Hampshire cap 2000. Awarded ACB contract for 2000-01
Opinions on cricket: 'Play to win. Never give up!'
Best batting: 86 Australia v Pakistan, Brisbane 1999-2000
Best bowling: 8-71 Australia v England, Brisbane 1994-95

2000 Season

	M	Inns	NO	Runs	HS	Avge	100s	50s	Ct	St	O	M	Runs	Wkts	Avge	Best	5wI	10wM
Test																		
All First	15	22	2	431	69	21.55	-	3	14	-	639.4	183	1620	70	23.14	6-34	5	-
1-day Int																		
NatWest	3	2	1	20	20	20.00	-	-	-	-	27	2	84	8	10.50	4-34	-	
B & H	4	3	0	13	7	4.33	-	-	-	-	32	1	112	5	22.40	2-6	-	
1-day Lge	13	13	1	151	34	12.58	-	-	5	-	113	15	438	25	17.52	4-23	-	

Career Performances

	M	Inns	NO	Runs	HS	Avge	100s	50s	Ct	St	Balls	Runs	Wkts	Avge	Best	5wI	10wM
Test	84	117	12	1613	86	15.36	-	4	64	-	23501	9505	366	25.96	8-71	16	4
All First	166	221	30	3170	86	16.59	-	9	123	-	42167	18127	683	26.54	8-71	31	4
1-day Int	149	86	25	769	55	12.60	-	1	53	-	8230	5709	230	24.82	5-33	1	
NatWest	3	2	1	20	20	20.00	-	-	-	-	162	84	8	10.50	4-34	-	
B & H	4	3	0	13	7	4.33	-	-	-	-	192	112	5	22.40	2-6	-	
1-day Lge	13	13	1	151	34	12.58	-	-	5	-	678	438	25	17.52	4-23	-	

WARREN, N. A.　　　　　　　Warwickshire

Name: <u>Nick</u> Alexander Warren
Role: Right-hand bat, right-arm
medium-fast bowler
Born: 26 June 1982, Moseley
Height: 5ft 11in **Weight:** 12st 7lbs
Nickname: Wazza
County debut: No first-team appearance
Parents: Lesley
Marital status: Single
Education: St Martins; Wheelers Lane Boys
School; Solihull Sixth Form College
Qualifications: 9 GCSEs, BTEC Sports
Science
Career outside cricket: 'Pilot'
Off-season: In Cape Town
Overseas tours: Warwickshire U19 to Cape
Town 1998-99; England U17 to Ireland 1999;
England U19 to Malaysia and (Youth World
Cup) Sri Lanka 1999-2000

Cricketers particularly admired: Allan Donald, Graeme Welch
Young players to look out for: Jim Troughton
Other sports played: Football

Other sports followed: Football (Birmingham City)
Injuries: Out for most of the season with ankle injury
Relaxations: Watching films; planes, music
Opinions on cricket: 'I haven't really played the game long enough.'

WARREN, R. J. Northamptonshire

Name: <u>Russell</u> John Warren
Role: Right-hand bat, wicket-keeper
Born: 10 September 1971, Northampton
Height: 6ft 2in **Weight:** 13st 4lbs
Nickname: Rab C, Rabbit
County debut: 1992
County cap: 1995
1st-Class 50s: 23
1st-Class 100s: 4
1st-Class 200s: 1
1st-Class catches: 97
1st-Class stumpings: 3
One-Day 100s: 1
Place in batting averages: 61st av. 34.75
(1999 56th av. 37.40)
Parents: John and Sally
Marital status: Single
Family links with cricket: 'Dad likes a bet.
Mum follows scores on Teletext'
Education: Whitehills Lower School; Kingsthorpe Middle and Upper Schools
Qualifications: 8 O-levels, 2 A-levels
Career outside cricket: 'Hustling on the baize'
Off-season: Training
Overseas tours: England YC to New Zealand 1990-91; Northamptonshire to Cape
Town 1993, to Zimbabwe 1995, to Johannesburg 1996, to Grenada 2000
Overseas teams played for: Lancaster Park, Christchurch, and Canterbury B, New
Zealand 1991-93; Riverside CC, Lower Hutt, New Zealand 1994-95; Petone CC,
Wellington, New Zealand 1995-96; Alma Marist CC, Cape Town, South Africa
1997-98
Cricketers particularly admired: Allan Lamb, Wayne Larkins
Young players to look out for: Mark Powell, Alec Swann
Other sports played: Golf, snooker
Other sports followed: Football (Manchester United and Northampton Town), rugby
(Northampton Saints), golf, snooker and horse racing ('mostly Nick Cook and John
Hughes tips!')
Relaxations: 'Music, having a bet'

Opinions on cricket: 'Smaller staffs. Scrap 2nd XI cricket.'
Best batting: 201* Northamptonshire v Glamorgan, Northampton 1996

2000 Season

	M	Inns	NO	Runs	HS	Avge	100s	50s	Ct	St	O	M	Runs	Wkts	Avge	Best	5wI	10wM
Test																		
All First	9	13	1	417	151	34.75	1	2	3	-								
1-day Int																		
NatWest	1	1	0	1	1	1.00	-	-	-	-								
B & H	2	2	0	33	23	16.50	-	-	4	-								
1-day Lge	5	5	1	23	10	5.75	-	-	5	-								

Career Performances

	M	Inns	NO	Runs	HS	Avge	100s	50s	Ct	St	Balls	Runs	Wkts	Avge	Best	5wI	10wM
Test																	
All First	88	142	17	4095	201 *	32.76	5	23	97	3							
1-day Int																	
NatWest	17	15	2	348	100 *	26.76	1	1	20	1							
B & H	14	13	1	128	23	10.66	-	-	15	-							
1-day Lge	82	71	11	1323	71 *	22.05	-	4	70	9							

WATKIN, S. L. Glamorgan

Name: <u>Steven</u> Llewellyn Watkin
Role: Right-hand bat, right-arm
medium-fast bowler
Born: 15 September 1964, Dyffryn, Rhondda
Height: 6ft 3in **Weight:** 12st 8lbs
Nickname: Watty, Banger
County debut: 1986
County cap: 1989
Benefit: 1998
Test debut: 1991
Tests: 3
One-Day Internationals: 4
50 wickets in a season: 9
1st-Class 50s: 1
1st-Class 5 w. in innings: 30
1st-Class 10 w. in match: 4
1st-Class catches: 66
One-Day 5 w. in innings: 1

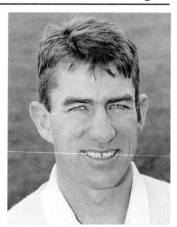

Place in batting averages: 200th av. 17.85 (1999 279th av. 8.60)
Place in bowling averages: 34th av. 22.22 (1999 59th av. 25.27)
Strike rate: 48.70 (career 57.27)
Parents: John (deceased) and Sandra
Wife and date of marriage: Caryl, 8 April 2000
Family links with cricket: Brothers play for local cricket teams
Education: Cymer Afan Comprehensive; Swansea College of Further Education;
South Glamorgan Institute of Higher Education
Qualifications: 8 O-levels, 2 A-levels, BA (Hons) Human Movement Studies
Career outside cricket: Cricket development officer
Off-season: Coaching
Overseas tours: British Colleges to West Indies 1987; England A to Kenya and
Zimbabwe 1989-90, to Pakistan and Sri Lanka 1990-91, to Bermuda and West Indies
1991-92; England to West Indies 1993-94
Overseas teams played for: Potchefstroom University, South Africa 1987-88;
Aurora, Durban 1991-92
Cricketers particularly admired: Richard Hadlee, Dennis Lillee, Ian Botham, Allan
Donald, Alec Stewart
Young players to look out for: Mark Wallace, Dave Harrison
Other sports played: Football (Welsh Boys' Clubs cap as goalkeeper)
Other sports followed: Football ('all Welsh football clubs'), rugby (Neath and
Maesteg)
Injuries: Out for three weeks with groin strain
Relaxations: Watching television, music, DIY, motor mechanics, 'a quiet pint'
Extras: Joint highest wicket-taker in English first-class cricket 1989 with 94 wickets
and took most (92) in 1993. Sister Lynda has played for Great Britain at hockey.
Players' Player of the Year and Glamorgan Player of the Year 1993. One of *Wisden*'s
Five Cricketers of the Year 1994. Began Glamorgan's match v Notts at Colwyn Bay
1999 with a spell of 5-0 off 17 balls, passing 800 first-class wickets in the process.
Scored maiden first-class 50 (51) v Gloucestershire at Cardiff 2000
Opinions on cricket: 'Two division cricket here to stay. But still too much cricket
being played and not enough rest and practice. Test players rested (Caddy and
Goughy) have shown how performances are raised with sufficient time off between
games.'
Best batting: 51 Glamorgan v Gloucestershire, Cardiff 2000
Best bowling: 8-59 Glamorgan v Warwickshire, Edgbaston 1988

---

91. Who took eight catches at Old Trafford in 1997 to
set a new England record in an Ashes Test?

2000 Season

	M	Inns	NO	Runs	HS	Avge	100s	50s	Ct	St	O	M	Runs	Wkts	Avge	Best	5wI	10wM
Test																		
All First	13	13	6	125	51	17.85	-	1	1	-	389.4	108	1067	48	22.22	6-26	2	-
1-day Int																		
NatWest	2	0	0	0	0	-	-	-	-	-	17.5	3	39	2	19.50	2-16	-	
B & H	6	3	0	11	10	3.66	-	-	1	-	51	12	139	9	15.44	3-7	-	
1-day Lge	5	4	2	3	2	1.50	-	-	2	-	37	2	162	6	27.00	2-28	-	

Career Performances

	M	Inns	NO	Runs	HS	Avge	100s	50s	Ct	St	Balls	Runs	Wkts	Avge	Best	5wI	10wM
Test	3	5	0	25	13	5.00	-	-	1	-	534	305	11	27.72	4-65	-	-
All First	251	280	102	1849	51	10.38	-	1	66	-	49199	23791	859	27.69	8-59	30	4
1-day Int	4	2	0	4	4	2.00	-	-	-	-	221	193	7	27.57	4-49	-	
NatWest	34	15	5	53	13	5.30	-	-	3	-	2165	1129	45	25.08	4-26	-	
B & H	43	24	11	100	15	7.69	-	-	9	-	2439	1556	57	27.29	4-31	-	
1-day Lge	151	64	24	265	31 *	6.62	-	-	25	-	6655	4765	183	26.03	5-23	1	

WATKINSON, M.   Lancashire

Name: Michael Watkinson
Role: Right-hand bat, right-arm
medium or off-spin bowler
Born: 1 August 1961, Westhoughton
Height: 6ft 1½in **Weight:** 13st
Nickname: Winker
County debut: 1982
County cap: 1987
Benefit: 1996 (£209,000)
Test debut: 1995
Tests: 4
One-Day Internationals: 1
1000 runs in a season: 1
50 wickets in a season: 7
1st-Class 50s: 50
1st-Class 100s: 11
1st-Class 5 w. in innings: 27
1st-Class 10 w. in match: 3
1st-Class catches: 156
One-Day 100s: 2
One-Day 5 w. in innings: 3
Place in batting averages: (1999 115th av. 28.75)

Place in bowling averages: (1999 116th av. 34.41)
Strike rate: (career 64.69)
Parents: Albert and Marian
Wife and date of marriage: Susan, 12 April 1986
Children: Charlotte, 24 February 1989; Liam, 27 July 1991
Education: Rivington and Blackrod High School, Horwich
Qualifications: 8 O-levels, HTC Civil Engineering
Career outside cricket: Draughtsman
Overseas tours: England to South Africa 1995-96
Cricketers particularly admired: Clive Lloyd, Imran Khan
Other sports followed: Football
Relaxations: Watching Bolton Wanderers
Extras: Played for Cheshire in Minor Counties Championship and in NatWest Trophy (v Middlesex) 1982. Man of the Match in the first Refuge Assurance Cup final 1988 and in B&H Cup final 1990. Resigned the Lancashire captaincy during the 1997-98 off-season. 2nd XI captain and coach
Best batting: 161 Lancashire v Essex, Old Trafford 1995
Best bowling: 8-30 Lancashire v Hampshire, Old Trafford 1994

2000 Season

	M	Inns	NO	Runs	HS	Avge	100s	50s	Ct	St	O	M	Runs	Wkts	Avge	Best	5wI	10wM
Test																		
All First																		
1-day Int																		
NatWest																		
B & H	1	1	0	8	8	8.00	-	-	-	-	5	0	26	1	26.00	1-26	-	
1-day Lge	3	2	0	42	33	21.00	-	-	1	-	24	1	122	3	40.66	2-46	-	

Career Performances

	M	Inns	NO	Runs	HS	Avge	100s	50s	Ct	St	Balls	Runs	Wkts	Avge	Best	5wI	10wM
Test	4	6	1	167	82 *	33.40	-	1	1	-	672	348	10	34.80	3-64	-	-
All First	308	459	49	10939	161	26.68	11	50	156	-	47806	24960	739	33.77	8-30	27	3
1-day Int	1	0	0	0	0	-	-	-	-	-	54	43	0	-	-	-	-
NatWest	46	40	7	1064	130	32.24	1	7	12	-	2681	1751	46	38.06	3-14	-	-
B & H	73	53	12	837	76	20.41	-	4	22	-	3740	2636	88	29.95	5-44	2	
1-day Lge	236	189	38	3262	121	21.60	1	9	59	-	8730	7113	225	31.61	5-46	1	

---

92. Who bowled England to victory at Headingley
in 1981 with figures of 8-43?

WEEKES, L. C.   Northamptonshire

Name: <u>Lesroy</u> Charlesworth Weekes
Role: Right-hand bat, right-arm fast bowler
Born: 19 July 1972, Montserrat
Height: 6ft 2in **Weight:** 16st
Nickname: Weeksey
County debut: 2000 (Yorkshire)
1st-Class 5 w. in innings: 2
1st-Class catches: 17
Strike rate: 23.00 (career 48.33)
Parents: Winifred and Franklyn
Marital status: Single
Children: Keisha, 15 August 1998
Education: Plymouth School; Montserrat
High School; Montserrat Sports College
Qualifications: 5 GCSEs, NCA coaching
award
Career outside cricket: Football
Off-season: 'Training; coaching future young
players'
Overseas teams played for: Leeward Islands
Cricketers particularly admired: Curtly Ambrose, Sir Viv Richards, Darren Gough
Young players to look out for: Sylvester Joseph, Liam Dickinson
Other sports played: Football, basketball
Other sports followed: Football (Manchester United)
Relaxations: 'Watching young cricketers play'
Extras: Played league cricket in Yorkshire. Played for Lincolnshire in the NatWest
1997 and for Yorkshire Board XI in the NatWest 1999. Made debut for Yorkshire 2000
v West Indians at Headingley, taking a career best 6-56. Left Yorkshire at end of 2000
season and has joined Northamptonshire for 2001
Best batting: 46 Leeward Islands v Guyana, Berbice 1993-94
Best bowling: 6-56 Yorkshire v West Indians, Headingley 2000

2000 Season

	M	Inns	NO	Runs	HS	Avge	100s	50s	Ct	St	O	M	Runs	Wkts	Avge	Best	5wI	10wM
Test																		
All First	1	2	0	20	10	10.00	-	-	-	-	23	10	56	6	9.33	6-56	1	-
1-day Int																		
NatWest																		
B & H																		
1-day Lge																		

Career Performances

	M	Inns	NO	Runs	HS	Avge	100s	50s	Ct	St	Balls	Runs	Wkts	Avge	Best	5wI	10wM
Test																	
All First	23	34	5	473	46	16.31	-	-	17	-	3190	1764	66	26.72	6-56	2	-
1-day Int																	
NatWest	2	2	0	8	8	4.00	-	-	1	-	58	66	0	-		-	-
B & H																	
1-day Lge																	

WEEKES, P. N. *Middlesex*

Name: <u>Paul</u> Nicholas Weekes
Role: Left-hand bat, off-spin bowler
Born: 8 July 1969, Hackney, London
Height: 5ft 10in **Weight:** 12st 10lbs
Nickname: Weekesy, Twiddles
County debut: 1990
County cap: 1993
1000 runs in a season: 1
1st-Class 50s: 29
1st-Class 100s: 10
1st-Class 5 w. in innings: 3
1st-Class catches: 131
One-Day 100s: 3
Place in batting averages: 177th av. 20.33
(1999 73rd av. 34.50)
Place in bowling averages: (1999 128th
av. 38.69)

Strike rate: 74.14 (career 86.82)
Parents: Robert and Carol
Marital status: Partner Christine
Children: Cherie, 4 September 1993; Shyann, 3 May 1998
Family links with cricket: Father played club cricket
Education: Homerton House Secondary School, Hackney; Hackney College
Qualifications: 3 O-levels, NCA and senior cricket coach
Career outside cricket: Coach for Middlesex MCB
Overseas tours: England A to India 1994-95; BWIA to Trinidad 1999
Overseas teams played for: Newcastle University, NSW 1989; Sunrise, Zimbabwe 1990
Cricketers particularly admired: Courtney Walsh
Young players to look out for: Stephen Peters
Other sports played: 'Try to play football. Best goal-hanger in the country – strike
rate fantastic'

Other sports followed: Boxing

Relaxations: 'Don't get much time to relax. If possible, listening to music; having a good time with friends'

Extras: Scored 50 in debut innings for both 2nd and 1st teams. Took two catches whilst appearing as 12th man for England in the second Test against West Indies at Lord's in 1995

Best batting: 171* Middlesex v Somerset, Uxbridge 1996

Best bowling: 8-39 Middlesex v Glamorgan, Lord's 1996

2000 Season

	M	Inns	NO	Runs	HS	Avge	100s	50s	Ct	St	O	M	Runs	Wkts	Avge	Best	5wI	10wM
Test																		
All First	8	13	1	244	39	20.33	-	-	8	-	86.3	20	242	7	34.57	2-32	-	-
1-day Int																		
NatWest	3	3	1	84	71 *	42.00	-	1	2	-	2.5	0	13	0	-		-	-
B & H	1	1	0	4	4	4.00	-	-	1	-	5	0	25	2	12.50	2-25	-	
1-day Lge	13	12	2	204	43	20.40	-	-	7	-	63.5	3	308	15	20.53	4-26	-	

Career Performances

	M	Inns	NO	Runs	HS	Avge	100s	50s	Ct	St	Balls	Runs	Wkts	Avge	Best	5wI	10wM
Test																	
All First	143	224	25	6400	171 *	32.16	10	29	131	-	14152	6739	163	41.34	8-39	3	-
1-day Int																	
NatWest	19	19	3	501	143 *	31.31	2	2	6	-	928	662	19	34.84	3-35	-	
B & H	32	29	6	727	77	31.60	-	5	10	-	1430	1034	30	34.46	3-32	-	
1-day Lge	151	127	17	2706	119 *	24.60	1	11	64	-	5121	4335	162	26.75	4-26	-	

WELCH, G. Derbyshire

Name: Graeme Welch

Role: Right-hand bat, right-arm medium-fast bowler

Born: 21 March 1972, County Durham

Height: 6ft **Weight:** 13st

Nickname: Pop

County debut: 1992 (one-day, Warwickshire), 1994 (first-class, Warwickshire)

County cap: 1997 (Warwickshire)

50 wickets in a season: 1

1st-Class 50s: 8

1st-Class 5 w. in innings: 4

1st-Class 10 w. in match: 1

1st-Class catches: 30

Place in batting averages: 216th av. 16.57 (1999 185th av. 21.73)

Place in bowling averages: (1999 94th av. 29.90)

Strike rate: 312.00 (career 60.54)

Parents: Jean and Robert

Wife and date of marriage: Emma, 4 October 1997

Family links with cricket: Father Robert plays club cricket in Durham. Brother Barrie plays club cricket in Leeds

Education: Hetton Primary; Hetton Comprehensive

Qualifications: 9 GCSEs, City & Guilds in Sports and Leisure, senior coaching award

Career outside cricket: 'Anything'

Overseas tours: Warwickshire to Cape Town 1992 and 1993; England XI to New Zealand (Cricket Max) 1997

Overseas teams played for: Avendale, Cape Town 1991-93; Wellington Collegians 1994-95; Johnsonville CC, New Zealand 1995-96; Wellington 1997

Cricketers particularly admired: Allan Donald, Andy Moles, Brian Lara, Dominic Ostler, Tim Munton

Young players to look out for: Mark Wagh, Tony Frost

Other sports played: Football, 'PlayStation'

Other sports followed: Football (Newcastle United)

Relaxations: 'Few beers in "The Brook". Playing PlayStation. Spending time with wife Emma'

Extras: Played for England YC v Australian YC 1991. Has taken two hat-tricks in the 2nd XI, against Durham in 1992 and against Worcestershire. Axa Equity and Law Winner's Medal 1994. Britannic Assurance Winner's Medal 1994. Warwickshire's most improved player in 1994. Left Warwickshire at the end of the 2000 season and has joined Derbyshire for 2001

Best batting: 84* Warwickshire v Nottinghamshire, Edgbaston 1994

Best bowling: 6-115 Warwickshire v Lancashire, Blackpool 1997

2000 Season

	M	Inns	NO	Runs	HS	Avge	100s	50s	Ct	St	O	M	Runs	Wkts	Avge	Best	5wl	10wM
Test																		
All First	7	8	1	116	55	16.57	-	1	1	-	156	32	564	3	188.00	1-56	-	-
1-day Int																		
NatWest	3	2	0	52	41	26.00	-	-	-	-	30	0	160	0	-	-	-	-
B & H	1	1	0	29	29	29.00	-	-	-	-	2	0	9	2	4.50	2-9	-	
1-day Lge	11	10	0	201	55	20.10	-	1	4	-	87	10	304	7	43.42	2-32	-	

Career Performances

	M	Inns	NO	Runs	HS	Avge	100s	50s	Ct	St	Balls	Runs	Wkts	Avge	Best	5wI	10wM
Test																	
All First	78	109	18	1895	84 *	20.82	-	8	30	-	11140	6236	184	33.89	6-115	4	1
1-day Int																	
NatWest	16	11	2	139	41	15.44	-	-	-	-	858	530	9	58.88	4-31	-	
B & H	22	16	4	241	55 *	20.08	-	1	1	-	895	704	22	32.00	3-20	-	
1-day Lge	73	57	19	854	71	22.47	-	3	16	-	2659	2040	51	40.00	3-37	-	

WELLS, A. P. Kent

Name: Alan Peter Wells
Role: Right-hand bat, right-arm medium bowler
Born: 2 October 1961, Newhaven
Height: 6ft **Weight:** 13st 3lbs
Nickname: Godfrey – 'the really old one in *Dad's Army*!'
County debut: 1981 (Sussex), 1997 (Kent)
County cap: 1986 (Sussex), 1997 (Kent)
Benefit: 1995 (Sussex)
Test debut: 1995
Tests: 1
One-Day Internationals: 1
1000 runs in a season: 11
1st-Class 50s: 101
1st-Class 100s: 45
1st-Class 200s: 1
1st-Class catches: 227
One-Day 100s: 8
Place in batting averages: 205th av. 17.47 (1999 84th av. 32.66)
Strike rate: (career 115.30)
Parents: Ernest William Charles and Eunice Mae
Wife and date of marriage: Melanie Elizabeth, 26 September 1987
Children: Luke William Peter, 29 December 1990; Daniel Allan Christian, 24 June 1995
Family links with cricket: Father, Billy, played for many years for local club and had trial for Sussex. Eldest brother Ray plays club cricket; brother Colin played for Sussex, Derbyshire and Somerset and is now cricket manager at Derbyshire
Education: Tideway Comprehensive, Newhaven
Qualifications: 5 O-levels, NCA coaching certificate
Career outside cricket: Selling for international telecom brokers
Off-season: MCC tour to Namibia

Overseas tours: Unofficial England XI to South Africa 1989-90; England A to South Africa 1993-94 (vice-captain), to India 1994-95 (captain)
Overseas teams played for: Border, South Africa 1981-82
Cricketers particularly admired: Graham Gooch
Young players to look out for: James Hockley
Other sports followed: Football (Tottenham Hotspur)
Injuries: Out for 'two to three weeks' with infection of right knee
Relaxations: Good wine, cooking, spending time with family, reading books and articles on wine
Extras: Played for England YC v India 1981. Banned from Test cricket for five years in 1990 for joining tour of South Africa; suspension remitted in 1992. Scored a century in each of his first two matches as acting-captain of Sussex and won both matches. Won top batting award for Sussex 1989-93. His book, *A Captain's Year*, is a diary beginning with the England A tour of South Africa in 1993-94. Scored a century in both innings against Kent at Hove in 1995, the first Sussex player to do so since C.B. Fry. Left Sussex after 15 years during the 1996-97 off-season and joined Kent in 1997. Struck six sixes off successive deliveries (five from one over) v Durham in the AXA League at Canterbury 1998
Opinions on cricket: 'Far more competitive and intense at the end of the season than ever before, due to two divisions – a great improvement. Pitches still haven't improved. A very healthy batch of English seamers around the country – more than before. The same cannot be said of the batters or spinners – due to pitches? Nice to see the young Windies batters struggling on our pitches – perhaps a good argument not to have overseas batters. Surely they'll only improve if exposed to our conditions and be better prepared when they tour against England.'
Best batting: 253* Sussex v Yorkshire, Middlesbrough 1991
Best bowling: 3-67 Sussex v Worcestershire, Worcester 1987

2000 Season

	M	Inns	NO	Runs	HS	Avge	100s	50s	Ct	St	O	M	Runs	Wkts	Avge	Best	5wI	10wM
Test																		
All First	12	19	2	297	60*	17.47	-	2	3									
1-day Int																		
NatWest	2	2	0	7	7	3.50	-	-	1	-								
B & H	2	2	0	70	36	35.00	-	-	-	-								
1-day Lge	11	11	1	284	90	28.40	-	2	1	-								

93. When did a Tudor and a Stewart first appear
in a Test match for England?

Career Performances

	M	Inns	NO	Runs	HS	Avge	100s	50s	Ct	St	Balls	Runs	Wkts	Avge	Best	5wl	10wM
Test	1	2	1	3	3 *	3.00	-	-	-	-							
All First	376	628	81	21099	253 *	38.57	46	101	227	-	1153	820	10	82.00	3-67	-	-
1-day Int	1	1	0	15	15	15.00	-	-	-	-							
NatWest	39	36	7	1045	119	36.03	3	5	14	-	6	1	0	-		-	-
B & H	69	65	8	1737	111 *	30.47	1	14	17	-	60	72	3	24.00	1-17	-	
1-day Lge	257	237	27	6405	127	30.50	4	38	73	-	62	69	4	17.25	1-0	-	

WELLS, V. J. Leicestershire

Name: Vincent (Vince) John Wells
Role: Right-hand bat, right-arm medium
bowler, occasional wicket-keeper,
county captain
Born: 6 August 1965, Dartford
Height: 6ft **Weight:** 13st 4lbs
Nickname: Vinny, Wellsy, Both
County debut: 1987 (Kent), 1992
(Leicestershire)
County cap: 1994 (Leicestershire)
One-Day Internationals: 9
1000 runs in a season: 2
1st-Class 50s: 39
1st-Class 100s: 11
1st-Class 200s: 3
1st-Class 5 w. in innings: 3
1st-Class catches: 106
One-Day 100s: 3
One-Day 200s: 1

One-Day 5 w. in innings: 2
Place in batting averages: 103rd av. 28.89 (1999 85th av. 32.66)
Place in bowling averages: 79th av. 28.17 (1999 142nd av. 47.30)
Strike rate: 58.04 (career 54.11)
Parents: Pat and Jack
Wife and date of marriage: Deborah Louise, 14 October 1989
Children: Harrison John, 25 January 1995; Molly Louise, 2 June 1996
Family links with cricket: Brother plays club cricket for Chestfield
Education: Downs School, Dartford; Sir William Nottidge School, Whitstable
Qualifications: 1 O-level, 8 CSEs, junior and senior coaching certificates
Off-season: 'Organising benefit for 2001 season'
Overseas tours: Leicestershire to Jamaica 1993, to Bloemfontein 1994 and 1995,

to Western Transvaal 1996, to Durban 1997, to Barbados 1998, to Anguilla 2000; England to Australia 1998-99 (CUB Series), to Sharjah (Coca-Cola Cup) 1998-99
Overseas teams played for: Parnell, Auckland 1986; Avendale, Cape Town 1986-89, 1990-91; Potchefstroom University, North West Transvaal 1996-97; Cornwall CC, Auckland 1998-99
Cricketers particularly admired: James Whitaker, Phil Simmons, Mike Kasprowicz, Anil Kumble – 'all play hard, practise hard and all respect the game; top people'
Young players to look out for: James Ormond
Other sports followed: Football (Chelsea and Leicester)
Injuries: Out for one week with a rib injury; for one week with a neck injury
Relaxations: 'Good food, pint of Guinness, spending time with my family and walking Jasper the dog'
Extras: Was a schoolboy footballer with Leyton Orient. Scored 100 not out on NatWest debut v Oxfordshire. Left Kent at the end of 1991 season to join Leicestershire. Missed 1992 NatWest final owing to viral infection. Hat-trick against Durham, 1994. Scored 201 not out against Berkshire in the 1996 NatWest Trophy. Member of England's 1999 World Cup squad and was reserve wicket-keeper. Captain of Leicestershire since retirement of James Whitaker during 1999 season. Granted a benefit for 2001
Opinions on cricket: 'People should realise how lucky we are to be playing this game for a living. Two divisions have made the end of the season – big games for virtually all sides, which has to be a good thing.'
Best batting: 224 Leicestershire v Middlesex, Lord's 1997
Best bowling: 5-18 Leicestershire v Nottinghamshire, Worksop 1998

2000 Season

	M	Inns	NO	Runs	HS	Avge	100s	50s	Ct	St	O	M	Runs	Wkts	Avge	Best	5wI	10wM
Test																		
All First	15	19	0	549	98	28.89	-	4	8	-	222.3	48	648	23	28.17	4-54	-	-
1-day Int																		
NatWest	2	2	0	65	60	32.50	-	1	-	-	7	1	31	1	31.00	1-11	-	
B & H	3	3	0	75	40	25.00	-	-	1	-	5.3	0	28	0	-		-	
1-day Lge	15	14	0	303	81	21.64	-	2	3	-	99.1	8	396	14	28.28	3-32	-	

Career Performances

	M	Inns	NO	Runs	HS	Avge	100s	50s	Ct	St	Balls	Runs	Wkts	Avge	Best	5wI	10wM
Test																	
All First	160	246	18	7708	224	33.80	14	39	106	-	13149	6486	243	26.69	5-18	3	-
1-day Int	9	7	0	141	39	20.14	-	-	7	-	220	189	8	23.62	3-30	-	
NatWest	21	20	4	658	201	41.12	2	3	1	-	887	536	23	23.30	3-30	-	
B & H	39	33	3	739	90	24.63	-	3	13	-	1543	1128	38	29.68	6-25	1	
1-day Lge	136	129	12	2912	101	24.88	2	12	30	-	4415	3418	121	28.24	5-10	1	

WELTON, G. E. Nottinghamshire

Name: <u>Guy</u> Edward Welton
Role: Right-hand opening bat
Born: 4 May 1978, Grimsby
Height: 6ft 1in **Weight:** 13st 7lbs
Nickname: Trigger, Giggs, Welts
County debut: 1997
1st-Class 50s: 6
1st-Class 200s: 1
1st-Class catches: 16
One-Day 100s: 1
Place in batting averages: 77th av. 32.09
(1999 205th av. 19.75)
Parents: Robert and Diana
Marital status: Single
Family links with cricket: Father is a
qualified cricket coach and keen club
cricketer
Education: Keelby Primary; Healing
Comprehensive; Grimsby College of Technology; Nottingham Trent University
Qualifications: 9 GCSEs, BTEC in Business and Finance, senior level cricket coach
Overseas tours: England U17 to Holland 1995; Nottinghamshire to South Africa 1998
Overseas teams played for: Randfontein CC, Johannesburg, South Africa 1996-97;
Willetton CC, Perth, Western Australia 1997-98; Coolbinia CC, Perth 1998-99
Cricketers particularly admired: David Gower, Viv Richards, Steve Waugh,
Sachin Tendulkar, Mark Lavender
Other sports played: Football ('youth trainee at Grimsby Town Football Club 1994-96')
Relaxations: Music and going to the gym
Extras: Completed a two-year YTS with Grimsby Town Football Club where he made
one first-team appearance as a substitute. Played cricket for England U14, U15 and
U17. Won the Lord's Taverners' Young Player Award in 1993 and was MCC Young
Cricketer 1994-95. Was 12th man for England at Lord's and The Oval against West
Indies in 1995. Scored maiden first-class century v Warwickshire at Edgbaston 2000,
going on to score 200* and become Nottinghamshire's youngest ever double
centurion; in the process he shared in a first-wicket stand of 406* with Darren Bicknell
(180*) that broke several records, including that for the highest Nottinghamshire
partnership for any wicket, formerly 398 by Arthur Shrewsbury and William Gunn v
Sussex at Trent Bridge 1890, and that for the highest unbeaten partnership in
Championship history
Best batting: 200* Nottinghamshire v Warwickshire, Edgbaston 2000

2000 Season

	M	Inns	NO	Runs	HS	Avge	100s	50s	Ct	St	O	M	Runs	Wkts	Avge	Best	5wI	10wM
Test																		
All First	13	23	2	674	200 *	32.09	1	3	8	-	1	0	1	0	-	-	-	-
1-day Int																		
NatWest	1	1	0	16	16	16.00	-	-	-	-								
B & H																		
1-day Lge	8	8	0	154	42	19.25	-	-	4	-								

Career Performances

	M	Inns	NO	Runs	HS	Avge	100s	50s	Ct	St	Balls	Runs	Wkts	Avge	Best	5wI	10wM
Test																	
All First	33	60	3	1436	200 *	25.19	1	6	16	-	6	1	0	-	-	-	-
1-day Int																	
NatWest	1	1	0	16	16	16.00	-	-	-	-							
B & H																	
1-day Lge	23	23	1	453	104 *	20.59	1	1	8	-							

WESTON, R. M. S.   Middlesex

Name: <u>Robin</u> Michael Swann Weston
Role: Right-hand bat, leg-break bowler
Born: 7 June 1975, Durham
Height: 6ft **Weight:** 12st 6lbs
County debut: 1995 (Durham),
1998 (Derbyshire), 2000 (Middlesex)
1st-Class 50s: 6
1st-Class 100s: 3
1st-Class catches: 28
Place in batting averages: 192nd av. 18.88
(1999 71st av. 34.91)
Strike rate: (career 93.50)
Parents: Kathleen Mary (deceased) and
Michael Philip
Marital status: Single
Family links with cricket: Father played for
Durham (and played rugby union for
England); brother Philip plays for
Worcestershire

Education: Bow School; Durham School; Loughborough University
Qualifications: 10 GCSEs, 4 A-levels, degree in Economics with Accountancy, basic
cricket coaching certificate

Overseas tours: England U18 to South Africa 1992-93, to Denmark 1993; England U19 to Sri Lanka 1993-94
Overseas teams played for: Fremantle, Western Australia 1996-98; Parnell CC, Auckland 1999-2000
Cricketers particularly admired: 'Anyone at the highest level'
Young players to look out for: Kevin Dean, Melvyn Betts
Other sports played: Golf, rugby union (Loughborough Students 1994-96, England U18 1993)
Other sports followed: Football (Sunderland AFC)
Relaxations: Most sports, listening to music and socialising with friends
Extras: Became youngest to play for Durham 1st XI, in Minor Counties competition, aged 15 in 1991. Released by Durham at the end of the 1997 season and joined Derbyshire. Scored maiden first-class century v Essex at Chelmsford 1999 and followed up with centuries in the next two Championship matches. NBC Denis Compton Award 1999. Left Derbyshire at the end of 1999 season and joined Middlesex for 2000. 2nd XI Championship Player of the Year 2000
Opinions on cricket: 'The two-league system seems to be creating more interest in the game, which can only be a good thing. If we are to continue to improve our standing in the world we *must* address the standard of our wickets.'
Best batting: 156 Derbyshire v Somerset, Derby 1999
Best bowling: 1-15 Derbyshire v Hampshire, Derby 1999

2000 Season

	M	Inns	NO	Runs	HS	Avge	100s	50s	Ct	St	O	M	Runs	Wkts	Avge	Best	5wI	10wM
Test																		
All First	6	10	1	170	39	18.88	-	-	3	-								
1-day Int																		
NatWest																		
B & H	1	1	0	18	18	18.00	-	-	-	-								
1-day Lge	6	6	0	56	28	9.33	-	-	2	-								

Career Performances

	M	Inns	NO	Runs	HS	Avge	100s	50s	Ct	St	Balls	Runs	Wkts	Avge	Best	5wI	10wM
Test																	
All First	41	72	3	1726	156	25.01	3	6	28	-	187	104	2	52.00	1-15	-	-
1-day Int																	
NatWest	6	6	1	103	56	20.60	-	1	1	-							
B & H	1	1	0	18	18	18.00	-	-	-	-							
1-day Lge	28	27	2	464	56	18.56	-	2	6	-							

WESTON, W. P. C. Worcestershire

Name: William <u>Philip</u> Christopher Weston
Role: Left-hand opening bat, left-arm
medium bowler
Born: 16 June 1973, Durham
Height: 6ft 4in **Weight:** 13st 9lbs
Nickname: Sven, Reverend, Wesso
County debut: 1991
County cap: 1995
1000 runs in a season: 3
1st-Class 50s: 37
1st-Class 100s: 14
1st-Class 200s: 1
1st-Class catches: 71
One-Day 100s: 1
Place in batting averages: 223rd av. 15.82
(1999 138th av. 26.38)
Strike rate: (career 229.75)
Parents: Kathleen Mary (deceased) and
Michael Philip

Wife and date of marriage: Sarah, 30 September 2000
Family links with cricket: Brother plays for Middlesex. Father played Minor
Counties cricket for Durham (and rugby union for England)
Education: Bow School, Durham; Durham School
Qualifications: 9 GCSEs, 4 A-levels, coaching certificates
Career outside cricket: Cricket development for Worcestershire CCC
Off-season: 'Coaching around Worcestershire for the club'
Overseas tours: England U18 to Canada 1991; England YC to New Zealand 1990-91;
England U19 to Pakistan 1991-92 (captain); Worcestershire to Zimbabwe 1996
Overseas teams played for: Melville, Perth 1992-94 and 1996-97;
Swanbourne, Perth 1995-96
Cricketers particularly admired: 'Everyone who makes the most of their talent'
Young players to look out for: Kadeer Ali
Other sports followed: Rugby union, football (Sunderland AFC)
Injuries: Out for three months with a knee operation ('ruined season')
Relaxations: 'Spending time with Sarah; travelling, cinema, property'
Extras: Played for Northants 2nd XI and Worcs 2nd XI in 1989. Scored century for
England YC v Australian YC 1991. Cricket Society's Most Promising Young Cricketer
1992. Worcestershire Uncapped Player of the Year 1992. Member of Whittingdale
Fringe Squad 1993
Opinions on cricket: 'The English domestic game and the development of its players
is being ruined by the lack of quality pitches we play on. Hard surfaces with even

bounce allowing an equal contest between bat and ball are not too much to ask for, are they? Without them, we are wasting our time.'

Best batting: 205 Worcestershire v Northamptonshire, Northampton 1997
Best bowling: 2-39 Worcestershire v Pakistanis, Worcester 1992

2000 Season

	M	Inns	NO	Runs	HS	Avge	100s	50s	Ct	St	O	M	Runs	Wkts	Avge	Best	5wI	10wM
Test																		
All First	10	19	2	269	58 *	15.82	-	2	1	-								
1-day Int																		
NatWest																		
B & H																		
1-day Lge	7	6	0	100	47	16.66	-	-	2	-								

Career Performances

	M	Inns	NO	Runs	HS	Avge	100s	50s	Ct	St	Balls	Runs	Wkts	Avge	Best	5wI	10wM
Test																	
All First	144	253	25	7685	205	33.70	15	37	71	-	919	599	4	149.75	2-39	-	-
1-day Int																	
NatWest	8	8	0	103	31	12.87	-	-	1	-							
B & H	21	20	2	234	54 *	13.00	-	1	9	-							
1-day Lge	79	66	8	1342	125	23.13	1	4	16	-	6	2	1	2.00	1-2	-	

WHARF, A. G. Glamorgan

Name: <u>Alexander</u> George Wharf
Role: Right-hand bat, right-arm fast bowler; all-rounder
Born: 4 June 1975, Bradford
Height: 6ft 4in **Weight:** 15st 7lbs
Nickname: Gangster
County debut: 1994 (Yorks), 1998 (Notts), 2000 (Glamorgan)
County cap: 2000 (Glamorgan)
1st-Class 50s: 3
1st-Class 100s: 2
1st-Class 5 w. in innings: 1
1st-Class catches: 21
Place in batting averages: 161st av. 21.92 (1999 235th av. 16.08)
Place in bowling averages: 63rd av. 25.40 (1999 131st av. 39.22)
Strike rate: 41.59 (career 54.60)
Parents: Derek and Jane
Marital status: 'Live with partner and little boy Tristan'
Children: Tristan Jack Busfield Wharf, 15 November 1997

Family links with cricket: 'Father played local league cricket and brother Simon started playing again after 13 years'
Education: Marshfields First School; Preistman Middle School; Buttershaw Upper School; Thomas Danby College
Qualifications: 6 GCSEs, City and Guilds in Sports Management, NCA coaching award, junior football coaching award
Off-season: 'Training and working on my game'
Overseas tours: Various pre-season tours with Yorkshire and Notts, including Yorkshire to Cape Town 1994-95, to Guernsey 1996
Overseas teams played for: Somerset West, Cape Town 1993-95; Johnsonville CC, Wellington, New Zealand 1996-97; Universities, Wellington 1998-99
Cricketers particularly admired: Ian Botham, Steve Waugh, Glenn McGrath, Vasbert Drakes, Steve James, Steve Watkin
Young players to look out for: David Lucas, Guy Welton
Other sports played: Football
Other sports followed: Football (Manchester United)
Injuries: Out for one game with sore shins; for two Championship games and five one-dayers with a bruised heel
Relaxations: 'Relaxing with family; watching the little one grow'
Extras: Attended Dennis Lillee coaching school, Chennai (Madras), during winter 1997-98. Scored 78 for Notts v Glamorgan at Colwyn Bay 1999, having arrived at the wicket with his side on 9 for 6. Left Nottinghamshire at end of the 1999 season and joined Glamorgan for 2000 on a three-year contract. Scored maiden first-class century (100*) v Oxford Universities at The Parks 2000. Returned maiden first-class five-wicket return (5-68) v Sussex at Colwyn Bay 2000. Returned second innings figures of 4-9 from 10 overs v West Indians at Cardiff 2000. Awarded Glamorgan cap 2000
Opinions on cricket: 'I try to keep my opinions to myself and just get on with it!'
Best batting: 101* Glamorgan v Northamptonshire, Northampton 2000
Best bowling: 5-68 Glamorgan v Sussex, Colwyn Bay 2000

94. Which Nottinghamshire opener scored centuries in three consecutive Test matches on the 1986-87 tour?

2000 Season

	M	Inns	NO	Runs	HS	Avge	100s	50s	Ct	St	O	M	Runs	Wkts	Avge	Best	5wI	10wM
Test																		
All First	10	15	2	285	101 *	21.92	2	-	5	-	256.3	51	940	37	25.40	5-68	1	-
1-day Int																		
NatWest	3	2	0	6	6	3.00	-	-	-	-	30	5	79	6	13.16	3-18	-	
B & H	4	3	0	23	15	7.66	-	-	-	-	33.4	3	147	4	36.75	3-37	-	
1-day Lge	11	5	0	20	5	4.00	-	-	2	-	79	5	350	8	43.75	2-37	-	

Career Performances

	M	Inns	NO	Runs	HS	Avge	100s	50s	Ct	St	Balls	Runs	Wkts	Avge	Best	5wI	10wM
Test																	
All First	38	56	7	849	101 *	17.32	2	3	21	-	4805	2943	88	33.44	5-68	1	-
1-day Int																	
NatWest	4	3	0	18	12	6.00	-	-	-	-	228	117	6	19.50	3-18	-	
B & H	10	7	0	71	20	10.14	-	-	2	-	556	468	13	36.00	4-29	-	
1-day Lge	32	20	8	217	38 *	18.08	-	-	6	-	1246	1005	23	43.69	3-26	-	

WHARTON, L. J.   Derbyshire

Name: Lian James Wharton
Role: Left-hand bat, slow left-arm bowler
Born: 21 February 1977, Derby
Height: 5ft 9in **Weight:** 10st 9lbs
Nickname: Tetley, The King
County debut: 2000
1st-Class 5 w. in innings: 1
1st-Class catches: 2
Place in bowling averages: 127th av. 38.66
Strike rate: 82.00 (career 82.00)
Parents: Pete and Di
Marital status: Single
Education: Ravensdale School;
Ecclesbourne; Mackworth College
Qualifications: 9 GCSEs, BTEC National
Computer Studies
Career outside cricket: Salesman; indoor
cricket umpire
Off-season: 'Going to Australia to play grade cricket for Mereweather CC in
Newcastle'
Overseas teams played for: Mereweather CC, Newcastle, NSW 2000-01
Cricketers particularly admired: Phil Tufnell, Ian Botham, Shane Warne, Stewart
Edge, Ian Fraser, Daniel Vettori, Rory Williams, Andrew Williams

Young players to look out for: James Dakin, George Moulds, Chris Windmill, Trevor Smith, Luke Sutton, Steve Stubbings, Tom Lungley
Other sports played: Indoor cricket ('train with England squad'), golf, football, tennis, 'spoof'
Other sports followed: Football (Derby County), basketball (Derby Storm)
Relaxations: Reading, going to the cinema, socialising, sleeping
Extras: Had match figures of 10-58 from 37 overs on debut for Derbyshire 2nd XI. Recorded maiden first-class five-wicket return (5-96, including spell of 5-6 from 47 balls) v West Indians at Derby 2000, finishing with match figures of 9-179
Opinions on cricket: 'Tea should be longer than 20 minutes. More day/night games – maybe a league. Two divisions has made a good improvement to the game. Relegation and promotion can go down to the last match, so there are no meaningless games. This should help improve the competitive nature of English cricketers. John the Chef should be the chef for every first-class county! Awesome!'
Best batting: 7 Derbyshire v West Indians, Derby 2000
Best bowling: 5-96 Derbyshire v West Indians, Derby 2000

2000 Season

	M	Inns	NO	Runs	HS	Avge	100s	50s	Ct	St	O	M	Runs	Wkts	Avge	Best	5wI	10wM
Test																		
All First	7	9	4	15	7	3.00	-	-	2	-	164	42	464	12	38.66	5-96	1	-
1-day Int																		
NatWest																		
B & H																		
1-day Lge	7	4	4	8	7 *	-	-	-	2	-	46	2	216	6	36.00	3-29	-	

Career Performances

	M	Inns	NO	Runs	HS	Avge	100s	50s	Ct	St	Balls	Runs	Wkts	Avge	Best	5wI	10wM
Test																	
All First	7	9	4	15	7	3.00	-	-	2	-	984	464	12	38.66	5-96	1	-
1-day Int																	
NatWest																	
B & H																	
1-day Lge	7	4	4	8	7 *	-	-	-	2	-	276	216	6	36.00	3-29	-	

95. Brisbane's Test venue is usually known as 'the Gabba'.
What is this short for?

WHILEY, M. J. A. Leicestershire

Name: Matthew (Matt) Jeffrey Allen Whiley
Role: Right-hand bat, left-arm
fast bowler
Born: 6 May 1980, Nottingham
Height: 6ft 4in **Weight:** 14st 10lbs
Nickname: Ding, Oggy
County debut: 1998 (Nottinghamshire)
1st-Class catches: 1
Strike rate: (career 163.50)
Parents: Paul and Barbara
Marital status: Girlfriend Lynsey Barber
Family links with cricket: 'Dad played club
cricket for Notts Harrington CC'
Education: Whitegate Primary School,
Clifton; Harry Carlton Comprehensive
School, East Leake
Qualifications: 8 GCSEs, Level 1 coaching
certificate
Career outside cricket: 'None as yet!'
Off-season: 'Fitness training and lying on a beach in Australia. Practising on the
Warloo'
Overseas tours: England U19 to New Zealand 1998-99; Nottinghamshire to
Johannesburg 1999
Overseas teams played for: Manawatu-Foxton CC and Horowhenua District Cricket
Association, both New Zealand 1997-98
Cricketers particularly admired: Dennis Lillee, Paul Reiffel, Graham Dilley,
Paul Franks
Players to look out for: Wayne Noon, Vicram Atri
Other sports played: 'Match preparation football in the Chris Waddle mould, hugging
the left flank'
Other sports followed: Football (Man Utd)
Relaxations: 'The Warloo, shopping'
Extras: Visited the Dennis Lillee MRF Pace Foundation, February 2000. Awarded
Nottinghamshire 2nd XI cap September 2000. Came second in the Freeserve Speedster
Challenge; bowled the fastest delivery (86.6 mph) but was adjudged to have bowled a
no-ball. Released by Nottinghamshire in the 2000-01 off-season and has joined
Leicestershire for 2001
Opinions on cricket: 'I am constantly told by one of my coaches (GD) that it is a
bowler's game, but I am not convinced.'
Best bowling: 1-44 Nottinghamshire v Oxford University, The Parks 1999

2000 Season

	M	Inns	NO	Runs	HS	Avge	100s	50s	Ct	St	O	M	Runs	Wkts	Avge	Best	5wI	10wM
Test																		
All First	1	2	0	0	0	0.00	-	-	1	-	13.3	2	76	0	-		-	-
1-day Int																		
NatWest																		
B & H																			
1-day Lge																		

Career Performances

	M	Inns	NO	Runs	HS	Avge	100s	50s	Ct	St	Balls	Runs	Wkts	Avge	Best	5wI	10wM
Test																	
All First	3	4	1	0	0 *	0.00	-	-	1	-	327	244	2	122.00	1-44	-	-
1-day Int																	
NatWest																	
B & H																	
1-day Lge																	

WHITE, C.   Yorkshire

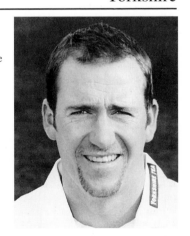

Name: Craig White
Role: Right-hand bat, right-arm
fast-medium bowler, cover fielder
Born: 16 December 1969, Morley, Yorkshire
Height: 6ft 1in **Weight:** 11st 11lbs
Nickname: Chalky, Bassey
County debut: 1990
County cap: 1993
Test debut: 1994
Tests: 12
One-Day Internationals: 29
1st-Class 50s: 33
1st-Class 100s: 8
1st-Class 5 w. in innings: 9
1st-Class catches: 116
One-Day 100s: 2
One-Day 5 w. in innings: 2
Place in batting averages: 247th av. 12.50
(1999 226th av. 17.96)
Place in bowling averages: 12th av. 17.20 (1999 63rd av. 25.80)
Strike rate: 37.80 (career 49.23)
Parents: Fred Emsley and Cynthia Anne

Wife and date of marriage: Elizabeth Anne, 19 September 1992
Family links with cricket: Father played for Pudsey St Lawrence
Education: Kennington Primary; Flora Hill High School; Bendigo Senior High School (all Victoria, Australia)
Off-season: Touring Kenya, Pakistan and Sri Lanka with England
Overseas tours: Australian YC to West Indies 1989-90; England A to Pakistan 1995-96, to Australia 1996-97; England to Australia 1994-95, to India and Pakistan (World Cup) 1995-96, to Zimbabwe and New Zealand 1996-97, to South Africa and Zimbabwe 1999-2000 (one-day series), to Kenya (ICC Knockout Trophy) 2000-01, to Pakistan and Sri Lanka 2000-01
Overseas teams played for: Victoria, Australia 1990-91
Cricketers particularly admired: Graeme Hick, Mark Waugh, Brian Lara
Other sports followed: Leeds RFC, motocross, golf, tennis
Relaxations: Playing guitar, reading, gardening and socialising
Extras: Recommended to Yorkshire by Victorian Cricket Academy, being eligible to play for Yorkshire as he was born in the county. 'Fred Trueman and I are the only Yorkshire players to debut in the 1st XI before the 2nd XI.' Formerly bowled off-spin. Called up for one-day series v South Africa and Zimbabwe 1999-2000 after injury to Andrew Flintoff. Took 5-21 and scored 26 in second One-Day International v Zimbabwe at Bulawayo in February 2000, winning the Man of the Match award. Took National League hat-trick (Fleming, Patel, Masters) v Kent at Headingley 2000. England's leading wicket-taker in the NatWest Triangular Series v Zimbabwe and West Indies 2000 with 11 wickets. Recorded maiden Test five-wicket return (5-57) in fourth Test v West Indies on his home ground of Headingley 2000, following up with 5-32 in the fifth Test at The Oval
Best batting: 181 Yorkshire v Lancashire, Headingley 1996
Best bowling: 8-55 Yorkshire v Gloucestershire, Gloucester 1998
Stop press: Scored 93 in England's first innings in the first Test at Lahore 2000-01, in the process sharing, with Graham Thorpe, in a new record sixth-wicket partnership for England in Tests v Pakistan (166); also took 4-54 in Pakistan's only innings of the match

2000 Season

	M	Inns	NO	Runs	HS	Avge	100s	50s	Ct	St	O	M	Runs	Wkts	Avge	Best	5wI	10wM
Test	4	6	1	62	27	12.40	-	-	1	-	81.3	14	236	13	18.15	5-32	2	-
All First	7	9	1	100	27	12.50	-	-	1	-	157.3	32	430	25	17.20	5-32	2	-
1-day Int	6	3	0	50	21	16.66	-	-	4	-	39	3	151	11	13.72	3-34	-	
NatWest	2	2	0	42	26	21.00	-	-	-	-	12	0	51	1	51.00	1-12	-	
B & H	6	6	1	142	45	28.40	-	-	-	-	44	7	190	8	23.75	5-25	1	
1-day Lge	7	5	1	36	14	9.00	-	-	-	-	44.5	4	126	14	9.00	4-14	-	

Career Performances

	M	Inns	NO	Runs	HS	Avge	100s	50s	Ct	St	Balls	Runs	Wkts	Avge	Best	5wI	10wM
Test	12	18	1	228	51	13.41	-	1	4	-	1300	688	24	28.66	5-32	2	-
All First	169	259	36	6678	181	29.94	8	33	116	-	14574	7781	296	26.28	8-55	9	-
1-day Int	29	22	1	330	38	15.71	-	-	8	-	1266	890	40	22.25	5-21	1	
NatWest	24	21	5	722	113	45.12	1	5	9	-	1079	674	21	32.09	3-38	-	
B & H	37	33	7	616	57 *	23.69	-	2	11	-	1620	1193	40	29.82	5-25	1	
1-day Lge	122	107	15	2242	148	24.36	1	7	36	-	3759	2715	119	22.81	4-14	-	

WHITE, G. W. — Hampshire

Name: <u>Giles</u> William White
Role: Right-hand bat, leg-break bowler
Born: 23 March 1972, Barnstaple, Devon
Height: 6ft **Weight:** 12st
Nickname: Chalky
County debut: 1991 (Somerset),
1994 (Hampshire)
County cap: 1998 (Hampshire)
1000 runs in a season: 1
1st-Class 50s: 29
1st-Class 100s: 7
1st-Class catches: 84
Place in batting averages: 108th av. 28.46
(1999 105th av. 30.29)
Strike rate: 39.50 (career 70.55)
Parents: John and Tina
Wife and date of marriage: Samantha,
25 September 1999
Family links with cricket: Father played club cricket for Exeter CC
Education: Sandford Primary School, Devon; Exeter Cathedral School; Millfield
School; Loughborough University
Qualifications: 10 O-levels, 3 A-levels, BA (Hons) Sports Management, Computing
diploma, coaching certificates
Off-season: 'Melbourne for month of December'
Overseas tours: Millfield School to Australia 1989; Hampshire to Anguilla, Cork and
Guernsey
Overseas teams played for: Waverley, Sydney 1990-91; Tigers Parrow, Cape Town
1994-95; Techs Mutual CC, Cape Town 1995-96; Rygersdaal, Cape Town 1996-97;
Wanneroo, Perth 1997-98
Cricketers particularly admired: Peter Hartley, Shane Warne, Darren Lehmann,
Robin Smith, Peter Bowler

Young players to look out for: Chris Tremlett, Lawrence Prittipaul, Simon Francis
Other sports played: Golf, squash
Other sports followed: Football (Southampton FC)
Injuries: Out for one game with a calf injury
Relaxations: Pubs, music, travel, friends, family
Extras: Hants Exiles Young Player of the Year 1997. Played for Somerset before joining Hants. Carried bat twice in 2000 season – for 78* v Somerset at Southampton (the first time by a Hampshire player since Paul Terry at Headingley in 1994); for 80* v Kent at Portsmouth
Opinions on cricket: 'Wickets need to improve. More time needed between games for practice. Should be two up, two down rather than three.'
Best batting: 156 Hampshire v Sri Lanka, Southampton 1998
Best bowling: 3-23 Hampshire v Nottinghamshire, Trent Bridge 1999

2000 Season

	M	Inns	NO	Runs	HS	Avge	100s	50s	Ct	St	O	M	Runs	Wkts	Avge	Best	5wI	10wM
Test																		
All First	18	32	4	797	96	28.46	-	5	14	-	13.1	1	58	2	29.00	2-2	-	-
1-day Int																		
NatWest	4	4	0	67	28	16.75	-	-	-	-								
B & H	4	4	1	45	27	15.00	-	-	1	-								
1-day Lge	13	12	0	147	27	12.25	-	-	4	-	1.4	0	9	0	-		-	-

Career Performances

	M	Inns	NO	Runs	HS	Avge	100s	50s	Ct	St	Balls	Runs	Wkts	Avge	Best	5wI	10wM
Test																	
All First	103	177	15	5222	156	32.23	7	29	84	-	635	456	9	50.66	3-23	-	-
1-day Int																	
NatWest	11	11	0	159	69	14.45	-	1	6	-	72	45	1	45.00	1-45	-	
B & H	16	15	1	232	56	16.57	-	1	2	-							
1-day Lge	77	74	5	1550	76	22.46	-	9	24	-	22	23	0	-		-	-

WHITE, R. A.   Northamptonshire

Name: <u>Robert</u> Allan White
Role: Right-hand opening bat, leg-spin bowler
Born: 15 October 1979, Chelmsford
Height: 5ft 11in **Weight:** 13st
Nickname: Whitey ('nothing too original')
County debut: 2000
1st-Class catches: 2
Parents: Dennis and Ann

Marital status: Single
Family links with cricket: 'Grandfather on Essex committee for many years. Dad flailed the willow and brother travels the local leagues high and low'
Education: Spratton Hall; Stowe School; St John's College, Durham University; Loughborough University
Qualifications: 10 GCSEs, 3 A-levels
Career outside cricket: 'Geological politician'
Off-season: 'A mixture of studying for my Politics degree and enjoying my time at university, not necessarily in that order'
Cricketers particularly admired: Ian Botham, Graham Gooch, Shane Warne
Other sports played: Snooker, darts, tennis
Other sports followed: Football (West Ham), rugby (Northampton Saints)
Relaxations: '*Fifteen To One* followed by *Countdown* is always compelling viewing'
Extras: Northamptonshire League Young Player of the Year and Youth Cricketer of the Year 1999
Opinions on cricket: 'There's far too much pessimism about English cricket today. The English game is in a transitional stage, but plenty of talented players are being produced.'
Best batting: 20 Northamptonshire v Oxford Universities, The Parks 2000

2000 Season

	M	Inns	NO	Runs	HS	Avge	100s	50s	Ct	St	O	M	Runs	Wkts	Avge	Best	5wI	10wM
Test																		
All First	1	2	0	31	20	15.50	-	-	2	-								
1-day Int																		
NatWest																		
B & H																		
1-day Lge																		

Career Performances

	M	Inns	NO	Runs	HS	Avge	100s	50s	Ct	St	Balls	Runs	Wkts	Avge	Best	5wI	10wM
Test																	
All First	1	2	0	31	20	15.50	-	-	2	-							
1-day Int																	
NatWest																	
B & H																	
1-day Lge																	

WHITTICASE, P.   Leicestershire

Name: Philip (<u>Phil</u>) Whitticase
Role: Right-hand bat, wicket-keeper
Born: 15 March 1965, Wythall, Birmingham
Height: 5ft 8in **Weight:** 12st
Nickname: Boggy, Rat
County debut: 1984
County cap: 1987
Benefit: 1997
50 dismissals in a season: 2
1st-Class 50s: 17
1st-Class 100s: 1
1st-Class catches: 309
1st-Class stumpings: 14
Parents: Larry Gordon and Ann
Wife and date of marriage: Karen,
12 October 1996
Children: Amy, 25 September 1997;
Jade, 18 November 2000
Family links with cricket: Grandfather and father were both wicket-keepers in local cricket
Education: Belle Vue Middle School; Crestwood Comprehensive
Qualifications: 6 O-levels, Diploma in Sports Psychology, Advanced, Level III and Staff Level II coaching qualifications
Off-season: 'Coaching staff and Excellence, Grace Road'
Overseas tours: Rutland Tourists to South Africa 1989; Leicestershire CCC to Montego Bay, to Bloemfontein
Overseas teams played for: South Bunbury, Western Australia 1982, 1984
Cricketers particularly admired: Dennis Amiss, Alan Knott, Bob Taylor
Young players to look out for: Darren Stevens, James Ormond
Other sports played: Football, golf
Other sports followed: Football (Birmingham City)
Relaxations: Reading (criminal psychology), all sports, keeping fit
Extras: Played schoolboy football for Birmingham City. Was Derek Underwood's last first-class victim. Lost seven teeth after being struck in the mouth by a bouncer from Neil Williams in Leicestershire's game against Essex in April 1995. Is 2nd XI captain
Opinions on cricket: 'The introduction of the two division system has produced more competitive cricket throughout the year, which is beneficial to the players but also the public. The involvement of agents is a little worrying, as some clubs are feeling the pinch and are therefore being priced out of the market. I hope this does not lead to an elite section of clubs, with the others going by the wayside.'
Best batting: 114* Leicestershire v Hampshire, Bournemouth 1991

2000 Season (did not make any first-class or one-day appearances)

Career Performances

	M	Inns	NO	Runs	HS	Avge	100s	50s	Ct	St	Balls	Runs	Wkts	Avge	Best	5wl	10wM
Test																	
All First	132	174	40	3113	114 *	23.23	1	17	309	14	5	7	0	-	-	-	-
1-day Int																	
NatWest	13	6	1	67	32	13.40	-	-	14	-							
B & H	29	19	7	313	45	26.08	-	-	29	4							
1-day Lge	69	45	9	413	38	11.47	-	-	56	4							

WIDDUP, S. *Yorkshire*

Name: Simon Widdup
Role: Right-hand bat, right-arm bowler, occasional wicket-keeper
Born: 10 November 1977, Doncaster, South Yorks
Height: 6ft **Weight:** 11st 11lbs
Nickname: Widds, Posh Spice, Reardo
County debut: 2000
1st-Class catches: 6
Place in batting averages: 226th av. 15.46
Strike rate: 15.00 (career 15.00)
Parents: Eric and Maggie
Marital status: Single
Family links with cricket: Great uncle Richard Knowles Tyldesley played for Lancashire in 1920s and was *Wisden* Cricketer of the Year 1925
Education: Saltersgate Infants/Middle School, Doncaster; Ridgewood Comprehensive School, Doncaster; Danum Sixth Form School, Doncaster
Qualifications: 11 GCSEs, 1 A-level, Level 1 and 2 coaching awards
Overseas tours: England Schools U15 to South Africa 1993; England U17 to Holland (ICC Youth Tournament) 1995
Overseas teams played for: Curtin University CC, Perth 1997-98
Cricketers particularly admired: Graeme Hick, Steve Waugh, Gary Fellows
Young players to look out for: John Sadler
Other sports played: Golf (16 handicap)
Other sports followed: Football (Doncaster Rovers FC, Arsenal FC)
Relaxations: 'Music (Stereophonics, Stone Roses), eating out, spending time with my girlfriend'

Extras: *Daily Telegraph* Young Cricketer of the Year 1992. Set Yorkshire League opening partnership record 1994. Set Yorkshire 2nd XI opening partnership record 1998. Abbot Ale Cup winner with Doncaster Town CC 1998. Has Yorkshire 2nd XI cap

Opinions on cricket: 'Better pitches for batters to play. Game is bowler-friendly. Need this to improve technique and strokemaking to take into the Test arena.'

Best batting: 44 Yorkshire v Somerset, Scarborough 2000
Best bowling: 1-22 Yorkshire v Somerset, Scarborough 2000

2000 Season

	M	Inns	NO	Runs	HS	Avge	100s	50s	Ct	St	O	M	Runs	Wkts	Avge	Best	5wI	10wM
Test																		
All First	9	14	1	201	44	15.46	-	-	6	-	2.3	0	22	1	22.00	1-22	-	-
1-day Int																		
NatWest																		
B & H																		
1-day Lge	4	4	0	49	38	12.25	-	-	2	-								

Career Performances

	M	Inns	NO	Runs	HS	Avge	100s	50s	Ct	St	Balls	Runs	Wkts	Avge	Best	5wI	10wM
Test																	
All First	9	14	1	201	44	15.46	-	-	6	-	15	22	1	22.00	1-22	-	-
1-day Int																	
NatWest																	
B & H																	
1-day Lge	4	4	0	49	38	12.25	-	-	2	-							

WILLIAMS, R. C. J.   Gloucestershire

Name: <u>Richard</u> Charles James Williams
Role: Left-hand bat, wicket-keeper
Born: 8 August 1969, Bristol
Height: 5ft 10in **Weight:** 11st
Nickname: Reg
County debut: 1990
County cap: 1996
1st-Class 50s: 5
1st-Class catches: 108
1st-Class stumpings: 16
Parents: Michael (deceased) and Angela
Marital status: Single
Family links with cricket: Father played local club cricket

Education: Clifton College Preparatory School; Millfield School
Qualifications: PE Diploma, NCA junior coaching award
Overseas tours: Gloucestershire to Namibia 1990, to Kenya 1991, to Sri Lanka 1992-93; Romany CC to Durban & Cape Town 1993; Gloucestershire Gypsies to Zimbabwe 1994-95, to South Africa 1995-96
Overseas teams played for: Manicaland, Zimbabwe 1990-91
Cricketers particularly admired: Andy Brassington, Jack Russell, David Gower
Other sports followed: Football, hockey, squash, snooker
Relaxations: 'Eating out, pubs and clubs, strutting my funky stuff'
Extras: Rapid Cricketline 2nd XI

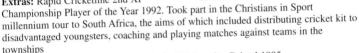

Championship Player of the Year 1992. Took part in the Christians in Sport millennium tour to South Africa, the aims of which included distributing cricket kit to disadvantaged youngsters, coaching and playing matches against teams in the townships
Best batting: 90 Gloucestershire v Oxford University, Bristol 1995

2000 Season

	M	Inns	NO	Runs	HS	Avge	100s	50s	Ct	St	O	M	Runs	Wkts	Avge	Best	5wI	10wM
Test																		
All First	2	3	1	76	43	38.00	-	-	11	1								
1-day Int																		
NatWest																		
B & H																		
1-day Lge	2	2	0	2	2	1.00	-	-	1	-								

Career Performances

	M	Inns	NO	Runs	HS	Avge	100s	50s	Ct	St	Balls	Runs	Wkts	Avge	Best	5wI	10wM
Test																	
All First	39	50	9	788	90	19.21	-	5	108	16							
1-day Int																	
NatWest																	
B & H	1	0	0	0	0	-	-	-	1	-							
1-day Lge	21	9	2	78	19	11.14	-	-	21	4							

WILLIAMSON, D.   Leicestershire

Name: Dominic Williamson
Role: Right-hand bat, right-arm
medium bowler
Born: 15 November 1975, Durham City
Height: 6ft 2in **Weight:** 11st
Nickname: Woky, Midge, Burt Picker, Watto
County debut: 1996
1st-Class catches: 5
One-Day 5 w. in innings: 2
Strike rate: 61.20 (career 70.64)
Parents: Dorothy and Gerard
Marital status: Single
Family links with cricket: Father and brother
Mark play/played for Kimblesworth CC
Education: Easington C of E Primary
School, Co. Durham; St Leonards RC
Comprehensive, Co. Durham; Durham Sixth
Form Centre
Qualifications: 9 GCSEs, 3 A-levels
Career outside cricket: 'Property developer'
Overseas tours: Leicestershire CCC to Holland 1996, 1998, to Guernsey 1997, 1998,
to Barbados 1998
Overseas teams played for: Ashburton CC, Australia 1994, 1996; Klerksdorp CC,
South Africa 1996-97
Cricketers particularly admired: Brian McMillan, Shane Warne, Steve Waugh,
Glenn McGrath, Stuart Smith
Other sports played: Squash, golf, football 'and PlayStation'
Other sports followed: Football (Newcastle United)
Extras: Winner of the Leicestershire 2nd XI Bowler of the Year award in 1997. Most
Improved Uncapped Player of the Year award 1998. Received the first 'free hit' for a
no-ball bowled in National League, v Hampshire at Leicester 1999; he despatched
John Stephenson's delivery for four. Released by Leicestershire at the end of the 2000
season
Best batting: 47 Leicestershire v Surrey, Guildford 2000
Best bowling: 3-19 Leicestershire v Glamorgan, Leicester 1997

---

96. What was the significance of Dean Headley's appearance
at Old Trafford in 1997?

2000 Season

	M	Inns	NO	Runs	HS	Avge	100s	50s	Ct	St	O	M	Runs	Wkts	Avge	Best	5wI	10wM
Test																		
All First	3	5	3	116	47	58.00	-	-	-	-	51	7	178	5	35.60	3-65	-	-
1-day Int																		
NatWest	1	1	0	0	0	0.00	-	-	-	-	2	1	1	2	0.50	2-1	-	
B & H																		
1-day Lge	6	4	0	27	12	6.75	-	-	2	-	24.2	0	121	7	17.28	3-32	-	

Career Performances

	M	Inns	NO	Runs	HS	Avge	100s	50s	Ct	St	Balls	Runs	Wkts	Avge	Best	5wI	10wM
Test																	
All First	9	13	4	273	47	30.33	-	-	5	-	989	529	14	37.78	3-19	-	-
1-day Int																	
NatWest	6	3	2	36	19 *	36.00	-	-	-	-	264	180	10	18.00	5-37	1	
B & H	5	2	0	17	11	8.50	-	-	-	-	198	203	3	67.66	2-49	-	
1-day Lge	50	38	11	327	39	12.11	-	-	15	-	1552	1185	55	21.54	5-32	1	

WILSON, E. J. — Warwickshire

Name: Elliot James Wilson
Role: Right-hand bat, right-arm medium bowler
Born: 10 November 1979, Hertford
Height: 5ft 9in **Weight:** 11st 4lbs
Nickname: Dwarf, Elly Tot, Pigeon, Buffy
County debut: No first-team appearance
Parents: Tom and Pam
Marital status: Single
Education: Alleyn Court School; The Deanes School; South East Essex College; Stamford College
Qualifications: 9 GCSEs, BTEC National Diploma in Sports Science, HND Sports Science
Career outside cricket: 'Coaching for Lincolnshire Cricket Board. Barman at "The Periwig", Stamford'
Overseas tours: Bishen Bedi Trust to Sharjah 1999
Overseas teams played for: Bishen Bedi Cricket Coaching Trust, New Delhi 1998-99
Cricketers particularly admired: Darren Gough, Allan Donald, Dermot Reeve, Michael Atherton, Michael Vaughan

Young players to look out for: Justin Bishop, Ricky Anderson, Ian Bell, Richard Howitt, Graham Napier
Other sports played: Football (West Ham Schoolboy)
Other sports followed: Rugby, football (Southend United)
Relaxations: 'Time spent with long-term partner Emma back home in Stamford'
Extras: Represented ECB XI v Sri Lanka U19 2000. Took 7-61 on debut for Lincolnshire v Cambridgeshire 2000
Opinions on cricket: 'This being my first season, I only have a brief knowledge of the rigours of county cricket. From what I have played, what everyone says about there being too much cricket is true. We must have more time between matches and more time for tea and lunch.'

WILSON, E. J. Worcestershire

Name: <u>Elliott</u> James Wilson
Role: Right-hand bat
Born: 3 November 1976, London
Height: 6ft 3in **Weight:** 14st
Nickname: Winko, Willow, Wils
County debut: 1998
1st-Class 50s: 7
1st-Class 100s: 3
1st-Class catches: 18
Place in batting averages: 122nd av. 26.86 (1999 64th av. 35.73)
Parents: Alec and Faye
Marital status: Single
Family links with cricket: 'Father is keen cricket fan and is chairman of my club at home (Saffron Walden). Rest of family wanted me to play rugby (they're New Zealanders)'

Education: Felsted Prep School; Felsted School; Durham University
Qualifications: 10 GCSEs, 3 A-levels
Career outside cricket: 'Final year of Business/Politics degree to be completed'
Off-season: Playing grade cricket for Mount Lawley, Perth
Overseas tours: Felsted School to Australia 1996-97; British Universities to South Africa 1999
Overseas teams played for: Pinetown CC, Durban 1995-96; Claremont, Cape Town
Cricketers particularly admired: Nick Knight ('same school'), Glenn McGrath
Young players to look out for: Duncan Catterall, Chris Liptrot, Kabir Ali, Kadeer Ali, Depesh Patel, Ryan Driver, James Pipe

Other sports played: Rugby (Eastern Counties) and hockey (East of England) while at school; tennis (LTA Junior doubles finalist)
Other sports followed: All sports
Relaxations: Going to the gym; catching up with friends
Extras: Broke Nick Knight's school record at Felsted with 1200 runs in 16 innings at an average of 120 in 1995 ('but that's now been beaten'). Scored 950 runs in first ten 2nd XI Championship games in 1996, while scoring more than 3000 runs in the season. Essex League Batsman of the Year in 1996. Worcestershire Uncapped Player of the Year 1999. Played in Durham University's BUSA Championship winning side 1999. Carried his bat for 104* out of 182 in first innings of Championship match v Middlesex at Worcester 2000
Opinions on cricket: 'Two divisions much better – increased importance of every game. Quality of playing and practice wickets at Worcester has been shocking. Well played England!'
Best batting: 116 Worcestershire v Middlesex, Worcester 1999

2000 Season

	M	Inns	NO	Runs	HS	Avge	100s	50s	Ct	St	O	M	Runs	Wkts	Avge	Best	5wl	10wM
Test																		
All First	17	31	2	779	104 *	26.86	2	4	9	-								
1-day Int																		
NatWest	2	2	0	21	21	10.50	-	-	-	-								
B & H	3	1	1	24	24 *	-	-	-	-	-								
1-day Lge	12	12	1	131	38	11.90	-	-	4	-								

Career Performances

	M	Inns	NO	Runs	HS	Avge	100s	50s	Ct	St	Balls	Runs	Wkts	Avge	Best	5wl	10wM
Test																	
All First	31	58	4	1416	116	26.22	3	7	18	-							
1-day Int																	
NatWest	2	2	0	21	21	10.50	-	-	-	-							
B & H	3	1	1	24	24 *	-	-	-	-	-							
1-day Lge	24	23	1	386	62	17.54	-	2	10	-							

97. At Adelaide in 1986-87, England selected three Leicestershire players in the Test side. Who were they?

WILTON, N. J. Sussex

Name: <u>Nicholas</u> James Wilton
Role: Right-hand bat, wicket-keeper
Born: 23 September 1978, Pembury
Height: 5ft 11in **Weight:** 12st
Nickname: Pops
County debut: 1998
1st-Class 50s: 1
1st-Class catches: 37
1st-Class stumpings: 2
Place in batting averages: 215th av. 16.66
(1999 241st av. 15.60)
Parents: Graham and Susan
Marital status: Single
Family links with cricket: 'Dad played local
club cricket. Brother plays club and school
cricket'

Education: St Johns C of E Primary School,
Crowborough; Beacon Community College,
Crowborough; City of Westminster College
Qualifications: 5 GCSEs, CFS in Sports Studies, GNVQ (Advanced) Leisure and
Tourism, ECB Level 1 coaching award
Career outside cricket: 'Coach or something involved in sport'
Off-season: 'Training hard for next season'
Overseas tours: England U19 to South Africa (inc Youth World Cup) 1997-98
Cricketers particularly admired: Alan Knott, Jack Russell, Ian Healy
Young players to look out for: Mike Yardy
Other sports played: Football (Sussex U10 and U11); 'I'll have a go at most things;
touch rugby's improving'
Other sports followed: Football (Arsenal FC)
Injuries: Out for three weeks with slipped disc in lower back
Relaxations: 'Cinema, music; spending time with girlfriend Amy'
Extras: Played for Sussex U10 to U19. Retained and registered by Sussex in 1997
while spending a season with the MCC Young Cricketers. Has represented England at
U14, U17 and U19 levels. Part of the England U19 squad which won the Youth World
Cup in South Africa 1998. Had shoulder operation in 1999 to cure recurring
dislocation problem
Opinions on cricket: 'Two divisional cricket has led to competitive cricket all year
round and a high standard, as every game has something riding on it. Day/night cricket
is a massive crowd-puller and great to play in. More needed to increase the level of
interest in the game.'
Best batting: 55 Sussex v Leicestershire, Arundel 1999

2000 Season

	M	Inns	NO	Runs	HS	Avge	100s	50s	Ct	St	O	M	Runs	Wkts	Avge	Best	5wI	10wM
Test																		
All First	8	11	2	150	46	16.66	-	-	19	-								
1-day Int																		
NatWest																		
B & H	3	2	1	10	7 *	10.00	-	-	2	-								
1-day Lge	10	7	1	8	3 *	1.33	-	-	4	3								

Career Performances

	M	Inns	NO	Runs	HS	Avge	100s	50s	Ct	St	Balls	Runs	Wkts	Avge	Best	5wI	10wM
Test																	
All First	16	25	4	352	55	16.76	-	1	37	2							
1-day Int																	
NatWest																	
B & H	3	2	1	10	7 *	10.00	-	-	2	-							
1-day Lge	13	9	1	18	7	2.25	-	-	9	3							

WINDOWS, M. G. N. — Gloucestershire

Name: <u>Matthew</u> Guy Newman Windows
Role: Right-hand bat, left-arm medium bowler
Born: 5 April 1973, Bristol
Height: 5ft 7in **Weight:** 11st 7lbs
Nickname: Steamy, Nik Nak, Bedos
County debut: 1992
County cap: 1998
1000 runs in a season: 2
1st-Class 50s: 29
1st-Class 100s: 10
1st-Class catches: 61
Place in batting averages: 49th av. 37.21 (1999 65th av. 35.55)
Strike rate: (career 58.50)
Parents: Tony and Carolyn
Marital status: 'Shacked up'
Family links with cricket: Father (A.R.) played for Gloucestershire (1960-69) and Cambridge University
Education: Clifton College Prep; Clifton College; Durham University
Qualifications: 9 GCSEs, 3 A-levels, BA (Hons) Sociology (Dunelm)
Career outside cricket: Training with Rowan Dartington Ltd, stockbrokers

Off-season: 'Studying for my stockbroking exams under the tutelage of Catherine Standen'

Overseas tours: Clifton College to Barbados 1991; England U19 to Pakistan 1991-92; Durham University to South Africa 1992-93; England A to Zimbabwe and South Africa 1998-99; Gloucestershire's annual pre-season tour to South Africa

Overseas teams played for: Gold Coast Dolphins, Queensland 1996-97

Cricketers particularly admired: David Boon, Courtney Walsh, David Milne

Other sports played: Rackets (British Open runner-up 1997)

Relaxations: Reading and travelling

Extras: Played for Lincolnshire and in England U19 home series v Sri Lanka 1992. Scored 71 on county debut v Essex in 1992. Gloucestershire Young Player of the Year 1994. Set record for highest individual score for Durham University (218*). Gloucestershire Player of the Year 1998. His 107 v Essex at Bristol 2000 was his third successive 100 against the county. 'Part of the one-day triumph of the Glorious Gloucesters'

Best batting: 184 Gloucestershire v Warwickshire, Cheltenham 1996

Best bowling: 1-6 Combined Universities v West Indians, The Parks 1995

2000 Season

	M	Inns	NO	Runs	HS	Avge	100s	50s	Ct	St	O	M	Runs	Wkts	Avge	Best	5wI	10wM
Test																		
All First	19	31	3	1042	166	37.21	2	6	5	-								
1-day Int																		
NatWest	5	4	0	47	23	11.75	-	-	-	-								
B & H	7	7	3	170	53 *	42.50	-	1	2	-								
1-day Lge	16	15	1	195	61	13.92	-	1	2	-								

Career Performances

	M	Inns	NO	Runs	HS	Avge	100s	50s	Ct	St	Balls	Runs	Wkts	Avge	Best	5wI	10wM
Test																	
All First	96	171	12	5456	184	34.31	10	29	61	-	117	111	2	55.50	1-6	-	-
1-day Int																	
NatWest	15	14	3	233	43 *	21.18	-	-	3	-							
B & H	14	14	5	317	53 *	35.22	-	1	3	-							
1-day Lge	81	74	6	1315	72	19.33	-	4	26	-	48	49	0	-	-	-	-

98. At Headingley in 1977, who became the first batsman to score his 100th first-class century in a Test match?

WOOD, J.   Lancashire

Name: John Wood
Role: Right-hand bat, right-arm
fast-medium bowler
Born: 22 July 1970, Crofton, Wakefield
Height: 6ft 3in **Weight:** 16st
Nickname: Woody
County debut: 1992 (Durham)
County cap: 1998 (Durham)
50 wickets in a season: 1
1st-Class 50s: 2
1st-Class 5 w. in innings: 11
1st-Class catches: 23
Place in batting averages: 252nd av. 12.06
(1999 274th av. 9.92)
Place in bowling averages: 74th av. 27.81
(1999 36th av. 22.36)
Strike rate: 58.12 (career 53.38)
Parents: Brian and Anne
Wife and date of marriage: Emma Louise, 30 October 1994
Children: Alexandra Mae, 7 April 1996; Joseph Samuel, 3 July 1998
Family links with cricket: 'Father played local league cricket for many years; brother plays for Spen Victoria in Bradford League'
Education: Crofton Junior School; Crofton High School; Wakefield District College; Leeds Polytechnic
Qualifications: 6 O-levels, BTEC Diploma Electronic Engineering, HND Electrical and Electronic Engineering, senior cricket coach
Overseas tours: Durham CCC to South Africa 1994-95
Overseas teams played for: Griqualand West Cricket Union, South Africa 1990-91; TAWA, Wellington and Wellington B, New Zealand 1993-95
Cricketers particularly admired: Wasim Akram, David Boon, Wayne Larkins
Young players to look out for: Steve Harmison, David Sales, Darren Stevens
Other sports played: Golf
Other sports followed: Football (Newcastle United, Leeds United), rugby league (Wakefield Trinity)
Relaxations: Golf, swimming
Extras: Played in the Bradford League. Made his debut for Durham (Minor Counties) in 1991. Durham Players' Player of the Year 1998. Left Durham at the end of the 2000 season and has joined Lancashire for 2001
Opinions on cricket: 'Just improve the wickets and all will be fine.'
Best batting: 63* Durham v Nottinghamshire, Chester-le-Street 1993
Best bowling: 7-58 Durham v Yorkshire, Headingley 1999

2000 Season

	M	Inns	NO	Runs	HS	Avge	100s	50s	Ct	St	O	M	Runs	Wkts	Avge	Best	5wl	10wM
Test																		
All First	10	15	0	181	44	12.06	-	-	2	-	319.4	66	918	33	27.81	5-36	3	-
1-day Int																		
NatWest	2	2	0	11	7	5.50	-	-	-	-	10.3	3	27	2	13.50	1-12	-	
B & H	6	5	1	38	28 *	9.50	-	-	-	-	43.3	5	130	12	10.83	4-26	-	
1-day Lge	11	9	4	75	28 *	15.00	-	-	3	-	87	6	345	8	43.12	2-29	-	

Career Performances

	M	Inns	NO	Runs	HS	Avge	100s	50s	Ct	St	Balls	Runs	Wkts	Avge	Best	5wl	10wM
Test																	
All First	88	132	20	1335	63 *	11.91	-	2	23	-	13880	8519	260	32.76	7-58	11	-
1-day Int																	
NatWest	9	4	1	20	8 *	6.66	-	-	-	-	429	279	8	34.87	2-22	-	
B & H	17	11	3	86	28 *	10.75	-	-	1	-	868	541	22	24.59	4-26	-	
1-day Lge	71	50	18	333	28 *	10.40	-	-	13	-	3081	2517	66	38.13	4-17	-	

WOOD, M. J. Somerset

Name: <u>Matthew</u> James Wood
Role: Right-hand bat, right-arm off-spin bowler
Born: 30 September 1980, Exeter
Height: 5ft 11in **Weight:** 11st 5lbs
Nickname: Woody
County debut: No first-team appearance
Parents: James and Trina
Marital status: Single
Education: St Joseph's Primary, Exmouth; Exmouth Community College; Exeter University
Qualifications: 8 GCSEs, 2 A-levels, Level 2 cricket coach
Overseas tours: West of England U15 to West Indies 1995
Cricketers particularly admired: Nick Folland, Saeed Anwar
Other sports played: Football
Other sports followed: Football (Liverpool FC)
Relaxations: Music
Extras: Has played for Devon

WOOD, M. J.   Yorkshire

Name: <u>Matthew</u> James Wood
Role: Right-hand bat, off-spin bowler
Born: 6 April 1977, Huddersfield
Height: 5ft 9in **Weight:** 12st
Nickname: Chud, Ronnie
County debut: 1997
1000 runs in a season: 1
1st-Class 50s: 6
1st-Class 100s: 4
1st-Class 200s: 1
1st-Class catches: 33
Place in batting averages: 195th av. 18.28
(1999 253rd av. 13.66)
Parents: Roger and Kathryn
Marital status: Single
Family links with cricket: 'Father played for
local team Emley. Mum made the teas and
sister Caroline scored'

Education: Emley First School; Kirkburton Middle School; Shelley High School and
Sixth Form Centre
Qualifications: 9 GCSEs, 2 A-levels, NCA coaching award
Overseas tours: England U19 to Zimbabwe 1995-96; Yorkshire CCC to West Indies
1996-97, to Cape Town 1997, 1998; MCC to Kenya 1999, to Bangladesh 1999-2000
Overseas teams played for: Somerset West CC, Cape Town 1994-95, Upper Hutt
United CC, Wellington, New Zealand 1997-98
Cricketers particularly admired: Martyn Moxon, Darren Lehmann, Matthew
Maynard, Michael Slater, 'Yorkshire CCC staff'
Young players to look out for: David Sales, Ryan Sidebottom, Matthew Hoggard
Other sports played: Football (Kirkburton FC), 'occasional golfer'
Other sports followed: Football (Emley FC, Liverpool FC)
Relaxations: Watching films, socialising with friends, eating out
Extras: Played for England U17 against India 1994. Spent two years at the Yorkshire
Academy before graduating to the full staff in 1996. Has Yorkshire 2nd XI cap. Scored
81 on first-class debut v Lancashire at Headingley in 1997. Scored 1000 runs in first
full season 1998
Opinions on cricket: 'Neutral groundsmen employed by the ECB to prevent doctored
pitches to suit home team. Hopefully this would see better pitches and games going
into day four. Two divisions has certainly spiced up county cricket and provided more
interest and should continue.'
Best batting: 200* Yorkshire v Warwickshire, Headingley 1998

2000 Season

	M	Inns	NO	Runs	HS	Avge	100s	50s	Ct	St	O	M	Runs	Wkts	Avge	Best	5wl	10wM
Test																		
All First	11	17	3	256	100 *	18.28	1	-	5	-								
1-day Int																		
NatWest	1	1	0	43	43	43.00	-	-	-	-								
B & H	6	4	1	82	59	27.33	-	1	1	-								
1-day Lge	6	4	0	73	31	18.25	-	-	3	-								

Career Performances

	M	Inns	NO	Runs	HS	Avge	100s	50s	Ct	St	Balls	Runs	Wkts	Avge	Best	5wl	10wM
Test																	
All First	48	81	9	1889	200 *	26.23	5	6	33	-							
1-day Int																	
NatWest	2	2	1	68	43	68.00	-	-	-	-							
B & H	6	4	1	82	59	27.33	-	1	1	-							
1-day Lge	22	15	2	307	65 *	23.61	-	2	7	-							

WOOD, N. T.   Lancashire

Name: <u>Nathan</u> Theodore Wood
Role: Left-hand opening bat
Born: 4 October 1974, Dewsbury, Yorkshire
Height: 5ft 7in **Weight:** 10st 5lbs
Nickname: Rodders, Woderwick, Hot Rod
County debut: 1996
1st-Class 50s: 5
1st-Class 100s: 1
1st-Class catches: 5
Place in batting averages: (1999 152nd av. 25.00)
Parents: Barry and Janet
Marital status: Single
Family links with cricket: Father played first-class and Test cricket (Yorkshire, Derbyshire, Lancashire and England). Uncle (Ron) played first-class cricket (Yorkshire)
Education: Altrincham Prep School; William Hulme's Grammar School; 'The Stiffs'
Qualifications: 8 GCSEs, cricket coaching award
Overseas tours: England U18 to South Africa 1992-93, to Denmark 1993; England U19 to Sri Lanka 1993-94; Lancashire CCC to India and South Africa 1997, to South Africa 1998, 1999

Cricketers particularly admired: Sir Don Bradman, Sir Garfield Sobers, Viv Richards
Young players to look out for: Owais Shah
Other sports played: Football
Other sports followed: Football (Manchester United)
Relaxations: 'Getting some TLC'
Extras: Played in junior 'One-Day Internationals' against Zimbabwe, India, South Africa and Sri Lanka. Played in U19 'Tests' against West Indies and Sri Lanka. Set opening partnership record for Lancashire 2nd XI of 340 with P.C. McKeown. Shared in record first-wicket partnership for Lancashire in matches against Surrey (259 with M.A. Atherton) 1997. Released by Lancashire at the end of the 2000 season
Best batting: 155 Lancashire v Surrey, The Oval 1997

2000 Season

	M	Inns	NO	Runs	HS	Avge	100s	50s	Ct	St	O	M	Runs	Wkts	Avge	Best	5wI	10wM
Test																		
All First	1	1	0	27	27	27.00	-	-	-	-								
1-day Int																		
NatWest																		
B & H																		
1-day Lge																		

Career Performances

	M	Inns	NO	Runs	HS	Avge	100s	50s	Ct	St	Balls	Runs	Wkts	Avge	Best	5wI	10wM
Test																	
All First	30	45	5	1179	155	29.47	1	5	5	-	92	154	0	-	-	-	-
1-day Int																	
NatWest																	
B & H																	
1-day Lge	1	1	0	23	23	23.00	-	-	-	-							

99. Who captained England in their successful
Ashes campaign in 1970-71?

WRIGHT, A. S.   Leicestershire

Name: <u>Ashley</u> Spencer Wright
Role: Right-hand opening bat, right-arm
medium bowler
Born: 21 October 1980, Grantham
Height: 5ft 11in **Weight:** 11st 7lbs
Nickname: Ash
County debut: No first-team appearance
One-Day 100s: 1
Parents: Keith and Anna
Marital status: Single
Family links with cricket: Father very keen
cricketer and senior coach; brother Luke
played for Leicester U15
Education: Redmile Primary School;
Belvoir High School; King Edward VII,
Melton Mowbray
Qualifications: 10 GCSEs, coaching award
Career outside cricket: 'Cricket is the only
thing I want to do'
Cricketers particularly admired: 'All the Leicestershire players'
Young players to look out for: Darren Stevens
Other sports played: Squash
Other sports followed: Football (Leicester City, Notts County, Notts Forest)
Relaxations: Music, cinema, going to gym, going out
Extras: Hit a highest score of 158 against Staffordshire U15. Won the Livingstone
Cup for outstanding batting performance in the 2nd XI 1999. Played for Leicestershire
Board XI in the NatWest 1999 and 2000

2000 Season (did not make any first-class or one-day appearances)

Career Performances

	M	Inns	NO	Runs	HS	Avge	100s	50s	Ct	St	Balls	Runs	Wkts	Avge	Best	5wI	10wM
Test																	
All First																	
1-day Int																	
NatWest	2	2	0	175	112	87.50	1	1	-	-							
B & H																	
1-day Lge																	

YARDY, M. H.   Sussex

Name: <u>Michael</u> Howard Yardy
Role: Left-hand bat, left-arm medium-fast
bowler
Born: 27 November 1980, Pembury, Kent
Height: 6ft 1in **Weight:** 13st 7lbs
Nickname: Yards
County debut: 1999 (one-day),
2000 (first-class)
Place in batting averages: 277th av. 9.14
Marital status: Single
Family links with cricket: Brother works for
Gray Nicolls and plays club cricket
Education: St Pauls School, Hastings;
William Parker School, Hastings
Qualifications: 5 GCSEs, 2 A-levels
Off-season: Fitness training at University of
Brighton
Overseas tours: Sussex U19 to Barbados
1998, to Cape Town 1999
Overseas teams played for: Cape Town CC 1999
Cricketers particularly admired: Michael Bevan, Chris Adams, James Kirtley,
Matthew Hayden
Young players to look out for: Nick Wilton, Paul Havell, Tim Ambrose, Matt Prior,
Dominic Clapp
Other sports played: Football (William Parker School – Goodyear National Cup
winners 1997)
Other sports followed: Football (West Ham), American football (New York Giants)
Injuries: Out for one month with side strain
Relaxations: Sleeping, cooking
Extras: Played in the Sussex U15 side that won the U15 County Championship 1996,
the U16 side that won the U16 County Championship in 1997 and the U19 side that
were runners-up in the NAYC Two-Day Cup 1997. Represented England U17 1998.
Played for Sussex Board XI in 1999 NatWest
Opinions on cricket: 'Shouldn't have an opinion – haven't played enough and my
records don't help my opinion so far!!'
Best batting: 25 Sussex v New Zealand A, Hove 2000

> 100. Which bowler made his Test debut in the sixth Test of the
> 1970-71 series and currently holds the record for most wickets
> taken in Tests between England and Australia?

2000 Season

	M	Inns	NO	Runs	HS	Avge	100s	50s	Ct	St	O	M	Runs	Wkts	Avge	Best	5wI	10wM
Test																		
All First	4	8	1	64	25	9.14	-	-	-	-	29	7	84	0	-		-	-
1-day Int																		
NatWest	2	2	0	28	15	14.00	-	-	4	-	16	1	76	1	76.00	1-46	-	
B & H																		
1-day Lge	1	0	0	0	0	-	-	-	-	-	3	0	15	0	-		-	-

Career Performances

	M	Inns	NO	Runs	HS	Avge	100s	50s	Ct	St	Balls	Runs	Wkts	Avge	Best	5wI	10wM
Test																	
All First	4	8	1	64	25	9.14	-	-	-	-	174	84	0	-		-	-
1-day Int																	
NatWest	3	3	0	28	15	9.33	-	-	4	-	108	90	1	90.00	1-46	-	
B & H																	
1-day Lge	1	0	0	0	0	-	-	-	-	-	18	15	0	-		-	-

YATES, G.   Lancashire

Name: Gary Yates
Role: Right-hand bat, off-spin bowler
Born: 20 September 1967,
Ashton-under-Lyne
Height: 6ft 1in **Weight:** 12st 10lbs
Nickname: Sweaty, Yugo, Pearly,
Backyard, Zippy
County debut: 1990
County cap: 1994
1st-Class 50s: 4
1st-Class 100s: 3
1st-Class 5 w. in innings: 5
1st-Class catches: 35
Place in batting averages: (1999 297th
av. 4.16)
Place in bowling averages: (1999 39th
av. 22.50)
Strike rate: 57.11 (career 73.88)
Parents: Alan and Patricia
Marital status: Single
Children: Francis Leonard George, 1 May 1999
Family links with cricket: Father played in Lancashire Leagues

Education: Manchester Grammar School
Qualifications: 6 O-levels, Australian Cricket Coaching Council coach
Career outside cricket: 'Rep with family business (Digical Ltd), selling diaries, calendars and business gifts'
Overseas tours: Lancashire to Tasmania and Western Australia 1990, to Western Australia 1991, to Johannesburg 1992, to Barbados and St Lucia 1992, to Calcutta 1997, to Cape Town 1997-98; MCC to Bangladesh 1999-2000
Overseas teams played for: South Barwon, Geelong, Australia 1987-88; Johnsonville, Wellington, New Zealand 1989-90; Western Suburbs, Brisbane 1991-92; Old Selbornian, East London, South Africa 1992-93; Hermanus CC, South Africa 1995-96
Cricketers particularly admired: Michael Atherton, Ian Botham, John Emburey
Young players to look out for: Chris Schofield
Other sports followed: All sports, especially football (Manchester City), golf, motor rallying
Relaxations: Playing golf, watching football and good films, eating
Extras: Played for Worcestershire 2nd XI in 1987. Made debut for Lancashire 2nd XI in 1988 and taken on to county staff in 1990. Scored century on Championship debut v Nottinghamshire at Trent Bridge. Rapid Cricketline Player of the Month April/May 1992
Best batting: 134* Lancashire v Northamptonshire, Old Trafford 1993
Best bowling: 6-64 Lancashire v Kent, Old Trafford 1999

2000 Season

	M	Inns	NO	Runs	HS	Avge	100s	50s	Ct	St	O	M	Runs	Wkts	Avge	Best	5wI	10wM
Test																		
All First	3	3	0	10	7	3.33	-	-	3	-	85.4	28	192	9	21.33	4-91	-	-
1-day Int																		
NatWest	2	0	0	0	0	-	-	-	4	-	18	0	75	4	18.75	2-35	-	
B & H	2	1	0	1	1	1.00	-	-	-	-	3	0	12	0	-	-	-	
1-day Lge	5	2	0	7	4	3.50	-	-	2	-	22	0	103	2	51.50	2-36	-	

Career Performances

	M	Inns	NO	Runs	HS	Avge	100s	50s	Ct	St	Balls	Runs	Wkts	Avge	Best	5wI	10wM
Test																	
All First	78	102	35	1705	134 *	25.44	3	4	35	-	13152	6760	178	37.97	6-64	5	-
1-day Int																	
NatWest	19	9	5	82	34 *	20.50	-	-	5	-	1146	669	16	41.81	2-15	-	
B & H	34	15	3	135	26	11.25	-	-	6	-	1566	1093	35	31.22	3-42	-	
1-day Lge	101	44	22	346	38	15.72	-	-	25	-	3546	2930	98	29.89	4-34	-	

ZUIDERENT, B. Sussex

Name: Bastiaan (<u>Bas</u>) Zuiderent
Role: Right-hand bat, right-arm off-spin bowler
Born: 3 March 1977, Utrecht, Holland
Height: 6ft 3in **Weight:** 14st 2lbs
Nickname: Diggler
County debut: 1999 (one-day)
One-Day Internationals: 5
Parents: Eduard and Jaqueline
Marital status: 'Lovely girlfriend Kelly'
Family links with cricket: 'Cousin J.J. plays for Holland'
Education: Van Oldebarnevelt School, Rotterdam; Erasmiaans Gymnasium, Rotterdam; University of Amsterdam
Qualifications: Level 1 coaching
Career outside cricket: 'Just cricket at the moment; still desire to become a doctor'
Off-season: 'Relaxing, holidays, prepare for next season, visit family and friends back in Holland'
Overseas tours: Tours with various Holland sides to Denmark, Kenya and South Africa; Holland to India and Pakistan (World Cup) 1995-96, to Malaysia (ICC Trophy) 1998
Overseas teams played for: VOC Rotterdam 1989-97; Wits Technicon, Johannesburg 1997; VRA Amsterdam 1998
Cricketers particularly admired: Martin Crowe, Steven Lubbers
Young players to look out for: J.J. Esmeijer (Holland), Matthew Prior
Other sports played: Football, golf, skiing, squash, tennis
Other sports followed: Football ('PSV Eindhoven!!')
Injuries: Out for four/five weeks with ankle ligament damage
Relaxations: Watching films, playing golf, shopping
Extras: Has represented Holland at various levels since the age of 12. Player of the Tournament, International Youth Tournament, Denmark 1993. Scored 54 v England in 1995-96 World Cup, becoming the second youngest player (after Sachin Tendulkar) to score 50 in a World Cup. Scored 99 (run out) for Holland v Worcestershire in NatWest Trophy 1997, winning the Man of the Match award. Played for Brighton & Hove in their Sussex League and Challenge Cup winning season 2000, scoring an unbeaten century in the cup final
Opinions on cricket: 'Keep making one-day game more and more interesting for the big crowds, i.e. music entertainment. Great game!!!'

2000 Season

	M	Inns	NO	Runs	HS	Avge	100s	50s	Ct	St	O	M	Runs	Wkts	Avge	Best	5wI	10wM
Test																		
All First																		
1-day Int																		
NatWest																		
B & H	1	1	0	2	2	2.00	-	-	-	-								
1-day Lge	7	6	0	127	68	21.16	-	1	3	-								

Career Performances

	M	Inns	NO	Runs	HS	Avge	100s	50s	Ct	St	Balls	Runs	Wkts	Avge	Best	5wI	10wM
Test																	
All First																	
1-day Int	5	5	1	91	54	22.75	-	1	4	-							
NatWest	4	4	0	133	99	33.25	-	1	1	-	12	15	0	-		-	-
B & H	2	2	0	3	2	1.50	-	-	1	-							
1-day Lge	9	8	0	151	68	18.87	-	1	5	-							

STOP PRESS

BASSANO, C. W. G.   Derbyshire

Name: <u>Christopher</u> Warwick Godfrey Bassano
Role: Right-hand bat, right-arm leg-spin or medium bowler; slip, gully or cover fielder
Born: 11 September 1975, East London, South Africa
Extras: Represented Tasmania U16, U17 and U19 and was in Tasmania Sheffield Shield squad 1994-95 – 1998-99. Played for Torquay (1994) and Old Bristolians (1998-2000) in England, as well as for Gloucestershire 2nd XI (2000)

POOLEY, J. C.   Middlesex

Name: <u>Jason</u> Calvin Pooley
Role: Left-hand bat, right-arm slow bowler
Born: 8 August 1969, Hammersmith, London
Extras: Made county debut in 1989 and was capped in 1995. Was Rapid Cricketline 2nd XI Championship Player of the Year 1989. Toured Pakistan with England A in 1995-96. Re-registered by Middlesex for 2001 and is 2nd XI coach

NOTE: <u>Martin</u> Lloyd Love (right-hand bat; Queensland) replaces Simon Katich as Durham's overseas player for 2001

QUIZ ANSWERS

1. David Lloyd and Dennis Amiss (Chief Executive at Warwickshire)
2. Geoff Lawson
3. Nasser Hussain and Graham Thorpe at Edgbaston
4. John Arlott's
5. Doug Walters
6. Graeme Hick
7. Arnie Sidebottom of Yorkshire; father of Ryan Sidebottom, also of Yorkshire
8. Mike Whitney
9. John Edrich (175 in England's second innings)
10. Phil DeFreitas, Darren Gough and Devon Malcolm
11. John Emburey
12. Bob Cowper
13. The Ashes were not played for
14. John Dyson (102 in Australia's first innings)
15. Bruce Reid (he was rested for the fifth Test)
16. Robin Smith (stumped by Healy, off May)
17. Glenn McGrath (7-76), Michael Kasprowicz (7-36) and Phil Tufnell (7-66)
18. Neil Hawke (caught by Cowdrey at first slip)
19. It was the same as the result of the first ever Test match, which it commemorated: Australia beat England by 45 runs
20. Ian Botham
21. Tim Robinson (he scored 148)
22. He was out handled the ball (for 133)
23. Jack Russell in 1989 (128*); Ian Healy in 1993 (102*)
24. He won the toss is all five Tests
25. Greg Chappell
26. Gladstone Small and Phil DeFreitas
27. An MCC groundstaff member, he caught Allan Border while fielding as substitute
28. Mark Waugh
29. Richie Benaud
30. Paul Allott
31. Allan Border (125)
32. The pitch was vandalised
33. Michael Slater's
34. Mike Denness (188 in the sixth Test at Melbourne in 1974-75)
35. Alan Davidson (it was his 186th Test wicket)
36. In the first Test at Trent Bridge on the 1981 tour
37. Eddie Hemmings
38. John Crawley
39. Derek Randall
40. Barry Jarman
41. Graham Gooch's
42. David Boon (164*, 101, 107)
43. Mike Brearley
44. Bob Holland
45. Kim Barnett
46. Glenn McGrath's
47. Martin McCague and Mark Ilott
48. Derek Underwood
49. Jeff Thomson
50. He recorded six ducks; the most in any Test series

51. Paul Reiffel (6-71 in 1993)
52. Tony Greig
53. Terry Alderman (42 in 1981; 6 Tests)
54. Michael Atherton (finished with 105 in 451 minutes)
55. Peter Taylor
56. Mark Waugh
57. Brian Statham (Barry Shepherd caught by Trueman)
58. The ball struck the foot of Allan Lamb at silly point and rebounded to Gower
59. Norman Cowans
60. Old Trafford
61. Steve Waugh
62. Dirk Wellham
63. David Gower
64. Peter Sleep
65. Graham Gooch
66. Steve Waugh (108 and 116)
67. Andrew Caddick
68. They became the first brothers to score a century each in the same Test innings (I.M 118; G.S. 113)
69. 87 balls
70. Mark Taylor
71. Allan Lamb
72. They constituted a single session of play
73. Graham Dilley
74. Allan Border
75. Jeff Thomson (Graham Gooch caught by Phillips)
76. Alan Knott
77. Ian Healy, Stuart MacGill and Colin Miller
78. Bob Massie
79. Rod Marsh (110* in the Centenary Test at Melbourne 1976-77)
80. Richard Ellison
81. Brian Johnston (he died the following January)
82. Michael Atherton
83. Terry Alderman
84. Steve Waugh
85. David Gower
86. Adam and Ben Hollioake
87. Bobby Simpson; Ken Barrington
88. Mike Gatting's
89. He set a world record for dismissals in a series with 28 (all caught)
90. Allan Border's
91. Alec Stewart
92. Bob Willis
93. At Perth in 1998-99 (Alex Tudor and Alec Stewart)
94. Chris Broad (162, 116, 112)
95. Woolloongabba
96. It was his Test debut and the first time three generations of the same family had played Test cricket
97. David Gower, James Whitaker and Phil DeFreitas
98. Geoffrey Boycott (191)
99. Raymond Illingworth
100. Dennis Lillee (167 in 29 Tests)

THE UMPIRES

BENSON, M. R.

Name: <u>Mark</u> Richard Benson
Born: 6 July 1958, Shoreham, Sussex
Height: 5ft 10in
Nickname: Benny
Wife and date of marriage: Sarah Patricia, 20 September 1986
Children: Laurence, 16 October 1987; Edward, 23 June 1990
Education: Sutton Valence School
Other sports played: Golf
Other sports followed: Football (Chelsea)
Relaxations: Bridge
Appointed to 1st-Class list: 2000
County as player: Kent
Role: Left-hand bat
County debut: 1980
County cap: 1981
Benefit: 1991 (£174,619)
Test debut: 1986
Tests: 1
One-Day Internationals: 1
1000 runs in a season: 11
1st-Class 50s: 99
1st-Class 100s: 47
1st-Class 200s: 1
1st-Class catches: 140
One-Day 100s: 5
Overseas tours: None

Highlight of playing career: 'Finished first-class career with batting average in excess of 40'
Extras: Scored 1000 runs in first full season. Kent captain 1991-95. Captained England in two one-day matches against Holland in 1993
Opinions on cricket: 'I think it is a great shame that in this great sport professional cricketers will cheat fellow professionals (i.e. not "walking"). How would a pro golfer be treated by fellow professionals if he was caught cheating? Even in snooker a player will call a foul on himself even if the referee hasn't seen the infringement.'
Best batting: 257 Kent v Hampshire, Southampton 1991
Best bowling: 2-55 Kent v Surrey, Dartford 1986

	M	Inns	NO	Runs	HS	Avge	100s	Ct	St	Runs	Wkts	Avge	Best	5wI	10wM
Test	1	2	0	51	30	25.50	-	-	-						
All First	292	491	34	18387	257	40.23	48	140	-	493	5	98.60	2-55	-	-

BURGESS, G. I.

Name: <u>Graham</u> Iefvion Burgess
Born: 5 May 1943, Glastonbury, Somerset
Education: Millfield School
Appointed to 1st-Class list: 1991
County as player: Somerset
Role: Right-hand bat, right-arm
medium bowler
County debut: 1966
County cap: 1968
Testimonial: 1977
1st-Class 100s: 2
1st-Class 5 w. in innings: 18
1st-Class 10 w. in match: 2
1st-Class catches: 120
Extras: Played Minor Counties cricket for
Wilts 1981-82 and for Cambs 1983-84
Best batting: 129 Somerset v
Gloucestershire, Taunton 1973
Best bowling: 7-43 Somerset v Oxford University, The Parks 1975

First-Class Career Performances

	M	Inns	NO	Runs	HS	Avge	100s	Ct	St	Runs	Wkts	Avge	Best	5wI	10wM
Test															
All First	252	414	37	7129	129	18.90	2	120	-	13543	474	28.57	7-43	18	2

CLARKSON, A.

Name: Anthony (Tony) Clarkson
Born: 5 September 1939, Killinghall,
North Yorkshire
Height: 6ft
Wife's name: Cheryl
Children: André, 5 September 1964;
Chantal, 27 May 1967; Pierre, 1 May 1969
Family links with cricket: Father was a
league professional
Education: Killinghall C of E; Harrogate
Grammar School; Leeds College of Building;
Bradford Polytechnic; Brunel College, Bristol
Career outside cricket: Architectural, civil
engineering and surveying consultant
Other sports followed: Golf and rugby
('especially league')
Relaxations: Golf, DIY, and gardening
Appointed to 1st-Class list: 1996
Counties as player: Yorkshire, Somerset
Role: Right-hand bat, right-arm off-spin bowler
County debut: 1963 (Yorkshire), 1965 (Somerset)
County cap: 1969 (Somerset)
1000 runs in a season: 2
1st-Class 100s: 2
1st-Class catches: 52
Extras: First English player to score a century in the Sunday League
Best batting: 131 Somerset v Northamptonshire, Northampton 1969
Best bowling: 3-51 Somerset v Essex, Yeovil 1967

First-Class Career Performances

	M	Inns	NO	Runs	HS	Avge	100s	Ct	St	Runs	Wkts	Avge	Best	5wI	10wM
Test															
All First	110	189	12	4458	131	25.18	2	52	-	367	13	28.23	3-51	-	-

CONSTANT, D. J.

Name: <u>David</u> John Constant
Born: 9 November 1941,
Bradford-on-Avon, Wiltshire
Height: 5ft 7in
Nickname: Connie
Wife's name: Rosalyn
Children: Lisa, 6 July 1966;
Julie, 21 February 1969
Family links with cricket: Father-in-law,
G.E.E. Lambert, played for Gloucestershire
Education: Grove Park Secondary Modern
Off-season: Bowls
Other sports followed: Football (Millwall)
Interests/relaxations: 'Six grandchildren and
bowls'
Appointed to 1st-Class list: 1969
First appointed to Test panel: 1971
Tests umpired: 36
One-Day Internationals umpired: 32
Other umpiring highlights: Stood in 1975, 1979 and 1983 World Cups
Counties as player: Kent, Leicestershire
Role: Left-hand bat, slow left-arm bowler
County debut: 1961 (Kent), 1965 (Leicestershire)
1st-Class 50s: 6
1st-Class catches: 33
Extras: County bowls player for Gloucestershire 1984-86 (outdoors). Also represented
Somerset at indoor version of the game in the Liberty Trophy
Best batting: 80 Leicestershire v Gloucestershire, Bristol 1966
Best bowling: 1-28 Leicestershire v Surrey, The Oval 1968

First-Class Career Performances

	M	Inns	NO	Runs	HS	Avge	100s	Ct	St	Runs	Wkts	Avge	Best	5wI	10wM
Test															
All First	61	93	14	1517	80	19.20	-	33	-	36	1	36.00	1-28	-	-

COWLEY, N. G.

Name: <u>Nigel</u> Geoffrey Cowley
Born: 1 March 1953, Shaftesbury, Dorset
Height: 5ft 6½in
Marital status: Divorced
Children: Mark Antony, 14 June 1973;
Darren James, 30 October 1976
Family links with cricket: Darren played
Hampshire Schools U11, U12, U13; Natal
Schools 1993, 1994, 1995; and toured India
with South Africa U19 1996
Education: Duchy Manor, Mere, Wilts
Off-season: Cricket coach at Durban High
School
Other sports played: Golf (8 handicap)
Other sports followed: Football
(Liverpool FC)
Appointed to 1st-Class list: 2000
Players to watch for the future: Graeme
Swann
Counties as player: Hampshire, Glamorgan
Role: Right-hand bat, off-spin bowler
County debut: 1974 (Hampshire), 1990 (Glamorgan)
County cap: 1978 (Hampshire)
Benefit: 1988 (£88,274)
1000 runs in a season: 1
50 wickets in a season: 2
1st-Class 50s: 36
1st-Class 100s: 2
1st-Class 5 w. in innings: 5
1st-Class catches: 105
Overseas tours: Hampshire to Barbados 1985, 1986, 1987, to Dubai 1989
Overseas teams played for: Paarl CC, 1982-83; Amanzimtoti, 1984-96
(both South Africa)
Extras: Played for Dorset 1972. NatWest Man of the Match award
Best batting: 109* Hampshire v Somerset, Taunton 1977
Best bowling: 6-48 Hampshire v Leicestershire, Southampton 1982

First-Class Career Performances

	M	Inns	NO	Runs	HS	Avge	100s	Ct	St	Runs	Wkts	Avge	Best	5wI	10wM
Test															
All First	271	375	62	7309	109*	23.35	2	105	-	14879	437	34.04	6-48	5	-

DUDLESTON, B.

Name: Barry Dudleston
Born: 16 July 1945, Bebington, Cheshire
Height: 5ft 9in
Nickname: Danny
Wife and date of marriage: Louise Wendy, 19 October 1994
Children: Sharon Louise, 29 October 1968; Matthew Barry, 12 September 1988; Jack Nicholas, 29 April 1998
Family links with cricket: 'Dad was a league cricketer'
Education: Stockport School
Career outside cricket: Managing director of Sunsport Tours & Travel
Off-season: Holiday, office and Sri Lanka
Other sports played: Golf
Other sports followed: All sports
Relaxations: Bridge, red wine
Appointed to 1st-Class list: 1984
First appointed to Test panel: 1991
Tests umpired: 2
One-Day Internationals umpired: 3
Other umpiring highlights: Has acted as third umpire in 15 Tests
Players to watch for the future: James Foster
Counties as player: Leicestershire, Gloucestershire
Role: Right-hand opening bat, slow left-arm bowler, occasional wicket-keeper
County debut: 1966 (Leicestershire), 1981 (Gloucestershire)
County cap: 1969 (Leicestershire)
Benefit: 1980 (Leicestershire; £25,000)
1000 runs in a season: 8
1st-Class 100s: 31
1st-Class 200s: 1
1st-Class catches: 234
One-Day 100s: 4
Overseas tours: Kent (as guest player) to West Indies 1972; D.H. Robins' XI to West Indies 1973; Wisden XI to West Indies 1984; MCC to Kenya 1993
Overseas teams played for: Rhodesia 1975-80
Highlight of playing career: 'Winning County Championship [with Leicestershire]'
Extras: Played for England U25. Holder with John Steele of the highest first-wicket partnership for Leics, 390 v Derbys at Leicester in 1979. Fastest player in Rhodesian cricket history to 1000 first-class runs in Currie Cup; second fastest ever in Currie Cup
Opinions on cricket: 'My team-mate Duncan Fletcher is doing a great job.'

Best batting: 202 Leicestershire v Derbyshire, Leicester 1979
Best bowling: 4-6 Leicestershire v Surrey, Leicester 1972

First-Class Career Performances

	M	Inns	NO	Runs	HS	Avge	100s	Ct	St	Runs	Wkts	Avge	Best	5wI	10wM
Test															
All First	295	501	47	14747	202	32.48	32	234	7	1365	47	29.04	4-6	-	-

EVANS, J. H.

Name: Jeffrey (Jeff) Howard Evans
Born: 7 August 1954, Llanelli
Height: 5ft 8in
Wife and date of marriage: Christine,
29 December 1983
Children: Rhian, 9 February 1986;
Siân, 3 September 1987
Education: Llanelli Boys Grammar School;
Dudley College of Education
Career outside cricket: Teacher; financial
consultant
Off-season: Independent Financial Adviser –
Inter Alliance; occasional supply teaching;
cricket coaching
Other sports played: 'Used to play team
squash and coach rugby in local league'
Other sports followed: 'Most sports, rugby
in particular'
Relaxations: Keeping fit, walking, cycling, skiing
Appointed to 1st-Class list: 2001
Umpiring highlights: Kent v New Zealanders 1999; Essex v Zimbabweans 2000;
Worcestershire v West Indies 2000; England U19 v Sri Lanka U19 2000
Players to watch for the future: Ian Hunter, James Pipe
County as player: Did not play first-class cricket. Played club and association cricket
in South Wales as a right-hand bat
Highlight of playing career: 'Playing alongside Winston Davis for Llanelli in the
early 1980s'
Extras: Coach to Welsh Schools Cricket Association team on tour to Australia 1993.
Taught in the Gwendraeth Grammar School – 'the old "Outside Half factory"'
Opinions on cricket: 'Would like to see more honesty throughout the game.'

Did not play first-class cricket

HAMPSHIRE, J. H.

Name: <u>John</u> Harry Hampshire
Born: 10 February 1941, Thurnscoe, Yorks
Height: 6ft
Nickname: Hamps
Wife and date of marriage: Judith Ann,
5 September 1964
Children: Ian Christopher, 6 January 1969;
Paul Wesley, 12 February 1972
Family links with cricket: Father (J.) and
brother (A.W.) both played for Yorkshire
Education: Oakwood Technical High School,
Rotherham
Other sports followed: Most sports
Relaxations: Gardening and cooking
Appointed to 1st-Class list: 1985
First appointed to Test panel: 1989
International panel: 1999 –
Tests umpired: 13
One-Day Internationals umpired: 16
Other umpiring highlights: Umpired four Tests in Pakistan 1989-90. Toured
Bangladesh 1999-2000 with MCC (as umpire). Stood in Coca-Cola Cup, Sharjah
2000. Umpired NatWest final 2000
Counties as player: Yorkshire, Derbyshire
Role: Right-hand bat, leg-spin bowler
County debut: 1961 (Yorkshire), 1982 (Derbyshire)
County cap: 1963 (Yorkshire), 1982 (Derbyshire)
Benefit: 1976 (Yorkshire)
Test debut: 1969
Tests: 11
1000 runs in a season: 15
1st-Class 50s: 142
1st-Class 100s: 43
1st-Class 5 w. in innings: 2
1st-Class catches: 445
One-Day 100s: 7
Overseas tours: MCC (England) to Australia and New Zealand 1970-71
Overseas teams played for: Tasmania, 1966-69, 1977-79
Extras: Captained Yorkshire 1979-80. Scored a century (107) at Lord's on Test debut
(v West Indies 1969); the only England player to have done so. Manager/coach of the
Zimbabwe squad for their first Test matches against India and New Zealand 1992-93
Best batting: 183* Yorkshire v Surrey, Hove 1971
Best bowling: 7-52 Yorkshire v Glamorgan, Cardiff 1963

First-Class Career Performances

	M	Inns	NO	Runs	HS	Avge	100s	Ct	St	Runs	Wkts	Avge	Best	5wI	10wM
Test	8	16	1	405	107	26.86	1	9	-						
All First	577	924	112	28059	183*	34.55	43	445	-	1637	30	54.56	7-52	2	-

HARRIS, M. J.

Name: <u>Michael</u> John Harris
Born: 25 May 1944, St Just-in-Roseland, Cornwall
Height: 6ft 1in
Nickname: Pasty
Wife and date of marriage: Danielle Ruth, 10 September 1969
Children: Jodie, Richard
Education: Gerrans Comprehensive
Career outside cricket: Sports teacher
Other sports followed: Squash, golf
Appointed to 1st-Class list: 1998
Counties as player: Middlesex, Notts
Role: Right-hand bat, leg-break bowler, wicket-keeper
County debut: 1964 (Middlesex), 1969 (Notts)
County cap: 1967 (Middlesex), 1970 (Notts)

1000 runs in a season: 11
1st-Class 50s: 98
1st-Class 100s: 40
1st-Class 200s: 1
1st-Class catches: 288
1st-Class stumpings: 14
Overseas teams played for: Eastern Province 1971-72; Wellington 1975-76
Extras: Shared Middlesex then-record first-wicket partnership of 312 with Eric Russell v Pakistanis at Lord's 1967. Scored nine centuries in 1971 to equal Nottinghamshire county record, scoring two centuries in a match twice and totalling 2238 runs for the season at an average of 50.86
Best batting: 201* Nottinghamshire v Glamorgan, Trent Bridge 1973
Best bowling: 4-16 Nottinghamshire v Warwickshire, Trent Bridge 1969

First-Class Career Performances

	M	Inns	NO	Runs	HS	Avge	100s	Ct	St	Runs	Wkts	Avge	Best	5wI	10wM
Test															
All First	344	581	58	19196	201*	36.70	41	288	14	3459	79	43.78	4-16	-	-

HOLDER, J. W.

Name: John Wakefield Holder
Born: 19 March 1945, St George, Barbados
Height: 6ft
Nickname: Benson, Hod
Wife's name: Glenda
Children: Christopher, 1968; Nigel, 1970
Family links with cricket: None
Education: St Giles Boys School;
Combermere High School, Barbados;
Rochdale College
Off-season: Keeping fit
Other sports followed: Football
(Manchester United)
Relaxations: Keeping fit and watching
wildlife documentaries
Appointed to 1st-Class list: 1983
First appointed to Test panel: 1988
Tests umpired: 10
One-Day Internationals umpired: 17
Other umpiring highlights: Umpired four Tests in Pakistan 1989-90
Players to watch for the future: Alex Tudor
County as player: Hampshire
Role: Right-hand bat, right-arm fast bowler
County debut: 1968
50 wickets in a season: 1
1st-Class 5 w. in innings: 5
1st-Class 10 w. in match: 1
1st-Class catches: 12
Extras: Championship hat-trick v Kent at Southampton 1972
Opinions on cricket: 'I can see the day coming when umpires in international cricket
as they are now will become redundant. TV technology is so advanced and
commentators are so critical of mistakes that I think TV technology will be used more
and more widely and eventually the TV umpire will make all the decisions. When that
happens, for me the game will become far more impersonal.'
Best batting: 33 Hampshire v Sussex, Hove 1971
Best bowling: 7-79 Hampshire v Gloucestershire, Gloucester 1972

First-Class Career Performances

	M	Inns	NO	Runs	HS	Avge	100s	Ct	St	Runs	Wkts	Avge	Best	5wI	10wM
Test															
All First	47	49	14	374	33	10.68	-	12	-	3415	139	24.56	7-79	5	1

HOLDER, V. A.

Name: <u>Vanburn</u> Alonza Holder
Born: 8 October 1945, St Michael, Barbados
Height: 6ft 3in
Nickname: Van
Wife's name: Christine
Children: James Vanburn, 2 September 1981
Education: St Leonard's Secondary Modern;
Community High
Off-season: 'Working'
Other sports followed: Football (Liverpool)
Relaxations: Music. Doing crosswords
Appointed to 1st-Class list: 1991
Players to watch for the future: Ben
Hollioake, Alex Tudor, Steve Harmison
County as player: Worcestershire
Role: Right-hand bat, right-arm
fast-medium bowler
County debut: 1968
County cap: 1970
Benefit: 1979
Test debut: 1969
Tests: 40
1st-Class 50s: 4
1st-Class 100s: 1
1st-Class 5 w. in innings: 38
1st-Class 10 w. in match: 3

1st-Class catches: 98
Overseas tours: West Indies to England 1969, 1973, 1975 (World Cup), 1976, to
India, Sri Lanka and Pakistan 1974-75, to Australia 1975-76, to India and Sri Lanka
1978-79 (vice-captain); Rest of the World to Pakistan 1973-74
Overseas teams played for: Barbados 1966-78
Extras: Made his debut for Barbados in the Shell Shield competition in 1966-67. Won
John Player League with Worcestershire 1973 and County Championship 1974. Played
in West Indies 1975 World Cup winning side
Best batting: 122 Barbados v Trinidad, Bridgetown 1973-74
Best bowling: 7-40 Worcestershire v Glamorgan, Cardiff 1974

First-Class Career Performances

	M	Inns	NO	Runs	HS	Avge	100s	Ct	St	Runs	Wkts	Avge	Best	5wI	10wM
Test	40	59	11	682	42	14.20	-	16	-	3627	109	33.27	6-28	3	-
All First	311	354	81	3559	122	13.03	1	98	-	23183	948	24.45	7-40	38	3

JESTY, T. E.

Name: <u>Trevor</u> Edward Jesty
Born: 2 June 1948, Gosport, Hampshire
Height: 5ft 9in
Nickname: Jets
Wife and date of marriage: Jacqueline,
12 September 1970
Children: Graeme Barry, 27 September
1972; Lorna Samantha, 7 November 1976
Family links with cricket: Daughter played
for England XI 2000
Education: Privett County Secondary
Modern, Gosport
Off-season: Cricket coaching
Other sports followed: Football (Arsenal)
Relaxations: Gardening, reading
Appointed to 1st-Class list: 1994
Players to watch for the future:
Giles White, Jason Brown

Counties as player: Hampshire, Surrey, Lancashire
Role: Right-hand bat, right-arm medium bowler
County debut: 1966 (Hampshire), 1985 (Surrey), 1988 (Lancashire)
County cap: 1971 (Hampshire), 1985 (Surrey), 1990 (Lancashire)
Benefit: 1982 (Hampshire)
One-Day Internationals: 10
1000 runs in a season: 10
50 wickets in a season: 2
1st-Class 50s: 110
1st-Class 100s: 33
1st-Class 200s: 2
1st-Class 5 w. in innings: 19
1st-Class catches: 265
1st-Class stumpings: 1
One-Day 100s: 7
Overseas tours: International XI to West Indies 1982; joined England tour to
Australia 1982-83; Lancashire to Zimbabwe 1989
Overseas teams played for: Border, South Africa 1973-74; Griqualand West 1974-76,
1980-81; Canterbury, New Zealand 1979-80
Highlights of playing career: 'Winning Championship with Hampshire in 1973.
Playing against Australia for England in one-day match on 1982-83 tour'
Extras: One of *Wisden*'s Five Cricketers of the Year 1983
Best batting: 248 Hampshire v Cambridge University, Fenner's 1984
Best bowling: 7-75 Hampshire v Worcestershire, Southampton 1976

First-Class Career Performances

	M	Inns	NO	Runs	HS	Avge	100s	Ct	St	Runs	Wkts	Avge	Best	5wI	10wM
Test															
All First	490	777	107	21916	248	32.71	35	265	1	16075	585	27.47	7-75	19	-

JONES, A. A.

Name: <u>Allan</u> Arthur Jones
Born: 9 December 1947, Horley, Surrey
Height: 6ft 4in
Nickname: Jonah
Marital status: Single
Education: St John's College, Horsham
Career outside cricket: Sports tours
Off-season: 'Enjoying life'
Other sports played: Golf
Other sports followed: Football (Arsenal)
Relaxations: English history, reading,
cooking
Appointed to 1st-Class list: 1985
First appointed to Test panel: 1996
One-Day Internationals umpired: 1
Other umpiring highlights: Has acted as
third umpire in numerous Tests. Has umpired
at Hong Kong Sixes
Players to watch for the future: Ed Joyce
Counties as player: Sussex, Somerset, Middlesex, Glamorgan
Role: Right-hand bat, right-arm fast bowler
County debut: 1964 (Sussex), 1970 (Somerset), 1976 (Middlesex), 1980 (Glamorgan)
County cap: 1972 (Somerset), 1976 (Middlesex)
50 wickets in a season: 4
1st-Class 5 w. in innings: 23
1st-Class 10 w. in match: 3
1st-Class catches: 50
Overseas teams played for: Northern Transvaal 1971-72; Orange Free State 1976-77;
Auckland (Birkenhead)
Highlight of playing career: '9-51 v Sussex 1972'
Extras: Won two Championship medals with Middlesex (1976 and 1977).
Represented MCC v Australians 1977. Was on stand-by for England tour of India
1976-77. Was the first person to play for four counties
Opinions on cricket: 'Groundsmen should be appointed and retained by ECB and not
their counties, to achieve higher standard of pitches and more uniformity. Second XI
should be scrapped; integrate club sides into counties to bring on younger players and

revive more interest in amateur game, thus creating more money for schools of excellence.'

Best batting: 33 Middlesex v Kent, Canterbury 1978
Best bowling: 9-51 Somerset v Sussex, Hove 1972

First-Class Career Performances

	M	Inns	NO	Runs	HS	Avge	100s	Ct	St	Runs	Wkts	Avge	Best	5wI	10wM
Test															
All First	214	216	68	799	33	5-39	-	50	-	15414	549	28.07	9-51	23	3

JULIAN, R.

Name: Raymond Julian
Born: 23 August 1936, Cosby, Leicestershire
Height: 5ft 11in
Nickname: Julie
Wife and date of marriage: Megan, 3 April 1993
Children: Peter Raymond, 1 February 1958; John Kelvin, 13 October 1960; David Andrew, 15 October 1963; Paul Anthony, 22 September 1967; Karen (stepdaughter), 27 June 1972
Family links with cricket: Father and two brothers all played local cricket. Two sons play local cricket
Education: Cosby Primary School, Leicestershire; Wigston Secondary Modern
Career outside cricket: Cricket coach, decorator and gardener
Off-season: Holidays abroad and watching England tour in Sri Lanka
Other sports played: Ex-first-class football referee (one FA Cup match; also linesman in old Southern League 1960-72)
Other sports followed: Football (Leicester City FC), boxing, rugby (Leicester Tigers)
Relaxations: Gardening, holidays, travel
Appointed to 1st-Class list: 1972
International panel: 1996
One-Day Internationals umpired: 5
Other umpiring highlights: Has acted as third umpire in eight Tests. Stood in 1998 B&H, 1999 B&H Super Cup and 2000 NatWest finals. Has umpired AON Trophy final and U19 and U17 finals. Umpired Oxford University v Cambridge University 1981, 1989, 1996. Awarded the PCA Umpires' Cup 1998-2000 ('good hat-trick')

Players to watch for the future: Matthew Hoggard, Simon Guy, Usman Afzaal, Jason Brown
County as player: Leicestershire
Role: Right-hand bat, wicket-keeper
County debut: 1953
County cap: 1961
1st-Class 50s: 2
1st-Class catches: 381
1st-Class stumpings: 40
Overseas tours: MCC to West Africa 1975-76 (as reserve wicket-keeper and umpire)
Highlight of playing career: 'Scoring my first first-class 50 at Lord's, June 1959'
Extras: Played for the Army 1955-57. Member of MCC. 'This season will be my 50th in cricket – Leicestershire 21 years and umpire for 29 years'
Opinions on cricket: 'Pleased we are into four-day cricket and have two divisions. Makes it more enjoyable at the end of the season.'
Best batting: 51 Leicestershire v Worcestershire, Worcester 1962

First-Class Career Performances

	M	Inns	NO	Runs	HS	Avge	100s	Ct	St	Runs	Wkts	Avge	Best	5wl	10wM
Test															
All First	192	288	23	2581	51	9.73	-	381	40						

KITCHEN, M. J.

Name: <u>Mervyn</u> John Kitchen
Born: 1 August 1940, Nailsea, Somerset
Education: Blackwell Secondary Modern, Nailsea
Appointed to 1st-Class list: 1982
First appointed to Test panel: 1990
International panel: 1995-99
Tests umpired: 20
One-Day Internationals umpired: 27
Other umpiring highlights: Stood in 1983 World Cup. Was third umpire for two Tests in 1994
County as player: Somerset
Role: Left-hand bat, right-arm medium bowler
County debut: 1960
County cap: 1966
Testimonial: 1973

1000 runs in a season: 7
1st-Class 50s: 68
1st-Class 100s: 17
1st-Class catches: 157
One-Day 100s: 1
Best batting: 189 Somerset v Pakistanis, Taunton 1967
Best bowling: 1-4 Somerset v Sussex, Taunton 1969

First-Class Career Performances

	M	Inns	NO	Runs	HS	Avge	100s	Ct	St	Runs	Wkts	Avge	Best	5wl	10wM
Test															
All First	354	612	32	15230	189	26.25	17	157	-	109	2	54.50	1-4	-	-

LEADBEATER, B.

Name: Barrie Leadbeater
Born: 14 August 1943, Leeds
Height: 6ft
Nickname: Leady
Marital status: Widowed
Wife and date of marriage: Jacqueline
(deceased 1997), 18 September 1971
Children: Richard Barrie, 23 November
1972; Michael Spencer, 21 March 1976;
Daniel Mark Ronnie, 19 June 1981
Education: Brownhill County Primary;
Harehills Secondary Modern, Leeds
Career outside cricket: HGV driver
Other sports followed: Table tennis, golf,
snooker, football (Leeds United)
Relaxations: 'Taking care of my family'
Appointed to 1st-Class list: 1981
One-Day Internationals umpired: 5
Other umpiring highlights: Stood in 1983 World Cup. Chairman of the First-Class
Umpires' Association
County as player: Yorkshire
Role: Right-hand opening bat, right-arm medium bowler, slip fielder
County debut: 1966
County cap: 1969
Benefit: 1980 (joint benefit with G.A. Cope)
1st-Class 50s: 27
1st-Class 100s: 1

1st-Class catches: 82
Overseas tours: Duke of Norfolk's XI to West Indies 1970
Overseas teams played for: Johannesburg Municipals 1978-79
Extras: Took part in London Marathon 1997, 1998, 2000
Opinions on cricket: 'Disappointed in players who lack self-control and professional pride and set bad examples to young players and public alike. Public should be regularly and properly informed during stoppages in play. Stoppages for bad light cause more frustration for public, players and, not least, umpires and a change in regulations may be needed soon if the game is to retain its support and credibility. The recent theory of the wicket-keeper standing between the leg stump and the return crease when the slow left-arm bowler is operating over the wicket should be made illegal. It is grossly negative and against the spirit of the game.'
Best batting: 140* Yorkshire v Hampshire, Portsmouth 1976
Best bowling: 1-1 Yorkshire v Middlesex, Headingley 1971

First-Class Career Performances

	M	Inns	NO	Runs	HS	Avge	100s	Ct	St	Runs	Wkts	Avge	Best	5wI	10wM
Test															
All First	147	241	29	5373	140*	25.34	1	82	-	5	1	5.00	1-1	-	-

LLOYDS, J. W.

Name: <u>Jeremy</u> William Lloyds
Born: 17 November 1954, Penang, Malaya
Height: 5ft 11in
Nickname: Jerry
Wife and date of marriage: Janine, 16 September 1997
Children: Kaeli, 16 November 1991
Family links with cricket: Father played cricket in Malaya. Brother Chris played for Somerset 2nd XI
Education: Curry Rivel Primary School; St Dunstan's Prep School; Blundell's School, Tiverton
Career outside cricket: Coaching and setting up Western Province Youth Programme 1992-95 in South Africa. Coach at St Stithian's, Johannesburg 1995-98
Off-season: 'Working at whatever comes up!'
Other sports played: Golf (6 handicap)

Other sports followed: Golf, football (Tottenham Hotspur), American football (San Francisco 49ers), Formula One and saloon car racing, rugby (Bath)
Relaxations: 'Reading, music and spending time at home with my family'
Appointed to 1st-Class list: 1998
One-Day Internationals umpired: 1
Other umpiring highlights: Has acted as third umpire in one Test
Counties as player: Somerset, Gloucestershire
Role: Left-hand bat, off-spin bowler
County debut: 1979 (Somerset), 1985 (Gloucestershire)
County cap: 1982 (Somerset), 1985 (Gloucestershire)
1000 runs in a season: 3
1st-Class 50s: 62
1st-Class 100s: 10
1st-Class 5 w. in innings: 13
1st-Class 10 w. in match: 1
1st-Class catches: 229
Overseas tours: Somerset to Antigua 1982; Gloucestershire to Barbados 1985, to Sri Lanka 1987
Overseas teams played for: St Stithian's Old Boys, Johannesburg 1978-79; Toombull DCC, Brisbane 1980-82; North Sydney District 1982-83; Alberton, Johannesburg 1984; Preston CC, Melbourne 1986; Orange Free State 1987; Fish Hoek CC, Cape Town 1988-92
Highlight of playing career: 'Winning 1983 NatWest final'
Extras: Highest score in Brisbane Premier League 1980-81 (165). Britannic Player of the Month July 1987. Gloucestershire Player of the Year 1987. Leading run-scorer in Western Province Cricket League 1988, 1989
Opinions on cricket: 'Too much overseas influence on how to play the game in England. We have more variations in wickets and weather conditions than in most other countries. Yes, take the best of what they have and work it into our game. Also, too much emphasis on all the various levels of coaching certificates. We have been dragged too far away from the *basics* – batting, bowling and fielding. The game hasn't really changed – but people have.'
Best batting: 132* Somerset v Northamptonshire, Northampton 1982
Best bowling: 7-88 Somerset v Essex, Chelmsford 1982

First-Class Career Performances

	M	Inns	NO	Runs	HS	Avge	100s	Ct	St	Runs	Wkts	Avge	Best	5wI	10wM
Test															
All First	267	408	64	10679	132*	31.04	10	229	-	12943	333	38.86	7-88	13	1

MALLENDER, N. A.

Name: <u>Neil</u> Alan Mallender
Born: 13 August 1961, Kirk Sandall, Doncaster
Height: 6ft
Nickname: Ghostie
Marital status: Divorced
Children: Kirstie, 12; Dominic, 9; Jacob 4
Education: Beverley Grammar School
Other sports played: Golf (3 handicap), 'also enjoy training at gym'
Other sports followed: Most sports
Relaxations: Most sports
Appointed to 1st-Class list: 1999
Players to watch for the future: Simon Francis, Mike Smethurst
Counties as player: Northamptonshire, Somerset
Role: Right-hand bat, right-arm medium-fast bowler

County debut: 1980 (Northamptonshire), 1987 (Somerset)
County cap: 1984 (Northamptonshire), 1987 (Somerset)
Benefit: 1994 (Somerset)
Test debut: 1992
Tests: 2
50 wickets in a season: 6
1st-Class 50s: 10
1st-Class 100s: 1
1st-Class 5 w. in innings: 36
1st-Class 10 w. in match: 5
1st-Class catches: 111
One-Day 5 w. in innings: 3
Overseas tours: England YC to West Indies 1979-80
Overseas teams played for: Kaikorai, Dunedin, New Zealand; University, Wellington, New Zealand; Otago, New Zealand 1983-84 – 1992-93
Highlight of playing career: 'England debut'
Extras: Represented England U19 1980-81. Took 5-50 on Test debut v Pakistan at Headingley in 1992
Best batting: 100* Otago v Central Districts, Palmerston North 1991-92
Best bowling: 7-27 Otago v Auckland, Auckland 1984-85

First-Class Career Performances

	M	Inns	NO	Runs	HS	Avge	100s	Ct	St	Runs	Wkts	Avge	Best	5wI	10wM
Test	2	3	0	8	4	2.66	-	-	-	215	10	21.50	5-50	1	-
All First	345	396	122	4709	100*	17.18	1	111	-	24654	937	26.31	7-27	36	5

PALMER, K. E.

Name: Kenneth (<u>Ken</u>) Ernest Palmer
Born: 22 April 1937, Winchester
Height: 5ft 10in
Nickname: Pedlar
Wife and date of marriage: Jacqueline,
24 September 1994
Children: Gary Vincent, 1 November 1965
Family links with cricket: Father played
club cricket and did the cricketer's double 13
times. Son played for Somerset, as did
brother Roy, also a Test umpire
Education: Southbroom Secondary Modern,
Devizes
Other sports followed: Football (Manchester
United) and rugby (Bath and England)
Relaxations: Car enthusiast
Appointed to 1st-Class list: 1972
First appointed to Test panel: 1978
International panel: 1994
Tests umpired: 22
One-Day Internationals umpired: 22
Other umpiring highlights: Has acted as third umpire in four Tests. Has umpired five
B&H finals and four NatWest finals. Stood in 1979 and 1983 World Cups
Players to watch for the future: Jason Brown, Marcus Trescothick
County as player: Somerset
Role: Right-hand bat, right-arm fast-medium bowler; all-rounder
County debut: 1955
County cap: 1958
Testimonial: 1968
Test debut: 1964-65
Tests: 1
1000 runs in a season: 1
50 wickets in a season: 2
100 wickets in a season: 4
1st-Class 50s: 27

1st-Class 100s: 2
1st-Class 5 w. in innings: 46
1st-Class 10 w. in match: 5
1st-Class catches: 156
Overseas tours: Commonwealth XI to Pakistan 1962; International Cavaliers to West Indies 1963-64
Overseas teams played for: Old Maristonian, South Africa 1964-65
Extras: Won Carling Single Wicket Competition 1961. Did the 'double' in 1961 (114 wickets, 1036 runs). With Bill Alley holds the Somerset record for sixth-wicket partnership – 265 v Northants at Northampton 1961. Called into Test side while coaching in South Africa 1964-65. Won Man of the Match Award for Somerset v Lancashire 1967. 'Pleased to become an MCC member for services to cricket'
Best batting: 125* Somerset v Northamptonshire, Northampton 1961
Best bowling: 9-57 Somerset v Nottinghamshire, Trent Bridge 1963

First-Class Career Performances

	M	Inns	NO	Runs	HS	Avge	100s	Ct	St	Runs	Wkts	Avge	Best	5wl	10wM
Test	1	1	0	10	10	10.00	-	-	-	189	1	189.00	1-113	-	-
All First	314	481	105	7771	125*	20.66	2	156	-	18485	866	21.34	9-57	46	5

PALMER, R.

Name: Roy Palmer
Born: 12 July 1942, Hampshire
Height: 6ft 3in
Nickname: Arp
Wife and date of marriage: Alyne,
5 November 1983
Children: Nick, 7 October 1968
Family links with cricket: Brother of Ken
Palmer, Test umpire and former Somerset
player; nephew Gary also played for
Somerset
Education: Southbroom Secondary Modern,
Devizes
Relaxations: DIY, reading, golf
Appointed to 1st-Class list: 1980
First appointed to Test panel: 1992
Tests umpired: 2
One-Day Internationals umpired: 8
Other umpiring highlights: Stood in 1983 World Cup
County as player: Somerset

Role: Right-hand bat, right-arm fast-medium bowler
County debut: 1965
50 wickets in a season: 1
1st-Class 50s: 1
1st-Class 5 w. in innings: 4
1st-Class catches: 25
Extras: Won two Man of the Match Awards in the Gillette Cup
Best batting: 84 Somerset v Leicestershire, Taunton 1967
Best bowling: 6-45 Somerset v Middlesex, Lord's 1967

First-Class Career Performances

	M	Inns	NO	Runs	HS	Avge	100s	Ct	St	Runs	Wkts	Avge	Best	5wI	10wM
Test															
All First	74	110	32	1037	84	13.29	-	25	-	5439	172	31.62	6-45	4	-

SHARP, G.

Name: George Sharp
Born: 12 March 1950, West Hartlepool,
County Durham
Height: 5ft 11in
Nickname: Sharpy, Blunt, Razor, Toffee
Wife and date of marriage: Audrey,
14 September 1974
Children: Gareth James, 27 June 1984
Education: Elwick Road Secondary Modern,
Hartlepool
Career outside cricket: Watching all sports
Off-season: Working as joint director with
GSB Loams Ltd for soils and top dressing
Other sports played: Golf (8 handicap)
Other sports followed: Football (Newcastle
Utd and Middlesbrough), rugby
(Northampton Saints)
Relaxations: Golf; 'spend a lot of time in the
gym during the off-season'
Appointed to 1st-Class list: 1991
International panel: 1996 –
Tests umpired: 12
One-Day Internationals umpired: 19

Other umpiring highlights: Has acted as third umpire in Tests. Has umpired three
B&H finals and one NatWest final. Stood in Singer Trophy (India, Sri Lanka,

Pakistan), Singapore 1996. Umpired in tournament between Pakistan, Sri Lanka and New Zealand in Sharjah 1997
County as player: Northamptonshire
Role: Right-hand bat, wicket-keeper
County debut: 1967
County cap: 1973
Benefit: 1982
1st-Class 50s: 21
1st-Class catches: 565
1st-Class stumpings: 90
Overseas tours: England Counties XI to Barbados and Trinidad 1975
Best batting: 98 Northamptonshire v Yorkshire, Northampton 1983
Best bowling: 1-47 Northamptonshire v Yorkshire, Northampton 1980

First-Class Career Performances

	M	Inns	NO	Runs	HS	Avge	100s	Ct	St	Runs	Wkts	Avge	Best	5wl	10wM
Test															
All First	306	396	81	6254	98	19.85	-	565	90	70	1	70.00	1-47	-	-

SHEPHERD, D. R.

Name: <u>David</u> Robert Shepherd
Born: 27 December 1940, Bideford, Devon
Height: 5ft 10in
Nickname: Shep
Marital status: Single
Family links with cricket: Brother played for MCC Young Professionals and Devon
Education: Barnstaple Grammar School; St Luke's College, Exeter
Career outside cricket: Teacher. Family business – post office/newsagent
Off-season: ICC umpiring abroad
Other sports followed: Rugby, football
Relaxations: Stamp collecting
Appointed to 1st-Class list: 1981
First appointed to Test panel: 1985
International panel: 1994 –
Tests umpired: 52

One-Day Internationals umpired: 92
Other umpiring highlights: Umpired the MCC Bicentenary Test, England v Rest of the World, at Lord's in 1987. With Dickie Bird and Steve Bucknor was one of the first

umpires officially sponsored by the ICC. Has stood in each World Cup since 1983, including the 1995-96 final between Australia and Sri Lanka in Lahore and the 1999 final between Australia and Pakistan at Lord's. Has umpired numerous domestic finals. Received National Grid/ICC 'bronze award' in March 1998 for long-service as a Test umpire. Umpired 50th Test, India v South Africa, Mumbai (Bombay) February 2000, receiving ICC 'silver award' to acknowledge this achievement. Known for his superstition regarding 'Nelson' score 111, and multiples – 222, 333 etc

County as player: Gloucestershire
Role: Right-hand bat, right-arm medium bowler
County debut: 1965
County cap: 1969
Benefit: 1978 (joint benefit with J. Davey)
1000 runs in a season: 2
1st-Class 50s: 55
1st-Class 100s: 12
1st-Class catches: 95
One-Day 100s: 2
Extras: Played Minor Counties cricket for Devon 1959-64. First player to score a century for Gloucestershire on his first-class debut, v Oxford University 1965. Was awarded the MBE in 1997 for services to cricket
Best batting: 153 Gloucestershire v Middlesex, Bristol 1968
Best bowling: 1-1 Gloucestershire v Northamptonshire, Gloucester 1968

First-Class Career Performances

	M	Inns	NO	Runs	HS	Avge	100s	Ct	St	Runs	Wkts	Avge	Best	5wI	10wM
Test															
All First	282	476	40	10672	153	24.47	12	95	-	106	2	53.00	1-1	-	-

STEELE, J. F.

Name: <u>John</u> Frederick Steele
Born: 23 July 1946, Stafford
Height: 5ft 10in
Nickname: Steely
Wife and date of marriage: Susan,
17 April 1977
Children: Sarah Jane, 2 April 1982;
Robert Alfred, 10 April 1985
Family links with cricket: Uncle Stan
played for Staffordshire. Brother David
played for Northamptonshire, Derbyshire and
England. Cousin Brian Crump played for
Northamptonshire and Staffordshire
Education: Endon School, Stoke-on-Trent;
Stafford College
Career outside cricket: Work study officer.
Fireman with Staffordshire Fire Brigade
Other sports followed: Soccer (Stoke City,
Port Vale), golf

Relaxations: Music and walking
Appointed to 1st-Class list: 1997
Counties as player: Leicestershire, Glamorgan
Role: Right-hand bat, slow left-arm bowler
County debut: 1970 (Leicestershire), 1984 (Glamorgan)
County cap: 1971 (Leicestershire), 1984 (Glamorgan)
Benefit: 1983 (Leicestershire)
1000 runs in a season: 6
1st-Class 50s: 69
1st-Class 100s: 21
1st-Class 5 w. in innings: 16
1st-Class catches: 414
Overseas teams played for: Springs HSOB, Northern Transvaal 1971-73; Pine Town
CC, Natal 1973-74, 1982-83; Natal 1975-76, 1978-79
Extras: Played for England U25. First-wicket record partnership for Leicestershire of
390 with Barry Dudleston v Derbyshire at Leicester 1979. Won two Man of the Match
Awards in the Gillette Cup and four in the Benson and Hedges Cup. Won the award for
the most catches in a season in 1984 and was voted Natal's Best Bowler in 1975-76
Best batting: 195 Leicestershire v Derbyshire, Leicester 1971
Best bowling: 7-29 Natal B v Griqualand West, Umzinto 1973-74
                 7-29 Leicestershire v Gloucestershire, Leicester 1980

First-class career performances

	M	Inns	NO	Runs	HS	Avge	100s	Ct	St	Runs	Wkts	Avge	Best	5wI	10wM
Test															
All First	379	605	85	15053	195	28.94	21	414	-	15793	584	27.04	7-29	16	-

WHITE, R. A.

Name: <u>Robert</u> Arthur White
Born: 6 October 1936, Fulham
Height: 5ft 9in
Nickname: Knocker
Wife: Janice
Children: Robin and Vanessa
Education: Chiswick Grammar School
Career outside cricket: Fireworks salesman
Off-season: Working
Other sports followed: All sports – golf, football, ice hockey and horse racing in particular
Relaxations: Theatre-going
Appointed to 1st-Class list: 1982
Players to watch for the future: 'All of them'
Counties as player: Middlesex, Nottinghamshire
Role: Left-hand bat, off-break bowler
County debut: 1958 (Middlesex), 1966 (Nottinghamshire)
County cap: 1963 (Middlesex), 1966 (Nottinghamshire)
Benefit: 1974 (Nottinghamshire)
1000 runs in a season: 1
50 wickets in a season: 2
1st-Class 50s: 50
1st-Class 100s: 5
1st-Class 5 w. in innings: 28
1st-Class 10 w. in match: 4
1st-Class catches: 190
Extras: Made independent coaching trips to South Africa 1959, 1960, 1966, 1967, 1968. Together with M.J. Smedley, put on 204 for the seventh wicket, then a Nottinghamshire record, v Surrey at The Oval 1967
Best batting: 116* Nottinghamshire v Surrey, The Oval 1967
Best bowling: 7-41 Nottinghamshire v Derbyshire, Ilkeston 1971

First-Class Career Performances

	M	Inns	NO	Runs	HS	Avge	100s	Ct	St	Runs	Wkts	Avge	Best	5wl	10wM
Test															
All First	413	642	105	12452	116*	23.18	5	190	-	21138	693	30.50	7-41	28	4

WHITEHEAD, A. G. T.

Name: <u>Alan</u> Geoffrey Thomas Whitehead
Born: 28 October 1940, Butleigh, Somerset
Appointed to 1st-Class list: 1970
First appointed to Test panel: 1982
Tests umpired: 5
One-Day Internationals umpired: 13
Other umpiring highlights: Stood in the
1979 and 1983 World Cups. Acted as third
umpire in the fifth Test against Australia at
Edgbaston 1993 and in two Tests in 1994
County as player: Somerset
Role: Left-hand bat, slow left-arm bowler
County debut: 1957
1st-Class 5 w. in innings: 3
1st-Class catches: 20
Best batting: 15 Somerset v Hampshire,
Southampton 1959
Best bowling: 6-74 Somerset v Sussex,
Eastbourne 1959

First-Class Career Performances

	M	Inns	NO	Runs	HS	Avge	100s	Ct	St	Runs	Wkts	Avge	Best	5wl	10wM
Test															
All First	38	49	25	137	15	5.70	-	20	-	2306	67	34.41	6-74	3	

WILLEY, P.

Name: Peter Willey
Born: 6 December 1949, Sedgefield,
County Durham
Height: 6ft 1in
Nickname: Will, 'many unprintable'
Wife and date of marriage: Charmaine,
23 September 1971
Children: Heather Jane, 11 September 1985;
David, 28 February 1990
Family links with cricket: Father played
local club cricket in County Durham
Education: Seaham Secondary School,
County Durham
Other sports followed: All sports
Relaxations: Gardening, dog walking
Appointed to 1st-Class list: 1993
International panel: 1996 –
Tests umpired: 20

One-Day Internationals umpired: 18
Other umpiring highlights: Stood in the 1999 World Cup and in the 1999 Benson
and Hedges Super Cup final
Counties as player: Northamptonshire, Leicestershire
Role: Right-hand bat, off-break bowler
County debut: 1966 (Northamptonshire), 1984 (Leicestershire)
County cap: 1971 (Northamptonshire), 1984 (Leicestershire)
Benefit: 1981 (Northamptonshire; £31,400)
Test debut: 1976
Tests: 26
One-Day Internationals: 26
1000 runs in a season: 10
50 wickets in a season: 2
1st-Class 50s: 101
1st-Class 100s: 43
1st-Class 200s: 1
1st-Class 5 w. in innings: 26
1st-Class 10 w. in match: 3
1st-Class catches: 235
One-Day 100s: 9
Overseas tours: England to Australia and India 1979-80, to West Indies 1980-81,
1985-86; unofficial England XI to South Africa 1981-82
Overseas teams played for: Eastern Province, South Africa 1982-85

Extras: Became youngest player ever to play for Northamptonshire at 16 years 180 days v Cambridge University in 1966. Leicestershire captain 1987. Played for Northumberland in 1992
Best batting: 227 Northamptonshire v Somerset, Northampton 1976
Best bowling: 7-37 Northamptonshire v Oxford University, The Parks 1975

First-Class Career Performances

	M	Inns	NO	Runs	HS	Avge	100s	Ct	St	Runs	Wkts	Avge	Best	5wl	10wM
Test	26	50	6	1184	102*	26.90	2	3	-	456	7	65.14	2-73	-	-
All First	559	918	121	24361	227	30.56	44	235	-	23400	756	30.95	7-37	26	3

THE BROADCASTERS

Name: Abdul Qadir
Born: 15 September 1955, Lahore, Pakistan
Height: 5ft 7in
Marital status: Married
Children: Rehman Qadir; Imran Qadir;
Sulaiman Qadir; Usman Qadir; Noor Fatima;
Noor Amina
Family links with cricket: Son Imran Qadir
represented Pakistan in the U15 World Cup
1996; son Sulaiman Qadir represented
Pakistan U17 in the ICC U17 Asia
tournament 2000 and was selected for the
squad to contest the U17 Asia Cup in
Bangladesh 2001
Education: Government College, Lahore
Career outside cricket: Property
construction; advertising; Imran Qadir Sports
International; Imran Qadir School

Other sports played: Football, hockey, chess
Other sports followed: Tennis
Relaxations: 'When I am alone I love to read poetry'
Broadcasting career: Has worked for Pakistan Radio. Commentated on 1999 World
Cup for Zee TV
Highlight of broadcasting career: 'According to Zee TV officials, I was the best
commentator, and they gave me a prize'
Newspapers and magazines contributed to: Has written for *Jang*, a leading
newspaper also published in England; for *Nawa-i-waqt* and many other magazines
Books published: None so far, although books on cricket, yoga, travel and poetry are
to be published
Players to watch for the future: 'My 7-year-old son Usman Qadir is very promising,
even at this age ready for every challenge'
County as player: Did not play county cricket
Role: Right-hand bat, leg-spin bowler
Test debut: 1977-78
Tests: 67
One-day Internationals: 104
1st-Class 100s: 2
1st-Class 5 w. in innings: 70
1st-Class 10 w. in match: 19
1st-Class catches: 76
One-Day 5 w. in innings: 2
Overseas tours: Pakistan to India 1979-80, 1986-87, to England 1982, 1987, to

Australia 1983-84, to New Zealand 1984-85, 1988-89, to Sri Lanka 1985-86, to West Indies 1987-88
Overseas teams played for: Punjab; Lahore Cricket Association; Habib Bank Limited; Carlton CC, Melbourne 1998-99
Extras: Has taken more Test wickets (236) than any other Pakistan spin bowler. Pride of Performance Life Achievement Gold Medal from PCB. Life membership of MCC. Ryder Medal for Victoria district cricketer of the year 1998-99 (72 wickets, av. 15.40). Played for Hanging Heaton in the Bradford League and for Stenhousemuir in Scotland
Opinions on cricket: 'Cricket is a gentleman's game. Today gambling and fixing have polluted it a lot. It should be rooted out completely. Everyone should think it over and try their utmost to get rid of it without any prejudice. Otherwise people will begin to forget this historic game. ICC should take the necessary measures.'
Best batting: 112 Lahore v Bahawalpur, Bahawalpur 1975-76
Best bowling: 9-49 Habib Bank v Rawalpindi, Rawalpindi 1982-83

First-Class and International Career Performances

	M	Inns	NO	Runs	HS	Avge	100s	Ct	St	Runs	Wkts	Avge	Best	5wI	10wM
Test	67	77	11	1029	61	15.59	-	15	-	7742	236	32.80	9-56	15	5
All First	198	234	40	3636	112	18.74	2	76	-	21017	897	23.43	9-49	70	19
1-day Int	104	68	26	641	41*	15.26	-	21	-	3453	132	26.15	5-44	2	

Name: <u>Jonathan</u> Philip Agnew
Born: 4 April 1960, Macclesfield
Height: 6ft 4in
Wife's name: Emma
Children: Jennifer, 1985; Rebecca, 1988
Education: Uppingham School
Relaxations: 'Eating good food and drinking good wine amongst friends'
First broadcast for: BBC Radio Leicester 1987
Broadcasting career: Became Sports Producer at Radio Leicester in 1989. Became BBC Cricket Correspondent in 1991
Highlight of broadcasting career: 'Interviewing Nelson Mandela'
Newspapers and magazines contributed to: *Today, Daily Express, Wisden Cricket Monthly*

Books published: Include *8 Days A Week* (1988); *Over to You, Aggers* (1997); current editor of *B&H Cricket Year*
County as player: Leicestershire
Role: Right-hand bat, right-arm fast bowler
County debut: 1978
County cap: 1984
Test debut: 1984
Tests: 3
One-day Internationals: 3
50 wickets in a season: 6
100 wickets in a season: 1
1st-Class 50s: 2
1st-Class 5 w. in innings: 37
1st-Class 10 w. in match: 6
1st-Class catches: 39
One-Day 5 w. in innings: 2
Career strike rate: 53.17
Overseas tours: England to India 1984-85
Overseas teams played for: Essendon, Melbourne; Parramatta, Sydney
Highlight of playing career: 'Returning to play NatWest semi-final for Leicestershire after two years in retirement'
Extras: One of *Wisden*'s Five Cricketers of the Year 1988
Opinions on cricket: 'Need more overseas players – two per county. The sooner the

two divisional Championship is scrapped – and regional cricket introduced – the better.'

Best batting: 90 Leicestershire v Yorkshire, Scarborough 1987
Best bowling: 9-70 Leicestershire v Kent, Leicester 1985

First-Class and International Career Performances

	M	Inns	NO	Runs	HS	Avge	100s	Ct	St	Runs	Wkts	Avge	Best	5wI	10wM
Test	3	4	3	10	5	10.00	-	-	-	373	4	93.25	2-51	-	-
All First	218	232	49	2118	90	11.57	-	39	-	19485	666	29.25	9-70	37	6
1-day Int	3	1	1	2	2*	-	-	1	-	120	3	40.00	3-38	-	

ALLOTT, P. J. W.   SkySports

Name: <u>Paul</u> John Walter Allott
Born: 14 September 1956, Altrincham
Height: 6ft 4in
Wife's name: Pamela
Children: Ben and Susie
Family links with cricket: Father
captain/secretary of Ashley CC for 40 years
Education: Altrincham Grammar School;
Bede College, Durham
First broadcast for: BBC Radio 5 (radio);
BBC 1 (TV)
Broadcasting career: BBC 1993-94;
BBC/Sky 1994-95; Sky Sports 1995-
Newspapers and magazines contributed to:
The Guardian, The Cricketer
County as player: Lancashire
Role: Right-hand bat, right-arm fast-medium
bowler

County debut: 1978
County cap: 1981
Benefit: 1990
Test debut: 1981
Tests: 13
One-Day Internationals: 13
50 wickets in a season: 5
1st-Class 50s: 10
1st-Class 5 w. in innings: 30
1st-Class catches: 134
Career strike rate: 59.61

Overseas tours: England to India and Sri Lanka 1981-82, to India 1984-85
Overseas teams played for: Wellington 1985-87
Extras: Scored 52* in his first Test innings, v Australia at Old Trafford 1981
Best batting: 88 Lancashire v Hampshire, Southampton 1987
Best bowling: 8-48 Lancashire v Northamptonshire, Northampton 1981

First-Class and International Career Performances

	M	Inns	NO	Runs	HS	Avge	100s	Ct	St	Runs	Wkts	Avge	Best	5wI	10wM
Test	13	18	3	213	52*	14.20	-	4	-	1084	26	41.69	6-61	1	-
All First	245	262	64	3363	88	16.98	-	134	-	16665	652	25.55	8-48	30	-
1-day Int	13	6	1	15	8	3.00	-	2	-	552	15	36.80	3-41	-	

BAXTER, P. A. S.   BBC Test Match Special

Name: Peter Alastair St John Baxter
Born: 8 January 1947, Derby
Height: 5ft 11in
Marital status: Separated
Children: Claire, 8 November 1983; Jamie,
5 July 1986
Family links with cricket: 'Son Jamie in
Bedfordshire U15 squad!'
Education: Wellington College, Berkshire
Other sports followed: Rugby union
First broadcast for: Radio Hilversum
(Holland) 1970, reading the football results
Broadcasting career: British Forces
Broadcasting Service (Aden) 1965. BBC
Radio Outside Broadcasts, September 1965.
Became Cricket Producer, BBC Radio, March
1973

Highlights of broadcasting career: 'First
Test match commentary, Calcutta 1984-85. Organisation of radio coverage of 1999
World Cup'
Books published: *Test Match Special, TMS 2* and *TMS 3*; *From Brisbane to Karachi,
Views from the Boundary*; *More Views from the Boundary*; *From Arlott to Aggers*;
World Cup: Cricket's Clash of the Titans; *Cricket's Greatest Battles*; *Out of the
Rough*
Players to watch for the future: Stephen Peters, Jason Brown, Jamie Baxter
County as player: Did not play first-class cricket
Highlight of playing career: 'Taking eight wickets in a school game on an impossibly
wet pitch'

Opinions on cricket: 'The ECB should not lose sight of the fact that they are running the game of cricket, with all the commercial and televisual distractions around.'

Did not play first-class cricket

BENAUD, R.   Channel 4

Name: Richard (<u>Richie</u>) Benaud
Born: 6 October 1930
Wife and date of marriage: Daphne,
26 July 1967
Family links with cricket: 'Lou Benaud, my father, a leg-spin bowler and all-rounder, was an outstanding country cricketer in New South Wales in the 1920s and early 1930s and then played in Sydney for Central Cumberland first and other grades from 1937-38 to 1956. Aged 43, he was in the team when I made my first-grade debut in 1946.'
Education: Parramatta High School
Career outside media: 'With Daphne, as Benaud and Associates Pty Ltd, International Sports Consultants'
Other sports played: 'Tennis and soccer up to age 21; since then, golf and horse racing'
Other sports followed: Golf, soccer, rugby league, rugby union, Australian Rules. 'The first match I ever watched in England was in 1953 when Alf Ramsey was at full back for Tottenham Hotspur'
Relaxations: 'Golf, horse racing, reading and the occasional glass of Montrachet or Lynch-Bages'
Broadcasting career: BBC Radio 1960. BBC Television 1963-99; Channel 4 Television 2000 – ; Channel 9 Television 1977 –
Newspapers and magazines contributed to: Journalist with *The Sun* (Sydney newspaper) 1956-68. Freelance journalist 1968 –
Books published: *Way of Cricket* (1961); *A Tale of Two Tests* (1962); *Spin Me a Spinner* (1963); *The New Champions* (1965); *Willow Patterns* (1969); *Benaud on Reflection* (1984); *The Appeal of Cricket* (1995); *Anything but ... An Autobiography* (1998)
County as player: Did not play county cricket
Role: Right-hand bat, leg-spin bowler
Test debut: 1951-52
Tests: 63

1st-Class 100s: 23
1st-Class 5 w. in innings: 56
1st-Class 10 w. in match: 9
1st-Class catches: 254
Overseas tours: Australia to England 1953, 1956, 1961 (captain), to West Indies 1954-55, to Pakistan 1956-57, 1959-60 (captain), to India 1956-57, 1959-60 (captain), to South Africa 1957-58
Overseas teams played for: Cumberland, Sydney; New South Wales 1948-49 – 1963-64
Extras: Captain of Australia 1958-59 – 1963-64 (28 Tests). Awarded OBE 1961. One of *Wisden*'s Five Cricketers of the Year 1962
Best batting: 187 Australians v Natal, Pietermaritzburg 1957-58
Best bowling: 7-18 New South Wales v MCC, Sydney 1962-63

First-Class and International Career Performances

	M	Inns	NO	Runs	HS	Avge	100s	Ct	St	Runs	Wkts	Avge	Best	5wI	10wM
Test	63	97	7	2201	122	24.45	3	65	-	6704	248	27.03	7-72	16	1
All First	259	365	44	11719	187	36.50	23	254	-	23371	945	24.73	7-18	56	9
1-day Int															

BISHOP, I. R. Channel 4

Name: <u>Ian</u> Raphael Bishop
Born: 24 October 1967, Port of Spain, Trinidad
Height: 6ft 5in
Wife and date of marriage: Jahan, 9 October 1993
Family links with cricket: 'My uncle, Renwick Bishop, represented West Indies U19'
Education: Belmont Boys' Primary School; Belmont Secondary School
Other sports played: 'Soccer for my former school'
Other sports followed: All sports, football (Manchester United)
Relaxations: Reading, television
Broadcasting career: Cana Radio; 6.10 Radio; BBC Radio. Channel 4 Television; TWI

Highlight of broadcasting career: 'Covering the West Indies v England series in 2000 with Channel 4'
Newspapers and magazines contributed to: *Trinidad Newsday* (newspaper)
Players to watch for the future: Ravi Rampaul (Trinidad)
County as player: Derbyshire
Role: Right-hand bat, right-arm fast bowler
County debut: 1989
County cap: 1990
Test debut: 1988-89
Tests: 43
One-Day Internationals: 84
50 wickets in a season: 2
1st-Class 50s: 3
1st-Class 100s: 2
1st-Class 5 w. in innings: 23
1st-Class 10 w. in match: 1
1st-Class catches: 50
One-Day 5 w. in innings: 2
Career strike rate: 48.36
Overseas tours: West Indies to England 1988, to Australia 1988-89, to Pakistan 1990-91, to Australia 1992-93
Overseas teams played for: Trinidad and Tobago 1987-1999
Highlight of playing career: 'West Indies beating Australia by one run in Adelaide 1992-93'
Extras: Topped 1990 first-class bowling averages in England with 59 wickets at 19.05. Played for Tynedale CC in Northumberland and Reigate Priory in Surrey
Best batting: 111 Trinidad and Tobago v Barbados, Port of Spain 1996-97
Best bowling: 7-34 Derbyshire v Hampshire, Portsmouth 1992

First-Class and International Career Performances

	M	Inns	NO	Runs	HS	Avge	100s	Ct	St	Runs	Wkts	Avge	Best	5wI	10wM
Test	43	63	11	632	48	12.15	-	8	-	3909	161	24.27	6-40	6	-
All First	159	211	41	2639	111	15.52	2	50	-	12665	549	23.06	7-34	23	1
1-day Int	84	44	19	405	33*	16.20	-	12	-	3128	118	26.50	5-25	2	

BLOFELD, H. C. BBC Test Match Special

Name: <u>Henry</u> Calthorpe Blofeld
Born: 23 September 1939, Hoveton, Norfolk
Height: 6ft
Wife's name: Bitten
Children: Suki, 1 September 1963
Education: Eton College; Cambridge University
Relaxations: Shooting, reading, bridge, collecting books
First broadcast for: Radio Jamaica, January 1971 (radio); Grenada TV 1960s (TV)
Broadcasting career: BBC Radio's *Test Match Special* 1972 –
Newspapers and magazines contributed to: *The Times, The Guardian, The Daily Telegraph, Independent, The Observer, Daily Sketch, Daily Mirror, Independent on Sunday*
Books published: *Cricket in Three Moods;*

The Packer Affair; Wine, Women and Wickets; Caught Short of the Boundary; My Dear Old Thing; On the Edge of My Seat (1991); *One Test After Another; Cakes and Bails; "It's Just Not Cricket"* (1999); *A Thirst for Life*
County as player: Norfolk; also Cambridge University
Role: Right-hand opening bat
1st-Class 50s: 2
1st-Class 100s: 1
1st-Class catches: 11
Overseas tours: Arabs to Barbados 1966-67
Highlight of playing career: '104* for Public Schools against Combined Services at Lord's 1956'
Extras: Cambridge Blue 1959
Best batting: 138 Cambridge University v MCC, Lord's 1959

First-Class Career Performances

	M	Inns	NO	Runs	HS	Avge	100s	Ct	St	Runs	Wkts	Avge	Best	5wl	10wM
Test															
All First	17	32	1	758	138	24.45	1	11	-	15	0	-	-	-	-
1-day Int															

BOTHAM, I. T.  SkySports

Name: <u>Ian</u> Terence Botham
Born: 24 November 1955, Heswall, Cheshire
Height: 6ft 2in
Wife and date of marriage: Kathryn,
31 January 1976
Children: Liam James, 26 August 1977;
Sarah Lianne, 3 February 1979; Rebecca
Kate, 13 November 1985
Education: Buckler's Mead Secondary
School, Yeovil
Other sports played: Football (Scunthorpe,
England Amateurs), golf
Other sports followed: Football
(Chelsea FC), rugby union (Newcastle)
Relaxations: Shooting, fishing
First broadcast for: '606'
Broadcasting career: Sky 1995 –
Highlight of broadcasting career: 'Seeing
Bob Willis and Paul Allott commentating on a One-Day International at Brisbane in
their underwear as the air-conditioning had broken down!'
Newspapers and magazines contributed to: Numerous, currently *The Mirror*
Books published: Include *High, Wide and Handsome*, written with Frank Keating;
It Sort of Clicks, in collaboration with Peter Roebuck; *Cricket My Way*, with Jack
Bannister; *Botham: Don't Tell Kath*; *The Botham Report* (1997)
Players to watch for the future: Michael Vaughan, Matthew Hoggard
Counties as player: Somerset, Worcestershire, Durham
Role: Right-hand bat, right-arm fast-medium bowler
County debut: 1974 (Somerset), 1987 (Worcs), 1992 (Durham)
County cap: 1976 (Somerset), 1987 (Worcs), 1992 (Durham)
Benefit: 1984 (Somerset)
Test debut: 1977
Tests: 102
One-Day Internationals: 116
1000 runs in a season: 4
50 wickets in a season: 7
100 wickets in a season: 1
1st-Class 50s: 97
1st-Class 100s: 36
1st-Class 200s: 2
1st-Class 5 w. in innings: 59
1st-Class 10 w. in match: 8

1st-Class catches: 352
One-Day 100s: 7
One-Day 5 w. in innings: 3
Career strike rate: 54.31
Overseas tours: England to Pakistan and New Zealand 1977-78, to Australia 1978-79, to Australia and India 1979-80, to West Indies 1980-81 (captain), to India 1981-82, to Australia 1982-83, to West Indies 1985-86, to Australia 1986-87, to New Zealand 1991-92, to Australia and New Zealand (World Cup) 1991-92
Overseas teams played for: Queensland
Highlights of playing career: 'Any time England beat the Aussies'
Extras: Captain of England in 12 Test matches. One of *Wisden*'s Five Cricketers of the Year 1978. BBC Sports Personality of the Year 1981. Awarded the OBE in 1992
Opinions on cricket: 'Getting better.'
Best batting: 228 Somerset v Gloucestershire, Taunton 1980
Best bowling: 8-34 England v Pakistan, Lord's 1978

First-Class and International Career Performances

	M	Inns	NO	Runs	HS	Avge	100s	Ct	St	Runs	Wkts	Avge	Best	5wI	10wM
Test	102	161	6	5200	208	33.54	14	120	-	10878	383	28.40	8-34	27	4
All First	402	617	46	19399	228	33.97	38	352	-	31942	1172	27.25	8-34	59	8
1-day Int	116	106	15	2113	79	23.21	-	36	-	4139	145	28.54	4-31	-	

COLVILE, C. E. N.

Name: <u>Charles</u> Edward Neate Colvile
Born: 29 March 1955, Rochester, Kent
Height: 6ft 4in
Wife and date of marriage: Alison Jane,
11 April 1981
Children: Raoul, 1986; Robyn, 1988;
Zara, 1990; Sasha, 1993
Education: Westminster School, London
First broadcast for: BBC Radio 4 *PM* 1976
(radio); BBC *Breakfast Time* (TV)
Broadcasting career: Began broadcasting
career doing a Saturday afternoon sports
report on *PM* in 1976. Radio Oxford 1977.
Radio 4 continuity announcer 1978. BBC
Radio Sport/*Today* Sports Correspondent
1982. BBC *Breakfast Time* 1985. LWT 1988.
BSB/BSkyB 1990 –
Highlight of broadcasting career: 'Some
would think commentating on Warne's 1994-95 MCG hat-trick, but being a good
Surrey boy, Stewart's two hundreds v West Indies in Barbados in 1993-94'
County as player: Did not play first-class cricket
Extras: Supports Surrey CCC

Did not play first-class cricket

EMBUREY, J. E.

SkySports

Name: <u>John</u> Ernest Emburey
Born: 20 August 1952, London
Height: 6ft 2in
Wife and date of marriage: Susie,
20 September 1980
Children: Clare, 1 March 1983;
Chloë, 31 October 1985
Education: Peckham Manor Secondary
School
Career outside media: Coach
Other sports played: Football, squash
Other sports followed: Golf, football
(Millwall FC)
Relaxations: Reading, fishing
First broadcast for: Talk Sport 1999 (radio);
Sky TV 1998 (TV)
Broadcasting career: Cricket analyst for Sky
TV since 1998
Highlight of broadcasting career: 'Studio cricket analyst during riot at West Indies v
Australia One-Day International in Barbados 2000'
Newspapers and magazines contributed to: *Evening Standard*
Books published: *Emburey*; *Spinning in a Fast World*
Players to watch for the future: Jason Brown, Andrew Strauss, Stephen Peters
Counties as player: Middlesex, Northamptonshire
Role: Right-hand bat, off-spin bowler
County debut: 1973 (Middlesex), 1996 (Northamptonshire)
County cap: 1977 (Middlesex)
Benefit: 1986 (Middlesex)
Testimonial: 1995 (Middlesex)
Test debut: 1978
Tests: 64
One-Day Internationals: 61
50 wickets in a season: 17
1st-Class 50s: 55
1st-Class 100s: 7
1st-Class 5 w. in innings: 72
1st-Class 10 w. in match: 12
1st-Class catches: 460
One-Day 5 w. in innings: 3
Career strike rate: 70.21
Overseas tours: England to Australia 1978-79, 1986-87, to Australia and India

756

1979-80, to West Indies 1980-81, 1985-86, to India and Sri Lanka 1981-82, 1992-93, to Pakistan, Australia and New Zealand 1987-88

Overseas teams played for: Prahran, Melbourne 1997-98; St Kilda, Melbourne 1979-80, 1984-85; Stellenbosch University, Cape Town 1982-83; Western Province, South Africa 1982-83, 1983-84; Fish Hoek, Cape Town 1983-84

Highlight of playing career: 'Appointment as England captain 1988'

Extras: One of *Wisden*'s Five Cricketers of the Year 1984. Captain of England in two Tests v West Indies 1988

Opinions on cricket: 'Two-division Championship has been good for the game – benefits will not materialise for a few years. Points structure of the current system is excellent. Not convinced that three up and three down in the Championship is right, though there were some entertaining matches at the end of the 2000 season. There is still room though for teams to contrive results if they are in promotion and relegation situations. There is not too much cricket played by the bread-and-butter county cricketers. They should enjoy playing the game, rather than keep criticising a game that earns them a living.'

Best batting: 133 Middlesex v Essex, Chelmsford 1983

Best bowling: 8-40 Middlesex v Hampshire, Lord's 1993

First-Class and International Career Performances

	M	Inns	NO	Runs	HS	Avge	100s	Ct	St	Runs	Wkts	Avge	Best	5wI	10wM
Test	64	96	20	1713	75	22.53	-	34	-	5646	147	38.40	7-78	6	-
All First	513	644	130	12021	133	23.38	7	460	-	41958	1608	26.09	8-40	72	12
1-day Int	61	45	10	501	34	14.31	-	19	-	2346	76	30.86	4-37	-	

FOWLER, G.   SkySports/BBC Test Match Special

Name: Graeme Fowler
Born: 20 April 1957, Accrington, Lancashire
Height: 5ft 9½in
Wife and date of marriage: Sarah,
14 February 1995
Children: Katherine Elizabeth, 4 August
1994; Georgina Ruby, 29 September 1995
Education: Accrington Grammar School for
Boys; College of St Hild and St Bede,
Durham University
Career outside media: Senior cricket coach,
Durham University Cricket Centre of
Excellence since October 1996
Relaxations: Gardening, music, playing
drums (1999 and 2000 for the Mark Butcher
Band at the Royal Albert Hall; 1991 for Roy
Harper Band on a live CD called *Unhinged*)

First broadcast for: BBC Radio 4 1987 (radio); Sky Sports 1995 (TV)
Broadcasting career: Part of Radio 4 *Test Match Special* team since 1996. Part of
Sky Sports cricket commentary team since 1997
Highlights of broadcasting career: 'Any with Henry Blofeld'
Newspapers and magazines contributed to: *Sunday Telegraph*, *Wisden Cricket
Monthly*
Books published: *Fox on the Run* (1986; Channel 4 Sports Book of the Year)
Players to watch for the future: James Foster
Counties as player: Lancashire, Durham
Role: Left-hand opening bat, right-arm medium bowler
County debut: 1979 (Lancashire), 1993 (Durham)
County cap: 1981 (Lancashire)
Benefit: 1991 (Lancashire; £152,000)
Test debut: 1982
Tests: 21
One-Day Internationals: 26
1000 runs in a season: 8
1st-Class 50s: 85
1st-Class 100s: 34
1st-Class 200s: 2
1st-Class catches: 154
1st-Class stumpings: 5
One-Day 100s: 9
Overseas tours: England to Australia 1982-83, to New Zealand and Pakistan 1983-84,
to India 1984-85

Overseas teams played for: Scarborough, Perth 1979-1980, 1986-1988; Kingsborough, Hobart 1981
Highlights of playing career: '201 v India, Madras 1984-85; 106 v West Indies, Lord's 1984'
Extras: First Englishman to score a Test double century in India
Opinions on cricket: 'Technology should be fully embraced. Full tours should be abolished and replaced by a world league. Needs to be semi-professional to allow all cricketers the chance – not just a few professionals – with half the current first-class fixtures. County clubs should be limited companies not private members' clubs. The game is run indirectly and directly by people who know very little about it.'
Best batting: 226 Lancashire v Kent, Maidstone 1984
Best bowling: 2-34 Lancashire v Warwickshire, Old Trafford 1986

First-Class and International Career Performances

	M	Inns	NO	Runs	HS	Avge	100s	Ct	St	Runs	Wkts	Avge	Best	5wI	10wM
Test	21	37	0	1307	201	35.32	3	10	-	11	0	-	-	-	-
All First	292	495	27	16663	226	35.60	36	154	5	366	10	36.60	2-34	-	-
1-day Int	26	26	2	744	81*	31.00	-	4	2						

FRINDALL, W. H. BBC Test Match Special

Name: William (<u>Bill</u>) Howard Frindall
Born: 3 March 1939, Epsom, Surrey
Height: 5ft 10½in
Wife and date of marriage: Deborah Margaret, 29 February 1992
Children: Alice Katharine, 24 January 1996
Family links with cricket: Father played village cricket in Surrey – took 9-45 for Walton Heath *c*1946
Education: Reigate Grammar School; Kingston upon Thames School of Art (Architecture Department)
Other sports played: Hockey in the RAF ('badly')
Other sports followed: None – 'don't have the time!'
Relaxations: Blind cricket (President of British Blind Sport since 1984); drawing and painting (oil and watercolour); gardening ('under my wife's supervision'); cats; philately

First broadcast for: BBC Radio (radio) – Worcestershire v West Indians 1966 (first Test match was England v West Indies, Old Trafford 1966); BBC2 (TV) Rothmans Cavaliers v Surrey, Cheam 1968

Broadcasting career: Set all questions for *Sporting Chance* (BBC Radio) 1965-67. Has scored all home Tests (and some overseas series) for *Test Match Special* since June 1966. Involved with BBC2's coverage of John Player League 1969-75 (captions and scorer). Interviews and reports for BBC Forces Radio (c1970-c1985) and BBC Wiltshire Sound (since 1996)

Highlight of broadcasting career: 'Wait for my memoirs! Possibly when John Arlott left early and I imitated him on *TMS*'

Newspapers and magazines contributed to: *The Times*, *The Daily Telegraph*, *The Guardian*, *Daily Mail*, *Daily Express*, *Daily Mirror*, *The Sun*, *The Observer*, *Sunday Telegraph*; Cricket Correspondent of *Mail on Sunday* 1987-89; currently cricket statistician to *The Times*

Books published: *The Wisden Book of Test Cricket* (1979; 5th edition 2000); *The Wisden Book of Cricket Records* (1981; 4th edition 1998); *The Guinness Book of Cricket Facts and Feats* (1983; 4th edition 1996); *England Test Cricketers* (1989); *Ten Tests for England* (1989); *Gooch's Golden Summer* (1991); *A Tale of Two Captains* (1992); *Playfair Cricket World Cup Guide* (1996); *Limited-Overs International Cricket: the complete record* (1997); *NatWest Playfair Cricket World Cup 1999* (1999); *Playfair Cricket Annual* (1986-; ed)

Players to watch for the future: Alice Frindall (aged 5)

County as player: Did not play first-class cricket but has played for Hampshire 2nd XI (1972) and for a host of sides, including (in benefits) Yorkshire, Essex, Kent and Warwickshire

Role: Right-hand bat, right-arm medium-fast bowler ('was fast-medium')

Overseas tours: Many, including MCC to USA 1992, to Canada 1994; Lord's Taverners to Portugal 1988, to Gibraltar 1992

Overseas teams played for: Several, including Crusaders, Australia 1982-83

Highlights of playing career: 'Taking 9-21 (all bowled) for Oxford Clergy. Clean bowling Ian Botham in a benefit match'

Extras: Awarded honorary Doctor of Technology by Staffordshire University in 1998 for services to cricket statistics. President BBC Cricket Club. Cricket archivist to Sir Paul Getty

Opinions on cricket: 'Wait for the memoirs.'

Did not play first-class cricket

Name: <u>Graham</u> Alan Gooch
Born: 23 July 1953, Leytonstone
Height: 6ft
Wife and date of marriage: Brenda,
23 October 1976
Children: Hannah; Megan and Sally (twins)
Family links with cricket: Father played
club cricket for East Ham Corinthians.
Second cousin Graham Saville played for
Essex and managed England U19
Education: Cannhall School and Norlington
Junior High School, Leytonstone; Redbridge
Technical College
Other sports followed: Football (West Ham)
Relaxations: Relaxing at home
First broadcast for: *TMS* at Sabina Park,
Jamaica 1995 (radio); Sky (TV)
Broadcasting career: Has made appearances
on Sky and Channel 4 and contributed to *TMS* but only became a *TMS* regular in
2000. Took part in Australia's Channel 9 coverage of Australia v West Indies at
Adelaide 2000-01
Highlight of broadcasting career: 'Appearing in a muck sweat on TV for pre-match
comments after a rapid shower and change having played squash with David Craven –
lesson learned!'
Books published: Include *Out of the Wilderness* (1988); *Test of Fire* (1990);
Captaincy (1992); *Gooch: My Autobiography*, with Frank Keating (1995)
Players to watch for the future: Matthew Hoggard, Alex Tudor
County as player: Essex
Role: Right-hand bat, right-arm medium bowler
County debut: 1973
County cap: 1975
Benefit: 1985 (£153,906)
Testimonial: 1995
Test debut: 1975
Tests: 118
One-Day Internationals: 125
1000 runs in a season: 20
1st-Class 50s: 217
1st-Class 100s: 115
1st-Class 200s: 12
1st-Class 300s: 1

1st-Class 5 w. in innings: 3
1st-Class catches: 555
One-Day 100s: 41
One-Day 5 w. in innings: 1
Career strike rate: 76.36
Overseas tours: England to Australia 1978-79, 1990-91 (captain), 1994-95, to Australia and India 1979-80, to West Indies 1980-81, 1989-90 (captain), to India and Sri Lanka 1981-82, to India and Pakistan (World Cup) 1987-88, to New Zealand 1991-92 (captain), to Australia and New Zealand (World Cup) 1991-92 (captain), to India 1992-93 (captain)
Overseas teams played for: Western Province, South Africa 1982-84
Highlights of playing career: 'Captaining England for the first time. Captaining England to victory over West Indies at Sabina Park 1990. Captaining Essex to first ever trophy (and scoring a century), B&H 1979'
Extras: Captained England in 34 Test matches. One of *Wisden*'s Five Cricketers of the Year 1980. Awarded OBE 1991
Best batting: 333 England v India, Lord's 1990
Best bowling: 7-14 Essex v Worcestershire, Ilford 1982

First-Class and International Career Performances

	M	Inns	NO	Runs	HS	Avge	100s	Ct	St	Runs	Wkts	Avge	Best	5wI	10wM
Test	118	215	6	8900	333	42.58	20	103	-	1069	23	46.47	3-39	-	-
All First	581	990	75	44846	333	49.01	128	555	-	8457	246	34.37	7-14	3	-
1-day Int	125	122	6	4290	142	36.98	8	45	-	1516	36	42.11	3-19	-	

GOWER, D. I.   SkySports

Name: <u>David</u> Ivon Gower
Born: 1 April 1957, Tunbridge Wells, Kent
Height: 6ft
Wife and date of marriage: Thorunn, 1992
Children: Alexandra, 25 September 1993; Samantha, 28 May 1996
Education: King's School, Canterbury; University College London
Career outside media: Director – David Gower Media, David Gower Promotions, uvine.com – the Internet Wine Exchange
Other sports played: Tennis, skiing
Relaxations: Wildlife, safaris, photography, music
First broadcast for: *Test Match Special* on England's 1989-90 tour of West Indies (radio); Channel 9 (Australia) during 1991-92 World Cup (TV)
Broadcasting career: 1994-99: commentator for BBC TV; presenter *Gower's Cricket Monthly* (BBC TV) and *David Gower's Cricket Weekly* (Radio 5). 1995 – : Team captain on *They Think It's All Over* (BBC TV). 1999 – : Presenter *Sky Sports International Cricket*

Highlight of broadcasting career: 'Brian Lara's 375 in Antigua'

Newspapers and magazines contributed to: *Sunday Telegraph, Sunday Express, The Daily Telegraph, The Times, Daily Express, The Sun, Wisden Cricket Monthly*; currently writes for *Skylines* (BA magazine)

Books published: Include *Anyone for Cricket* (1979); *With Time to Spare* (1980); *Heroes and Contemporaries* (1983); *A Right Ambition* (1986); *Gower: The Autobiography* (1992)

Counties as player: Leicestershire, Hampshire

Role: Left-hand bat

County debut: 1975 (Leicestershire), 1990 (Hampshire)

County cap: 1977 (Leicestershire), 1990 (Hampshire)

Benefit: 1987 (Leicestershire; £121,546)

Test debut: 1978

Tests: 117

One-Day Internationals: 114

1000 runs in a season: 13

1st-Class 50s: 136

1st-Class 100s: 51

1st-Class 200s: 2

1st-Class catches: 282

1st-Class stumpings: 1

One-Day 100s: 19

Overseas tours: England to Australia 1978-79, 1982-83, 1986-87, 1990-91, to Australia and India 1979-80, to West Indies 1980-81, 1985-86, to India and Sri Lanka 1981-82, to New Zealand and Pakistan 1983-84, to India 1984-85

Overseas teams played for: Claremont-Cottesloe, Western Australia 1977-78

Highlight of playing career: 'Ashes 1985'

Extras: Captain of England in 32 Test matches. One of *Wisden*'s Five Cricketers of the Year 1979. Awarded OBE in 1992

Opinions on cricket: 'Two main things to aim for: a world Test championship and a streamlined first-class set-up in England.'

Best batting: 228 Leicestershire v Glamorgan, Leicester 1989

Best bowling: 3-47 Leicestershire v Essex, Leicester 1977

	M	Inns	NO	Runs	HS	Avge	100s	Ct	St	Runs	Wkts	Avge	Best	5wI	10wM
Test	117	204	18	8231	215	44.25	18	74	-	20	1	20.00	1-1	-	-
All First	448	727	70	26339	228	40.08	53	282	1	227	4	56.75	3-47	-	-
1-day Int	114	111	8	3170	158	30.77	7	44	-	14	0	-	-	-	-

HOLDING, M. A. *SkySports*

Name: <u>Michael</u> Anthony Holding
Born: 16 February 1954, Kingston, Jamaica
Height: 6ft 3in
Education: Kingston College HS
Counties as player: Lancashire, Derbyshire
Role: Right-hand bat, right-arm fast bowler
County debut: 1981 (Lancashire),
1983 (Derbyshire)
County cap: 1983 (Derbyshire)
Test debut: 1975-76
Tests: 60
One-Day Internationals: 102
50 wickets in a season: 3
1st-Class 50s: 14
1st-Class 5 w. in innings: 39
1st-Class 10 w. in match: 5
1st-Class catches: 124
One-Day 5 w. in innings: 3
Career strike rate: 49.97

Overseas tours: West Indies to Australia 1975-76, 1979-80, 1981-82, 1984-85, to England 1976, 1980, 1984, to New Zealand 1979-80, 1986-87, to India 1983-84
Overseas teams played for: Jamaica 1972-89; Tasmania 1982-83; Canterbury, New Zealand 1987-88
Extras: One of *Wisden*'s Five Cricketers of the Year 1977
Best batting: 80 Derbyshire v Yorkshire, Chesterfield 1985
Best bowling: 8-92 West Indies v England, The Oval 1976

First-Class and International Career Performances

	M	Inns	NO	Runs	HS	Avge	100s	Ct	St	Runs	Wkts	Avge	Best	5wI	10wM
Test	60	76	10	910	73	13.78	-	22	-	5898	249	23.68	8-92	13	2
All First	222	283	43	3600	80	15.00	-	124	-	18233	778	23.43	8-92	39	5
1-day Int	102	42	11	282	64	9.09	-	30	-	3034	142	21.36	5-26	1	

HUGHES, S. P. Channel 4

Name: <u>Simon</u> Peter Hughes
Born: 20 December 1959, Kingston, Surrey
Height: 5ft 10in
Wife and date of marriage: Tanya,
June 1994
Children: Callum, March 1998;
Nancy, September 2000
Family links with cricket: Father keen club
player and coach. Uncle once hit ball over
school pavilion
Education: Latymer Upper School,
Hammersmith; Durham University
Other sports played: Football, golf, tennis
Other sports followed: Formula One
Relaxations: Modern novels, Hammond
organ

First broadcast for: LBC 1983 (radio); BBC
1991 – NatWest semi-final (TV)
Broadcasting career: 1988: Two winters writing and reading sports news on GLR.
1992-98: Commentary and interviews for BBC TV. 1999: Began with Channel 4 as
'the Analyst'
Newspapers and magazines contributed to: *Independent* (1986-93), *The Daily
Telegraph* (1994 –)
Books published: *From Minor to Major* (1992); *A Lot of Hard Yakka* (1997; Sports
Book of the Year); *Yakking Around the World* (2000); *Jargonbusting: the Analyst's
Guide to Test Cricket* (2001)
Players to watch for the future: Callum Hughes (aged 3)
Counties as player: Middlesex, Durham
Role: Right-hand bat, right-arm fast-medium bowler
County debut: 1980 (Middlesex), 1992 (Durham)
County cap: 1981 (Middlesex)
Benefit: 1991 (Middlesex; £110,000)
50 wickets in a season: 2
1st-Class 50s: 1
1st-Class 5 w. in innings: 10
1st-Class catches: 50
One-Day 5 w. in innings: 1
Career strike rate: 62.18
Highlight of playing career: 'Bowling the last over in pouring rain to win the 1986
B&H Cup'
Extras: Played in Championship and Gillette Cup winning sides in first season 1980

Opinions on cricket: 'Writing and talking about cricket is much easier than playing it.'
Best batting: 53 Middlesex v Cambridge University, Fenner's 1988
Best bowling: 7-35 Middlesex v Surrey, The Oval 1986

First-Class Career Performances

	M	Inns	NO	Runs	HS	Avge	100s	Ct	St	Runs	Wkts	Avge	Best	5wI	10wM
Test															
All First	205	226	70	1776	53	11.38	-	50	-	15139	466	32.48	7-35	10	-
1-day Int															

LANE, T. P.   BBC Test Match Special

Name: Timothy (<u>Tim</u>) Paul Lane
Born: 18 September 1951
Height: 5ft 8in
Marital status: Single
Children: Samantha, 5 June 1979
Family links with cricket: Fierce backyard rivalry with two brothers
Education: St Patrick's College; St Brendan's College; Devonport High School (Tasmania); University of Tasmania ('studied science; failed through lack of interest')
Other sports played: 'Competed in the 1984 Australian Olympic marathon trial; missed selection by a mere 80 minutes – it was a public participation run'
Other sports followed: 'Hopelessly irrational supporter of Carlton ("The Blues") in the Australian Football League'

Relaxations: 'House, garden, some very slow jogging (which justifies the over-indulgence that inevitably follows)'
First broadcast for: 7AD – 'a country station in Tasmania with a very small, tolerant audience' (radio); ABC, Tasmania (TV)
Broadcasting career: Started part-time with ABC in 1973, joining full-time staff two years later. Transferred to Melbourne 1979, working in TV until 1989 before switching to radio and becoming a member of the international cricket commentary team, covering every series in Australia since. Has covered every Olympic Games since 1984 and every Commonwealth Games since 1982. Also broadcast Australian Rules out of Melbourne, covering approximately 50 games per season
Highlight of broadcasting career: 'Broadcasting Cathy Freeman's victory in the 400 metres at the Sydney Olympics

County as player: Did not play first-class cricket but played second grade for Devonport, Tasmania in 1972 ('the call of broadcasting saved me further embarrassment')

Role: Right-hand bat, left-arm over-the-wrist spinner

Highlight of playing career: 'Represented Australian Media XI at Centurion Park and in Karachi'

Players to watch for the future: Damien Martyn – 'ready to blossom for Australia; Victoria's Michael Klinger looks a long-range tip'

Opinions on cricket: 'Obviously it is flourishing in Australia, but it would be healthier as an international game if there were greater evenness across the range of competing nations. That can only be achieved by greater attention to development in some of the struggling countries. There seems to be a crisis of confidence in umpiring brought on by a combination of the pressure of TV scrutiny and by pressure from players on the field. The first is now unavoidable, the second could be attended to by more courageous administration (refereeing etc). And, of course, there is the issue of match-fixing, although I don't see this as necessarily being as threatening to the game's popularity as do most observers. Not that it's anything to be proud of, but sport as entertainment seems to transcend the kind of judgment that the most discerning might make about an event's credibility.'

Did not play first-class cricket

LLOYD, D. SkySports

Name: David Lloyd
Born: 18 March 1947, Accrington, Lancashire
Height: 6ft
Wife's name: Diana ('second marriage')
Children: Graham, Sarah, Steven, Ben
Family links with cricket: Son Graham plays for Lancashire CCC
Education: Accrington Secondary Technical School, Oswaldtwistle
Other sports played: 'Played soccer in teenage years for Burnley B, Rossendale Utd, Accrington Stanley'
Other sports followed: Football, golf
Relaxations: Golf, flyfishing, wine and draught beer
First broadcast for: *Test Match Special* (radio); BSB, 'which soon merged with BSkyB' (TV)

Highlight of broadcasting career: 'Every day in the box' ('What could be better?! Best seat in the house, chatting with your pals and having fun')

Newspapers and magazines contributed to: *The Daily Telegraph*

Books published: *Anything But Murder*, autobiography with Alan Lee; *G'day, Ya Pommie B...*; *Out of the Rough*, with Jonathan Agnew and Peter Baxter

Players to watch for the future: Stephen Harmison, Usman Afzaal, Chris Schofield, Andrew Flintoff, Alex Tudor, Gary Keedy, Matthew Hoggard

County as player: Lancashire

Role: Left-hand bat, slow left-arm bowler

County debut: 1965

County cap: 1968

Testimonial: 1978

Test debut: 1974

Tests: 9

One-Day Internationals: 8

1000 runs in a season: 11

1st-Class 50s: 93

1st-Class 100s: 37

1st-Class 200s: 1

1st-Class 5 w. in innings: 5

1st-Class 10 w. in match: 1

1st-Class catches: 334

One-Day 100s: 7

Career strike rate: 65.81

Overseas tours: England to Australia 1974-75

Highlights of playing/coaching career: '214* England v India 1974. Coaching England and putting a structure in place – identified need for central contracts. Winning in Sharjah and playing small part in helping team in beating India, Pakistan, South Africa, Australia and New Zealand in international competition'

Opinions on cricket: 'Central contracts for England players will be a very significant development in the re-emergence of the England team. Match fixing and everything that goes with it has, on the face of it to the general public, been treated far too lightly. Pitches in England need to improve dramatically and a "standard" cricket ball (Kookaburra) should be used in cricket at first-class level. Indoor stadiums should be high on the agenda for people entrusted with the development of the game in England. ECB to provide less money to county clubs and much more to premier league development.'

Best batting: 214* England v India, Edgbaston 1974

Best bowling: 7-38 Lancashire v Gloucestershire, Lydney 1966

First-Class and International Career Performances

	M	Inns	NO	Runs	HS	Avge	100s	Ct	St	Runs	Wkts	Avge	Best	5wI	10wM
Test	9	15	2	552	214*	42.46	1	11	-	17	0	-	-	-	-
All First	407	652	74	19269	214*	33.33	38	334	-	7172	237	30.26	7-38	5	1
1-day Int	8	8	1	285	116*	40.71	1	3	-	3	1	3.00	1-3	-	

Name: <u>Simon</u> John Mann
Born: 1 November 1963, Bristol
Height: 5ft 11in
Marital status: Single
Education: Queen Elizabeth's Hospital,
Bristol; Birmingham University; London
College of Printing
Other sports played: Rugby (Bristol Schools
XV – 'on one occasion I played opposite
Stuart Barnes; by the time he had finished, I
knew it was time to give up')
Other sports followed: Football ('there is
only one football team in Bristol')
First broadcast for: Capital Radio, London,
reading the sports news (radio); BBC TV,
reporting for *Cricket Focus* (TV)
Broadcasting career: 1988-90: News and
sports reporter with Capital Radio. 1990-

2000: BBC Sport; 'last summer was my first as an official member of the *Test Match Special* commentary team although I'd commentated for *TMS* during the 1995-96 World Cup and England's tour of Zimbabwe'. 2000 – : Freelance ('offers welcome')
Highlight of broadcasting career: 'Commentating on the closing overs of the South Africa v Australia World Cup semi-final for BBC TV. It was an exciting, unpredictable one-day game with a dramatic and bizarre finish. It's a shame they are not all like that'
Newspapers and magazines contributed to: *The Guardian*
Players to watch for the future: Adam Gilchrist
County as player: Did not play first-class cricket; North London CC since 1986
Role: Right-hand bat, 'bowler of very occasional slow left-arm filth'
Overseas tours: David Hopps' XI to Sri Lanka 1997
Opinions on cricket: 'The rules for one-day cricket need to be updated constantly to provide players with new challenges and make the game less formulaic. The third umpire will become as important as, if not more important than, the two in the middle in decision-making. The role television plays will inevitably increase. At the moment, it is absurd that three million people at home know a batsman is out/not out but the umpire in the middle, using the fallible naked eye, has made the incorrect decision. What's wrong with a qualified umpire, sitting in the stand, actually making the right decision? I love Test cricket, but matches must restart when the rain stops. Covers must cover the whole ground and be flexible enough to be removed within 15 minutes.'

Did not play first-class cricket

Name: <u>Victor</u> James Marks
Born: 25 June 1955, Middle Chinnock, Somerset
Height: 5ft 9in
Wife and date of marriage: Anna, 9 September 1978
Children: Amy, 27 November 1979; Rosie, 8 November 1987
Family links with cricket: 'Father was a dangerous village cricketer'
Education: Blundell's School, Tiverton; Oxford University
Career outside media: Teaching ('but not since 1981')
Other sports played: Golf, Rugby fives, social tennis
Other sports followed: Rugby, golf, Somerset CCC

Relaxations: Golf ('but it's not very relaxing'), writing for *The Observer*
First broadcast for: BBC *TMS* in India 1984, 'filling in for indisposed Mike Selvey' (radio)
Broadcasting career: *TMS* 'for last decade or so'; TV 'very rarely'
Newspapers and magazines contributed to: *The Observer*, *The Cricketer* magazine
Books published: *Somerset County Cricket Scrapbook* (1984); *Marks Out of XI* (1985); *TCCB Guide to Better Cricket* (1987); *The Ultimate One-Day Cricket Match*, with Robin Drake (1988); *The Wisden Illustrated History of Cricket* (1989); *My Greatest Match*, with Bob Holmes (1994)
County as player: Somerset; also Oxford University
Role: Right-hand bat, off-spin bowler
County debut: 1975
County cap: 1979
Benefit: 1988
Test debut: 1982
Tests: 6
One-Day Internationals: 34
1000 runs in a season: 2
50 wickets in a season: 8
1st-Class 50s: 73
1st-Class 100s: 5
1st-Class 5 w. in innings: 40
1st-Class 10 w. in match: 5

1st-Class catches: 145
One-Day 5 w. in innings: 2
Career strike rate: 73.33
Overseas tours: England to Australia 1982-83, to New Zealand and Pakistan 1983-84, to India 1984-85
Overseas teams played for: Western Australia 1986-87; Bayswater Morley, Perth 1981-82, 1986-87
Extras: Oxford Blue 1975, 1976, 1977, 1978; captain of Oxford University 1976-77
Best batting: 134 Somerset v Worcestershire, Weston-super-Mare 1984
Best bowling: 8-17 Somerset v Lancashire, Bath 1985

First-Class and International Career Performances

	M	Inns	NO	Runs	HS	Avge	100s	Ct	St	Runs	Wkts	Avge	Best	5wI	10wM
Test	6	10	1	249	83	27.66	-	-	-	484	11	44.00	3-78	-	-
All First	342	500	90	12419	134	30.29	5	145	-	28591	859	33.28	8-17	40	5
1-day Int	34	24	3	285	44	13.57	-		8	-	1135	44	25.79	5-20	2

MARTIN-JENKINS, C. D. A.   BBC Test Match Special

Name: <u>Christopher</u> Dennis Alexander Martin-Jenkins
Born: 20 January 1945, Peterborough
Height: 6ft 3in
Wife and date of marriage: Judy, 17 April 1971
Children: James, Robin and Lucy
Family links with cricket: James captains Radley in *The Cricketer* Cup; Robin plays for Sussex
Education: Marlborough College; Cambridge University
Other sports played: Rugby fives (Cambridge 1966, 1967), golf ('gross underachiever')
Other sports followed: 'All ball games, and I have played most of them with amateur relish'
Relaxations: Music, the family, the open air
Broadcasting career: First broadcast as a freelance sports reporter in the late 1960s. BBC 1970-81 and 1984-91 (Cricket Correspondent 1973-81 and 1984-91; occasional commentator on BBC TV 1981-91). Freelance commentator 1992 –

Highlight of broadcasting career: 'Describing England winning the Ashes with monotonous regularity'
Newspapers and magazines contributed to: *The Daily Telegraph* (Cricket Correspondent 1991-99), *The Times* (Cricket Correspondent 1999 –), *The Cricketer* (Assistant Editor 1966-70; Editor 1981-91)
Books published: Numerous, including *The Complete Who's Who of Test Cricketers* and *Ball by Ball: the Story of Cricket Broadcasting*
County as player: Did not play first-class cricket but played for Surrey 2nd XI and Surrey Club and Ground
Role: Right-hand bat, right-arm medium bowler ('until 21'), off-spin bowler ('since')
Highlights of playing career: 'Reached final of Surrey Single Wicket, defeating two Test players en route. Dismissed Alvin Kallicharran with unplayable long-hop, Surrey 2nd XI v Warwickshire 2nd XI, The Oval 1971'
Extras: Captain of Marlborough College 1963. Played three years for Cambridge University Crusaders
Opinions on cricket: 'Please read *The Times*!'

Did not play first-class cricket

MAXWELL, J. E.   BBC Test Match Special

Name: James (Jim) Edward Maxwell
Born: 28 July 1950, Sydney
Height: 5ft 8in
Wife and date of marriage: Madonna, 28 March 1987
Children: Hamish, 20 June 1990; Oliver, 11 March 1994
Family links with cricket: 'Distant cousin on my mother's side was Gerry Weigall, an eccentric English cricketing person of the Golden Age. My great-grandfather W. S. Trickett was one of the early trustees of the SCG and president of the NSWCA. My father bowled undisguised googlies and was secretary of I Zingari Australia'
Education: Cranbrook School, Sydney; 'life and the racetrack (Randwick mainly)'
Other sports played: Golf ('four games in

the Royal Sydney Pennant team a long while ago – two won, two lost; now off 11, going north')

Other sports followed: 'Hockey and rugby union are my main alternative commentary sports'

Relaxations: Golf, reading, theatre, Australian Brandenburg Orchestra ('spectator only'), gardening, socialising, inventing games

First broadcast for: ABC in April 1973, cricket from December 1973 (radio); ABC in 1975 as commentator/presenter (TV)

Broadcasting career: Has covered over 140 Tests on radio 'and more one-dayers than I can remember'. Has also covered rugby league, rugby union and hockey (at Olympics, Commonwealth Games and Champions Trophy) on radio and TV and has covered snooker and table tennis on TV. Has filled a variety of roles as presenter/interviewer on *ABC Radio Grandstand*, and has several years' experience working in news on sport TV. Editor of *ABC Cricket Book* since 1988. Has created a variety of audio-cassettes for ABC, most recently a history of Australia v West Indies cricket 1930-99

Highlight of broadcasting career: 'Describing the batting of the Waugh twins at Sabina Park in 1995 when Australia regained the Frank Worrell Trophy'

Publications contributed to: *B&H Cricket Year* 1999, 2000; *Wisden Australia* 1999, 2000-01

Books published: *The First Sixty Years* (ABC 1994)

Players to watch for the future: Marlon Samuels, Shane Watson (Tasmania)

County as player: Did not play first-class cricket but played club cricket for Old Cranbrookians CC (Sydney) and Australian Old Collegians

Role: Right-hand bat, off-spin bowler, occasional wicket-keeper

Overseas tours: Several, including Australian Old Collegians World Tour 1972

Highlight of playing career: 'Hitting Don Shepherd for six off a serious inside edge at Swansea in 1972, playing for Australian Old Collegians'

Opinions on cricket: 'Australia's positive approach to Test cricket, in particular, needs to be emulated by other nations if the five-day game is to prosper, given the young generation's salivation at the instant form of the game. The four-year rotation needs to be reviewed so that Australia and South Africa can play a five-Test series somewhere. The ICC needs to be given a stronger powerbase to take uniform decisions in the long-term interest of the game – e.g. developing a higher standard of umpiring, and technology that can be universally applied. More ICC funds [should be] spent on revitalising the game in existing countries like England and the West Indies.'

Did not play first-class cricket

NICHOLAS, M. C. J.   Channel 4

Name: <u>Mark</u> Charles Jefford Nicholas
Born: 29 September 1957, London
Height: 6ft
Family links with cricket: Grandfather
(F.W.H.) played for Essex as batsman and
wicket-keeper and toured with MCC. Father
played for Navy
Education: Bradfield College
Other sports followed/played: Most –
football, golf, fives, squash
Newspapers and magazines contributed to:
The Daily Telegraph
Broadcasting career: Presenter and
commentator with Sky until 1999; with
Channel 4 1999 –
County as player: Hampshire
Role: Right-hand bat, right-arm medium
bowler

County debut: 1978
County cap: 1982
Benefit: 1991 (£174,260)
1000 runs in a season: 10
1st-Class 50s: 81
1st-Class 100s: 35
1st-Class 200s: 1
1st-Class 5 w. in innings: 2
1st-Class catches: 215
One-Day 100s: 1
Overseas tours: England B to Sri Lanka 1985-86 (captain); England A to Zimbabwe
and Kenya 1989-90 (captain)
Best batting: 206* Hampshire v Oxford University, The Parks 1982
Best bowling: 6-37 Hampshire v Somerset, Southampton 1989

First-Class Career Performances

	M	Inns	NO	Runs	HS	Avge	100s	Ct	St	Runs	Wkts	Avge	Best	5wI	10wM
Test															
All First	377	620	89	18262	206*	34.39	36	215	-	3235	72	44.93	6-37	2	-
1-day Int															

Name: <u>Dermot</u> Alexander Reeve
Born: 2 April 1963, Kowloon, Hong Kong
Height: 6ft
Marital status: Single
Children: Emily Kaye, 14 September 1988
Family links with cricket: 'Dad and brothers
Mark and Phil played at school. Mark plays
for Stanmore CC'
Education: King George V School,
Hong Kong
Career outside media: After-dinner speaker
and company director
Other sports played: 'Still play football for
North Curry FC; love my golf; swim and
boxercise for fun'
Other sports followed: Football (Man Utd),
'most sports except motor racing and horse
racing'

Relaxations: 'Three months in the winter in Western Australia; beach, golf, wine,
guitar'
Broadcasting career: Commentated on a few games for BBC TV and Sky while still
playing. Covered 1994-95 Ashes tour for Sky. Covered 1999 World Cup for BBC.
Channel 4 1999 –
Highlight of broadcasting career: 'Sharing the commentary box with Richie'
Newspapers and magazines contributed to: *The Times*, *Daily Mirror*, *The Cricketer*;
'writing for IC24 on the net this year'
Books published: *Winning Ways* (1996)
Players to watch for the future: David Sales, Ian Blackwell, Matthew Hoggard,
Steffan Jones, Robert Key, Matt Bulbeck
Counties as player: Sussex, Warwickshire, Somerset
Role: Right-hand bat, right-arm medium bowler
County debut: 1983 (Sussex), 1988 (Warwickshire), 1998 (one-day, Somerset)
County cap: 1986 (Sussex), 1989 (Warwickshire)
Benefit: 1996 (Warwickshire)
Test debut: 1991-92
Tests: 3
One-Day Internationals: 29
1000 runs in a season: 2
50 wickets in a season: 2
1st-Class 50s: 52
1st-Class 100s: 6

1st-Class 200s: 1
1st-Class 5 w. in innings: 8
1st-Class catches: 200
One-Day 100s: 1
One-Day 5 w. in innings: 1
Career strike rate: 64.76
Overseas tours: England to New Zealand 1991-92, to India and Pakistan (World Cup) 1995-96
Overseas teams played for: Hong Kong
Highlight of playing career: 'Being told by Graham Gooch I was in the team for my England debut'
Extras: Awarded OBE 1996. One of *Wisden*'s Five Cricketers of the Year 1996
Opinions on cricket: 'One neutral umpire for Tests has certainly helped. I would like to see more use of the third umpire – e.g. each team can have four referrals per innings if they feel a wrong decision has been given. It would slow play slightly but be great for the crowd with the big screen, great for TV audiences and reverse the odd bad decision. I would still like to see a domestic 20-over competition played in the evening. We must attract a new audience who perhaps work nine-to-five and are busy at weekends. Make this competition more dynamic by allowing a side to lose 15 wickets per innings.'
Best batting: 202* Warwickshire v Northamptonshire, Northampton 1990
Best bowling: 7-37 Sussex v Lancashire, Lytham 1987

First-Class and International Career Performances

	M	Inns	NO	Runs	HS	Avge	100s	Ct	St	Runs	Wkts	Avge	Best	5wI	10wM
Test	3	5	0	124	59	24.80	-	1	-	60	2	30.00	1-4	-	-
All First	241	322	77	8541	202*	34.86	7	200	-	12232	456	26.82	7-37	8	-
1-day Int	29	21	9	291	35	24.25	-	12	-	820	20	41.00	3-20	-	

RUSCOE, S.   Channel 4

Name: Sybil Ruscoe
Born: 8 August 1960, Wem, Shropshire
Height: 5ft 3in
Marital status: Single
Family links with cricket: 'My dad played local club cricket in Shropshire. My mum knitted cricket sweaters and made fine cricket teas'
Education: Adams School, Wem
Other sports played: Skiing, golf, hockey ('had to retire from hockey at 17 after injury – blood clot on the brain')
Other sports followed: All sports, football (Stoke City)
Relaxations: Travel ('have trekked across Iceland and Chile'), poetry, the First World

War, Shropshire, all music ('but especially Bob Marley, soul, Wyclef Jean, Miles Davis'), P.G. Wodehouse, *Daily Telegraph* crossword, laughing with friends

First broadcast for: Radio Wyvern, Worcester (radio); BBC TV – Top of the Pops (TV)

Broadcasting career: Local independent and BBC radio, including Radio One *Breakfast Show* with Simon Mayo and Radio 5 Live. Channel 4 cricket

Highlights of broadcasting career: 'Meeting Muhammad Ali at the Atlanta Olympics in 1996. Presenting a three-hour radio show from the Lord's Pavilion. Interviewing the anti-apartheid campaigner, the late Archbishop Trevor Huddleston'

Newspapers and magazines contributed to: *The Daily Telegraph*, *Wolverhampton Express & Star*, *Newport & Market Drayton Advertiser*, *North Shropshire Journal*

Books published: 'Currently writing a semi-autobiographical cricket/media novel'

Players to watch for the future: Gary Pratt, Ian Pattison, Ben Platt (Shropshire)

County as player: Did not play first-class cricket but is an 'enthusiastic beach and garden cricketer – useful leg-spinner'

Highlights of playing career: 'Reverse-sweeping Henry Olonga on Southend beach. Facing Allan Donald at Edgbaston. Fielding with Michael Slater at the Oswestry Disabled Cricket Club. Being complimented by Lord Cowdrey on my batting style at Arundel'

Opinions on cricket: 'The ECB, counties and MCC should all be putting even more effort into making cricket as "inclusive" as possible. Too often certain sections of people still feel excluded from the game. We should all – from broadcasters to players – be campaigning for more cricket in schools.'

Did not play first-class cricket

SELVEY, M. W. W. BBC Test Match Special

Name: <u>Michael</u> Walter William Selvey
Born: 25 April 1948, London
Height: 6ft 2in
Wife and date of marriage: Sarah,
23 October 1992
Children: Nichola, 12 May 1975 ('by first
marriage'); Joshua, Adam and Hannah,
9 January 1997 (triplets)
Education: Battersea Grammar School;
University of Manchester; Cambridge
University
Other sports played: Golf (6 handicap)
Other sports followed: 'Most that do not
involve horses, cars, footballers, wrestlers,
attempts to beat people senseless, or pastimes
masquerading as sport'
Relaxations: Golf, gym, kids, pub, guitar,
harmonica, reading, cooking, music
First broadcast for: *Test Match Special*, India 1985 (radio); BBC – John Player
League (TV)
Broadcasting career: Regular summariser for *TMS* since 1985
Highlights of broadcasting career: 'Any England win. Any great player in top form'
Newspapers and magazines contributed to: *The Guardian* (Cricket Correspondent
1987 –), *Wisden Cricket Monthly*
Books published: *The Ashes Surrendered* (1989)
Players to watch for the future: Joshua, Adam and Hannah Selvey
Counties as player: Surrey, Middlesex, Glamorgan; also Cambridge University
Role: Right-hand bat, right-arm fast-medium bowler
County debut: 1968 (Surrey), 1972 (Middlesex), 1983 (Glamorgan)
County cap: 1973 (Middlesex), 1983 (Glamorgan)
Test debut: 1976
Tests: 3
50 wickets in a season: 6
100 wickets in a season: 1
1st-Class 50s: 4
1st-Class 5 w. in innings: 38
1st-Class 10 w. in match: 4
1st-Class catches: 80
One-Day 5 w. in innings: 2
Career strike rate: 58.90
Overseas tours: England to Australia and India 1976-77

Overseas teams played for: University-St Helier, Auckland 1978-80
Highlight of playing career: 'Taking 3-6 in first 20 balls in Tests'
Extras: Cambridge Blue 1971
Opinions on cricket: 'Not what it was, blah, blah … young players of today, blah, blah … pitches, blah, blah … spinners, blah, blah … money, blah, blah … in my day, blah blah … zzzzzz. All rubbish of course. Greatest improvements are in fielding, which is phenomenal, and the capacity to chase targets, which is equally so. Pleased that England pace bowlers have finally understood the standards required.'
Best batting: 67 Middlesex v Zimbabwe, Bulawayo 1980-81
Best bowling: 7-20 Middlesex v Gloucestershire, Gloucester 1976

First-Class and International Career Performances

	M	Inns	NO	Runs	HS	Avge	100s	Ct	St	Runs	Wkts	Avge	Best	5wI	10wM
Test	3	5	3	15	5*	7.50	-	1	-	343	6	57.16	4-41	-	-
All First	278	278	88	2399	67	12.62	-	80	-	20582	772	26.66	7-20	38	4
1-day Int															

THOMSON, J. R.   BBC Test Match Special

Name: Jeffrey (<u>Jeff</u>) Robert Thomson
Born: 16 August 1950, Bankstown, Sydney
Family links with cricket: Father played for Bankstown district, Sydney. Four brothers all played grade cricket
Education: Punchbowl High School, Bankstown
Broadcasting career: Worked for Queensland radio station 4IP in the 1970s as a public relations executive
Books published: Include *Thommo*, with David Frith (1980)
County as player: Middlesex
Role: Right-hand bat, right-arm fast bowler
County debut: 1981 (only season)
Test debut: 1972-73
Tests: 51
One-Day Internationals: 50
1st-Class 50s: 2
1st-Class 5 w. in innings: 28
1st-Class 10 w. in match: 3
1st-Class catches: 61
One-Day 5 w. in innings: 1

Overseas tours: Australia to England 1975, 1977, 1985, to West Indies 1977-78 (vice-captain), to New Zealand 1981-82, to Pakistan 1982-83
Overseas teams played for: Bankstown-Canterbury, Sydney; New South Wales 1972-73 – 1973-74; Queensland 1974-75 – 1985-86
Extras: First Queensland bowler to take 300 Sheffield Shield wickets
Best batting: 61 Queensland v Victoria, Brisbane 1974-75
Best bowling: 7-27 Queensland v Western Australia, Brisbane 1984-85

First-Class and International Career Performances

	M	Inns	NO	Runs	HS	Avge	100s	Ct	St	Runs	Wkts	Avge	Best	5wI	10wM
Test	51	73	20	679	49	12.81	-	20	-	5602	200	28.01	6-46	8	-
All First	187	216	64	2065	61	13.58	-	61	-	17864	675	26.46	7-27	28	3
1-day Int	50	30	6	181	21	7.54	-	9	-	1942	55	35.30	4-67	-	

WILLIS, R. G. D.   SkySports

Name: Robert (<u>Bob</u>) George Dylan Willis
Born: 30 May 1949, Sunderland
Height: 6ft 6in
Family links with cricket: Brother, David, kept wicket for Blackheath CC
Education: Royal Grammar School, Guildford
Other sports played: Football (kept goal for Guildford City)
Newspapers and magazines contributed to: Include *Wisden Cricket Monthly*
Books published: Include *Diary of a Cricket Season* (1979); *Cricket Revolution* (1981)
Counties as player: Surrey, Warwickshire
Role: Right-hand bat, right-arm fast bowler
County debut: 1969 (Surrey), 1972 (Warwickshire)
County cap: 1972 (Warwickshire)
Benefit: 1981 (Warwickshire; £44,951)
Test debut: 1970-71
Tests: 90
One-Day Internationals: 64
50 wickets in a season: 5
1st-Class 50s: 2
1st-Class 5 w. in innings: 34
1st-Class 10 w. in match: 2

1st-Class catches: 134
One-Day 5 w. in innings: 4
Career strike rate: 53.37
Overseas tours: England to Australia and New Zealand 1970-71, 1974-75, to West Indies 1973-74, 1980-81 (vice-captain; returned early, injured), to Australia and India 1976-77, 1979-80 (vice-captain), to Pakistan and New Zealand 1977-78, 1983-84 (captain), to Australia 1978-79 (vice-captain), 1982-83 (captain), to India and Sri Lanka 1981-82 (vice-captain)
Extras: Captained England in 18 Test matches. One of *Wisden*'s Five Cricketers of the Year 1978. Awarded MBE 1982
Best batting: 72 Warwickshire v Indians, Edgbaston 1982
Best bowling: 8-32 Warwickshire v Gloucestershire, Bristol 1977

First-Class and International Career Performances

	M	Inns	NO	Runs	HS	Avge	100s	Ct	St	Runs	Wkts	Avge	Best	5wl	10wM
Test	90	128	55	840	28*	11.50	-	39	-	8190	325	25.20	8-43	16	-
All First	308	333	145	2690	72	14.30	-	134	-	22468	899	24.99	8-32	34	2
1-day Int	64	22	14	83	24	10.37	-	22	-	1968	80	24.60	4-11	-	

THE 2000 SEASON

ROLL OF HONOUR 2000

PPP HEALTHCARE CHAMPIONSHIP

Division One

		P	W	L	D	T	Bt	Bl	Pts
1	Surrey (1)	16	9	2	5	0	44	41	213
2	Lancashire (2)	16	7	1	8	0	35	42	193
3	Yorkshire (6)	16	7	2	7	0	36	48	188
4	Leicestershire (3)	16	4	3	9	0	42	39	165
5	Somerset (=4)	16	2	4	10	0	41	40	145
6	Kent (=4)	16	4	4	8	0	18	42	140
7	Hampshire (7)	16	3	9	4	0	20	48	112
8	Durham (8)	16	2	9	5	0	27	41	112
9	Derbyshire (=9)	16	2	6	8	0	19	44	111

The bottom three counties were relegated to Division Two for the 2001 season

Division Two

		P	W	L	D	T	Bt	Bl	Pts
1	Northamptonshire (13)	16	7	4	5	0	39	45	188
2	Essex (12)	16	5	2	9	0	28	41	165
3	Glamorgan (14)	16	5	3	8	0	27	41	160
4	Gloucestershire (18)	16	6	4	6	0	20	42	158
5	Worcestershire (15)	16	5	5	6	0	25	42	151
6	Warwickshire (=9)	16	2	3	11	0	47	35	150
7	Nottinghamshire (17)	16	2	4	10	0	41	43	148
8	Middlesex (16)	16	2	6	8	0	36	46	138
9	Sussex (11)	16	3	6	7	0	31	39	134

The top three counties were promoted to Division One for the 2001 season

Yorkshire, Hampshire and Derbyshire were deducted eight points for a poor pitch

NORWICH UNION NATIONAL LEAGUE

Division One

		P	W	L	T	NR	Pts
1	Gloucestershire (I/4)	16	9	6	0	1	38
2	Yorkshire (I/5)	16	9	7	0	0	36
3	Northamptonshire (II/3)	16	9	7	0	0	36
4	Leicestershire (I/6)	16	7	6	2	1	34
5	Kent (I/3)	16	7	7	0	2	32
6	Somerset (II/2)	16	7	8	0	1	30
7	Worcestershire (I/2)	16	6	8	0	2	28
8	Lancashire (I/1)	16	6	8	1	1	28
9	Sussex (II/1)	16	5	8	1	2	26

The bottom three counties were relegated to Division Two for the 2001 season

Division Two

		P	W	L	T	NR	Pts
1	Surrey (II/6)	16	11	3	0	2	48
2	Nottinghamshire (II/5)	16	11	4	0	1	46
3	Warwickshire (I/7)	16	10	5	1	0	42
4	Middlesex (II/7)	16	8	5	1	2	38
5	Essex (I/9)	16	7	7	0	2	32
6	Glamorgan (II/4)	16	7	7	2	0	32
7	Durham (II/9)	16	5	11	0	0	20
8	Hampshire (I/8)	16	5	11	0	0	20
9	Derbyshire (II/8)	16	2	13	0	1	10

The top three counties were promoted to Division One for the 2001 season

NATWEST TROPHY

Winners: Gloucestershire
Runners-up: Warwickshire

BENSON AND HEDGES CUP

Winners: Gloucestershire
Runners-up: Glamorgan

2000 AVERAGES (all first-class matches)

BATTING AVERAGES – including fielding
Qualifying requirements: 6 completed innings

Name	Matches	Inns	NO	Runs	HS	Avge	100s	50s	Ct	St
M.G.Bevan	12	18	3	1124	174	74.93	5	1	2	-
M.H.Richardson	6	11	2	642	212*	71.33	1	4	1	-
S.Chanderpaul	5	9	3	418	161*	69.66	2	1	3	-
D.S.Lehmann	16	23	1	1477	136	67.13	4	9	8	-
M.W.Goodwin	8	12	2	651	194	65.10	3	1	3	-
P.D.Bowler	18	26	5	1305	157*	62.14	5	4	8	-
J.L.Langer	16	27	3	1472	213*	61.33	5	7	25	-
M.L.Hayden	15	22	0	1270	164	57.72	4	6	21	-
R.Dravid	16	25	3	1221	182	55.50	2	8	15	-
S.G.Law	16	27	2	1385	189	55.40	5	6	19	-
R.C.Irani	17	29	7	1196	168*	54.36	1	9	2	-
A.D.Brown	16	23	5	935	295*	51.94	2	4	16	-
M.T.G.Elliott	13	21	0	1076	177	51.23	4	4	19	-
D.P.Ostler	16	24	2	1096	145	49.81	2	7	19	-
L.R.Prittipaul	4	6	0	298	152	49.66	1	1	1	-
M.R.Ramprakash	17	28	4	1183	120*	49.29	4	7	15	-
R.J.Bailey	13	19	4	728	118	48.53	2	5	4	-
A.Habib	17	23	1	1038	172*	47.18	2	8	8	-
N.H.Fairbrother	15	23	5	823	138	45.72	2	3	16	-
K.J.Barnett	11	16	2	640	118*	45.71	2	3	8	-
M.A.Wagh	9	16	3	592	137	45.53	2	3	4	-
J.P.Crawley	15	22	1	951	156	45.28	5	-	6	-
P.A.J.DeFreitas	14	18	3	677	123*	45.13	1	4	1	-
U.Afzaal	16	26	3	1018	151*	44.26	3	4	9	-
V.S.Solanki	16	28	2	1138	161*	43.76	2	8	23	-
M.J.Powell	17	26	2	1046	145	43.58	2	8	10	-
S.M.Katich	16	28	3	1089	137*	43.56	3	5	21	-
M.E.Trescothick	12	19	2	738	105	43.41	1	5	11	-
M.P.Vaughan	13	21	1	866	155*	43.30	2	4	2	-
M.A.Butcher	16	25	4	891	191	42.42	2	3	13	-
D.G.Cork	14	17	4	542	200*	41.69	1	2	10	-
J.M.Dakin	9	12	1	458	135	41.63	1	3	2	-
A.L.Penberthy	15	21	2	785	116	41.31	1	5	10	-
W.S.Kendall	18	31	3	1156	161	41.28	3	5	17	-
S.P.James	17	28	2	1070	309*	41.15	3	2	5	-
M.Burns	15	20	1	775	160	40.78	2	5	3	-
T.L.Penney	13	18	4	569	100*	40.64	1	2	8	-
I.J.Ward	16	25	3	894	158*	40.63	3	3	4	-
A.F.Giles	13	14	3	444	128*	40.36	1	1	4	-
C.J.Adams	16	26	3	913	156	39.69	1	7	15	-
N.V.Knight	10	15	0	593	233	39.53	1	1	7	-
J.Cox	17	26	1	983	171	39.32	3	3	6	-

Name	Matches	Inns	NO	Runs	HS	Avge	100s	50s	Ct	St
G.D.Rose	15	18	5	510	124	39.23	2	1	4	-
D.A.Leatherdale	17	30	5	975	132*	39.00	2	7	9	-
D.R.Brown	16	22	6	622	203	38.87	1	2	11	-
M.A.Atherton	18	29	1	1068	136	38.14	3	6	15	-
D.L.Hemp	17	24	2	834	129	37.90	1	5	9	-
K.A.Parsons	15	22	2	745	193*	37.25	2	1	17	-
M.G.N.Windows	19	31	3	1042	166	37.21	2	6	5	-
W.W.Hinds	11	19	1	669	150	37.16	3	3	11	-
A.D.R.Campbell	8	10	2	292	150*	36.50	1	1	11	-
N.Shahid	9	12	0	434	80	36.16	-	3	13	-
D.J.G.Sales	13	20	0	713	276	35.65	1	5	9	-
A.D.Shaw	12	18	5	462	88*	35.53	-	3	29	4
W.K.Hegg	17	23	5	639	128	35.50	1	4	39	6
J.N.Snape	15	20	3	598	69	35.17	-	4	8	-
G.A.Hick	14	24	2	773	122	35.13	3	3	16	-
D.D.J.Robinson	12	19	3	561	93*	35.06	-	4	5	-
A.Flintoff	13	19	1	631	119	35.05	1	4	12	-
A.Dale	17	27	3	837	81	34.87	-	5	8	-
R.J.Warren	9	13	1	417	151	34.75	1	2	3	-
J.E.R.Gallian	16	26	3	796	150	34.60	3	-	23	-
D.J.Bicknell	16	28	3	858	180*	34.32	2	2	3	-
R.W.J.Howitt	6	10	2	274	118*	34.25	1	1	-	-
M.P.Maynard	15	22	1	716	119*	34.09	2	5	17	2
Q.J.Hughes	6	10	3	237	119	33.85	1	1	-	-
A.Flower	7	10	1	300	116*	33.33	1	-	16	1
N.C.Johnson	7	8	0	266	83	33.25	-	3	6	-
A.J.Strauss	17	28	2	862	111*	33.15	1	3	6	-
M.J.DiVenuto	16	25	3	725	92*	32.95	-	6	12	-
B.F.Smith	17	23	2	686	111*	32.66	2	2	10	-
M.A.Roseberry	11	20	3	549	139*	32.29	1	2	3	-
A.J.Stewart	10	15	1	451	124*	32.21	2	-	24	1
P.A.Cottey	16	23	0	740	154	32.17	2	2	8	-
P.A.Nixon	18	25	7	578	134*	32.11	1	3	47	2
R.R.Montgomerie	17	30	2	899	133	32.10	2	4	17	-
G.E.Welton	13	23	2	674	200*	32.09	1	3	8	-
M.P.Dowman	17	29	3	833	140	32.03	2	4	11	-
S.C.Ganguly	14	21	0	671	99	31.95	-	6	10	-
S.D.Stubbings	18	32	4	889	135*	31.75	1	4	4	-
D.Ripley	13	18	3	475	56	31.66	-	3	38	4
S.L.Campbell	12	20	0	629	146	31.45	1	4	13	-
J.W.Cook	11	17	1	502	137	31.37	2	1	4	-
M.P.Bicknell	15	18	2	500	79*	31.25	-	4	5	-
S.P.Titchard	11	19	2	530	141*	31.17	1	3	-	-
S.B.Styris	5	9	1	247	72	30.87	-	1	4	-
U.B.A.Rashid	15	22	3	585	110	30.78	1	4	6	-
G.J.Whittall	7	11	1	304	89	30.40	-	2	2	-
I.J.Harvey	10	14	1	395	79	30.38	-	4	10	-
R.G.Smalley	6	10	1	272	83	30.22	-	1	6	4
R.R.Sarwan	9	16	2	423	59*	30.21	-	3	2	-

Name	Matches	Inns	NO	Runs	HS	Avge	100s	50s	Ct	St
C.H.Gayle	8	14	1	392	128	30.15	1	2	5	-
A.R.Danson	6	9	2	211	117*	30.14	1	-	4	-
M.J.Powell	18	28	0	843	128	30.10	2	4	11	-
J.E.Morris	13	20	0	601	115	30.05	1	3	7	-
A.J.Hollioake	16	23	0	689	80	29.95	-	3	27	-
J.J.Porter	6	10	0	297	93	29.70	-	4	-	-
R.C.Russell	16	23	3	593	110*	29.65	1	2	50	4
M.B.Loye	12	18	1	504	93	29.64	-	3	1	-
M.V.Fleming	14	18	2	471	47	29.43	-	-	4	-
N.J.Speak	14	24	5	552	89*	29.05	-	4	3	-
G.D.Lloyd	16	22	1	608	126	28.95	1	2	20	-
V.J.Wells	15	19	0	549	98	28.89	-	4	8	-
A.McGrath	10	14	1	375	133	28.84	1	1	8	-
B.C.Lara	10	18	0	519	176	28.83	2	1	15	-
G.M.Hamilton	13	16	2	402	125	28.71	1	2	7	-
T.R.Gripper	6	11	2	258	66*	28.66	-	2	5	-
G.W.White	18	32	4	797	96	28.46	-	5	14	-
P.R.Pollard	14	24	1	652	123*	28.34	1	5	3	-
A.J.Tudor	14	16	6	283	64*	28.30	-	1	5	-
C.M.Tolley	6	9	1	223	60	27.87	-	2	2	-
D.J.Millns	8	11	4	195	50*	27.85	-	1	2	-
E.C.Joyce	6	8	1	195	51	27.85	-	1	7	-
A.P.Grayson	17	31	2	807	144	27.82	1	5	10	-
I.D.Blackwell	18	23	2	582	109	27.71	1	2	6	-
P.J.Prichard	17	31	3	775	96	27.67	-	5	10	-
M.H.W.Papps	5	10	2	220	63	27.50	-	1	2	1
S.D.Peters	16	28	6	602	77*	27.36	-	4	12	-
M.V.Nagamootoo	9	16	2	381	100	27.21	1	-	2	-
L.D.Sutton	10	16	1	407	79	27.13	-	2	20	1
S.J.Rhodes	18	28	6	591	103	26.86	1	1	54	1
E.J.Wilson	17	31	2	779	104*	26.86	2	4	9	-
A.S.Rollins	16	24	0	636	100	26.50	1	4	19	-
C.P.Schofield	17	22	2	528	70*	26.40	-	4	6	-
D.A.Kenway	15	27	1	685	136	26.34	1	3	13	1
P.J.Franks	13	18	1	447	60	26.29	-	3	5	-
D.S.Lucas	10	12	5	184	46*	26.28	-	-	3	-
D.L.Maddy	17	25	1	630	102	26.25	1	4	16	-
N.D.Burns	16	21	4	445	67*	26.17	-	3	36	1
C.G.Taylor	12	22	3	492	104	25.89	1	-	8	-
S.D.Thomas	17	20	7	336	52	25.84	-	1	2	-
N.M.K.Smith	17	20	2	464	87	25.77	-	4	8	-
M.J.Walker	15	25	4	536	61	25.52	-	1	12	-
P.D.Collingwood	16	27	0	681	111	25.22	1	4	19	-
V.J.Craven	8	11	1	251	58	25.10	-	2	6	-
G.P.Swann	16	24	0	597	72	24.87	-	3	8	-
D.Byas	17	26	2	596	84	24.83	-	2	22	-
J.J.B.Lewis	16	28	2	645	115	24.80	1	4	8	-
J.I.Englefield	6	11	1	248	90	24.80	-	1	3	-
O.A.Shah	12	20	0	489	76	24.45	-	3	7	-

Name	Matches	Inns	NO	Runs	HS	Avge	100s	50s	Ct	St
A.F.G.Griffith	11	21	1	486	130	24.30	1	2	5	-
I.D.K.Salisbury	16	19	6	313	57*	24.07	-	2	6	-
C.M.W.Read	16	23	3	479	56*	23.95	-	3	40	-
W.G.Khan	3	6	0	143	74	23.83	-	1	-	-
J.C.Scuderi	9	13	2	261	51	23.72	-	1	-	-
G.P.Thorpe	11	16	0	376	115	23.50	1	1	9	-
R.D.Jacobs	8	14	2	281	78	23.41	-	1	23	2
A.N.Aymes	13	22	5	398	74*	23.41	-	3	32	6
R.C.Driver	11	20	4	372	64	23.25	-	2	2	-
E.T.Smith	11	18	0	415	175	23.05	1	-	6	-
K.P.Dutch	5	7	0	160	91	22.85	-	2	9	-
R.S.C.Martin-Jenkins	15	23	1	499	86	22.68	-	2	4	-
I.D.Fisher	6	10	2	181	68*	22.62	-	1	1	-
G.P.Sulzberger	6	11	0	248	60	22.54	-	1	8	-
M.A.Ealham	11	14	1	293	83	22.53	-	2	3	-
D.R.Hewson	11	21	1	448	67	22.40	-	3	5	-
J.P.Pyemont	11	15	1	313	124	22.35	1	-	5	-
A.Singh	5	7	0	156	79	22.28	-	1	1	-
D.P.Fulton	14	24	1	512	115	22.26	1	1	29	-
M.J.Chilton	10	14	1	286	46	22.00	-	-	10	-
A.G.Wharf	10	15	2	285	101*	21.92	2	-	5	-
R.D.B.Croft	14	17	4	282	56	21.69	-	2	4	-
S.K.Warne	15	22	2	431	69	21.55	-	3	14	-
G.M.Fellows	14	20	4	341	46	21.31	-	-	8	-
A.Pratt	7	10	1	191	38	21.22	-	-	7	-
A.R.K.Pierson	6	9	3	126	48	21.00	-	-	3	-
R.W.T.Key	17	29	1	584	83	20.85	-	5	4	-
M.P.Speight	11	18	1	354	55	20.82	-	1	29	-
D.I.Stevens	15	22	0	457	78	20.77	-	2	6	-
P.Johnson	12	19	2	353	100	20.76	1	-	9	-
R.L.Johnson	15	23	3	414	69	20.70	-	2	13	-
A.D.Mascarenhas	16	24	1	473	100	20.56	1	2	3	-
R.A.Smith	17	29	0	595	61	20.51	-	3	3	-
R.J.Turner	18	26	2	492	75	20.50	-	2	39	-
J.S.Laney	14	25	1	489	81	20.37	-	2	12	-
M.C.J.Ball	9	14	2	244	53	20.33	-	1	13	-
P.N.Weekes	8	13	1	244	39	20.33	-	-	8	-
D.C.Nash	17	24	2	445	75*	20.22	-	1	32	4
I.J.Sutcliffe	12	17	1	319	53	19.93	-	2	11	-
P.C.L.Holloway	13	20	1	377	113	19.84	1	1	9	-
M.N.Lathwell	9	14	1	257	54*	19.76	-	1	4	-
J.N.Batty	13	16	2	276	100*	19.71	1	-	29	7
A.F.Gofton	6	7	1	117	47*	19.50	-	-	-	-
S.M.Guy	6	9	2	136	42	19.42	-	-	21	2
M.T.E.Peirce	14	24	1	446	86	19.39	-	2	3	-
T.H.C.Hancock	15	22	1	407	85	19.38	-	1	7	-
W.Phillip	6	11	3	155	67*	19.37	-	1	22	1
S.D.Udal	12	21	3	346	85	19.22	-	1	8	-
P.D.Trego	7	8	1	134	62	19.14	-	1	3	-

Name	Matches	Inns	NO	Runs	HS	Avge	100s	50s	Ct	St
A.W.Evans	4	6	0	114	58	19.00	-	1	-	-
M.E.Cassar	14	20	2	341	77*	18.94	-	1	1	-
R.M.S.Weston	6	10	1	170	39	18.88	-	-	3	-
S.J.Lacey	11	17	4	242	55*	18.61	-	1	1	-
J.C.Adams	10	17	0	313	98	18.41	-	2	6	-
M.J.Wood	11	17	3	256	100*	18.28	1	-	5	-
Saqlain Mushtaq	12	14	2	217	66	18.08	-	2	8	-
D.R.Law	15	23	3	360	68*	18.00	-	2	6	-
M.M.Patel	14	16	1	269	60	17.93	-	1	13	-
M.P.Smethurst	16	19	10	161	66	17.88	-	1	3	-
S.L.Watkin	13	13	6	125	51	17.85	-	1	1	-
K.Newell	13	21	1	356	64	17.80	-	1	5	-
Kabir Ali	10	15	3	213	50*	17.75	-	1	5	-
S.W.Weenink	6	9	2	124	72*	17.71	-	1	4	-
A.P.Cowan	14	20	6	245	67	17.50	-	1	4	-
A.P.Wells	12	19	2	297	60*	17.47	-	2	3	-
S.R.Lampitt	18	27	8	331	56*	17.42	-	1	12	-
M.J.McCague	7	11	0	191	72	17.36	-	1	2	-
K.J.Piper	16	18	3	260	69	17.33	-	1	28	3
C.E.W.Silverwood	9	11	1	173	48	17.30	-	-	1	-
P.J.Hartley	9	11	5	103	23*	17.16	-	-	-	-
C.D.Crowe	8	8	2	103	30	17.16	-	-	4	-
M.W.Alleyne	16	24	0	410	126	17.08	1	-	14	-
K.M.Krikken	10	13	0	221	51	17.00	-	1	18	2
P.J.Martin	9	11	3	134	40	16.75	-	-	2	-
N.J.Wilton	8	11	2	150	46	16.66	-	-	19	-
G.Welch	7	8	1	116	55	16.57	-	1	1	-
N.Peng	8	14	0	231	98	16.50	-	1	1	-
G.W.Flower	7	13	2	180	76*	16.36	-	1	10	-
R.J.Cunliffe	9	14	0	229	74	16.35	-	1	10	-
F.A.Rose	8	11	1	162	48	16.20	-	-	-	-
W.L.Law	8	11	1	161	85	16.10	-	1	4	-
S.V.Carlisle	6	7	0	112	65	16.00	-	1	6	-
W.P.C.Weston	10	19	2	269	58*	15.82	-	2	1	-
M.J.Cawdron	6	8	0	125	32	15.62	-	-	1	-
R.J.Blakey	12	18	1	264	56	15.52	-	1	41	2
S.Widdup	9	14	1	201	44	15.46	-	-	6	-
R.K.Illingworth	10	12	2	154	44*	15.40	-	-	5	-
A.J.Harris	11	14	4	153	39	15.30	-	-	4	-
M.J.Birks	6	7	0	107	32	15.28	-	-	8	2
J.A.H.Marshall	5	9	0	133	69	14.77	-	1	11	-
M.A.Gough	7	12	0	176	33	14.66	-	-	3	-
C.E.L.Ambrose	6	10	2	117	36*	14.62	-	-	1	-
J.A.Daley	10	17	0	247	50	14.52	-	1	4	-
S.J.Cook	7	10	0	145	43	14.50	-	-	2	-
B.L.Hutton	10	15	2	188	55	14.46	-	1	8	-
A.R.C.Fraser	15	22	6	227	30	14.18	-	-	4	-
A.C.Morris	8	12	1	154	60	14.00	-	1	4	-
M.N.Bowen	4	6	0	83	24	13.83	-	-	2	-

Name	Matches	Inns	NO	Runs	HS	Avge	100s	50s	Ct	St
T.M.Smith	10	13	2	152	53*	13.81	-	1	4	-
M.M.Betts	11	18	4	192	55	13.71	-	1	7	-
J.D.Middlebrook	11	15	0	201	45	13.40	-	-	5	-
J.D.P.Oram	4	7	0	93	27	13.28	-	-	1	-
M.C.Ilott	10	13	4	119	25	13.22	-	-	4	-
D.M.Cousins	16	23	7	210	29*	13.12	-	-	3	-
D.Gough	10	13	3	131	23*	13.10	-	-	3	-
T.A.Munton	16	22	7	191	52	12.73	-	1	7	-
C.White	7	9	1	100	27	12.50	-	-	1	-
W.J.House	6	10	1	112	35	12.44	-	-	3	-
B.W.Gannon	8	10	4	74	28	12.33	-	-	3	-
T.R.Ward	7	10	1	110	39	12.22	-	-	8	-
G.Chapple	16	19	1	218	41	12.11	-	-	4	-
J.Wood	10	15	0	181	44	12.06	-	-	2	-
G.Keedy	13	15	3	144	34	12.00	-	-	2	-
J.Ormond	12	15	7	95	30*	11.87	-	-	1	-
C.A.Sayers	6	8	2	71	46	11.83	-	-	4	-
I.Mohammed	4	6	0	71	24	11.83	-	-	1	-
T.J.Mason	10	14	2	140	52*	11.66	-	1	4	-
S.J.Renshaw	4	7	1	69	26	11.50	-	-	1	-
P.Aldred	11	14	1	149	38	11.46	-	-	4	-
C.C.Lewis	5	7	0	80	24	11.42	-	-	6	-
A.Kumble	12	16	0	181	56	11.31	-	1	3	-
I.N.Flanagan	4	8	0	89	23	11.12	-	-	7	-
N.Hussain	10	16	1	166	33	11.06	-	-	7	-
B.C.Hollioake	10	14	1	142	29	10.92	-	-	8	-
S.J.W.Lewis	6	10	1	98	26	10.88	-	-	2	-
A.R.Caddick	10	15	2	141	21*	10.84	-	-	3	-
J.P.Taylor	7	10	1	96	27	10.66	-	-	3	-
B.J.Hyam	15	24	0	256	53	10.66	-	1	49	6
S.R.G.Francis	9	13	7	64	30*	10.66	-	-	1	-
N.Killeen	10	15	1	144	38*	10.28	-	-	1	-
P.S.Jones	15	16	4	122	56*	10.16	-	1	4	-
A.J.Sexton	4	7	0	71	36	10.14	-	-	3	-
J.M.M.Averis	5	7	1	60	25*	10.00	-	-	1	-
M.K.Davies	5	8	0	79	25	9.87	-	-	2	-
A.A.Donald	8	9	2	69	18	9.85	-	-	3	-
G.D.McGrath	14	15	3	112	55	9.33	-	1	3	-
M.H.Yardy	4	8	1	64	25	9.14	-	-	-	-
S.J.E.Brown	14	21	12	82	19	9.11	-	-	2	-
J.J.Bates	4	6	0	54	17	9.00	-	-	5	-
S.J.Harmison	11	15	3	104	33*	8.66	-	-	2	-
A.Sheriyar	11	11	3	69	17	8.62	-	-	-	-
N.C.Phillips	5	9	0	76	29	8.44	-	-	3	-
P.C.R.Tufnell	16	21	9	100	19	8.33	-	-	4	-
N.A.M.McLean	9	17	2	122	29	8.13	-	-	-	-
R.J.Kirtley	16	22	4	146	26*	8.11	-	-	5	-
J.Lewis	17	23	2	169	38	8.04	-	-	4	-
D.A.Cosker	12	15	4	88	14*	8.00	-	-	9	-

Name	Matches	Inns	NO	Runs	HS	Avge	100s	50s	Ct	St
M.J.Rawnsley	9	13	0	102	18	7.84	-	-	5	-
J.D.Lewry	17	24	5	149	39	7.84	-	-	5	-
R.D.King	9	12	4	62	21	7.75	-	-	-	-
M.J.Saggers	14	17	5	91	24	7.58	-	-	3	-
R.D.Stemp	11	11	5	45	11	7.50	-	-	7	-
M.J.Hoggard	16	18	4	103	20*	7.35	-	-	3	-
R.J.Logan	6	8	1	51	24	7.28	-	-	1	-
A.D.Patterson	8	10	1	67	20*	6.70	-	-	17	-
J.P.Stephenson	10	15	0	96	19	6.40	-	-	7	-
A.D.Mullally	8	12	2	60	12	6.00	-	-	-	-
P.M.Such	12	13	4	53	14	5.88	-	-	3	-
D.D.Masters	16	20	7	71	21	5.46	-	-	4	-
C.D.Collymore	6	9	3	29	14	4.83	-	-	1	-
C.A.Walsh	6	9	3	26	7	4.33	-	-	-	-
K.J.Dean	12	15	3	49	22	4.08	-	-	-	-
A.S.Bones	4	7	0	24	7	3.42	-	-	-	-
J.F.Brown	10	14	5	30	11	3.33	-	-	-	-
E.S.H.Giddins	12	11	3	25	14	3.12	-	-	3	-
D.E.Malcolm	7	10	1	24	8	2.66	-	-	1	-
T.F.Bloomfield	10	8	2	16	4*	2.66	-	-	-	-
Kadeer Ali	4	7	0	13	8	1.85	-	-	1	-
T.P.Cotterell	8	10	4	7	5*	1.16	-	-	2	-
P.M.Hutchison	7	8	2	3	3*	0.50	-	-	3	-

BOWLING AVERAGES
Qualifying requirements: 10 wickets taken

Name	Overs	Mdns	Runs	Wkts	Avge	Best	5wI	10wM
C.A.Walsh	242.2	106	457	40	11.42	6-74	3	1
R.J.Sidebottom	134.2	46	300	24	12.50	6-16	4	1
G.D.McGrath	415.4	132	1057	80	13.21	8-41	6	3
M.Mbangwa	211.5	86	428	30	14.26	6-14	2	1
Saqlain Mushtaq	451.2	127	1016	66	15.39	7-11	6	2
A.R.Caddick	329.4	98	848	55	15.41	7-64	5	2
P.J.Martin	236.2	83	464	30	15.46	7-67	3	-
G.P.Sulzberger	189.3	61	458	28	16.35	5-55	1	-
I.J.Harvey	254.2	79	658	40	16.45	6-19	3	1
A.D.Mullally	343.5	105	832	49	16.97	9-93	5	1
O.T.Parkin	108	30	291	17	17.11	4-14	-	-
C.White	157.3	32	430	25	17.20	5-32	2	-
M.P.Bicknell	413.2	115	1052	60	17.53	9-47	3	1
K.J.Dean	246	57	785	44	17.84	8-52	4	-
G.J.Whittall	106	31	290	16	18.12	3-14	-	-
M.M.Betts	354	91	832	44	18.90	7-30	1	1
I.D.K.Salisbury	380.3	101	984	52	18.92	8-60	3	2
D.Gough	324.1	62	949	50	18.98	6-63	2	-
H.H.Streak	156.1	50	346	18	19.22	6-87	2	-
A.Flintoff	135.2	49	290	15	19.33	4-18	-	-
D.M.Cousins	510.4	142	1318	67	19.67	5-123	1	-

Name	Overs	Mdns	Runs	Wkts	Avge	Best	5wI	10wM
M.J.Saggers	425.2	99	1148	57	20.14	7-79	2	-
L.J.Hamilton	94	22	287	14	20.50	5-55	1	-
J.F.Brown	517.5	142	1258	61	20.62	7-78	4	2
M.P.Smethurst	378.1	90	1161	56	20.73	7-37	3	-
A.M.Smith	250.4	70	623	30	20.76	5-52	1	-
J.Lewis	562.3	169	1506	72	20.91	8-95	4	-
S.R.Lampitt	412.5	108	1173	56	20.94	7-45	2	-
D.G.Cork	356.4	94	886	42	21.09	6-41	1	-
M.J.Cawdron	199.5	64	534	25	21.36	6-25	2	1
K.P.Dutch	143.4	45	366	17	21.52	6-62	1	-
S.J.E.Brown	442.2	110	1208	56	21.57	7-51	4	-
G.M.Hamilton	313.4	80	866	40	21.65	5-22	1	-
S.L.Watkin	389.4	108	1067	48	22.22	6-26	2	-
A.L.Penberthy	131	30	358	16	22.37	5-54	1	-
C.E.L.Ambrose	207.1	65	403	18	22.38	4-30	-	-
M.R.Strong	84.2	15	269	12	22.41	4-46	-	-
J.P.Taylor	212.3	50	540	24	22.50	6-27	1	1
A.J.Tudor	304.3	71	1071	47	22.78	7-48	3	-
N.A.M.McLean	271.3	68	803	35	22.94	5-30	2	-
P.C.R.Tufnell	738.3	255	1500	65	23.07	6-48	3	-
A.F.Giles	526.4	163	1200	52	23.07	8-90	5	2
S.K.Warne	639.4	183	1620	70	23.14	6-34	5	-
A.R.C.Fraser	474.3	150	1111	48	23.14	6-64	1	-
D.R.Tuffey	116	23	373	16	23.31	5-74	1	-
M.E.Cassar	212.2	54	702	30	23.40	6-76	1	-
J.C.Scuderi	120	28	333	14	23.78	4-58	-	-
J.N.Snape	113.3	44	239	10	23.90	3-70	-	-
G.Chapple	431.5	101	1175	49	23.97	6-42	1	-
R.C.Irani	407.3	120	1008	42	24.00	5-79	1	-
D.D.Masters	435.2	104	1161	48	24.18	6-27	3	-
C.D.Collymore	126.4	40	369	15	24.60	3-18	-	-
R.D.King	195.1	45	618	25	24.72	3-28	-	-
R.J.Kirtley	521.4	138	1559	63	24.74	6-41	4	-
J.D.Middlebrook	281.1	68	771	31	24.87	6-82	1	1
A.P.Cowan	398.5	98	1175	47	25.00	5-54	2	-
B.C.Strang	187.3	59	452	18	25.11	5-68	1	-
M.M.Patel	570.3	202	1157	46	25.15	6-77	2	-
A.Kumble	498.3	139	1133	45	25.17	6-44	2	1
B.W.Gannon	201.5	38	732	29	25.24	5-58	1	-
C.R.Pimlott	93	31	303	12	25.25	3-42	-	-
J.Ormond	380.3	75	1116	44	25.36	6-50	3	-
A.G.Wharf	256.3	51	940	37	25.40	5-68	1	-
P.M.Hutchison	129.3	32	420	16	26.25	3-62	-	-
M.J.Hoggard	501.4	134	1323	50	26.46	5-50	2	-
A.A.Donald	205.3	61	530	20	26.50	4-59	-	-
D.A.Leatherdale	154	34	508	19	26.73	3-17	-	-
M.V.Fleming	278.1	72	753	28	26.89	4-77	-	-
S.B.Styris	115.4	27	325	12	27.08	3-45	-	-
G.Keedy	478	142	1005	37	27.16	6-56	1	1

Name	Overs	Mdns	Runs	Wkts	Avge	Best	5wI	10wM
S.D.Udal	350.3	104	818	30	27.26	5-58	1	-
M.W.Alleyne	254.5	72	684	25	27.36	6-49	1	-
M.Burns	132.2	33	387	14	27.64	3-11	-	-
J.Wood	319.4	66	918	33	27.81	5-36	3	-
M.C.Ilott	283.2	85	724	26	27.84	3-37	-	-
P.R.Reiffel	233.3	60	586	21	27.90	5-62	1	-
E.S.H.Giddins	285.5	92	813	29	28.03	5-15	1	-
A.Dale	240.4	54	645	23	28.04	5-25	2	-
V.J.Wells	222.3	48	648	23	28.17	4-54	-	-
C.P.Schofield	374	80	1102	39	28.25	5-48	1	-
A.D.Mascarenhas	313.5	88	796	28	28.42	4-52	-	-
D.E.Malcolm	184.1	46	541	19	28.47	5-45	1	-
R.L.Johnson	473	129	1429	50	28.58	6-71	2	-
R.D.Stemp	398.2	140	946	33	28.66	5-123	1	-
S.D.Thomas	488	93	1612	56	28.78	5-43	2	-
M.A.Ealham	271.5	67	703	24	29.29	5-35	1	-
P.M.Such	422.4	101	1055	36	29.30	7-167	3	1
C.E.W.Silverwood	292.3	80	762	26	29.30	4-60	-	-
D.J.Millns	226.1	42	880	30	29.33	5-58	1	-
M.J.McCague	129.4	20	412	14	29.42	5-52	1	-
J.D.Lewry	524.4	137	1569	53	29.60	6-66	3	-
P.J.Franks	393.4	81	1247	42	29.69	7-56	2	-
C.D.Crowe	185.3	50	453	15	30.20	4-55	-	-
R.S.G.Anderson	234.4	56	729	24	30.37	6-34	3	1
S.J.Cook	137	41	335	11	30.45	4-13	-	-
A.J.Harris	384.3	62	1358	44	30.86	6-110	4	-
F.A.Rose	153	32	527	17	31.00	4-63	-	-
A.C.Morris	183.1	43	562	18	31.22	3-48	-	-
T.A.Munton	439.3	122	1093	35	31.22	7-34	2	-
N.M.K.Smith	310.4	70	875	28	31.25	5-66	1	-
G.D.Rose	332.3	79	908	29	31.31	5-74	1	-
S.J.Harmison	304.1	69	822	26	31.61	4-74	-	-
N.Killeen	288.3	84	697	22	31.68	3-14	-	-
P.S.Jones	403.4	88	1294	40	32.35	5-41	1	-
D.A.Cosker	429.5	141	944	29	32.55	4-82	-	-
D.S.Lucas	271.5	57	888	27	32.88	4-61	-	-
G.P.Swann	467.3	92	1366	41	33.31	6-118	2	-
P.A.J.DeFreitas	459.2	122	1105	33	33.48	4-41	-	-
P.D.Trego	165.1	34	603	18	33.50	4-84	-	-
M.A.Robinson	228	77	537	16	33.56	3-88	-	-
D.R.Law	291.4	50	1042	30	34.73	5-78	1	-
J.O.Grove	192.5	27	733	21	34.90	5-90	1	-
R.D.B.Croft	586.1	153	1432	40	35.80	5-26	2	-
T.F.Bloomfield	222.3	35	834	23	36.26	4-46	-	-
R.S.C.Martin-Jenkins	360.1	75	1202	33	36.42	5-94	1	-
P.Aldred	203.3	44	624	17	36.70	4-97	-	-
I.D.Fisher	211.1	48	588	16	36.75	3-40	-	-
B.C.Hollioake	117.5	25	407	11	37.00	4-41	-	-
R.K.Illingworth	221.5	72	483	13	37.15	3-34	-	-

Name	Overs	Mdns	Runs	Wkts	Avge	Best	5wI	10wM
S.P.Jones	104	12	374	10	37.40	4-47	-	-
A.Sheriyar	278.2	59	1048	28	37.42	4-51	-	-
B.P.Martin	133	35	378	10	37.80	3-43	-	-
M.V.Nagamootoo	328.4	93	801	21	38.14	4-12	-	-
D.R.Brown	268.2	49	917	24	38.20	5-87	1	-
N.C.Johnson	158.5	44	500	13	38.46	4-28	-	-
A.Richardson	368.2	96	1040	27	38.51	4-69	-	-
L.J.Wharton	164	42	464	12	38.66	5-96	1	-
S.J.Lacey	241.5	68	626	16	39.12	4-84	-	-
P.D.Collingwood	214.2	61	474	12	39.50	2-21	-	-
S.R.G.Francis	170.2	37	602	15	40.13	4-95	-	-
K.A.Parsons	150.4	41	443	11	40.27	5-13	1	-
Kabir Ali	219	41	811	20	40.55	4-114	-	-
T.C.Hicks	147	29	570	14	40.71	5-54	1	-
R.J.Logan	133.1	33	453	11	41.18	5-61	1	-
U.B.A.Rashid	343.5	84	994	23	43.21	5-103	1	-
J.P.Stephenson	172.1	33	566	13	43.53	4-68	-	-
M.C.J.Ball	243.1	58	658	15	43.86	3-31	-	-
I.D.Blackwell	411.3	123	1010	23	43.91	4-18	-	-
A.P.Grayson	178	39	443	10	44.30	3-55	-	-
J.M.Dakin	211.4	39	641	14	45.78	2-20	-	-
P.J.Hartley	204.2	33	697	15	46.46	3-91	-	-
T.J.Mason	239.3	55	710	14	50.71	3-38	-	-

THE PRIMARY CLUB

PO Box 12121
London NW1 9WS
Tel: 0171 267 3316
Fax: 0171 485 6808

Derek Underwood, the patron of the Primary Club, qualified for membership in some style in 1965. Playing for Kent against the South Africans he was out first ball twice in the same match.

However, members do not have to be playing Test or county cricket when the ultimate disaster strikes in order to qualify for the club. As long as you are out first ball at ANY level of cricket you are eligible to join The Primary Club.

Why join? The Primary Club is a charity (Registered Charity No. 285285) and all profits from subscriptions, donations and the range of items for sale (ties, sweaters, shirts, mugs, umbrellas, etc.) go to pay for sporting and recreational facilities for the blind and partially sighted. All the club's workers are volunteers.

For many of us sport is an important part of our every day lives; for the blind and partially sighted, sport can mean so much more. The confidence and sense of achievement they get from mastering a physical skill helps them a great deal in tackling the problems of their lives.

MEMBERSHIP APPLICATION

Name

Address

Joining subscription:	
To include City tie – £12	
To include Club tie – £12	
To include City & Club tie – £18	
To include Bow tie – £12	
Lady, to include brooch – £6	
DONATION	
TOTAL REMITTANCE TO: 'THE PRIMARY CLUB' £	

Please photocopy this form rather than spoil the book

TIES AND OTHER ITEMS FOR MEMBERS

The City tie has several small reproductions of the club emblem embroidered on navy blue fabric – the Club tie has a single larger one on green. A colour leaflet of the full range of clothing and other items will be sent to members.

DEED OF COVENANT

If you wish to consider making a donation under a 4 year (or more) charitable deed of covenant, please tick the box, but do not include this donation in your present remittance. Further details and a form of deed will then be sent to you. Such a deed does not increase the cost to you of your donation but enables the Club to recover income tax.

PCA AWARD WINNERS

HAYTER CUP (PCA Player of the Year)
Sponsored in 1999 & 2000 by
Fleming Premier Banking

1970	Mike Procter and Jack Bond
1971	Lance Gibbs
1972	Andy Roberts
1973	Peter Lee
1974	Barry Stead
1975	Zaheer Abbas
1976	Peter Lee
1977	Mike Procter
1978	John Lever
1979	John Lever
1980	Robin Jackman
1981	Richard Hadlee
1982	Malcolm Marshall
1983	Ken McEwan
1984	Richard Hadlee
1985	Neal Radford
1986	Courtney Walsh
1987	Richard Hadlee
1988	Graeme Hick
1989	Jimmy Cook
1990	Graham Gooch
1991	Waqar Younis
1992	Courtney Walsh
1993	Steve Watkin
1994	Brian Lara
1995	Dominic Cork
1996	Phil Simmons
1997	Steve James
1998	Mal Loye
1999	Stuart Law
2000	Marcus Trescothick

ARLOTT CUP
(PCA Young Player of the Year)

1990	Mike Atherton
1991	Dominic Cork
1992	Mark Lathwell
1993	Malachy Loye
1994	John Crawley
1995	Andy Symonds
1996	Chris Silverwood
1997	Ben Hollioake
1998	Andrew Flintoff
1999	David Sales
2000	Matthew Hoggard

HAROLD GOLDBLATT UMPIRES' CUP
Sponsored in 2000 by Andersen Consulting

1997	Peter Willey
1998	Ray Julian
1999	Ray Julian
2000	Ray Julian

PCA SPECIAL MERIT AWARD
Sponsored in 2000 by JLT

1997	Lord Cowdrey
1998	Dickie Bird
1999	David English
2000	The Primary Club

SLAZENGER SHEER INSTINCT
INDIVIDUAL PERFORMANCE AWARD

1997	Alistair Brown
1998	Graeme Hick
1999	Mark Alleyne
2000	Alec Stewart

INDEX OF PLAYERS BY COUNTY

*denotes not registered for the 2001 season. Where a player is known to have moved in the off-season he is listed under his new county.

DERBYSHIRE

ALDRED, P.
BAILEY, R.J.
BASSANO, C.W.G.
CORK, D.G.
DEAN, K.J.
DIVENUTO, M.J.
DOWMAN, M.P.
DUMELOW, N.R.C.
ILLINGWORTH, R.K.
KHAN, R.M.
KHAN, Z.M.
KRIKKEN, K.M.
LACEY, S.J.*
LUNGLEY, T.
MARSH, A.J.
MUNTON, T.A.
PIERSON, A.R.K.
PYEMONT, J.P.
SAXELBY, M.*
SHAH, K.Z.*
SMITH, T.M.
SPENDLOVE, B.L.
STUBBINGS, S.D.
SUTTON, L.D.
TITCHARD, S.P.
WELCH, G.
WHARTON, L.J.

DURHAM

ALI, S.M.*
BRIDGE, G.D.
BRINKLEY, J.E.
BROWN, S.J.E.

COLLINGWOOD, P.D.
DALEY, J.A.
DAVIES, M.A.
GOUGH, M.A.
HARMISON, S.J.
HATCH, N.G.
HUNTER, I.D.
KATICH, S.M.*
KILLEEN, N.
LAW, D.R.
LEWIS, J.J.B.
LOVE, M.L.
PATTISON, I.
PENG, N.
PHILLIPS, N.C.
PRATT, A.
PRATT, G.J.
ROBINSON, R.*
SPEAK, N.J.
SPEIGHT, M.P.
SYMINGTON, M.J.

ESSEX

ANDERSON, R.S.G.
BISHOP, J.E.
COWAN, A.P.
FLANAGAN, I.N.*
FOSTER, J.S.
GRAYSON, A.P.
HUSSAIN, N.
HYAM, B.J.
ILOTT, M.C.
IRANI, R.C.
JEFFERSON, W.I.
LAW, S.G.

MCGARRY, A.C.
MASON, T.J.
NAPIER, G.R.
PETERS, S.D.
PETTINI, M.L.
PHILLIPS, T.J.
PRICHARD, P.J.
ROBINSON, D.D.J.
SHARIF, Z.
SUCH, P.M.
THOMPSON, D.J.*

GLAMORGAN

CHERRY, D.D.
COSKER, D.A.
CROFT, R.D.B.
DALE, A.
DAVIES, A.P.
ELLIOTT, M.T.G.*
EVANS, A.W.
HARRISON, D.S.
JAMES, S.P.
JONES, S.P.
LAW, W.L.*
MAHER, J.P.
MAYNARD, M.P.
NEWELL, K.
PARKIN, O.T.
POWELL, M.J.
SHAW, A.D.
THOMAS, I.J.
THOMAS, S.D.
WALLACE, M.A.
WATKIN, S.L.
WHARF, A.G.

INDEX OF PLAYERS BY COUNTY

GLOUCESTERSHIRE

ALLEYNE, M.W.
AVERIS, J.M.M.
BALL, M.C.J.
BARNETT, K.J.
BRESSINGTON, A.N.
CAWDRON, M.J.
COTTERELL, T.P.
CUNLIFFE, R.J.
FORDER, D.J.
GANNON, B.W.
HANCOCK, T.H.C.
HARDINGES, M.A.
HARVEY, I.J.
HEWSON, D.R.
LEWIS, J.
MOHAMMED, I.*
RUSSELL, R.C.
SMITH, A.M.
SNAPE, J.N.
SUTLIFF, M.D.R.
TAYLOR, C.G.
WILLIAMS, R.C.J.
WINDOWS, M.G.N.

HAMPSHIRE

ADAMS, J.H.K.
AYMES, A.N.
BRUNNSCHWEILER, I.
FRANCIS, J.D.
FRANCIS, S.R.G.
HAMBLIN, J.R.C.
HARTLEY, P.J.*
JOHNSON, N.C.
KENDALL, W.S.
KENWAY, D.A.

LANEY, J.S.
MASCARENHAS, A.D.
MORRIS, A.C.
MORRIS, Z.C.
MULLALLY, A.D.
PRITTIPAUL, L.R.
RENSHAW, S.J.*
SAVIDENT, L.*
SEXTON, A.J.
SHAH, I.H.
SMITH, R.A.
STEPHENSON, J.P.
TREMLETT, C.T.
UDAL, S.D.
VAN DER GUCHT, C.G.
WARNE, S.K.*
WHITE, G.W.

KENT

ADAMS, K.
BANES, M.J.
CULLINAN, D.J.
DRAVID, R.*
EALHAM, M.A.
FERLEY, R.S.
FLEMING, M.V.
FULTON, D.P.
GOLDING, J.M.
HEADLEY, D.W.*
HOCKLEY, J.B.
JONES, G.O.
KEY, R.W.T.
KHAN, A.
LAZENBURY, P.S.
MARSH, S.A.*
MASTERS, D.D.
MCCAGUE, M.J.
NIXON, P.A.

PATEL, M.M.
PHILLIPS, B.J.
SAGGERS, M.J.
SCOTT, D.A.*
SMITH, E.T.
TROTT, B.J.
WALKER, M.J.
WELLS, A.P.

LANCASHIRE

ANDERSON, J.M.
ATHERTON, M.A.
AUSTIN, I.D.
CHAPPLE, G.
CHILTON, M.J.
CRAWLEY, J.P.
DRIVER, R.C.
FAIRBROTHER, N.H.
FLINTOFF, A.
GANGULY, S.C.*
GREEN, R.J.
HAYNES, J.J.
HEGG, W.K.
HOGG, K.W.
KEEDY, G.
LLOYD, G.D.
MARTIN, P.J.
MCKEOWN, P.C.*
MURALITHARAN, M.
ROBERTS, T.W.
SCHOFIELD, C.P.
SCUDERI, J.C.
SMETHURST, M.P.
WATKINSON, M.
WOOD, J.
WOOD, N.T.*
YATES, G.

INDEX OF PLAYERS BY COUNTY

LEICESTERSHIRE

ADSHEAD, S.J.
BOSWELL, S.A.J.
BURNS, N.D.
CROWE, C.D.
DAKIN, J.M.
DEFREITAS, P.A.J.
GRIFFITHS, P.
HABIB, A.
KHAN, A.A.*
KUMBLE, A.*
LEWIS, C.C.*
MADDY, D.L.
MALCOLM, D.E.
MARSH, D.J.
ORMOND, J.
SMITH, B.F.
STELLING, W.F.
STEVENS, D.I.
SUTCLIFFE, I.J.
WARD, T.R.
WELLS, V.J.
WHILEY, M.J.A.
WHITTICASE, P.
WILLIAMSON, D.*
WRIGHT, A.S.

MIDDLESEX

ALLEYNE, D.
BATT, C.J.*
BLOOMFIELD, T.F.
BROWN, M.J.
BRYAN, R.B.
COOK, S.J.
CREESE, M.L.
DALRYMPLE, J.W.M.
FLEMING, S.P.
FRASER, A.R.C.
HEWITT, J.P.
HUNT, T.A.
HUTTON, B.L.
JOYCE, E.C.
KEEGAN, C.B.
LANGER, J.L.*
LARAMAN, A.W.
MAUNDERS, J.K.
NASH, D.C.
POOLEY, J.C.
ROSEBERRY, M.A.
SHAH, O.A.
STRAUSS, A.J.
TUFNELL, P.C.R.
WEEKES, P.N.
WESTON, R.M.S.

NORTHAMPTONSHIRE

BAILEY, T.M.B.
BLAIN, J.A.R.
BROWN, J.F.
CASSAR, M.E.
COOK, J.W.
COUSINS, D.M.
COVERDALE, P.S.
DAVIES, M.K.*
DOBSON, M.C.
GOODE, C.M.
HAYDEN, M.L.*
HUSSEY, M.E.K.
INNES, K.J.
LOYE, M.B.
MACLEAN, R.A.
PANESAR, M.S.

PAYNTER, D.E.
PENBERTHY, A.L.
POWELL, M.J.
RIPLEY, D.
ROLLINS, A.S.
SALES, D.J.G.
STRONG, M.R.
SWANN, A.J.
SWANN, G.P.
TAYLOR, J.P.
WADE, J.
WARREN, R.J.
WEEKES, L.C.
WHITE, R.A.

NOTTINGHAMSHIRE

AFZAAL, U.
BICKNELL, D.J.
BLEWETT, G.S.
BOWEN, M.N.*
CLOUGH, G.D.
FRANKS, P.J.
GALLIAN, J.E.R.
HARRIS, A.J.
HAYWOOD, G.R.*
HEWISON, C.J.
JOHNSON, P.
LOGAN, R.J.
LUCAS, D.S.
MALIK, M.N.
MILLNS, D.J.
MORRIS, J.E.
NEWELL, M.
NOON, W.M.
PIETERSEN, K.P.
RANDALL, S.J.
READ, C.M.W.

INDEX OF PLAYERS BY COUNTY

REIFFEL, P.R.*
SMITH, G.J.
STEMP, R.D.
TOLLEY, C.M.
WELTON, G.E.

SOMERSET

BLACKWELL, I.D.
BOWLER, P.D.
BULBECK, M.P.L.
BURNS, M.
CADDICK, A.R.
COX, J.
DUTCH, K.P.
GAZZARD, C.M.
GROVE, J.O.
HOLLOWAY, P.C.L.
JARVIS, P.W.*
JOHNSON, R.L.
JONES, I.
JONES, P.S.
KENNIS, G.J.*
KERR, J.I.D.
LATHWELL, M.N.
PARSONS, K.A.
ROSE, G.D.
TREGO, P.D.
TRESCOTHICK, M.E.
TUCKER, J.P.
TURNER, R.J.
WOOD, M.J.

SURREY

AMIN, R.M.
BATTY, G.J.
BATTY, J.N.

BICKNELL, M.P.
BISHOP, I.E.
BROWN, A.D.
BUTCHER, G.P.
BUTCHER, M.A.
CARBERRY, M.A.
GIDDINS, E.S.H.
GREENIDGE, C.G.
HOLLIOAKE, A.J.
HOLLIOAKE, B.C.
MURTAGH, T.J.
PATTERSON, M.W.
PORTER, J.J.
RAMPRAKASH, M.R.
RATCLIFFE, J.D.
SALISBURY, I.D.K.
SAMPSON, P.J.
SAQLAIN MUSHTAQ
SCOTT, B.J.M.
SHAHID, N.
STEWART, A.J.
THORPE, G.P.
TUDOR, A.J.
WARD, I.J.

SUSSEX

ADAMS, C.J.
AMBROSE, T.R.
BATES, J.J.*
BEVAN, M.G.*
CARPENTER, J.R.
CLAPP, D.A.
COTTEY, P.A.
DAVIS, M.J.G.
GOODWIN, M.W.
GREENFIELD, K.
HAVELL, P.M.R.

HOUSE, W.J.
HUMPHRIES, S.*
KHAN, W.G.*
KIRTLEY, R.J.
LEWRY, J.D.
MARTIN-JENKINS, R.S.C.
MONTGOMERIE, R.R.
PATTERSON, A.D.*
PEIRCE, M.T.E.*
PRIOR, M.J.
RASHID, U.B.A.
ROBINSON, M.A.
TAYLOR, B.V.
WILTON, N.J.
YARDY, M.H.
ZUIDERENT, B.

WARWICKSHIRE

ALTREE, D.A.*
BELL, I.R.
BETTS, M.M.
BROWN, D.R.
CARTER, N.M.
DAGNALL, C.E.
DONALD, A.A.*
DRAKES, V.C.
FRANKLIN, G.D.
FROST, T.
GILES, A.F.
HEMP, D.L.
KNIGHT, N.V.
OSTLER, D.P.
PENNEY, T.L.
PIPER, K.J.
POWELL, M.J.
RICHARDSON, A.
SHEIKH, M.A.

INDEX OF PLAYERS BY COUNTY

SIERRA, R.E.
SMITH, N.M.K.
SPIRES, J.A.
TAHIR, N.
TROUGHTON, J.O.
WAGG, G.G.
WAGH, M.A.
WARREN, N.A.
WILSON, E.J.

WORCESTERSHIRE

ALI, KABIR
ALI, KADEER
BICHEL, A.J.
BOULTON, N.R.
CATTERALL, D.N.
HICK, G.A.
LAMPITT, S.R.
LEATHERDALE, D.A.
LIPTROT, C.G.
MCGRATH, G.D.*
PATEL, D.
PIPE, D.J.
POLLARD, P.R.
RAWNSLEY, M.J.
RHODES, S.J.
SHERIYAR, A.
SINGH, A.
SOLANKI, V.S.
SPIRING, K.R.
WESTON, W.P.C.
WILSON, E.J.

YORKSHIRE

BAKER, T.M.
BLAKEY, R.J.
BYAS, D.
CRAVEN, V.J.
DAWSON, R.K.J.
ELSTUB, C.J.
FELLOWS, G.M.
FISHER, I.D.
GOUGH, D.
GUY, S.M.
HAMILTON, G.M.
HARDEN, R.J.*
HOGGARD, M.J.
HUTCHISON, P.M.
INGLIS, J.W.*
LAMBERT, G.A.
LEHMANN, D.S.
LUMB, M.J.
MCGRATH, A.
MIDDLEBROOK, J.D.
RAMSDEN, G.
RICHARDSON, S.A.
SIDEBOTTOM, R.J.
SILVERWOOD, C.E.W.
STEAD, R.A.
TAYLOR, C.R.
VAUGHAN, M.P.
WHITE, C.
WIDDUP, S.
WOOD, M.J.